D0287120

Norway

Anthony Ham

Miles Roddis

Contents

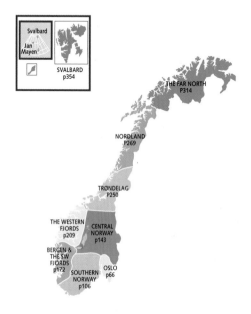

Destination Norway

Norway is, quite simply, breathtakingly beautiful. No matter how many pictures you've seen, nothing can prepare you for that first moment that you stand amid the precipitous, over-whelming view of the Norwegian fjords. From eyrie-like lookout points hundreds of metres above the water to the deck of a slow boat cruising between cliffs and remote rural villages, Norway's fjords are truly astonishing.

But there's so much more to Norway than 'just' fjords, although they alone would be sufficient reason to visit.

From the white-timbered villages along the picturesque southern coast to the frontier beauty of northern Arctic regions, Norway has an extraordinary diversity of landscapes, taking in vast forests, rugged peaks, dramatic glaciers, expansive icefields and wild Arctic tundra. Countless exceptional hiking trails carry you almost instantly away from the clamour of modern life and into some of the last great wilderness areas left in Europe, while every-thing from white-water rafting, skiing and climbing, to dog-sledding and parasailing, will surely satisfy the thrill seeker in you.

If your idea of a holiday is somewhat less energetic, you'll not want to miss the epic journey of the Hurtigruten coastal ferry, which transports you from the enchanting Unesco World Heritage–listed city of Bergen, all the way to remote little Kirkenes deep in the Arctic. En route, you'll encounter some of the best Norway has to offer, from spectacular islands such as the Lofoten and captivating towns like Trondheim and Tromsø, to a delicious sense that you're heading to the ends of the earth but doing so in considerable comfort.

Yes, Norway is expensive. But with such stunning natural beauty and some of the friendliest people in northern Europe, Norway is one place you can't afford to miss.

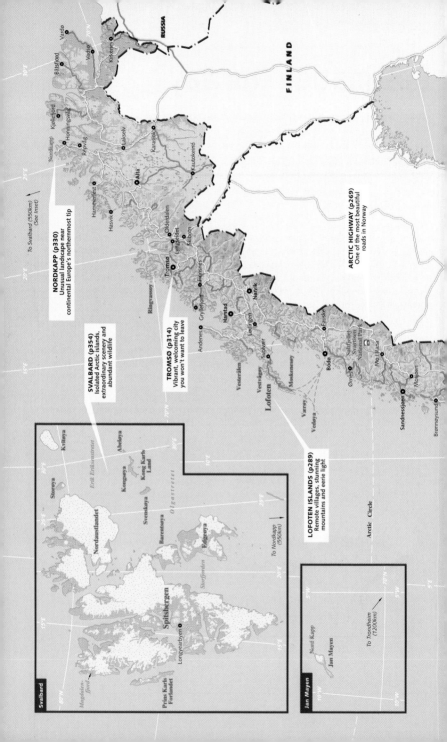

Svalbard

Storøya

Kvitøya

Abeløya

Kongsøya

Nordaustlandet

Svenskøya

Kong Karls Land

Barentsøya

Edgeøya

Erik Eriksenstretet

Olgastretet

Storfjorden

To Nordkapp
(550km)

Spitsbergen

Longyearbyen

Magdalena-fjorden

Prins Karls Forland

Jan Mayen

Nord-Kapp

Jan Mayen

To Trondheim
(1200km)

To Svalbard (550km)
(See inset)

NORDKAPP (p330)
Unusual landscape near
continental Europe's northernmost tip

SVALBARD (p354)
Isolated Arctic islands,
extraordinary scenery and
abundant wildlife

TROMSØ (p314)
Vibrant, welcoming city
you won't want to leave

LOFOTEN ISLANDS (p289)
Remote villages, stunning
mountains and eerie light

ARCTIC HIGHWAY (p269)
One of the most beautiful
roads in Norway

RUSSIA

FINLAND

Vardø

Vadsø

Båtsfjord

Kirkenes

Kjøllefjord

Honningsvåg

Skarsvåg

Repvåg

Laksely

Karasjok

Hammerfest

Hasvik

Alta

Kautokeino

Øksfjord

Skaidi

Olderdalen

Lyngseidet

Tromsø

Finnsnes

Ringvassøy

Andenes

Gryllefjord

Harstad

Narvik

Lødingen

Sortland

Fauske

Vesterålen

Svolvær

Saltfjellet-
Svartisen
National Park

Bodø

Ørnes

Mo i Rana

Moskenesøy

Lofoten

Vestvågøy

Mosjøen

Varøy

Værøy

Vedøya

Sandnessjøen

Brønnøysund

Arctic Circle

TRONDHEIM (p252)
Gateway to the north, sacred cathedral and lovely vibe

ÅLESUND (p237)
Art Nouveau city in a beautiful location

GEIRANGER (p234)
Breathtaking fjord traversed by slow boats

BRYGGEN (p177)
Captivating, World Heritage-listed houses along the waterfront

HARDANGERFJORD (p189)
Orchards and snow-capped peaks by the water's edge

PREIKESTOLEN (p206)
The world's best lookout above Lysefjord

RØROS (p152)
World Heritage-listed village, log cabins and charming atmosphere

JOTUNHEIMEN NATIONAL PARK (p167)
Beautiful summit of Norway, glaciers and walking trails

OSLO-BERGEN RAILWAY (p13)
Scenic rail journey through the best of Norway

GRIMSTAD (p119)
Delightful white-timbered village, picturesque harbour and quiet streets

ELEVATION

1800m
1500m
1200m
900m
600m
300m
0

To Jan Mayen (1200km)
(See inset)

NORWEGIAN SEA

NORTH SEA

SWEDEN

GULF OF BOTHNIA

BALTIC SEA

STOCKHOLM

OSLO

Skagerrak

100 km
60 miles

Norway is a remarkable country with lots to offer. You can start at **Røros** (p152), a charming old town in a little-visited corner of Norway, and move onto **Grimstad** (p119), a pretty harbour with narrow streets and white-timbered houses. The **Oslo–Bergen railway** (p13) offers a spectacular scenic adventure, while **Preikestolen** (p206) provides a magnificent view. **Trondheim** (p252) is Norway's third-largest city, most famous for its sacred cathedrals. The fjords are purely spectacular – visit **Hardangerfjord** (p189), a pristine fjord system cutting deep into the Norwegian interior, or Norway's most photographed fjord, **Geiranger** (p234). Up north visit the **Nordkapp** (p332), a dramatic landform close to continental Europe's northernmost tip, and **Trømso** (p316), a lively city.

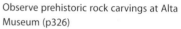

Observe prehistoric rock carvings at Alta Museum (p326)

INGRID RODDIS

LEE FOSTER

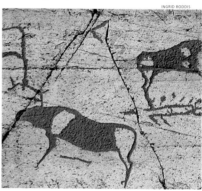

Admire Munch's famous painting *The Scream* at the National Gallery in Oslo (p72)

Clamber up to see the awesome view at Jotunheimen National Park (p167)

ANDERS BLOMQVIST

NED FRIARY

Discover the historic waterfront
buildings at Bryggen (p177), Bergen

GLENDA BENDURE

Take in the long and winding road,
Trollstigen (p231)

Explore the pretty coastal town of Ålesund (p237)

ANDERS BLOMQVIST

DAVID TIPL

See the spectacular frozen Tana River (p337) in Finnmark

CHRISTIAN ASLUND

Join a Svalbard tour (p356) – walk leaders carry
a gun for protection against polar bears

NED FRI

Visit the quaint seaside village of Lofoten Islands, such as Reine (p300), once voted
the most scenic place in Norway

Getting Started

Norway is extremely well developed, but unless you've decided to blow the massive inheritance sitting in your bank account, prior knowledge and careful planning can make your hard-earned kroner go a lot further. Because of the vast distances involved, you're unlikely to be able to visit all of Norway's myriad sights, so doing some research before you go will help to make the most of this exceptional destination.

WHEN TO GO

Norway is at its best and brightest from May to September. Late May is particularly pleasant – flowers are blooming, fruit trees blossoming, daylight hours are growing longer and most hostels and tourist sites are open but uncrowded. North of the Arctic Circle, the true midnight sun is visible at least one day a year, and at Nordkapp it stays out from 13 May to 29 July. In Lofoten, it's visible from 28 May to 14 July.

In general, the mountainous inland areas experience warmer summers and colder winters than the typically milder coastal areas, and temperatures over 30°C in summer and below -30°C in winter aren't uncommon. At any time of the year, be aware that extremes of temperature are always possible.

For climate details of major centres across Norway, see p337.

In addition to climatic factors, visitors should also consider the tourist season, which coincides with European school holidays and runs roughly from mid-June to mid-August. During this period, public transport runs frequently; tourist offices, hostels, summer hotels and tourist sites are open their longest hours; and most upmarket hotels offer better summer rates. There's also a 'shoulder' season, running from mid-May to mid-June and mid-August to early September, when these places are open shorter hours. Unless you're an avid skier or hope to glimpse the aurora borealis, Norway's cold dark winters can be trying for visitors – public transport runs infrequently; most hostels and camping grounds are closed; and tourist sites, museums and tourist offices open only limited hours, if at all.

For a list of public and school holidays in Norway, see p380.

DON'T LEAVE HOME WITHOUT...

In general, you'll need to pack no more for Norway than you would any other European holiday, but there are some particular things which you won't regret having:

- Nice shoes – many Norwegians often consider shoes to be the mark of a person.
- Sturdy hiking boots – hiking in sandals is a recipe for disaster.
- One alternative to jeans and trainers (sneakers) – Norwegians dress casually, but you'll need something more for a night out.
- A jacket, jersey (sweater) or anorak (windbreaker) that can be added or removed, even in summer.
- A sleeping sheet, a warm, but lightweight sleeping bag and/or your own sheets – most hostels and camping huts charge extra for bed linen (p368).
- A rail pass of some description (see p390) – why pay full price when you don't have to?
- Plenty of patience if you're driving – getting anywhere in a hurry can be a frustrating business on Norwegian roads (see p401).

COSTS & MONEY

Norway is expensive. You'll pay for everything from coffee refills to crossing bridges and using tunnels, from visiting churches to answering nature's call in public toilets.

If you stay in camping grounds (or, even better, camp in the open air – see p369) and prepare your own meals, you could squeeze by on around Nkr200 to Nkr220 per person per day. Staying in hostels that include breakfast (or eating breakfast at a bakery), having lunch at an inexpensive restaurant and picking up supermarket items for dinner, you can probably manage on Nkr350 per day.

Staying at a hotel that includes a buffet breakfast, eating a light lunch and an evening meal at a moderately priced restaurant, you can expect to spend at least Nkr600 per person per day if you're doubling up and Nkr750 if you're travelling alone. Once you factor in transport (a rail pass significantly reduces costs but rail lines don't extend north beyond Bodø), entertainment (concert and cinema tickets usually start from Nkr50, but can be Nkr150) and alcohol (nightclub cover charges start from Nkr70), you'll find yourself struggling to keep within a Nkr1000 daily limit. If you rent a car, Nkr1500 is a more likely minimum.

HOW MUCH?

Cup of coffee with pastry: Nkr50

Adult entry to museum: Nkr40 to Nkr75

Oslo–Bergen train one-way: Nkr670

'Norway in a Nutshell' 24-hour tour: Nkr1735

One-day car rental: from Nkr440

LONELY PLANET INDEX

Litre of petrol: Nkr9.50 to Nkr10.75

Litre of bottled water: Nkr8

Bottle of beer: Nkr15

Souvenir T-shirt: Nkr99

Street snack – hot dog: Nkr15

TRAVEL LITERATURE

Norway has a rich selection of books which make for great pre-departure reading or an accompaniment to long, lazy cruises through the fjords. Apart from the main online bookstores, you might also want to try **The Scandinavia Connection** (www.scandinavia-connection.co.uk).

Summer Light: A Walk Across Norway, by Andrew Stevenson, is an affectionate and luminous account of a walk from Oslo to Bergen which captures the essence of Norway.

Letters from High Latitudes, by Lord Dufferin, evokes a mid-19th-century sailing trip around the Arctic, including Jan Mayen, Svalbard and mainland Norway, with extensive references to the more romantic aspects of Norwegian history.

Barry Lopez, the author of *Arctic Dreams*, wrote a classic, ethereal and haunting treatment of Arctic regions, including references to the Sami culture.

A readable account of travelling through the Norwegian highlands accompanied by mountain myths is *The Fellowship of Ghosts: A Journey Through the Mountains of Norway*, by Paul Watkins.

Rowing to Latitude: Journeys Along the Arctic's Edge, by Jill Fredston, documents the harsh richness of Norway's arctic coasts by an author who rowed her way almost along its length.

An amusing, honest account of an American woman's time spent as an expat in Karmøy is *Island Soul: A Memoir of Norway*, by Patti Jones Morgan.

Letters on Sweden, Norway & Denmark, by Mary Wollstonecraft, recounts several emotion-filled months in late-18th-century Scandinavia with a pervasive and endearing tone of the Englishwoman abroad.

Neither Here nor There: Travels in Europe, by Bill Bryson, revisits, after almost three decades, an early-1970s backpacking trip from Norway's Arctic Circle to the island of Capri in Italy made by one of travel literature's funniest writers.

INTERNET RESOURCES

The Internet is a great place to find out more about Norway, and Norwegian-language websites usually have a UK or US flag or some other

TOP TENS

SIGHTS FOR CHILDREN

▪ Hunderfossen Familiepark (p148) – fairy-tale palaces and plenty of activities in Lillehammer.

▪ Atlantic Ocean Park (p239) – a four million litre aquarium and marine highlights in Ålesund.

▪ Musk Ox & Elk Safaris (p158) – expeditions in search of Norway's unusual animals in Oppdal.

▪ White-water rafting (p160) – custom-designed excursions for families in Sjoa.

▪ The myths of Seljord (p140) – Norway's answer to Loch Ness with a host of local myths.

▪ Dog-sledding (p372) – an age-old way of exploring the northern winter wonderland.

▪ Children's Art Museum (p85) – children's artwork from around the world in Oslo.

▪ Bobsled run (p146) – hurtling down the mountain at (almost) Olympic speed in Lillehammer.

▪ Children's Museum (p202) – themed activities-focused museum just for kids in Stavanger.

▪ Dyrepark (p123) – a favourite holiday destination for Norwegian children with a funfair and zoo in Kristiansand.

REGIONAL FESTIVALS & EVENTS

▪ Røros Market (p155) – held on the last Tuesday of February this annual market dates back to 1644.

▪ Vinterfestuka (p279) – in March in Narvik – a busy week of winter events.

▪ Sami Easter Festival (p348) – held in Easter at Kautokeino where weddings, cultural events and the reindeer racing world championship take place.

▪ Bergen International Festival (p184) – held at end of May with 12 days of dance, music and folklore.

▪ Extremesport Week (p192) – held in late June in Voss with high-adrenaline thrills.

▪ Molde Jazz Festival (p243) – held in July, this is a premier music festival with international acts.

▪ Olavsfestdagene (p259) – this is held in late July with processions and music to honour St Olav in Trondheim.

▪ St Olav Festival (p264) – held on 29 July in Stiklestad – it is a medieval market, modern-day Vikings and famous outdoor pageant.

▪ Nordlands Music Festival (p285) – held in early August in Bodø – a 10-day festival of symphony orchestras, jazz, rock and folk.

▪ Christmas Festival (p148) – two weeks of sleigh rides, Christmas parties, Santa visits and Christmas lighting held in Lillehammer.

FJORDS

▪ Geirangerfjord (p234) – precipitous, popular and one of Norway's signature images.

▪ Sognefjorden (p211) – arguably Norway's most beautiful network of fjords.

▪ Lysefjord (p206) – plunging cliffs, cruises and death-defying lookout points.

▪ Nærøyfjorden (p214) – one of Norway's narrowest and prettiest fjords.

▪ Magdalenefjord (p366) – remote Svalbard fjord that you'll probably have to yourself.

▪ Hardangerfjord (p189) – rolling hills and lovely villages climbing up from the bank.

▪ Eidfjord (p197) – most spectacular branch of Hardangerfjord.

▪ Trollfjord (p292) – breathtakingly steep fjord on Lofoten.

▪ Vestfjord (p289) – sheltered bays and pretty villages separating Lofoten from the mainland.

▪ Jøssingfjord (p128) – surprisingly vertiginous fjord in the flatlands of the south.

place to click so you can get information in English. Tourist offices in most cities and even many smaller towns have websites with practical information; see the individual town entries throughout the book.

Fjord Norway (www.fjordnorway.com) Everything you need to know about Norway's star attraction.

Kulturnett (www.kulturnett.no) Includes listing of over 850 museums and other cultural sites.

Lonely Planet (www.lonelyplanet.com) Latest travel news, succinct summaries on Norway, postcards from other travellers and the Thorn Tree bulletin board.

Norway.Com (www.norway.com) Comprehensive practical and tourist-oriented site.

Norwegian Tourist Board (www.visitnorway.com) Comprehensive site ranging from the practical to the inspirational.

The Norway Post (www.norwaypost.no) Up-to-the-minute news on Norway in English with an emphasis on travel and culture.

Itineraries

CLASSIC ROUTES

NORWAY IN MICROCOSM
Two Weeks

After a couple of days exploring **Oslo's** (p71) many galleries and museums, take the scenic Oslo–Bergen railway, often billed as one of the most spectacular rail journeys on earth. From Oslo, the line climbs gently through forests, plateaus and ski centres to the vast **Hardangervidda Plateau** (p138). At Myrdal, take the Flåmsbanen railway, down to **Flåm** (p211), from where fjord cruises head up the incomparable **Sognefjord** (p211). From Gudvangen, **Voss** (p189), where thrill seekers will love the easily accessible adventure activities on offer. Beyond Voss, the railway passes through different landscape until you reach **Bergen** (p174).

Bergen is a delight with its timbered houses, wonderful fish market and a cosmopolitan air. Bergen could act as a launch pad for a trip south to **Stavanger** (p198), an appealing place. Stavanger also serves as a base for trips to **Lysefjord** (p206), including the walk up to the dramatic Preikestolen or Pulpit Rock. En route back to Bergen you could linger for a while in **Hardangerfjord** (p189) where **Ulvik** (p194) and **Eidfjord** (p197) stand out among Norway's most worthwhile fjord-side towns.

The route from Oslo to Bergen can be done in two days as part of the 'Norway in a Nutshell' tour. If you've more time, a week is advisable. A circuit from Bergen to Stavanger and returning via Lysefjord and Hardangerfjord will add another week to the journey. If you're returning to Oslo, the entire itinerary takes in around 1570km.

THE HEART OF NORWAY &
THE BEST OF THE FJORDS
Three Weeks

Central Norway is the sort of place which seduces all who visit. A short train or bus ride from **Oslo** (p94), **Lillehammer** (p145) host of the 1994 Winter Olympics and it is one of central Norway's most pleasing spots with a wealth of Olympic sites. From here you'd be seriously miscalculating if you didn't factor in a detour to World Heritage-listed **Røros** (p152), arguably Norway's most enchanting village. Here you'll find painted timber houses, sloping pedestrianised streets and an evocative old mine, not to mention an old world charm that can be hard to leave behind. A little further north, **Trondheim** (p252) is a delightful coastal capital.

From Trondheim, make your way to pretty **Ålesund** (p237) or stop off in **Åndalsnes** (p231), starting point for the beautiful roads south into the Western Fjords. The Trollstigen Rd, with steep gradients, waterfalls and hairpin bends, takes you past **Romsdal** (p231), with 1.5km-high vertical cliffs – the highest in Norway. Other highlights on your way south include: the similarly precipitous and much-photographed **Geirangerfjord** (p234); following the fantastic chasm of Norangsdalen to lovely Norangsfjorden, dominated by some of the most impressive mountains in Norway; and gorgeous Fjærland, a veritable Shangri-la of fjords, glaciers and peaks. From Geiranger, there's easy access to **Lom** (p165), the starting point for the Sognefjellet Rd, northern Europe's highest, and passing through the extraordinarily beautiful **Jotunheimen National Park** (p167). The road leads down to **Sognefjord** (p211) where you'll find good connections on to Voss, Bergen and Oslo.

Keeping up a brisk pace, you could accomplish this 1475km journey in 10 days, but two to three weeks would enable you to linger in each place a little longer. This would be especially worthwhile in Røros, Trondheim, Ålesund and any of the countless, spectacular fjords.

ROADS LESS TRAVELLED

NORWAY'S FAR NORTH   Three Weeks

Northern Norway is true frontier territory country, although to get there you'll need to start along well-trodden paths. **Bergen** (p188) is the starting point of the Hurtigruten coastal ferry which runs all the way to **Kirkenes** (p341). The wonderful **Lofoten Islands** (p289) is high in Norway's list of most breathtaking places; **Kabelvåg** (p294), **Henningsvær** (p295), Nusfjord and Moskenesøy will initiate you into the delightfully backwoods-feel of the Lofoten. The **Vesterålen** (p303) archipelago also contains some little-visited gems, including Nyksund and Stø.

Returning to the mainland, energetic **Tromsø** (p314) is an antidote to lonely northern nights, a great place to return after excursions offshore to Karlsøy or inland to the **Lyngen Alps** (p322). Or experience the equally dramatic but even quieter fishing villages of **Senja** (p322). In your pursuit of solitude include visits to the **Øvre Dividal National Park** (p323) and the rock carvings of Alta. If you're in the area, don't miss Nordkapp for novelty value before venturing to the **Nordkyn Peninsula** (p335), some salmon fishing at **Tana Bru** (p337) and go to the Sami cultural centres of **Kautokeino** (p346) and **Karasjok** (p349), as well as the **Reisa National Park** (p349).

Finally, to get so far off-the-beaten track that you'll almost fall off the end of the earth, there's no place quite like **Svalbard** (p352), a place of rare and stark beauty that is the Arctic in essence.

A minimum timeframe for this journey would be three weeks, but it could easily take a month, especially if you take time out to do a spot of hiking. Travelling by the coastal steamer is picturesque and none-too-fast, adding time (and countless postcard-like memories) to the trip.

NORWAY'S SECRET SOUTH

One Week

Such is the Norwegian love of exploring their own country, that getting off the beaten track can be difficult. Being among the few *foreign* visitors is, however, relatively easy in Norway's south while everybody else rushes to the well-worn routes along the western coast. **Tønsberg** (p108) is Norway's oldest town, making it worth a quick look en route along the coast to the wonderful white-timbered towns of **Kragerø** (p113), **Risør** (p115), **Grimstad** (p119) and **Lillesand** (p120), any one of which could absorb long lazy days by the beach or fill an afternoon of meandering through narrow lanes crawling up from the harbours. **Arendal** (p116) doesn't get many foreign visitors but is a lovely seaside town with a delightful old quarter, while **Sandefjord** (p111) just has one stand-out attraction – the Norwegian Whaling Museum – where you'll learn things you probably never knew about whaling from the Norwegian perspective and still leave unconvinced.

Kristiansand (p121) shouldn't detain you long, but it is the place to seek transport up into the forested hills of Setesdalen, where you'll find **Evje** (p139), a centre for geological curiosities and, further north, some excellent roadside **folk museums** (p141). The folk tales of **Seljord** (p139), home of Selma the Serpent and a community of decidedly cranky trolls are for those who long for a land where fairytales which you thought existed only in the imagination could just come true. One of Norway's most stirring wartime legends finds a dramatic setting in **Rjukan** (p135), a gateway to appealing hiking and cycling expeditions.

A week is the shortest possible time needed to accomplish this 650km journey. The route along the coast promises countless tempting detours which could prolong the time necessary, while for the routes up through the interior of southern Norway, more infrequent public transport is another possible factor if you're not driving.

TAILORED TRIPS

UNESCO WORLD HERITAGE–LISTED NORWAY   Two Weeks

The drafters of Unesco's World Heritage list must have been tempted simply to list the whole country! As it is, they chose five sites which, if you visit them all, will see you travelling through large swathes of northern and western Norway. Starting in **Bergen** (p174), a stroll down to the waterfront will take you to the wonderful old trading warehouses of **Bryggen** (p177), 58 of which have made it onto the Unesco list and which wind back from the harbourside in delight-

fully but dangerously rickety narrow lanes. Northwest of Bergen and after passing some of Norway's finest fjord scenery, you'll find the 12th-century stave church in **Urnes** (p219), Norway's oldest and one of its most fairytale constructions by the banks of the Sognefjord. From there, cross the towering peaks of the Norwegian interior and head for **Røros** (p152), a postcard-pretty village which captures the essence of central Norway of yesteryear. From there, it's a long, but astonishingly beautiful haul up to **Alta** (p324), home to up to 3000 Stone- and Iron-Age rock carvings and one of the earliest open-air history books.

ADVENTUROUS NORWAY   Six Weeks

Norway's wilderness regions are so vast that many start where people's backyards end. Even **Oslo** (p84), Norway's sprawling capital, has ample hiking and cycling trails seemingly miles from anywhere but starting just beyond the last metro stop. Serious hikers won't want to miss the trails into the Hardangervidda National Park or to the summit of Gausta (1883m) from **Rjukan** (p135), where you can also indulge in a spot of rail-biking, bungee-jumping and more skiing. **Sjoa** (p159) may be small but its rapids attract white-water rafting and river-board enthusiasts and experts from across the globe, while **Oppdal** (p157) promises more rafting, not to mention hang-gliding and skiing. The **Jotunheimen National Park** (p167) is the undoubted hiking capital of Norway with end-

less trails through Norway's highest and most picturesque country, where you can also enjoy some summer skiing to cool off. **Voss** (p189) is one, big high-energy rush with parachut-ing, parasailing, rafting and bungee jumping. Other fine national parks where hiking off into the pristine wilderness is almost an imperative include: **Rondane** (p161); **Dovrefjell-Sunndalsfjella** (p163), home to musk ox and reindeer; **Jostedalsbreen** (p163), with its vast icecap and the opportunity for kiting (glacier windsurfing on skis); **Rago** (p277); **Reisa** (p349); **Saltfjellet-Svartisen** (p274); and **Stabbursdalen** (p334), the world's northernmost pine forest.

18

The Authors

ANTHONY HAM
Coordinating Author

Ever since his uncle and aunt gave him his first book on Norway almost 20 years ago, and ever since his parents made him green with envy by recounting in heartless detail their trip to the fjords, Anthony has had a long-distance love-affair with the country. Although more accustomed to sunnier climes – he lives in Madrid and has travelled extensively in Europe, Africa and the Middle East – he has always been driven by a somewhat contradictory passion for lively cities and the great places of solitude on the planet. Norway fitted the bill on both counts. Anthony wrote the introductory chapters, Oslo, Southern Norway, Central Norway, Bergen & the Southwestern Fjords chapters.

My Favourite Trip

I'd start in Oslo whose museums and galleries (p71) offer a microcosm of the Norwegian world. I'd meander my way south-west along the southern coast with its fabulous white towns and delightful yacht harbours, particularly Kragerø (p113), Risør (p115), Arendal (p116) and Grimstad (p119). After a brief pause in Kristiansand (p121), I'd head for cosmopolitan Stavanger (p198), en route taking Rv44 between Egersund and Flekkefjord. From Stavanger, I'd scale the heights of Preikestolen (p206) for a view over the stunning Lysefjord (p206), before working my way up to charming Bergen (p174) via Ulvik and Eidfjord – the best of Hardangerfjord. Heading east, I'd spend as long as I could in the Jotunheimen National Park (p167), sweep down to Lillehammer (p145) and then end up in Røros (p152) where I'd be happy to spend the rest of my days.

MILES RODDIS

A distant camping holiday deep in the forests of Finland, an even more distant Swedish girlfriend and a mental image of cliffs, fretted fjords and lush green grass; such were the pulls that tempted Miles to take on this assignment, north of the Arctic circle.

Miles, who has written or contributed to over 25 LP books, usually writes about Mediterranean lands these days. So these chill breaths of Scandinavian air came as a tonic – though a little less rain would be welcome next time round, God, if that's all right with You... Miles wrote the Western Fjords, Trøndelag, Norland, The Far North and Svalbard chapters.

Snapshot

Norwegians live a comfortable life, just don't tell them that we said so. By any measure, Norway's social welfare system is one of the most impressive in the world and Norwegians of all ages find themselves borne along on a raft of benefits, including (but by no means restricted to) a government-sponsored university education, generous holiday leave, free medical care, up to a year's paid maternity leave and a guaranteed pension – perhaps the ultimate in cradle-to-grave care. When the long-standing rule of the left-leaning Labour Party came to an end in 2001, even the new centre-right government knew that the welfare system was sacrosanct.

The largesse of the state, however, has prompted fears (and angst-ridden debates) among many Norwegians they are perceived as lazy by the outside world (who, it must be said, are largely jealous of Norway's nanny state, although less so of the prohibitively high taxes paid by Norwegians). The other concern among Norwegians is that many of their number have come to take the easy life for granted; one recent study showed that Norwegians on average work less than 160 days per year. What with longer term concerns about how long the bounty of Norway's oil riches will last (oil exports account for around 30% of Norway's GDP), an increasing number of Norwegians cast an anxious eye towards the future.

Another issue which casts a shadow over the normally sunny dispositions of Norwegians is uncertainty over Norway's place in the world. Norwegians love to travel, often ranging to enviably far reaches of the earth. Norway is also one of the largest per capita donors of foreign aid and its government is actively involved in peacemaking initiatives across the globe. And yet, Norway takes a grim pride in thumbing its nose at international opinion, most (in)famously with its stance on whaling. Immigration is minimal. And Norwegians have always voted, against the wishes of their government, to remain outside the EU (although a July 2004 poll suggested that support for membership had risen to just above 50%), fearing that a loss of independence will follow hot on the heels of integration. Many also fear a threat to their high standard of living.

To understand these many contradictory impulses and the propensity of Norwegians to be wary and defensive, one need only to cast an eye over Norway's history. For too many centuries, Norway was forced to cede sovereignty and become minor inhabitants in someone else's kingdom. Norway was also, until the discovery of oil in the 1960s, one of the poorest countries in Europe – they waited a long, long time to be this wealthy. You'll meet Norwegians who bristle with indignation at the mere thought that directives on daily life should be made from Brussels (or anywhere else for that matter), even as many – particularly urban-dwellers and southerners – recognise that Norway cannot remain forever isolated from the larger world economy. Most realise that they may soon be left with little choice.

FAST FACTS

Population: 4,577,500

GDP per capita: US$37,700 (3rd highest in the world)

Inflation: 2.5%

Unemployment rate: 4.5%

Life expectancy: 81.8 years (women) and 75.9 years (men)

External debt: 0

No. of tourists annually: 4.5 million

Oil wealth: 14th largest reserves in the world, 6th largest producer, and 3rd biggest oil exporter

No. of doctors/nurses per 100,000 people: 413/1840 (compared with 162/500 in UK)

Proportion of country covered by forests: 27%

History

Norway's history tells a very different story from the stable, peaceful country you'll encounter when you visit. From the rampant and almost mythical Vikings, to a seemingly endless cycle of wars with its neighbours and with itself, Norway's stability and independence was extremely hard-won throughout a history soaked in blood.

EARLY HISTORY

Norway during the ice age must have been a pretty bleak place. That said, it was probably preferable to Siberia, from where the first humans to arrive in Norway came around 11,000 years ago. The ancient hunting culture which they brought with them, known as the Komsa, was the forerunner of the Sami (p34), a people who, true to their Siberian origins, still inhabit the cold northern regions of Scandinavia and northwestern Russia. Another site of early settlement was around Trondheim, where the coastal Fosna people pursued a hunting, fishing and herding lifestyle.

After the ice receded, people of the Nøstvet-Økser culture of central Europe began migrating to southern Scandinavia, particularly along the southern Norwegian coast. This nomadic, hunter-gatherer people, although of mixed European descent, were most likely tall, blonde-haired, blue-eyed and spoke a Germanic language, the predecessor of modern Scandinavian languages.

Around 2500 BC, the wonderfully named Battle-Axe, Boat-Axe and Funnel-Beaker cultures (named after the stone tools they used) entered southern Norway from what is present-day Sweden. The paucity of naturally occurring metals ensured that the most significant Bronze Age relics are rock carvings which portray ships and religious symbols – clearly the Scandinavians were already a seafaring people. The Scandinavians traded amber for metals, particularly bronze, from mainland Europe.

During the later years of the Roman Empire, Rome provided Norway with fabric, iron implements and pottery. Iron tools allowed farmland to be cleared of trees, larger boats were built with the aid of iron axes and a cooling climate saw the establishment of more permanent structures built from stone and turf. By the 5th century, the Norwegians had learned how to smelt their own iron from ore found in the southern Norwegian bogs. The runic alphabet also arrived, probably from a Germanic source, and it can still be seen on stone slabs throughout the region.

After the fall of the Roman Empire, a period of migration and fighting between several regions ensued. By AD 700, much of Norway was divided into small, independent, non-confederated kingdoms ruled by *jarls* (earls). What would become Norway was known to mainland Europeans only as the Norovegr (North Way), the trade route which led from Oslofjord westward along the southern coast.

THE VIKING ERA

Norway's greatest impact on world history undoubtedly came during the glory and infamy of the Viking Age, which was to last almost 500 years.

DID YOU KNOW?

Under the 9th century Viking system of compensation for murder, a slave was worth half the value of a peasant, who was, in turn, worth half that of a landlord. A landlord was worth 25% the value of a chieftain and one-eighth that of a king.

A good overview of Norwegian history written without academic jargon can be found at www.cs.ucsb.edu/~ansa /norway/history/history2 .html.

9000 BC	AD 793
First humans arrive in Norway from Siberia	Start of Viking era with attack on St Cuthbert's monastery in Britain

The years of Viking supremacy began innocently enough. In the 8th century, Norway had become overpopulated; polygamy had led to an excess of male heirs and land was being divided into ever-smaller plots. The solution for many young men was to seek their fortune across the sea, made easier by the fact that most had seafaring in their blood.

One of the earliest accounts of Norse seafaring came in the *Anglo Saxon Chronicle* for 787, wherein it was noted that three ships came to Britain from Hordaland (Heredalande), piloted by sailors who were described as Northmen. In the 780s Norwegian farmers peacefully settled in Orkney and Shetland.

These first historical records of Norse seagoing activity gave little hint of what was to come. While the advance parties caused scarcely a ripple, Nordic shipbuilders at home were developing a fast and manoeuvrable sailing vessel which had a heavy keel, up to 16 pairs of oars and a large square sail. In short, for the first time a boat had been built which was sufficiently sturdy for ocean crossings.

The Oxford History of the Vikings, by Peter Sawyer, is one of the best and most comprehensive accounts of the Viking era, with updated scholarly research, loads of illustrations and plenty of vivid accounts of Viking exploits.

Thus equipped, the Viking Age began in earnest in 793. St Cuthbert's monastery on the island of Lindisfarne, off the coast of Northumberland in Britain was plundered, followed a year later by the plundering of Jarrow, also in Northumberland. The trickle became a wave in 795 when a fleet of 100 Viking ships set their sights on southern Wales. Although they were successfully resisted by King Maredydd, the monasteries of neighbouring Ireland presented easy targets and yielded a great deal of loot.

Many Vikings believed that the Christian monasteries they encountered were a threat to their pantheist traditions. In the more lawless regions of Britain and Ireland, they destroyed Christian communities and slaughtered monks, who could only wonder what sin they had committed to invite the heathen hordes. Despite the sacking of monasteries at both Applecross and Iona, however, the Viking predilection for war did not prevent them from enjoying a relatively peaceful coexistence with the Celts in the Western Isles of Scotland.

After their early raids, the Vikings attacked Britain, Ireland and the continent in great fleets, terrorising, murdering, enslaving, assimilating or displacing local populations. The Viking reach was extraordinary. Many coastal regions of northern Norway, Britain, Ireland, France (Normandy was named for these Northmen), Russia (as far east as the river Volga), Moorish Spain (Seville was raided in 844), and the Middle East (they even reached Baghdad) all came under the Viking sway. Well-defended Constantinople (Istanbul) proved a bridge too far – the Vikings attacked six times but never took the city. Such rare setbacks notwithstanding, the Viking raids transformed Scandinavia from an obscure backwater on Europe's northern fringe to an all-too-familiar place capable of striking fear at the very heart of the continent.

For all of their destruction elsewhere, Viking raids increased standards of living at home. Emigration freed up farmland and fostered the emergence of a new merchant class, while raiding parties returned with slaves who provided farm labour.

During the 9th and 10th centuries, Norwegian farmers also crossed the Atlantic to settle the Faroes, Iceland and Greenland. By the year 1000, almost five centuries before Columbus, Leifur Eiríksson, the son of

872

Battle at Hafrsfjord; Harald Hårfagre unites Norway for first time

995

First Christian church constructed in Norway

THE LEGEND OF THE VIKINGS

Few historical people have captured the imagination quite like the Vikings. Immortalised in modern cartoons (*Asterix* and *Hagar the Horrible* to name just a few), the real-life Vikings were no laughing matter.

The Vikings spread across Europe with war on their minds and returned home with slaves in their formidable, low Norse longboats. These boats, over 30m long and which could travel at up to 12 knots (24km/h), gave birth to the Viking legend, enabling them to cover distances remarkable in a time when, for most people, the known world extended only to the near horizon.

The raiders were invariably followed by settlers travelling in smaller cargo boats called *knerrir* (singular *knörr*). These sturdy little craft, scarcely 18m in length with little freeboard, were designed to carry great loads. Journeys in them must have been crowded, uncomfortable and often frightening.

Perhaps the most curious aspect of Viking voyages, however, was the navigational tool they employed to travel through uncharted territory. Norse sagas mention a mysterious device known as a *solarsteinn*, or 'sunstone', which allowed navigation even when the sky was overcast or the sun was below the horizon and celestial navigation was impossible.

It is now generally agreed that the *solarsteinn* was a crystal of *cordierite*, which is found around Scandinavia and has natural polarising qualities. When observed from below and rotated, light passing through the crystal is polarised blue when the long axis is pointed toward the source of the sunlight.

That the Vikings were centuries ahead of their time is evident in the fact that, even today, jet planes flying over polar regions, where magnetic compasses are unsuitable, use a sky compass which determines the position of the sun by filtering sunlight through an artificial polarising lens.

Eiríkur Rauðe (Eric the Red), had explored the coast of North America, which he named Vinland, or the 'land of wine'.

THE FIRST UNIFICATION OF NORWAY

While the Vikings were ranging far and wide, at home a decisive civil war sea-battle was raging in 872 at Hafrsfjord near Haugesund; see the boxed text, p205. The demographic consequences were considerable, with as many as 20,000 people emigrating from Norway to Iceland to escape the victorious king Harald Hårfagre (Fair-Hair), son of Svarta-Halvdan (Halvdan the Black). Politically, Harald's victory produced far-reaching consequences as he unified a number of separate realms into the Kingdom of Norway.

The reign of Harald Hårfagre was such an odd and entertaining time, at least for historians, that it was recorded for posterity in the *Heimskringla*, the Norwegian Kings Saga, by the Icelander, Snorre Sturluson.

According to Snorre, Harald's unification of Norway was inspired by a woman who taunted the king by refusing to have relations with a man whose kingdom wasn't even as large as tiny Denmark. Through a series of confederations and trade agreements, he extended his rule as far north as Trondheim, which was founded in 997 at the mouth of the Nid River. Soon thereafter, it became the first capital of the new kingdom. His foreign policies were equally canny, and he even sent one of his sons, Håkon, to be reared in the court of King Athelstan of England. There is no record of whether the woman in question was sufficiently impressed.

DID YOU KNOW?

Contrary to modern representations, Vikings didn't have horns on their helmets, which could just mean that Hagar the Horrible is an imposter.

1024

Olav II founded the Church of Norway

1030

King/St Olav killed at Battle of Stiklestad

The king did, however, marry 10 wives and fathered a surfeit of heirs, thereby creating serious problems over succession. The one who managed to rise above them all was Erik, his last child and only son with Ragnhild the Mighty, daughter of the Danish King Erik of Jutland. The ruthless Erik rose to power by eliminating all of his legitimate brothers except Håkon (who was safe in England). Together with a host of squabbling illegitimate brothers, Erik, whose reign was characterised by considerable ineptitude, then proceeded to squander his father's hard-won Norwegian confederation. When Håkon returned from England to sort out the mess as King Håkon den Gode (Håkon the Good), Erik was forced to flee to Britain where he took over the throne of York as King Erik Blood-Axe.

MEDIEVAL NORWAY

King Håkon the Good, who had been baptised a Christian during his English upbringing, brought the new faith with him to Norway. His attempts to introduce it into his realm, accompanied by missionaries and a bishop from Britain, met with limited success. This was particularly true in Trondheim, where the subjects appeared to be utterly preoccupied with drinking and toasting Þór (Thor), Oðinn (Odin) and Freyr. Although the missionaries were eventually able to replace the names of the gods with those of Catholic saints, they failed to control the pagan practice of blood sacrifice. When Håkon the Good was defeated and killed in 960, Norwegian Christianity all but disappeared.

It was revived briefly during the reign of King Olav Tryggvason (Olav I), a Viking who had converted to Christianity in England. Being a good Viking, Olav decided that only force would work to convert his countrymen to the truth. Unfortunately for the king, his intended wife, Queen Sigrid of Sweden, refused to convert to Christianity. Olav cancelled the marriage contract and Sigrid married the pagan king Svein Forkbeard of Denmark. Together they orchestrated Olav's death in a great Baltic sea-battle, then took Norway as their own.

Christianity was finally cemented in Norway by King Olav Haraldsson, Olav II, who was also converted in England. There, he and his Vikings allied themselves with King Ethelred and managed to save London from a Danish attack under King Svein Forkbeard by destroying London Bridge (from whence we derive the song 'London Bridge is Falling Down'). Succeeding where his namesake had failed, Olav II helped construct Norway's first Christian church, at Mosterhamn on the island of Bømlo, Hardanger in 995, and founded the Church of Norway in 1024. He even managed to bring Christianity to recalcitrant Trondheim.

However, no Scandinavian monarch of the time could ever rest comfortably in his bed. King Canute (Knut) of Denmark was eyeing Norway for possible annexation and, in 1028, Knut invaded the country, forcing King Olav II to flee. Although Olav later returned, a popular farmers' uprising in Trøndelag led to his death at the decisive Battle of Stiklestad in 1030. For Christians, this amounted to martyrdom and the king was thereafter canonised as a saint. Indeed, the great Nidaros Cathedral in Trondheim stands as a memorial to Olav and, until the Protestant reformation, the cathedral served as a destination for pilgrims from all over

Gunnar's Daughter, by Sigrid Undset, gives a somewhat racier edge to Viking history in the form of a historical novel rich in Norwegian folk tales and good old-fashioned Viking raids.

DID YOU KNOW?

The word 'Viking' is derived from vik, which in Old Norse referred to a bay or cove, a reference to Vikings' anchorages during raids.

A site for Viking-junkies, Explore North (www.ex plorenorth.com/vikings .html) has links ranging from the quirky to the informative with heavy doses of Norse gods, Norse mythology and conspiracy theories.

Europe (see the boxed text, p254). Apart from rising to the lofty heights of sainthood, Olav is also remembered for having forged a lasting identity for Norway as an independent kingdom.

Canute's brief reign was followed by four generations of kings who ruled Norway as a semiautonomous nation. Although King Olav Kyrre (Olav the Peaceful) founded Bergen and Stavanger around 1070, none has captured the attention of historians quite like Harald III (Harald Hardråda, or Harald 'Hard-Ruler'), half-brother of St Olav. After establishing a base by founding Oslo in 1043, Harald III raided throughout the Mediterranean before mounting an ill-fated invasion of England in 1066. His death at the hands of King Harold of England at the Battle of Stamford Bridge is generally regarded as the end of the Viking Age and expansionism, although Viking power abroad didn't begin to wane significantly until the 13th century.

Den Kongelige Norske Sankt Olavs Orden (www .saintolav.com) has everything you ever wanted to know (and probably a few things you didn't) about St Olav; some of it's a bit hagiographic but the 'History of Norway' section is good for understanding the history of the Norwegian monarchy.

THE RISE & FALL OF NORWEGIAN KINGDOMS

The 12th century cemented Norway's Christian identity with stone and stave churches constructed throughout the land. Of the few buildings which still stand, the oldest is at Urnes, on Lustrafjorden, which dates from around 1130.

Although stuttering, Viking expansionism had yet to completely die out. In 1107, the Viking king, Sigurd I (the Crusader), led an expedition of 60 ships to the Holy Land. Three years later, he captured Sidon. Successes abroad did not translate into peace at home. Sigurd died in 1130 and the rest of the century was fraught with brutal civil wars over succession to the throne. These disputes culminated in a crucial naval battle (1184) at Fimreite, on Sognefjord, where a host of wealthy and influential citizens were slaughtered. The victorious King Sverre, a churchman turned warrior, paved the way for medieval Norway's so-called 'Golden Age' which saw Bergen claim the title of national capital.

For a while Norway enjoyed a period of relative peace and prosperity resulting from trade between coastal towns and the German-based Hanseatic League (see the boxed text, p177).

In 1261 and 1262, respectively, Greenland and Iceland voluntarily joined the Kingdom of Norway. Lingering disputes with Scotland were resolved in 1266 when the Western Isles and the Isle of Man were sold to the Scots, marking the beginning of the loss of Norwegian territory.

Haakon V built brick and stone forts, one at Vardø to protect the north from the Russians, and another at Akershus in 1308 to defend Oslo harbour. The transfer of the national capital from Bergen to Christiania (formerly Oslo) soon followed. Haakon V's successor, his grandson Magnus, son of Haakon's daughter and a Swedish duke, was elected to the Swedish crown in 1319; the two kingdoms united that year and the royal line of Harald Hårfagre came to an end, ushering in a period of decline which would last for 200 years – Norway became just another province of Denmark.

In August 1349, the Black Death arrived on an English ship via Bergen. The bubonic plague would eventually kill one-third of Europe's population. During this tragic period, land fell out of cultivation, towns were

1349

Black Death devastates one-third of population

1720

Sweden defeated ending 150 years of war with Norway

ruined, trading activities faltered and the national coffers decreased by 65%. In Norway, as much as 80% of the nobility perished. Because their peasant workforce had also been decimated, the survivors were forced to return to the land, forever changing the Norwegian power-base.

By 1387, Norway had lost control of Iceland and 10 years later, Queen Margaret of Denmark formed the Kalmar Union of Sweden, Denmark and Norway, with Eric of Pomerania as king. Margaret's neglect of Norway continued into the 15th century, when trade links with Iceland were broken and the Greenland colonies mysteriously disappeared without trace.

The loss of independence was compounded by the increasingly powerful Hanseatic traders who created a very lopsided trade situation in favour of the Germans. They did, however, import vital commodities for Norwegian use, and the port of Bergen was largely sustained by the export of dried cod from Nordland. In 1427, the Hanseatic traders in Bergen got word of an impending pirate raid on the port and cleared out; when the attack came, the Norwegian defences were overwhelmed and it was eight years before the Germans returned to re-establish their trade.

In 1469, Orkney and Shetland were pawned – supposedly a temporary measure – to the Scottish Crown by the Danish-Norwegian King Christian I, who had to raise money for his daughter's dowry. Just three years later, the Scots annexed both island groups. In 1523, the Swedes seceded from the Union, installing the first Vasa king and setting the stage for a prolonged period of war.

REFORMATION, WAR & POLITICAL UNION

In 1537, the Reformation replaced the incumbent Catholic faith with Lutheran Protestantism. Some 22 years later, Christian III broke the Hanseatic grip on trade in Bergen, which spawned a diversification in the mercantile population as Dutch, Danish and Scottish traders brought wealth and expertise to the city and created a comfortable Norwegian middle class.

In the late 16th century, a series of disputes began between the Danish Union and Sweden, including the Seven Years War between 1563 and 1570, and the Kalmar War between 1611 and 1614, both of which were played out partly on Norwegian soil. Trondheim, for example, was repeatedly captured and recaptured by both sides. During the Kalmar War, a two-pronged invasion of Norway was mounted from Scotland. In Gudbrandsdalen, a grassroots effort by local farmers succeeded in defeating one of these expeditions (see the boxed text, p161).

It was during this period that exploration of the Arctic was first wedded to commercial gain, laying the foundations for many of Norway's modern and most controversial industries. Whalers, sealers and walrus hunters from various nations were followed closely by trappers in search of fox pelts.

In two further wars during the mid-17th century, Norway lost a good portion of its territory to Sweden. The Great Nordic War with the expanding Swedish Empire was fought in the early 18th century, and in 1716 the Swedes occupied Christiania (Oslo). Trondheim was besieged by the Swedes in the winter of 1718–19, but the effort was abandoned

1814	1854
Norway ceded to Sweden; First Norwegian constitution by Norwegian rebels	Norway's first railway, from Oslo to Eidsvoll, completed

after the death of the Swedish emperor, Karl XII. The Swedes were finally defeated in 1720, ending over 150 years of war.

Despite attempts to re-establish trade with Greenland through the formation of Norwegian trading companies in Bergen in 1720, Danish trade restrictions scuppered the nascent economic independence. As a consequence, Norway was unable to weather the so-called 'Little Ice Age', from 1738 to 1742. The failure of crops ensured a period of famine and the death of one-third of Norwegian cattle, not to mention thousands of people.

During the Napoleonic wars, Britain blockaded Norway, causing the Danes to surrender on 14 January 1814. The subsequent Treaty of Kiel presented Norway to Sweden in a 'Union of the Crowns'. Tired of having their territory divided up by foreign kings, a contingent of farmers, businesspeople and politicians gathered at Eidsvoll Verk in April 1814 to draft a new constitution and elect a new Norwegian king. The business was completed on 17 May 1814, a date still celebrated as Norway's national day. It didn't last long. Sweden forced the new king, Christian Frederik, to yield and accept the Swedish choice of monarch, Karl Johan. War was averted by a compromise which provided for devolved Swedish power. Disputes between Norway and Denmark ensued over ownership of the colonies of Iceland, Greenland and the Faroe Islands (this issue wasn't resolved until 1931, when the World Court settled in favour of Denmark).

After centuries of war and living under foreign occupation, Norway enjoyed a major cultural revival in the 19th century. This flowering of musical and artistic expression was led by poet and playwright Henrik Ibsen, composer Edvard Grieg and artist Edvard Munch. This period also saw the development of a unique Norwegian dialect known as *landsmål* (or *Nynorsk*). Norway's first railway, from Oslo (King Karl Johan changed the name back from Christiania in order to wipe off that vestige of the Danish union) to Eidsvoll, was completed in 1854, and Norway began looking at increased international trade, particularly of fish and whale products.

A rapidly increasing population, combined with the fact that Norway was one of the poorest corners of Europe, brought about a period of mass emigration to North America. Between 1825 and 1925, over 750,000 Norwegians re-settled in the USA and Canada.

THE KINGDOM OF NORWAY

In 1905, a constitutional referendum was held. As expected, virtually no-one in the country favoured continued union with Sweden. The Swedish king Oskar II was forced to recognise Norwegian sovereignty, abdicate and re-instate a Norwegian constitutional monarchy, with Haakon VII on the throne, whose descendants rule Norway to this day with decisions on succession remaining under the authority of the *Storting* (parliament). Oslo was declared the national capital of the new and independent Kingdom of Norway.

The first three decades of the 20th century brought a flurry of technological advances and world-firsts. In 1911, the Norwegian explorer Roald Amundsen reached the South Pole. In 1913, Norwegian women became

In Their Own Words: Letters from Norwegian Immigrants, by Solveig Zempel, is a sometimes grim, sometimes uplifting collection of letters from Norwegians in America from 1870, casting light on the difficulties of life in Norway in the early 19th century.

The Hollywood producers may have brushed lightly over the fine details of historical accuracy in *The Heroes of Telemark* (1965), but this landmark episode in the history of Norwegian resistance does at least have Kirk Douglas swashbuckling all over the screen.

1905	1920
Kingdom of Norway becomes independent under constitutional monarchy after referendum	*Storting* elected to join the newly formed League of Nations

among the first in Europe to be given the vote. Prior to 1914, hydro-electric projects sprang up all around the country and prosperous new industries emerged to drive the increasingly healthy export economy. Despite Norway's neutrality during WWI, the German forces sank quite a few Norwegian merchant ships.

In 1920, Norwegian territory was extended for the first time in several centuries with the signing of the Svalbard Treaty, which took effect in 1925. The 1920s brought new innovations, including the development of factory ships which allowed processing of whales at sea and caused an increase in whaling activities, especially around Svalbard and in the Antarctic; for more information on whaling, see the boxed text, p58.

Also in 1920, the *Storting* voted to join the newly formed League of Nations, a move which was opposed only by the communist-inspired Labour Party, an increasingly militant and revolutionary party which dominated the *Storting* by 1927. From the late 1920s, the effects of the Great Depression in the USA reverberated around the world and brought economic hardship to Norway. By December 1932, there was 42% unemployment and farmers were hit especially hard by the economic downturn.

WWII & ITS AFTERMATH

By 1933, the doctrine of fascism had begun to spread throughout Europe and the former Norwegian defence minister Vidkun Quisling formed a Norwegian fascist party, the Nasjonal Samling. After the Germans invaded Norway on 9 April 1940, King Håkon and the royal family fled first to Elverum (see the boxed text, p152), then Britain and thence to the US capital, Washington DC (where they stayed for the duration of the war), while British, French, Polish and Norwegian forces fought a desperate rearguard action.

Six southern towns were burnt out, and despite some Allied gains, the British were out on a limb and were ordered to abandon Arctic Norway to its fate. In Oslo, the Germans established a puppet government under Vidkun Quisling, whose name entered the lexicon as a byword for those who betray their country.

However, over the next five years, the Norwegian resistance network distinguished itself in sabotaging German designs, often through the assistance of daring Shetland fishermen who smuggled arms across the sea to western Norway. Among the most memorable acts of defiance was the famous commando assault of February 1943 on the heavy water plant at Vemork, which was involved in the German development of an atomic bomb (see the boxed text, p134).

The Germans exacted bitter revenge on the local populace and 1500 Norwegians died during the period of occupation. Among the civilian casualties were 630 Norwegian Jews who were sent to central European concentration camps. Serbian and Russian prisoners of war were coerced into slave labour on construction projects in Norway, and many perished from the cold and an inadequate diet. The high number of worker fatalities during the construction of the arctic Highway through the Saltfjellet inspired its nickname, the *blodveien* (blood road).

DID YOU KNOW?

The 1925 Svalbard treaty granting Norwegian sovereignty over the islands of Svalbard came with the provision that mineral residency rights be opened up to more than 20 signatories of the treaty, countries which included the USSR, Australia, Canada, India, Japan, the USA and most EU countries.

DID YOU KNOW?

The first Allied victory of WWII occurred in late May 1940 in Norway, when a British naval force re-took Narvik and won control over this strategic iron ore port. It fell again to the Germans on 9 June.

9 April 1940	1945
Nazi Germany invades Norway and government goes into exile	Russian army retreats from Arctic Norway after German surrender

THOSE GENEROUS GERMANS

Shortly following the German invasion of Norway in 1940, the commander-in-chief of the occupying forces, General von Falkenhorst, issued the following declaration:

I have been given the task of protecting the land of Norway against attack from the Western powers. The Norwegian government has refused several offers of co-operation. The Norwegian people must now themselves decide over the destiny of their country. If this announcement is complied with, such as it was with great understanding by the Danish people in the same situation, Norway will be spared from the horrors of war.

If resistance should be offered and the hand offered in peaceful intention should be refused, I shall be forced to proceed with the sharpest and most ruthless means to break the resistance.

Anyone who supports the issued mobilisation order of the fled former government or spreads false rumours will be court-martialled.

Every civilian caught with weapon in hand will be SHOT.

Anyone destroying constructions serving the traffic and military intelligence or municipal devices will be SHOT.

Anyone using weapons contrary to international law will be SHOT.

The German army, victorious in many battles, the great and powerful air force and navy will see to it that my announcement will be carried through.

The German Commander-in-Chief von Falkenhorst – Infantry General

Finnmark suffered particularly heavy destruction and casualties during the war. The Germans constructed submarine bases in Altafjorden and elsewhere, which were used to attack convoys headed for Murmansk and Arkhangelsk in Russia, hoping to disrupt the supply of armaments to the Russians.

Norway 1940, by Francois Kersaudy, uses the mid-1940 German invasion of Norway as a springboard for an impassioned coverage of the Norwegian theatre of war with an emphasis on how Norwegians were betrayed by their Allies.

In early 1945, with the Germans facing an escalating two-front war and seeking to delay the Russian advance into Finnmark, the German forces adopted a scorched-earth policy and utterly devastated northern Norway, burning fields, forests, towns and villages. Shortly after the German surrender of Norway, Quisling was executed by firing squad, other collaborators were packed off to prison and on 7 May, the Russian army withdrew from Arctic Norway.

Although the communist party made gains in postwar elections, the Iron Curtain remained in place at the Russian border. Severe wartime rationing didn't end until 1952, by which time major reconstruction works (including many destroyed villages) were underway, particularly to rebuild Arctic Norway. In addition, the merchant navy and whaling fleet bounced back.

In 1946, Norway became a founding member of the UN. Ever conscious of its proximity to Russia, the country also joined NATO in 1949. Closer links with other Scandinavian countries developed after the formation of the Nordic Council in 1952.

MODERN NORWAY

Oil was discovered in the North Sea in the late 1960s and the economy boomed, transforming Norway from one of Europe's poorest countries to one of its richest. Since then, successive socialist Labour governments

1946	late 1960s
Norway becomes founding member of UN	Oil discovered, making Norway one of Europe's richest countries

have used the oil windfalls (and punitively high income tax rates and service user-fees) to foster one of the most extensive social welfare systems in history with free medical care and higher education, as well as generous pension and unemployment benefits. It all adds up to what the government has claimed is the 'most egalitarian social democracy in western Europe'.

In 1960, Norway joined the European Free Trade Association (EFTA), but in 1972, Norwegians narrowly voted against joining the European Economic Community (EEC). Through the 1980s, a strong Norwegian economy prevented increased unemployment and social decay, and the results of 1972 were repeated in 1994 with a vote against joining the EEC's successor, the European Union (EU). The 'no' vote was due especially to the concerns of traditional family farms and fishing interests which hoped to avoid competition with their larger and more technologically advanced EU counterparts. For more on Norway and the EU, see p19.

Norway: Elites on Trial, by Knut Heidar, may be a bit dry and academic but it remains one of the finest and most detailed descriptions of modern Norway with an emphasis on its evolving relationship with the EU.

1972	**1994**
Norwegians vote against joining the EEC	Norwegians vote against joining EU for second time

The Culture

THE NATIONAL PSYCHE

Norwegians are at once fiercely independent and keen to engage with the world. You'll encounter people who take reluctant but defiant pride in their government's controversial stance on commercial whaling, seeing threats not to the animals but to a traditional Norwegian industry and Norwegian freedom of action. You'll find even more who agonise over whether Norway should join the EU, fearful of the sovereignty they will lose, yet aware that they have a responsibility to engage with their neighbours to the south and east. But above all else you'll find Norwegians who speak numerous languages, have travelled widely and who love nothing more than to welcome visitors to their country.

Perhaps not surprisingly given the beauty of their country, Norwegians love the great outdoors. They take very seriously the ancient law of *allemansretten* or 'every man's right', whereby public access to wild areas is guaranteed, and they'll actively encourage you to do likewise; many even refuse to remain housebound through depressingly long winters. That's not to say that they don't welcome summer – they do, they almost worship it with a frenetic awareness that it may only last for two months and with an eagerness that only those who have lived through the long Norwegian winter can truly understand. Norwegians are generally good-natured, but in summer they positively glow with infectious good humour – it's a great time to be here. That this has always been true was summed up by the playwright, Henrik Ibsen (see the boxed text, p44): He who wishes to understand me must know Norway. The magnificent but severe natural environment surrounding people up there in the north forces them to keep to their own. That is why they become introspective and serious, they brood and doubt – and they often lose faith. There, the long, dark winters come with their thick fogs enveloping the houses – oh, how they long for the sun!

Norwegians believe above all in fairness yet are often wary of non-white immigrants and are sometimes ready with negative remarks about Sweden. Norway has been consistently voted the world's most liveable country, yet many Norwegians grumble that things are not as they used to be.

> 'Perhaps not surprisingly given the beauty of their country, Norwegians love the great out-doors'

LIFESTYLE

The lifestyle of Norwegians has been heavily influenced (some critics would say socially engineered) by government welfare programmes. Whatever your position on the subject, the results are undeniably impressive. It's not just we who think so – Norway again came first in 2004 on the UN Human Development Index, which ranks countries according to life expectancy, education and income, making it officially the most liveable country in the world.

Work & Family Life

Norway's legendary programme of government-funded social benefits has two primary foci: the family and equality between men and women (for further information see p38). Although early welfare payments for families were aimed at providing 'a mother's wage', protecting a woman's right to remain at home without relying on her husband's income, the focus has shifted since the 1970s toward protecting the right of both men and women to work outside the home. This has manifested in everything from paid leave to heavily subsidised childcare. Paid maternity leave is based on a compulsory nine-week minimum, with the full-pay provisions extending to 42 weeks – the highest in Europe. Fathers are granted four weeks, of which 78% take advantage. Each parent is also entitled to an additional one year's unpaid, but job-protected, leave (civil servants get three years) or to work part-time and receive full pay for up to two years. There are also government grants of over Nkr32,000 upon the birth of a child and family allowance income support during the child's life.

All in all, Norway's a great place to have a baby and start a family. Perhaps because of this reason, Norway has one of the highest fertility rates (1.9 children per family) in Europe, compared to a 1.45 average elsewhere in the EU.

There have, nonetheless, been changes in the family demographics in recent years, with the average age (27.5) of first-time mothers increasing, a decline in marriage rates (5.6 per 1000 people), a rise in de facto relationships (49% of children are born outside wedlock), and an increase in the numbers of single mothers (22% of children grow up in single-parent households). These new realities, most of which are protected under the welfare system, have begun a perceptible shift away from the traditional nuclear family which has always provided the bedrock of Norwegian society. Partly this change is because of the greater choice which rising Norwegian incomes (US$43,350 per capita, the third highest in the world) have enabled and partly because of a decline in churchgoing among the young. Perhaps the most noticeable impact has been not upon immediate family units – which have diversified rather than been replaced and the double-income-two-kids model remains the norm – but on traditional, extended families whereby the requirement to care for elderly relatives seems to have transferred from family members to the state.

Like in most Western countries, Norway has an ageing population and an average life expectancy of close to 80 years, trends which have profound implications for future governments to fund social welfare provisions at their present generous levels. Although the retirement age is set at 67 for men and women, pensions are guaranteed for the remainder of a person's life.

If you've ever in an idle moment perused the boards of a real estate agent, you'll agree that house prices can be prohibitive. They're also taxed as a luxury. Undeterred, Norwegians continue to push the rates of home ownership above 80% of the population.

DID YOU KNOW?

A staggering 83% of working-age Norwegians has completed education beyond secondary level and 26% hold higher degrees.

Education

Education is compulsory (and has been since 1889!), with the public system heavily funded and private schools actively discouraged. Students at secondary level have a range of choices, from traditional academic programmes to vocational training. Many also choose to study in cities other than their home town, contributing to a situation wherein children leave home and become relatively independent much earlier than in most southern European countries. Education, including university studies, are free.

The policy of choice extends to members of the Sami culture, with conscious efforts undertaken to preserve their traditional culture – Sami students study cultural studies and can do some course-work in the Sami language. Non-Norwegian speakers also have access to subsidised special education programmes.

> **RUSSING AROUND**
>
> An unusual tradition for students graduating from high school is called *russ*. When a student becomes *russ*, or *rødruss*, he or she dons red overalls and a red beret and, by virtue of this status, is permitted for a time to raise all sorts of holy hell. Although the line is drawn at actual property damage, other sorts of mischief – unrestrained noise, partying, removable graffiti and general obnoxiousness – are permitted and even encouraged. This may go on for several weeks around the end of the school year. Most of it's good-natured adolescent fun, but if you're trying to sleep, you may not get the joke.

There are four main universities: the University of Oslo (the oldest); the University of Bergen; the Norwegian University of Science & Technology in Trondheim; and the University of Tromsø. There are also around 40 regional and specialist colleges.

Traditional Culture

Norway is a decidedly modern country and, apart from vestiges in remote rural areas, its cultural traditions are only visible in the country's excellent folk museums, folk performances and, if you're very lucky, some weddings.

One of the most evident elements is the *bunad*, the elaborate regional folk costumes. Each district has developed their own unique designs which exhibit varying degrees of colour and originality. Although they remained in everyday use until after WWII in traditional regions such as Setesdal and parts of Telemark, they're now something of a novelty and are dusted off mainly for weddings and other festive events.

The intricate embroidery work on these lovely creations was traditionally performed by shepherdesses and milkmaids while tending their livestock. Nowadays, these elaborate costumes are produced only by a few serious seamstresses and embroiderers and the purchase of a *bunad* represents a major financial commitment. The Norwegian Folk Museum in Oslo features displays of these memorable costumes, but the best place to observe them is in Oslo during the 17 May National Day celebrations, when men and women from all over the country turn up in the traditional dress of their heritage areas.

POPULATION

DID YOU KNOW?

Traditional Norwegian homes belonging to peasants were built of wood, but wealthier Norwegians displayed their means by constructing palatial but cold and draughty stone dwellings.

Norway has one of the lowest population densities (around 12%) in Europe. Traditionally a rural society of remote and rural farmsteads (which remain a feature, albeit diminished, of the Norwegian countryside), there's an irreversible trend of urbanisation underway and 75% of the population now live in urban areas (compared with 93% in the UK, 84% in Germany and 89% in the Netherlands).

Nordic

Most of Norway's population is considered to be of Nordic stock; these people are thought to have descended from central and northern European tribes who migrated northward around 8000 years ago; modern Nordic peoples are in fact the indigenous peoples of southern and central Scandinavia. The Nordic physical stereotype – a tall sturdy frame, light hair and blue eyes – does have some basis in fact with nearly 70% of Norwegians having blue eyes, higher than anywhere else in the world outside Scandinavia.

FOLKLORE & LEGENDS

To the first-time visitor, it can seem as if the Vikings belong irretrievably to the past and Norway can seem the archetype of the modern, rationalist society. Think again. Nowhere else in Europe does a tradition of folktales and legends survive to such an extent.

Mythical Creatures

Perhaps the most Norwegian of Norway's supernatural beings is the troll, thought to have emerged in Norway at the close of the last ice age. Trolls inhabit gloomy forests, moonlit lakes, deep fjords, snowy peaks and roaring waterfalls. They're predominantly creatures of shadow and darkness; any troll who is exposed to direct sunlight will turn to stone.

Trolls, which can live for hundreds of years, come in all shapes and sizes, some large, some small, but nearly all have four fingers and toes on each hand and foot, as well as long, crooked noses and bushy tails. Some have multiple heads, with up to three eyes per head. They also have a strange predilection for harassing billy goats and a violent aversion to the sound of church bells. Despite being known for having a short fuse and getting decidedly cranky, they're generally kind to humans.

A larger version of the troll was the giant, and according to legend, the world was created from the body of the giant Ymir of Jotunheimen (home of the giants), after his death at the hand of the Norse god Oðinn.

Elves, who normally live stream-side in the deepest forests, also come in both good and bad varieties. They only emerge at night-time, when there's no risk or danger of turning to stone, and it's said that the sites of their nocturnal festivities and dances are marked by luxuriant rings of grass.

Other elusive creatures include *hulder*, who steal milk from summer pastures; the frightening draugen, a headless fisherman who foretells drownings with a haunting wail; and the *vetter* (wights), who serve as the guardian spirits of the wildest coastlines. Serpents also existed in Viking mythology, but at least one is still with us today – the mysterious Selma the Serpent (see the boxed text, p140). Despite attempts by practitioners of Wicca to rehabilitate the image of their much-maligned art, witches remain powerful forces of evil in popular Norwegian folklore and are capable of all sorts of heinous behaviour.

Folk Tales

The valleys in western and northern Norway are rich sources of folk tales, sagas and myths, many of them explaining curious geographic features. In the north, they're an especially rich part of Nordland coastal culture.

In one story, a lonely island-dwelling giantess shouted across the water to a giant named Blåmann (blue man) on the mainland, asking him to marry her. He agreed, provided she brought the island along with her. Sadly, by the time she'd packed everything up, the sun rose and she turned to stone, as did Blåmann, who'd stayed out too long waiting for her. The island became known as Gygrøy (giantess island), but local fisherfolk renamed it Landegode (the good land), lest the giantess take offence. Landegode's distinctive profile is a familiar landmark on the ferry between Bodø and Kjerringøy, while poor old Blåmann is now an icecap.

Another legend involves Hestmannen (the Horseman), who attempted to shoot the princess Lekamøya with an arrow when she wouldn't marry him. Her father, the king of Sømna, threw down his hat as a distraction, and the result was Torghatten, a hat-shaped peak that looks as if it's been pierced through, on Torget island south of Brønnøysund. Hestmannen himself is a knobbed peak on the island of Hestmanna, located further north and accessible from the town of Mo I Rana.

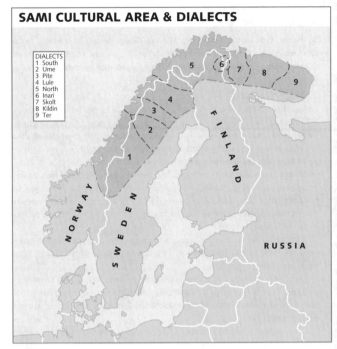

SAMI CULTURAL AREA & DIALECTS

DIALECTS
1 South
2 Ume
3 Pite
4 Lule
5 North
6 Inari
7 Skolt
8 Kildin
9 Ter

Arctic Council (www
.arctic-council.org/saami
.html) contains
informative links to Sami
cultural and political sites
in the wider Scandinavian
context.

Sami

Norway's 40,000 indigenous Sami people (formerly known as Lapps)
make up the country's largest ethnic minority and can reasonably claim
to be Norway's longest-standing residents. Now primarily inhabiting
the far northern region of Finnmark (scattered groups live in Nordland,
Trøndelag and Hedmark), this hardy, formerly nomadic people has for
centuries occupied northern Scandinavia and northwestern Russia, living
mainly by herding domestic reindeer. The total population of around
60,000 Sami forms an ethnic minority in four countries – Norway, Sweden, Finland and Russia (above map). The Sami refer to their traditional
lands as Sápmi, or Samiland.

Reindeer herding was successfully modernised in the 1980s and 1990s,
and is now a major capital earner. In addition to reindeer herding, modern Sami engage in fishing, agriculture, trade, small industry and the
production of handicrafts, in addition to most other trades and profes-
sions in Norwegian society as a whole.

For details on Sami religion, see p38.

POLITICAL ORGANISATIONS

In addition to the Sami parliament, which convenes in Karasjok and
is elected by direct ballot every four years, the Norwegian Sami people
also belong to the **Saami Council** (www.saamicouncil.net), which was founded in
1956 to foster cooperation between political organisations in Norway,
Sweden, Finland and Russia. The Norwegian Sami also participate in
the **Arctic Council** (www.arctic-council.org) and the World Council of Indigenous
Peoples (WCIP), which encourages solidarity and promotes information

THE SAMI'S HISTORICAL STRUGGLE

Although it is believed that the forerunners of the Sami migrated to Norway from Siberia, the oldest written reference to the Sami was penned by the Roman historian Tacitus in AD 98. In AD 555, the Greek Procopius referred to Scandinavia as Thule, the furthest north, and its peoples as *skridfinns*, who hunted, herded reindeer and travelled about on skis. The medieval Icelandic sagas confirm trading between Nordic peoples and the Sami, and the trader Ottar, who 'lived further north than any other Norseman', served in the court of English King Alfred the Great and wrote extensively about his native country and its indigenous peoples.

During this era, the Sami lived by hunting and trapping in small communities or bands known as *siida*. Each community occupied their own designated territory. While 17th- and 18th-century colonisation of the north by Nordic farmers presented conflicts with this system, many of the newcomers found that the Sami way of life was better suited to the local conditions and adopted their dress, diet, customs and traditions.

Around 1850, reforms were introduced which restricted the use of the Sami language in schools. From 1902, it became illegal to sell land to any person who couldn't speak Norwegian, and this policy was practised zealously, particularly in the early 20th century. However, there was an about turn after WWII when official policy began promoting internal multiculturalism. By the 1960s, the Sami's right to preserve and develop their own cultural values and language were enshrined across all government spectra. Increasingly, official policy viewed the Sami as Norwegian subjects but also an ethnic minority and separate people. Their legal status improved considerably and the government formed two committees: the Samekulturutvalget to deal with Sami cultural issues, and the Samerettsutvalget to determine the legal aspects of the Sami status and resource ownership.

In 1988, the Norwegian government passed an enlightened constitutional amendment stating: 'It is the responsibility of the authorities of the State to create conditions enabling the Sami people to preserve and develop its language, culture and way of life.' It also provided for the creation of an elected 39-member Sami parliament, or **Sameting** (www.samediggi.no), to serve as an advisory body to bring Sami issues to the national parliament (similar bodies also exist in Finland and Sweden).

In early 1990, the government passed the Sami Language Act, which gave both the Sami language and Norwegian equal status. Later the same year, Norway ratified the International Labour Organisation proposition No 169, which guaranteed the rights of indigenous and tribal peoples.

exchange between indigenous peoples in the various member countries. The **Nordic Sami Institute** (☎ 78 48 80 00; info@nsi.no) at Kautokeino was established in 1974 and seeks to promote Sami language, culture and education, as well as promote research, economic activities and environmental protection. It's funded by the Nordic Council of Ministers.

In Tromsø in 1980, the Saami Council's political programme adopted the following principles:

We, the Sami, are one people, whose fellowship must not be divided by national boundaries. We have our own history, tradition, culture and language. We have inherited from our forebears a right to territories, water and our own economic activities. We have an inalienable right to preserve and develop our own economic activities and our communities, in accordance with our own circumstances and we will together safeguard our territories, natural resources and national heritage for future generations.

SPORT

For thousands of years, skis were the only practical means of winter transport in much of Norway, and as a result, it is in winter sports that Norwegians have excelled. In fact, the people of Telemark invented the graceful

Telemark turn (see the boxed text, p376) and the word slalom is derived from the Norwegian words *sla låm*, or 'slope track', which originally referred to a nordic ski competition that wove over hill and dale, dodging thickets! In 1928, 1932 and 1936, Sonja Henie was the Olympic figure skating gold medallist; speed-skater Johann Koss won three gold medals at the Viking Ship Arena in Hamar. At the 1998 Olympics, cross-country skier, Bjoern Daehlie, won his seventh gold medal, making him the most successful athlete in Winter Olympics history.

In winter, big ski-jumping events normally take place at Holmenkollen near Oslo, and other winter events occur at the Olympic venues in Hamar and Lillehammer.

Football is another hugely popular winter sport. In the 1990s the Norwegian men's national football (soccer) team maintained a top-20 FIFA ranking, although by September 2004 this had fallen to 38th. After qualifying for the 1994 and 1998 World Cups (at the latter they even defeated Brazil) they then failed to qualify for both the 2002 World Cup and 2004 European Championships, casting a pall of gloom over the sport in Norway. The bulk of Norway's national team stars play for Premier League teams in the UK (Ole Gunnar Solskjær scored the dramatic winner for Manchester United in the 1999 European Champions League Final), while back at home, Trondheim's Rosenberg team has dominated domestic competition.

However, it's the Norwegian women's national team that has strutted the world stage with most success, clinching the Women's World Cup in 1995, the gold medal at the Sydney Olympics in 2000 and now ranks third in the world rankings of women's footballing nations. Their best-known players were Heidi Stoere, who played 151 times for Norway between 1980 and 1997, and Bente Nordby, the goalkeeper who saved US superstar Mia Hamm's penalty en route to a famous tournament victory.

DID YOU KNOW?

After finishing second to Germany in Nagano in 1998, Norway topped the medal count in the Salt Lake City 2002 Winter Olympics, taking home 13 gold medals in a total medal count of 25.

MULTICULTURALISM

The thing that strikes many first-time visitors to Norway is how positively monocultural it all is. Norway's complicated approach to immigration sends out numerous conflicting messages. Immigration is strictly controlled and only bona fide refugees (ie those who have applied for and been granted refugee status with the UN elsewhere), not asylum seekers are admitted. While there is an argument to be made that the policy is, especially given Norway's wealth, mean-spirited and geared towards maintaining social homogeneity, it's also true that few nations contribute as much money to foreign aid and refugee programmes as does the Norwegian government.

Eugenics and the Welfare State, by Gunnar Broberg and Nils Roll-Hansen, is a disturbing historical account of Norwegian attitudes to foreigners and its implications for multiculturalism in Norway.

Those that *are* allowed into Norway – mostly from Somalia, Bosnia, Kosovo, Sri Lanka and other seriously troubled areas – are overwhelmingly concentrated in Oslo and arrive with the knowledge that the government is keen to repatriate them as soon as possible. In May 2004, the Norwegian prime minister Kjell Magne Bondevik rejected a plan to turn empty, disused churches into mosques, claiming that it was not 'the most natural' solution.

The deeply rooted Norwegian belief in fairness also came to the fore with widespread outrage in August 2001 when the Norwegian ship Tampa was refused entry to Australian waters because it had rescued some 400 asylum seekers off the Australian coast. There was more hand-wringing eight months earlier when a mixed-race youth was stabbed to death outside his Oslo home in Norway's first racially motivated murder.

If you're suffocating from all the sameness, visit Oslo's Grønland District, behind the Oslo S train station and which is, depending on your perspective, an immigrants' ghetto or a refreshingly heterogeneous and multicultural place.

A PRAIRIE HOME COMPANION

While modern Norway has a wary relationship with immigrants from non-European cultures, Norwegian emigration to the USA from the 19th century has fostered a flourishing Norwegian culture in the diaspora. The unofficial voice of Norwegian-American culture is the radio show *A Prairie Home Companion (PHC)*. First broadcast in 1974 in the heavily ethnic-Norwegian state of Minnesota, it's now one of the most popular shows on the US National Public Radio network, a two-hour Saturday evening ritual for some three million listeners in Norway, equal to two-thirds the population of Norway!

Comedic sound effects and interludes of old-time and folk music frame skits with characters like Guy Noir Private Eye and the cultured cowboys Dusty and Lefty; faux advertisements pitch Bertha's Kitty Boutique (for persons who care about cats) and the Ketchup Advisory Board. The annual joke show teems with titters about Norwegians (and other ethnicities, which would be politically incorrect without Public Radio's upscale imprimatur), and *PHC* is not above occasional excretory humour.

The show's Norwegian heart is the weekly news from Lake Wobegon (also a classic book by the same name), a tiny, fictional town in Minnesota's wind- and snow-swept north, where 'all the women are strong, all the men are good looking, and all the children are above average'. Taciturn Norwegian bachelor farmers observe the world from the Chatterbox Café, and locals ice-fish, eat *lutefisk* and fill the Church of Our Lady of Perpetual Responsibility. The town's best-known landmark is the Tomb of the Unknown Norwegian, and its leading civic organisation is the Sons of Knute.

PHC's Norwegian-ness is all the more remarkable given that its host, originator and chief writer, Garrison Keillor, is of Scottish descent. He also contributes to the *New Yorker* and *Time* magazines.

Emigration from Norway

No discussion of multiculturalism would be complete without mentioning the phenomenon of Norwegian emigration (800,000 to the USA and Canada alone in the 19th and early 20th centuries). Across the world you'll find people with Norwegian ancestry, many of whom visit Norway in search of their origins. If your story is a part of Norway's history, check out the excellent pamphlet *How to Trace Your Ancestors in Norway*, available on the Internet at www.ide-as.com/fndb/howto.html; the website also has excellent advice and links to websites where you can refine your search.

Other sources of help include the **Norwegian Emigrant Museum** (Norsk Utvandrermuseum; ☎ 62 57 48 50; www.museumsnett.no/emigrantmuseum) in Hamar and the **Norwegian Emigration Centre** (☎ 51 53 88 60; www.emigrationcenter.com) in Stavanger.

A Prairie Home Companion (http//:prairiehome.publicradio.org) is the site for Norway's favourite radio programme, with excerpts from archived episodes and how to get into the Lake Wobegon experience.

RELIGION

Some 86% of the Norwegian population nominally belongs to the Church of Norway, with the remainder (mostly in Oslo) comprising other Christian denominations, including around 40,000 Roman Catholics, as well as over 50,000 Muslims and around 1000 Jews.

Christianity

Christianity in Norway dates back over a thousand years and one of the country's earliest kings, Olav II was canonised by the Catholic Church. However, modern Norwegian Christianity has been most influenced by the German reformer Martin Luther, whose Protestant doctrines were adopted in Norway in 1537.

Today, the Church of Norway is the national denomination of Protestant Evangelical Lutheranism and the Norwegian constitution states:

'All inhabitants of the Realm shall have the right to free exercise of their religion. The Evangelical-Lutheran religion shall remain the official religion of the State. The inhabitants professing it are bound to bring up their children in the same.' So much for complete freedom of religion!

Like in the UK, the King of Norway is also the official head of the Church and has the final say in all controversial decisions. This power was dramatically exercised in 1961, when King Olav V appointed the country's first woman priest and again in 1993, when King Harald V sanctioned the first female bishop. Even more controversial was the occasion in the 1970s when a bishop and quite a few priests quit after the *Storting* (parliament), with royal sanction, passed a liberal abortion law. A good proportion of the populace scarcely noticed the issue, but a few more pious parishioners decided that the Church was Christian in name more than practice and withdrew.

While the average Norwegian attends church about twice a year and the organisation funds missions around the world, as many as 5000 Norwegians leave the official church annually, most of them advocating a separation of church and state.

Sami

Historically, the Sami religious traditions were characterised mainly by a relationship to nature and its inherent god-like archetypes. In sites of special power, particularly prominent rock formations, people made offerings to their gods and ancestors to ensure success in hunting or other endeavours. Intervention and healing were effected by shamanic specialists, who used drums and small figures to launch themselves onto out-of-body journeys to the ends of the Earth in search of answers. As with nearly all indigenous peoples in the northern hemisphere, the bear, as the most powerful creature in nature, was considered a sacred animal.

Historically, another crucial element in the religious tradition was the singing of the *joik* (also spelt *yoik*), or 'song of the plains'. Each person had his or her own melody or song which conveyed not their personality or experiences, but rather their spiritual essence. So powerful and significant was this personal mantra that the early Christian missionaries considered it a threat to their efforts and banned it as sinful.

Although most modern Sami profess Christianity, elements of the old religion have recently made a limited comeback.

WOMEN IN NORWAY

According to the UN, Norway is one of the best places in the world to be a woman. In the 2004 Gender-Related Development Index (an adjunct of the overall Human Development Index), Norway ranked first in the world. In addition to a raft of beneficial social welfare provisions, Norway has a female labour force participation rate of nearly 80%, well above the EU and Organisation for Economic Cooperation and Development (OECD) average (60%). Some 79% of married women with children under the age of six work in paid employment, although more than half of these (53%) work part-time. In 2003 there were 102 women in primary, secondary or tertiary education for every 94 men.

In spite of such positive statistics, there remain areas where Norwegian women are far from equal with their male counterparts. In the field of employment, women's annual incomes (US$31,356) still lag behind those of men (US$42,340) even though equal pay is mandated by law under gender equality legislation. In March 2002, on the occasion of International Women's Day, the government announced that 40% of

DID YOU KNOW?

To be officially considered Sami, a person must speak Sami as their first language, consider themselves a member of the Sami community and live in accordance with that society, or have a parent who satisfies either condition.

DID YOU KNOW?

In the 1993 election all three party leaders were women, and, after the 2001 elections, 36.4% of national MPs were women (compared with 48.8% in Rwanda, 45% in Sweden, 17.9% in the UK and just 14.3% in the USA).

board members of companies would have to be women (in 2002, just 6.6% of board members in public stock companies were women); less than 20% of senior leadership positions in universities and other areas of the public sector were held by women. Domestic violence also remains a serious problem; in 2002, 10,000 women sought medical treatment as a result of abuse in the home.

ARTS
Literature
MEDIEVAL NORSE LITERATURE
Norwegian literature dates over a thousand years to the sagas of the Vikings. The two mainstays of the genre are skaldic poetry (the *skalds*, the metaphoric and alliterative works of Norwegian court poets in the 9th and 10th centuries) and eddic poetry (named after the *Edda*, the most important collection of medieval Icelandic literature). The latter, which combines Christian with pre-Christian elements, is the most extensive source of information on Norse mythology, but it wasn't written down until Snorre Sturluson recorded it in the 13th century, long after the Christianisation of both Norway and Iceland. Its subject matter includes the story of the origin, history and end of the world, instructions on writing poetry, and a series of disconnected aphorisms attributed to the god Oðinn. Apart from the *Edda* itself, there are three forms of eddic poetry: legendary sagas, heroes' sagas, and didactic poetry.

NORWAY'S NOBEL PRIZE WINNERS
Near the end of the 19th century, Norwegian literature gained international prominence with the work of 'four great ones': Henrik Ibsen (1828–1906; see the boxed text, p44), Bjørnstjerne Bjørnson (1832–1910), Alexander Kjelland (1849–1906) and Jonas Lie (1833–1908). Although Ibsen receives the most attention today, the prolific Bjørnson became hugely popular with his story *Trust and Trial* in 1857. His considerable body of work documented vignettes of rural life (for which he was falsely accused of romanticising the lot of rural Norwegians), before turning his attention to social problems in the hope of promoting industrialisation in Norway. In 1903, he was the first Norwegian writer to be awarded the Nobel Prize for Literature.

www.norway.org.uk /culture/ is an excellent government site with details of upcoming cultural events to recent news and comprehensive cultural background information.

Sigrid Undset (1882–1949) received the Nobel Prize in 1920 and is often cited as the most significant female writer in Norwegian literature. Undset began her career with a series of books on the plight of poor and middle-class women and between 1920 and 1922, she published the *Kristin Lavransdottir* trilogy, a historical novel set in 14th century Scandinavia. Although much more optimistic than her earlier work, Undset continued to criticise the fact that women must subject their will and sexuality to social and religious standards. *Kristin Lavransdottir* was followed by the *Master of Hestviken* series, which was also set in medieval times.

www.ibsen.net has everything you needed to know about Norway's foremost playwright with an exhaustive encyclopaedia section and loads of links.

A generation after these writers, the work of the hugely controversial Knut Hamsun (1859–1952), who won the Nobel Prize in 1928, can be divided into three periods. Most of his early work, including his great novels *Hunger* (1890) and *Mysteries* (1892), features romantic heroes, tragic love stories and psychological examination. Later, Hamsun wrote a number of social novels which praised rural life and criticised industrialisation and urbanisation, notably *The Growth of the Soil* (1917). Hamsun's elitism, his appreciation of Germanic values and his idealisation of rural life led him to side with the Nazis in WWII, forever darkening his reputation with Norwegians. Only now is he being recognised as belonging to the tradition of Dostoevsky and Joyce as a significant contributor to literary modernism.

CONTEMPORARY LITERATURE

The vast corpus of contemporary Norwegian literature has yet to be translated into English. Knud Faldbakken's *Twilight Country*, and its sequel *Sweetwater*, portray futuristic apocalyptic visions, which stand in stark contrast to *The Sleeping Prince* which retells the fairy-tale *Sleeping Beauty* from a woman's perspective.

Herrbjørg Wassmo, one of several prominent modern female writers, received the Nordic Prize for Literature in 1987. Her books centre around the plight of women and damaged children in Norwegian society. *Dina's Book* tells the eponymous heroine's story in 1840s Norway, while *The House with the Blind Glass Windows* is set in and after WWII.

Another accessible and increasingly world-renowned author is Jostein Gaarder. His first bestselling novel, *Sophie's World* (1991) sold over 15 million copies and has been translated into over 40 languages. The novel addresses serious philosophical and religious issues with multiple layers of narrative and all seen through the eyes of a young adult. Other Gaader works, including *The Solitaire Mystery* and *The Christmas Mystery* similarly rely on the voice of a child protagonist who must solve some riddle to determine his or her destiny. More recently, *That Same Flower* purports to be the translation of a letter from Floria Aemilia to her lover Saint Augustine. In this feminist guise – giving Augustine's asceticism and ideals a distinctly unusual twist – Gaarder raises familiar issues such as the existence of God and the point of human life.

Jan Kjærstad's *The Seducer* (2003) somehow manages to combine the necessary recipes for a bestseller – a thriller with a love affair and a whiff of celebrity – with seriously good writing that won the 1999 Nordic Prize for Literature and a host of other international prizes. Trailing in its wake are searing critical portraits of many aspects of Norwegian society.

Music

CLASSICAL MUSIC

The 19th century was an extraordinarily rich time for Norwegian music. Edvard Grieg (see the boxed text, p181) gained world renown, which still holds as one of history's greatest composers. The considerable talent of his contemporaries, Halfdan Kierulf and Johan Svendsen, saw the 1870s and 1880s labelled the 'Golden Age' of Norwegian music. However, the virtuoso violinist Ole Bull (see the boxed text, p180), known throughout Europe as the 'Nordic Paganini', had an arguably more significant role to play. Bull is credited with critically encouraging the careers of Edvard Grieg, Henrik Ibsen (see the boxed text, p44), bringing the Hardanger-area folk fiddlers to Bergen concert halls and reviving Europewide interest in Norwegian folk music. His impact upon Norwegian culture is difficult to overestimate. Indeed, Bull and Grieg were central to the nascent sense of a Norwegian identity separate from the rest of Scandinavia, which followed Norwegian independence in 1905.

Classical music remains very much alive in Norway with fine philharmonic orchestras in Oslo, Bergen (which dates from 1765), Trondheim and Stavanger and the Norwegian Opera Company (established in 1958). In addition to Grieg, watch out for the works of other Norwegian composers such as David Monrad Johansen, Geirr Tveitt, Fartein Valen and Pauline Hall, with more recent works, many of which

Dollar Road, by Kjartan Flogstad, is an expansive portrayal of the transformation of small-town Norway from a rural to an industrialised society and written in an engaging, magic-realist style.

Norwegian Folk Tales, by Peter Christen Asbjornsen and Jørgen Moe, is a colourful and definitive gathering of trolls, elves, witches and princesses; anything else written by the authors is also worth tracking down.

bear unmistakable traces of folk music roots, by Hanson, Kvandal and Søderlind also possible.

MODERN FOLK, JAZZ & FUSION
For those who like their music with a more contemporary twist, Norwegian jazz saxophonist Jan Garbarek is one of the world music scene's hottest properties, having recorded in collaboration with Pakistani qawwali superstar Nusrat Fateh Ali Khan and Sami *(Ragas & Sagas)* and with the acclaimed Tunisian oud player, Anouar Brahem *(Ustad Shaukat Hussein-Madar)*. His other works, include *Twelve Moons* and *I Took up the Runes*. Another wonderful fusion of Norwegian folk music, this time with the Senegalese kora player Solo Cissokho, *From Senegal to Setesdal* is well worth picking up. Knut Reierstad and Hans Fredrik Jacobsen have also distinguished themselves by wedding traditional Norwegian music to the Nepalese sounds of Vajra on *Himalaya Blues*.

If you prefer your folk music to be uncontaminated by foreign sounds, the following contemporary works should satisfy: Tore Bruvoll and Jon Anders Halvorsen's traditional Telemark songs *(Nattsang)*; the live Norwegian performances of Bukkene Bruse (heavy on the Hardanger fiddle; *Spel*); Rusk's impressively wide repertoire of music from southeastern Norway *(Rusk)*; Sigrid Moldestad and Liv Merete Kroken who bring classical training to bear on the traditional fiddle *(Spindel)*; while Sinikka Langeland's *Runoja* draws on ancient runic music.

The haunting music of the Sami people of northern Norway is also enjoying a revival. Recent Sami artists such as Aulu Gaup, Mari Boine Persen and Nils Aslak Valkeapääs have performed, recorded and popularised traditional and modern versions of the traditional *joik*, or personal songs; Boine in particular has enjoyed international airtime. For further information on the role of music in Sami culture, see p38 and the boxed text, p348.

All right, if we must. No discussion of Norwegian music would be complete without mentioning A-ha, the big Norwegian band of the 1980s.

MUSIC FESTIVALS
Norway has some excellent music festivals which include jazz festivals in Molde, Kongsberg and Oslo; blues festivals in Notodden and Voss; a chamber music festival in Risør; a Scandinavian-oriented contemporary music festival in Oslo; and the diverse musical charms of Bergen's International Festival.

www.norwayfestivals .com/index.cfm has a fairly exhaustive list of Norway's multitude of festivals, most of which have a strong cultural bent, including literature, music and theatre.

Architecture
Norway's vast timber resources provided the raw material for much of Norway's traditional architecture. In the far north, where both wood and stone were in short supply, the early nomadic Sami ingeniously built their homes of turf which provided excellent insulation against the cold.

Most larger religious buildings were also constructed in stone and employed strong Anglo-Saxon influences (Christianity was, after all, imported into Norway from England). Notable exceptions include the Gothic-style Nidaros Cathedral in Trondheim and the Romanesque Stavanger Cathedral.

Other places of significant architectural distinction include the 58 charming Unesco World Heritage–listed trading warehouses of Bryggen in Bergen and the Art Nouveau splendour of Ålesund, which was completely rebuilt after a devastating fire in 1904.

However, if Norway can be said to have made one stand-out contribution to world architecture, it is undoubtedly the stave church. Seemingly conceived by a whimsical, child-like imagination, the stave church is an ingenious adaptation to unique local conditions. Originally dating from the late Viking Age, these ornately worked wooden houses of worship are among the oldest surviving wooden buildings on Earth, albeit heavily restored. Named for their vertical supporting posts, these churches are distinguished by detailed carved designs, dragon-headed gables resembling the prows of classic Viking ships and by their undeniably beautiful, almost Asian forms. Of the 500 to 600 which were originally built, only about 20 of those that remain retain many of their original components. The most exquisite stave churches are at Heddal, the Fantoft Stave Church near Bergen, Ringebu and, the oldest of them all, the Unesco World Heritage–listed Urnes Stave Church. For more information about stave church construction, see the boxed text, p219.

After all the destruction wrought by WWII, Norway's architecture was governed by functionalist necessity rather than any coherent sense of style. Nowhere is this exemplified more than in the 1950, red-brick Oslo Rådhus.

For a comprehensive run-down on historical and contemporary Norwegian architecture, visit the excellent Norwegian Museum of Architecture.

Painting & Sculpture

Folk art has been part of Norwegian life since the ancient hunters told their stories in carved stone, with the most accessible remnants including the rock carvings of Alta and the stylised Bronze Age artefacts uncovered with the *Oseberg* ship.

Centuries later, 19th century Norway gave birth to two extraordinary talents: painter Edvard Munch (see the boxed text, p43) and sculptor Gustav Vigeland (see the boxed text, p80). So individual was their style, however, that their unique works had little effect on future Norwegian artistic directions.

Gustav Vigeland – The Sculptor and His Works, by Ragna Thus Stan, is the definitive summary of the life and work of one of the world's most innovative sculptors.

During the early 20th century, the impressionist Henri Matisse inspired several ardently decorative Norwegian artists. Axel Revold, Per Krohg and Alf Rolfsen soon came to be known as the 'fresco brothers'. Another pupil of Matisse, Henrik Sørensen, served unofficially as the 'club's' fourth member.

During the postwar years, the brooding forests of Jakob Weidemann, the constructivist paintings of Gunnar S Gundersen, and the literal (nonfigurative) sculptures of Arnold Haukeland and Åse Texmon Rygh dominated the visual arts scene.

Edvard Munch, by JP Hodin, is a terrific introduction to the life and work of Norway's pre-eminent painter, with examples of his work and anecdotes from the author who was a contemporary of Munch.

By the 1990s, the arts were receiving substantial government funding. Among those who benefited were Olav Jensen, Anne Dolven, Ørnulf Opdahl, Bjørn Tufta, Håvard Vikhagen and Andres Kjær, most of whose work represented a return to abstract and expressionist forms, with harsh depictions of the Norwegian landscape the norm. Norwegian sculptors who distinguished themselves in the 1990s included Bård Breivik, who studied the relationships between humans and their tools, and Per Inge Bjørlo, whose woodcuts and linotype prints depict in primitive form both people and animals. Odd Nerdrum's provocative paintings have also brought him to the attention of many people, both home and abroad.

For the best overview of Norwegian art, visit the National Gallery in Oslo, the Rogaland Art Museum or the Bergen Art Museum. The best collections of contemporary Norwegian art are on display at National Museum of Contemporary Art, the Astrup Fearnley Museum and the Henie-Onstad Art Centre, all of which are in Oslo.

EDVARD MUNCH

Edvard Munch (1863–1944), Norway's most renowned painter and one of Europe's great mas-ters, was a tortured soul. His acquaintance with the darker emotions began with his Christiania (Oslo) childhood: his mother died of tuberculosis when Edvard was just five, his elder sister likewise succumbed at the age of 15, and his younger sister was diagnosed with mental illness as a young girl.

Munch spent his early years as a painter in Paris where he was greatly influenced by the French Realist school, and there he produced his first great work, *The Sick Child,* a portrait of his sister Sophie shortly before her death. So provocative was the painting that professional criticism was largely negative.

After returning to Christiania, he fell in with a bohemian crowd whose influence exacerbated his natural tendency for darker themes. He returned to Paris, where he learned of the death of his father, and in 1890, he produced the haunting painting *Night,* depicting a lonely figure in a dark window. The following year he finished *Melancholy* and began sketches of what would be his best known work, *The Scream,* which graphically represents Munch's own inner torment.

In 1892, Munch moved to Berlin where he buried himself in a cycle of angst-ridden, atmos-pheric themes that he would collectively entitle *Frieze of Life – A Poem about Life, Love and Death.* The series included *Starry Night, Moonlight, The Storm, Vampire, Ashes, Anxiety* and *Death in the Sickroom.* His obsession with darkness and doom went from dominating his work to casting a long shadow over his life. Alcoholism, chronic emotional instability and a tragic love affair culminated in the 1907 work, *Death of Marat,* and, a year later, he checked into a Copenhagen mental health clinic for eight months.

After leaving the clinic, Munch returned to Norway, where he settled on the coast at Kragerø. It became clear that Munch's postclinic work was to be altogether different, dominated by a sun-nier, more hopeful disposition dedicated to humans in harmony with their landscape. Perhaps the most emblematic of Munch's paintings from this period is *History,* which portrays an elderly man beneath a spreading oak tree, relating the history of humanity to a young child.

Upon his death, Munch bequeathed his body of works to the City of Oslo, and they're now on display at the National Gallery, the Munch Museum and Bergen Art Museum, although not always as securely as art lovers would hope – see the boxed text, p73.

Cinema

Norway has a small but internationally acclaimed film industry. Spear-heading the industry's claims to international recognition, is Nils Gaup, who received an Oscar nomination for *The Pathfinder,* which is based on a medieval legend and presented in the Sami language. Gaup's next film, *Håkon Håkonsson,* was funded by Disney and told the story of a 19th century Norwegian Robinson Crusoe who set off for the South Seas.

The prolific Arne Skouen, a *Dagbladet* newspaper columnist who made 17 films between 1948 and 1968, was similarly honoured with an Oscar nomination for *Nine Lives,* a story set during the German occupation and which follows a soldier put ashore on the stormy northern coast of Norway as he attempts to reach neutral Sweden.

Another of Norway's premier directors is Anja Breien, who launched her successful career in the mid-1970s with *Jostedalsrypa,* portraying a young 14th century Norwegian girl who was the only survivor of the Black Death in the western Norwegian valley, Jostedalen. Since then, Breien has made an acclaimed trilogy *Wives, Wives 10 Years After* and *Wives III,* with a fourth instalment planned for 2005. Breien's greatest critical successes, however, are probably *Next of Kin,* which was featured at the Cannes Film Festival in 1979, and *Witch Hunt,* which took awards at the Venice Film Festival in 1982.

Wives, Wives 10 Years After and *Wives III,* directed by Anja Breien, is a trilogy about three Norwegian women who return to their school reunions and discuss their lives offering fascinating insights into the evolving experiences of Norwegian women.

HENRIK IBSEN

Henrik Johan Ibsen, Norway's most famous playwright, was born in Skien in 1828. By the age of 15, difficult family circumstances had forced him to Grimstad where he worked as a pharmacist's apprentice. In his spare time, Ibsen, who failed both Greek and mathematics and thereafter abandoned plans to become a doctor, wrote poetry which caught the eye of the violinist Ole Bull (see the boxed text, p180) who steered the impressionable young Ibsen toward the theatre.

Ibsen worked for six years with the theatre in Bergen, followed by five years in Christiania (Oslo), where he acquired a sharp eye for theatrical technique. His masterpiece during this period, *The Pretenders* (1863), takes place in 13th century Norway, with King Håkon Håkonsson expressing anachronistic dreams of national unity.

From 1864, Ibsen lived and studied in Rome, Dresden and Munich, decrying the small-mindedness of Norwegian society of the day; so disenchanted was he by his homeland that he wouldn't return home until 1891, at the age of 63. In his later works, notably *Brand* (1866), *Emperor and Galilean* (1873), *Pillars of Society* (1877), the highly provocative *Ghosts* (1881), *An Enemy of the People* (1882), *The Wild Duck* (1884) and *Hedda Gabler* (1890), he achieved a more realistic dialogue and came to be known as the father of modern Norwegian drama.

Above all others, however, the enormously popular *Peer Gynt* (1867) was Ibsen's international breakthrough, especially when set to the music of Edvard Grieg. In this enduring epic, an ageing hero returns to his Norwegian roots after wandering around the world and is forced to face his own soul. As he looks back on a wasted life of travel and his fruitless search for truth, his essence peels away like the skin of an onion, ultimately revealing no core to his personality.

In the similarly acclaimed *The Doll's House* (1879), Ibsen successfully explored the doctrine of critical realism and the experiences of the individual in the face of the majority. As his protagonist Nora puts it: 'I will have to find out who is right, society or myself.' As a result, Nora has become a symbol for women who sacrifice family life to struggle for equality and liberation.

In his last drama, the semi-autobiographical *When We Dead Awaken*, Ibsen describes the life of the estranged artist, sculptor Professor Rubek, who returns to Norway in his later years but finds no happiness, having forsaken his only love and his youth to misplaced idealism.

Ibsen became a partial invalid after suffering a heart attack in 1901 and died five years later.

The strong social context of Norwegian film-making also found expression in the works of Marius Holst, who made the 1995 Berlin Festival winner, *Blue Angel*, depicting childhood conflicts in Oslo; and Berit Nesheim's *Frida*, known for its searing portrayal of adolescence. A lighter view of childhood is evident in the work of Ivo Caprino, who specialises in animation and Norwegian fairy tales, notably the humorous cartoon film, *Pinchcliff Grand Prix*.

Of the international films which have been shot in Norway, Sigrid Undset's *Kristin Lavransdottir*, which starred the Norwegian actress Liv Ullman and was directed by Sweden's Ingmar Bergman, is probably the most famous. The film *Black Eyes*, by Russian director Nikita Michalkhov, was filmed in the spectacular landscapes around Kjerringøy in Nordland.

Theatre & Dance

Traditional folk dancing and singing is enjoying something of a resurgence in popularity and numerous festivals feature these elements. Ring dances such as roundels, pols, reinlenders, polkas and mazurkas fell into disuse in the 18th century, but they re-emerged around the time of independence in 1905, when the country was seeking a distinctive national identity. Today, troupes of *leikarringer* (folk dancers) practise all over the country and compete in *kappleiker* (dance competitions), which attract large audiences. These festivities are often accompanied by traditional instruments such as the unique Hardanger fiddle, which derives its distinctive sound from four or five sympathetic strings stretched out beneath the usual four strings. The best place to catch performances of live folklore in summer is Bergen.

Oslo, Bergen and other larger towns have theatre, opera and ballet companies. Classical performances take place in summer in Bergen, including a number of evocative outdoor settings, but elsewhere most are in winter, when outdoor activities are limited, and sadly, few visitors are around to enjoy them.

Environment

THE LAND

The simple facts of Norway's geography – a land area of 385,155 sq km and borders with Sweden, Finland and Russia – only tell a small part of the country's spectacular natural history.

The Coast

A good place to start forming a picture of Norway's unique landforms is by looking at a map. Seeming to wrap itself around Scandinavia like a protective shield from the freezing Arctic, Norway's coastline – 57,000km long – appears to have shattered under the strain, riven as it is with islands and fjords (long, narrow inlets of the sea bordered by high, steep cliffs) cutting deep fissures inland.

Although Norwegian geological history stretches back 1.8 billion years when the Pre-Cambrian rocks in southern Norway were a late addition to the Baltic Shield (the core of the European continent), the process of fjord formation is decidedly more recent. During the glacial periods of the past 1.8 million years, the elevated highland plateaus subsided at least 700m due to an ice sheet up to 2000m thick. The movement of this ice, which was driven by gravity down former river courses, gouged out the fjords and valleys and created the surrounding mountains by sharpening peaks and exposing high cliffs of bare rock. The bulk of the ice melted about 8800 years ago, with the end of the last ice age, and Norway is currently experiencing an interglacial period. As a result, only a few remnant icecaps and valley glaciers remain on the mainland.

Some of the islands along the far northern coast – notably Lofoten and Vesterålen – are largely comprised of granite and gneiss. Another island of the far north, Svalbard, is geologically independent from the rest of Europe and sits on the Barents continental plate deep in the polar region. While the remainder of Norway's ice fields struggle to survive, Svalbard still experiences dramatic glaciation. Sedimentary rock layers in Svalbard include fossils and coal.

However Norway's geology may have evolved, the process has certainly proved profitable. In the North Sea lie two rift valleys which contain upper Jurassic shale bearing the rich deposits of oil and gas that are now being exploited, making Norway one of the world's largest exporters of petroleum products.

Inland

If you think Norway is spectacular now, try to imagine what it must have been like 450 million years ago when the Caledonian Mountain Range, which ran along the length of Norway, was as high as the present-day Himalayas. With time, ice and water eroded them down to their current altitude. Before you get too disappointed, remember that mountain ranges, some capped with Europe's largest glaciers and ice fields, cover more than half the land mass – great news for tourists and adventure seekers, less so for farmers with less than 3% of Norwegian soil suitable for agriculture. Norway's highest mountains are in the Jotunheimen National Park where Galdhøpiggen soars to a 'mere' 2469m.

A little known fact about Norway is that it contains some of the highest waterfalls and glacial streams in the world, hardly surprising given its combination of mountains and wet climate. Some authorities place the

Northern Lights: The Science, Myth, and Wonder of Aurora Borealis, by Calvin Hall et al, combines hard science with historical legend to help unlock one of Norway's great mysteries.

glacial stream Utigårdsfossen, which flows into Nesdalen and Lovatnet from Jostedalsbreen (not readily accessible to tourists) as the second or third highest in the world at 800m, with a greatest vertical drop of 600m. However, most listings count the following Norwegian waterfalls among the 10 highest in the world: Mongefossen in Romsdal (774m; now dry due to hydroelectric developments); Mardalsfossen in Eikesdal (655m); and Tyssestrengene (646m in multiple cascades), near Odda.

There's one final natural phenomenon which fascinates us all: nearly a third of Norway lies north of the Arctic Circle, which links places at which there is at least one full day when the sun never sets and one day when it never rises.

No Man's Land, by Martin Conway, is one of the finest works on Norway's exotic Arctic wonderland detailing the history of Svalbard from its discovery to the present day.

WILDLIFE

Despite sparse wildlife populations when compared with neighbouring Sweden and Finland, Norway's diverse landscapes and altitude ranges harbour a wide variety of species, including a number of signature creatures such as the reindeer, elk, lemming and musk oxen.

For excellent catalogues of natural history books and field guides, including some Scandinavian titles try the following:

Adventurous Traveler Bookstore (☎ 800 282 3963; www.adventuroustraveler.com; based in the USA)

Andrew Isles Natural History Books (☎ 03-9510 5750; www.andrewisles.com; based in Australia)

Subbuteo Natural History Books (☎ 0870-0109 700; www.wildlifebooks.com; based in the UK)

Animals

Norway's unique settlement pattern, which spreads the human population thinly throughout the country, limits wildlife habitat and restricts numbers, but there's still plenty to see.

LAND MAMMALS

The smaller mammal species are the most prevalent, although you're unlikely to see them unless you get away from the main roads and hiking routes.

Hare (Arctic hares) are found throughout the country, typically on moors or mountain grassland and sometimes in woodland. *Pinnsvin* (hedgehogs) are found south of Trøndelag. In southern Norway, forested and lake-studded areas support a good-sized *bever* (beaver) population, while *grevling* (badgers) are found in the river valleys and woods and *oter* (otters) frequent wooded watercourses and in the sea (except in north Finnmark).

Vesel (weasels) and *røyskatt* (stoats) are widespread in all districts; northern varieties turn white in winter, when they're known as ermine and are trapped for their fur. The more solitary *jerv* (wolverine), a larger cousin of the weasel, inhabits high mountain forests and low alpine areas, mainly near marshes and lakes in Nordland, eastern and central Norway. *Skogmår* (pine martens) are found in many damp forested areas south of Finnmark. Mink also like water and inhabit forested areas as far north as Tromsø.

Lemen (lemmings), which occupy mountain areas through 30% of the country, stay mainly around 800m altitude in the south and lower in the north. They measure up to 10cm and have soft orange-brown and black fur, beady eyes, a short tail and prominent upper incisors. If you encounter a lemming in the mountains, it may become enraged, hissing,

ARCTIC PHENOMENA

The Aurora Borealis

There are few sights as mesmerising as an undulating aurora. Although these appear in many forms – pillars, streaks, wisps and haloes of vibrating light – they're most memorable when they appear as pale curtains wafting on a gentle breeze. Most often, the Arctic aurora appears as a faint green or light rose but, in periods of extreme activity, can change to yellow or crimson.

The visible aurora borealis, or northern lights (in the southern hemisphere, the corresponding phenomenon is called the aurora australis), are caused by streams of charged particles from the sun, the solar wind, which are directed by the Earth's magnetic field towards the polar regions. Because the field curves downward in a halo surrounding the magnetic poles, the charged particles are drawn earthward. Their interaction with electrons in nitrogen and oxygen atoms in the upper atmosphere (about 160km above the surface) releases the energy creating the visible aurora. During periods of high activity, a single auroral storm can produce a trillion watts of electricity with a current of one million amps.

The Inuit (Eskimos) call the lights *arsarnerit* ('to play with a ball'), as they were thought to be ancestors playing ball with a walrus skull. It was believed that the lights could be attracted by whistling or repelled by barking like a dog. The Inuit also attach spiritual significance to the lights, and some believe that they represent the capering of unborn children; some consider them gifts from the dead to light the long polar nights and others see them as a storehouse of events, past and future.

The best time of year to catch the northern lights in Norway is from October to March, although you may also see them as early as August. Oddly enough, Svalbard is actually too far north to catch the greatest activity.

Midnight Sun & Polar Night

Because the Earth is tilted on its axis, the polar regions are constantly facing the sun at their respective summer solstices and are tilted away from it in the winter. The Arctic and Antarctic circles, at 66° 33′ north and south latitude respectively, are the southern and northern limits of constant daylight on the longest day of the year.

The northern half of mainland Norway, as well as Svalbard and Jan Mayan, lie north of the Arctic Circle but, even in southern Norway, the summer sun is never far below the horizon. Between late May and mid-August, nowhere in the country experiences true darkness and in Trondheim, for example, the first stars aren't visible until mid-August.

Conversely, winters here are dark, dreary and long, with only a few hours of twilight to break the long polar nights. In Svalbard, not even a twilight glow can be seen for over a month. During this period of darkness, many people suffer from SAD syndrome, or 'seasonal affective disorder'. Its effects may be minimised by using special solar spectrum light bulbs for up to 45 minutes

squeaking and attempting to attack! There's also *skoglemen* (a forest-dwelling version of lemmings), which is found near the Swedish border between Hedmark and Finnmark.

Norway's larger land mammals are what travellers get most excited about.

From the forests of the far south to southern Finnmark, *elg* (elk; moose in the USA) are fairly common, although given the Norwegian fondness for elk meat, they wisely tend to stay clear of people and roads.

After being hunted to the brink of extinction, the downright pre-historic *moskus-okse* (musk oxen) were re-introduced into Dovrefjell National Park from Greenland in the 1940s and have since extended their range to the Femundsmarka National Park near Røros. For more information, see the boxed text, p164.

Elk- and/or musk ox-viewing safaris are an easy way to catch sight of these striking and elusive creatures in Oppdal, Dombås, Evje and Hovden, among other places.

after waking up. Not surprisingly, most northern communities make a ritual of welcoming the sun the first time it peeks above the southern horizon.

Town	Latitude	Midnight Sun	Polar Night
Bodø	67° 18′	4 Jun to 8 Jul	15 Dec to 28 Dec
Svolvær	68° 15′	28 May to 14 Jul	5 Dec to 7 Jan
Narvik	68° 26′	27 May to 15 Jul	4 Dec to 8 Jan
Tromsø	69° 42′	20 May to 22 Jul	25 Nov to 17 Jan
Alta	70° 00′	16 May to 26 Jul	24 Nov to 18 Jan
Hammerfest	70° 40′	16 May to 27 Jul	21 Nov to 21 Jan
Nordkapp	71° 11′	13 May to 29 Jul	18 Nov to 24 Jan
Longyearbyen	78° 12′	20 Apr to 21 Aug	26 Oct to 16 Feb
Ny Ålesund	78° 55′	16 Apr to 25 Aug	22 Oct to 20 Feb

Fata Morgana

If the aurora inspires wonder, the Fata Morgana may prompt a visit to a psychiatrist. The clear and pure Arctic air doesn't cause distant features to appear out of focus. As a result, depth perception becomes impossible and the world takes on a strangely two-dimensional aspect where distances are indeterminable. Early explorers meticulously laid down on maps and charts islands, headlands and mountain ranges that were never seen again. An amusing example of distance distortion is described in the enigmatic book *Arctic Dreams*, by Barry Lopez:

> A Swedish explorer had all but completed a written description in his notebook of a craggy headland with two unusually symmetrical valley glaciers, the whole of it a part of a large island, when he discovered what he was looking at was a walrus.

Fata Morganas are apparently caused by reflections off water, ice and snow, and when combined with temperature inversions, create the illusion of solid, well-defined features where there are none. On clear days off the outermost coasts of Lofoten, Vesterålen, northern Finnmark and Svalbard, you may well observe inverted mountains or nonexistent archipelagos of craggy islands resting on the horizon. It's difficult indeed to convince yourself, even with an accurate map, that they're not really there!

Also unsettling are the sightings of ships, large cities and forests, where there could clearly be none. Normal visibility at sea is just under 18km, but in the Arctic, sightings of islands and features hundreds of kilometres distant are frequently reported.

Wild *reinsdyr* (reindeer) exist in large herds, usually above the tree line and sometimes as high up as 2000m across Central Norway, especially on the Hardangervidda plateau where you'll find Europe's largest herd, but also in Jotunheimen, Dovrefjell and inland areas of Trøndelag. The reindeer of Finnmark are owned by the Sami and most are driven to the coast at the start of summer, then back to the interior in winter. The smaller *svalbardrein* (Svalbard caribou) is native only to Svalbard.

State of the Environment Norway (www.environ ment.no) is a comprehensive site covering everything from bio-diversity and international agreements to statistics and Svalbard.

MARINE MAMMALS

The seas around Norway are rich fishing grounds, due to the ideal summer conditions for the growth of plankton. This wealth of nutrients also attracts baleen whales, which feed on the plankton, as well as toothed whales and seals, who feed mainly on the fish that eat the plankton. For more whale species see p52.

Minkehval (minke whales), one of the few whale species which is not endangered, measure around seven to 10m long and weigh between five and 10 tonnes. They're baleen whales, which means that they have plates of whalebone baleen rather than teeth, and migrate between the Azores area and Svalbard.

Between Ålesund and Varangerhalvøya, it's possible to see *knolhval* (humpback whales), toothed whales which measure up to 15m and weigh up to 30 tonnes. These are among the most acrobatic whales and often leap about and flap their flukes before sounding. They're also among the most vocal of whales, producing deep songs that can be heard and recorded hundreds of kilometres away.

Spekkhogger (killer whales), or orcas, are the top sea predators and measure up to 7m and weigh an astonishing five tonnes. There are around 1500 off the coast of Norway, swimming in pods of two or three. They eat fish, seals, dolphins, porpoise and whales (such as minke), which may be larger than themselves.

The long-finned *grindhval* (pilot whale), about 6m long, may swim in pods of up to several hundred and range as far north as Nordkapp. *Hvithval* (Belugas), which are up to 4m long, are found mainly in the Arctic Ocean and travel in pods of five to 10 or more.

The grey and white *narhval* (narwhal), which grows up to 3.5m long, is best recognised by the peculiar 2.7m spiral ivory tusk which projects from the upper lip of the males. This tusk is in fact one of the whale's two teeth and was prized in medieval times. Narwhal live mainly in the Arctic Ocean in pods of 15 to 20 and occasionally head upstream into freshwater.

Norway also has bottlenose, white-beaked, Atlantic white-sided and common dolphins.

Marine Mammals of the North Atlantic, by Carl Christian Kinze, is an excellent field guide to Norway's 51 marine mammals.

THE TRUTH ABOUT LEMMINGS

Few creatures have been so unjustly maligned as the humble lemming. We've all heard tales of hundreds of thousands of lemmings diving off cliffs to their deaths in a ritual of mass suicide. Some people also maintain that their bite is fatal and that they spread disease among the human population.

All you need to know about lemmings? Actually, no. Firstly, although lemmings can behave aggressively and ferociously (sometimes even when neither threatened nor cornered), there's no evidence that their bite is any more dangerous than that of other rodents, nor are they particularly prone to spreading any sort of disease.

As for their self-destructive behaviour, lemmings are known for their periodic mass movements every five to 20 years, when a particularly prolific breeding season results in overpopulation. Thanks to the increased numbers, the vegetation is decimated and food sources grow scarce, forcing lemming swarms (the last such plague was in 2001) to descend from the high country in search of other, less crowded high ground. Most meet an undistinguished fate, squashed on roads or eaten by predators and domestic animals. Indeed, for a couple of years following a lemming population surge, there will also be an increase in the population of such predators as foxes, buzzards and owls.

Quite often, however, the swarms head for the sea, and often do face high cliffs. When the press of their numbers builds up near the back of the ranks, the leaders may be forced over the edge. Also, inclement weather when crossing fjords or lakes can result in mass drownings. As unpleasant as the phenomenon may be, particularly for the lemmings, there's no evidence to suggest that lemmings are prone to suicide.

However, not all lemmings join the rush to near-certain death. The clever, more aggressive individuals who remain in the hills to guard their territories grow fat and happy, living through the winter under the snow and breeding the following year. Females as young as 15 days can become pregnant and most individuals give birth to at least two litters of five each year, thereby ensuring the survival of the species.

Seals are commonly seen near the seashore throughout Norway and even in some inland fjords. The main species include *steinkobbe* (harbour seals), *havert* (grey seals), *ringsel* (ringed seals), *grønlandssel* (harp seals), *klappmyss* (hooded seals) and *blåsel* (bearded seals). The much larger *hvalross* (walrus), which in Norway lives only in Svalbard, measures up to nearly 4m and weighs up to 1450kg. They're best identified by their ivory tusks, which are elongated canine teeth and can measure up to 1m long in the males. Although they were once heavily hunted for their ivory and blubber, since they became a protected species in 1952, their Svalbard population increased to around 1000.

FISH

Centuries of fishing have severely depleted fish stocks among species which were once the mainstays of the Norwegian economy. *Sild* (herring), *hellefisk* (halibut) and *lysing* (hake) have all been over-fished and are no longer abundant. Among freshwater fish, *laks* (salmon) are the most widespread and a large sport angling community ensures that the stocks are kept as healthy as possible. However, diseases are now spreading from farmed fish to the wild stocks, creating major problems in some areas; see the boxed text, p373 for information on how to protect salmon.

Cod: A Biography of the Fish that Changed the World, by Mark Kurlansky, is a lively and wonderfully idiosyncratic book, which is also hugely informative with everything you needed to know about the humble cod.

BIRDS

Norway makes an excellent venue for ornithologists, but the country attracts so many nesting species and permanent residents that it would be impossible to discuss them all in detail.

The best bird-watching sites include Revtangen (coastal Rogaland), Utsira (off the Rogaland coast), Fokstumyra (in Dovrefjell), Femundsmarka National Park (Hedmark), Runde (near Ålesund, with over 350,000 nesting pairs of sea birds), the islands of Nordland (especially Lovund, Træna, Røst, Værøy and Bleiksøya), Øvre Pasvik National Park (eastern Finnmark) and Svalbard (for visiting migratory species in summer).

The greatest bird populations in Norway are along the coastline, where millions of sea birds nest in coastal cliff faces and feed on fish and other sea life. The most prolific species include terns, *havsule* (gannets), *alke* (razorbills), *lundefugl* (puffins), *lomvi* and *teist* (guillemots), *havhest* (fulmar), *krykkje* (kittiwake), *tjuvjo* and *fjelljo* (skuas) and *alkekonge* (little auk).

The most dramatic of Norway's raptors is the lovely *havørn* (white-tailed eagle), the largest northern European raptor, with a wingspan of up to 2.5m, of which there are now at least 500 nesting pairs along the Nordland coast, as well as in parts of Troms and Finnmark. The *fjellvåk* (rough-legged buzzard) lives by hunting lemmings and voles in Arctic and alpine tundra areas. There are also about 500 pairs of *kongeørn* (golden eagle) in higher mountain areas. The rare *fiskeørn* (osprey) has a maximum population of 30 pairs and is seen only in heavily forested areas; your best chances of seeing one is in Stabbursdalen and Øvre Pasvik National Parks.

There are also at least four species of owls: *jordugle* (short-eared owls), found on marshy moors; *spurveugle* (pygmy owls), which like coniferous forests; *snøugle* (snowy owls), which prefer alpine tundra; and *hubro* (eagle owls), which reside in northern and mountain forests.

Especially in southern Norway, you'll also find the usual European variety of woodland birds. Very few of the spectacular *sidensvans* (waxwings) breed in Norway, but in winter they arrive from Russia in large numbers and may be observed in woods, parks and gardens.

Among the largest woodland birds are the *fjellrype* (ptarmigan) and two species of *orrfugl* and *jerpe* (grouse). The *skotsk lirype* (red grouse) prefers treeless moors and tundra while the bizarre *tiur* (capercaillie), which resembles a wild turkey or a modest peacock, struts around in coniferous forests.

The standout species among Norway's host of wading and water birds include the *storlom* (black-throated wading bird), *smålom* (red-throated diver) called 'loons' in North America, *horndykker* (horned grebes), *åkerrikse* (corncrakes) and Norway's national bird, the *fossekall* (dipper), which lives near and makes its living by diving into mountain streams.

ENDANGERED SPECIES

Centuries of hunting and accelerating human encroachment have pushed numerous animal species to the brink of extinction, although some have begun to make a recovery thanks to bans on hunting.

Bjørn (brown bears) have been persecuted for centuries, and while some remain in forested valleys along the Swedish border between Hedmark and Finnmark, Norway's only permanent population is in Øvre Pasvik National Park in eastern Finnmark.

Isbjørn (polar bears), the world's largest land carnivore, are found only in Svalbard, spending much of their time on pack or drift ice. Since the ban on hunting came into force in 1973, their numbers have increased to over 5000. Despite weighing up to 720kg and measuring up to 2.5m long, polar bears are swift and manoeuvrable, thanks to the hair on the soles of the their feet which facilitates movement over ice and snow and provides additional insulation. A polar bear's diet consists mostly of seals, beached whales, fish and birds, and only rarely do they eat reindeer or other land mammals (including humans). Polar bear milk contains 30% fat (the richest of any carnivorous land mammal), which allows newborn cubs to grow quickly and survive extremely cold temperatures. Thanks to this rich diet, one polar bear's liver contains enough vitamin D to kill a human who might be stupid enough to eat it.

As in most places, *ulv* (wolves) aren't popular with farmers or reindeer herders and hunters, and only a few still exist in the country (around Hamar and in Finnmark). They occasionally wander in from Russia and are normally shot due to a perceived risk of rabies.

A rare forest-dweller is the solitary lynx, Europe's only large cat.

Sadly, many years of whaling in the North Atlantic and Arctic oceans have reduced several whale species to perilously small populations. Apart from the minke whale, there's no sign that the numbers will ever recover in this area.

The endangered *seihval* (sei whale), a baleen whale, is found off the coast of Finnmark and is named because its arrival corresponds with that of the *sei* (pollack), which also comes to feast on the seasonal plankton. They measure up to 18m and weigh up to 30 tonnes (calves measure up to 5m at birth). The annual migration takes the *sei* from the seas off northwest Africa and Portugal (winter), up to the Norwegian Sea and southern Barents Sea in summer.

The *finhval* (fin whale) measures 24m and can weigh up to 80 tonnes. These whales were a prime target after the Norwegian Svend Føyn developed the exploding harpoon in 1864 and unregulated whalers left only a few thousand in the North Atlantic. Fin whales are also migratory, wintering between Spain and southern Norway and spending summer in northern Norway, Jan Mayen and Svalbard.

Spermsetthval (sperm whales), which measure up to 19m and can weigh up to 50 tonnes, are characterised by their odd squarish profile. They subsist mainly on fish and squid and usually live in pods of 15 to

'Isbjørn (polar bears), the world's largest land carnivore, are found only in Svalbard, spending much of their time on pack or drift ice'

20. Their numbers were depleted by whalers after whale oil and the valuable spermaceti wax from their heads. Fortunately, the fish-rich shoals off Vesterålen attract quite a few sperm whales and they're predictably observed on boat tours.

The largest animal on earth, the *blåhval* (blue whale), measures around 28m and weighs in at a staggering 110 tonnes. Although they can live to 80 years old, 50 is a more common upper limit. Heavily hunted for its oil, the species finally received protection from the International Whaling Commission in 1967 (far too late!). Prior to 1864, there were between 6000 and 9000, but only a few hundred remain in the world's oceans (although Norwegian estimates put the number at some 11,000). There has recently been some evidence that a few hardy blue whales are making a comeback in the northeast Atlantic.

The *grønlandshval* (bowhead whale), or Greenland right whale, was virtually annihilated by the end of the 19th century for its baleen, which was used in corsets, fans and whips. It was also targeted because they are slow swimmers and float when dead. In 1679, Svalbard had around 25,000 bowheads, but only a handful remain and worldwide numbers are critically low.

Plants

In general, Norwegian flora is typical of that in temperate climates, and includes around 250 species of flowering plants.

Alpine and arctic flowers dominate in the highlands and northern areas, while fertile areas at low elevation have well-mixed woodland, where the tree species include conifers, ash, elm, lime, oak, beech, Norway maple and alder. Fruit trees, such as apple and plum, are cultivated in sheltered coastal areas, particularly around Hardangerfjord. In mountainous areas of western Norway, the conifer- and birch-dominated woodlands climb to between 900m and 1200m. Offshore islands are less wooded, and in northern Nordland, Troms and southern Finnmark, the tree line may be as low as 200m to 300m.

Around the periphery of the high plateaus and around southern Norway, the forests include Scots pine, Norway spruce, aspen, silver birch, hazel, black alder, mountain ash, and in the higher altitudes, dwarf birch, willow and juniper.

Between the dwarf trees and the snow line, the main vegetation types are mosses, fungi and lichens. Mountain grasses grow mainly in boggy areas and high in the mountains, near the summer snow line, you'll find saxifrage and a range of smaller tundra plants.

Despite the harsh Arctic conditions, short growing season, severe winters, low precipitation, poor soils and prevailing permafrost, Svalbard has around 165 species of tiny ground-loving plants, including dwarf willow and polar birch and a variety of tundra flowers and lichens.

Hikers will find a profusion of berries, most of which grow low to the ground and ripen between mid-July and early September. The most popular edible varieties are blueberries (huckleberries), which grow on open uplands; blue swamp-loving bilberries; red high-bush and low-bush cranberries; muskeg crowberries; and the lovely amber-coloured cloudberries. The last, which are considered a delicacy, are known locally as *moltebær*, and grow one per stalk on open swampy ground. In the Arctic regions of neighbouring Sweden and Finland, nearly everyone takes to the outdoors in droves to pick this delicious bounty, but in Norway, some cloudberry patches are zealously guarded. For rules on picking cloudberries, see p60.

DID YOU KNOW?

Possibly the largest animal to ever inhabit the earth, the longest blue whale ever caught measured 33.58m; 50 people could fit on its tongue alone.

The Whaling Season – An Inside Account of the Struggle to Stop Commercial Whaling, by Kieran Mulvaney, is a passionate account of whaling by an experienced Greenpeace activist.

NATIONAL PARKS

Norway's 22 national parks (see the boxed text, p55 and map below) have been established to preserve wilderness areas and to protect wildlife and distinctive natural features of the landscape. In many cases, they don't protect any specific features, but rather, attempt to prevent development of remaining wild areas. As a result, park boundaries don't necessarily coincide with the incidence of spectacular natural features or ecosystem boundaries, but simply follow contour lines around uninhabited areas.

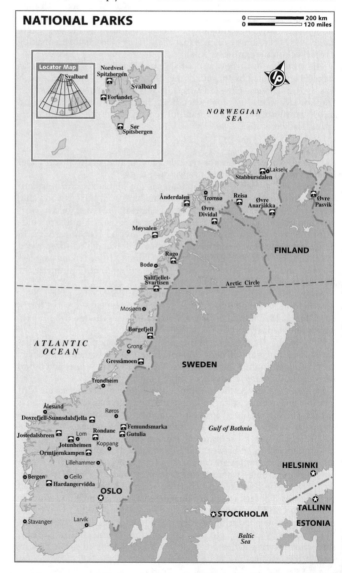

NATIONAL PARKS

National Park	Features	Size	Activities	Best time	Page
Børgefjell	alpine vegetation	1447 sq km	bird-watching	Jun-Aug	p253
Dovrefjell-Sunndalsfjella	musk ox, reindeer, Snøhetta (2286m) highlands, Fokstumyra Marshes	4367 sq km	hiking, climbing, bird-watching, wildlife safaris	May-Sep	p163
Femundsmarka	glaciers, highlands, musk ox, reindeer	390 sq km	hiking, boat trips	mid-Jun–Aug	p157
Forlandet	water-bird, seal & walrus breeding grounds	640 sq km	bird-watching	Jul-Aug	p366
Gressåmoen	first growth spruce forest	182 sq km	bird-watching	May-Sep	p253
Gutulia	primeval old growth forest	19 sq km	bird-watching	May-Sep	
Hardangervidda	vast upland plateau, largest wild reindeer herd in Europe	3422 sq km	Nordic skiing, hiking	Jun-Aug	p136
Jostedalsbreen	Jostedalsbreen icecap (487 sq km), glaciers	1230 sq km	hiking, ice-climbing, kiting, boat trips	Jun-Aug	p220
Jotunheimen	Norway's highest mountains	1145 sq km	hiking	Jul-Aug	p167
Møysalen	Lofoton's last wilderness, Møysalen Peak (1262m)	51.2 sq km	-	Jul-Aug	
Nordvest Spitzbergen	Kongsbreen ice field, Magdalene-fjord, archaeological sights, caribou & marine mammal breeding grounds	3560 sq km	hiking, kayaking	Jul-Aug	p366
Ormtjernkampen	old growth pine forest, birch forest	9 sq km	-	Jun-Aug	
Rago	high peaks, plunging valleys & waterfalls, abuts Swedish national parks	167 sq km	hiking	Jul-Aug	p277
Reisa	dramatic Reisa Gorge, waterfalls, wildlife	803 sq km	hiking	Jun-Aug	p349
Rondane	reindeer, Rondane massif, archaeological sites	580 sq km	hiking, wildlife safaris	Jun-Aug	p161
Saltfjellet-Svartisen	straddles Arctic Circle, upland moors, icecaps, Sami archaeological sites	2105 sq km	hiking	Jul-Aug	p274
Stabbursdalen	world's northernmost pine forest	98sq km	hiking	Jul-Aug	p334
Sør Spitsbergen	Norway's largest park, 65% ice coverage, sea bird breeding grounds	5300 sq km	-		
Øvre Anarjåkka	birch & pine forests, bogs, lakelands	1399 sq km	-	Jul-Aug	
Øvre Dividal	wild park, Arctic rhododendron & heather, wolverine	743 sq km	hiking, dog-sledding		p323
Øvre Pasvik	boreal forest, last Norwegian habitat of brown bear	119 sq km	hiking		p345
Ånderdalen	bogs, coastal pine & birch forests (some trees over 500 years old)	69 sq km	-	Jul-Aug	

The focus is very much on preservation, rather than on the managed interaction between humans and their environment, although a few interpretation centres do exist. By 2008, up to 15% of Norway is expected to lie within protected areas.

Compared to their counterparts in the USA, Britain and elsewhere, Norwegian national parks are very low profile and pleasantly lack the traffic and overdeveloped tourist facilities which have turned parks in many countries into little more than transplanted (or seasonal) urban areas. Some parks, particularly Jotunheimen and Rondane, are increasingly suffering from overuse but, in most parks, erosion, pollution and distress to wildlife are kept to a minimum.

Regulations governing national parks, nature reserves and other protected areas are – not surprisingly in Norway – quite strict. In general, there are no restrictions on entry to the national parks, nor are there any fees, but drivers must nearly always pay a toll to use roads leading into the parks. Dumping rubbish, removing plant, mineral, or fossil specimens, hunting or disturbing wildlife, and using motorised off-road vehicles are all prohibited.

Further national park information is available at local tourist offices and also from the **Directorate for Nature Management** (☎ 73 58 05 00; www.dirnat .no) in Trondheim.

> UN Environment Programme (www.unep .net) is a UN environment network which is great for getting an overview on the low-down on Norway's environmental record.

ENVIRONMENTAL ISSUES

Norway has a generally excellent record when it comes to environmental policies. Industrial waste is highly regulated, recycling is popular, there's little rubbish along the roadsides and general tidiness takes a high priority in both urban and rural environments.

There is, as ever, another side to the story. Loss of habitat has placed around 900 species of plants and animals on the endangered or threatened species lists (see p52). Although many animals are now protected, sport-hunting and fishing are more popular here than in most other European countries. The past sin of over-fishing has also come back to haunt the economy. Most controversial of all, however, has been Norway's internationally unpopular stance on whaling and sealing which has raised international ire and resulted in boycotts on Norwegian products.

Wilderness Areas

Norway may have one of the lowest population densities in Europe, but thanks to its settlement pattern which is unique in Europe, and favoured scattered farms over villages, even the most remote areas are inhabited and a large proportion of the population is rural. This factor, combined with a national appreciation – in summer, some would say that this appreciation is elevated to the level of obsession – of fresh air and outdoor recreation, has ensured that most Norwegians have kept some contact with nature.

It has also meant that the natural world has been greatly altered by human activities. The landscape is crisscrossed by roads which connect remote homes, farmsteads and logging areas to more populated areas; all but a couple of major rivers have been dammed for hydroelectric power; most Norwegian families own holiday homes beside lakes, around ski slopes or in areas of natural beauty; and even the wild-looking expanses of Finnmarksvidda and the huge peninsulas that jut into the Arctic Ocean serve as vast reindeer pastures. As a result, apart from the upland ice fields and the national parks, real wilderness in Norway is limited to a few forested mountain areas along the Swedish border, scattered parts of Hardangervidda and most of Svalbard.

Recycling

Recycling is popular and Norwegians strongly support sorting of household waste – paper, glass, plastics, tyres, car batteries and organic matter – for collection and travellers are encouraged to do likewise. A deposit scheme for glass bottles has been a success and about 96% of beerglass and soft-drink bottles are now returned. Supermarkets give money back for returned aluminium cans and plastic bottles (usually Nkr1 to Nkr1.50). There is also a pre-paid recycling charge on automobiles sold in Norway, which ensures that they're turned into scrap metal rather than roadside eyesores when their life is over.

Forestry

Although no forestry operation can be entirely environmentally sound, overall, Norway has one of the world's most sustainable forestry policies and much of the current visible damage to the forests is due to agricultural clearing and timber over-exploitation between the 17th and 20th centuries.

Today, Norway's productive forests cover around 25% of the national area. Currently, numerous small forestry operations, mostly in eastern Norway, cut about 8.4 million cu metres annually. Clear-felling is practised in some areas but it's thankfully both rare and on a small scale. In general, operations employ selective cutting to prevent soil erosion and unsightly landscape degradation. In addition, companies immediately re-seed the cuts, planting a total of around 50 million seedlings annually.

Fishing & Marine Resources

Norway's most controversial environmental issues – among both Norwegians and international conservationists – involve marine mammal hunting, fishing rights and declining fish stocks.

COMMERCIAL FISHING

It's fair to say that Norwegians usually view the critical depletion of fish stocks in Norwegian waters through the prism of economic self-interest, rather than as a strictly environmental concern. Throughout recorded history, the seas off the Norwegian coast have provided bountiful fishing opportunities and thereby providing a critical backbone to the Norwegian economy. Still Norway's second largest export earner, it was one of Norway's few commercial resources in the days before oil – the essential context to understanding many of Norway's environmental policies as they relate to marine life.

A major factor in the success of Norwegian offshore fisheries has always been the amount of warm Gulf Stream water entering the northern seas, although this varies from year to year. The larger the volume of warm water, the greater the growth of plankton in the far north and the greater the amounts of food available to fish and marine mammals.

Until about 25 years ago, deep-sea fishing in the area was pretty much a free-for-all. Ideal ocean conditions, wedded to the development of sonar which located schools of herring and other commercially valuable fish, ensured that during the 1960s, the Norwegian fishing community enjoyed particularly high catches. Such a bounty, however, came at a cost, and by the late 1970s, herring stocks were nearly wiped out. In addition, over-fishing depleted stocks of cod all across the North Atlantic, from Newfoundland's Grand Banks (Canada) to northern Norway.

Stung into action by the threat to tens of thousands of livelihoods, on 1 January 1977 Norway established a 200 nautical mile offshore economic

'Today, Norway's productive forests cover around 25% of the national area'

SAVE THE WHALES?

No Norwegian environmental issue inspires more international fervour and emotion than that of renewed whaling in the North Atlantic.

In 1986, as a result of worldwide campaigns expressing critical concern over the state of world whale populations, the International Whaling Commission imposed a moratorium on whale hunting. Although it has largely held, two key elements in recent years have placed the moratorium under considerable threat.

The first has been the decision by the three major whaling nations – Norway, Japan and Iceland – to either resume commercial whaling or, in the case of Japan and Iceland, to threaten a withdrawal from the Commission and a full-scale resumption of commercial whaling in 2006 unless the moratorium is replaced by a management plan which allows some whaling.

Norway resumed commercial whaling of minke whales in 1993 in defiance of an international whaling ban. While Norway supports the protection of threatened species, the government contends that minke whales, with a northeast Atlantic population of anything between 70,000 and 200,000, can sustain a limited harvest. The Norwegian government issued a quota of 753 in 1999, a figure which fell to 549 by 2001. In contrast to the campaigns of the 1970s and 1980s which led to the moratorium, the international political response to these developments has been muted, although conservation groups, especially Greenpeace and the World Wildlife Fund, have expressed vociferous opposition.

The second development threatening world whale stocks is a concerted campaign which has seen nations with no history of whaling – including Mauritania, Ivory Coast, Benin, Surinam, Grenada, Tuvalu and even land-locked Mongolia – joining the Commission. The result has seen a change from nine pro-whaling votes out of 55 in 2000 to 21 out of 57 in 2003. Allegations that pro-whaling votes have been rewarded with development aid have been denied by the Japanese.

Norway, for its part, sees the moratorium as unnecessary and outdated. It counters historical evidence, which indicates that whalers in this region have had no qualms about hunting their prey to the verge of extinction, by claiming that modern whalers have a better and more informed perspective, that they adhere to a more sensible quota system and that they now adopt more humane methods of killing. The Norwegians claim that they support only traditional, family-owned operations and have neither the intention nor desire to return to industrial whaling. Many Norwegians also feel that conservationists are mainly city folk who have a sentimental relationship with animals and are out of touch with reality, reflecting a 'quasi-religious fervour which projects human relationships and emotions onto wild sea creatures'. Japan and Norway resumed trading in whale meat in May 2004. Whale meat is openly sold in fish markets (especially Bergen) – a good moment to decide where you stand on the issue.

In addition to hunting, a major threat to Norwegian whales comes from chemical pollution, particularly the PCBs which are suspected of damaging cetacean reproductive and immune systems, a phenomenon which has already led to numerous deaths from viral infections.

For further information on whales and marine conservation, contact **Greenpeace UK** (☎ 020-7865 8100; www.greenpeace.org.uk); or the more radical **Whale and Dolphin Conservation Society** (☎ 0870 870 0027; www.wdcs.org). The northern Norwegian perspective is available from **High North Alliance** (www.highnorth.no). For the Norwegian government's take on the issue, see the website of the **Ministry of Fisheries'** (www.odin.dep.no) or visit the Whaling Museum in Sandefjord.

zone, which was extended to Svalbard later that year and to Jan Mayen in 1980. The country now has agreements with the EU, Russia, the Faroe Islands, Iceland, Greenland and Poland to set quotas.

Almost three decades of intensive conservation measures later, including strict quotas, the herring fishery industry is again thriving. Cod fishing regulations are now in place; it will be many years before the numbers return. Fishing and aquaculture (fish farming) remain the foundation of Norway's coastal economy, providing work for almost 22,000 people in the fishing fleet, and a host of secondary industries – shipbuilding, fish feed, processing, packaging, fishing gear and the transportation of fish products. With an annual catch of over three million tonnes, Norway is the 10th largest fishing nation in the world.

The aquaculture industry, which has thrived for at least two decades and was born out of the depletion of wild fish stocks, concentrates mainly on Atlantic salmon and trout, but there has also been experimentation with Arctic char, halibut, catfish and scallops. Currently, fish farming amounts to 460,000 tonnes of fish per annum, but the export of pen-raised salmon and trout constitutes 55% of the value of Norway's fish exports.

This ready-made alternative to ocean fishing does carry attendant and potentially serious consequences. The main drawback is that diseases in captive stock have spread to wild stock whenever fish escape from the pens, thereby threatening wild populations. Escapes have been reduced in recent years, but it remains an issue of major concern, resulting in greater government regulation.

'With an annual catch of over three million tonnes, Norway is the 10th largest fishing nation in the world'

SEALING

Seal hunting, perhaps because of its shocking visual images, almost rivals whaling in earning the condemnation of environmentalists around the world. In Norway, seal hunting is restricted to two species, the harp seal and hooded seal, and the purpose is ostensibly to cull a growing population. This is mainly because the fishing community wishes to restrict the competition between fishing boats and marine mammals who depend on fish and eat up to 2.5kg per day. Sealing also provides a livelihood for people in Norway and several other North Atlantic countries.

Sealing occurs only on a very small scale, mainly for fur and meat, but it may successfully be argued that it's a cruel business. To mitigate protests, regulations limit seal hunters to only two tools: a rifle and a *hakapik*, or gaff; the former is for adult seals and the latter for pups (which may not be hunted while still suckling). Hunters are also required to take courses and shooting tests before each sealing season.

In late 2001, plans for tourist seal-hunting trips caused worldwide consternation.

Food & Drink

We'd love to tell you otherwise but Norwegian food is downright bland, often heavy and difficult to digest. To make matters worse, prices of food and drink in Norway may inspire you to finally commence that diet programme you've been planning. The key is to think in krone and avoid converting the Norwegian price into your home currency or you may wind up emaciated.

High-quality Norwegian food does exist, with seafood a stand-out highlight and game meats a distinctive and consistently honourable exception to the generally depressing picture.

For a full list of Norwegian food names, see the Menu Decoder and Food Glossary at the end of this chapter.

STAPLES & SPECIALTIES
Seafood

If there's one Norwegian contribution to international cuisine which at least one Lonely Planet author couldn't live without, it's salmon. Where other Norwegian foods will quickly empty your wallet without adequate compensations for taste, salmon (grilled or smoked) remains blissfully cheap, although this applies only to farmed salmon; wild salmon is considerably more expensive. The quality is consistently top-notch. An excellent salmon dish, *gravat laks* is made by marinating salmon in sugar, salt, brandy and dill.

Norwegian National Recipes: An Inspiring Journey in the Culinary History of Norway, by Arne Brimi, is an exhaustive and highly readable study of Norwegian food covering all of Norway's regions and written by one of Norway's premier chefs.

Other Norwegian freshwater seafood specialties which are recommended include brown trout (only in the south), perch, Arctic char, Arctic grayling, bream, tench and eel.

The most common ocean fish and seafood that you're likely to eat are cod (often dried), boiled or fresh shrimps, sprat, haddock, mackerel, capelin, sandeel, ling, ocean perch and coalfish. The ugly but inexplicably lovable catfish is, sadly, rather delicious, as is the blenny. Herring (once the fish of the poor masses, it's now considerably more expensive and normally served pickled in onions, mustard or tomato sauce), is still served in some places, but are becoming rarer while wild stocks recover. Norwegians rave about fish soup, a thin, creamy and slightly fish-flavoured soup. It may contain a shrimp or two if you're lucky.

Other Specialties

Potatoes feature prominently in nearly every Norwegian meal and most restaurants serve boiled, roasted of fried potatoes with every dish. Other vegetables that turn up with some regularity are cabbage (often stewed), turnip, carrots, swedes (rutabagas), cauliflower and broccoli.

The country's main fruit-growing region is around Hardangerfjord, where strawberries, plums, cherries, apples and other orchard fruits proliferate. Edible wild berries include strawberries, cranberries, black currants, red currants, blueberries, raspberries and the most prized, cloudberries; warm cloudberry jam with ice cream is simply fantastic!

Norwegian cheeses have come to international attention as a result of the mild but tasty Jarlsberg, a white cheese first produced in 1860 on the Jarlsberg estate in Tønsberg.

Every Thursday from September to May, many Bergen restaurants serve *raspeballer*, a powerful traditional meal with salted meat, potatoes and mashed turnip – an acquired taste perhaps, but hearty winter food.

Eating Habits

The Norwegian day starts with coffee (always!), a boiled egg and some sort of bread or dry crispbread (normally Ryvita) topped with cheese, cucumber, tomato and a type of pickled herring.

For lunch, most people opt for a sandwich or a slice of bread topped with sardines, shrimp, ham, olives, cucumber, egg or whatever. In the mid-afternoon, Norwegians often break for a snack of coffee, and one of the highlights of the day, waffles with cream and jam. Unlike the firm Belgian waffles, which are better known abroad, Norwegian waffles are flower-shaped and are soft and normally strongly flavoured with cardamom.

The Norwegian Kitchen, by K Innli (ed), brings together over 350 favourite recipes of members of the Association of Norwegian Chefs.

The main meal is eaten some time between 4pm and 6pm. Usually the only hot meal of the day, it normally includes a meat, seafood or pasta dish, with boiled potatoes, a scoop of vegetables and perhaps even a small salad or green garnish. Note that Norwegians often take full advantage of long summer days and often eat out considerably later.

DRINKS

If Norway has a national drink, it's coffee, and it's almost universally drunk in such staggering quantities that one can only wonder how people can remain so calm under the influence of so much caffeine. Most Norwegians drink it black and strong, but foreigners requiring milk and/or sugar are normally indulged.

Authentic Norwegian Cooking, by Astrid Karlsen Scott, has an emphasis on the practical and has been endorsed by none other than Ingrid Espelid, the Betty Crocker or Delia Smith of Norway.

Teas and infusions are also available all over the country, as are the usual range of fizzy drinks and mineral water, but they're much cheaper in supermarkets.

Alcoholic Drinks

Beer is not far behind coffee in the popularity stakes. It's available in some supermarkets and also in bulk at eminently reasonable prices from the beer outlets of the state monopoly shops known as Vinmonopolet (fondly known as just pole), the only place where wine and spirits may be purchased.

Beer is commonly sold in bars in 400mL (around Nkr50 on average) or 500mL (around Nkr60) glasses (about 30% and 15% less than a British pint, respectively). The standard Norwegian beer is pils lager, with an alcohol content of around 4%, and it's still brewed in accordance with the 16th-century German purity law. The most popular brands are the

---

AQUAVIT

Only the Norwegians would make an alcoholic drink from potatoes. The national spirit, *aquavit* (or *akevitt*) is a potent dose of Norwegian culture made from the potato and caraway liquor. The name is derived from the Latin *aqua vitae*, the 'living waters'. Although caraway is an essential ingredient, various modern distilleries augment the spicy flavour with any combination of orange, coriander (cilantro), anise, fennel, sugar and salt! The confection is aged for three to five years in 500L oak barrels that have previously been used to age sherry.

Perhaps the most esteemed version of this libation is *Linje Aquavit*, or 'line aquavit', which first referred to stores that had crossed the equator. In the early days, ships carried oak barrels of *aquavit* abroad to trade, but the unsold barrels were returned to Norway and offered for sale. When it was discovered that the product had improved with age and travel, these leftovers became a highly prized commodity. Today, bottles of *Linje Aquavit* bear the name of the ship involved, its route and the amount of time the barrels have aged at sea.

THE TROUBLE WITH ALCOHOL

Norway must be one of the few countries in the world where the population actually voted *for* prohibition (in a 1919 referendum)! The ban on alcohol remained in force until 1927, by which time half the Norwegian population was involved either in smuggling or illegally distilling home brew, including no doubt many who had voted in favour of the ban. The state monopoly system emerged as an alternative method of restricting alcohol, but even today, that seems to have little effect on the amount of illegal distilling which continues. If you're offered any home-made swill, remember that the effects can be diabolical!

Norway's official attitude toward alcohol continues to border on paranoia. Alcohol sales are strictly controlled and a few towns have even implemented virtual prohibition. In some places, including parts of Telemark, drinking beer in public actually incurs a fine of Nkr2000 and/or prison time!

The legal drinking age is 18 years for beer and wine and 20 for spirits.

---

lagers *Ringsnes* in the south and *Mack* in the north. *Munkholm* is a fairly pleasant alcohol-free beer. Note that when friends go out drinking, people generally buy their own drinks rather than rounds.

CELEBRATIONS

The main celebratory dish is *lutefisk* (dried cod) which is, thankfully, reserved for Christmas when Norwegians can't get enough of it. The cod is dried and then soaked, producing a gelatinous sauce. It's definitely an acquired taste.

For other Christmas dishes and delicacies, see the boxed text, p381.

WHERE TO EAT & DRINK

Hotel breakfasts in Norway often consist of a gargantuan buffet which includes English, American, Continental and Scandinavian options all on one groaning table. If you're staying somewhere where breakfast is not included, your best bet is a bakery where bread, pastries, sandwiches and bagels are relatively well-priced. The next best advice if you're trying to save money is to shop in supermarkets, Norway's last bastion of reasonable prices; for nationwide opening hours, see inside the front cover of this book. Some supermarkets have reasonably priced delicatessens where you can pick up salads sold by the kilogram, or grilled chickens for around Nkr30.

DID YOU KNOW?

In Svalbard, alcohol is available duty-free, but it's rationed for residents and visitors must present a valid plane ticket.

Pizzas also feature prominently in the local diet. Peppe's Pizza is Norway's standout pizza chain with creative pizzas (from Nkr134) a cut above the rest and servings large enough for two; their lunch-time buffets (around Nkr100) are especially good.

If you love fresh fish, any of Norway's fish markets are fabulous places to eat. Among the best are in Stavanger, Kristiansand, and above all others, Bergen. In summer in even the smallest fishing village, you can often buy fresh shrimp direct from the fishing boats for around Nkr60 to Nkr80/kg.

Meals at moderately priced restaurants are typically Nkr80 to Nkr120, though some may feature a *dagens rett* (daily special) for as little as Nkr70.

More upmarket restaurants tend to have reasonably high standards, with prices for main dishes rarely below Nkr200 and often considerably higher. If money is no object, some such places offer three- to five-course meals (from Nkr350 up to Nkr475) which are usually of the highest quality.

Quick Eats
Petrol stations normally sell several types of hot dogs, just about the cheapest hot meal you can buy; garnish and sauce costs no extra. *Gatekjøkken* (food wagons or kiosks) also serve hot dogs, burgers, chips, pizza slices and the like for Nkr20 to Nkr60.

VEGETARIANS & VEGANS
While vegetarianism isn't big in Norway, nearly every restaurant offers some sort of vegetarian option, even if it's just a cheese and onion omelette or a pasta with cream sauce. Oslo, Bergen and other cities have European-style cafés that have a range of creative and inexpensive dishes, normally including several vegetarian options.

WHINING & DINING
Eating out in Norway with children couldn't be easier. Many restaurants offer children's menus, with smaller portions and prices to match. Most of those that don't are willing to serve a smaller portion if you ask.

For more information on travelling with children in Norway, see p376.

EAT YOUR WORDS
If menus in Norway make you break out in a cold sweat, turn to p412 to start learning some elementary Norwegian.

DID YOU KNOW?

It is often claimed, backed by authoritative research surveys, that *Pizza Grandiosa*, a marginally satisfying brand of frozen pizza, is in fact Norway's national dish.

Useful Phrases
Table for ..., please.
Et bord til ..., takk.　et boo-rr til ... tuhk
Can I see the menu, please?
Kan jeg få menyen, takk.　kuhn yay for me-nü-yön tuhk
I'd like today's special, please.
Jeg vil gjerne ha dagens rett, takk.　yay vil ya-rrnö hah dah-göns rret takk
What does it include?
Hva inkluderer det?　vah in-kloo-de-rre rde?
Is service included in the bill?
Er bevertninga iberegnet?　arr bö-vart-ning-uh ee-bö-rray-nöt?
Not too spicy, please.
Ikke for sterkt krydra, takk.　ik-kö fo shtarrkt krrüd-drruh tuhk
I don't eat meat.
Jeg spiser ikke kjøtt.　yay spi-sörr ik-kö cher-t
I don't eat chicken or fish or ham.
Jeg spiser verken kylling eller fisk eller skinke.　yay spee-sörr varr-kön chül-ling el-lörr fisk el-lö shing-kö

TRAVEL YOUR TASTEBUDS

- Reindeer – a beef-like meat served in expensive restaurants (a fillet will cost at least Nkr250), but what will you tell the kids?
- Whale – leave your environmental credentials at the door.
- Brown cheese – Gudbrandsdalsost (also known as *gjetost* or *brunost*) is made from the whey of goat's and/or cow's milk and has a slightly sweet flavour and a decidedly off-putting caramel-coloured appearance.
- Reconstituted cod, mackerel or saithe balls – a staple for older folk.
- Cod tongues – enormously popular in Lofoten and nowhere else.
- Fermented trout – this is, how shall we put it, utterly disgusting.

NORWAY'S TOP FIVE

- Torget (p175) is a harbourside fish market with loads of atmosphere and the freshest seafood you'll find.

- Bølgen & Moi (p125) has superb fish and shellfish soup and other seafood and overlooks a charming fish harbour.

- Fossheim Turisthotell (p166) was founded by renowned chef Arne Brimi, his legacy of wild trout, reindeer, elk and ptarmigan lives on.

- Hamnøy Mat og Vinbu (p301) is a family-run restaurant where local specialties are home-cooked and it has the best fish cakes in Norway.

- Isqueen (p303) is a beached whaler-turned-restaurant with incomparable Arctic food and wonderful views.

Menu Decoder

DAIRY PRODUCTS
gudbrands dalsost – sweet brown goat cheese
mysost – brown whey cheese
pultost – soft fermented cheese, often with caraway seeds
rømmegrot – delicious sour cream variant upon porridge, traditionally served at Christmas

SOUPS, MIXED DISHES & DRINKS
dagens rett – today's special
fårikål – lamb in cabbage stew
gløgg – Christmas drink which may or may not be fermented with cinnamon, raisins, almonds, ginger, cloves, cardamon and other spices with juices
koldtbord – buffet of cold dishes (fish, meat, cheese, salad and a sweet)
lapskaus – thick stew of diced meat, potatoes, onions and other vegetables
pytt i panne – eggs with diced potato and meat
suppe – soup
svele – pancake speciality served with strawberries and cream

MEAT
bankebiff – slices/chunks of beef simmered in gravy
bidos – traditional reindeer meat stew served at Sami weddings
dyrestek – roast venison
kjøttkake – small hamburger steak
kjøttpålegg – cold meat cuts
lam(mebog) – (shoulder of) lamb
postei – meat pie
reinsdyrstek – roast reindeer
spekemat – cured meat (lamb, beef, pork, reindeer, often served with scrambled eggs)
spekepølse – air-dried sausage
syltelabb – boiled, salt-cured pig's trotter

SEAFOOD
bacalao – fish dish using cod
fiskebolle – fish ball
fiskegrateng – fish casserole
gaffelbitar – salt- and sugar-cured sprat/herring fillets
gravlaks – salt- and sugar-cured salmon with dill and creamy sauce
klippfisk – salted and dried cod
lutefisk – stockfish treated in lye solution, boiled

rakefisk – cured and fermented fish (often trout)
(røyke)laks – (smoked) salmon
saltfish – preserved cod that is filleted; salted and dried for around three weeks
sildesalat – salad with slices of herring, cucumber, onions, etc
spekesild – salted herring, often served with pickled beetroot, potatoes and cabbage

Food Glossary

MEAT & POULTRY

kjøtt	meat
kylling	chicken
oksekjøtt	beef
pølse	sausage
skinke	ham
sauekjøtt	lamb/mutton
svinekjøtt	pork

VEGETABLES

grøn(n)saker	vegetables
løk	onion
potet	potato
sopp	mushroom
tomat	tomato

SEAFOOD

brisling	sprat/sardine
fisk	fish
hellefisk	halibut
hvalbiff	whale steak
lysing	hake
makrell	mackerel
reker	shrimps
sild	herring
torsk	cod
tunfisk	tuna

FRUIT

ananas	pineapple
appelsin	orange
banan	banana
druer	grapes
eple	apple
frukt	fruit
jordbær	strawberries

BREAKFASTS & BREADS

bocadillos	filled rolls
brød	bread
egg	eggs
grøt	porridge, cereal
helkornbrød	wholemeal bread
honning	honey
loff	white bread
rundstykke	roll
shillingsboller	pastry bun
syltetøy	jam

DAIRY PRODUCTS

fløte	cream
ost	cheese
smør	butter
skyr	Icelandic yoghurt

DESSERTS, CAKES & COOKIES

goro	variety of biscuit
is	ice cream
kake	cake
krumkake	variety of biscuit
pannekake	pancake
sjokolade	chocolate
strull	variety of biscuit

DRINKS

jus	fruit juice
kaffe	coffee
melk	milk
rødvin	red wine
hvitvin	white wine
te	tea
vann	water
øl	beer

OSLO

Oslo

CONTENTS

Norway's capital and largest city (population 521,900) creeps up on you and makes you very glad you came. Possessed of a staid reputation and by no measure Scandinavia's most beautiful city, low-key Oslo nonetheless has lots to see and do – it just doesn't make such a big fuss about it.

Oslo's list of world-class museums is truly staggering, gathering together a microcosm of Norway's rich cultural past and present. Those who've always dreamed of the Vikings or of joining one of the great Norwegian polar explorations will fall in love with Bygdøy. This peninsula also boasts the finest folk museum in the country, one which showcases the extraordinary diversity of Norwegian culture. Art lovers will adore the National Gallery – Edvard Munch's world renowned *The Scream*, which is part of its collection, is one of Europe's most haunting masterpieces – as well as the Munch Museum, while those with an eye for the innovative won't want to miss the array of provocative works by sculptor Gustav Vigeland. Add to this a medieval fortress, shady parks and the buzzing café-bar-restaurant districts of Grünerløkka and Aker Brygge, and you'll soon discover that there's much to like about Norway's capital.

Oslo sits at the head of the Skagerrak Strait inlet known as Oslofjord, while the Nordmarka (North Woods) to the north of the city provide a green belt for hiking and skiing, which makes Oslo a very liveable city for lovers of the outdoors. The charming village of Drøbak and the larger towns of Fredrikstad and Halden also lie in one of Norway's least-visited areas to the southeast, offering rewarding day trips.

HIGHLIGHTS

- Admiring the exceptional **artworks** (p71) of master painter Edvard Munch and renowned sculptor Gustav Vigeland

- Ranging across the lovely Bygdøy Peninsula, home to wonderful **museums** (p81)

- Catching the rhythm of Oslo's August **Jazz Festival** (p86) – a great time to be in the city

- Starting the afternoon in one of **Grünerløkka's cafés or bars** (p90) and finding yourself still there early the next morning

- Strolling the quaint streets of **Gamlebyen** (p98) in Fredrikstad

- Catching a ferry along the Oslofjord to the charming timbered village of **Drøbak** (p96)

AREA: 8903 SQ KM	HIGHEST ELEVATION: FJELLSJØKAMPEN 812M	POPULATION: 1,267,200

OSLO REGION

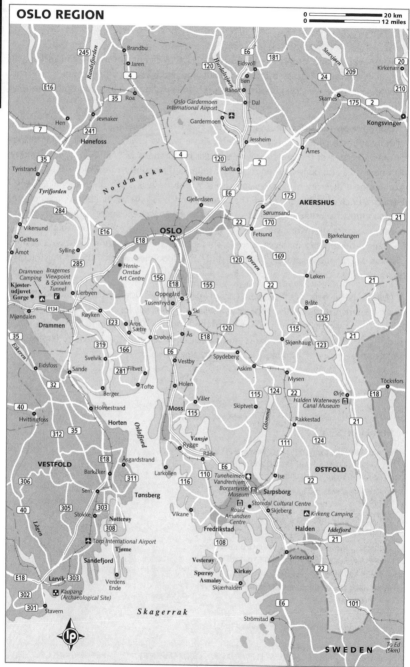

0 ⟞⟞⟞⟞⟞⟞⟞⟞ 20 km
0 ⟞⟞⟞⟞⟞⟞⟞⟞ 12 miles

Randsfjorden

Brandbu
245
Jaren
4

Hurdalsjøen

E6
181
Eidsvoll
120
Bøn
Råholt
Dal

Storsjøen
20
Kirkenær
24
209
210
Skarnes
175
2

Kongsvinger

E16
35
Roa

Oslo Gardermoen
International Airport
Gardermoen

Jessheim

Hen
7
241
Jevnaker
Hønefoss

Ârnes

4
120
Kløfta
2

Tyristrand
35

Nordmarka

Nittedal
E6
Gjelleråsen

175
AKERSHUS

Tyrifjorden
284

Sørumsand
170
Fetsund

21

Vikersund
Geithus
 Âmot
Sylling
E16
285

OSLO
E18

22

Bjørkelangen

Drammen
Camping
Bragernes
Viewpoint
& Spiralen
Tunnel
Kjøster-
udjuvet
Gorge
E134
Mjøndalen
Drammen
35
Eikeren
Eidsfoss
Sande
32
40
Hvittingfoss
312
35

Henie-
Onstad
Art Centre
156
E18
155
Lierbyen
Røyken
E23
Âros
Sætre
319
166
Svelvik
281
Filtvet
Berger
Tofte
Holmestrand
Horten
Ostofjord

Oppegård
TusenFryd
Ski
Âs
E18
Drøbak
E6
Vestby
Holen
Moss
115
Vâler
Rygge
Râde

Øyeren
120
169

Løken
22

Brâte
125

Skjønhaug
Skiptvet
123
115
21

Spydeberg
Askim
Mysen
124
22
Glomma
Skjeberg

Ørje
Halden Waterways
Canal Museum
E18

Töcksfors

Rakkestad
21

111
124

Vansjø
116
110
Tuneheimen
Vandrerhjem
Borgarsyssel
Museum
Stondal Cultural Centre
Roald
Amundsen
Centre

ØSTFOLD
Ise
22
Sarpsborg

VESTFOLD
E18
Âsgardstrand
Barkåker
311
Sem
303
306
Larkollen
Tønsberg

Stokke
305
40
Løken
308
Nøtterøy
Torp International Airport
Tjøme
Sandefjord
E18
Larvik
303
302
301
Stavern
Kaupang
(Archaeological Site)
Verdens
Ende

Vikane
Fredrikstad
108

Vesterøy
Spærøy
Asmaløy
Kirkøy
Skjærhalden

Skagerrak

Halden
Iddefjord
21
Svinesund
22

Kirkeng Camping
Skjeberg
Halden

E6
101
Strömstad

To Ed
(5km)
SWEDEN

HISTORY

The name Oslo is derived from the words *Ás*, the Old Norse name for the Norse Godhead, and *lo*, which meant 'pasture', yielding roughly 'the fields of the gods'.

The city was originally founded in 1048 by King Harald Hardråda (Harald Hard-Ruler; see p23), whose son Olav Kyrre (Olav the Peaceful) set up a cathedral and a corresponding bishopric here. In the late 13th century, King Håkon V created a military presence by building the Akershus Festning (Fortress, see p83) in the hope of deterring the Swedish threat from the east. After the mid-14th-century bubonic plague wiped out half of the country's people, Norway united with Denmark and, from 1397 to 1624, Norwegian politics and defence were handled from Copenhagen. Oslo slipped into obscurity. In 1624, it burned to the ground. It was resurrected by King Christian IV, who rebuilt it on a more easily defended site and renamed it Christiania, after his humble self.

For three centuries, the city held on as a seat of defence. In 1814, the framers of Norway's first constitution designated it the official capital of the new realm, but their efforts were effectively nullified by Sweden, which had other ideas about Norway's future and unified the two countries under Swedish rule. In 1905, when that union was dissolved, the stage was set for Christiania to flourish as the capital of modern Norway. It reverted to its original name, Oslo, in 1925 and the city has never looked back.

ORIENTATION

Oslo's central train station (Oslo Sentralstasjon or Oslo S) sits at the eastern end of the city centre, with the Galleri Oslo Bus Terminal not far away to the northeast. From Oslo S the main street, Karl Johans gate, forms a ceremonial axis westward through the heart of the city to the Royal Palace. Most sights, including the harbourfront and Akershus Festning (Fortress), are within a 15-minute walk of Karl Johans gate, as are the majority of hotels and *pensions*. Many of the sights outside the centre, including Vigeland Park and the Munch Museum, are just a short bus or tram ride away. The Bygdøy Peninsula is a mere 10-minute ferry ride across the harbour.

Maps

The tourist offices distribute a detailed and free city plan. Unless you're heading out to the suburbs, it should be sufficient. On the reverse side is a map of the T-bane system and an inset covering Holmenkollen.

INFORMATION
Bookshops

Ark Bokhandel (Map pp74-6; ☎ 22 47 32 00; Øvre Slottsgate 23-25; ☿ 10am-8pm Mon-Fri, 10am-6pm Sat) Highly recommended, with a good English-language and stationery section; other branches around town.

Nomaden (Map pp74-6; ☎ 23 13 14 15; Uranienborgveien 4; ☿ 10am-6pm Mon-Fri, 10am-4pm Sat) Travel books, maps and gear.

Norli (Map pp74-6; ☎ 22 00 43 00; www.norli.no; Universitetsgata 20-24; ☿ 9am-7pm Mon-Fri, 10am-4pm Sat) Largest bookshop in Norway.

Ringstrøms Bookshop (Map pp74-6; Ullevålsveien 1; ☿ 10am-4pm Mon-Fri, 10am-2pm Sat) Second-hand and antiquarian books and CDs.

Tanum Libris (Map pp74-6; ☎ 22 41 11 00; www.tanum .no; Karl Johans gate 43; ☿ 10am-8pm Mon-Fri, 10am-6pm Sat) Another branch at Oslo S train station.

Tronsmo (Map pp74-6; ☎ 22 99 03 99; Kristian Augusts gate 19; ☿ 9am-5pm Mon-Wed, 9am-6pm Thu & Fri, 10am-4pm Sat) Alternative bookshop with feminist, gay, lesbian and political works.

Emergency

Ambulance (☎ 113)
Fire (☎ 110)
Police (Map pp74-6; ☎ 112, ☎ 22 70 54 00; Henrik Ibsens gate 10)

Internet Access

Arctic Internet Café (Map pp74-6; ☎ 22 17 19 40; Oslo S; per 30/60 min Nkr30/50; ☿ 8am-midnight)

Deichmanske Bibliotek (Municipal Library; Map pp74-6; ☎ 22 03 29 00; Henrik Ibsens gate 1; free but time-limited access; ☿ 10am-6pm Mon-Fri, 9am-2pm Sat Jun-Aug & 10am-8pm Mon-Fri, 9am-3pm Sat Sep-May)

Galleriet i Café (Map pp74-6; Galleri Oslo Bus Terminal; per 30/60 min Nkr30/50; ☿ 10am-11pm Mon-Fri, noon-10pm Sat & Sun)

QBA (Map pp72; ☎ 22 35 24 60; Olaf Ryesplass 4; per hr Nkr80; ☿ 8am-1am Mon-Fri, 11am-1am Sat & Sun) Pricey, but offers free access for laptop wireless users.

Sam Telecom (Map pp74-6; ☎ 22 11 41 04; Hausmanns gate 6; per 30/60 min Nkr20/30; 10am-8pm Mon-Fri, noon-6pm Sat)

Studenten (Map pp74-6; ☎ 23 42 56 80; Karl Johans gate 45; per 15/30/60 min Nkr20/30/55; ☿ 11am-11pm Mon-Thu, 11am-9pm Fri & Sat, noon-11pm Sun)

OSLO IN....

Two Days

Start your day with a stroll through the centre of town, passing by the elegant **Stortinget** (parliament building, p82) and **Oslo Cathedral** (p82), which are both along the busy pedestrian thoroughfare of **Karl Johans gate** (p69). From the waterfront Aker Brygge district, take a ferry to **Bygdøy** (p81) with its exceptional museums. And don't miss the **National Gallery** (p72) located at Universitetsgata in central Oslo.

By night, head to the **Grünerløkka** (p90) district where the bars, cafés, restaurants and feel-good vibe are infectious. Also treat yourself to a night in the opulent **Grand Hotel** (p88).

Four Days

Follow the two-day itinerary, but with the extra time you can linger in the medieval **Akershus Castle and Fortress** (p83). You'll also have time for the excellent **Munch Museum** (p72), **Vigeland Park** (p73) and **Vigeland Museum** (p73). Make space in your schedule as well for an evening at one of the harbourside restaurants in **Aker Brygge** (p90).

One Week

A week in Oslo will allow you to enjoy some of the more specialist museums on offer – the **Historical Museum** (p77), **Children's Art Museum** (p85), **Ibsen Museum** (p78) and **National Museum for Contemporary Art** (p77) are among the best – as well as a stroll through the **Botanical Garden** (p83) featuring alpine plants. Ranging a bit further, head for the **Holmenkollen ski jump** (p84) and **Tryvannstårnet** (p84) observation tower, or take a longer day-trip to **Drøbak** (p96) or experience delightful **Gamlebyen** (p98), the old quarter of Fredrikstad.

Use-It (Map pp74-6; ☎ 22 41 51 32; Møllergata 3; free access; ⊙ 9am-6pm Mon-Fri, 11am-5pm Sat Jun-Aug, shorter hours rest-of-year)

Laundry

A-Snarvesk (Map pp72; Thorvald Meyers gate 18; wash/dry Nkr45/25; ⊙ 10am-8pm Mon-Fri, 10am-3pm Sat)
Majorstua Myntvaskeri (Map p72; Vibes gate 15; ⊙ 9am-8pm Mon-Fri, 8am-3pm Sat) Located 1km north of the Royal Palace.
Selva As (Map pp74-6; Ullevålsveien 15; wash/dry Nkr40/25; ⊙ 8am-9pm Mon-Fri, 8am-3pm Sat)

Left Luggage

Oslo S has various sizes of lockers which cost from Nkr20 to Nkr30 per 24 hours.

Libraries

Deichmanske Bibliotek (Municipal Library; Map pp74-6; ☎ 22 03 29 00; Henrik Ibsens gate 1; ⊙ 10am-6pm Mon-Fri, 9am-2pm Sat Jun-Aug & 10am-8pm Mon-Fri, 9am-3pm Sat Sep-May) Largest public library in Norway; reading room with foreign newspapers and magazines.

Medical Services

Jernbanetorget Apotek (Map pp74-6; ☎ 22 41 24 82; Fred Olsens gate) A 24 hour pharmacy opposite Oslo S.
Oslo Kommunale Legevakten (Oslo Emergency Clinic;

Map pp74-6; ☎ 22 11 80 80; Storgata 40; ⊙ 24 hr) Casualty and emergency medical clinic .
Tannlegesvakten (Map p72; ☎ 22 67 30 00; Tøyen Senter, Kollstadgata 18; ⊙ 11am-2pm, 7-10pm) Recommended dental practice.

Money

You'll find banks scattered all over town and most have ATMs which accept international cards; most have branches along or just off Karl Johans gate near Oslo S.

The tourist office and post office in Oslo S change money (into Norwegian kroner only) at a less advantageous rate (usually 3% less than banks).

American Express (Map pp74-6; ☎ 22 98 37 35; Fridtjof Nansens plass 6; ⊙ 10am-4.30pm Mon-Fri, 10am-3pm Sat) Offers the best rates with no commission on Amex travellers cheques and around 1% for most of the other brands of travellers cheques.

Post

Main post office (Map pp74-6; ☎ 23 14 90 00; cnr Prinsens & Kongens gates) Surprisingly small for a central post office. To receive mail, have it sent to Poste Restante, Oslo Sentrum Postkontor, Dronningens gate 15, 0101 Oslo. You'll find convenient post office branches at Oslo S, at Solli plass, and on Grensen.

Telephone & Fax

Telekort card phones and coin phones are found throughout the city. Coin phones take Nkr1 to Nkr20 coins, but you'll need at least Nkr3 for a local call.

Faxes can be sent from post offices.

Telehuset (Map pp74-6; ☎ 22 00 30 40; Karl Johans gate 41a; ✆ 10am-5pm Mon-Fri, 9am-3pm Sat) For information on mobile phones this is a good place to visit.

Toilets

In this city full of expensive public toilets, there are still several daytime options for free relief: the 3rd floor of the Glasmagasinet arcade on Stortorvet; upstairs in the Paléet arcade at Karl Johans gate 37–43; and in the Deichmanske Bibliotek, Henrik Ibsens gate 1. Alternatively, visit a museum or hold on until lunch time and use the restaurant facilities. Toilets at Oslo S and the Galleri Oslo bus terminal cost Nkr10.

Tourist Information

Den Norske Turistforening (DNT; Norwegian Mountain Touring Club; Map pp74-6; ☎ 22 82 28 22; www.dntoslo.no; Storgata 3; ✆ 10am-4pm Mon-Wed & Fri, 10am-6pm Thu, 10am-2pm Sat, open 1 hr earlier in summer) Provides information, maps and brochures on hiking in Norway and sells memberships which include discounted rates on the use of mountain huts along the main hiking routes. You can also book some specific huts and pick up keys.

Oslo Promotion Tourist Office (Map pp74-6; ☎ 24 14 77 00; www.visitoslo.com; Fridtjof Nansens plass 5; ✆ 9am-7pm Jun-Aug, 9am-5pm Mon-Sat Apr, May & Sep, 9am-4pm Mon-Fri Oct-Mar) Located just north of the

Rådhus (Town Hall). Look out for its us the monthly *What's On in Oslo.*

Tourist office (Map pp74-6; Jernbanetorget 1, Osl ✆ 8am-11pm May-Aug, 8am-11pm Mon-Sat Sep, 8am-5pm Mon-Sat Oct-Apr) This is in busy Oslo S, where they deal only with Oslo information, sell the Oslo Pass and help book accommodation.

Use-It (Map pp74-6; ☎ 22 41 51 32; www.use-it.no; Møllergata 3; ✆ 9am-6pm Mon-Fri Jul-Aug, 11am-5pm Mon-Fri Sep-Jun) The exceptionally helpful and savvy Ungdomsinformasjonen (Youth Information Office better known as Use-It) is aimed at (but not restricted to) a backpackers market. It makes (free) bookings for inexpensive or private accommodation and provide information on anything from current events to hitching possibilities. Free guided tours and barbecues from July to mid-August are also organised here. The office offers free condoms, Internet access and phone calls. Use-It also publishes *Streetwise*, a comprehensive and user-friendly guide to doing Oslo on the cheap.

Travel Agencies

Kilroy Travels (Map pp74-6; ☎ 02633; Nedre Slottsgate 23; ✆ 10am-6pm Mon-Fri, 10am-3pm Sat) Specialises in student and youth travel and discounted stand-by tickets.

SIGHTS

Oslo may not be Europe's prettiest capital city, but it does have a wonderful array of museums, most of which radiate out from the banks of Oslofjord.

Art Galleries & Museums

Oslo has a fine collection of galleries and exhibition spaces. From the signature work of Edvard Munch through the Impressionists

---

OSLO PASS & OSLO PACKAGE

To do a circuit of even a few Oslo sites, it's worth picking up the Oslo Pass, which covers not only museum and swimming pools admissions, but also includes free parking in city council car parks and free transport on all city buses, ferries, trams, T-bane lines and local Norwegian State Railways (NSB) trains (excluding night buses and trams). It also entitles holders to discounts on sightseeing tours, theatre tickets and car hire. The brochure *Oslo Pass*, available from the tourist offices, has a full list of entitlements.

The Oslo Pass costs Nkr195/285/375 for one/two/three days (Nkr75/95/125 for children under 16). A one-day family card for two adults and two children costs Nkr395. The card is sold at tourist offices, some hotels and Narvesen kiosks. It's great value if you're doing a lot of sightseeing in a short period of time, especially if you have a car and wish to leave it parked for a few days. Note, however, that students and senior travellers pay half price at most museums and other sites, meaning that it may be cheaper to buy a public transport pass and pay separate museum admissions.

The Oslo Package gets you the Oslo Pass plus a hotel room (up to two children included free), and breakfast. It costs from Nkr490 to Nkr1200 per person per day and can be reserved by calling ☎ 23 10 62 62 or accessing www.visitoslo.com.

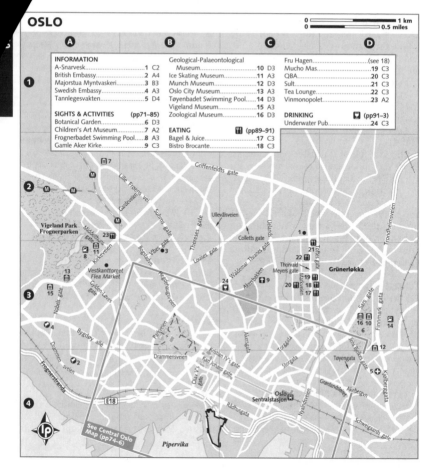

OSLO

0 — 1 km
0 — 0.5 miles

INFORMATION
A-Snarvesk.................................1 C2
British Embassy...........................2 A4
Majorstua Myntvaskeri.................3 B3
Swedish Embassy.........................4 A3
Tannlegesvakten.........................5 D4

SIGHTS & ACTIVITIES   (pp71–85)
Botanical Garden.........................6 D3
Children's Art Museum.................7 A2
Frognerbadet Swimming Pool......8 A3
Gamle Aker Kirke........................9 C3

Geological-Palaeontological
    Museum..............................10 D3
Ice Skating Museum....................11 A3
Munch Museum..........................12 D3
Oslo City Museum.......................13 A3
Tøyenbadet Swimming Pool......14 D3
Vigeland Museum.......................15 A3
Zoological Museum.....................16 D3

EATING   🍴 (pp89–91)
Bagel & Juice..............................17 C3
Bistro Brocante...........................18 C3

Fru Hagen...............................(see 18)
Mucho Mas................................19 C3
QBA..20 C3
Sult...21 C3
Tea Lounge...............................22 C3
Vinmonopolet...........................23 A2

DRINKING   🍷 (pp91–3)
Underwater Pub.........................24 C3

Vigeland Park
Frognerparken

Vestkanttorget
Flea Market

See Central Oslo
Map (pp74–6)

Pipervika

---

to many other big international and Norwegian names, there's more than enough to keep art lovers occupied for a couple of days of art appreciation.

NATIONAL GALLERY

One of Oslo's major highlights is the **National Gallery** (Nasjonalgalleriet; Map pp74-6; ☎ 22 20 04 04; www.nasjonalgalleriet.no; Universitetsgata 13; admission free; 🕙 10am-6pm Mon, Wed & Fri, 10am-8pm Thu, 10am-4pm Sat, 11am-4pm Sun). It houses the nation's largest collection of Norwegian art, including works from the Romantic era and more-modern works from 1800 to WWII. Some of Edvard Munch's best known creations are on display, including his most renowned work, *The Scream*; see

the boxed text, p73. There's also an impressive collection of European art with works by Gauguin, Picasso, El Greco and many of the Impressionists: Manet, Degas, Renoir, Matisse, Cézanne and Monet.

For more on Edvard Munch, see the boxed text, p43.

MUNCH MUSEUM

Edvard Munch (1863–1944) fans won't want to miss the **Munch Museum** (Munch-museet; Map p72; ☎ 23 24 14 00; www.munch.museum.no; Tøyengata 53; adult/child Nkr60/30, free with Oslo Pass; 🕙 10am-6pm Jun–mid-Sep, 10am-4pm Tue-Fri, 11am-5pm Sat & Sun mid-Sep–May), which is dedicated to his life's work and has most of the pieces not contained in the National Gallery. Despite

ANDERS BLOMQVIST

An outdoor café in the square on Karl Johans Gate (p89), Olso

Bronze and granite sculptures by Gustav
Vigeland in Oslo's Vigeland Park (p73)

BILL BACHMANN

ANDERS BLOMQVIST

Royal Palace (p69), Oslo

JON DAVISON

The Viking Ship Museum (p78), Bygdoy Peninsula, Olso

Stave church at the Norwegian Folk Museum (p78), Oslo

DEANNA S

DEANNA SWANEY

The Norwegian flags are out in force in Oslo for National Day celebrations (p379) on 17 May

ONCE WAS CARELESS, TWICE IS...

On 12 February 1994, the day of the opening ceremony of the Winter Olympics in Lillehammer, Norwegians woke to the news that arguably the nation's most prized cultural possession, *The Scream* by Edvard Munch, had been stolen from the National Gallery in Oslo. There was nothing hi-tech about this deeply embarrassing incident – a patrolling police officer discovered the theft (carried out by breaking a window and using wire cutters) when he found a ladder propped up against the gallery wall. In place of the painting was a note: 'Thanks for the poor security.'

The nation was appalled, even more so when the authorities received a ransom demand of $US1 million from people with ties to the anti-abortion movement. A Lutheran minister who had helped plan anti-abortion protests during the Olympics claimed that the painting would be returned if Norwegian national television broadcast a graphic film showing a foetus being aborted.

Finally, after almost three months, the Norwegian police discovered four fragments of the painting's frame in the northern Oslo suburb of Nittedal. Within days, Edvard Munch's master-work, which was painted on fragile paper, was found undamaged in a hotel in Asgardstrand, about 40 miles south of Oslo. Three Norwegians were arrested and Norwegians breathed a huge collective sigh of relief.

Fast forward 10 years. On 22 August 2004, two masked, armed men walked into the Munch Museum, threatened a guard, detached another version of *The Scream* (Edvard Munch painted four versions) as well as another Munch masterpiece, *Madonna*, and made off in a getaway car, all within five minutes and in front of startled gallery visitors. No alarms went off, the police took 15 minutes to arrive and, astonishingly, the paintings were uninsured; gallery officials claimed that the paintings were simply priceless.

At the time of writing, Norwegian police were still hunting for the missing paintings and thieves, not to mention wondering how this could have been allowed to happen a second time.

the artist's tendency towards tormented visions, all is not grey. Yes, you'll see works including *The Sick Child* and *The Maiden & Death*, but lighter themes, such as *The Sun* and *Spring Ploughing*, are also represented. With over 5000 drawings and paintings bequeathed to the City of Oslo by Munch himself, this is a landmark collection, although one which is critically diminished by the August 2004 theft of two of Munch's most important works; see the boxed text, above. To get there, take the T-bane to Tøyen, followed by a five-minute signposted walk.

FROGNERPARKEN & VIGELAND PARK

Frognerparken, which has as its centerpiece **Vigeland Park** (Map p72; ⊙ year-round), is an extraordinary open-air showcase of work by Norway's best-loved sculptor, Gustav Vigeland (see the boxed text, p80). Vigeland Park is brimming with nearly 212 granite and bronze Vigeland works. His highly charged work ranges from entwined lovers and tranquil elderly couples to contempt-ridden beggars. His most renowned work, *Sinataggen* (the 'Little Hot-Head'), portrays a London child in particularly ill humour.

It's a great place to visit in the evening after other city sites have closed.

Near the southern entrance to the park lies **Oslo City Museum** (Map p72; Oslo Bymuseum; ☎ 23 28 41 70; Frognerveien 67; adult/child Nkr40/20, free with Oslo Pass; ⊙ noon-4pm Wed-Sun, noon-7pm Tue) housed in the 18th-century Frogner Manor (built on the site of a Viking-era manor); it contains exhibits of minor interest on the city's history.

Frognerparken itself attracts Oslo locals with its broad lawns, ponds, stream and rows of shade trees. On a sunny afternoon it's ideal for picnics, strolling or lounging on the grass.

To get there, take tram No 12 or 15, marked Frogner, from the city centre.

VIGELAND MUSEUM

For an in-depth look at Gustav Vigeland's work, visit **Vigeland Museum** (Map p72; ☎ 22 54 25 30; www.vigeland.museum.no; Nobels gate 32; adult/child Nkr40/20, free with Oslo Pass; ⊙ 11am-5pm Tue-Sun Jun-Aug, noon-4pm Tue-Sun Sep-May), opposite the southern entrance to Frognerparken. It was built by the city in the 1920s as a home and workshop for the sculptor, in exchange for the donation of a significant proportion of

OSLO

CENTRAL OSLO

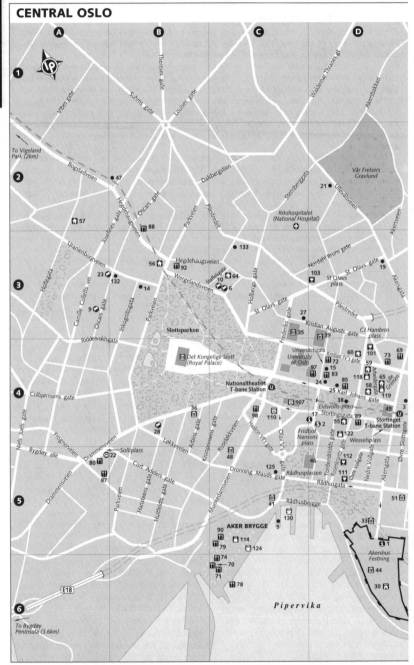

A **B** **C** **D**

1

VP

Vibes gate
Suhms gate
Thereses gate
Louises gate
Waldemar Thranes gt
Akersbakken

To Vigeland
Park (2km)

2

Bogstadveien
Dalbergstien
Sternbergata
21 ● Ulleysveien
Akersveien

Rikshospitalet
(National Hospital)
●

Vår Frelsers
Gravlund

● 47

57

Josefines gate
Oscars gate
Hegdehaugsveien
88

3

Uranienborgveien
Holtegata
Camille Colletts vei
Oscars gate
Incognitogata
Parkveien

Hegdehaugsveien
56
92
Staffeldsgata
10 ▢ 64
● 6

● 133

Holbergs gate

St Olavs gate

Nordahl Bruns gate
103
St Olavs
plass
19
St Olavs gate
Akersgata

23 ● 132
● 14
9 ●

Wergelandsveien
St Olavs gate
Pilestredet

27 ●

4

Riddervoldsgata
Colbjørnsens gate
Niels Juels gate
Frognerveien
Bygdøy allé
Drammensveien

Slottsparken

Det Kongelige Slott
(Royal Palace)

Kristian Augusts gate
35
39

Universitetsgata
University
of Oslo
97
24 ●

Kristian IV's gate
72
● 15
83
85
118

CJ Hambros
plass
60 ▢ 101
59
73
69

Karl Johans gate

Nationaltheatret
T-bane Station
107

38 ●
Stortingsgata 89
17 Eidsvolls plass
55
2

Stortinget
T-bane Station
49
3

49 ●

Fredriks gate
Lille Grensen

36
98
110

Sollisplass
80 22
87

28

Løkkeveien
Arbins gate
Kronprinsens gate
Ruseløkkveien
Haakon VII's gate
Olav V's gate

48

Cort Adelers gate
Hansteens gate
Hultbdts gate

Dronning Mauds gate
Munkedamsveien

Fridtjof
Nansens
plass

122
Rosenkrantz gate
Tordenskiolds gate

Wesselsplass
112
111
Øvre Vollgate
Nedre Vollgate
Akersgata
Øvre Slottsgate

125
Rådhusplassen
46

Rådhusgata

51

5

41
130
5

AKER BRYGGE

90
79
114
124

74
70
71

78

33

Akershus
Festning

44

30

1

6

E18

To Bygdøy
Peninsula (3.6km)

Pipervika

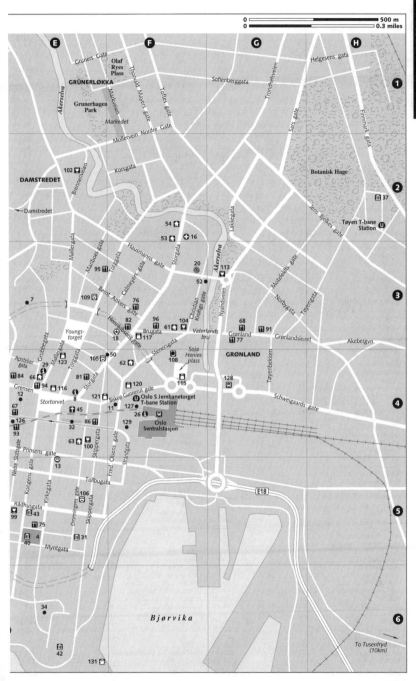

his life's work, and it contains his early collection of statuary and monuments to public figures, as well as plaster moulds, woodblock prints and sketches. When he died in 1943, his ashes were deposited in the tower, and four years later the museum was opened to the public.

EMANUEL VIGELAND MUSEUM
Few visitors realise that Gustav Vigeland's brother Emanuel was also an accomplished artist: many Norwegians feel that he actually produced work superior to that of his better-known sibling. For a taste of his work, check out the stained-glass in the Oslo Cathedral, then visit this **museum** (Map p79; ☎ 22 14 57 88; www.emanuelvigeland.museum.no; Grimelundsveien 8; adult/child Nkr30/15, free with Oslo Pass; ☼ noon-4pm Sun) dedicated to his work; it's just a pity that it's not open longer hours. To get there, take the T-bane (line 1) to Slemdal.

ASTRUP FEARNLEY MUSEUM
This **museum** (Astrup Fearnley Museet; Map pp74-6; ☎ 22 93 60 60; www.afmuseet.no; Dronningens gate 4; adult/child Nkr50/25, free with Oslo Pass & Tue; ☼ 11am-5pm Tue, Wed & Fri, 11am-7pm Thu, noon-5pm Sat & Sun) offers a changing programme of modern Norwegian and international art exhibitions; check out *What's On in Oslo* for details of what's showing.

NATIONAL MUSEUM OF CONTEMPORARY ART
Featuring the National Gallery's collections of post-WWII Scandinavian and international art is the **National Museum of Contemporary Art** (Museet for Samtidskunst; Map pp74-6; ☎ 22 86 22 10; Bank plassen 4; adult/child Nkr40/free; ☼ 10am-5pm Tue, Wed & Fri, 10am-8pm Thu, 11am-5pm Sat, 11am-5pm Sun). Some of the collection is definitely an acquired appreciation, but it does provide a timely reminder that Norwegian art didn't cease with Edvard Munch.

STENERSEN MUSEUM
This **museum** (Stenersenmuseet; Map pp74-6; ☎ 23 49 36 00; Munkedamsveien 15; adult/child Nkr40/20, free with Oslo Pass; ☼ 11am-5pm Wed & Fri-Sun, 11am-7pm Tue & Thu) contains three formerly private collections of works by Norwegian artists from 1850 to 1970. The museum and much of the art, which includes works by Munch, were a gift to the city by Rolf E Stenersen. Other collections displayed in the museum were

provided by Oslo residents Amaldus Nielsen and Ludvig O Ravensberg.

HENIE-ONSTAD ART CENTRE
In Høvikodden, west of the centre, lies one of Norway's best private art collections, the **Henie-Onstad Art Centre** (Henie-Onstad Kunstsenter; Map p79; ☎ 67 80 48 80; Høvikodden; admission free; ☼ 11am-7pm Tue-Thu, 11am-6pm Fri-Sun), founded in the 1960s by Norwegian figure skater Sonja Henie and her husband Niels Onstad. The couple actively sought out collectible works of Joan Miró and Pablo Picasso, as well as assorted Impressionist, abstract, Expressionist and modern Norwegian works. It all comes together pretty well, and when you've seen enough art you can head downstairs for a look at Sonja's various skating medals and trophies. From Jernbanetorget, take any bus towards Sandvika and get off at Høvikodden.

Other Museums
ICE SKATING MUSEUM
This **museum** (Skøytemuseet; Map p72; ☎ 22 43 49 20; Middelthuns gate 26; adult/child Nkr20/10, free with Oslo Pass; ☼ 10am-2pm Tue & Thu, 11am-2pm Sun) is dedicated to speed- and figure-skating in Norway. Featured are historical skating apparatus and information on such Norwegian champions as speed skater Johann Olav Koss and figure skater Sonja Henie. It makes a nice complement to the Olympic sites in Lillehammer (p145) and Hamar (p150).

HISTORICAL MUSEUM
The highly recommended **Historical Museum** (Historisk Museet; Map pp74-6; ☎ 22 85 99 64; University of Oslo, Frederiks gate 2; adult/child Nkr40/free; ☼ 10am-4pm Tue-Sun mid-May–mid-Sep, 11am-4pm Tue-Sun rest-of-year) is actually three museums under one roof. Most interesting is the ground floor **National Antiquities Collection** (Oldsaksamlingen), with displays of Viking-era coins, jewellery and ornaments. Look out for the 9th-century **Hon treasure**, the largest such find in Scandinavia (2.5kg). A section on medieval religious art includes the doors and richly painted ceiling of the Ål stave church (built around 1300). The 2nd level has an Arctic exhibit and the Myntkabinettet, a collection of the earliest Norwegian coins from as early as AD 995. The 2nd level and top floor hold the **Ethnographic Museum**, with changing exhibitions on Asia, Africa and the Americas.

NORWEGIAN SCIENCE & TECHNOLOGY MUSEUM, NORWEGIAN COMMUNICATIONS MUSEUM

Visitors with a scientific bent will enjoy a visit to the **Norwegian Science & Technology Museum** (Norsk Teknisk Museum & Telemuseum; Map p79; ☎ 22 79 60 00; www.tekniskmuseum.no; Kjelsåsveien 143; adult/child Nkr75/30, free with Oslo Pass; ☯ 10am-6pm mid-Jun–mid-Aug, shorter hours rest-of-year), near Lake Maridal. It houses an extensive technical library and an interactive learning centre for scientific research and experimentation. Possibly of more interest for the lay visitor is the adjacent **Norwegian Communications Museum** (Norsk Telemuseum; Map p79; ☎ 22 22 05 05; Kjelsåsveien 143; adult/child Nkr75/35, free with Oslo Pass; ☯ 10am-6pm mid-Jun–mid-Aug, shorter hours rest-of-year), which charts communications in Norway from Viking beacons to modern Internet technology. However, it's probably only worth it if you have the Oslo Pass. Take bus No 22, 25 or 37 to Kjelsås station or tram No 12 or 15 to Kjelsås Allé.

THEATRE MUSEUM

This **museum** (Teatermuseet; Map pp74-6; ☎ 22 42 65 09; Christiania Torv 1; adult/child Nkr25/15; ☯ 11am-3pm Wed, noon-4pm Thu & Sun) is housed in the first town hall (Rådhus) of old Christiania (1641). The building is itself of as much interest as the exhibits, which chart the history of Oslo theatre from 1800.

IBSEN MUSEUM

Housed in the last residence of Norwegian playwright Henrik Ibsen (see the boxed text, p44) is the **Ibsen Museum** (Ibsen-Museet; Map pp74-6; ☎ 22 12 35 50; Arbins gate 1; adult/child Nkr50/20, free with Oslo Pass; ☯ hourly guided tours noon-2pm Tue-Sun). The study remains exactly as he left it and other rooms have been restored in the style and colours popular in Ibsen's day. This is a must-see for Ibsen fans who are continuing on to his birthplace, Skien (p135), or Grimstad, (p119) where the eminent playwright spent his formative years.

NORWEGIAN MUSEUM OF ARCHITECTURE

Near the Akershus Fortress, this **museum of architecture** (Norsk Arkitekturmuseum; Map pp74-6; ☎ 22 42 40 80; www.arkitektur.museum.no; Kongens gate 4, Kvadraturen; admission free; ☯ 11am-6pm Mon-Fri, noon-4pm Sat & Sun), contains a permanent exhibition of 1000 years of fine Norwegian architecture and construction, as well as temporary exhibits on various aspects of modern Norwegian design. One of its main attractions is that it provides a contemporary antidote for those with an overdose of folk museums and traditional architecture.

NORWEGIAN FOLK MUSEUM

Norway's largest open-air museum and one of Oslo's premier attractions is this **folk museum** (Norsk Folkemuseum; Map p79; ☎ 22 12 37 00; www.norskfolkemuseum.no; Museumsveien 10; adult/child Nkr75/20 mid-May–mid-Sep, free with Oslo Pass, Nkr55/20 rest-of-year; ☯ 10am-6pm mid-Jun–mid-Sep, 11am-3pm Mon-Fri, 11am-4pm Sat & Sun rest-of-year). The museum includes more than 140 buildings, mostly from the 17th and 18th centuries, which have been gathered from around the country and are clustered according to region of origin. Paths wind past old barns, elevated *stabbur* (raised storehouses) and rough-timbered farmhouses with sod roofs sprouting wildflowers. The Gamlebyen (Old Town) section is a reproduction of an early-20th-century Norwegian town and includes a village shop and old petrol station; in summer (daily except Saturday) you can see weaving and pottery-making demonstrations. Another highlight is the restored stave church, built around 1200 in Gol and shifted to Bygdøy in 1885.

The exhibition hall near the main entrance includes exhaustive displays on Norwegian folk art, historic toys, festive costumes from around the country (including dress for weddings, christenings and burials), the Sami culture of Finnmark, domestic and farming tools and appliances, as well as visiting exhibits. Sunday is a good day to visit, as folk music and dancing is staged at 2pm (in summer). From Wednesday to Saturday from July to mid-August, there are Norwegian evenings of folk tales (in English) and folk dancing (adult/child Nkr195/50, including museum tour) at 5.30pm.

It's the definitive guide to traditional Norwegian culture – don't miss it.

VIKING SHIP MUSEUM

This captivating **museum** (Vikingskipshuset; Map p79; ☎ 22 13 52 80; Huk Aveny 35; adult/child Nkr40/20, free with Oslo Pass; ☯ 9am-6pm May-Sep, 11am-4pm Oct-Apr) houses three Viking ships excavated from the Oslofjord region and, upstairs, there's a good general exhibit on Vikings – it's the

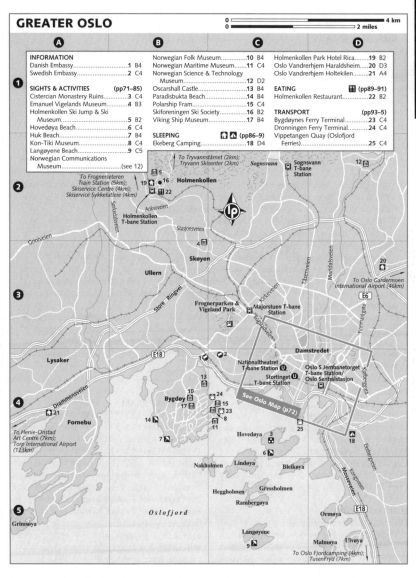

GREATER OSLO

0 ————————— 4 km
0 ————————— 2 miles

INFORMATION
Danish Embassy..............................1 B4
Swedish Embassy............................2 C4

SIGHTS & ACTIVITIES   (pp71–85)
Cistercian Monastery Ruins...........3 C4
Emanuel Vigelands Museum..........4 B3
Holmenkollen Ski Jump & Ski
    Museum.....................................5 B2
Hovedøya Beach.............................6 C4
Huk Beach......................................7 B4
Kon-Tiki Museum...........................8 C4
Langøyene Beach...........................9 C5
Norwegian Communications
    Museum..............................(see 12)

Norwegian Folk Museum...............10 B4
Norwegian Maritime Museum........11 C4
Norwegian Science & Technology
    Museum...................................12 D2
Oscarshall Castle...........................13 B4
Paradisbukta Beach.......................14 B4
Polarship Fram..............................15 C4
Skiforeningen Ski Society..............16 B2
Viking Ship Museum.....................17 B4

SLEEPING   (pp86–9)
Ekeberg Camping..........................18 D4

Holmenkollen Park Hotel Rica........19 B2
Oslo Vandrerhjem Haraldsheim......20 D3
Oslo Vandrerhjem Holtekilen.........21 A4

EATING   (pp89–91)
Holmenkollen Restaurant...............22 B2

TRANSPORT   (pp93–5)
Bygdøynes Ferry Terminal.............23 C4
Dronningen Ferry Terminal.............24 C4
Vippetangen Quay (Oslofjord
    Ferries)...................................25 C4

best summation of Viking history brought to life you'll find anywhere. The ships had been drawn ashore and used as tombs for nobility, who were buried with all they expected to need in the hereafter: jewels, furniture, food, servants, intricately carved carriages and sleighs, tapestries and fierce-looking figures. Built of oak in the 9th century, these

Viking ships were buried in blue clay, which preserved them amazingly well.

The impressive *Oseberg*, buried in 834, is festooned on prow and stern with elaborate dragon and serpent carvings, measures 22m and required 30 oarsmen. The burial chamber beneath it held the largest collection of Viking-age artefacts ever uncovered

GUSTAV VIGELAND

The Norwegian sculptor Gustav Vigeland (1869–1943) was born to a farming family near Mandal in the far south of the country. As a child and teenager he became deeply interested in Protestant-ism, spirituality, woodcarving and drawing – a unique combination that would dominate his life's work. In 1888, Vigeland secured an apprenticeship to sculptor Brynjulf Bergslien. The following year he exhibited his first work at the State Exhibition of Art. It was the break he needed, bring-ing his talents to national and international attention.

In 1891 he travelled to Copenhagen and then to Paris and Italy, where he worked with vari-ous masters; he was especially inspired by the work of French sculptor Auguste Rodin. When his public grants ran out he returned to Norway to make a living working on the restoration of the Nidaros Cathedral in Trondheim and producing commissioned portraits of prominent Norwegians.

In 1921, the City of Oslo recognised his talents and built him a spacious studio in which to work; in return, he would bequeath to the city all his subsequent works, as well as his original models and sketches. It was an offer the sculptor couldn't refuse.

The highlight of Vigeland Park is the 14m-high granite Monolith, which crowns the park's highest hill. This incredible production required three stone carvers working daily from 1929 to 1943 and was carved from a single stone pillar quarried from Iddefjorden in southeastern Norway. It depicts a writhing mass of 121 detailed human figures, both entwined with and undermining each other in their individual struggle to reach the top. The circle of steps around it supports rows of stone figures. The figures, together with the pillar, have been interpreted in many ways: as a phallic representation, the struggle for existence, yearnings for the spiritual spheres and transcendence of cyclic repetition.

Leading down from the plinth bearing this column is a series of steps supporting sculptures depicting people experiencing the full range of human emotions and activities. The numerous sculptures dominating the surrounding park carry the artist's themes from the realist to the lu-dicrous. The result is truly one of Norway's artistic highlights and, best of all, there are no signs admonishing you to keep your distance.

in Scandinavia, but had been looted of all jewellery. The sturdier 24m-long *Gokstad*, built around 890, is the finest remaining ex-ample of a Viking longship, but when it was unearthed its corresponding burial chamber had also been looted and few artefacts were uncovered. Of the third ship, the *Tune*, only a few boards and fragments remain.

KON-TIKI MUSEUM

This worthwhile **museum** (Map p79; ☎ 23 08 67 67; Bygdøynes; adult/child Nkr40/20, free with Oslo Pass; ☒ 9.30am-5.45pm Jun-Aug, shorter hours rest-of-year) is dedicated to the balsa raft which Norwe-gian explorer Thor Heyerdahl sailed from Peru to Polynesia in 1947. The museum also displays the totora reed boat *Ra II*, built by Aymara people on the Bolivian island of Suriqui in Lake Titicaca. Heyerdahl used it to cross the Atlantic in 1970. For a full run-down on the life of this extraordinary explorer who achieved a lot in his lifetime, see the boxed text, p110.

POLARSHIP FRAM

Opposite the *Kon-Tiki* Museum lies the **Polarship Fram** (Map p79; ☎ 23 28 29 50; www.fram .museum.no; adult/child Nkr30/15, free with Oslo Pass; ☒ 9am-6.45pm mid-Jun–Aug, shorter hours rest-of-year), launched in 1892. This is similarly a ship with history. From 1893 to 1896 Fridtjof Nansen's North Pole expedition took the 39m schooner *Fram*, meaning 'forward', to Russia's New Siberian Islands, and en route back to Norway the team passed within only a few degrees of the North Pole it-self. Later, it was used by Roald Amundsen (see the boxed text, p364) in 1911 to land on the Ross Ice Shelf before he struck out on foot for the South Pole. Otto Sverdrup also sailed it around southern Greenland to Canada's Ellesmere Island between 1898 and 1902. You can clamber around inside the boat and imagine how it must have felt to be trapped in the polar ice. The museum also includes an interesting rundown on the history of polar exploration.

NORWEGIAN MARITIME MUSEUM

This **museum** (Norsk Sjøfartsmuseum; Map p79; ☎ 24 11 41 50; Bygdøynesveien 37; adult/child Nkr40/free; ⏰ 10am-6pm mid-May–Aug, 10.30am-4pm Fri-Wed, 10am-6pm Thu Sep–mid-May) depicts Norway's relationship with the sea, including the fishing and whaling industry, the seismic fleet (which searches for oil and gas), shipbuilding and wreck salvaging. Outside the museum there's a seamen's memorial commemorating the 4700 Norwegian sailors killed in WWII, and alongside it is Roald Amundsen's ship *Gjøa*, the first ship to completely transit the North–West Passage (from 1903 to 1906). Other features of the museum include Norway's largest collection of maritime art, a dried cod display and a film with scenic footage of the Norwegian coastline and the underwater realm. The top-floor balcony of the larger wing opens onto a view over the islands of Oslofjord.

ZOOLOGICAL MUSEUM & GEOLOGICAL-PALAEONTOLOGICAL MUSEUM

By Oslo's botanical gardens, the university's **Zoological Museum** (Zoologisk Museum; Map p72; ☎ 22 85 17 00; Sars gate 1; adult/child combined ticket with Geological Museum Nkr40/20; ⏰ 11am-4pm Tue-Sun) has well-presented displays of stuffed wildlife from Norway and elsewhere, including a special exhibit on Arctic wildlife. The adjacent **Geological-Palaeontological Museum** (Geologisk Museum; Map p72; ☎ 22 85 17 00; Sars gate 1; adult/child combined ticket with Zoological Museum Nkr40/20; ⏰ 11am-4pm Tue-Sun) contains displays on the history of the solar system and Norwegian geology, as well as examples of myriad minerals, meteorites and moon rocks. The palaeontological section includes a 10m-long iguanodon skeleton and a nest of dinosaur eggs.

SKI MUSEUM

At the Holmenkollen ski jump, the **Ski Museum** (Map p79; ☎ 22 92 32 00; www.skiforeningen .no; Kongeveien 5; adult/child Nkr50/25; ⏰ 9am-8pm Jun-Aug, 10am-4pm Jan-Apr & Oct-Dec, 10am-5pm May & Sep) leads you through the 4000-year history of nordic and downhill skiing in Norway. Of particular interest are the exhibits on the Antarctic expeditions of Amundsen and Scott, and Fridtjof Nansen's slog across the Greenland icecap (you'll see the boat he constructed from his sled and canvas tent to

row the final 100km to Nuuk). You can also see get a taste of it feels to win the Olympic downhill in the ski simulator.

Admission to the Ski Museum includes a visit to the **ski jump tower** (see p81). Part of the route to the top of the tower is served by a lift, but you're on your own for the final 114 steep steps. To get to the museum, take T-bane line 1 to Holmenkollen, then follow signs uphill.

Bygdøy Peninsula

The Bygdøy Peninsula holds some of Oslo's top attractions. You can rush around all the sights in half a day, but allotting a few extra hours will be more rewarding.

Although only minutes from central Oslo, Bygdøy maintains its rural character. The royal family maintains a summer home here, as do many of Oslo's well-to-do residents.

Ferries (Map p79; ☎ 23 35 68 90; No 91) operate from early April to early October, making the 15-minute run to Bygdøy (adult/child Nkr20/10, free with the Oslo Pass) every 30 to 40 minutes from 8.45am with the last crossing returns from Bygdøy at around 6.30pm in April and September, 9.15pm in summer, with earlier final departures the rest of the year. The ferries leave from Rådhusbrygge 3 (opposite the Rådhus) and stop first at Dronningen ferry terminal, from where it's a 10-minute walk to the Norwegian Folk Museum (see p78) and a 15-minute walk to the Viking Ship Museum (see p78). Beyond the ships it's a further 20 minutes to Bygdøynes where the *Kon-Tiki*, *Polarship Fram* and Norwegian Maritime museums (see p80) are clustered; the route is signposted and makes a pleasant walk. Alternatively, you can also take bus No 30 to the folk museum from Jernbanetorget.

OSCARSHALL CASTLE

This **castle** (Oscarshall Slott; Map p79; ☎ 22 56 15 39; Oscarshallsveien; adult/child Nkr50/20, free with Oslo Pass; ⏰ noon-4pm Thu, Fri & Sun late May–early Sep, guided tours hourly noon-3pm), designed by Johan Henrik Nebelong to reflect a blend of romantic and English neogothic styles, was constructed as a residence for King Oscar I from 1847 to 1852. It's probably the least interesting of Bygdøy's attractions, but is worth a brief detour to view from the outside if you're passing by.

THE NOBLE NOBELS

Most Nobel prizes – physics, chemistry, medicine, literature, peace and economics – are awarded every October in Stockholm, but the most prestigious prize of all, the Peace Prize, is reserved for Oslo. Each year on 10 December, the Oslo Rådhus becomes a focus of world attention as it honours individuals who have successfully encouraged or brought peace to tumultuous areas of the world.

In his will in 1895, Alfred Nobel, the Swedish founder of the prize (who, somewhat perversely, was also credited with the invention of dynamite), stipulated that the responsibility for the Peace Prize be delegated to a committee appointed by the Norwegian *Storting* (Parliament). It's thought by many that his intentions may have been to foment growing Norwegian agitation against the Swedish-Norwegian union. Since 1901, when the first Peace Prize was awarded to Jean Henri Dunant, the Swiss founder of the International Red Cross, the presentation ceremony has been held in Oslo.

Although the Norwegian *Storting* appoints the five-member committee that determines the winner of the Peace Prize, the parliamentary delegates have no say in the committee's decisions. Nominations are made by eminent international jurists, academics, former Nobel Peace Prize winners and the Nobel Committee members themselves. Nominations must be submitted by 1 February each year.

Once the 100 or so names have been put forward, the committee goes to work, painstakingly investigating the merits of each nominee. Eventually, a shortlist is formed from which the winner is selected. The prize has been awarded to such luminaries as Martin Luther King, Jr (1964); Mother Teresa (1979); the 14th Dalai Lama, Tenzin Gyatso (1989); Mikhail Gorbachev (1990); Aung San Suu Kyi (1991); Nelson Mandela (jointly with FW de Klerk 1993); and Jimmy Carter (2002). The Peace Prize can also be awarded to organisations, with winners including Amnesty International (1977), the International Campaign to Ban Landmines (1997); and Médecins Sans Frontières (1999).

Rarely are such decisions so clear-cut and invariably they attract significant controversy, most notably by awarding the prize to Henry Kissinger and Le Duc Tho (1973); Yitzhak Rabin, Shimon Perez and Yasser Arafat (1994); Northern Ireland's John Hume and David Trimble (1998); Kofi Annan and the UN (2001); and Shirin Ebadi (2003), a female human rights lawyer from Iran.

Some time in 2005, a **Nobel Peace Center** (Map pp74-6; www.nobelpeacecenter.org) is due to open on the Aker Brygge waterfront.

Churches

OSLO CATHEDRAL

Dating from 1697, the **Oslo Cathedral** (Domkirke; Map p74-6; ☎ 22 31 46 00; Stortorget 1; admission free; ☒ 10am-4pm) is worth seeing for its elaborate stained-glass by Emanuel Vigeland (brother of Gustav Vigeland) and painted ceiling (completed between 1936 and 1950). The exceptional altarpiece, a 1748 model of the *Last Supper and the Crucifixion* by Michael Rasch, was an original feature of the church (from 1700), but it was moved all over the country before being returned from Prestnes church in Majorstue in 1950. The organ front and pulpit were both part of the original construction. Occasionally, concerts are held in the church (Nkr100).

The **bazaar halls** (Basarhallene; Map pp74-6), around the back of the church, date from 1858 and are currently used by summer handicraft sales outlets.

GAMLE AKER KIRKE

This medieval stone **church** (Map p72; ☎ 22 69 35 82; Akersbakken 26; admission free; ☒ noon-2pm Mon-Sat), located north of the centre on Akersbakken, dates from 1080 and is Oslo's oldest building. Lutheran services are held at 9am and 11am on Sunday. Take bus No 37 from Jernbanetorget to Akersbakken then walk up past the churchyard.

Stortinget (Parliament)

Norway's yellow-brick **parliament building** (Map pp74-6; ☎ 23 31 35 96; Karl Johans gate 22; admission free; guided tours in Norwegian & English 10am & 1pm, in German 11.30am mid-Jun–mid-Aug, Sat only rest-of-year), right in the centre of town and staring up the hill towards the royal palace, is one of Europe's more charming parliaments. Dating from 1866, it is particularly striking from the outside, giving architectural soul to the otherwise undistinguished city centre.

Oslo Town Hall

This twin-towered **town hall** (Rådhus; Map pp74-6; ☎ 22 46 16 00; Fridtjof Nansens plass; adult/child Nkr40/free, free Sep-May or with Oslo Pass; ☺ 9am-5pm May-Aug, 9am-4pm Sep-Apr), completed in 1950 to commemorate the city's 900th anniversary, houses the city's political administration. Something of an Oslo landmark, its red brick functionalist exterior is unusual, if not particularly imaginative. The entrance is lined with wooden reliefs from Norse mythology and the interior halls and chambers are decorated with splashy and impressive frescoes and paintings by some of Norway's most prominent artists. It's here that the Nobel Peace Prize is awarded on 10 December each year (see the boxed text, p82). The building's interior features an important fusion of ancient mythology and modern governance. You can view the main hall for free from the front corridor. Guided tours (in English) are available at 10am, noon and 2pm Monday to Friday and on weekends in June and July (no extra charge).

Akershus Castle & Fortress

Strategically located on the eastern side of the harbour, dominating the Oslo harbourfront, are the medieval castle and fortress (*slott* and *festning*) and is arguably Oslo's architectural highlight.

When Oslo was named capital of Norway in 1299, King Håkon V ordered the construction of Akershus to protect the city from external threats. Since it suffered repeated fires, sieges and battles, the fortress was reconstructed to withstand the increased fighting power of the day, including the 1559 addition of the Munk gun tower. Between 1580 and the mid-18th century, it was further fortified with moats and reinforced ramparts.

When Oslo was rebuilt after the 1624 fire, the city, renamed Christiania, was shifted to the less vulnerable and more defensible site behind the protective fortress walls. By 1818, the need for defence had been superseded by the need for space and most of the outer rampart was destroyed to accommodate population growth. From 1899 to 1963 it underwent major renovations and, nowadays, the park-like grounds serve as a venue for concerts, dances and theatrical productions – a far cry from its warlike origins and a welcome departure from its grim history. Note, however, that this complex remains a military installation and may be closed to the public whenever there's a state function.

In the 17th century, Christian IV renovated **Akershus Castle** (Akershus Slott; Map pp74-6; ☎ 22 41 25 21; adult/child Nkr40/10; ☺ 10am-4pm Mon-Sat, 12.30-4pm Sun May–mid-Sep, guided tours 11am, 1pm & 3pm Mon-Sat & 1pm & 3pm Sun) into a Renaissance palace, although the front remains decidedly medieval. In its dungeons you'll find dark cubbyholes where outcast nobles were kept under lock and key (one dungeon still holds a rather miserable-looking model wrapped in sackcloth), while the upper floors contained sharply contrasting lavish banquet halls and staterooms.

The chapel is still used for army events, and the crypts of King Håkon VII and Olav V lie beneath it. The guided tours are led by university students in period dress and, while not compulsory, they do offer an entertaining anecdotal history of the place that you won't get by wandering around on your own.

Entry to the expansive **fortress** (Festning; Map pp74-6; admission free; ☺ 6am-9pm) is through a gate at the end of Akersgata or over a drawbridge spanning Kongens gate at the southern end of Kirkegata. After 6pm in winter, use the Kirkegata entrance.

The **Akershus Fortress Information Centre** (Map pp74-6; ☎ 23 09 39 17; ☺ 9am-5pm Mon-Fri & 11am-5pm Sat & Sun mid-Jun–mid-Aug, closes 1hr earlier rest-of-year), inside the main gate, has an exhibit entitled *New Barricades* which recounts the history of the Akershus complex. At 1.30pm, you can watch the changing of the guard at the fortress.

Just outside the northern wall of the fortress, **Christiania Bymodell** (Map pp74-6; ☎ 22 33 31 47; admission free; ☺ noon-5pm Tue-Sun) features a terrific 10m by 15m model of old Christiania in 1840, and a multimedia display of its history from its founding in 1624 up until 1900.

Parks & Gardens

Oslo's **Botanical Garden** (Botanisk Hage; Map p72; ☎ 22 85 17 00; Sars gate 1; admission free; ☺ 7am-8pm Mon-Fri, 10am-8pm Sat & Sun Apr-Sep, 7am-5pm Mon-Fri & 10am-5pm Sat & Sun Oct-Mar) features over 1000 alpine plants from around the world, as well as sections dedicated to vegetation from both

OSLO

temperate and tropical regions. Specimens in the aromatic garden are accompanied by text in both print and braille.

Damstredet District

The skewed wooden homes of the Damstredet district (Map pp74-6), some dating back to the early 19th century, add a splash of character amid Oslo's otherwise modern and run-of-the-mill architecture. This rather quirky looking neighbourhood north of the city centre provides a pronounced counterpoint to the deprived and dreary suburb of Akerselva, just east across the river.

Holmenkollen District

The **Holmenkollen Ski Jump**, perched on a hilltop overlooking Oslo, offers a panoramic view of the city and doubles as a concert venue. During Oslo's annual ski festival, held in March, it draws the world's best ski jumpers.

Tryvannstårnet District

The **Tryvannstårnet observation tower** (Map p79; ☎ 22 14 67 11; Voksenkollen; adult/child Nkr40/20; ⏰ 10am-5pm May-Sep, 10am-4pm Oct-Apr), north of the ski jump, sits at 538m and overlooks the suburban wilderness of Nordmarka. A lift zips you to the top and a 20,000-sq-km view as far as snowcapped Mt Gausta to the west, the Oslofjord to the south and the boundless Swedish forests to the east. From the Holmenkollen T-bane station, take the scenic ride to the end of the line at Frognerseteren and look for the signposted walking route.

ACTIVITIES
Climbing

The best local climbing is on the pre-bolted faces of Kolsåstoppen, which is accessible on T-bane line 3 to Kolsås. Otherwise, climbers can head for the indoor climbing wall at **Villmarkshuset** (Map pp74-6; ☎ 22 05 05 22; post@veggivegg.no; Christian Krohgs gate 16; per 2 hr before/after 4pm Nkr45/80; ⏰ 10am-10pm Mon-Thu, 10am-8pm Fri, 10am-6pm Sat, noon-8pm Sun, shorter hours mid-Jun–mid-Aug). It also offers bouldering (Nkr45 for two hours) and can proffer advice on outdoor climb spots.

For general information about climbing and gear, try also **Skandinavisk Høyfjellsutstyr** (Map pp74-6; ☎ 23 33 43 80; www.shu.no; Bogstadveien 1; ⏰ 9am-6pm Mon-Wed & Fri, 9am-7pm Thu, 9am-4pm Sat).

Cycling

The tourist office has free cycling maps '*Sykkelkart Oslo*', which trace the bicycle lanes and paths throughout the city, while *Idrett og friluftsliv i Oslo* covers the Oslo hinterland. It also has a pamphlet *Opplevelsesturer i Marka* which contains six possible cycling and/or hiking itineraries within reach of Oslo.

For Norway-wide cycling information and maps, contact **Syklistenes Landsforening** (Map pp74-6; ☎ 22 47 30 30; post@slf.no; Storgata 23C; ⏰ 10am-5pm Mon-Fri, 10am-2pm Sat mid-Jun–mid-Aug, shorter hours rest-of-year).

For details of renting bicycles in Oslo, see p95.

Hiking

A network of trails with a total length of around 1200km leads off into Nordmarka from Frognerseteren (at the end of T-bane line 1), including a good trail down to the lake Sognsvann, 6km northwest of the centre at the end of T-bane line 5. There's also an excellent network of hiking trails around the lake itself; the pleasant route around the lake takes less than an hour. On hot days, the eastern shore offers refreshing swimming, while the wilder western shore is a bit better for relative solitude. Other hiking routes radiate out into the hills beyond (see p84 for more information).

A more urban, but mostly green two-hour walk will take you along the Akerselva river from the Kjelsås tram stop to Vaterlands bru (bridge), right in the heart of Grønland. Other hikes are outlined in two maps produced by Park og Idrettsvesenet and available from the tourist office.

Avid hikers may want to stop by the **DNT office** (Map pp74-6; ☎ 22 82 28 22; Storgata 3; ⏰ 10am-4pm Mon-Wed & Fri, 10am-6pm Thu, 10am-2pm Sat, open 1hr earlier mid-Jun–mid-Aug), which maintains several mountain huts in the Nordmarka region and can provide information and maps covering longer-distance hiking routes throughout Norway.

Ice Skating

At the **Narvisen outdoor ice rink** (Map pp74-6; ☎ 22 30 30 33; Karl Johans gate), you can skate for free whenever it's cold enough to freeze over (usually from around November to March). Skates may be hired from the ice rink for around Nkr40.

Skiing

Oslo's ski season is roughly from December to March, and the area has over 2400km of prepared nordic tracks (1000km in Nordmarka alone), many of them floodlit. Easy-access tracks begin right at the end of T-bane lines 1 and 5. **Skiservice Centre** (Map p79; ☎ 22 13 95 04; www.skiservice.no; Tryvannsveien 2), at Voksenkollen station, one T-bane stop before Frognerseteren, hires out snowboards and nordic skis. The downhill slopes at **Tryvann Skisenter** (Map p79; ☎ 22 13 64 50) are open in the ski season. **Skiforeningen** (Ski Society; Map p79; ☎ 22 92 32 00; holmenkollen@skiforeningen.no; www.skiforeningen.no; Kongeveien 5) can provide further information on skiing options, or check out www.holmenkollen.com.

Swimming

ISLANDS & BEACHES

If the weather hots up, there are a few reasonable beaches within striking distance of central Oslo. Ferries to half a dozen islands in the Oslofjord region leave from Vippetangen Quay, southeast of Akershus Fortress. Boats to Hovedøya and Langøyene are relatively frequent in summer (running at least hourly), while other islands are served less often.

The southwestern shore of otherwise rocky Hovedøya (Map p79), the nearest island to the mainland, is popular with sunbathers. The island is ringed with walking paths to old cannon emplacements and the 12th-century **Cistercian monastery ruins**. Take boat No 92 and 93.

South of Hovedøya lies the undeveloped island of Langøyene (Map p79), with superb swimming from rocky or sandy beaches (one on the southeastern shore is designated for nude bathing). Boat No 94 will get you there.

The Bygdøy Peninsula has two popular beaches, **Huk** (Map p79) and **Paradisbukta** (Map p79), which can be reached on bus No 30 from Jernbanetorget to its last stop. While there are some sandy patches, most of Huk comprises grassy lawns and large smooth rocks which are ideal for sunbathing. Separated into two beaches by a small cove, the beach on the northwestern side is open to nude bathing. If Huk seems too crowded, a 10-minute walk through the woods north of the bus stop leads to the more secluded Paradisbukta.

POOLS

Oslo has two outdoor municipal swimming pools: **Frognerbadet Swimming Pool** (Map p72; ☎ 23 27 54 50; Frognerparken; adult/child Nkr50/25, free with Oslo Pass; ☼ mid-May–mid-Aug) and **Tøyenbadet Swimming Pool** (Map p72; ☎ 23 30 44 70; Helgesens gata 90; adult/child Nkr50/25, free with Oslo Pass), which is near the Munch Museum.

OSLO FOR CHILDREN

Oslo's wealth of museums and more-staid attractions find necessary light relief in Oslo's two child-inspired museums which range from the inspirational to the downright fun. Oslo's National Constitution Day celebrations (17 May; see p86) is known mainly as a time for celebration of the family and reverence for child-like fun and children's interests.

Children's Art Museum

If you have a particular affinity for your friends' refrigerator art displays, visit the **Children's Art Museum** (Barnekunstmuseet; Map p72; ☎ 22 46 85 73, Lille Frøens vei 4; adult/child Nkr50/30; ☼ 11am-4pm Tue-Thu & Sun late Jun–early Aug, shorter hours rest of-year, closed early Aug–mid-Sep), located near the Frøen T-bane station. If you're in a certain frame of mind, this collection of children's work from 180 countries – textiles, sculpture, paintings and drawings – can be pleasantly inspiring for kids, as well as adults.

TusenFryd

Children, and many of their parents, love **TusenFryd** (Map p79; ☎ 64 97 64 97, Vinterbro; height over/under 140cm Nkr225/195; ☼ 10.30am-7pm mid-Jun–Sep, shorter hours rest-of-year), where there's swimming, carousels, a fantasy farm, an excellent new wooden rollercoaster which creates zero gravity 12 times each circuit, and various other rides for little and big kids to enjoy. You'll find it 10km south of Oslo, just off the E6. The TusenFryd bus departs from the Galleri Oslo bus terminal nine times daily from 10am to 4pm (adult/child Nkr35/25).

TOURS

If you have limited time, organised city tours will give you a taste of what the city Oslo has to offer, although this will probably just leave you wishing that you had more time!

Oslo & Oslofjord

Båtservice Sightseeing (☎ 23 35 68 90; www.boat sightseeing.com; Pier 3, Rådhusbrygge) does a tidy 7½-hour city tour to the Bygdøy museums, Vigeland Park and the Holmenkollen ski jump, plus a cruise of the Oslofjord for a reasonable Nkr465 (late May to early September only). It also does a range of other tours and fjord cruises of shorter duration, including a 50-minute mini-cruise on Oslofjord (Nkr100, free with the Oslo Pass) and a two-hour cruise (Nkr185, or Nkr315 for an evening prawn buffet).

HM Kristiansen Tours (Map pp74-6; ☎ 23 15 73 00; www.hmk.no; Hegdehaugsveien 4) offers two/three/ four-hour tours (adult Nkr190/260/320, child Nkr90/130/160) around Oslo from mid-May to September. The four-hour tour takes in Vigeland Park, most of the museums on Bygdøy, the city centre and Holmenkollen, while the three-hour version includes most of the same places (except Holmenkollen) plus the National Gallery.

City Sightseeing (☎ 22 95 54 14; www.citysightseeing .com; May-Dec) promises a similar deal. Its 1½-/ two-/three-hour tours (Nkr190/230/250) really just offer a city overview from the bus window, although the three-hour version does allow 1½ hours at the Munch Museum. The tourist office has a list of pick-up points.

Probably of more interest is **Oslo Pride City Sightseeing** (☎ 97 10 47 42; www.citysightsee ing.no; mid-May–mid-Sep), Oslo's version of the hop-on-hop-off phenomenon. Two-day tickets cost Nkr150/75 per adult/child and cover the overwhelming proportion of city sights, which you can explore at your own pace. The tourist office has a list of stops that this tour company goes to.

Oslo Promenade (adult/child Nkr80/free; ☎ 5.30pm Mon, Wed & Fri Jun-Aug) is a guided evening walk through the centre of Oslo; the guides are knowledgeable and entertaining, making this a good option for getting an insider's view of Oslo. The walks start from in front of the Rådhus (Town Hall).

Norway in a Nutshell

The popular 'Norway in a Nutshell' day tours cost adult/child under 16 Nkr1735/ Nkr867.50, and may be booked through any tourist office or travel agency, or directly through NSB. For more information regarding this tour see p404.

FESTIVALS & EVENTS

Oslo's most festive annual event is surely the 17 May **National Constitution Day** celebration, when Oslo residents, whose roots spring from all over Norway, descend on the Royal Palace dressed in the finery of their native districts; see also p85.

In mid-March, the **Holmenkollen Ski Festival** attracts nordic skiers and ski jumpers from around the world. During the last weekend in July there's the **Summer Parade**, an indoor and outdoor contemporary music festival. August sees the **Oslo International Jazz Festival** (www.oslojazz.no), with great live jazz at venues across the city for six days; it doesn't quite have the caché of its counterpart in Molde but its accessibility does draw a substantial following. In October, there's the Scandinavia-oriented **Ultima Contemporary Music Festival** (☎ 22 42 99 99).

For details on these and other festivals, visit www.visitoslo.com.

SLEEPING

Oslo has a good range of accommodation, but booking ahead is nonetheless a good idea in summer.

Budget

Norway's camping grounds and budget accommodation tend to be a tram or bus ride away from the centre.

HOSTELS

Oslo also has some good HI-affiliated hostels. Sleeping bags aren't allowed at most; you must have HI regulation sheets or there is the option of hiring sheets for Nkr50 per visit.

YMCA Sleep-In (Map pp74-6; ☎ 22 42 10 66; fax 22 20 83 97; Grubbegata 4; mattress Nkr130; ⌛ mid-Jul–mid-Aug, reception 8-11am & 5-11.30pm) As basic as they come, the YMCA summer hostel, a 10-minute walk from Oslo S, is still a good central budget choice. Not surprisingly in this expensive city, it fills up quickly and you need a sleeping bag. Beds consist of mattresses on the floor in large dorms. Basic kitchen facilities are available.

Anker Hostel (Map pp74-6; ☎ 22 99 72 10; www.anker hostel.no; Storgata 55; dm in 4-/6-bed room Nkr170/145, d from Nkr430) This traveller-savvy hostel boasts an international atmosphere, spick-and-span rooms, laundry, luggage room, kitchen and a small bar. Breakfast costs Nkr60. It's

---

IN SEARCH OF THE CHEAPEST BED

Cheap beds in Oslo come at a premium, but there are four good services to help you track one down.

The best service is that operated by **Use-It** (Map pp74-6; ☎ 22 41 51 32; www.use-it.no; Møllergata 3), the Oslo Youth Information Service. It will help with bookings at hostels and private homes (dorms from Nkr120); there's no minimum stay and bookings are free. If you'll arrive in Oslo outside of the opening hours, contact them beforehand and ask for suggestions and phone numbers so you can book directly.

Staff at the official tourist offices (Oslo S and Fidtjof Nansens plass; see p71) also book rooms in private homes (two nights minimum stay) for prices a little cheaper than the hostels, as well as unfilled hotel rooms at discounted rates. A Nkr50 booking fee applies.

Den Norske Turistforening (Map pp74-6; DNT; Norwegian Mountain Touring Club; ☎ 22 82 28 22; www .dntoslo.no; Storgata 3) has lists of around 40 locally owned huts in Nordmarka. Among them are better-known staffed huts, where beds must be booked in advance and you can expect to pay Nkr185/240 for DNT members/nonmembers; most such huts are at least 10km from the centre.

One final option is **Bed & Breakfast Norway** (☎ 22 67 30 80; rominorg@online.no; www.bbnorway .com), which can track down one of the 16 B&Bs in the capital.

---

a very well-run place that comes highly recommended. To get there, take bus No 30–32, or tram No 11, 12, 13, 15 or 17 from Jernbanetorget to Hausmanns gate.

Oslo Vandrerhjem Haraldsheim (Map p79; ☎ 22 22 29 65; post@haraldsheim.oslo.no; Haraldsheimveien 4; dm from Nkr175, s/d with shared bathroom Nkr320/460, with private bathroom Nkr340/500) This hostel is 4km from the city centre, has 24-hour reception and 270 beds, mostly in clean four-bed dorms. There are kitchen and laundry facilities. Prices include breakfast. Take tram No 12, 15 or 17, or bus No 31 or 32 to Sinsenkrysset, then walk five minutes uphill.

Oslo Vandrerhjem Holtekilen (Map p79; ☎ 67 51 80 40; oslo.holtekilen.hostel@vandrerhjem.no; Michelets vei 55, Stabekk; dm Nkr180, s/d with shared bathroom Nkr280/460) This hostel is 9km west of Oslo and is fairly good value, but you'll also have to factor the bus fare into your costs, as the area is too far out to be included in day cards or the Oslo Pass. Breakfast is included. Take bus No 151, 153, 161, 162, 252 or 261 to Kveldroveien, or local train to Stabekk and cross the footbridge over the E18.

Oslo Vandrerhjem IMI (Map pp74-6; ☎ 22 98 62 00; oslo.imi.hostel@vandrerhjem.no; Staffelsgata 4; dm incl breakfast Nkr190; s/d with shared bathroom incl breakfast Nkr295/470; ✆ Jun–mid-Aug) This is ideal if you want to be close to the centre. You can look forward to decent accommodation, which is used for students the rest of the year. There's a kitchen and laundry facilities.

PENSION
Cochs Pensjonat (Map p79; ☎ 23 33 24 00; www.cochs pensjonat.no; Parkveien 25; s/d with shared bathroom Nkr390/540, s/d with private bathroom from Nkr490/640) This is a good choice with attractive, renovated rooms in a pleasant part of town, not far from the Royal Palace. The rooms with private bathroom are tidy, if a touch overpriced compared with what you can get elsewhere in Oslo.

CAMPING
Oslo Fjordcamping (Map p79; ☎ 22 75 20 55; mail@ oslocamping.no; Ljansbrukveien 1; tent site without/with car Nkr130/150, static caravans rental Nkr300) Oslo's best camping ground is this family-friendly place by the Oslofjord, which doesn't seem to attract the loud-and-young in such prolific numbers as the rest of the sites in the Oslo vicinity. There are showers, a kiosk selling simple snacks, and a nearby restaurant. It's 9km south of the city; take bus No 83.

Ekeberg Camping (Map p79; ☎ 22 19 85 68; mail@ ekebergcamping.no; Ekebergveien 65; tent sites 10-2 persons Nkr130-190; ✆ late May–early Aug) Nestled on a scenic knoll southeast of the city, Ekeberg Camping promises one of the best views over Oslo. Perhaps for that reason, it can get seriously crowded and facilities aren't as well maintained as they could be. Take bus No 34 or 46 from Jernbanetorget to Ekeberg (10 min). Prices rise by 10% in peak periods.

OSLO

Those who prefer wild camping can take T-bane line 1 to Frognerseteren at the edge of the Nordmarka or line 5 to Sognsvann. You can't camp at Sognsvann itself, but walk a kilometre or two into the woods and you'll find plenty of natural camp sites where you can pitch a tent for free.

Mid-Range

Oslo has plenty of hotels, with the best deals usually offered by those forming part of one of the hotel pass networks; see p371 for details. Five members of the Tulip Inn/ Rainbow chain of hotels offer reasonably good-value weekend and summer rates (identified via their email address).

Rica Travel Hotel (Map pp74-6; ☎ 22 00 33 00; rica .travel.hotel.oslo@rica.no; Arbeidergata 4; s/d mid-Jun–mid-Aug & Sat & Sun Nkr695/945, Nkr950/1290 rest-of-year; 🖳) This is a good-value business hotel. Rooms are modern and compact (some are larger than others) yet pleasant, and have all the mod-cons to ensure a pleasant stay. It also has a few 'kombi-rooms' (single rooms with an extra sofa bed) which go from Nkr795. The central location is also a winner.

Anker Hotel (Map pp74-6; ☎ 22 99 75 10; www.anker -hotel.no; Storgata 55; s/d mid-Jun–mid-Aug Nkr690/890, Sat & Sun Nkr590/790, rest-of-year Nkr 830/1080; 🖳) This is a particularly good choice for those who don't want to be in the busy downtown area but still be within walking distance; it's also close to the hip Grünerløkka restaurant and bar area. Rooms are modern and attractive, and staff members are friendly.

Hotel Bondeheimen (Map pp74-6; ☎ 23 21 41 00; booking@bondeheimen.com; Rosenkrantz gate 8; s/d mid-Jun–mid-Aug from Nkr750/830, Sat & Sun Nkr750/990, rest-of-year Nkr1095/1295) This central hotel is a terrific option, with attractive rooms and friendly staff. The older rooms (with 1980s Scandinavian pine-wood furniture) are slowly being renovated and all are highly recommended.

Hotel Spectrum (Map pp74-6; ☎ 23 36 27 00; spec trum@rainbow-hotels.no; Brugata 7; s/d mid-Jun–mid-Aug & Sat & Sun Nkr630/790, rest-of-year Nkr1075/1325; 🖳) This middle-of-the-road Rainbow Hotel is central and comfortable, although some of the rooms are starting to show their age. Still a good choice nonetheless.

Cecil Hotel (Map pp74-6; ☎ 23 31 48 00; cecil@rain bow-hotels.no; Stortingsgata 8; s/d mid-Jun–mid-Aug & Sat & Sun Nkr660/840, rest-of-year Nkr1175/1425; 🖳) This hotel has a great location just a stone's

throw from *Stortinget*; the entrance is on Rosen-krantz gate. Rooms are modern, quiet and well-appointed and there's an excellent breakfast buffet.

Hotell Astoria (Map pp74-6; ☎ 24 14 55 50; astoria@ rainbow-hotels.no; Dronningens gate 21; s/d mid-Jun–mid-Aug & Sat & Sun Nkr475/625, rest-of-year Nkr585/735) Just 100m south of the central Karl Johans gate and not far from the bus and train stations, this place is one of the cheapest Rainbow hotels, with tidy rooms, although some are bigger than others. Most rooms look onto a large courtyard.

Hotel Terminus (Map pp74-6; ☎ 22 05 60 00; termin us@rainbow-hotels.no; Stenersgata 10; s/d mid-Jun–mid-Aug & Sat & Sun Nkr630/790, rest-of-year Nkr1075/1325; 🖳) Tulip Inn/Rainbow's best summer value is Hotel Terminus, just 200m north of Oslo S. The comfortable rooms have full amenities and a touch more character than most. What's more, the breakfast is above average and complimentary coffee, tea and fruit are available throughout the day. Highly recommended.

Top End

Hotel Bristol (Map pp74-6; ☎ 22 82 60 00; booking@ bristol.no; Kristian IV's gate 7; s/d mid-Jun–mid-Aug & Sat & Sun Nkr995/1195, rest-of-year from Nkr1350/2030; 🖳 🅿) Hotel Bristol is the one of the best top-end hotels in Oslo, with delightful, stylish rooms which come with polished floorboards, period furniture, bathtubs (some rooms) and most modern luxuries.

Grand Hotel (Map pp74-6; ☎ 23 21 20 00; grand@rica .no; Karl Johans gate 31; s/d mid-Jun–mid-Aug & Sat & Sun from Nkr995/1250, rest-of-year Nkr1845/1995; 🖳) Brimming with period character, the regal

Grand Hotel oozes charm and an old-world elegance. The rooms are beautifully appointed and classy without being over-done. Also highly recommended.

Holmenkollen Park Hotel Rica (Map p79; ☎ 22 92 20 00; www.holmenkollenparkhotel.no; Kongeveien 26; s Nkr1600-1950, d Nkr 1600-2100) To really pamper yourself, head uphill to this historic hotel, near the Holmenkollen ski jump. In 1891, Dr Ingebrigt Christian Lund Holm opened a castle-like sanatorium here with one of the finest views in Oslo. The rooms in this architecturally distinguished building have understated but unmistakable character.

EATING
Oslo has Norway's biggest range of places to eat, all of which are open for lunch and dinner daily unless otherwise stated.

Nearly all the hotels set up elaborate breakfast buffets for their guests and most of them are open to nonresidents from Nkr80 to Nkr100. This is the best option for anyone who wants to start the day with a good-value feast.

If you can't face any more herring or scrambled eggs for breakfast, there are good bakeries all across Oslo where coffee and a pastry goes for around Nkr50. Most open from 7.30am to 4pm or 5pm Monday to Friday (10am to 5pm on Saturday).

Central Oslo
Paléet Food Court (Map pp74-6; ☎ 22 41 22 63; Karl Johans gate 37; meals Nkr75-95) One of the more pleasant food courts in Norway, this base-ment gathering of restaurants includes In-dian, Japanese (sushi from Nk75), Thai and Italian food, as well as baguettes (Nkr43) and grilled meat and fish (from Nkr95).

Salsa (Map pp74-6; ☎ 22 41 20 60; Nedre Slottsgate 15; dishes from Nkr32) The Salsa restaurant, with outdoor seating, is a good, no-frills choice and serves reasonable tapas and *bocadillos* (filled rolls).

Peppe's Pizza (Map pp74-6; ☎ 23 31 12 80; Karl Johans gate 1; pizzas from Nkr134; Stortingsgata 4 (Map pp74-6); Hegdehaugsveien 31 (Map pp74-6); Observatoriegata (Map pp74-6); Aker Brygge (Map pp74-6) The recom-mended Norwegian pizzeria chain, offers large pizzas, lasagne (Nkr93) and lunch-time buffets (Nkr95).

Café Norrøna (Map pp74-6; ☎ 23 31 80 00; Grensen 19; lunch buffet Nkr148, salad/soup buffet Nkr98/78; 11am-4.30pm mid-May–mid-Sep, until 6pm rest-of-year) If

you're craving salad or vegetables, this café is fantastic with lunch buffets that your body will thank you for after all of those hot dogs.

Stortorvets Gjæstgiveri (Map pp74-6; ☎ 23 35 63 60; Grensen 1; starters Nkr70-130, mains Nkr145-245) This historic place has far more ambience than most Oslo restaurants can muster, serv-ing well-prepared traditional Norwegian delicacies in a delightful old Oslo build-ing. The reindeer carpaccio (Nkr130) is particularly good. They also have live jazz some Saturday afternoons.

A Touch of France (Map pp74-6; ☎ 23 10 01 60; Øvre Slottsgate 16; starters Nkr75-150, mains Nkr185-289) If you're missing Paris, A Touch of France is not a bad approximation of a Parisian streetside café, with outdoor tables, com-munal dining tables and an informal at-mosphere. The food also wouldn't shame a Parisian chef, especially the shellfish platter (Nkr375).

Onkel Donald Kafé-Bar (Map pp74-6; ☎ 23 35 63 10; Universitetsgata 26; snacks & sandwiches Nkr39-89, light meals Nkr98-131, mains Nkr179-198) This is one of the most chic places in Oslo, with a buzzy ambience, stylish dining area and very good Norwegian food. It stays open late (until 3am most nights), when it morphs into an equally hip bar.

Rust (Map pp74-6; ☎ 23 20 22 10; Hegehaugsveien 22; snacks & light meals Nkr54-127, mains Nkr136-198) In an attractive part of Oslo, Rust comes highly recommended. It has a bohemian retro décor, nice outdoor terrace, friendly waiters and all-round good feel, not to mention tasty food.

Engebret Café (Map pp74-6; ☎ 22 82 25 25; Bank plassen 1; sandwiches Nkr59-89, starters Nkr125-145, mains Nkr245-345; lunch & dinner Mon-Sat) First founded beside the Christiania Theatre in 1857, Engebret Café was the city's first 'theatre café' and attracted both actors and writers. Today it retains a cultured and classy atmosphere with high quality Norwegian and international cuisine, spe-cialising in fish dishes.

Gamle Rådhus (Map pp74-6; ☎ 22 42 01 07; Nedre Slottsgate 1; starters Nkr98-145, mains Nkr245-285) Housed in an historic 1641 building, this is Oslo's oldest restaurant. The dark, cosy atmosphere is enhanced by an English-style pub and roaring fire. If you've always wanted to try the glutinous fish dish *lute-fisk* (dried cod), pop in here in the weeks

THE AUTHOR'S CHOICE

Better known as just 'Løkka', the formerly downmarket workers' district of Grünerløkka is one of Oslo's best-kept secrets and is fast becoming one of the city's trendiest neighbourhoods. It's the sort of place that doesn't see too many tourists, but if you lived in Oslo you'd keep on returning here for its good restaurants and hip cafés and bars. Many restaurants turn into bars by night and stay open until 3am on weekends.

Tea Lounge (Map p72; ☎ 22 37 07 05; Thorvald Meyers gate 33B; sandwiches & salads Nkr72) This place is a gem. The Art Deco façade sets the scene for a hip and happening place that does light meals, great coffee and iced teas, and a host of alcoholic beverages. It's ideal at any time of the day or night and stays open until 3.30am in summer.

before Christmas, when they make up big batches of it.

Also recommended:

Vegeta Vertshus (Map pp74-6; ☎ 22 83 42 32; Munkedamsveien 3B; small/large plates Nkr90/100, buffets Nkr145) Hearty vegetarian buffets, including wholegrain pizza, casseroles and salads.

Sushi Nam King (Map pp74-6; ☎ 22 20 19 40; Torggata 24; sushi Nkr36-165, mains Nkr145-249; ☺ 4-11.30pm Mon-Sat, 4-10.30pm Sun) Japanese–Korean hybrid that's ideal for a sushi fix .

Far East (Map pp74-6; ☎ 22 20 56 28; Bernt Ankers gate 4; lunch specials Nkr78, mains Nkr78-158) Excellent and filling Thai or Vietnamese food.

There are a couple of great budget choices around the university. At **University Café** (Map pp74-6; Universitetsgata; dinner for students/others Nkr40/50), in the basement of the law school, you'll enjoy basic meals in generous portions. Discerning students pack out **BIT** (Map pp74-6; Universitetsgata; ☺ 8am-7pm Mon-Fri, 10am-5pm Sat), which does great baguettes (Nkr36 to Nkr42), calzone (Nkr42) and ciabatta (Nkr39 to Nkr42); **Kaffe & Krem** (Map pp74-6; Drammensveien 30; Solli plass); and **Baker Hansen** (Map pp74-6; Akersgata 47), which does great bagels.

Aker Brygge

Aker Brygge, the old shipyard turned trendy shopping complex west of the main harbour, has a food court (from 11am to 10pm) with various eateries including Noodle Bar (Map pp74-6) with Chinese dishes, a baked-potato stall and other options.

Reker (fresh shrimp) are sold from boats near Aker Brygge while the best-value fresh produce comes from the market stalls around Grønlandstorg.

ICA Gourmet Supermarket & Café (Map pp74-6; Holmens gate 7, Aker Brygge; ☺ 9am-10pm Mon-Fri, 9am-8pm Sat) At the rear of Aker Brygge, ICA will get you salivating. On offer, filled baguettes (Nkr40), whole grilled chicken (Nkr45.50), as well as wok or pasta dishes and sushi. You can eat inside, but takeaway works out a bit cheaper and is infinitely more pleasant.

Albertine (Map pp74-6; ☎ 21 02 36 30; Stranden 3; snacks Nkr34-95, light meals Nkr95-135, mains Nkr189-225; ☺ breakfast, lunch & dinner) Probably the most pleasant of the waterfront eateries, Albertine offers bistro-style food and a front-row seat to watch the world go by.

Big Horn Steak House (Map pp74-6; ☎ 22 83 83 63; Fjordaléen 6; steaks Nkr159-436) The US-style Big Horn Steak House specialises in steaks of various sizes. Ask any Norwegian for their favourite place for steaks and chances are that many will send you here.

Also recommended:

Beach Club (Map pp74-6; ☎ 22 83 83 82; Bryggetorget 14; burgers Nkr85-135; ☺ breakfast, lunch & dinner) Great for a sunny afternoon; serves full American breakfast (Nkr105).

Café Sorgenfri (Map pp74-6; ☎ 21 50 10 90; Bryggetorget 14; lunch & light meals Nkr69-155, starters Nkr75-115, mains Nkr195-245) Varied menu and pleasant outdoor tables.

Herbern Marina (Map pp74-6; ☎ 22 83 19 90; Stranden 30; light meals Nkr79-113, 0.4L beer from Nkr57) Surprisingly reasonable prices right out on the water.

Grünerløkka

Sult (Map p72; ☎ 22 87 04 67; Thorvald Meyers gate 26; dishes Nkr79-179) The popular and informal Sult perfectly captures the Grünerløkka vibe with an imaginative menu replete with superb fish and pasta dishes. It's always packed so get there early and wait for a table in the attached bar (appropriately called Tørst).

Bagel & Juice (Map p72; ☎ 22 37 05 80; Thorvald Meyers gate 44; bagels Nkr31-58; ☺ breakfast, lunch & dinner) This bright and cheery place does terrific bagels, a huge range of fresh juices (Nkr32 to Nkr40) and good coffee (Nkr20 to Nkr34).

Mucho Mas (Map p72; ☎ 22 37 16 09; Thorvald Meyers gate 36; starters Nkr39-85, mains around Nkr110) It may not look like much from the outside, but this is one of Norway's best Mexican restaurants. The full Mexican repertoire is on offer, including tacos, nachos and burritos; all dishes are offered in meat or vegetarian versions. You'll also find well-priced beer to help put out the fire. Credit cards aren't accepted.

Bistro Brocante (Map p72; ☎ 22 35 68 71; Thorvald Meyers gate 40; lunch specials Nkr59-135, starters Nkr38-96, mains 164-285) Another very good choice, this informal French-inspired café serves delicious meals, including salads (Nkr98 to Nkr115) and quiche (Nkr93). The outdoor tables are at a premium in summer.

Fru Hagen (Map p72; ☎ 22 35 67 87; Thorvald Meyers gate 40; mains Nkr75-159) Next door to Bistro Brocante, this trendy and arty place serves international-style meals until 9.30pm, then turns into a popular upmarket bar. Here too, you'll have to fight (or be patient) for an outdoor table.

QBA (Map p72; ☎ 22 35 24 60; Olaf Ryes plass 4; snacks & light meals Nkr29-79; ⏰ 8-1am Mon-Fri, 11-1am Sat & Sun) This is another very cool hang-out that turns into a bar popular with trendy students, especially on Friday night. It offers wireless Internet access for those with laptops and serves a wide range of drinks, nachos, wraps, salads and bruschetta.

Around Oslo S & Grønland

The Oslo City Shopping Centre has a food court (Map pp74-6; including bakeries, a baked potato and grill joint, and Chinese and Mexican restaurants) which open until 9pm weekdays and 6pm on Saturday. They're fine for a quick, cheap meal, but come with that unmistakably sterile shopping centre ambience.

Anyone over 18 can buy beer at Oslo supermarkets until 8pm from Monday to Friday and 6pm on Saturday. For wine or spirits, you'll have to be at least 20 years old and visit the **Vinmonopolet** (Map pp74-6; Kirkeveien 64, Oslo City Shopping Centre, Møllergata 10 & Elisenbergveien 37; ⏰ 10am-5pm Mon-Wed, 10am-6pm Thu, 10am-6pm Fri, 10am-2pm Sat).

The Grønland district and the back streets west of Storgata are also brimming with inexpensive ethnic supermarkets where you'll find otherwise unavailable items such as fresh herbs and African, Asian and Middle Eastern ingredients.

Teddy's Soft Bar (Map pp74-6; ☎ 22 17 36 00; Brugata 3A; light meals around Nkr75; ⏰ lunch & dinner Mon-Sat) Teddy's Soft Bar is a local institution and has scarcely changed since it opened in the 1950s. On offer are light, typically Norwegian meals – try the *pytt i panne* (Nkr88), which is essentially eggs with diced potato and meat.

Punjab Tandoori (Map p74-6; ☎ 22 17 20 86; Grønlandsleiret 24; lunch specials Nkr75, mains around Nkr60) Near the Grønland T-bane station, this place has simply presented Indian fare – curry, dal, samosas and tasty curries – that won't be too hot unless you ask them to be. The lunch special includes chicken tandoori with rice and nan.

Baker Brun (Map p74-6; ☎ 22 17 51 26; Grønland 12) One of our favourite bakeries – it has a few tables and great breads and pastries (there are other Baker Brun branches around town).

Supermarkets abound around Oslo. Only the small ones classed as kiosks can open on Sundays. Some of the more central choices include the following:

Kiwi (Map pp74-6 Oslo S (Jernbanetorget), Storgata; ⏰ 9am-9pm Mon-Fri, 9am-8pm Sat)

Rimi (Map pp74-6; Gunerius Shopping Centre, Storgata; ⏰ 8am-10pm Mon-Sat)

Oslo Helsekost (Map pp74-6; ☎ 22 42 96 00; Akersgata 32; ⏰ 9am-5pm Mon-Wed & Fri, 9am-6pm Thu, 10am-3pm Sat) Small health-food store selling organic produce and wholesome snacks.

Holmenkollen

Holmenkollen Restaurant (Map p79; ☎ 22 13 92 00; Holmenkollveien 119; mains Nkr199-289, 3-course summer menu Nkr425) This highly regarded restaurant, uphill from the Holmenkollen T-bane station (line No 1), offers fine food and views. You can enjoy the same view and simpler meals at the adjacent cafeteria for around Nkr120.

DRINKING & ENTERTAINMENT

The tourist office's free monthly brochure *What's On in Oslo* lists current concerts, theatre and special events, but the best publication for night owls is the free *Streetwise*, published annually in English by Use-It (p71).

Pubs, Discos & Nightclubs

Oslo isn't the most exciting of European cities by night. Indeed, the famed Spanish movie director Pedro Almodovar, an icon of dynamic Madrid in the 1980s, complained a decade later that the Spanish capital was

OSLO

in danger of becoming 'as boring as Oslo'. If only Oslo were indeed *that* boring!

That said, it doesn't take too long to find the pulse of Oslo and most nights from Wednesday through to Saturday can get pretty lively by Norwegian standards with happy, noisy crowds without too much that will stay long in the memory. *Streetwise* has a good listing for the latest cool spots.

Note that many Oslo night spots have an unwritten dress code which expects patrons to be relatively well turned out – at the very least, don't show up in grubby gear and hiking boots. For most bars and clubs that serve beer and wine, you must be over 18 years of age, but many places, especially those that serve spirits, impose a higher age limit. On weekends, most Oslo night spots remain open until at least 3am.

Beer prices for half-litres typically range from Nkr50 to Nkr65, but some places (usually grim and inhabited by wary elbow-on-the-bar locals) charge as little as Nkr29 for those travellers watching their kroner. Bars and clubs in the centre tend to be pricey (you'll want to drink slowly with a half-litre of beer able to fetch Nkr99!), while those

east of the centre and north of Oslo S are generally more downmarket.

The cheapest places we found are **Lille Laila** (Map pp74-6; cnr Brugata & Christian Krohgs gate; half-litre inside/outside Nkr29/34), where you may just want to pay the extra Nk5 to get outside and away from the depressing bar; and **Stargate** (Map pp74-6; Grønlandsleiveret 2; half-litre Nkr36) which is just (but only just) a touch more pleasant, with a down-to-earth drinking-den atmosphere.

Another very agreeable spot a bit closer to the centre is the jazzy **Café Con Bar** (Map pp74-6; ☎ 22 05 02 00; Brugata 11; ☺ 11am-1am Mon-Thu, 11am-3am Fri & Sat, noon-3am Sun), which has an infectiously energetic vibe most nights. A hip place is **Onkel Donald Kafé-Bar** (Map pp74-6; ☎ 23 35 63 10; Universitetsgata 26; see p89).

Once billed by the British magazine *The Face* as one of the three best clubs in the world, **Skansen** (Map pp74-6; ☎ 22 42 28 88; Rådhusgata 25; cover charge Nkr50; ☺ Wed-Sun) closed for a few years and never quite recovered its soul. Then again, it's still a lively spot (housed in a former public lavatory) which resounds to the beats of house, funk, jazz and techno with a regular cast of well-known DJs on Fridays and Saturdays.

LIVE MUSIC IN OSLO

Oslo has a fitful live music scene, although few places have regular programmes; Wednesday to Saturday is when you're most likely to catch something (apart from a cold if you're smoking outside in winter). Cover charges of around Nkr60 or Nkr70 normally apply.

Jazz is a recurring theme and most bars host live performances during Oslo's August Jazz Festival (p86).

Far and away the best place for jazz is **Blå** (Map pp74-6; ☎ 22 20 91 81, Brenneriveien 9C), where you can catch outstanding new artists and bands before they hit the big time.

Café Con Bar (Map pp74-6; ☎ 22 05 02 00; Brugata 11) has live music some Saturdays and a big jazz sound from 10pm to 2am on Sunday nights. **Herr Nilsens Pub** (Map pp74-6; ☎ 22 33 54 05; CJ Hambros plass 5; cover charge Nkr70) is a pleasant hang-out for the over-30s crowd and from 11pm to 2am on Saturday, you can ease into your night with a dose of smooth live jazz. Somewhat more frenetic and unpredictable is **Smuget** (Map pp74-6; ☎ 22 42 52 62, Rosenkrantz gate 22; cover charge Nkr65/75 weekdays/weekends), a reliable hot spot with a pounding disco and live jazz, rock and blues.

Rock fans may want to check out **Elm Street Rock Café** (Map pp74-6; ☎ 22 42 14 27; Dronningens gate 32) that's always popular, but especially on Wednesdays, when there are often live shows.

For something completely different, the **Underwater Pub** (Map pp72; ☎ 22 46 05 26, Dalsbergstien 4) is notable on Tuesday and Thursday, when students of the State School of Opera lubricate their vocal chords and treat patrons to their favourite arias. Yes, the ceiling really is the surface of the sea!

Irish folk bands perform a few times a week at **Dubliner** (Map pp74-6; ☎ 22 33 70 05; Rådhusgata 28; cover charge Nkr60), a friendly and authentic Irish pub with the usual wood-panelling, friendly bar staff and ample pints of Guinness (Nkr62).

The Belfast-like barricades outside say it all at **Blitz** (Map pp74-6; ☎ 22 11 23 49; Pilestredet 30C), the home of Oslo's rebellious bohemian scene. It also features a book café and live concerts.

GAY & LESBIAN OSLO

Oslo's gay scene is pretty changeable, but one perennial favourite is **London Pub** (Map pp74-6; ☎ 22 70 87 00; CJ Hambros plass 5; cover charge Nkr50). Not your average English pub, this dark but popular (mainly male) gay bar has DJs, a disco and a piano bar. It's a good spot to find out where the latest cool places are. Also worth checking out is *Streetwise*, the free Oslo guide published by Use-It, (p71) which has a 'Gay Guide' covering cafés, pubs, clubs, bookstores and other activities or services of interest. There's also a **gay and lesbian helpline** (☎ 22 11 33 60). For more information on gay issues, see p380.

For a cool bar scene, check out Thorvald Meyers gate and the surrounding streets in Grünerløkka, where there are many restaurants which turn decidedly funky after the kitchen closes; see p90 for some ideas to get you started. Particularly worth lingering in are the following:

Sult (Map p72; ☎ 22 87 04 67; Thorvald Meyers gate 26)

Tea Lounge (Map p72; ☎ 22 37 07 05; Thorvald Meyers gate 33B)

Fru Hagen (Map p72; ☎ 22 35 67 87; Thorvald Meyers gate 40)

QBA (Map p72; ☎ 22 35 24 60; Olaf Ryes plass 4)

Concerts

Keep your ear to the ground in summer to hear about outdoor concerts at Vigeland Park – a weird-and-wonderful venue.

The city's largest concert halls, **Oslo Spektrum** (Map pp74-6; ☎ 22 05 29 00; Sonja Henies plass 2) and **Rockefeller Music Hall** (Map pp74-6; ☎ 22 20 32 32; Torggata 16), host a wide range of artists and events, including internationally known musicians.

Den Norske Opera (Map pp74-6; ☎ 81 54 44 88; Storgata 23; tickets from Nkr300) is Oslo's opera company and stages opera, ballet and classical concerts every month, except for July.

You may also want to check out the alternative dance and theatre scene at the café-style **Black Box** (Map pp74-6; ☎ 22 10 40 20; Stranden 3), in the Aker Brygge complex.

The **National Theatre** (Nationaltheatret; Map pp74-6; ☎ 22 00 14 00; Stortingsgata 15) is Norway's showcase theatre venue and has a lavish rococo hall. It was constructed specifically as a venue for the works of Norwegian playwright Henrik Ibsen, whose works are still performed here.

Cinema

Saga Kino (Map pp74-6; ☎ 82 03 00 00; Stortingsgata 28) The six-screen Saga Kino cinema shows first-run movies, including Hollywood fare, in their original language; the entrance is on Olav V's gate.

Filmens Hus (Map pp74-6; ☎ 22 47 45 00; Dronningens gate 16) Filmens Hus screens old classics and international festival winners most days.

SHOPPING

Oslo excels in upmarket shopping and there are many fine shops on Grensen and Karl Johans gate. For art, try the galleries on Frognerveien.

Oslo Sweater Shop (Map pp74-6; ☎ 22 42 42 25; Biskop Gunnerus gate 3; ☯ 8am-10pm Mon-Sat, 1-7pm Sun) Traditional Norwegian sweaters are popular purchases and the Oslo Sweater Shop has good prices and selections.

Husfliden (Map pp74-6; ☎ 24 14 12 80; Lille Grensen 7) Husfliden is a larger shop selling quality Norwegian clothing and crafts, with items ranging from carved wooden trolls to elaborate folk costumes.

Vestkanttorget flea market (Amaldus Nilsens plass; ☯ 10am-4pm Sat) If you're happy with pot luck and sifting through heaps of junk, take a chance here. It's at the plaza which intersects Professor Dahls gate, a block east of Vigeland Park and it's a more-than-pleasant way to pass a Saturday morning.

Also recommended:

Heimen Husflid (Map pp74-6; ☎ 23 21 42 00; Rosenkrantz gate 8) Clothing and crafts.

Unique Design (Map pp74-6; ☎ 22 42 97 60; Rosenkrantz gate 13) Good for sweaters.

GETTING THERE & AWAY
Air

Oslo's Gardermoen International Airport (☎ 64 81 20 00) opened in October 1998 and has a motorway and high-speed rail link to the city centre (see p95). For details of international services, see p387.

Domestic flights also depart from here and include services (with sample one-way fares) to: Ålesund (Nkr553), Bergen (Nkr739), Røros (from Nkr430, daily except Saturday), Stavanger (Nkr739), Tromsø (Nkr808) and Trondheim (Nkr553).

BUS TRAVEL

Destination	Departures	Cost	Duration
Åndalsnes	2 daily	Nkr390/570 (day/night)	7hr
Arendal	3 daily	Nkr340	4hr
Bergen	3 daily	Nkr640	11½hr
Kristiansand	8 daily	Nkr380	5½hr
Lillehammer	4 daily	Nkr250	3hr
Røros	3 daily	Nkr465	6hr
Stavanger	up to 5 daily *	Nkr720	9½hr
Trondheim	3 daily	Nkr610	8½hr

* change at Kristiansand

KLM, Widerøe, SAS Braathens and Ryanair also operate 'Oslo' services to/from Torp Airport, some 123km southwest of Oslo. See p95 for details of getting there.

Boat

For details of international ferry services, see p393.

Ferries operated by **DFDS Seaways** (Map pp74-6; ☎ 22 41 90 90; Vippetangen 2), and **Stena Line AS** (Map pp74-6; ☎ 02010; Jernbanetorget 2) connect Oslo with Denmark from the Vippetangen Quay off Skippergata. Bus No 60 stops within a couple of minutes walk of the terminal.

Color Line Ferries (Map pp74-6; ☎ 81 00 08 11; Øvre Slottsgate 12A) run to/from Hirtshals (Denmark) and Kiel (Germany); they dock at Hjortneskaia, west of the central harbour. Take tram No 10 or 13 from Oslo S, or the Color Line bus which leaves Oslo S one hour before boat departures.

Bus

Long-distance buses arrive and depart from the **Galleri Oslo Bus Terminal** (Map pp74-6; Schweigaards gate 8, Galleri Oslo); the train and bus stations are linked via a convenient overhead walkway for easy connecting services.

Nor-Way Bussekspress (☎ 82 02 13 00, 81 54 44 44; www.nor-way.no) has the biggest range of services.

During summer, more-popular routes attract special summer prices which promise substantial discounts. These include Bergen (Nkr265), Trondheim (Nkr290) and Røros (Nkr290).

International services also depart from the bus terminal. For details of schedules and prices, see p399.

Car & Motorcycle

The main highways into the city are the E6 from the north and south, and the E18 from the east and west. Each time you enter Oslo, you must pass through (at least) one of 19 toll stations and pay Nkr15 to Nkr25.

Hitching

When leaving Oslo it's generally best to take a bus or train to the outskirts of the city in your direction of travel and start hitching from there (see p404).

To hitch to Bergen, take bus No 161 to its final stop and wait beside the E16 towards Hønefoss. For Trondheim, take T-Bane line 5 (direction: Vestli) to Grorud and wait beside Rv4, which connects to the E6 north. For the south coast and Stavanger, take bus No 31 or 32 to the Maritim petrol station.

Train

All trains arrive and depart from Oslo S in the city centre. It has **reservation desks** (Map pp74-6; ☉ 6am-11pm, international 6.30am-11pm) and an **information desk** (☎ 81 50 08 88) which provides details on routes and timetables throughout the country.

There are frequent train services around Oslofjord (eg Drammen, Skien, Moss, Fredrikstad and Halden).

For details of international schedules and prices, see p390.

GETTING AROUND

Oslo has an efficient public transport system with an extensive network of buses, trams, underground trains and ferries. In addition to single-trip tickets, day and transferable

TRAIN TRAVEL

Destination	Departures	Cost	Duration
Åndalsnes	up to 3 daily	Nkr644	5½hr
Arendal	3 daily	Nkr250	3½hr
Bergen	5 daily	Nkr670	6½-8hr
Kristiansand	4 daily	Nkr531	4½hr
Lillehammer	11-17 daily	Nkr282	2¼hr
Røros	up to 3 daily	Nkr582	5hr
Stavanger	up to 5 daily	Nkr783	8hr
Trondheim	4 daily	Nkr748	6½hr

All fares are in 2nd-class seats; 2nd-class sleepers cost an additional Nkr150

eight-trip tickets are also available. Children aged four to 16 and seniors over 67 years of age pay half price on all fares.

The Oslo Pass (see the boxed text, p71) includes access to all public transport options within the city, however with the exception of night buses and trams. Bicycles can be carried on trams and trains for an additional Nkr10. The automatic fine for travelling without a ticket is a rather punitive Nkr750.

Trafikanten (Map pp74-6; ☎ 177, 81 50 01 76; Jernbanetorget; ⏱ 7am-8pm Mon-Fri, 8am-6pm Sat & Sun) is located below Oslo S tower and provides free schedules and a public transport map, *Sporveiskart Oslo*.

To/From the Airport

Flybussen (☎ 177, 22 17 70 30; www.flybussen.com) is the airport shuttle to Gardermoen International Airport at Gardermoen, 50km north of Oslo. It departs from the bus terminal at Galleri Oslo three or four times hourly from 4.05am to 9.50pm. The trip costs Nkr100/160 one-way/return (valid one month) and takes 40 minutes. **Flybussekspressen** (☎ 177) connects Gardermoen with Majorstua (Nkr110), Bekkestua (Nkr130), Ski (Nkr150) and other places, one to four times hourly.

FlyToget (☎ 81 50 07 77; www.flytoget.no) rail services leave Asker station for Gardermoen (Nkr150, 24 minutes) every 20 minutes between 4.45am and midnight, with departures also from the National Theatre. In addition, most northbound **NSB** (☎ 81 50 08 88) intercity and local trains stop at Gardermoen (Nkr75, from 26 minutes, hourly but fewer on Saturday).

To get to/from Torp Airport, 123km southwest of Oslo and serviced by Ryanair among others (see p93), take the **Torp-Ekspressen** (☎ 81 50 01 76; adult/child Nkr130/70) bus between Galleri Oslo Bus Terminal and the airport (1½ hours). Departures from Oslo leave three hours before scheduled Ryanair departures, and leave from Torp after Ryanair flights arrive. Although the service operates primarily for Ryanair passengers (the bus will wait if the flight is delayed), passengers on other airlines may also use it. At other times, you'll need to take the hourly Telemarksekspressen bus (or a taxi; from Nkr150, 10 minutes) between the airport and Sandefjord train station from where there are connections to Oslo.

Bicycle

Renting a bicycle is more difficult in Oslo than it should be. The only place where bikes can be rented by the day is **Skiservice Sykkelutleie** (Map p79; ☎ 22 13 95 04; www.skiservice .no; Tryvannsveien 2; per day around Nkr175).

One innovative alternative if you don't plan on going too far is **Oslo Citybike** (☎ 22 02 34 88), a network of bikes which cyclists can borrow from bicycle stands around the city. Although access cards (Nkr50) last for 24 hours, you have to leave each bike after three hours (in practise, locals return the bikes and immediately release them again). Cards can be purchased from the tourist office (p71) and you'll need to leave a Nkr500 cash deposit.

Den Rustne Eike (Map pp74-6; ☎ 22 44 18 80; Oscars gate 32; 8am-4.30pm Mon-Fri, 10am-2pm Sat) can handle bike repairs.

For more cycling information see p84.

Boat

Ferries to the Oslofjord islands sail from Vippetangen Quay. The express boat **Princessin** (☎ 81 50 01 76; www.nbds.no) connects Oslo with Drøbak (Nkr62, 1½ hours, three weekly) and other Oslofjord stops en route: Ildjernet, Langåra and Håøya (which is a holiday spot offering fine swimming and camping). It departs from Aker Brygge pier.

For details of ferries to Bygdøy, see p81.

Bus & Tram

Bus and tram lines lace the city and extend into the suburbs. There's no central station, but most converge at Jernbanetorget in front of Oslo S. Most westbound buses, including those to Bygdøy and Vigeland Park, also stop immediately south of the National Theatre.

The frequency of service drops dramatically at night, but on weekends, night buses N12, N14 and N18 follow the tram routes until 4am or later; there are also weekend night buses (No 201 to 218). These services are called Nattlinjer and cost Nkr45 per ride (no passes are valid).

Tickets for most trips cost Nkr20 if you buy them in advance (7-Eleven, Narvesen, Trafikanten) or Nkr30 if you buy them from the driver. A day pass costs Nkr55.

Car & Motorcycle

Oslo has its share of one-way streets, which can complicate city driving a bit, but the streets are rarely as congested as in most European cities.

Metered street parking, identified by a solid blue sign with a white 'P', can be found throughout the city. Payment (up to Nkr44 per hour) is usually required from 8am to 5pm Monday to Friday, until 3pm Saturday. At other times, parking is free unless otherwise posted. The city centre also has 16 multistorey car parks, including those at Oslo City and Aker Brygge shopping centres; fees range from Nkr70 to Nkr200 per 24 hour period.

Note that the Oslo Pass includes parking at all municipal car parks; instructions for display come with the pass.

Taxi

Flagfall starts from Nkr45 plus Nkr12 to Nkr18 per kilometre. There are taxi stands at Oslo S, shopping centres and city squares, but any taxi with a lit sign is available for hire. Otherwise, phone **Norgestaxi** (☎ 08000) or **Oslo Taxi** (☎ 02323), but note that the meter starts running at the point of dispatch! Oslo taxis accept major credit cards.

T-Bane

The five-line Tunnelbanen underground system, better known as the T-bane, is faster and extends further from the city centre than most city bus lines. All lines pass through the Nationaltheatret, Stortinget and Jernbanetorget stations.

AROUND OSLO

DRØBAK

pop 11,200

Once Oslo's winter harbour, Drøbak is a cosy little village by the water's edge, home to enough clapboard timber buildings to warrant a day trip from the capital.

The helpful **tourist office** (☎ 64 93 50 87; Hanegata 4; ☼ 10am-5.30pm mid-Jun–mid-Aug) by the harbour has a wealth of information on Drøbak, including *Walks Around Drøbak* (free) to guide your rambling through the village.

In town, there are several small eateries around the pretty Torget sq and along nearby Storgata.

Sights

Drøbak is known as Oslo's 'Christmas town' and is renowned for its public decorations. There's also a Christmas shop, **Tregaardens Julehus** (☎ 64 93 41 78; www.julehuset .no; Torget 4; ☼ 10am-5pm Mon-Fri, 10am-3pm Sat Mar-Oct, 10am-7pm Mon-Fri & 10am-3pm Sat Nov, 10am-8pm Mon-Fri & 10am-4pm Sat Dec-Feb), which has a Father Christmas postbox for kids.

Saltvannsakvarium (☎ 64 93 09 74; Havnegata 4; adult/child Nkr30/10; ☼ 11am-7pm May-Aug, 11am-4pm Sep-Apr) lays claim to the title of the world's only *lutefisk* museum. Not far away, the small **Drøbak Båtforenings Maritime Samlinger** (☎ 64 93 09 74; Kroketønna 4; adult/child Nkr10/5; ☼ 11am-7pm May-Aug, 11am-4pm Sep-Apr) is a museum of maritime paraphernalia, including a number of boat engines.

Around 3km north of the centre, the **Follo Museum** (☎ 64 93 99 00; Belsjøvn; adult/child Nkr20/5; ☼ 11am-4pm Tue-Fri & noon-5pm Sat & Sun late May–early Oct) is an open-air museum with displays on the culture of this coastal region of Oslofjord, as well as displays on Roald Amundsen (see the boxed text, p364) who lived nearby.

The **Oscarsborg fortress**, on an offshore island and built in the 1850s, fired the shots that sank the German warship *Blücher* on 9 April 1940. Ferries (adult/child Nkr65/40, 45 minutes) to the island depart 14 times daily from the harbour from mid-June to mid-August.

Getting There & Away

The hourly bus No 541 travels between Oslo and Drøbak (Nkr62, one hour). Alternatively in July, the express boat **Princessin** (☎ 81 50 01 76; www.nbds.no) does one trip from Oslo's Aker Brygge pier daily Wednesday to Sunday (three times weekly in August), allowing at least 1½ hours in Drøbak before returning to Oslo. The one-way fare is Nkr62.

The new tunnel under Oslofjord, between Drøbak and Drammen, charges Nkr55 each way for a car (motorcycles free).

DRAMMEN

pop 90,000

Drammen is an industrial centre of more interest to businesspeople than tourists. With heavy port machinery and factories, it hardly jumps out at you as being worth a stop. It does, however, have a couple of quirky elements – Drammen was the start of the Royal Road to Bergen and it was the original home of the potato alcohol aquavit – which may warrant a detour. The **tourist office** (☎ 32 80 62 10; www.drammen.kommune.no; Bragernes Torg 6; ☼ 9am-5pm Mon-Fri & 11am-5pm Sat & Sun mid-Jun-mid Aug, 9am-4.30pm Mon-Fri rest-of-year) can be visited for further information.

Sights & Activities

Drammen has several buildings of note all of which are clustered close together in the old centre around the main thoroughfare Bragernes Torg: the historic **Stock Exchange** on Bragernes Torg (which now houses a McDonald's); the restored **Rådhus** on Engenes 1 (the city hall, a former courthouse and jail); the **fire station** in Bragernes Torg (now a bank); the lovely **Drammen Theatre** (☎ 32 21 31 00; Gamle Kirkeplass; ☼ for events only), built in 1870, burned down in 1993 and reopened in 1996; and the Gothic-style **Bragernes church** (Bragernes Torg) from 1871.

You can also see the house (from the outside only) where *aquavit* was first produced in 1804, on Sommerfrydveien, by merchant Johan Godtfried Schwencke in response to a royal decree that corn not be used to produce spirits. In late autumn, Drammen holds a national *aquavit* competition in which celebrities judge which is the best brand.

To get beyond the industry, worthwhile hikes take you up into the **Bragernesåsen** woodlands or the scenic 50m-deep **Kjøster-udjuvet Gorge**, just over 1km north of town. Hiking maps are available from the tourist office.

Sleeping & Eating

There's a good mix of cafés, restaurants, pubs and nightclubs either in or near Bragernes Torg.

Drammen Vandrerhjem & Davik Troika (☎ 32 26 77 00; fax 32 26 77 01; Fagerlibakken 1; dm/s/d Nkr220/350/550) This clean and friendly hostel offers high-standard dorms or even better hotel rooms in the attached Davik Troika if you decide to buck the trend and stay the night.

Getting There & Away

Trains run to Oslo every 30 minutes (Nkr70, 35 minutes) and buses depart once or twice every hour (Nkr75, 35 minutes).

AROUND DRAMMEN

Just outside Drammen is the remarkable 1650m-long **Spiralen tunnel** to the 200m-high summit of Bragernes, which affords a fabulous view over the city. The best part is the fact that the tunnel makes six spirals inside the hill en route to the top. If you don't have a car, go on a summer weekend, when bus No 41 does the trip three times daily from Bragernes Torg (Nkr21, 15 minutes).

Another interesting excursion will take you to Åmot, where the **Royal Blåfarveværk** (☎ 32 78 67 00; www.blaa.no; hourly tours Nkr50; ☼ noon-6pm mid-May–mid-Sep, noon-6pm Sun rest-of-year) was established by King Christian VII in 1773 to extract cobalt to produce blue pigments for the glass and porcelain industries. It's also worth looking at the large Haugfoss waterfall, the Mølla shop (which sells cobalt-blue glasswork), and the various art exhibitions in the attached **museum** (☎ 32 78 67 00; adult/child Nkr60/free; ☼ 10am-5pm mid-May–mid-Sep). Take the regular Nettbuss express bus No 100 or 101 from Drammen to Åmot (Nkr68, one hour) then change to bus No 105 (Nkr26, seven minutes).

ØSTFOLD

The Østfold region, the detached slice of Norway to the east of Oslofjord, is a mix of forest, pastoral farmland and small seaside villages which carry great historical significance and are well worth visiting.

FREDRIKSTAD

pop 96,600

Fredrikstad is home to one of the best-preserved fortress towns in Scandinavia, Gumlebyen with a modern waterfront district just across the water. It's this mix of the old and the new which gives Fredrikstad its charm. Once an important trading centre between mainland Europe and western Scandinavia, Fredrikstad also has a cathedral (1880) which contains stained glass work by Emanuel Vigeland; bizarrely, the steeple contains a lighthouse, which still functions at night.

Information

The Gamlebyen **tourist office** (☎ 69 30 46 00; turistkontoret@opplevfredrikstad.com; Tøhusgata 41; ☼ 9am-5pm Mon-Fri & 11am-5pm Sat & Sun mid-Jun–mid-Aug, 9am-4.30pm Mon-Fri mid-Aug–mid-Jun), in the old town (Gamlebyen) is complemented in the summer by the smaller **tourist office** (☎ 69 39 65 00; Dampskipsbrygga; ☼ 8am-9pm 15 Jun-15 Aug), at the marina. The latter also offers Internet access (per 15 minutes Nkr10).

Sights

GAMLEBYEN

The charming timbered houses, moats, gates and drawbridge of the Fredrikstad Gamlebyen (Old Town) are simply enchanting. It was first built in 1663 – as a primary trade outlet connecting southern Norway with mainland Europe, Fredrikstad was vulnerable to waterborne assaults – the old town began life as a military enclave which could be readily defended against Swedish aggression and attacks. The perimeter walls, once defended by the 200 cannons, now consist of grassy embankments

which make for a very pleasant stroll. The narrow cobbled streets have been similarly preserved, still lined with picturesque 17th-century buildings, many of which remain occupied today.

Among the finest old buildings in town, look out particularly for the old **convict prison** (Salveriet, 1731); the **stone storehouse** (1674–91), the oldest building in Gamlebyen and now a ceramics showroom; and **Balaklava** (1783), a historic building.

From mid-June to mid-August, the Gamlebyen **tourist office** (☎ 69 30 46 00) runs guided tours (adults/child Nkr75/35, one hour). They leave from the tourist office at 11am, 1pm and 3pm, and at noon and 4pm on Saturday and Sunday.

The **Fredrikstad Museum** (☎ 69 30 46 00; combined ticket with Isegran adult/senior/child Nkr40/20/10; ☼ 9am-5pm Mon-Fri & 11am-5pm Sat & Sun mid-Jun–mid-Aug, 9am-4.30pm Mon-Fri mid-Aug–mid-Jun) is housed in the same building as the tourist office in Gamlebyen and is well worth a browse. The downstairs area houses temporary exhibitions, while upstairs you'll find scale models of the old town and an interesting collection of relics from three centuries of Fredrikstad's civilian, military and industrial activities. Also on the top floor is a military museum.

ISEGRAN

Fredrikstad Museum has another section on **Isegran** (☎ 69 30 60 00; combined ticket with Fredrikstad Museum adult/senior/child Nkr40/20/10; ☼ noon-5pm Tue-Sun mid-Jun–mid-Aug), an islet across the Glomma. Norse sagas mention the 13th-century fortress of Isegran, which later became a further line of defence against Sweden in the mid-17th century. The **ruins** of a stone (originally wood) tower remain visible at the eastern end of the island. It's also the site of a small museum on local boatbuilding (from the time when boats were lovingly hand-crafted from wood). Boats run between Isegran and Gamlebyen or the modern centre (Nkr6). By road or on foot, access is from Rv108, about 600m south of Fredrikstad city centre.

HVALFANGER (WHALING) MUSEUM

This small whaling **museum** (☎ 69 32 44 21; Tolbodgaten; admission Nkr10; ☼ noon-4pm Wed-Sun Jun-July, Sat & Sun Aug) is run by proud old men only too keen to show you around the old photos, the formidable whaling guns once used in the Antarctic and the even more formidable penis of a blue whale. No English is spoken and all labels are in Norwegian.

KONGSTEN FESTNING

A 15-minute walk southeast of the Gamlebyen drawbridge (turn off Torsnesvien at Fredrikstad Motell & Camping; right) lies the flower-festooned **Kongsten Festning** (Fort). Dating from 1685, it once served as a lookout and warning post for the troops at nearby Gamlebyen. Although it can get overrun on summer weekends, this otherwise lonely and appealingly unkempt spot is a fun place to scramble around the turrets, embankments, walls and stockade, or just sit in the sun and soak up the silence.

Festivals & Events

The **Glomma Festival** (☎ 69 31 54 77; glommas@ glommafestivalen.no) runs during the second week in July, featuring a week of musical performances, ritual duels, a 'bathtub regatta' for creative vessels and a veteran sailing ship exhibition. It's a very popular festival so book ahead for accommodation.

Sleeping

GAMLEBYEN & SARPSBORG

Fredrikstad Motell & Camping (☎ 69 32 05 32; fax 69 32 36 66; Torsnesveien 3; tents without/with car Nkr100/155, caravan Nkr155-190, 2–4-person cabins Nkr260-Nkr360,

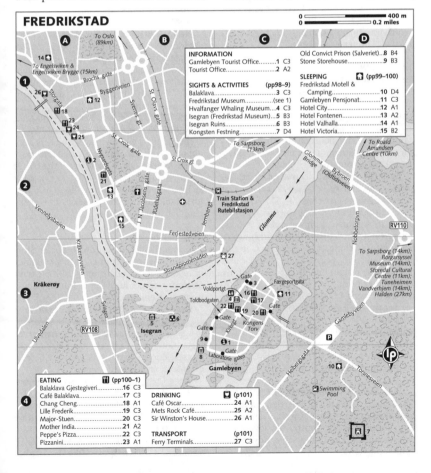

FREDRIKSTAD

0 —————— 400 m
0 —————— 0.2 miles

To Oslo (89km)
To Engelsviken & Engelsviken Brygge (15km)
Brochs gate
Byggerveien
St Olavs gate
Sverres gate
St Croix gate
Nygaardsgata
St Croix gt
J N Jacobsens gate
Riddersgata
Vennelysveien
Krakeroyveien
Ferjestedveien
Strandpromenaden
Kråkerøy
RV108
Svingen
Uvevdalen
Isegran
Voldportgt
Toldbodgaten
Gate
Gate
Gate
Gate
Kongsta
Kongens Torv
Laboratorie gaten
Gamlebyen
To Sarsborg (13km)
Glomma Bridge
Bybroen (Oldtidsvien)
Train Station & Fredrikstad Rutebilstasjon
Jernbanegt
Glomma
Nobbetorpvn
RV110
To Sarpsborg (14km); Borgarsyssel Museum (14km); Sforedal Cultural Centre (11km); Tuneheimen Vandverhjem (14km); Halden (27km)
Gamlebyveien
Heibergsgata
To Roald Amundsen Centre (10km)
Færgeportgata
Swimming Pool
Torsnesveien

INFORMATION
Gamlebyen Tourist Office..........1 C3
Tourist Office.............................2 A2

SIGHTS & ACTIVITIES   (pp98–9)
Balaklava....................................3 C3
Fredrikstad Museum...........(see 1)
Hvalfanger Whaling Museum...4 C3
Isegran (Fredrikstad Museum)...5 B3
Isegran Ruins.............................6 B3
Kongsten Festning....................7 D4

Old Convict Prison (Salveriet)..8 B4
Stone Storehouse.....................9 B3

SLEEPING   (pp99–100)
Fredrikstad Motell & Camping..........................10 D4
Gamlebyen Pensjonat..............11 C3
Hotel City.................................12 A1
Hotel Fontenen.......................13 A2
Hotel Valhalla..........................14 A1
Hotel Victoria.........................15 B2

EATING   (pp100–1)
Balaklava Gjestegiveri............16 C3
Café Balaklava........................17 C3
Chang Cheng...........................18 A1
Lille Frederik...........................19 C3
Major-Stuen............................20 C3
Mother India...........................21 A2
Peppe's Pizza..........................22 C3
Pizzanini.................................23 A1

DRINKING   (p101)
Café Oscar..............................24 A1
Mets Rock Café.......................25 A2
Sir Winston's House.................26 A1

TRANSPORT   (p101)
Ferry Terminals.......................27 C3

motel s/d Nkr400/500; (P)) This multifaceted but largely uninspiring place, in the grounds of Kongsten Fort, is nonetheless good for its proximity to the old town. From the centre, take any bus (eg No 362) headed for Torsnes.

Gamlebyen Pensjonat (☎ 69 32 20 20; www.gamlebyen-pensjonat.no; Smedjegaten 88; s/d with shared bathroom Nkr350/500; (P)) Housed in the renovated former artillery barracks, this place can have the feel of a student dormitory on summer weekends, but it's the only choice for budget travellers in the old town and, as such, represents decent value.

Tuneheimen Vandrerhjem (☎ 69 14 50 01; fax 69 14 22 91; Tuneveien 44; dm incl breakfast Nkr210, s/d with shared bathroom incl breakfast Nkr350/500; (P)) The nearest youth hostel to Fredrikstad is near Lake Tunevannet, 1km from Sarpsborg, which is in turn a 14km bus ride from Fredrikstad. Dinner is available.

NEW TOWN

Hotel Fontenen (☎ 69 30 05 00; fax 69 31 32 64; Nygaardsgata 9-11; s/d Nkr595/895 mid-Jun–mid-Aug & Sat & Sun, Nkr795/995 rest-of-year; (P)) One of the best-value mid-range places in town, this place has pleasant rooms, good breakfasts and a family feel. The polished floorboards and views of the cathedral (ask for a room at the front) are among the highlights.

Hotel City (☎ 69 38 56 00; www.hotelcity.no; Nygaardsgata 44/46; s/d Nkr750/950 mid-Jun–mid-Aug & Sat & Sun, Nkr1150/1350 rest-of-year; (P) (☐)) The upmarket option in the new town is excellent value in summer, with very good rooms. Surprisingly the leopard skin furnishings in some rooms come at no extra cost. It also has a nightclub, plus a pub, pizzeria, and two quality restaurants. Don't be put off by the drab exterior.

Hotel Victoria (☎ 69 38 58 00; www.hotelvictoria.no; Turngaten 3; s/d Nkr750/950 mid-Jun–mid-Aug & Sat & Sun, Nkr1250/1400 rest-of-year; (☐)) Opposite the cathedral grounds, this place is also better than it looks from the outside. Ageing but well-maintained, it offers attractive rooms just a short walk from the ferry to Gamlebyen.

Hotel Valhalla (☎ 69 36 89 50; www.hotelvalhalla.no; Valhallsgate 3; s/d Nkr595/795) High on a hill overlooking the town, but within easy walking distance of the centre, the lovely old wooden house has comfortable, tidy rooms and good views.

Eating
GAMLEBYEN

What the old town lacks in accommodation, it makes up for with restaurants.

Lille Frederik (Torvgaten; burgers from Nkr49; ☺ 11am-10pm Mon-Fri, 10am-10pm Sat, noon-10pm Sun) For burgers, snacks and coffee, Lille Frederik is just the place. It's hugely popular in summer when snackers descend on the outdoor tables like seagulls and queues can be long.

Peppe's Pizza (☎ 69 32 32 10; Torvgt 57; pizzas Nkr134-234, pasta from Nkr93; ☺ noon-11pm Mon-Fri, 11am-11.30pm Sat, noon-11.30pm Sun) The Italian food here is good, but the outdoor tables along the cobbled street are the ideal place to drink a beer and gaze across the river. Peppe's also does kid's meals (Nkr33 to Nkr66).

Major-Stuen (☎ 69 32 15 55; Voldportgata 73; starters Nkr65-129, mains Nkr129-245; ☺ noon-10pm) Another fine place in Gamlebyen, the recommended Major-Stuen has an international menu, but specialises in Norwegian dishes, including whale beef with fried onions, stewed cabbage and potatoes (Nkr225).

Café Balaklava (☎ 69 32 30 40; Færgeportgata 78; snacks Nkr79-89, desserts Nkr30-45; ☺ noon-10pm) is a charming, well-run place which is very popular and also has the excellent, more upmarket **Balaklava Gjestgiveri** (☎ 69 32 30 40; Faergeportgata; mains from Nkr150, 3-course dinner Nkr450; ☺ 6-11pm Mon-Sat) next door in a historic building, which specialises in Norwegian fish and beef dishes.

NEW TOWN

The Fredrikstad waterfront between Storgata and the water is lined with all manner of restaurants and bars, most with pleasant outdoor terraces ideal for a summer's afternoon or evening.

Pizzanini (☎ 69 30 03 00; Storgata 5; pizzas Nkr70-220, pasta Nkr84-125; ☺ noon-1am Sun-Thu & noon-2am Fri & Sat summer, 3pm-midnight winter) When other restaurants stand empty, this place always buzzes, due in part to its young vibe and extensive, well-priced menu.

Chang Cheng (☎ 69 31 71 77; Storgata 15; starters Nkr32-65, mains Nkr98-175; ☺ noon-11pm) Also reasonably priced, this busy Chinese restaurant is particularly good value at lunch time when it offers a special menu for Nkr68.

Mother India (☎ 69 31 22 00; Nygaardsgata 17; mains Nkr120-195; ☺ 2-10pm Mon-Fri, 3-11pm Sat & Sun)

This atmospheric Indian restaurant gets the thumbs up from locals and travellers alike for its attractive décor and good food.

Engelsviken Brygge (☎ 69 35 18 40, Engelsvikveien 6, Engelsviken; 3-course dinner around Nkr350) One of the best places in the area is this excellent quayside seafood restaurant, 15km north-west of Fredrikstad. The high-quality food include crab, mussels, catfish and halibut.

Drinking

The following three places all have breezy outdoor tables in summer.

Mets Rock Café (☎ 69 31 78 99; Dampskipsbrygga 12; ☺ 11am-3am Wed, Fri & Sat, 11am-2am Sun-Tue & Thu) On the river promenade, this place serves Mexican meals for around Nkr100 and it has a bar with a DJ playing rock music nightly from 10pm (only Wednesday, Friday and Saturday in summer). There's no cover charge but you must be over 20 years of age.

Café Oscar (☎ 69 39 66 20; Storgata 5; ☺ noon-2.30am Wed, Fri & Sat, noon-1.30am Sun-Tue & Thu) Also with a buzzy vibe, Café Oscar offers cover bands from 10.30pm Wednesday (free) and from 11.30pm Friday and Saturdays (cover charge Nkr60). Beer costs Nkr59.

Sir Winston's House (☎ 69 31 00 80; Storgata 17; ☺ noon-3am Wed, Fri & Sat, noon-2am Sun-Tue & Thu) Beside the river, this English-style pub serves fish and chips for Nkr95, and you can choose between 10 draught beers. On weekends it also offers DJ music (mostly 1960s, but some contemporary) and dancing.

Getting There & Away

Intercity buses arrive and depart from the **Fredrikstad Rutebilstasjon** (☎ 177) at the train station. Bus No 200 and 360 run to/from Sarpsborg (Nkr30, 25 minutes, twice hourly). Nor-Way Bussekpress has one to seven daily services between Oslo and Fredrikstad (Nkr147, 1¼ hours), with most buses continuing to Hvaler; there are also regular **Flybussekspressen** (☎ 177) services from Fredrikstad to Oslo Gardermoen International Airport (Nkr205, 2¼ hours, every hour or two).

Fredrikstad lies on the rail line between Oslo and Göteborg. Trains to/from Oslo (Nkr148, one hour) run about 10 times daily, but note that southbound international trains require a seat reservation for travelling to be valid.

For details of international boat departures, see p393.

Getting Around

To cross the Glomma to Gamlebyen, you can either trek over the high and hulking Glomma bridge or take the Nkr6 *Go'vakker Randi* ferry from Strandpromenaden. It operates from 5.30am to 11pm on weekdays (to 1am on Friday); from 7am to 1am on Saturday and from 9.30am to 11pm on Sunday.

From the train station it's a five-minute walk to the riverfront, where a ferry shuttles across the river Glomma to the main gate of Gamlebyen (Nkr6, two minutes) regularly between 5.30am and 11pm.

For a taxi, phone ☎ 69 36 26 00. Bicycle hire is available from the two tourist offices.

AROUND FREDRIKSTAD
Hvaler Skerries

Norwegian holiday-makers and artists love the Hvaler Skerries, an offshore archipelago of 833 forested islands and islets guarding the southern entrance to Oslofjord. The main islands of **Vesterøy**, **Spjærøy**, **Asmaløy** and **Kirkøy** are connected to the mainland by a toll road (Nkr55) and tunnel. Bus No 365 (Nkr58) runs all the way to Skjærhalden, at the far end of Kirkøy.

Hvaler **tourist office** (☎ 69 37 86 76; Skjærhalden; ☺ 10am-8pm mid-Jun–mid-Aug) can point you in the direction of the numerous sights dotted around the islands.

Above the coastline of Akerøy Island, accessible only by ferry (taxi boat), clings a well-preserved 17th-century coastal **fortress**, renovated in the 1960s. Admission is free and it's always open.

The mid-11th-century **stone church** (Skjærhalden; ☎ noon-4pm July, noon-4pm Sat 2nd half of Jun & 1st half of Aug) on the island of Kirkøy is one of the oldest in Norway. The church hosts a week-long music and arts festival in July.

The tourist office has a list of fully equipped private houses and chalets in Hvaler available for Nkr400 to Nkr700 per day or Nkr2700 to Nkr4500 per week.

Hvaler Kurs & Konferansesenter (☎ 69 37 91 28; fax 69 37 91 32; Skjærhalden; apt from Nkr500) offers excellent apartments for rent.

All year, the M/S *Hollungen* and M/S *Hvalerfergen II* sail roughly every hour from

Skjærhalden and through the Hvaler Skerries (Nkr45, one hour). Alternatively, you can sail with the scheduled ferry M/S *Vesleø II* between Skjærhalden, Koster (Sweden) and Strömstad (Sweden) from mid-June to mid-August for Nkr115/95 adult/child return.

Roald Amundsen Centre

The renowned and quite noted polar explorer Roald Amundsen, who in 1911 was the first man to reach the South Pole, was born in 1872 at Hvidsten, midway between Fredrikstad and Sarpsborg. Although the family moved to Oslo when Roald was still a small child, the family home in Hvidsten, which was the base for a small shipbuilding and shipping business, is now the **Roald Amundsen Centre** (☎ 69 34 83 26; www.roaldamundsen .no; admission free, tours adult/child Nkr40/20; ☉ 10am-8pm Mon-Fri, 11am-3pm Sun mid-May–mid-Aug), which is dedicated to the man's life and expeditions. Standing surrounded by these quiet fields of southern Norway, it seems perhaps not so surprising that Amundsen set off to seek adventure so far from home. The centre is signposted about 11km east of Fredrikstad, along the Rv111 towards Sarpsborg.

Borgarsyssel Museum

This excellent county **museum** (☎ 69 15 50 11; Kirkegata, Sarpsborg; adult/child Nkr40/20; ☉ 10am-5pm Tue-Sat & noon-5pm Sun mid-May–Aug) of Østfold lies in the town of Sarpsborg (14km northeast of Fredrikstad). The open-air display contains 30 period buildings from various parts of the country and includes a vast collection of cultural art and artefacts. There's also a **herb garden**, a **petting zoo** and the **ruins** of King Øystein's St Nikolas church, constructed in 1115 and destroyed by the Swedes in 1567. From Fredrikstad, trains and buses run frequently to Sarpsborg.

Storedal Cultural Centre

This **cultural centre** (☎ 69 16 92 67; Storedal; admission Nkr20; ☉ 10am-5pm Tue-Fri, noon-6pm mid-May–Aug) is 11km northeast of Fredrikstad. King Magnus the Blind was born here in 1117; he took the throne at 13 years of age and earned his nickname at 18 when he was blinded by an enemy in Bergen. A later owner of the farm, Erling Stordahl, who was also blind, developed a monument to King Magnus, as well as a centre dedicated to blind and other disabled people.

In the **botanic garden**, the various plants and herbs are identified in both script and Braille. The most intriguing feature is the *Ode til Lyset* (Ode to the Light), a 'sound sculpture' by Arnold Haukeland and Arne Nordheim which, using photo cells and a computer in the farmhouse, transmutes the slightest fluctuations in natural light into haunting, ever-changing music. To get there, follow Rv110 east for about 9km from Fredrikstad – the centre is 2.1km north of the main road.

Oldtidsveien

People have lived and worked in the Østfold region for thousands of years, and numerous examples of ancient stone works and rock paintings lie along the Oldtidsveien (Old Times Way), the old sunken road between Fredrikstad and Sarpsborg. At Solberg, there are three panels with around 100 figures dating back 3000 years. At Gunnarstorp are several 30m-wide **Bronze Age burial mounds** and several **Iron Age standing stones**. The site at Begby has well-preserved renditions of ships, men and animals, while Hunn has several **stone circles** and a series of **burial mounds** dating from 500 BC to AD 800. The **rock paintings** at Hornes clearly depict 21 ships complete with oarsmen. The sites are signposted off the E6, just south of Sarpsborg, but they may also be visited on a long day walk or bike ride from Fredrikstad.

HALDEN

pop 21,900

The soporific border town of Halden, at the end of Iddefjord between steep rocky headlands, possesses a hugely significant history as a cornerstone of Norwegian defence through centuries of Swedish aggression. With a pretty little harbour filled with yachts, a looming fortress rising up behind the town and a sprinkling of decent restaurants, this place makes a worthwhile detour.

History

Halden served as a garrison during the Hannibal Wars from 1643 to 1645. From 1644 it was fortified with a wooden stockade. In the 1658 Roskilde Treaty between Sweden and Denmark, Norway lost its Bohuslän province (and Bohus fortress), and Halden was left exposed as a border outpost requiring heavy defences. When attacks by

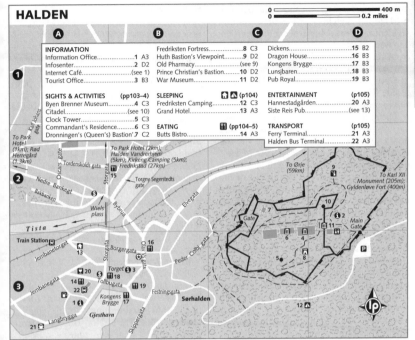

HALDEN

0 ——————— 400 m
0 ——————— 0.2 miles

INFORMATION		Fredriksten Fortress..................**8** C3	Dickens.............................**15** B2
Information Office....................**1** A3		Huth Bastion's Viewpoint..........**9** D2	Dragon House.....................**16** B3
Infosenter............................**2** D2		Old Pharmacy..........................(see 9)	Kongens Brygge.................**17** B3
Internet Café.........................(see 1)		Prince Christian's Bastion........**10** D2	Lunsjbaren.........................**18** B3
Tourist Office........................**3** B3		War Museum..........................**11** D2	Pub Royal...........................**19** B3
SIGHTS & ACTIVITIES (pp103–4)		SLEEPING (p104)	ENTERTAINMENT (p105)
Byen Brenner Museum............**4** C3		Fredriksten Camping..............**12** C3	Hannestadgården................**20** A3
Citadel................................(see 10)		Grand Hotel..........................**13** A3	Siste Reis Pub.....................(see 13)
Clock Tower...........................**5** C3			
Commandant's Residence..........**6** C3		EATING (pp104–5)	TRANSPORT (p105)
Dronning's (Queen's) Bastion'**7** C2		Butts Bistro..........................**14** A3	Ferry Terminal.....................**21** A3
			Halden Bus Terminal.............**22** A3

Swedish forces in 1658, 1659 and 1660 were scarcely repelled, the need for a better fortification became apparent, resulting in the fortress, which was begun in 1661.

In the midst of it all, in 1659 and 1716, the Halden resistance resorted to fire to drive out the enemy, a sacrifice honoured with a mention in the Norwegian national anthem, which includes the lines: '... we chose to burn our nation, lest we let it fall'. The fires also serve as a centrepiece for a museum on the town's history in the fortress.

Further attacks continued into the 19th century. In the first few years of the 20th century, Fredriksten Fortress was armed with increasingly powerful modern cannons, turret guns and howitzers. However, this firepower was removed during the 1906 negotiations for the dissolution of the Swedish–Norwegian union and the town nestled into life as a quiet seaside village.

Information

The Halden **tourist office** (☎ 69 19 09 80; www .visithalden.com; Torget 2; 9am-5.30pm Mon-Fri mid-Jun–mid-Aug, 9am-4.30pm Mon-Fri rest-of-year), just off

Torget, has some useful information. When it's closed, try the **information office** (☎ 69 18 14 78; Langbrygga; 8am-8pm Jul–mid-Aug) at the harbour, although they're more geared towards boating information. The latter also has Internet access (per 15 minutes Nkr20). For yacht mooring and other harbour information, call ☎ 69 18 12 73.

Sights
FREDRIKSTEN FORTRESS & MUSEUMS

Crowning the hilltop behind Halden is the 1661 **Fredriksten Fortress** (Fredriksten Festning; ☎ 69 18 54 11; www.museumsnett.no/hhs; adult/child Nkr50/20, incl all museums; 10am-5pm 18 May-Aug), which has resisted six Swedish sieges and never been captured.

To reach the fortress from the town, a half-overgrown cobbled footpath climbs from the top of Festningsgata in Sørhalden (a neighbourhood of 19th-century sea captains' cottages), up the unkempt lilac-covered slopes. The road for cars leads up from the same street.

On 28 July 1660 King Fredrik III of Denmark issued a declaration ordering a more sturdy fortification above Halden. The pentagonal citadel, as well as the adjoining Gyldenløve Fort, Stortårnet and Overberget, was constructed across two parallel hills from 1661 to 1671, and augmented between 1682 and 1701. Its crowning event came on 11 December 1718, when the warmongering Swede King Karl XII was shot dead on the site (a monument now marks the spot).

The museums in the castle grounds cover various facets of the fortress' history. Going down the hill from the ticket office, the **War Museum** contains a good overview of Halden's experiences of war from the centuries of Swedish aggression to the arrival of the Nazis. A tunnel leads up into **Prince Christian's Bastion** – the main vantage point for the fortress defenders. A broader sweep of Halden's history is outlined in the **Byen Brenner Museum** ('the town is on fire') exhibition about halfway down the main thoroughfare. Displays in the **old pharmacy** describe the history of pharmacology from early Norwegian folk remedies to early-20th-century apothecaries. It's housed in the former **Commandant's Residence**, constructed between 1754 and 1758 and damaged by fire in 1826. After renovation it was used as a powder laboratory, armoury and barracks. Note the Fredrik V monogram over the doorway.

In the former prison building near the lower entrance is the military section, displaying artefacts and describing the history of military conflict in Halden from the 17th century to WWII. Perhaps the most interesting sites are the **brewery**, which once produced up to 3000L of beer a day, and the **bakery ovens**, which baked bread for up to 5000 soldiers. There's also a multimedia presentation and shop at the Infosenter, just inside the main entrance of the fortress.

There are many intriguing old buildings dotted around the fortress, but even better are the **views** over Halden and the surrounding hills from alongside the cannons near the **Dronningen's (Queen's) Bastion**, **Clock Tower**, **Huth Bastion's Viewpoint** and the **citadel** (the outside of Prince Christian's Bastion). Note that the high bastions are barely fenced if at all.

Guided tours (adult/child Nkr50/25; ☉ noon, 1pm & 2pm Tue–Sat & noon, 1pm, 2pm & 3pm Sun mid-Jun–mid-Aug, noon, 1pm & 2pm Sat May–mid-Jun, noon, 1pm & 2pm Sun mid-Aug–end Sep) of the fortress and other buildings on the ground are in Norwegian or English.

Rød Herregård

Rød Herregård **manor** (☎ 69 18 54 11, Herregårdsveien; tours adult/child Nkr50/10; ☉ for tours noon, 1pm & 2pm Tue–Sat & noon, 1pm, 2pm & 3pm Sun mid-Jun–mid-Aug, noon, 1pm & 2pm Sat May–mid-Jun, noon, 1pm & 2pm Sun mid-Aug–end Sep), dating from 1733, has fine interiors, notable collections of both weapons and art, and one of the best gardens in Norway. It's 1.5km northwest of the town centre and is well-signposted.

Sleeping

Fredriksten Camping (☎ 69 18 40 32; fax 69 18 75 73; Fredriksten Festning; tent & car sites without/with electricity Nkr120/150, 4-/5-bed cabins Nkr350/400, showers Nkr10; [P]) A great location amid the trees and adjacent to the fortress makes this well-run place a winner. It also offers minigolf and, after the fortress closes and the crowds disappear, a quiet green spot to pitch a tent.

Halden Vandrerhjem (☎ 69 21 69 68; fax 69 21 66 03; Brødløs; dm/s/d/tr Nkr/125/160/295/345; mid-Jun–mid-Aug) The family-run hostel, at the suburban Tosterød school, offers standard rooms in pleasant surroundings on the edge of Halden. Take bus No 102–104 from Busterud Park (marked Gimle).

Park Hotel (☎ 69 21 15 00; www.park-hotel.no; Marcus Thranes gate 30; s/d Nkr790/890 mid-Jun–mid-Aug & Sat & Sun, Nkr1050/1260 rest-of-year; [P] [🖳]) The Park Hotel, 1.5km from the centre, has recently renovated rooms that represent the best summer value in town for its combination of attractively furnished, airy rooms and friendly staff.

Grand Hotel (☎ 69 18 72 00; fax 69 18 79 59, Jernbanetorget 1; s/d Nkr650/790 Fri & Sat, Nkr790/920 Sun-Thu mid-Jun–mid-Aug, Nkr890/990 Sun-Thu rest-of-year) The Grand Hotel, opposite the train station, is comfortable and functional rather than luxurious, but the location's good, as are the buffet breakfasts.

Eating

Around Gjesthavn (Guest Harbour), you'll find several pleasant restaurants with outdoor seating.

Kongens Brygge (☎ 69 18 75 22; Gjesthavn; pizzas Nkr130, mains from Nkr175; ☉ lunch & dinner) Right on the waterfront, this place has a cruisy atmosphere and a wonderful pontoon terrace open in summer. The pizzas are expensive but quite generous proportions bound to fill hungry travellers.

ANDERS BLOMQVIST

The Bryggen (p177), a huddle of wooden buildings on Bergen's waterfront.

JAN STROMME

Harbour area at night in winter, Bergen (p172)

Impressive, part Gothic, part Anglo-Norman Stavanger Cathedral (p198)

NED FRIARY

NED

Cyclists admire the view of Bergen from the top of Mt Føyen (p182)

Preikestolen (Pulpit Rock; p206) and the extraordinary view down Lysefjord (p206)

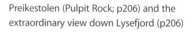

CHRISTIAN ASLUND

Skiing at the action-packed Voss (p189)

Dickens (☎ 69 18 35 33; Storgata 9; mains from Nkr110; ☺ lunch & dinner) The very popular Dickens offers a choice between outdoor seating (summer only) or the dining room in a 17th-century cellar. In summer it also has a lively pontoon terrace in Gjesthavn.

Pub Royal (☎ 69 18 00 80; Olav V's gata 1; pasta & sandwiches Nkr50-85, small/medium/large pizzas Nkr65/125/160, other mains Nkr160-190; ☺ lunch & dinner) This local favourite, just up the hill from the water, offers a varied atmosphere and extensive menu, and is popular with a younger crowd.

Other good choices:

Butts Bistro (☎ 69 17 20 12; Tollbugata 3; mains from Nkr110; ☺ 3pm-4am Fri & Sat, 3pm-midnight Sun-Thu) Unfortunately named, but good food and great on weekends for a midnight curry.

Dragon House (☎ 69 18 44 67; Borgergata 3; starters Nkr35, mains Nkr75-139, lunch menu Nkr65; ☺ lunch & dinner) Varied menu and decent food.

Lunsjbaren (☎ 69 17 60 95; Torget; sandwiches from Nkr29, snacks & burgers from Nkr45)

Drinking & Entertainment

Siste Reis Pub (☎ 69 17 61 45; Jernbanetorget 1; ☺ 3pm-midnight Sun-Thu, 2pm-3am Fri & Sat) At this popular pub in the Grand Hotel building beer costs only Nkr32 for 500mL (before 11pm). It has a chatty and chilled late-night ambience.

Hannestadgården (☎ 69 19 77 81; Tollbugata 5; beer garden ☺ 3pm-3am Mon-Fri & 1pm-3am Sat, nightclub ☺ 10pm-3am Fri & Sat, cover charge for nightclub Nkr50) This multi-purpose nightspot has an atmospheric beer garden, a piano bar, boisterous nightclub and regular concerts (cover charge Nkr70) throughout summer. It's probably the best night-time action you'll find in Halden.

Dickens (☎ 69 18 35 33; Storgata 9) If you prefer laidback music on a lazy summer's afternoon, head to Dickens where there's (free) jazz in the courtyard from 1.30pm to 3.30pm on Saturdays during July and August.

Getting There & Away

Trains between Oslo and Halden (Nkr191, 1¾ hours) run hourly from Monday to Friday and every second hour on weekends.

An average of four daily trains continue on to Göteborg and Malmö in Sweden. The long-distance bus terminal sits right at the harbour, with regular services (less on weekends) to Oslo and Fredrikstad.

For information on ferries to Sweden, see p394.

AROUND HALDEN
Halden Canal (Haldenkanalen)

East and north of Halden, a canal system connects the town with Göteborg, Sweden, for all but one short dry section (1.8km). The highlight is the Brekke Locks, a system of four locks between Femsjøen and Aspern (on the Halden–Strømsfoss run) which raise and lower the boats a total of 26.6m.

Canoe hire is available from **Kirkeng Camping** (☎ 69 19 92 98), 5km northeast of town in Aremark, if you prefer to explore under your own steam. You can pick up a boating and recreation map from the tourist office in Halden. For information on canal travel in larger private boats, contact **Båt & Motor a/s** (☎ 69 17 58 59).

The region is particularly popular with canoeists and boat owners from all around Norway, but visitors can get a quick taste on the tourist cruise boat called **M/S Turisten** (☎ 93 06 64 44), which follows the Haldenkanalen between Tistedal (east of Halden) and Strømsfoss (adult/senior/child return Nkr250/200/150, 3½ hours). The boat leaves Strømsfoss at 11am and begins its leisurely return from Tistedal at 3pm on Wednesday and Friday to Sunday from mid-June to mid-August. To reach the town of Tistedal, take bus No 103 or 106 (Nkr32, 18 minutes, twice hourly except late Saturday afternoon and Sunday).

On Thursdays during July, the service runs between Strømsfoss (11am) and Ørje (2pm, Nkr200/150/100, 2½ hours). On this latter trip, you can visit the **Halden Waterways Canal Museum** (Haldenvassdragets Kanalmuseum; ☎ 69 81 10 21; Ørje; adult/child Nkr50/20; ☺ noon-6pm Tue-Sun mid-Jun–mid-Aug), located right beside the canal.

Southern Norway

CONTENTS

When the weather turns warm, the rocky, island-studded south coast becomes a paradisiacal magnet for Norwegian holiday-makers and you could do a lot worse than join them.

The undoubted highlights of Norway's southern coast are the white towns and villages which nestle into the numerous rocky coves and bays. The prettiest of these are between Kristiansand and Larvik with charming white-timbered houses snaking their way in from waterfronts crowded with yachts. Among these, Grimstad, the one-time home of Henrik Ibsen, is arguably the most enchanting, retaining its village feel despite its considerable size and historical significance. Risør and Kragerø are similarly pretty-as-a-postcard with superb harbourside locations. Lillesand is another gem all dressed in white, so perfectly preserved as to appear like a model village.

Kristiansand, southern Norway's largest town, also has a pleasant old town, and is an attractive fishing harbour. Arendal, another larger town, is similarly sea-facing and with a wonderfully preserved old quarter, while the road between Egersund and Flekkefjord offers plunging cliffs and scenery that you'd normally associate with the fjord regions further north.

Sparsely populated and richly forested, southern Norway's delightful inland regions form a transition zone between the vast forests of Sweden, the sunny coastal regions and the precipitous mountains and fjords in the west with ample forests and few foreign visitors. It's worth seeking out the Heddal Stave Church, which is one of the finest of its kind in Norway, and the intriguing silver mines at Kongsberg. Picturesque Telemark and the delightfully quiet, rolling hills of Setesdalen will satisfy those seeking to escape the summer crowds along the coast. Rjukan is a gateway to the wonderful Hardangervidda National Park, while with a host of adventure activities and scenic countryside elsewhere, it's well worth lingering for a few days.

SOUTHERN NORWAY

HIGHLIGHTS

- Strolling through the narrow streets of the 'white towns' of **Risør** (p115), **Grimstad** (p119), **Lillesand** (p120) and **Kragerø** (p113)

- Exploring the beaches and offshore islands of Norway's sunshine coast along the **Skagerrak** (p119)

- Sitting back to enjoy a leisurely cruise through the scenic **Telemark canal system** (p133)

- Admiring the exquisite roof lines and paintings in the stave church at **Heddal** (p133)

- Scouring the surface of **Seljordvatn** (p139) in search of Selma the Serpent

- Taking a train through the royal silver mines near the pleasant town of **Kongsberg** (p130)

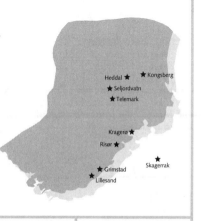

Heddal ★   ★ Kongsberg
★ Seljordvatn
★ Telemark
Kragerø ★
Risør ★
★ Skagerrak
★ Grimstad
★ Lillesand

| AREA: 31,628 SQ KM | HIGHEST ELEVATION: GAUSTA 1881M | POPULATION: 649,100 |

SOUTHERN NORWAY

Getting There & Away

The 586km-long Sørland rail line connecting Stavanger and Oslo (via Kristiansand) keeps mainly inland, but buses meet the trains and link the rail line with most southern towns. The E18/39 runs inland between Stavanger and Mandal, but from there to Oslo it follows the coast. There are also international ferry services from some towns (p393).

THE COAST

TØNSBERG

pop 44,700

Tønsberg is the oldest town in Norway. At first glance, this much-touted fact can result in disappointment for first-time visitors, as it's a largely modern town quietly getting about its business. Look a little closer, however, and you'll find enough Viking era ruins and timbered houses, not to mention a decrepit castle, to keep you occupied for an hour or two en route along the coast.

The **tourist office** (☎ 33 35 45 20; www.visittonsberg.com; Nedre Langatte 36; h9am-7pm Mon-Sat, 9am-3pm Sun mid-Jun–early Aug, 9.30am-3.30pm rest-of-year) is located on the Tønsberg Brygge waterfront, produces the excellent (and free) *Tønsberg Guide*.

History

In the *Saga of Harald Hårfagre* (p22), Snorre Sturluson mentions that Tønsberg existed

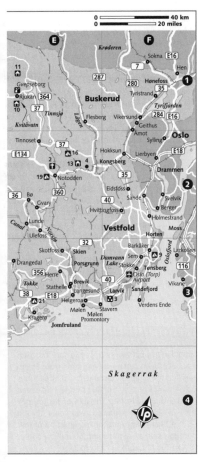

A CITY OF INVENTION

Tønsberg's history is not all Vikings and sea-farers and it was here that an eclectic range of inventions was born. Cheesemaking at the Jarlsberg Estate (formerly Sæheimir) began in 1860 and now Jarlsberg cheese is internationally renowned. The world's first bulk oil tanker was built in Tønsberg in 1878. In the mid-19th century, Svend Foyn, the 'father' of Norwegian sealing and whaling, turned Tønsberg into a base of operations and source of expertise for whalers in the Arctic and Antarctic waters. The exploding harpoon, which transformed modern whaling, was developed here. To round off the list of diverse Tønsberg in-novations, in 1953 Arne Gravdahl invented the sanitary pad.

Sights

TØNSBERG CASTLE

The 13th-century ruins of **Tønsberg** (Castrum Tunsbergis; ☎ 33 31 18 72; admission free, tower adult/child Nkr10/5; ☺ tower 11am-6pm late Jun–mid-Aug, shorter hours rest-of-year), spread across the 63m-high hill behind the town, was once one of the largest medieval fortifications in Norway. Size counted for little, however, in 1503 when the Swedes destroyed the fortress and little remains of the castle itself. Nonetheless, the modern (1888), 17m-high **Slotts-fjellstårnet tower**, provides a good viewpoint over the ruins. In front of the tower there's a bronze model of how the castle looked in 1500. Parts of the 600m-long outer wall remain intact, while the extant medieval stone foundations include **King Magnus Lagabøte's Keep**, the 1191 **Church of St Michael**, the **hall of King Håkon Håkonsson** and various **guard towers**. The park is always open.

RUINS

Atop the hill in the Haugar district, you'll find the **Viking-era grave mounds** of kings Olav and Sigrød. In the park off Kongsgaten lie the ruins of **Kongsgården**, the old Royal Court of King Håkon Håkonsson where the kings of Vestfold were elected, while at Storgaten 17 are the ruins of the medieval **Church of St Olav** (possibly based on the round church in Jerusalem) and which dates from 1207, as well as St Olav's monastery and several

prior to the Battle of Hafsfjord, which took place in 872. Tønsberg celebrated its 1100-year anniversary in 1971. The name, mean-ing 'farm hill', probably refers to the farm Haugar (now in the centre of town).

When King Harald Hårfagre divided the kingdom in the 9th century, he appointed his son, Bjørn Farmann, to rule over Vest-fold, and the court of Sæheimir, at Tøns-berg, became the seat of royal power. In the late medieval period it served as one of three Hanseatic trading posts in Norway, with ties to northern Germany. The town was de-stroyed by fire in 1535, after which it fell into decline. By the 17th century the town had recovered and by 1850, Tønsberg had the largest merchant fleet in Norway.

Viking-age graves. They all carry important historical weight, which compensates for the fact that they can be visually unexciting to the lay visitor.

VESTFOLD COUNTY MUSEUM

Standing at the foot of Slottsfjellet (Castle Rock) at the northern end of town, is **Vestfold County Museum** (Vestfold Fylkesmuseum; ☎ 33 31 29 19; www.vfm.no; Farmannsveien 30; adult/child Nkr40/5; ☺ 10am-5pm Mon-Sat, noon-5pm Sun mid-May–mid-Sep), located within a five-minute walk northwest of the train station. Highlights include displays on the excavation of the impressive *Oseberg* Viking ship (now shown in Oslo's Viking Ship Museum p78), a host of medieval artefacts from the local district, a collection of historic period-furnished farm buildings, and a section on Tønsberg's whaling history, including skeletons of both a sperm whale and a blue whale. The latter, measuring 23m long, is the largest whale skeleton on display in the world.

Sleeping

The tourist office has listings of holiday huts, cabins, cottages, guesthouses and private rooms for the Skerries, south of town, and details of how to get there.

Furustrand Camping (☎ 33 32 44 03; fax 33 32 74 03; Tareveien 11, Tolvsrød; tent sites Nkr100 plus per car/person Nkr 35/25, cabins from Nkr500) Campers should head 5.5km east of the centre; take bus No 111 or 116 to Tolvsrød (Nkr18). The compensation for the inconvenience is the beachfront location and reasonable facilities.

Tønsberg Vandrerhjem (☎ 33 31 21 75; tonsberg .hostel@vanderrhyjem.no; Dronning Blancasgata 22; dm Nkr195-220, s/d with shared bathroom Nkr350/450, s/d with private bathroom Nkr450/550; ☐ Ⓟ) This exceptionally well-run and friendly hostel is well equipped, clean and tidy and just a five-minute walk from the train station. Prices include a good breakfast.

Rainbow Hotel Brygga (☎ 33 34 49 00; www.rain bow-hotels.no/brygga; Nedre Langgate 40; s/d mid-Jun–mid-Aug & Sat & Sun Nkr725/960, rest-of-year

THOR HEYERDAHL

Larvik's favourite son was the intrepid and controversial Thor Heyerdahl (1914–2002), the quirky scientist, anthropologist and explorer.

He specialised in epic journeys. In 1947 he sailed 6000km in a balsawood raft, the *Kon-Tiki*, from Peru to Polynesia to prove that the South Pacific may have been settled by migrants from South America rather than Asia. His hotly disputed theories – backed up by discoveries of similarities of fauna and cultural artefacts in Polynesia and South America and by the fact that Pacific ocean currents run east–west – ran against the grain of conventional wisdom. The film of his journey won an Oscar in 1951 for Best Documentary and his exploits in the grim postwar years (during WWII, Heyerdahl won medals for bravery in resisting the Nazis) captured the imagination of millions across the world; his book describing the expedition sold an astonishing 60 million copies worldwide. To see the actual *Kon-Tiki* ship, visit the *Kon-Tiki* Museum in Oslo (p80).

Although also renowned as one of the first Europeans to excavate sites on Galapagos and Easter islands, Heyerdahl again grabbed international attention in 1970 when he crossed the Atlantic in a papyrus raft. His purpose was to prove that Columbus may not have been the first successful transatlantic navigator and that even the ancient Egyptians could have accomplished the voyage. His first raft, *Ra*, sank soon after setting out, but the dogged Heyerdahl was undeterred, successfully completing the crossing in *Ra II*.

In 1978, the indefatigable Heyerdahl sailed the *Tigris* from the Euphrates and Tigris rivers, down the Persian Gulf and across the Indian Ocean to Djibouti to prove how the ancient Sumerians travelled widely. When he was subsequently prevented from entering the Red Sea due to local conflicts, Heyerdahl set fire to his ship in a spectacular anti-war protest. In addition to his many roles of scientist and explorer, Heyerdahl was a fervent internationalist – his crew was always multinational and his boats flew the UN flag.

On the occasion of Heyerdahl's 75th birthday in 1989, a statue in his honour was unveiled at Tollerodden, east of Larvik's harbour. It's sculpted in blue larvikite, a beautiful 50 million-year-old type of granite which is quarried locally.

Heyerdahl, who believed to his dying day that the world's oceans ought to be considered one vast highway when studying ancient civilisations, died of cancer in northern Italy on 18 April 2002.

Nkr1210/1510; 🖳) This modern, waterfront hotel has pleasant (if smallish) rooms, great breakfasts and is popular with families.

Quality Hotel Tønsberg (☎ 33 00 41 00; tonsberg@ quality.choicehotels.no; s/d from Nkr700/900; 🖳 🐕) Another excellent option, this branch of the Quality Hotel chain has stylish (in a Nordic minimalist kind of way) rooms by the waterfront at the quieter, southern end of town.

Eating

For its size, Tønsberg has an unusually large number of restaurants, all of the establishments listed here are open for lunch and dinner daily.

Himmel & Hav (☎ 33 00 49 80; Tønsberg Brygge; tapas buffet Nkr198, mains Nkr115-275) This place is recommended for its excellent fish and seafood dishes and the various buffets the restaurant offers are well worth the money. Great live music can also be heard at night on summer weekends.

Brygga (☎ 33 31 12 70; Nedre Langgate 35; mains Nkr175-210) A slight step upmarket from the neighbouring Himmel & Hav, this is Norwegian and international cuisine at its most pleasant, particularly on the outdoor terrace. There's also good beer.

Esmeralda (☎ 33 31 91 91; Nedre Langgate 26C; salads Nkr75-100) This long-standing local favourite is brisk, bright and breezy with economical light meals on the terrace.

Peppe's Pizza (☎ 33 31 70 71; Nedre Langgate 26B; pizzas from Nkr134) Friendly Peppe's does its usual pizza thing in an atmospheric old house dating from 1700.

Away from the water, there are some popular choices for those with a taste for something a touch more exotic:

Bombay Tandoori (☎ 33 31 71 06; Ovre Langgate 36; mains from Nkr120) You'll smell this place before you see it and the food is excellent.

Fregatten (☎ 33 31 47 76; Storgaten 17; 2/6 sushi from Nkr45/50, mains Nkr99-219) Japanese, Chinese and Norwegian food are all served here.

Getting There & Away

The **Tønsberg Rutebilstasjon** (☎ 33 30 01 00; Jern-banegaten) is a block south of the train station. Nor-Way Bussekspress buses run between Tønsberg and Kristiansand (Nkr330, 4½ hours, one to two daily), via most coastal towns en route. There are also buses to Oslo (Nkr140, 1¾ hours).

Intercity trains run hourly between **Tøns-berg station** (☎ 81 50 08 88) and Oslo (Nkr168, 1½ hours).

SANDEFJORD

pop 39,400

This former whaling capital is worth a brief detour for one main reason: it's home to the world's only major museum dedicated to whaling.

The Sandefjord **tourist office** (☎ 33 46 05 90; www.visitsandefjord.com; Thor Dahls Gate 1; 🕒 9am-6pm Mon-Fri, 10am-4.30pm Sat, 12.30-4.30pm Sun mid-Jun–early Aug, 9am-4pm Mon-Fri rest-of-year) is just back from the waterfront.

The **Whaling Museum** (Hvalfangstmuseet; ☎ 33 48 46 50; www.hvalfangstmuseet.no; Museumsgaten 39; adult/child Nkr50/25; 🕒 10am-5pm Thu-Tue, 10am-7pm Wed late Jun–mid-Aug) puts across the Norwegian perspective of the whaling debate with an emphasis on history and a minimum of polemics. As such, it's an important opportunity to see the other side of the debate (see the boxed text, p58) in particular, over the rights and wrongs of one of Norway's oldest industries. The extensive archive of photos, equipment and information on marine life is complemented by the whaleboat *Southern Actor*, which is moored at the **harbour** (🕒 9.30am-5pm late Jun–mid-Aug); entry is by the same ticket.

Most buses running between Oslo or Sarpsborg and Kristiansand stop in the town of Sandefjord.

LARVIK

pop 23,000

Larvik is larger than it is attractive. It does, however, make a good base from which to explore the surrounding holiday areas. The town's main historical claim to fame is as the home town of Thor Heyerdahl (see the boxed text, p110), one of Norway's premier explorers.

Information

Laundrette (Guest Harbour) A coin-operated laundry is available at the Guest Harbour.

Tourist office (☎ 33 13 91 00; www.visitlarvik.no; Storgata 48; 🕒 8.30am-6pm Mon-Sat & 1-4pm Sun mid-Jun–early Aug, 9am-4pm Mon-Fri rest-of-year) Located opposite the ferry dock and the staff are typically helpful. They also offer Internet access (per 15 min Nkr20) and can advise about the archaeological dig at the ancient Viking town of Kaupang.

Sights

LARVIK MUSEUM

This **museum** (☎ 33 17 12 90; adult/child combined ticket Nkr40/10) consists of three parts.

The classic baroque timber **Herregården manor house** (Herregårdsletta 6; guided tours 12.30pm, 1.30pm & 2.30pm Tue-Sat mid-Jun–mid-Aug & Sun Jun–mid-Sep) was constructed in 1677 as the home of the Norwegian Governor General, Ulrik Frederik Gyldenløve, the Duke of Larvik; as the illegitimate son of King Fredrik IV of Denmark, Gyldenløve was given a dukedom and packed off to Norwegian obscurity. It's currently furnished in 17th- and 18th-century style.

Larvik Maritime Museum (Kirkestredet 5; ☺ noon-4pm Tue & Sat mid-Jun–mid-Aug & Sun Jun–mid-Sep), in a 1730 brick structure immediately east of the harbour, is home to a collection of maritime art, artefacts and quite a number of impressive model ships. There's also a small exhibition on the nearby Viking town of Kaupang (see p112).

Verkensgarorden (Nedre Fritzøegate 2; ☺ noon-4pm Tue-Sat mid-Jun–mid-Aug, noon-3pm Tue-Sat rest-of-year) has a collection of tools and implements from a local 17th-century sawmill and ironworks. There's also a permanent geological exhibition documenting the evolution of blue larvikite, a beautiful, locally quarried 50 million-year-old type of granite.

BØKESKOGEN

The 300-hectare **Bøkeskogen** (Beech Woods) north of the town centre form a pleasant green belt for strolling; watch out for the 80 (Viking-era is ancient) **Viking-era grave mounds** amid the greenery. The highest point affords a fine view over the forest, as well as the lake Farrisvatn.

KAUPANG

This a Viking town located 5km east of Larvik and dates from the 8th century when up to 600 people lived there. There is an archaeological dig, however most of the artefacts are on their way to Oslo. The town is still worth visiting. Contact the tourist office for more information.

Sleeping

Hovlandbanen Camping (☎ 33 11 44 22; Hovland; tent/caravan sites Nkr120/175, cabins from Nkr225, electricity per person Nkr25; ☺ Jun-Sep) For once, campers don't have to head too far into the backblocks as this camping ground is 1.5km north (uphill) from the harbour, next to a race track.

Lysko Gjestegaard (☎ 33 18 77 79; www.lysko-it.no; Kirkestredet 10; s/d from Nkr500/700; P) This quiet guesthouse, opposite the Maritime Museum at the eastern end of the harbour, is set in a lovely old timbered house and has self-catering facilities. Prices don't include breakfast.

Gyldenløve Hotel (☎ 33 18 25 26; fax 33 18 79 70; Storgata 26; s/d from Nkr600/750) With considerable charm, this renovated 1903 hotel represents a good choice right on the waterfront.

Quality Hotel Grand Farris (☎ 33 18 78 00; fax 33 18 70 45; Storgata 38; s/d from Nkr690/890; P ▯) Also overlooking the water, this is Larvik's finest with supremely comfortable rooms which helps you forgive the fact that it's something of an architectural eyesore.

Eating

Larvik nights can be quiet, but there are plenty of restaurants to choose from, even if they lack the waterfront position of other towns along the coast. All restaurants listed here are open for lunch and dinner daily.

Ferdinands Lillekjøkken (☎ 33 13 05 44; Storgata 32; mains from Nkr130) You'll find steak and seafood dinners served nightly at this fine restaurant.

Restaurant Hansemann (☎ 33 14 00 01; Kongegata 33; specials from Nkr85, mains from Nkr145) Catering to a range of budgets, Hansemann is known for its decent meat and fish dishes.

Jeppe's (☎ 33 18 08 08; Storgata 24; pizza & Mexican buffet Nkr110) Close to the centre, Jeppe's offers an exciting buffet on Wednesday, Friday and Saturday.

Bøkekroa Restaurant (☎ 33 18 10 53; Bøkeskogen) The food here is unremarkable, but it's still the place to be on Friday from 6.30pm to 10pm when jazz concerts set the pace for a mellow Larvik night. On Sunday morning breakfast is served, accompanied by choir music.

Getting There & Away

Nor-Way Bussekspressen buses pass through Larvik en route between Seljord (Nkr190, 2¼ hours, up to three times daily) and Tønsberg (Nkr75, one hour). For other destinations along the coast, you may need to change at Tønsberg or Arendal.

Local trains run up to 20 times daily between Oslo S (Central Station) and Larvik

(Nkr227, two hours). Some of these trains continue from Larvik to Skien (Nkr55, 45 minutes), where there are a few daily connections to Nordagutu on the Oslo–Stavanger rail line.

Color Line operates ferries to Fredrikshavn in Denmark (see p393).

Getting Around

The train and bus stations are side by side on Storgata.

The Vestfold region is fabulous for cycling and bike trails have been meticulously laid out from one end of the county to the other. The tourist office hires bicycles for Nkr120/550 per day/week and sells the indispensable three-part map *Sykkelkart Vestfold* for Nkr100.

AROUND LARVIK

The low-lying Brunlanes Peninsula, southwest of Larvik, has a few moderately interesting towns which are packed in summer with Norwegian holiday-makers who flood the coastal camping grounds. An alternative to the crowded beaches is the Numendalslågen for salmon fishing at Holmfoss or Brufoss; ask at the tourist office in Larvik (p111) for details and information regarding fishing licences.

BRUNLANES PENINSULA
Stavern

The pleasant little town of Stavern, just south of Larvik, has more life than the other towns on the peninsula. The pedestrian streets, lined with cafés and small private galleries, make for a pleasant stroll. Highlights include the mid-18th-century fort, **Fredriksvern Verft**, surrounded by block houses which once formed part of the fortress defences. Also worth visiting is the colourful 1756 **church** (☎ 33 19 99 75; Kommandør Herbsgata 1; admission free; ⏰ 11am-1pm Tue-Fri), Norway's first naval house of worship.

Stavern is also the start of the popular and attractive 33km-long Kyststien **coastal walk** to Ødegården on the western coast of Brunlanes. The Stavern **tourist office** (☎ 33 19 73 00; Havnegata 3; ⏰ 10am-4pm Wed-Sat & 1-4pm Sun mid-Jun–early Aug) provides route maps, *Kyststien i Larvik* (Nkr85).

For accommodation, try **Fredtun Folkehøyskole** (☎ 33 15 68 00; www.fredtun.no; Route 301; s/d Nkr300/500, s/d with shared bathroom Nkr265/550),

a decent mid-range option 1km south of town, or the very pleasant **Hotel Wassilioff** (☎ 33 11 36 00; www.wassilioff.no; Havnegata 1; s/d from Nkr750/900), which offers greater comfort just across the park from the water; at the latter, you pay an extra Nkr200 for sea views.

To get to and from Larvik (Nkr23, 15 minutes, once or twice hourly), use bus No 1.

Mølen

The Mølen Promontory is something of a geological oddity as it forms the end of the ice age **Ra moraine** (rock and silt pushed ahead of the glacier and deposited as a new landform) which extends from the lake Farrisvatn (which the moraine dammed) to the southwestern end of Brunlanes. According to the postcards sold in Mølen, this is the only place in this area that experiences big ocean-style waves. More often the sea is as flat as a millpond. The 230 stone cairns and heaps of boulders, which are laid out in parallel rows, are Iron Age burial mounds. The larger ones – particularly those in the shape of boats – were probably honoured nobles, while the nondescript heaps were for lesser mortals. It makes a nice day walk from Helgeroa, about 4km away along the Kyststien coastal walk (see left for details); to reach Helgeroa from Larvik (Nkr34), take bus No 1 (via Stavern; 40 minutes) or No 3 (direct; 20 minutes).

DAMVANN

Some 20km north of Larvik is the beautiful, haunting lake of Damvann surrounded by forests. Popular legend claims it to be the home a witch called Huldra, a woman of such exquisite beauty that it is said that any man who looked upon her was doomed. On Sunday in July, a modern-day version of **Huldra** (Ellen Dalen; ☎ 33 11 25 17) serves meals here from noon to 4pm. Access is difficult without a car; the nearest bus stop is at Kvelde (6km from the lake) on Numendalslågen Rd.

KRAGERØ
pop 5300

If you're working your way down the coast from Oslo, Kragerø is the first truly picturesque village you'll come to. Although it straggles out a bit along the waterfront, the narrow streets and whitewashed houses which climb the hill just back from the water are truly wonderful.

Kragerø has long served as a retreat for Norwegian artists and Edvard Munch (see the boxed text, p43) spent a few restorative fishing holidays here. While here, he wrote

'Many a sleepless night my thoughts and dreams go to Kragerø... Above blasts the wind from the sea, behind are the fragrant pines, and beyond, the waves breaking over the skerries. My regards to Kragerø, the pearl of the coastal towns.'

Clearly he was a better painter than a writer. A statue of Munch stands on the spot where he painted a winter sun over the sea. The tourist office (☎ 35 98 23 88; www.visitkragero.no; Torgaten 1; 9am-7pm Mon-Fri, 9am-6pm Sat & 9am-5pm Sun mid-Jun–mid-Aug, shorter hours rest-of-year) overlooks the water and has listings of pensions, apartments and private homes in Kragerø and in some of the quieter hamlets along the coast. For free Internet, head to the public library, between the tourist office and the pretty main square.

Sights & Activities

The Berg-Kragerø Museum (☎ 35 98 14 53; Lovisenbergveien 45; adult/child Nkr40/free; noon-6pm Jun–mid-Aug) on the southern shore of Hellefjord, 3km from the centre, occupies a 120-hectare estate with a country residence dated from 1803, gardens, walking tracks, a café and a gallery for visiting art and history exhibits.

For a great view over the town and its skerries, climb from Kragerø Stadium to the lookout point on Steinmann Hill.

For something a bit more quirky, you could always take a rail-bicycle ride along the 13km railway between Sannidal and Merkebekk. Rail-bikes (bicycles on bogies, called dressin in Norwegian) rent for Nkr60/220 per hour/day. Book through Støa Camping (below) or ask at the tourist office.

Sleeping

Kragerø Vandrerhjem (☎ 35 98 57 00; kragero.hostel@vandrerhjem.no; Lovisenbergveien 20; dm/s/d Nkr225/400/500; mid-Jun–mid-Aug) Prices at this fine HI hostel, about 2km from town, include breakfast and they serve dinner for Nkr100.

Støa Camping (☎ 35 99 02 61; spar.kivle@ngbutikk.net; Sannidal; tent sites Nkr120, cabins from Nkr225) Støa Camping is uninspiring, but more than

adequate and conveniently connected to the town by bus No 607 (Nkr26, 12 minutes).

Victoria Hotel (☎ 35 98 75 25; victoria@aco.no; PA Heuchtsgata 31; s/d Nkr780/1000) The finest place to stay in Kragerø, the attractive Victoria Hotel has well-appointed rooms and is a great base for your stay here.

Eating

Stim (☎ 35 98 30 00; Storgata 1; 2-course meal Nkr350) Stim is a highly recommended fish and fowl restaurant, with a contemporary international menu and fresh local produce.

El Paso Western Saloon (☎ 35 98 15 32; PA Heuchtsgata 31; lunches from Nkr75, mains Nkr85-229) This rather incongruous place attempts to fuse the Norwegian seaside with the badlands of West Texas. It nearly works and has become the tourist's choice for steaks, burgers, pizza, attempts at Mexican fare and other non-seafood dishes.

Amadeus Musikk Kafé (☎ 35 98 15 32; PA Heuchtsgata 31; mains around Nkr110) Equally improbable, this café isn't bad on a weekend evening when live performances are staged.

Kafe Edvard (☎ 35 98 15 50; Edvard Munchsvei 2; lunch specials from Nkr75) For simple Norwegian fare without the customary Norwegian price tag, this place is hard to beat.

Getting There & Away

The simplest approach is by rail from Oslo or Kristiansand to Neslandsvatn, where most trains are met by a connecting Drangedal Bilruter bus (☎ 35 99 81 00) to Kragerø. Nor-Way Bussekspress runs two to five buses daily to Oslo from Tangen, by the E18 (Nkr300, 3½ hours), where there are connecting buses to/from Kragerø. Coming from Kristiansand (Nkr180, 2½ hours) is similarly easy.

AROUND KRAGERØ
Jomfruland

Every summer, Norwegian tourists flock to the island of Jomfruland, just off the coast from Kragerø. Measuring around 10km long and up to 600m wide, the island is covered by forest and encircled by mostly sandy beaches. The landmark old (1869) and new (1937) lighthouses (☎ 35 99 11 79; adult/child Nkr20/10; noon-4pm Mon-Sat, noon-6pm Sun mid-Jun–mid-Aug) can be visited.

The appealing Jomfruland Camping (☎ 35 99 12 75; janne.riis@c2i.net; Åsvik brygge; tent sites from Nkr100, caravan sites with electricity Nkr175, 4-bed cabins Nkr450) is near the Åsvik brygge ferry terminal.

In summer, ferries between Kragerø and Jomfruland (Nkr32, 50 minutes) are run by **Kragerø Fjordbåtselskap** (☎ 35 98 58 58) up to three times daily.

RISØR
pop 4500

Risør, the 'White Town on the Skagerrak', is one of southern Norway's prettiest. Centred around the U-shaped harbour and surrounded by historic white houses (dating from 1650 to 1890), this is a great place to relax for a few days, amid the colourful fishing boats and private yachts. It's a place to wander and soak up the rustic charm. If you get bored by long, lazy days by the water, you probably shouldn't be here.

Information

Info Sør complex (☎ 37 11 90 00; www.infosor.no; 9am-6pm Mon-Fri, 10am-4pm Sat & noon-6pm Sun mid-Jun–mid-Aug, 9am-4pm rest-of-year) This large complex covers the region in general; it's out of town on the E18 near the Telemark boundary.

Library (Kragsgate 48A; 11am-3pm Mon-Fri & 11am-2pm Sat mid-Jun–mid-Aug, 11am-7pm Mon-Thu & 11am-2pm Fri & Sat rest-of-year) Free Internet access here.

Tourist office (☎ 37 15 22 70; Kragsgata 3; 10am-6pm Mon-Fri, 10am-4pm Sat & noon-6pm Sun mid-Jun–mid-Aug) Generous with time and information and just 50m west of the harbour.

Sights & Activities

RISØR AQUARIUM

The interesting **Risør Saltwater Aquarium** (Saltvannsakvariet; ☎ 37 15 32 82; Dampskipsbrygga; adult/child Nkr45/25; 11am-7pm mid-Jun–mid-Aug, shorter hours rest-of-year), on the quay in front of the Risør Hotel, is a small showcase of saltwater fish, crustaceans and shellfish common to Norway's south coast. Highlights include baby lobsters and the colourful cuckoo wrasse.

RISØR MUSEUM & RISØR KUNSTPARK GALLERY

For the lowdown on local geology, fishing and the 275-year history of Risør, check out the **Risør Museum** (☎ 37 15 17 77; Prestegata 9; adult/family Nkr30/50; 9am-4pm Mon-Fri & 9am-2pm Sat mid-Jun–mid-Aug). Ask for a loan of the explanatory booklet in English. Adjunct to the museum is the **Risør Kunstpark Gallery** (9am-4pm Mon-Fri & 9am-2pm Sat mid-Jun–mid-Aug)

which displays works by artists inspired by Risør's charm.

RISØR ART CENTRE

This innovative **art centre** (Risør Kunstforum; ☎ 37 15 63 83; www.kunstforum.no; Tjenngata 76; for courses mid-Jun–mid-Aug) runs a range of courses ranging from making handmade paper to watercolour painting. Courses start from Nkr1500 for three days, up to Nkr3300 for seven days; full accommodation/course packages are also available.

BOAT HIRE

To explore the offshore islands under your own steam (or horsepower), **Risør Båtformidling** (☎ 37 15 25 50) rents out small motorboats, while **Sørlandet Feriesenter** (☎ 37 15 40 80) also rents larger motorboats and canoes.

Festivals

To get summer rolling, the town hosts the **Risør Chamber Music Festival** in the last week of June, with a growing cast of local and international performers in attendance.

On the first weekend in August, Risør hosts the **Risør Wooden Boat Festival** (Trebåtfestival), which attracts old salts and other boat people from all over Norway. The festival encompasses a full programme of boat races, concerts and kids' activities; getting accommodation at this time can be difficult.

Sleeping

The tourist office can arrange rooms, houses and cabins.

Moen Camping (☎ 37 15 50 91; fax 37 15 17 63; Moen; tent sites Nkr100, cabins Nkr300-550) This well-run and well-equipped place is Risør's closest camping ground, 11km west of town off the E18. Regular buses (Risør to/from Arendal, Kristiansand and Oslo) run past the entrance.

Risør Kunstforum (☎ 37 15 63 83; kontor@kunstforum.no; Tjenngata 76; s/d/tr Nkr450/600/700) This appealing place, 1km west of the harbour, offers simple but adequate rooms with do-it-yourself breakfast, but the real attractions include art and sculpture classes (above).

Risør Hotel (☎ 37 14 80 00; www.risor-hotel.no; Tangengata 16; s/d from Nkr795/1095 mid-Jun–mid-Aug, Nkr550/850 rest-of-year) The Risør Hotel suffers from the lack of competition in town. Although probably the pick of a very limited choice, it lacks the attention to detail you'd expect for this price. The waterfront location is, however, a winner.

Det Lille Hotell (☎ 37 15 14 95; www.detlillehotel .no; s/d per night from Nkr1100/1350, per week from Nkr7700/9100) This interesting choice offers self-catering suites and apartments dotted around town. Most are in delightfully restored homes with period furnishings and ideal if you plan to spend a week here. Highly recommended for a splurge.

Eating

Around, or just back from the harbour, you'll find several moderately priced cafés and restaurants.

Café Excellensen (☎ 37 15 30 50; Torvet 1; dinner & drinks Nkr350; ❤ breakfast, lunch & dinner) This pleasant daytime café transforms into a pricey, but high-quality steakhouse in the evening.

Brasserie Krag (☎ 37 15 04 50; Kragsgata 12; mains Nkr89-198; ❤ lunch & dinner) This recommended restaurant has a fairly diverse selection on the menu and a laid-back ambience.

Brygge Pizza (☎ 37 15 00 99; Strandgata 2; pizzas from Nkr75; ❤ lunch & dinner) One of the few places with tables out on the water. A good option for those counting their kroner.

Risør Hotel (☎ 37 14 80 00; Tangengata 16; meals Nkr45-Nkr85; ❤ lunch & dinner) This restaurant has a lovely elevated terrace overlooking the water and good snacks and meals, as well as a more expensive à la carte menu.

Getting There & Away

Local buses link Risør with the rail line at Gjerstad (Nkr55, 45 minutes) several times daily. Nor-Way Bussekspress buses between Kristiansand (Nkr140, three hours) and Oslo (Nkr300, 3¾ hours) connect at Vinterkjær with local buses to/from Risør (Nkr26, 20 minutes).

AROUND RISØR

The Skerries, just offshore from Risør, are a popular excursion if you can tear yourself away from one of the harbourside cafés of Risør. The southernmost island of **Stangholmen**, with a pretty lighthouse dating from 1855, is the most popular, due in part to the fact that it's the only one of the islands with a restaurant: **Stangholmen Fyr Restaurant & Bar** (☎ 37 15 24 50; mains from Nkr200) in the lighthouse.

Any of the islands can be reached by ferries and water taxis. In summer, **ferries** (☎ 37 15 24 50) leave Tollbubrygga for Stangholmen

(Nkr35 return, twice hourly) from 10am to at least midnight.

LYNGØR

pop 100

Tiny Lyngør, consisting of several offshore islets near the village of Gjeving, isn't shy about the fact that it won the 1991 European competition for the tidiest town on the continent. Even if it weren't for that distinction, this picturesque little settlement would be worth a visit – part of its charm lies in the fact that visitors can't bring their vehicles across on the ferry.

Sleeping & Eating

Knatten Pensjonat (☎ 37 16 10 19; Odden; s/d Nkr550/750) If you want to enjoy Lyngør after the day-trippers have returned to the mainland, try this simple *pension*. It's a touch overpriced, but you're not exactly spoiled for choice. It's 300m from Holmen Quay.

Seilmakerfruens Kro (☎ 37 16 60 00; Ytre Lyngør; pizzas around Nkr150; ❤ lunch & dinner) This is the most reasonably priced eating choice on the island with decent pizzas and a few à la carte specialties.

Den Blå Lanterne (☎ 37 16 64 80; Holmen; ❤ lunch & dinner) The fact that many wealthy Norwegians have houses in Lyngør is reflected in the prices (fish soup starts from around Nkr300) at this high quality, but outrageously expensive place.

Getting There & Away

The **Lyngør Båtselskap ferry** (☎ 41 45 41 45) between Gjeving, Holmen and Lyngør leaves up to seven times daily on weekdays, four times on Saturday and at least once on Sunday (adult/child Nkr25/15).

For further information of the M/S *Patricia* ferry, see p118.

ARENDAL

pop 30,800

Arendal is one of the more attractive larger towns along Norway's southern coast. Its lively waterfront district (known as Pollen) is backdropped by timbered houses climbing up the hillsides, nowhere more delightfully than in the old district of Tyholmen. For those seeking greater communion with the sea than a harbourside café can offer, the offshore islands of Merdø, Tromøy and Hisøy are worthwhile excursions (p118).

Information

C & A Internet (Ostregata 9; ☺ noon-midnight; per hr Nkr35) Located opposite the Ting Hai Hotel, this place has good connections and stays open as long as there are customers.

Library (☎ 37 01 39 13; Torvet 6; ☺ 10am-6pm Mon-Sat) Like a lot of public libraries in Norway free (but time-limited) Internet access is available here.

Tourist office (☎ 37 00 55 44; info@arendal.com; www .arendal.com; Langbrygga 5; 9am-4pm Jun & Aug, 9am-6pm Mon-Sat & noon-6pm Sun Jul) This office was due to move a few months after we visited.

Sights & Activities

TYHOLMEN

Rising up behind the Guest Harbour (Gjeste-havn) is the old harbourside Tyholmen district which is home to a beautiful collection of 17th- to 19th-century timber buildings featuring neoclassical, rococo and baroque influences. In 1992, it was deservedly awarded the Europa Nostra prize for its expert restoration. Tyholmen was once separated from the mainland by a canal which was filled in after the great sailing era. There are plans to restore the canal and work is already underway.

Right on the harbour at the foot of the hill, stands the striking **town hall** (Rådhus; ☎ 37 01 30 00; Rådhusgata 10; admission free; ☺ 9am-3pm Mon-Fri). Originally a shipowner's home dating from 1815, it became the town hall in 1844. Inside, some late-19th-century modifications are unfortunate (the domed ceiling was flattened), but the elegant original staircase remains.

MUSEUMS

The **Aust-Agder Museum** (☎ 37 07 35 00; www.aust -agder.museum.no; Parkveien 16; adult/child Nkr25/15; ☺ 9am-3pm Mon-Fri, noon-3pm Sat) was first conceived in 1832, when the town authorities asked its globetrotting sailors to be on the lookout for items which may be of interest back home. The results of this search are now housed in the county museum, along with relics of Arendal's shipbuilding, timber and import-export trades. The most interesting exhibits are those covering the ill-fated final journey of the slave ship *Fredensborg*, which went down off Tromøy in 1768; sadly those African slaves who survived were rewarded by being sold in the Caribbean.

Also well worth a visit is **Arendal Town Museum** (☎ 37 02 59 25; Nedre Tyholmsvei 14; adult/ child Nkr20/10; ☺ 10am-3pm Tue-Fri & 10am-2pm Sat),

largely because it is a rare opportunity to see inside one of Arendal's charming old burghers' houses (Klöckers Hus).

CANOE HIRE

If you'd prefer to explore the outlying islands (p118), you can hire **canoes** (☎ 37 03 41 15; Stoaveien 41) per half day from Nkr125.

Festivals & Events

Arendal hosts a week-long **jazz and blues festival** (www.canalstreet.no) in late July – a great time to be in town. Tickets cost around Nkr25.

Sleeping

Arendal has a good sprinkling of mid-range hotels, but those on a tight budget will need to head out of town.

Nidelv Brygge og Camping (☎ /fax 37 01 14 25; Vesterveien 251, Hisøy; tent sites Nkr90 plus per adult/child Nkr15/10, caravan sites Nkr110, cabins Nkr250-750) Located on the Nidelv River at Hisøy, 6km west of Arendal, this reasonable camping ground can be reached on any bus (Nkr25, every half-hour) bound for Kristiansand or Grimstad. If you're driving, take the Rv420.

Ting Hai Hotel (☎ 37 02 22 01; fax 37 02 23 25; Østregate 5; s/d Nkr650/890) The Ting Hai Hotel has simple but tidy spacious rooms a few blocks up from the harbour.

Scandic Hotel (☎ 37 05 21 50; www.scandic-arendal .no; Friergangen 1; s/d Nkr790/990 mid-Jun–mid-Aug, Nkr690/790 Sat & Sun, Nkr1105/1305 rest-of-year) Similarly well-situated and comfortable, the modern Scandic Hotel sits just beneath the historic Tyholmen district, a stone's throw from the water.

Arendal Maritime Hotel (☎ 37 00 07 20; booking@ arendal-maritime-hotel.no; Vestregate 11; s/d from Nkr685/865) Up the hill and a bit further from the water, this reasonable place represents good mid-range value if the other places are full.

Clarion Tyholmen Hotel (☎ 37 07 68 00; tyholmen .hotel@eunet.no; Teaterplassen 2; s/d from Nkr890/1090) Undoubtedly Arendal's best hotel, the Clarion combines prime waterfront position with attractive, semi-luxurious rooms in a restored old building which seeks to emulate Tyholmen's old-world ambience.

Eating

Pollen boasts several atmospheric open-air restaurants and cafés. All are open for lunch and dinner daily.

Sjøloftet (☎ 37 01 90 00; Langebryggen 3; pizzas from Nkr150) At the northern end of Langebryggen and overlooking the water, Sjøloftet specialises in pizza and it's so popular in summer that outdoor tables are only for the patient.

Madam Reiersen (☎ 37 02 19 00; Nedre Tyholmsvei 3; mains Nkr125-245) This place offers more sophisticated fare than Sjøloftet, with an emphasis on pasta dishes; the food's good, but it costs a bit more than it should.

Ting Hai (☎ 37 02 22 01; Østregate 5; mains from around Nkr120) Away from the shore, this is one of Norway's better Chinese restaurants with cheerful service, generous servings and good food.

Café Det Lindvedske Hus (☎ 37 02 18 38; Nedre Tyholmsvei 7b; snacks & pasta Nkr45-95) There's a good choice of well-priced sandwiches, delicious snacks and pasta dishes at this American-run café, along side dining in atmospheric 200-year-old décor.

Café Sam (☎ 37 02 46 63; Havnegaten 8; snacks from Nkr15) Café Sam, on Torvet (the main square), does the usual ice cream and snacks, but it also has an attached bakery – ideal for self-caterers.

If you just want a tasty snack, the waterfront fish market sells inexpensive fish cakes.

Entertainment

Many of the restaurants around the water conveniently double as evening drinking spots. Other bars and discos stay open until around 2.30am.

For an outdoor drink in summer, **Fiskebrygge** (☎ 37 02 31 13; Nedre Tyholmsvei 1; ✆ 9am-2am Wed-Sun Apr-Sep) has a great location on the waterfront and serves a range of beer (from Nkr45) and cocktails (from Nkr79). Also right on the water, **Fishermans Pub** (☎ 37 02 88 70; Langbryggen 19; ✆ 8pm-2am) is a great spot to kick-start your evening, especially at the outdoor tables in summer.

For dancing the night away, **Club Papparazzi** (☎ 37 02 40 45; Friergangen 4-6; ✆ 9pm-4am), attracts a young-ish crowd drawn to the energetic music, while **Mammarazzi** (☎ 37 02 72 02; Langbryggen 15) struggles to rise above its kitsch name and generally succeeds – it's the disco of choice for tourists and locals alike. For something a little more chilled and sedate, try **Rubens Danserestaurant** (☎ 37 02 51 60; Friergangen 1; ✆ Fri & Sat).

Getting There & Away

Nor-Way Bussekspress buses between Kristiansand (Nkr102, 1½ hours, up to nine daily) and Oslo (Nkr340, four hours) call in several times daily at the Arendal Rutebilstasjon, a block west of Pollen harbour. Local buses connect Arendal with Grimstad (Nkr40, 30 minutes, hourly), Risør (Nkr78, 1¼ hours) and Kristiansand (Nkr98, 1½ hours, hourly).

Arendal is connected with the main rail system by a trunk line from Nelaug, but the **station** (☎ 37 02 20 03) lies a 10-minute walk through the Fløyheia tunnel or over the hill along Hylleveien and Iuellsklev.

M/S Patricia (☎ 37 08 55 78) sails from Arendal (Pollen) to Lyngør three times weekly in July (Nkr175/280 one-way/return).

For details of ferries from Arendal to Strömstad (Sweden), see p394.

For details of yacht mooring, contact **Arendal Gjestehavn** (☎ 37 01 31 47).

Getting Around

Town buses in Arendal charge Nkr20. **Sykkelsport** (☎ 37 02 39 60; cnr Nygaten & Vestre gates) rents bicycles for Nkr75 to Nkr120 per day. This is a great way to explore the islands and reach the bathing beaches on Hisøy and Tromøy.

AROUND ARENDAL

The 260-hectare island of **Merdø**, just off Arendal has been inhabited since the 16th century. One peculiarity is that the island bears the remnants of vegetable species introduced in the ballast of early sailing vessels. The **Merdøgård Museum** (☎ 37 07 35 00; adult/child Nkr25/10; ✆ noon-4.30pm mid-Jun–mid-Aug), housed in a historic 1736 sea captain's residence, is decked out in period furnishings. The admission fee includes hourly guided tours.

Ferry access to Merdø and Hove (on the island of Tromøy) is on the **M/F Merdø** (☎ 99 46 12 35; ✆ end Jun–mid-Aug). There are nine sailings between 9am and 5.30pm. At other times of the year, the **M/F Trau** (☎ 37 08 56 09; ✆ year-round) runs to Merdø, while the **Tromøy II** (☎ 90 06 12 35; www.skilsoferga .no; ✆ year-round) runs to Skilso on Tromøy. Fares are around Nkr20 to Nkr30.

The favoured bathing sites are on Tromøy, Spornes and Hove. The nearest access to Spornes is on the bus marked 'Tromøy Vest/ Øst', but you'll still have a 15-minute walk.

Alternatively, take a bike on the **M/S Skilsøy ferry** (☎ 37 00 55 44), which sails frequently between Arendal and the western end of Tromøy (Nkr15, 10 minutes).

On the islets of **Store** and **Lille Torungene** rise two grand lighthouses which have guided ships into Arendal since 1844. They're visible from the coasts of both Hisøy and Tromøy.

Popular beaches on **Hisøy** include Stølsvigen, Tangen and Vrageviga, but note that the bus runs only as far as Sandvigen. Kolbjørnsvik, on Hisøy, may be reached from Arendal (Nkr18, six minutes) on the frequent **M/S Kolbjørn III** (☎ 94 58 71 72).

GRIMSTAD

pop 9500

The white town of Grimstad is one of the loveliest on the Skagerrak coast and, what it lacks in surrounding scenery, it makes up for in the charm and overall enchantment of its narrow pedestrianised centre. Renowned as the sunniest spot in Norway, with an average of 266 hours of sunshine per month in June and July, Grimstad also has an unmistakably young vibe, thanks to its large student population.

History

Grimstad's low-key atmosphere, peacefulness and charm belies its past importance. Between 1865 and 1885, Grimstad was perhaps *the* greatest shipbuilding centre in the world. The oak forests that grew on the hillsides were chopped down and sawn into timbers to supply the booming industry; at one point the town had 40 shipyards, and 90 ships were under construction simultaneously.

During the same period, a land shortage caused local farmers to turn to fishing and many an inland farm homestead doubled as a shipbuilding workshop. By 1875, Grimstad had a home fleet of 193 boats.

Information

Guest harbour (Gjestehavn; ☎ 37 04 05 93; www.grimstadgjestehavn.no) A range of amenities are offered in its fierce competition with other villages to attract the yachting fraternity. There are public toilets, showers, a laundry (all open to land-lubbers) and wireless Internet access for those with suitably equipped laptops at some berths; for the latter, you can purchase a scratch card (24-hour use for Nkr150) from the tourist office.

Library (☎ 37 29 67 90; Storgata 44; ⏰ 10am-6pm Mon-Sat) Internet is available at the library for free.
Tourist office (☎ 37 04 40 41; www.grimstad.net; Smith Petersensgata 3; ⏰ 9am-6pm Mon-Fri, 10am-4pm Sat & Sun Jun-Aug) This office is friendly, helpful and just back from the water. It's the place to go for information on everything from theatre performances to Nordic sea-rafting.

Sights
IBSENHUSET & GRIMSTAD TOWN MUSEUM

Grimstad's favourite son was Henrik Ibsen (see the boxed text, p44). He arrived here in January 1844 and the house where he worked as a pharmacist's apprentice, and where he lived and first cultivated his interest in writing, has been converted into the **Grimstad Town Museum** (Grimstad By Museum; ☎ 37 04 46 53; Henrik Ibsens gate 14; adult/child Nkr35/10, child admission free Sun; ⏰ 11am-5pm Mon-Sat & 1-5pm Sun May–mid-Sep), which contains a re-created pharmacy and many of the writer's belongings. There's also a library with the writer's complete works. His 1861 poem *Terje Vigen* and his 1877 drama *Pillars of Society* take place in the Skerries offshore from Grimstad.

The eager young custodians of the museum can arrange **tours** (☎ 37 04 04 90) of the town's other Ibsen landmarks, as well as sights associated with well-known Norwegian author Knut Hamsun (p39), who lived at nearby Norholm from 1918 to 1952.

GRIMSTAD MARITIME MUSEUM

This important **museum** (Sjøfartsmuseet; ☎ 37 04 04 90; Hasseldalen; adult/child combined ticket with Grimstad By Museum, Nkr40/15; ⏰ 11am-5pm Mon-Sat, 1-5pm Sun May–mid-Sep), in the office of the 1842 Hasseldalen shipyard, provides a glimpse into Grimstad's history during 'the days of the white sails'. While you're there, it's worth climbing the short track from the end of Batteriveien up the hill Binabben for a view over Grimstad.

QUARRY THEATRE

One of the more unusual cultural experiences in Grimstad is run by Kristiansand-based **Agder Theater** (☎ 38 12 28 88; www.agder teater.no; tickets Nkr300), who perform in an old quarry up to six days a week in summer; the tourist office should also have a programme of upcoming performances. The quarry, 4km north of town, became infamous during WWII when red granite blocks for

SOUTHERN NORWAY

Hitler's 'Victory Monument' were taken from here; the monument was, of course, never built.

Sleeping

Grimstad Hytteutleie (☻ 37 25 10 65; fax 37 25 10 64; Grooseveien 103) This place can book holiday cabins in the area for one night (from Nkr350) or one week. For camping, at least nine nearby camping grounds are listed on the tourist office's website (www.grimstad.net).

Bie Appartement & Feriesenter (☎ 37 04 03 96; www.bieapart.no; off Arendalsveien; tent sites Nkr220, cabins Nkr500-1200; ⊉) The nearest camping option is friendly, well equipped and 800m northeast of the centre along Arendalsveien. It's not the most picturesque site in Norway, but being this close to Grimstad more than compensates.

Grimstad Vertshus & Kro (☎ 37 04 25 00; post@grimstad-vertshus.no; Grimstadtunet; s/d Nkr595/750) This cosy place is a fair hike into town and feels a bit out on a limb, but it's friendly and good value, especially considering the lack of mid-range options around the harbour.

Norlandia Sørlandet Hotel (☎ 37 09 05 00; www.norlandia.no/sorlandet; Televeien 21; s/d from Nkr705/850; ⊑) This modern hotel, around 3km west of the harbour, has fine rooms in a quiet woodland setting. Some of the upper rooms have views of the ocean.

Grimstad Hotell (☎ 37 25 25 25; www.grimstadhotell.no; Kirkegata 3; s/d Nkr675/845 Sun-Thu, Nkr1045/1245 Fri & Sat; ⊑) The stylish and very comfortable Grimstad Hotell is the only in-town hotel and comes with loads of charm in its restored old Grimstad house.

Eating

Apotekergården (☎ 37 04 50 25; Skolegata 3; mains from Nkr210; ☻ lunch & dinner) The highly recommended Apotekergården is an excellent gourmet restaurant with a breezy outdoor terrace and a cast of regulars who wouldn't eat anywhere else.

Dr Berg (☎ 37 04 44 99; Storgata 2; mains from Nkr145; ☻ lunch & dinner) With its eyrie-like perch overlooking the water, Dr Berg is a great place to try the local seafood.

Platebaren (☎ 37 04 21 88; Storgata 15; baguettes Nkr27-35, salads Nkr49; ☻ 9am-5pm Mon-Wed & Fri, 9am-7pm Thu & 9am-3pm Sat) This highly recommended coffee bar spills out into the street in summer and is a terrific place to tuck into

decent-sized snacks. Even better are the milk shakes (Nkr26), while coffee lovers swear by the iced coffee with ice cream (Nkr30).

Sam Berg (☎ 37 04 03 12; Storgata 9) Located at the harbour-end of the pedestrian zone, Sam Berg bakes bread and is great for those planning a picnic.

Getting There & Away

The Grimstad **Rutebilstasjon** (☎ 37 04 05 18) is on Storgata at the harbour. Nor-Way Bussekspress buses between Oslo (Nkr395, five hours) and Kristiansand (Nkr80, one hour) call at Grimstad three to five times daily. Nettbuss buses to/from Arendal run once or twice hourly (Nkr41, 30 minutes).

Getting Around

You can hire 21-speed bicycles from the tourist office for Nkr30/150 per hour/day; the daily rate drops to Nkr100 for more than one day, child seats cost Nkr20 and those with boats moored in Gjestehavn can rent the bikes for free.

LILLESAND

pop 6000

Lillesand, between Kristiansand and Arendal, has a pretty village centre of old whitewashed houses. There's a local **tourist office** (☎ 37 26 16 80; Rådhuset; ☻ 9am-6pm Mon-Fri, 10am-4pm Sat & noon-4pm Sun mid-Jun–mid-Aug) in the local town hall.

Sleeping & Eating

The tourist office can book self-catering cabins, private rooms and apartments from Nkr200.

Tingsaker Camping (☎ 37 27 04 21; fax 37 27 01 47; tent/caravan sites with car Nkr150, cabins Nkr750-950) This crowded camping ground, on the shore 1km east of the centre, is a typical seaside holiday resort with camping, caravans and a range of overpriced cabins.

Lillesand Hotel Norge (☎ 37 27 01 44; fax 37 27 30 70; Strandgata 3; s/d from Nkr795/1300, snacks & mains Nkr75-275) This fine, boutique hotel has been thoughtfully renovated to reflect the original 1837 construction and is loaded with period touches (particularly in the public areas) and character. There are rooms dedicated to King Alfonso XIII of Spain and author Knut Hamsun, both of whom stayed here, and there's an antiquarian library and good restaurant.

REBRANDING KRISTIANSAND

Not so long ago, Kristiansand was derided throughout Norway for its polluted air, foul coastline and dying salmon stream. However, in recent years local ingenuity has turned the city's reputation around. Industrial effluent is now cleaned in three massive sewage plants before it's released into the sea and the air pollutants are now filtered. The previously choking residue is now sold as concrete strengthener used on offshore oil rigs, netting millions of kroner annually. The small, redeveloped harbour area around the fish market now captures something of the intimate feel of many of the smaller towns along Norway's southern coast. The construction of new and stylish apartments along the waterfront has also helped to add to the aesthetic transformation, a process of which local residents are justifiably proud.

Getting There & Away

The most pleasant way to reach Lillesand is by boat from Kristiansand (see p124). There's also an hourly Nettbuss to Kristiansand (Nkr51), Grimstad (Nkr41) and Arendal (Nkr65).

KRISTIANSAND

pop 63,400

Busy Kristiansand, the fifth-largest city in Norway, has undergone something of a regeneration in recent years (see the boxed text, above) and it's now a pleasant place to spend a day or two. Norway's closest port to Denmark, and hence the first glimpse of the country for many ferry travellers from the south, Kristiansand has a charming small harbour around the fish market, a delightful old town, some good museums, an excellent children's park and good restaurants.

Orientation

Central Kristiansand's locally termed *kvadraturen*, the square grid pattern measuring six long blocks by nine shorter blocks was conceived by King Christian IV, who founded the city in 1641. This is one of the easiest Norwegian cities to find your way around. The rail, bus and ferry terminals form a cluster west of the city centre. Pedestrianised Markens gate serves as a focus for the central shopping and restaurant district,

while the fish market is at the southern tip of the centre.

Information

You can change money at the **post office** (cnr Rådhus & Markens gates) or at all the major banks (there are several on Markens gate).

Café.com Internet Café (Dronningens gate 56; per hr Nkr45; ☎ 11am-11pm Mon-Thu, 11am-3am Fri, noon-5am Sat, 1-11pm Sun)

Gjestehavn (Guest Harbour; ☎ 38 02 07 15; per wash/dry Nkr30/30) The Guest Harbour has laundry facilities.

Kristiansand Library (☎ 38 12 49 10; Rådhus gate 11; ☎ 10am-6pm Mon-Thu, 10am-4.30pm Fri, 10am-3pm Sat) The library offers free, time-limited Internet access.

Kristiansand og Oppland Turistforening (☎ 38 02 52 63; mail@kot.no; Kirkegata 15; ☎ 8.30am-3.30pm Mon-Wed & Fri, 8.30am-6pm Thu) For maps and information on hiking, huts and organised mountain tours in far southern Norway, contact this place.

Tourist office (☎ 38 12 13 14; www.sorlandet.com; Vestre Strandgate 32; ☎ 8.30am-6pm Mon-Fri, 10am-6pm Sat, noon-6pm Sun mid-Jun–mid-Aug; 8.30am-3.30pm Mon-Fri rest-of-year) The enthusiastic office has comprehensive information and friendly staff.

Sights

CHRISTIANSHOLM FORTRESS

The most prominent feature along the Strandepromenaden is the distinctive **Christiansholm Fortress** (Kristiansand Festning; ☎ 38 07 51 50; admission free; ☎ grounds 9am-9pm mid-May–mid-Sep). Built by royal decree between 1662 and 1672 to keep watch over the strategic Skagerrak Straits and protect the city from pirates and rambunctious Swedes, the construction featured walls up to 5m thick and an armoury buried within a concentric inner wall, all of which came at a price: it was financed by the 1550 local citizens, who were taxed and coerced into labour. It was connected to the mainland by a bridge over a moat (filled in during the 19th century) deep enough to accommodate tall ships.

The fortress served its purpose as a formidable deterrent – it was never taken by enemy forces. In 1872 the structure was damaged when a town fire burned the roof. More recently, a new roof with glass clerestory windows has been built, but a ring of eight bronze cannons, cast between 1666 and 1788, still menaces the offshore skerries. Free guided tours take place on Sundays from mid-June to mid-August; contact the tourist office for details.

KRISTIANSAND

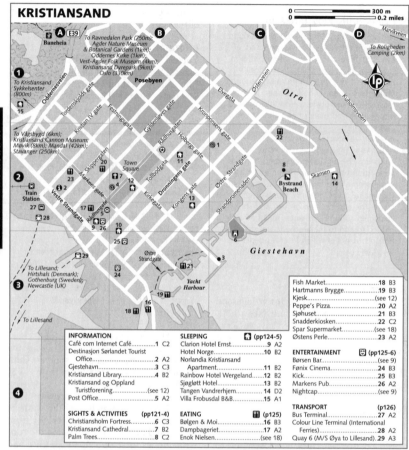

0 ————————— 300 m
0 ————————— 0.2 miles

SOUTHERN NORWAY

Baneheia

To Ravnedalen Park (750m);
Agder Nature Museum
& Botanical Gardens (1km);
Oddernes Kirke (1km);
Vest-Agder Folk Museum (4km);
Kristiansand Dyrepark (9km);
Oslo (330km)

Posebyen

To Kristiansand
Sykkelsenter
(800m)

To Vågsbygd (6km);
Kristiansand Cannon Museum;
Møvik (8km); Mandal (42km);
Stavanger (250km)

Town
Square

Train
Station

Østre
Strandgate

To Lillesand;
Hirtshals (Denmark);
Gothenburg (Sweden);
Newcastle (UK)

Yacht
Harbour

To Lillesand

Otra

Giestehavn

Ekvegata

Østerveien

Strandpromenaden

Bystrand
Beach

Skansen

Marvikveien

To Roligheden
Camping (2km)

Kuholmsveien

INFORMATION	
Café com Internet Café.............1	C2
Destinasjon Sørlandet Tourist	
Office...................................2	A2
Gjestehavn...........................3	C3
Kristiansand Library.................4	B2
Kristiansand og Oppland	
Turistforening...................(see 12)	
Post Office............................5	A2

SIGHTS & ACTIVITIES (pp121–4)	
Christiansholm Fortress..........6	C3
Kristiansand Cathedral............7	B2
Palm Trees............................8	C2

SLEEPING ⏏ (pp124–5)	
Clarion Hotel Ernst..................9	A2
Hotel Norge..........................10	B2
Norlandia Kristiansand	
Apartment...........................11	B2
Rainbow Hotel Wergeland......12	B2
Sjøgløtt Hotel........................13	B2
Tangen Vandrerhjem.............14	D2
Villa Frobusdal B&B................15	A1

EATING 🍴 (p125)	
Bølgen & Moi........................16	B3
Dampbageriet.......................17	A2
Enok Nielsen.....................(see 18)	

Fish Market..........................18	B3
Hartmanns Brygge.................19	B3
Kjesk.................................(see 12)	
Peppe's Pizza........................20	A2
Sjøhuset...............................21	B3
Snadderkiosken.....................22	C2
Spar Supermarket...............(see 18)	
Østens Perle.........................23	A2

ENTERTAINMENT 🎭 (pp125–6)	
Børsen Bar.........................(see 9)	
Fønix Cinema........................24	B3
Kick....................................25	B3
Markens Pub.........................26	A2
Nightcap...........................(see 9)	

TRANSPORT (p126)	
Bus Terminal.........................27	A2
Colour Line Terminal (International	
Ferries)...............................28	A2
Quay 6 (M/S Øya to Lillesand).29	A3

KRISTIANSAND CATHEDRAL

Built in a neogothic style in 1884, the **Kristiansand Cathedral** (Domkirke; ☎ 38 10 77 50; Kirkegata; admission free, tower Nkr20; ⏱ 10am-4pm Mon-Fri, 10am-2pm Sat mid-Jun–mid-Aug) has seating for 1800 people and is Norway's third-largest church. Guided tours (adult/child Nkr20/10) of the cathedral, including the tower, run at 11am and 2pm Monday to Saturday in summer. You might also catch some organ practice at 11am on weekdays in summer.

BANEHEIA & RAVNEDALEN PARKS

Baneheia and Ravnedalen, both north of the city centre, offer greenery and a network of lakeside **hiking** and **skiing tracks** for

those keen to escape the city for a while. Both **parks** were created between 1870 and 1880 by Kristiansand's city chairman, General Oscar Wergeland. Over a 30-year period, he oversaw the planting of 150,000 coniferous trees and transformed the area into a recreational green belt.

AGDER NATURE MUSEUM & BOTANICAL GARDEN

The winding paths through the established 50-hectare park at **Gimle Estate** (☎ 38 09 23 88; Gimleveien 23; adult/child Nkr40/15; ⏱ 10am-6pm Tue-Fri, noon-6pm Sat-Mon mid-Jun–mid-Aug, shorter hours rest-of-year) will lead you through a botanical garden containing a number of rare trees, shrubs, flowers, rocks, minerals and stuffed animals. The estate house has 19th-century period interiors and extraordinary teeth-like columns at the front, and there's also a historic rose garden dating from 1850. It's just over 1km from the centre, across the Oddernes bridge.

POSEBYEN

The Kristiansand **Posebyen** ('Old Town') takes in most of the 14 blocks at the northern end of the town's characteristic *kvadraturen*. It's worth taking a slow stroll around this enchanting quarter, whose name was given by French soldiers who came to *reposer* (French for relax). A scale model (with buildings around 1m high) of the city as it appeared when designed by Christian IV is on view at Vest-Agder Folk Museum (see right). The annual *Kristiansand* guide, published by the tourist office, includes a good section 'A Stroll through Posebyen' to guide your wandering.

KRISTIANSAND DYREPARK

Over the years, the former **Kristiansand zoo** (☎ 38 04 97 00; www.dyreparken.no; admission, incl all activities, adult Nkr85-240, child Nkr70-195, depending on season; ☼ 10am-7pm mid-May–Aug, shorter hours rest-of-year) has gradually expanded into one of Norway's most popular domestic attractions. Off the E18, 10km east of Kristiansand, it's probably *the* favourite holiday destination for children from around the country.

The funfair portion includes a log ride and pirate ship cruise, and the zoo portion offers a surprising variety of specimens, including the near-extinct golden lion tamarin. If you want to enjoy the water park, be sure to bring a swimming costume.

The real highlights, however, are the **Northern Wilderness** (Nordisk Vilmark), where visitors are transported over the habitat of moose, wolves, lynx and wolverines on elevated boardwalks; and **Cardamom Town** (Kardamomme By), named for a key ingredient in Scandinavian waffles, a fantasy village based on the popular children's stories of Thorbjørn Egner. The town, which vaguely suggests a setting in northern Africa, has been carefully laid out exactly as it appeared in the illustrated book. It's also possible to stay in the park (see p124).

To get there, take the Dyreparkbussen or local bus No M1 (adult/child Nkr23/12),

which operates more or less hourly throughout summer.

VEST-AGDER FOLK MUSEUM

Located 4km east of town on the E18, the open-air **Vest-Agder Folk Museum** (Vest-Agder Fylkesmuseum; ☎ 38 09 02 28; Vigeveien 22B; adult/child Nkr40/15; ☼ 10am-6pm Tue-Fri, noon-6pm Sat-Mon mid-Jun–mid-Aug, noon-5pm Sun rest-of-year) houses a collection of farmsteads and hamlets from the Setesdalen region. It also includes displays of traditional costumes, art and children's toys. Folk dancing performances are sometimes held in summer at 5pm on Wednesdays. There's also a scale model which is being built of Kristiansand Old Town and is due for completion in 2006.

SETESDALSBANEN

The 78km-long narrow-gauge railway between Kristiansand and Byglandsfjord was opened in 1896 to link Setesdalen with the coast. It was used to transport nickel from the Evje mines and local timber and barrel staves which were used in the salting and export of herring. Although competition from the normal-gauge state railway forced its closure in 1962, the **Setesdalsbanen Railway** (☎ 38 15 64 82; www.setesdalsbanen.no; adult/child return Nkr80/40; 15min one-way) still runs steam- or diesel-powered locomotives along the last 6km between Grovane (2km north of Vennesla) and Beihøldalen. In July, steam trains leave Grovane at 6pm Tuesday to Friday and diesel trains at noon on Thursday; from mid-June to the end of August, steam trains operate on Sunday at 11.30am and 2pm. NSB trains run up to four times daily from Kristiansand to Vennesla (Nkr28, 12 minutes), while Bus No 30 does the same trip (Nkr33).

KRISTIANSAND KANONMUSEUM

The **Kristiansand Cannon Museum** (☎ 38 08 50 90; Møvik; adult/child Nkr50/20; ☼ 11am-6pm mid-Jun–mid-Aug, 11am-3pm Mon-Wed, 11am-5pm Thu-Sun mid-May–mid-Jun & mid-Aug–Sep, 11am-5pm Sun Oct), 8km south of town, preserves the Germans' heavy Vara Battery, which, along with an emplacement at Hanstholm in Denmark, ensured marginal German control of the strategic Skagerrak Straits. At each end, four 337-tonne, 38cm cannons with a range of 55km (which was covered in two minutes) controlled traffic along either end

TROPICAL NORWAY?

Kristiansand sells itself as Norway's No 1 beach resort, a title it claims due to the decided lack of competition. However, it does have one feature which supports its claim above other coastal towns: five palm trees along the town beach (Bystrand). Not just any palm trees, but what locals claim to be the only palm trees in Norway. Before you start dreaming of long trunks, shady, swaying fronds and coconuts, we should point out that these are rather small and stunted. But they are palm trees nonetheless and that alone makes them special in Norway. In fact, so valuable are they that the city authorities take no chances. At the first hint of summer's end, the trees are whisked off to the town hall where a glass house protects these most cosseted of palm trees in conditions more suited to their species.

of the strait, while the unprotected middle zone was heavily mined. In the autumn of 1941, over 1400 workers and 600 soldiers occupied this site. Visitors to the current museum can see the big guns as well as bunkers, barracks, munitions storage (including some daunting 800kg shells) and a power generator.

THE SKERRIES

In summer, Kristiansand's archipelago of offshore skerries turns into one of the country's greatest sun-and-sea destinations for Norwegian holiday-makers, although it's little explored by foreign visitors.

The most popular island, **Bragdøy**, lies almost within spitting distance of the mainland and boasts a coastal museum, cultural centre and preservation workshop for wooden ships, as well as several nice walks and bathing sites. In the distance, you'll see the beautiful classic lighthouse **Grønningen Fyr**. During school holidays, you can sleep in a dorm bed in the **lighthouse** (☎ 38 08 55 66; saltebua@bragdoya.no; dm Nkr130).

Ferries (Nkr15) to the island run from Vågsbygd, around 8km south of central Kristiansand, three times daily Monday to Friday, with an additional sailing on Saturday, and three on Sunday.

In July, the **M/S Maarten** (☎ 38 10 83 84; www .ms-maarten.no; adult/child Nkr100/50, swimming Nkr80/ 40) offers 2½-hour cruises for sightseeing and/or swimming at noon daily.

M/S Øya (☎ 95 93 58 55; bjorlykkeas@c2i.net) sails from/to Lillesand (Nkr170/85 per adult/ child one way, Nkr300/170 return, three hours) once daily except Sunday from late June to early August.

Activities

Kristiansand is one of Norway's most popular beach-bathing venues, and if the cool waters of the Skagerrak don't put you off, you can join the locals on the sandy **Bystrand** (town beach).

Sleeping

Kristiansand can be booked solid during the July school holiday period so don't arrive in town without a reservation.

Kristiansand Dyrepark (☎ 38 04 98 00; info@ dyreparken.no; fantasy house Nkr2500-3400) One of Norway's more unusual sleeping options are the self-catering fantasy houses, that sleep up to five, in the Dyrepark (see p123). These charming products of a child-like imagination are fantastic for kids, but very often booked out in summer. Prices include two days' admission to the park.

Roligheden Camping (☎ 38 09 67 22; roligheden@ roligheden.no; Framnesveien; tent sites Nkr120 plus per person Nkr25, 4-person cabins from Nkr650; ☺ Jun-Aug) Tent campers are in luck at this well-run camping ground at a popular beach site 3km east of the centre. Take bus No 15 from the centre.

Tangen Vandrerhjem (☎ 38 02 83 10; kristiansand .hostel@vandrerhjem.no; Skansen 8; dm incl breakfast Nkr195, s/d incl breakfast from Nkr395/475; ☺ Jan-Nov; ▯ ℗) The huge Kristiansand HI hostel isn't Kristiansand's most distinguished architectural landmark, but the rather bland warehouse (10-minute walk northeast of the fortress) conceals simple, tidy rooms and friendly staff.

Clarion Hotel Ernst (☎ 38 12 86 00; www.ernst .no; Rådhusgate 2; s/d Nkr1025/1145 mid-Jun–mid-Aug, Nkr995/1245 rest-of-year; ▯) Although part of a chain, this luxurious hotel differs from most for its individually decorated rooms, which are spacious and with more character than other places. The excellent breakfast is served in the pleasant glass-roofed courtyard setting.

Rainbow Hotel Wergeland (☎ 38 17 20 40; werge land@rainbow-hotels.no; Kirkegata 15; s/d from Nkr890/ 1020; 💻) It doesn't get any more central than this attractive, modern hotel right next to the cathedral. The high-standard rooms also have a touch more charm than others in the Rainbow chain.

Also recommended:

Villa Frobusdal B&B (☎ 38 07 05 15; fax 38 07 01 15; Frobusdalen 2; s/d Nkr525/725) Rustic and cosy with a personal touch; 10 minutes' walk from centre.

Sjøgløtt Hotel (☎ /fax 38 02 21 20; sjoglott@sjoglott .no; Østre Strandgate 25; s/d with shared bathroom Nkr350/660, with private bathroom Nkr640/880) Small and intimate.

Norlandia Kristiansand Apartment (☎ 38 07 98 00; service@kristiansand.norlandia.no; Tollbodgata 46; 2-/4-bed apt from Nkr570/785) Small, self-catering student flats.

Hotel Norge (☎ 38 17 40 00; www.hotel-norge.no; Dronningens gate 5; s/d Nkr 890/1090 mid-Jun–mid-Aug, Nkr725/925 Sat & Sun; 💻) Well-appointed rooms, great mattresses and roof-top sun lounge.

Eating

Enok Nielsen (☎ 38 09 71 11; Fiskehallen; snacks Nkr44-125, mains Nkr95-228; 🕑 11am-late) Not quite as classy as Bølgen & Moi but with good food, this place next to the fish market entrance serves good bagels (Nkr58 to Nkr65), as well as shellfish salad (Nkr128) and mussels (Nkr136).

Snadderkiosken (☎ 38 02 90 29; Østre Strandgate 78a; dishes Nkr17-75; 🕑 9am-11.30pm Mon-Fri, 11.30am-11.30pm Sat & Sun, close 10.30pm Oct-Mar) Copy the locals and go to this kiosk, one of the best of its kind in Norway, near the town beach for a great meal deal. It has an extensive and great-value menu: hot dogs and baguettes start at Nkr17, hearty meatballs and mashed potatoes goes for Nkr50 and there's a big range of fish, chicken and meat dishes and snacks.

Dampbageriet (☎ 38 02 70 70; Rådhus gate 5; 🕑 8am-5pm Mon-Wed & Fri, 8am-7pm Thu, 8am-4pm Sat) If you're after sitting in a park by the water for a picnic, stop by and grab an enticing range of bagels, baguettes and pastries at Dampbageriet.

Spar Supermarket (🕑 9am-8pm Mon-Fri, 9am-6pm Sat) Located at the fish harbour, this supermarket does whole barbecued chickens to take away for a bargain Nkr29.90.

Two other excellent places by the waterfront to the east are the deservedly popular

Hartmanns Brygge (☎ 38 12 07 21; Østre Strandgate 2a; lunch specials Nkr59-145, fish soups Nkr95-169, mains Nkr235-255; 🕑 lunch & dinner), for high-quality beef, duck and fish dishes, and **Sjøhuset** (☎ 38 02 62 60; Østre Strandgate 12a; light meals & snacks Nkr75-149, starters Nkr82-98, mains Nkr172-249).

Also recommended:

Østens Perle (☎ 38 07 02 00; Markens gate 35; lunch specials Mon-Sat from Nkr69, mains Nkr79-179, Mongolian lunch buffet adult/child Nkr158/85; 🕑 2-11pm) Good Asian food.

Peppe's Pizza (☎ 38 07 20 70; Gyldenløves gate 7; pizzas for two from Nkr134) Ever-popular and excellent pizza chain.

Kjesk (☎ 38 10 86 10; Kirkegata 15; light meals Nkr45-135; 🕑 lunch & dinner Mon-Sat) Very cool coffee bar with great food.

Entertainment

Kick (☎ 38 02 62 44; Dronningens gate 8; 🕑 2pm-late) This outdoor café is one of the most popular hang-outs for young people which morphs into a disco with a DJ as the night wears on.

Markens Pub (☎ 38 02 06 99; Tollbodgata 3; 🕑 noon-late Mon-Sat, 6pm-late Sun) Markens Pub has disco music in the evening from

---

THE AUTHOR'S CHOICE

Fish market (☎ 38 12 24 50; 🕑 8am-5pm Mon-Sat) The freshest and best-value seafood around is sold here. The most atmospheric place to eat in Kristiansand is at this place at the charming small harbour. The vendors happily cook up fish soup or salmon, shrimps and fishcakes (Nkr40 to Nkr175) for you to enjoy, with a beer or two, on the outdoor patio.

Bølgen & Moi (☎ 38 17 83 00; Sjølystveien 1A; café light meals Nkr55-169; restaurant starters Nkr95-145, mains Nkr220-245; 🕑 café noon-10pm, restaurant 5-10pm Mon-Sat) For something a little more formal without straying from the fish harbour, try the super-cool Bølgen & Moi where you'll struggle to get an outdoor table on a summer's evening. The café's fish and shellfish soup (Nkr136) recently won the prize for the best fish soup in town and it also does great three-/four-/five-course menus (per person Nkr390/460/520). The restaurant also closes on Monday in winter. It also stays open as late as there are customers, although the kitchen may close.

Wednesday to Saturday and is a pleasant enough pub at other times.

Nightcap (☎ 38 12 86 00; Rådhus gate 2; ◷ 6pm-late) At the Clarion Hotel Ernst, this is a popular night spot for the 25- to 35-year-old crowd, but they won't check your ID if you over qualify. Also at the hotel is the classy and more sedate Børsen Bar.

Fønix Cinema (☎ 82 00 07 00; Vestre Strandgate 9) Take in a movie at this large venue.

Getting There & Away

Kristiansand is a transport hub for southern Norway.

BOAT

For information on ferries to Denmark, Sweden and the UK, see p393.

BUS

Nor-Way Bussekspress (☎ 81 54 44 44; www.nor-way .no) departures from Kristiansand:

Destination	Departures	Cost	Duration
Arendal	up to 9 daily	Nkr102	1½hr
Bergen (via Haukeligrend)	8.45am daily	Nkr610	12hr
Evje	1-2 daily	Nkr100	1hr
Flekkefjord	2-4 daily	Nkr200	2hr
Oslo	up to 9 daily	Nkr380	5½hr
Stavanger	2-4 daily	Nkr350	4½hr

CAR & MOTORCYCLE

With a vehicle, access to the E18, north of the centre, is via Vestre Strandgate; when arriving you'll most likely find yourself along Festningsgata. The city, like most of the southern Norwegian coast, is unfortunately surrounded with toll booths – sometimes you'll pay just to do a U-turn.

TRAIN

There are up to four trains daily to Oslo (Nkr531, 4½ hours) and up to five to Stavanger (Nkr379, three hours).

Getting Around

Kristiansand has a good bus system, with both route maps and timetables available from the tourist office and bus station. A short ride around the town centre costs Nkr15/10 per adult/child, while to sites further afield (eg Kristiansand Dyrepark) costs Nkr23/12.

For bicycle rental, **Sykkelsenter** (☎ 38 02 68 35; Grim Torv 3; per day/week Nkr150/500) has a range of bikes on offer.

MANDAL
pop 10,100

The white town of Mandal, Norway's southernmost town, is best known for the 800m-long beach, Sjøsanden. About 1km from the centre and backed by forests, the Copacabana it ain't, but it is Norway's finest stretch of sand, just crying out for a sunny Mediterranean climate. There's also an attractive old town of white clapboard buildings just north of the Mandalselva River. The **tourist office** (☎ 38 27 83 00; www.visitregionmandal .com; Bryggegaten 10, ◷ 9am-7pm Mon-Fri, 10am-4pm Sat & Sun Jun-Aug, 9am-4pm Mon-Fri Sep-May) is situated along the waterfront.

Sights
MANDAL MUSEUM

The moderately interesting town **museum** (☎ 38 27 30 00; Store Elvegata 5/6; adult/child Nkr15/free; ◷ 11am-5pm Mon-Fri, 11am-2pm Sat, noon-5pm Sun late Jun–mid-Aug), which displays a host of historical maritime and fishing artefacts and works by local artists, is elevated above the mundane by impressive exhibits of Mandal's favourite son, Gustav Vigeland (see the boxed text, p80).

VIGELAND HUS

The family home of Norway's finest sculptor has been converted into a small **museum** (☎ 38 27 83 00; adult/child Nkr20/free, ◷ noon-4pm Tue-Sun mid-Jun–mid-Aug) and exhibition space. The house has been decorated in a style approximating the days of the sculptor's early days and his workshop has been transformed into a gallery. Well worth a visit for those seeking an insight into this fine artist.

Festivals

The second week in August, when Mandal hosts the **Shellfish Festival** (www.skalldyrfes tivalen.no), is a great time to be in town. A seafood-lover's delight, fresh seafood is everywhere, as well as a range of musical performances.

Sleeping & Eating

Accommodation in Mandal tends to be rather expensive.

Sjøsanden Feriesenter (☎ 38 26 14 19; www .sjosanden-feriesenter.no; Sjøsandveien 1; tent sites without/with car Nkr120/140, d Nkr350-600, 2–6-person self-catering apts Nkr450-700) Location is everything here. Being just a few metres away from the beach Sjøsanden distinguishes this well-run place from the other camping grounds in the vicinity.

Kjøbmandsgaarden Hotel (☎ 38 26 12 76; www .kjobmandsgaarden.com; Store Elvegaten 57; s/d with shared bathroom Nkr475/700, with private bathroom Nkr725/980) With these prices, the owners clearly think more highly of their rooms than we do. The rooms are basic, but they are clean and located in an atmospheric old building from 1863.

First Hotel Solborg (☎ 38 27 21 00; tomerik.torres fold@firsthotels.no; Neseveien 1; s/d from Nkr675/975, main courses Nkr165-235; ☐ ☒) This flash hotel, only a 10-minute walk west of the beach, boasts an indoor pool, the best restaurant in town and a bar and Saturday disco called Soldekket. Oh yes, and the rooms at this place aren't at all bad either.

Biffen (☎ 38 26 52 08; Store Elvegate 47b; dishes from Nkr89) For a reasonably priced meal, French-inspired Biffen is a good option.

Dr Nielsen's (☎ 38 26 61 00; Store Elvegate 47a; mains from Nkr75) Any cravings for Greek salads and grilled meats will be satisfied here where they also do pasta, chicken and some fish dishes.

Getting There & Away
The Mandal Rutebilstasjon lies north of the river, just a short walk from the historic district. The Nor-Way Bussekspress coastal route between Stavanger (Nkr320, 3½ hours) and Kristiansand (Nkr80, 45 minutes) passes through Mandal two to four times daily.

LINDESNES
As the southernmost point in Norway (latitude 57° 58' 53" N), Lindesnes (literally 'arching land peninsula') provides an occasional glimpse of the power nature can unleash between the Skagerrak and the North Sea. Even better, as the brochures point out, 'the camera angles are better than at Nordkapp' (2818km away).

Rising above the cape is the evocative **Lindesnes Fyr** (☎ 38 25 77 35; www.lindesnesfyr.no; adult/child Nkr40/free; ☼ noon-6pm May, 10am-7pm Jun, 9am-9pm Jul & Aug, 11am-6pm Sep, noon-4pm Sun only Oct-Apr), a classic lighthouse. Inside the tower, there are exhibitions on the history of the lighthouse. The first lighthouse on the site (and the first in Norway) was fired up in 1655 using coal and tallow candles to warn ships off the rocks. The current electrical version, built in 1915, is visible up to 19½ nautical miles out to sea.

Also of interest is the **Lindesnes District Museum & Gustav Vigeland Gallery** (☎ 38 25 80 68; near E39 in Vigeland; adult/child Nkr30/free; ☼ 11am-5pm Mon-Sat, noon-5pm Sun late Jun–mid-Aug), which documents the history of the Lindesnes district and the inspiration behind the works of sculptor Gustav Vigeland.

Sleeping
Lindesnes Camping og Hytteutleie (☎ 38 25 88 74; www.lindesnescamping.no; Lillehavn; tent sites Nkr110, camper vans NKr350, cabins Nkr220-650) You'll find excellent modern facilities at this place, on the shore 3.5km northeast of Lindesnes Fyr. There's a small kiosk and kitchen facilities.

Lindesnes Gjestehus (☎ 38 25 97 00; fax 38 25 97 65; Spangereid; B&B per person Nkr300) About 11km north of the cape lies this simple but cosy guesthouse.

Getting There & Away
Buses from Mandal (Nkr53, one hour) travel to the lighthouse via Spangereid on Monday, Wednesday and Friday.

FLEKKEFJORD
pop 5600
Flekkefjord is a quiet place with a pretty old town (the town's history dates back to 1660 when it competed for power with Kristiansand). Once a significant herring port and later a major tannery, the town is now noted for having virtually no tidal variation (typically less than 10cm between high and low tides). The **tourist office** (☎ 38 32 21 31; fax 38 32 21 30; Elvegaten 15; ☼ 10am-6pm Mon-Fri, 10am-4pm Sat, noon-4pm Sun mid-Jun–mid-Aug, 9am-4pm Mon-Fri rest-of-year) isn't the best-stocked tourist office in the country, but they're eager to help.

Sights
Before setting out to explore the town, collect the pamphlet *A Tour of Flekkefjord* from the tourist office.

The richest source of old architecture is the **Hollenderbyen** (Dutch Town) district,

SOUTHERN NORWAY

with its narrow streets and old timber buildings. You'll find the **Flekkefjord Museum** (☎ 38 32 26 59; Dr Kraftsgata 15; adult/child Nkr20/free; ☺ 11am-5pm Mon-Fri, noon-3pm Sat & Sun Jun-Aug), housed in a home from 1724, but with 19th-century interiors.

One feature which stands out is the unusual octagonal log-built **Flekkefjord church** (Kirkegaten; admission free; ☺ 11am-5pm Mon-Sat Jul–mid-Aug), which was consecrated in 1833. Designed by architect H Linstow (he of the Royal Palace in Oslo), the octagonal theme continues throughout, with the columns, steeple and baptismal font all conforming to the eight-sided form.

Sleeping & Eating

Egenes Camping (☎ 38 32 01 48; fax 38 32 01 11; tent sites without/with car Nkr90/110 plus per person Nkr20, caravan sites Nkr120, 4-/6-person cabins from Nkr275/500, self-catering flats Nkr450-650) This spectacularly located camping ground is beside Lake Seluravatnet, 1km off the E39 and 5km east of Flekkefjord. There's boat and canoe hire and a good-value café (mains around Nkr75). Buses running from Flekkefjord (Nkr25, 10 minutes) towards Kristiansand pass within 1km of the site. Water-sports equipment is also available.

Maritim Fjordhotell (☎ 38 32 33 33; www.fjord hotellene.no; Sundegaten 9; s Nkr749-849, d Nkr899-1199) Flekkefjord's best hotel has a great waterfront position with stylish rooms and a decent restaurant (mains from Nkr110). The attached bar can get a little noisy on weekends.

Pizza Inn (☎ 38 32 22 22; Elvegaten; snacks Nkr59-105, pizza/pasta from Nkr159/115, mains Nkr149-179; ☺ lunch & dinner) This very pleasant harbourside restaurant has breezy outdoor tables to pass a summer's afternoon or cosy booths for a winter's evening. The service is good, as is the food.

Kaffebøsen (Elvegaten; ☺ 10am-4pm Mon-Wed & Fri-Sat, 10am-9pm Thu) For good coffee on the waterfront, try this laid-back and surprisingly cool place.

Getting There & Away

The Nor-Way Bussekspress bus between Kristiansand (Nkr200, two hours) and Stavanger (Nkr200, two hours) passes through Flekkefjord. Buses run to Jøssingfjord once or twice daily except Sunday (Nkr57, 40 minutes).

FLEKKEFJORD TO EGERSUND

If you have your own vehicle, forsake the E39 and take the coastal Rv44 to Egersund – one of southern Norway's most spectacular drives. You'll pass through barren, bouldered hills with a few forested sections, before descending to the pretty village of Åna Sira. Further along Jøssingfjord, around 32km west of Flekkefjord, you'll come across breathtaking, perpendicular rock scenery, including a fine waterfall and two 17th-century houses nestling under an overhanging cliff.

Some 30km southeast of Egersund and 2km south of Hauge, you'll also come across some picturesque timber homes and warehouses at **Sogndalsstrand**.

EGERSUND

pop 9500

Egersund, arranged around an island-dotted cove amid low hills, is probably the prettiest town along this stretch of coastline. It also has a long history (there has been a church here since at least 1292), as told in part on the ancient rune stones found in nearby Møgedal. The **tourist office** (☎ 51 49 27 44; www.reisemal-sydvest .no; Jernbaneveien 2; ☺ 8am-4pm Mon-Fri, 10am-6pm Sat Jun-Aug) isn't the finest the country has to offer, but it's fine for local information.

Sights

DALANE FOLK MUSEUM

The worthwhile museum is divided into two parts. The **Dalane Folkmuseum** (☎ 51 46 14 10; www.museumsnett.no/dalmus; Slettebø; adult/child Nkr20/10; ☺ 11am-5pm Mon-Sat, 1-6pm Sun mid-Jun–mid-Aug, 1-5pm Sun only rest-of-year) features a series of eight historic timber homes at Slettebø, 3.5km north of town along the Rv42. The StavangerExpressen bus (three to six daily except Sunday) runs right past the door. The other section is the **Egersund Fayance Museum** (☎ 51 46 14 10, Eia; adult/child Nkr20/10; ☺ 11am-5pm Mon-Sat, noon-6pm Sun mid-May–mid-Aug; 1-5pm Sun only rest-of-year), a walkable 1.5km northeast of town, which displays the history and wares of Egersund Fayance, the ceramic and porcelain firm which sustained the entire district from 1847 to 1979.

HISTORIC BUILDINGS

Nearly two-thirds of the original town was gutted by fire in 1843, after which Egersund was reconstructed with wide streets to thwart the spread of future fires and many buildings survive from this era. **Strandgaten**, a street of timber houses constructed after 1843, is well worth a stroll. **Skrivergården** (Strandgaten 58) was built in 1846 as the home of the local magistrate Christian Feyer. The town park opposite served as his private garden – half his luck. The **Bilstadhuset** (Nygaten 14) still has its original timberwork and includes a sailmaker's loft upstairs, but it's not open to the public.

EGERSUND KIRKE
This delightful wooden **church** (Torget; admission free; 🕙 11am-4pm Mon-Sat, 10am-3pm Sat, 12.30-3pm Sun mid-Jun–mid-Aug) on the water's edge should not be missed. The structure was built in the 1620s, but the carved altarpiece, a depiction of the baptism and crucifixion of Christ by Stavanger carpenter Thomas Christophersen and painted by artist Peter Reimers, dates back to 1607 and the baptismal font is dated 1583. The cross-shaped design, intimate balconies and wonderfully decorated pew doors are all worth lingering over. An English-language sheet handed out at the door details the church's history.

VARBERG
You'll get a fine view over the town centre from the summit of Varberg, the hill with the prominent TV mast. The path to the top will take you about 15 minutes from the centre of town.

Sleeping
Steinsnes Camping (🕿 51 49 41 36; fax 51 49 40 73; Tengs; tent sites Nkr110 plus per person Nkr25, cabins Nkr275-550) Egersund's most convenient camping ground is 3km north of Egersund; buses heading for Hellvik will get you there.

Grand Hotell (🕿 51 49 18 11; www.grand-egersund .no; Johan Feyersgate 3; s/d from Nkr585/785; 🖵) The Grand Hotell is a lovely old 19th-century building with stylish, renovated rooms although you pay more for those in the picturesque old, but refurbished wing.

Other places to try are the friendly **Blomsterbua Pensjonat** (🕿 40 40 79 95; Rundevollsveien 43; d Nkr250), run by students from school buildings (bed linen not provided) from late-June to mid-August, and **Egersund Hotel** (🕿 51 49 02 00; egersund.hotell@c2i.net; Årsdaddalen; s/d from Nkr500/650), which is 1km southeast of town along the Rv44, and comfortable and modern in a 1970s kind of way.

Eating
Vinstokken (🕿 51 49 06 60; Strandgaten 60; snacks Nkr70-155, mains from Nkr155) Vinstokken is a good-quality French restaurant in the historical district and just back from the water.

For something a little less refined, **Telegrafen** (🕿 51 49 80 00; Areneset; pizzas from Nkr115, slices from Nkr25; 🕙 lunch & dinner) is good for cheap pizzas, while **Havnehagen** (Gjestehavn, Strandgaten; snacks Nkr23-80; 🕙 lunch & dinner) is popular in summer for outdoor tables, baked potatoes and hamburgers (Nkr50).

Getting There & Away
Trains to/from Oslo (Nkr690, eight hours) run via Kristiansand three to six times daily. There are also numerous daily services to/from Stavanger (Nkr135, one hour). **Fjord Line** (🕿 81 53 35 00) runs international ferries between Bergen and Hanstholm in Denmark, via Egersund (but it's not available for transport between Bergen and Egersund). For details, see p393.

AROUND EGERSUND
For details of the route between Egersund and Flekkefjord, see p128.

If you're driving along the Rv42, **Terland Klopp**, 20km northeast of town, is a lovely 60m-long bridge from 1888. Constructed in 21 stone arches, it has been proposed for inclusion on Unesco's list of historical monuments.

Eigerøy Fyr (Midbrødøy; adult/child Nkr20/10; 🕙 11am-4pm Sun only July), the majestic 1855 lighthouse on Midbrødøy, is near the southwestern tip of Eigerøy island. There are great views at any time, but especially on stormy days. Take the Nord Eigerøy bus from the Rutebilstasjon and get off at the sign 'Eigerøy fyr' on the Rv502 (Nkr24, 15 minutes). From there, it's a 30-minute one-way walk down the Fyrvegen road to the lighthouse.

THE INTERIOR

The interior regions of southern Norway are covered by the steeply forested hillsides, high plateaus and lake-studded regions of Telemark (which gave its name to a graceful nordic ski manoeuvre; see the boxed text, p376) and Setesdalen.

KONGSBERG

pop 17,600

Kongsberg, founded in 1624, owes its existence to the discovery of one of the world's purest silver deposits in the nearby Numedal Valley. In the resulting silver rush, it briefly became the second-largest town in Norway, with 8000 inhabitants, including 4000 miners and 2000 farmers. These days, the town is attractive with cascading rapids running through the heart of town and, nearby, is the interesting Kongsgruvene (Royal Silver Mine).

History

The history of Kongsberg begins and ends with silver, which was discovered by two children with an ox in 1623. Their father attempted to sell the windfall, but the king's soldiers got wind of it and the family was arrested and forced to disclose the site of their discovery; it's almost certain that silver was discovered earlier, but by wiser individuals who kept it to themselves. Between 1623 and 1957, a total of 1.35 million kilogram of pure thread-like 'wire' silver

was produced for the royal coffers. Kongsberg is still home to the national mint, but the last mine – no longer able to turn a profit – closed in 1957.

Orientation & Information

Kongsberg is neatly split into old and new sections by the falls of the river Numedalslågen. The new eastern section takes in the main shopping district, the tourist office and the rail and bus terminals. In the older section west of the river lie the museum, church and HI hostel. The **tourist office** (☎ 32 29 90 50; www.visitkongsberg.no; Karschesgt 3; ☼ 9am-7pm Mon-Fri, 10am-4pm Sat & Sun mid-Jun–mid-Aug, shorter hours rest-of-year) is excellent with plenty of local information.

Sights

KONGSBERG KIRKE

Norway's largest baroque **church** (☎ 32 73 50 00; Kirketorget; adult/child Nkr30/10; ☼ 10am-4pm Mon-Fri, 10am-1pm Sat, 2-4pm Sun mid-May–mid-Aug, shorter hours rest-of-year), in the old town west of the river, was officially opened in 1761. The rococo-style interior features ornate chandeliers and

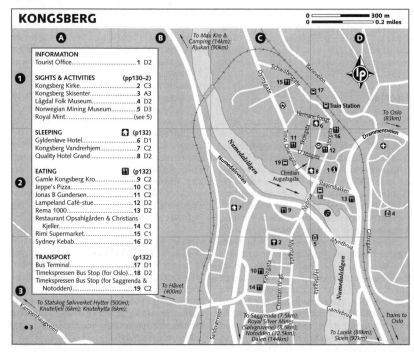

KONGSBERG

| 0 | 300 m |
| 0 | 0.2 miles |

INFORMATION
Tourist Office..............................**1** D2

SIGHTS & ACTIVITIES (pp130–2)
Kongsberg Kirke...........................**2** C3
Kongsberg Skisenter......................**3** A3
Lågdal Folk Museum......................**4** D3
Norwegian Mining Museum...........**5** D3
Royal Mint................................(see 5)

SLEEPING (p132)
Gyldenløve Hotel...........................**6** D1
Kongsberg Vandrerhjem..................**7** C2
Quality Hotel Grand **8** D2

EATING (p132)
Gamle Kongsberg Kro.....................**9** C2
Jeppe's Pizza..............................**10** C3
Jonas B Gundersen.........................**11** C2
Lampeland Café-stue.....................**12** D2
Rema 1000................................**13** D2
Restaurant Opsahlgården & Christians
   Kjeller...................................**14** C3
Rimi Supermarket..........................**15** C1
Sydney Kebab..............................**16** D2

TRANSPORT (p132)
Bus Terminal...............................**17** D1
Timekspressen Bus Stop (for Oslo)...**18** D2
Timekspressen Bus Stop (for Saggrenda &
   Notodden).............................**19** C2

To Max Kro & Camping (14km); Rjukan (90km)

Train Station

To Oslo (83km)

Schwabesgt
Banevelen
Dyrmyrgate
Numedalsveien
Numedalslågen
Hermann Fossgt
Linius Olsensgt
Stølegata
Storgata
Kirkegata
17 Malgata
Christian Augustsgata
Nybrua
Stasjonsbakken
Drammensveien
Myntbrua
Myntgata
Hyttegata
Clitregata
Numedalslågen
Gamlebrua

To Statskog Sølvverket Hytter (500m);
Knutefjell (6km); Knuthehytta (6km);

Kampenhaugveien

To Håvet (400m)

Sandsveien

To Saggrenda (7.5km);
Royal Silver Mines
(Sølvgruvene) (8.5km);
Notodden (32.5km);
Dalen (144km)

Christian IV vg

To Larvik (88km);
Skien (97km)

Trains to Oslo

● 3

an unusual altar that combines the altar-piece, high pulpit and organ pipes on a single wall. From June to August, there are organ recitals at 8pm every Wednesday.

NORWEGIAN MINING MUSEUM
Kongsberg hosts this worthwhile **mining museum** (Norsk Bergverksmuseum; ☎ 32 72 32 00; Hyttegata 3; adult/child Nkr50/10; ☺ 10am-5pm mid-May–Aug, noon-4pm Sep–mid-May) in an 1844 smelter. This museum tells the story of mining in Kongsberg with relics, models and mineral displays, and the old smelting furnaces still survive in the basement. In the same building, other sections include the Royal Mint, which was moved from Akershus Fortress in Oslo to the source of silver in 1686.

LÅGDAL FOLK MUSEUM
This **folk museum** (Lågdalsmuseet; ☎ 32 73 34 68; Tillischbakken 8-10; adult/child Nkr40/10; ☺ 11am-5pm mid-Jun–mid-Aug, 11am-5pm Sat & Sun mid-May–mid-Jun & mid-late Aug, 11am-3pm Mon-Fri mid-Aug–mid-Jun), a 10-minute walk southeast of the train station, houses a collection of 32 period farmhouses and miners' cottages, an indoor sampling of re-created 19th-century workshops and a local WWII resistance museum. In summer there are guided tours at 11am, 1.30pm and 3.30pm.

ROYAL SILVER MINES
Kongsberg's *raison d'être* is the profusion of silver mines in the surrounding district, especially those collectively known as Sølvgruvene. The main shaft of the largest mine plunges all of 1070m into the mountain, to a depth of 550m below sea level.

There are a variety of ways to explore the mines. The most frequent and popular **mine tour** leaves from the signposted Kongsgruvene, which lies about 700m from Saggrenda (8km south of Kongsberg). It begins with a 2.3km **rail ride** along the *stoll*, a tunnel which was painstakingly chipped through the mountain in order to drain water from the mines. Constructed without machinery or dynamite – the rock was removed by heating it with fire, then throwing water on the rock to crack it – the job progressed at the laborious pace of about 7cm per day and took 73 years (1782 to 1855) to complete! Inside, visitors are guided around some of the equipment used in the extraction of

silver, including an ingenious creaking and grinding lift which replaced 300m of the climb between the surface and work area on 65 wet and slippery ladders. The train departs hourly from 10am to 4pm daily July to mid-August (shorter hours mid-May to June and mid-August to September). Tours last for 1¼/1½ hours and cost Nkr100/125 for an adult, Nkr30/50 for a child. Be sure to bring warm clothing, as the underground temperatures can be rather chilly (6°C).

One possibility is the **two-hour guided walk** (Nkr225) through the 5km-long Underberg mine. This trip also ends with a 2.3km train ride. If you prefer staying above ground, you can follow the **miners' route** (Nkr50) to work taken by the miners, who left Kongsberg at 4am to begin their 15-hour work day. The route passes the waterworks which powered the underground machinery and lots of abandoned equipment, finishing up at the Saxony mine.

The most exciting option is the **'rope and torch' tour** (Nkr800), which begins with a 1km walk through Crown Prince Fredrik's tunnel. You must then abseil by torchlight down 112m into the mine (after a 'crash' course in abseiling), where you'll see vast mined areas and lots of historical equipment. These tours run just three times over summer; contact the Kongsberg tourist office for specific dates.

The Oslo–Notodden TIMExpressen bus runs from Kongsberg to Saggrenda (Nkr44, 10 minutes, hourly); you then walk for 15 minutes towards the mines.

Activities
Kongsberg's best hiking and cross-country skiing is found in the green, forested Knutefjell, immediately west of the town, and the Kongsberg tourist office sells the map *Kultur-og Turkart Knutefjell* (Nkr80), which details the hiking and skiing tracks.

From town, the most convenient route heads into the hills from the **Kongsberg Skisenter**, from there a stiff 6km climb to **Knutehytta hut** (☎ 32 73 12 83), at 695m in the heart of the range. In winter, the steepest part of the climb may be negotiated on the Skisenter's 1700m chairlift. An easier and slightly shorter route to Knutehytta leads north from Meheia, on the Notodden road (accessible on the Notodden buses). You can then return to town via the Skisenter.

Another option close to the Skisenter is **Statskog Sølvverket Hytter** (☎ 32 73 50 00; fax 32 73 50 01; cabins Nkr275-500) with 16 simple cabins with open fireplaces. In winter, transport to the Skisenter is by Skitaxi (Nkr30 one-way).

Tours
In summer the tourist office organises guided bus tours along part of the **Solvveien Silver Rd**, which once connected the mines at Kongsberg with the port at Drammen. Contact the tourist office for prices and departures as these vary with demand.

Festivals & Events
Kongsberg's best-known annual event is the popular four-day **Kongsberg Jazz Festival** (☎ 32 73 31 66; www.kongsberg-jazzfestival.no), which takes place in late June or early July.

Sleeping
Max Kro & Camping (☎ 32 76 44 05; fax 32 76 44 72; Jondalen; tent/caravan sites Nkr110/130, 4-/6-bed cabins Nkr350/500) The nearest camping ground to town, this reasonable if inconvenient place is 14km northwest of town on Rv37 towards Rjukan. To get there use the twice-daily Kongsberg–Rjukan Nor-Way Bussekspress bus (Nkr26, 15 minutes).

Kongsberg Vandrerhjem (☎ 32 73 20 24; kongsberg .hostel@vandrerhjem.no; Vinjesgata 1; dm/s/d incl breakfast Nkr200/425/500; P) Kongsberg's youth hostel is probably your best-value accommodation option, bridging the gap between budget and mid-range with comfortable rooms in a quiet, but accessible part of town.

Gyldenløve Hotel (☎ 32 86 58 00; www.gyldenlove .no; Hermann Fossgata 1; s/d mid-Jun–mid-Aug & Sat & Sun year-round Nkr710/875, Mon-Fri rest-of-year Nkr1250/ 1415; 🖳) One of Kongsberg's best hotels, the Gyldenløve has spacious rooms with some pleasing stylistic flourishes and polished floorboards.

Quality Hotel Grand (☎ 32 77 28 00; www.quality -grand.no; Christian Augustsgata 2; s/d mid-Jun–mid-Aug Nkr740/890, rest-of-year Nkr935/1075) Although a touch more expensive than the Gyldenløve Hotel, the Quality Hotel Grand, near the river, is a comfortable establishment with all mod cons. There's a weekend nightclub here in summer (Nkr80 cover charge).

Eating
All of the following places are open for lunch and dinner daily unless stated otherwise.

Gamle Kongsberg Kro (☎ 32 73 16 33; Thornesveien 4; mains Nkr155/259) This popular place, south of the river bridge, offers a varied, but rather expensive menu. The outdoor seating allows fine views of the upper river chutes.

Jonas B Gundersen (☎ 32 72 88 00; cnr Tinius Olsansgata & 17 Maigata; lunch Nkr54-98, pizza Nkr89-119, mains 99-209) At this good restaurant, menus look like vinyl records, there's an unmistakable New Orleans jazz feel and the food includes imaginative salads, Italian and Mexican dishes.

Jeppe's Pizza (☎ 32 73 15 00; Kirkegata 6; pizza from Nkr80, other dishes Nkr89-239) In the Old Town, Jeppe's also offers steaks, Mexican-style dishes, spare ribs and salads. The fish and chips are good and cost Nkr95.

Restaurant Opsahlgården & Christians Kjeller (☎ 32 76 45 00; Kirkegata 10; starters Nkr75-98, mains Nkr195-22; ☿ restaurant 5-10pm Mon-Sat, café 3-10pm Mon-Fri & 2-10pm Sat) A few doors up from Jeppe's, this fine dining restaurant is complemented by a pleasant café where lighter meals are available and outdoor tables in summer.

Other recommended places for a lighter meal or quick snack:

Sydney Kebab (☎ 32 76 88 58; Storgata 1; kebabs Nkr49-89, falafel Nkr49; ☿ until 4am Sat & Sun)
Lampeland Café-stue (☎ 32 73 31 30; Storgata 19) Coffee and snacks.
Rimi Supermarket (Schwabesgate 5) West of the train station; has a bakery.
Rema 1000 (Stasjonsbakken 4) Good grocery selection.

Getting There & Away
Trains connect Kongsberg with Oslo (Nkr142, 1½ hours, every two hours).

NSB (☎ 32 73 31 40) buses between Kongsberg and Larvik (Nkr168, 2¼ hours) run one to three times daily. **Nettbuss Telemark Timekspressen** (☎ 35 02 60 00) buses connect Kongsberg with Oslo (Nkr149, 1½ hours), Saggrenda (Nkr44, 10 minutes), and Notodden (Nkr75, 35 minutes) at least hourly throughout the day. Oslo-bound ones stop at Den Norske Bank (on Storgata); for Saggrenda and Notodden, they stop in front of the cinema (on Tinius Olsansgata).

Getting Around
The tourist office hires out bicycles for a cost of Nkr250 for the first day, then Nkr150 per day.

THE TELEMARK CANAL

The 105km-long Telemark Canal system, a series of lakes and canals which connect Skien and Dalen (with a branch from Lunde to Notodden), lifts and lowers boats a total of 72m in 18 locks. It was built for the timber trade from 1887 to 1892 by up to 400 workers. Most canal travellers bring their own boats (the return trip from Skien to Dalen costs Nkr750 per boat). See the boxed text, below, for details of canal cruises.

Notodden

pop 8300

The centre of industrial Notodden has little to recommend it but the surrounding area is one of Telemark's most visited places, thanks to the impressive Heddal stave church. This lovely and imposing structure, flanked by a tidy churchyard and gentle agricultural land, lies about 5km west of town on the E134.

For visitor information, contact the Notodden **tourist office** (☎ 35 01 50 00; www.notodden.kommune.no; Teatergate 3; 8am-3pm Mon-Fri mid-Jun–mid-Aug, 8am-3.30pm rest-of-year).

SIGHTS

The **Heddal Stave Church** (☎ 35 02 00 93; www.heddal-stavkirke.no; Heddal; adult/child Nkr30/free except for Sun services; ☉ 9am-7pm mid-Jun–mid-Aug, 10am-5pm mid-May–mid-Jun & mid-Aug–mid-Sep, shorter hours rest-of-year) is the largest of Norway's 28 remaining stave churches. It is another of Norway's signature images and one that seems to have sprung like a fairy tale from a child's imagination.

The church possibly dates from 1242, but parts of the chancel date from as early as 1147. In 1952 it was heavily restored.

As with all stave churches, it's constructed around Norwegian pine support pillars – in this case, 12 large ones and six smaller ones, all topped by fearsome visages – and has four carved entrance portals. Of special interest are the lovely 1668 'rose' paintings on the walls, a runic inscription in the outer passageway (which suggests that construction was completed on 25 October 1242) and the 'Bishop's chair', which was made of an old pillar in the 17th century. Its ornate carvings relate the pagan tale of the Viking Sigurd the Dragon-slayer, which has been reworked into a Christian parable involving Jesus Christ and the devil. The altarpiece originally dates from 1667, but was restored in 1908, and the exterior bell tower was added in 1850.

The displays in the adjacent building (where tickets are sold) describe the history of the church and its carvings and reveal the finer points of general stave church construction. For more information, see the boxed text, p219.

On Saturday, when weddings are held, it may be closed to the public. On Sunday

---

A SLOW BOAT THROUGH TELEMARK

Every day from June to mid-August, the ferry M/S *Telemarken* sets out to travel along the canals of Telemark between Akkerhaugen, 24km south of Notodden, and Lunde (Nkr225, 3¾ hours). It leaves Akkerhaugen/Lunde around 10am/1.50pm. If you only want to sail one way from Lunde to Akkerhaugen, buses leave from Notodden for Lunde (Nkr95, one hour) late morning and from Akkerhaugen to Notodden at around 5pm (6pm on weekends).

Six times weekly between mid-May and early September (daily from mid-June to mid-August), the sightseeing boats M/S *Victoria* (built in 1882) and M/S *Henrik Ibsen* (built in 1907) make the leisurely 11-hour journey between Skien and Dalen (Nkr330). Round trips, including one-way by boat from Skien to Dalen and return to Skien by bus (three hours), cost a total of Nkr560. In the opposite direction, you can take the **Telemark Bilruter** (☎ 35 06 54 00) bus from Skien back to Dalen (Nkr230, 3¼ hours, daily except Saturday mid-June to mid-August). Return tickets for all boats are 50% cheaper.

For further information, contact **Telemarkreiser** (☎ 35 90 00 30; info@telemarkreiser.no; www.visittelemark.com). They have the free *Ruteplan* which details 10 possible bus/ferry itineraries through Telemark.

A great way to see the canal is by canoe, kayak or bicycle, and the ferries will transport your own boat/bicycle for Nkr160/110 between Skien and Dalen. Canoe hire at **Gåsodden Camping** (☎ 35 54 50 77; Fjærekilen, Skien) costs Nkr225/60 per day/hour.

from Easter to November, services are held at 11am (visitors are welcome, but to avoid disruption, they must remain for the entire one-hour service); after 1pm the church is again open to the public.

From Notodden, Bus No 301 goes right by or take any bus heading for Seljord and Bondal.

The **Heddal Rural Museum** (Bygdetun; ☎ 35 02 08 40; Heddal; adult/child Nkr20/free; 🕑 11am-5pm mid-Jun–mid-Aug), 300m from the stave church, includes a collection of houses from rural Telemark.

FESTIVALS & EVENTS

Notodden is also famous for its hugely popular **Blues Festival** (☎ 35 02 76 50; nbf@bluesfest.no; www.bluesfest.no) in early August; tickets must be bought through **Billetservice** (☎ 81 53 31 33; www.billettservice.no).

SLEEPING

Notodden Camping (☎ 35 01 33 10; Reshjem-veien; tent sites without/with car Nkr80/120, caravan sites Nkr130, plus per person Nkr10, cabins Nkr350-450) Notodden Camping is an acceptable site 3km west along the E134, then 200m south on Reshjemveien. You'll be lucky to find a square inch of space at festival time. Take a bus from the centre in the direction of Seljord.

Nordlandia Telemark Hotel (☎ 35 01 20 88; fax 35 01 40 60; Torvet 8; s/d mid-Jun–mid-Aug Nkr790/890, Sat & Sun Nkr860/960) Part of the ScanPlus network,

THE HEROES OF TELEMARK

In 1933 in the USA it was discovered that 0.02% of all water molecules are 'heavy', meaning that the hydrogen atoms are actually deuterium, an isotope that contains an extra neutron. Heavy water weighs 10% more than normal water, boils at 1.4°C higher and freezes at 4°C higher than ordinary water – sufficient to stabilise nuclear fission reactions, making it invaluable in the production of the atom bomb.

During WWII in Norway the occupying Germans were aware that heavy water could be created by the process of electrolysis and, in the hope of eventually building an atom bomb, they set up a heavy-water production plant at Vemork, near Rjukan. Had they been allowed to continue, the war might have ended quite differently. Fortunately, between March and October 1942, Allied insurgents were able to gather intelligence and mount Operation Grouse, which turned out to be one of the most daring sabotage missions of the entire war.

The mission was launched in October 1942 when four Norwegians parachuted into Sognadal, west of Rjukan. They were to be joined a month later by 34 specially trained British saboteurs who would arrive in two gliders. The British insurgents had prepared for their landing at Skoland near Lake Møsvatnet, but one tow plane and its glider crashed into a mountain, and the other glider crashed on landing. All the British survivors were shot by the Germans.

Undeterred, the Norwegian group changed its mission name to Swallow and retreated to Hardangervidda, where they subsisted through the worst of the winter. On 16 February 1943 a new British-trained group called Gunnerside landed on Hardangervidda. Unfortunately a bliz-zard was raging and they wound up a long 30km march from their intended drop site. By the evening of 27 February the saboteurs were holed up at Fjøsbudalen, north of Vemork, waiting to strike. After descending the steep mountainside along the now-famous Sabotørruta (Saboteurs' Route), they crossed the gorge to the heavy-water plant, wire-clipped the perimeter fence and planted the explosives, which largely destroyed the facility. Some of the saboteurs retreated on skis to Hardangervidda then fled, in uniform and fully armed, into neutral Sweden, while the rest remained on the plateau, successfully avoiding capture.

The plant was rebuilt by the Germans, but on 16 November 1943, 140 US planes bombed Vemork, killing 20 Norwegians in the process. The Germans abandoned any hopes of producing heavy water in Norway and decided to shift their remaining stocks to Germany. The remaining saboteurs realised that this relocation procedure involved a ferry across the lake Tinnsjø and, on 19 February 1944, the night before the ferry was due to sail, they placed a timed charge on the boat. The following night, the entire project was literally blown out of the water.

In 1965 this intriguing story was made into the dramatic (but historically inaccurate) film *The Heroes of Telemark*, starring Kirk Douglas.

here you'll get a modern hotel room and a reasonable breakfast in this fairly bland building in the town centre.

GETTING THERE & AWAY
Between Kongsberg and Notodden, Timekspressen buses run once or twice an hour (Nkr75, 35 minutes).

Skien
pop 31,000
Industrial Skien is visited mainly by travellers along the Telemark Canal. There's not a lot to see, but Ibsen fans may want to pause here on their way elsewhere. The **tourist office** (☎ 35 90 55 20; info@grenland.no; Nedre Hjellegate 18; ⏰ 8.30am-7pm Mon-Fri, 10am-4pm Sat, 11am-4pm Sun mid-Jun–mid-Aug, 8.30am-4pm Mon-Fri rest-of-year) is helpful.

SIGHTS
Author and playwright Henrik Ibsen (see also the boxed text, p44) was born in Skien on 20 March 1828. In 1835 the family fell on hard times and moved out to the farm Venstøp, 5km north of Skien, where they stayed for seven years. The 1815 farmhouse has now been converted into a worthwhile **museum** (☎ 35 52 57 49; Venstøphøyda; adult/child Nkr40/20; ⏰ 10am-6pm mid-May–Aug). Buses from Skien run only twice daily.

SLEEPING & EATING
Skien Vandrerhjem (☎ 35 50 48 70; skien.hostel@vandrerhjem.no; Moflatveien 65; dm/s/d Nkr150/320/480) This well-equipped hostel is open year-round and has tidy rooms. Breakfast costs Nkr50 extra.
   Rainbow Høyers Hotell (☎ 35 90 58 00; hoeyers@rainbow-hotels.no; Kongensgate 6; s/d from Nkr690/890) This family-run place is an excellent choice with spacious, light and airy rooms right next to the harbour.
   Comfort Hotel Bryggeparken (☎ 35 91 21 00; bryggeparken@comfort.choicehotels.no; Langbryggene 7; s/d from Nkr640/840) Also right on the water, this modern place may lack the personal touch, but the rooms are modern and very comfortable. They also have a decent restaurant and waterfront café.
   Shanghai Restaurant (☎ 35 52 21 00; Kongensgate 20C; starters Nkr25-45, mains Nkr75-125, Sun buffet 3-8pm Nkr100; ⏰ lunch & dinner) For decent Chinese food at very reasonable prices, this place is hard to beat. They also do take away.

GETTING THERE & AWAY
Nor-Way Bussekspress buses run to Notodden (Nkr128, 1¾ hours) and Rjukan (Nkr232, 3¼ hours) once or twice daily. NSB trains run every hour or two from Skien to Larvik and Oslo (Nkr274, 1¾ hours).

Dalen
pop 790
The pretty town of Dalen is a jumping-off point for ferries along the Øst Telemark Canal system. Just outside town is the quiet 14th-century **Eidsborg Stave Church** (adult/child Nkr40/10; ⏰ 9am-4pm Mon-Fri Jun-Aug) with a single nave and dedicated to St Nicolas.
   Tourist information is dispensed by the **tourist office** (☎ 35 07 70 65; www.visitdalen.com).

SLEEPING & EATING
Buøy Camping (☎ 35 07 75 87; fax 35 07 77 01; tent sites Nkr130, s/d Nkr230/380, cabins Nkr475-700) This is a reasonable camping ground with hostel-style rooms and cabins.
   Dalen Hotel (☎ 35 53 70 00; www.dalenhotel.no; s/d from Nkr900/1150) The ornate Dalen Hotel, with its faint resonance of a stave church, first opened in 1894 and lies 1km from Dalen Brygge. It's a comfortable place to soak up an old-world atmosphere, although more so in the public areas than the rooms.

RJUKAN
pop 3600
The 6km-long town of Rujkan nestles into the deep, steep-sided Vestfjorddalen, hiding in the shadow of Telemark's highest and most-recognisable peak, Gausta (1881m). The location is stunning, tempered somewhat by the industrial plants at either end. The Rjukan hinterland also plays host to numerous outdoor activities that are definitely worth the effort.

History
Thanks to its founders, this hydroelectric company town was aesthetically planned and designed and, in the first 10 years after its founding in 1907, the industry supported 10,000 residents. In the early days, the administrators' homes occupied the highest slopes, where the sun shone the longest; below them were the homes of office workers and in the valley's dark depths dwelt the labourers. The builders of the Mår Kraftverk hydroelectric plant on the eastern limits

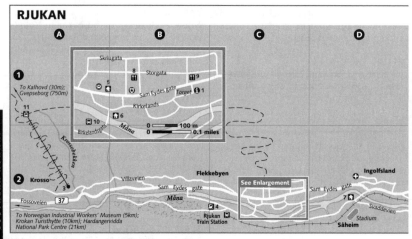

RJUKAN

of town clearly had an eye for records: its daunting wooden stairway consists of 3975 steps (it's the world's longest and is open to very fit visitors). The **tourist office** (☎ 35 09 12 90; www.visitrjukan.com; Torget 2; ☻ 9am-7pm Mon-Fri, 10am-6pm Sat & Sun late Jun–late Aug, 9am-3.30pm Mon-Fri rest-of-year) is the best of its kind in Telemark. It has knowledgeable staff, loads of brochures and an interactive computer screen outside the door.

Sights

NORWEGIAN INDUSTRIAL WORKERS' MUSEUM

This **museum** (Norsk Industriarbeidermuseet; ☎ 35 09 90 00; www.visitvemork.com; adult/child Nkr60/35; ☻ 10am-6pm mid-Jun–mid-Aug, 10am-4pm May–mid-Jun & mid-Aug–Sep, shorter hours rest-of-year) located 7km west of Rjukan, is in the Vemork power station, which was the world's largest when it was completed in 1911. These days it honours the Socialist Workers' Party, which reached its height of Norwegian activities in the 1950s. You won't want to miss the 30-minute film *If Hitler Had the Bomb* describing the epic events of war-time Telemark (see the boxed text, p134), nor the miniature power station in the main hall. There's also an interesting exhibition about the worldwide race in the 1930 and '40s to make an atom bomb. It consists of short films, touch screen exhibits, photos and dioramas.

Disabled travellers and seniors over 65 are permitted to drive up to the entrance; everyone else must park at the swinging bridge. In summer, a bus (adult/child Nkr20/10; 10am to 4pm mid-June to mid-August) runs up from the car park to the entrance. Otherwise, it's a 15-minute climb on foot.

HARDANGERVIDDA NATIONAL PARK CENTRE

About 21km west of Rjukan, this new **visitor centre** (☎ 35 09 57 00; www.hardangervidda-senter.no; Møsvatn; adult/child Nkr60/35; ☻ 10am-6pm Jul–mid-Sep, 10am-6pm Sat & Sun rest-of-year) features exhibitions on Norwegian reindeer, interactive computer displays, an interesting 3-D map, and a video. The children's room is particularly well presented.

KROSSOBANEN

The **Krossobanen Cable Car** (☎ 35 09 04 44; adult one-way/return Nkr35/70, child Nkr15/30, bike Nkr30; ☻ 10am-8pm mid-Jun–Sep, 10am-6pm Sat-Thu Jan–mid-Jun & Oct-Dec) was constructed in 1928 by Norsk Hydro to provide its employees with access to the sun. Long since renovated, it whisks tourists up to Gvepseborg (886m) for a view over the deep, dark recesses. It also operates as the trailhead for a host of hiking and cycling trails; ask at the tourist office for details.

Sleeping

Rjukan's town centre is pretty thin on standout accommodation options, but there are better choices up in the Gaustablikk area – ideal if you're here to hike.

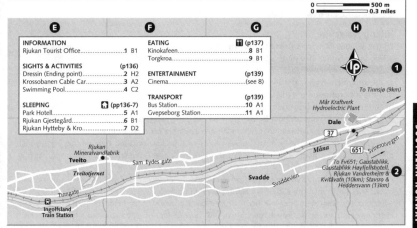

SOUTHERN NORWAY

RJUKAN & WEST

Rjukan Gjestegård (☎ 35 09 05 27; fax 35 09 09 96; Birkelandsgata 2; dm Nkr175, s/d with shared bathroom Nkr290/465) This centrally located guesthouse occupies the buildings of the old youth hostel. The location is good and it's not a bad choice if you want to be in town. Breakfast costs Nkr60.

Rjukan Hytteby & Kro (☎ 35 09 01 22; post@rjukan -hytteby.no; Brogata 9; 2-/4-/6-bed cabins Nkr650/850/ 950) Probably the best choice in town, Rjukan Hytteby & Kro sits in a pretty spot by the riverbank and has simple, tidy huts which seek to emulate the early-20th-century hydro-electric workers' cabins.

Park Hotell (☎ 35 08 21 88; www.parkhotell-rjukan .no; Sam Eydes gate 67; s/d from Nkr590/850) The most expensive hotel in the area in a place whose time has past. The tired, musty rooms are way overpriced; don't expect satellite TV or fluffy towels.

Krokan Turisthytte (☎ 35 09 51 31; fax 35 09 01 90; near Rv37; 4-bed cabins Nkr375-500) About 10km west of Rjukan, this historic place was built in 1869 as DNT's first hut. You're housed in museum-like 16th-century log cabins, and traditional meals include meat soup (Nkr50).

GAUSTABLIKK

A couple of places at the lake Kvitåvatn, off the Fv651 and 10km from town, provide a front-row view of Gausta and easy access to the Skipsfjell/Gaustablikk ski area; you'll need a car for access. For the busy winter season, contact **Gausta Booking** (☎ 45 48 51 51; www.gaustabooking.com) which can help you track down a spare hut.

Gaustablikk Høyfjellshotell (☎ 35 09 14 22; www .gaustablikk.no; s/d from Nkr760/960) With a prime location overlooking the lake and mountain, this pleasant mountain lodge has good facilities and meals. It also has apartments, half-board rates, a range of prices depending on the season and a programme of guided hiking tours.

Rjukan Vandrerhjem (☎ 35 09 20 40; fax 35 09 20 95; Gaustablikk; dm Nkr175, s/d/tr with shared bathroom Nkr300/430/480, d/tr with private bathroom Nkr505/555) The simple accommodation in this youth hostel is in a cosy pine lodge with six bunks per room in huts.

Eating

Central Rjukan doesn't have a huge choice for places to eat.

Kinokafeen (☎ 40 85 60 48; Storstulgate 1; mains Nkr150-279; ☽ lunch & dinner) Kinokafeen, at the cinema, has a pleasant ambience and offers a range of main courses, but also smaller dishes (Nkr50 to Nkr95) and ciabatta sandwiches (Nkr35).

Torgkroa (☎ 35 09 09 30; Sam Eydes gate 93; snacks from Nkr45, mains Nkr89-179) This straightforward and popular place on the square serves burgers, Chinese dishes and pizzas.

Rjukan Hytteby & Kro (☎ 35 09 01 22; Brogata 9; pizzas from Nkr130, lunch from Nkr59) This pizza and fast-food hang-out does everything from snacks to tacos, lasagna and kebabs.

SOUTHERN NORWAY

GETTING ACTIVE IN RJUKAN

Hiking & Cycling

To get an idea of what's possible, visit the tourist office to pick up the free *Rujkan – Cycling & Hiking Guide*, which has route suggestions.

The popular hiking track up Gausta (1881m) leads to DNT's **Gaustahytta** (☎ 35 09 41 50) at the summit, which it shares with an enormous NATO radio tower that severely disrupts the mountain's profile; before this gigantic structure was built it used to be known as Norway's most beautiful and impressive mountain. A road link, but unfortunately no public transport runs from the eastern end of Rjukan (just before the hydroelectric plant) to Stavsro at lake Heddersvann, at a height of 1173m. **Taxis** (☎ 35 09 14 00) are available for a cost of around Nkr240.

Allow all day for the hike, which leaves plenty of time for exploring the summit. The tourist office distributes a map of the Fv651, but the *Turkart Gausta Området* is a better option and is available for (Nkr50).

From Gvepseborg, the top station on the Krossobanen cable car, good walking or cycling tracks strike out onto the expansive Hardangervidda plateau, home to Europe's largest herd of wild reindeer. The main route, which can also be used by cyclists, leads 13km north to DNT's Helberghytta and the **Kalhoud Turisthytta** (☎ 35 09 05 10). An eight-hour walk takes you from Gvepseborg to Kalhovd, where you can catch a bus out or head on to connect with the ferry (Nkr110) to Mårbuhytta. From there it's a two-day hike west to **Mogen Turisthytta** (☎ 35 07 41 15), where you can catch the Møsvatn ferry (Nkr175) back to Skinnarbu, west of Rjukan on Rv37. For those seeking greater guidance, the tourist office organises guided expeditions for hikers and cyclists (adults Nkr655 to Nkr1245, children Nkr360 to Nkr665).

Alternatively you can follow the marked route which begins above Rjukan Fjellstue, just north of the Rv37. This historic track follows the Sabotørruta (Saboteurs' Route), the path taken by the members of the Norwegian Resistance during WWII (see the boxed text, p134). From late June until mid-August, guided hikes (adult/12-16/under-12 Nkr120/50/free) along the route can be arranged by calling ☎ 95 72 34 96 or alternatively through the tourist office.

The best map to use for any of these hikes is Statens Kartverk's *Hardangervidda Øst*, at a scale of 1:100,000 and available from the tourist office (Nkr125).

Swimming

There's a swimming pool across the Måna river.

Rail-biking

Ask the tourist office or call ☎ 45 48 38 99 for details about local trips by *dressin* (rail-bikes, or bicycles on bogies). The 10km-long trips (Nkr250) start at lake Tinnsjø and follow the disused rail line up the valley to Rjukan. There are shorter versions available for Nkr50 per hour.

Skiing

The **tourist office** (☎ 35 09 14 22; www.gaustablikk.no) has a wealth of information for winter-sports enthusiasts, with their brochure *Gaustablikk Skisenter* providing the definitive guide to all things white and powdery.

Lift tickets cost from Nkr255/1135 per day/week for adults, Nkr200/900 for children. Equipment rental for downhill/cross-country skiing starts from Nkr280/150 for the first day, while a snowboard can be had for Nkr300.

Bungee-jumping

If all of that doesn't provide sufficient excitement, you might prefer an even more rapid descent than skis can offer. In summer on Tuesdays and Thursdays at 5pm and Saturdays at 11am, the bungee ropes are unfurled for quite an adrenalin rush. It costs Nkr490 per jump. Contact ☎ 99 51 31 40 or the tourist office for details.

Entertainment

Park Hotell (☎ 35 08 21 88; Sam Eydes gate 67; ☿ 7pm-midnight Mon-Thu, 7pm-3am Fri & Sat) The bar (for reasons best known to the owners, it's called the Ammonia Bar) serves a nightly clientele which is mostly the local elbow-on-the-bar crowd, while the disco attracts the 18-to-25-crowd.

Rjukan Cinema (Rjukan Kino; Storstulgate 1) Changes films weekly.

Getting There & Away

A daily express bus connects Rjukan to Oslo (Nkr270, three hours) via Kongsberg (Nkr170, two hours).

Getting Around

Rjukan's linear distances will seem intimidating, but the local Bybuss runs from Vemork to the eastern end of the valley. Bike hire at the tourist office costs Nkr150/30 per day/hour.

SELJORD

pop 1200

Scenic little Seljord is a place of legend, known mainly as the home of Selma the Serpent, the Nessie-type monster that inhabits the depths of the lake Seljordvatn (see the boxed text, p140).

Hikers can also seek out the area's other enigmatic residents – the feuding troll women, Ljose-Signe, Glima and Tårån, who inhabit the surrounding peaks; we didn't see them but locals assured us that they're there. Seljord was also the inspiration for some of Norway's best-known folk legends, including Asbjørnsen and Moe's *The Three Billy Goats Gruff*, known the world over. The **tourist office** (☎ 35 06 59 88; www.seljordportalen.no; ☿ 8am-7pm Mon-Fri, 9am-6pm Sat & Sun mid-Jun–mid-Aug, 8am-7pm Mon–Fri only rest-of year) has lots of local information and revels in good troll stories. The tourist office keeps lists of rooms, cabins and houses for rent.

Sights

Other sights in Seljord with their own legends include the charming 12th-century Romanesque stone **church** (admission free; ☿ 11am-5pm mid-Jun–mid-Aug), built in honour of St Olav and located at the northern end of town. In the grounds, between the church and the churchyard wall, are two impressions reputedly made by two

mountain trolls who were so upset by the encroachment of Christianity that they pummelled the site with boulders.

Festivals & Events

On the second weekend of September, Seljord holds the **Dyrsku'n Festival**, which started in 1866 and is now Norway's largest traditional market and cattle show, attracting 60,000 visitors annually. If you want to experience the full measure of rural Telemark, don't miss it.

Sleeping & Eating

Seljord Camping og Badeplass (☎ /fax 35 05 04 71; tent sites Nkr110, cabins Nkr350-700; ☿ late Jun-late Aug) This pleasant camping ground beside the lake is the dock for monster boats on Seljordvatn (fares vary with the number of passengers).

Seljord Hotel (☎ 35 05 10 00; fax 35 05 10 01; s/d Nkr795/895) This comfortable hotel, on the main street in town, has well-appointed rooms that make a good base for exploring Telemark.

Sjøormkroa (☎ 35 05 05 02; mains Nkr89-149) You'll get a decent meal in this odd serpent-shaped building, on the E134 next to the lake.

Getting There & Away

Nor-Way Bussekspress (Haukeliekspressen) buses connect Seljord with Notodden (Nkr125, 1¼ hours) and Oslo (Nkr283, 3¼ hours) up to four times daily.

SETESDALEN

The forested hillsides and lake-filled mountain valleys of Setesdalen are home to some of southern Norway's most beautiful landscapes. Popular with outdoor enthusiasts (rafters, canoers, skiers, hikers and climbers), Setesdalen, one of Norway's most traditional and conservative regions, remains somewhat secluded and off the well-trodden tourist pathways.

For information on mountain hiking and huts in the Setesdalen area, contact the **Kristiansand og Oppland Turistforening** (☎ 38 02 52 63; Kirkegata 15) in Kristiansand.

Evje

pop 1370

Set alongside a lake and surrounded by forests, Evje is Setesdalen's southern gateway.

SELMA THE SERPENT

The first testimony to the existence of Selma the Serpent dates back to the summer of 1750, when Gunleik Andersson-Verpe of nearby Bø was 'attacked by a sea horse' while rowing across the lake. In 1880, Bjørn Bjørge and his mother Gunnhild reported killing a bizarre lizard while doing laundry in the lake. Nearly every summer since (Selma seems to prefer the warm weather), witnesses have sighted the fins and humps of this fast-moving lake creature. According to most observers, the creature measures the size of a large log, or slightly bigger. Some have described it as eel-like, while others have likened it to a snail, a lizard or a crocodile and have reported lengths of 25m, 30m and even 50m. Amateur videos filmed in 1988 and 1993 reveal a series of humps in the water, but their grainy nature renders the evidence inconclusive. Researchers generally remain open-minded, but have suggested that the lake is too small to support creatures more than about 7m long.

As with Scotland's famous Nessie, Selma has fuelled local folklore and drawn tourists to search the surface of the deep pine-rimmed lake Seljordvatn (14km long, 2km wide and 157m deep) for evidence. In 1977, Swedish freelance journalist Jan-Ove Sundberg scanned the lake with sonar equipment and detected several large objects moving in unison, then separating in several directions. In the summer of 1998, he returned with an 11-member team and spent 17 days trawling the lake with imaging equipment and even a mini-submarine outfitted with three underwater cameras, sonar and a gripping arm. According to Sundberg, 'The serpent does not fit any species known to humanity. It has several qualities not seen before, such as travelling on the surface at high speed and moving vertically up and down. It shows a back or a head or a neck or all three for long periods above the surface and travels very fast, maybe up to 25 knots.'

The Seljord Council and the lakeside camp site sponsored Sundberg's search for the beast, hoping that the publicity would result in a boost in tourism, and well it might. The village has already set up **Lake Serpent Centre** (Sjøormsenteret; ☎ 35 05 03 55; adult/child Nkr40/free; ☺ noon-6pm mid-Jun–mid-Aug), by the road through the centre of town, which offers the lowdown on Seljord's best-known resident. The village coat of arms has also been changed to depict a yellow Selma on a red background.

Its main attractions, apart from a pleasantly somnambulant air, are a range of outdoor activities and numerous opportunities for geologists to get all excited about the nearby mines and mineral deposits. The **information centre** (☎ 37 93 14 00; www.setesdal.com; ☺ 10am-4pm Mon-Fri, 10am-2pm Sat & Sun mid-Jun–mid-Aug, 10am-4pm Mon-Fri rest-of-year) Occupies the same lovely old log building as the bus terminal. Ask also about permits for mineral prospecting. They also offer free Internet access.

SIGHTS

Rock fans will enjoy the small **Evje Og Hornnes Museum** (☎ 37 93 07 94; adult/child/family Nkr25/15/60; ☺ 11am-4pm mid-Jun–mid-Aug), 2km west of town and across the river in Fennefoss. Displays include more than 100 different types of minerals found in the surrounding hills, as well as exhibits on local nickel mining and traditional rural life in Setesdalen.

For displays of local and worldwide minerals, the **Setesdal Mineral Park** (☎ 37 93 13 10; Hornnes; adult/child Nkr70/40; ☺ 10am-5pm mid-Jun–mid-Aug, shorter hours May–mid-Jun & mid-Aug–Oct) is about 10km south of Evje.

The **Flåt Nickel Mine** (☎ 37 93 03 71; adult/child Nkr50/30), once Europe's largest with a shaft 422m deep, was due to be opened for guided tours (not for the claustrophobic) not long after we visited; check at the Information Centre to find out the latest.

SLEEPING

Odden Camping (☎ 37 93 06 03; www.oddencamping .setesdal.com; tent sites without/with car Nkr70/120 plus per person Nkr10, caravan sites per 2 people Nkr140, 2–8-bed huts Nkr250-1000) This highly recommended camping ground is extremely well run and can be found in a postcard setting by the water just 200m south of town.

Neset Camping (☎ 37 93 40 50; www.nesetcamping .setesdal.com; tent sites from Nkr155 plus per person Nkr10, 4-/8-bed cabins Nkr450-600) Also in a picturesque, lush lakeside spot, Neset Camping is situated around 15km north of town along the Rv9 road.

Evje Vandrerhjem (☎ 37 93 11 77; tim@troll-moun tain.no; tent sites/teepees per person Nkr50/80, caravan sites Nkr100, dm/d Nkr150/300, 5-bed cabins Nkr550; P 🖳) This energetic youth hostel, 7km north of town is a good, modern hostel run by the Setesdal Rafting & Activity Centre. In addition to the host of activities on offer (see the boxed text below), there is also a climbing wall (Nkr100).

Revsnes Hotell (☎ 37 93 43 00; www.revsneshotell .no; Byglandsfjord; s/d from Nkr 650/900, 3-course din ner Nkr275; P 🖳) Evje's best hotel is 12km north of town, set by the lovely lake By glandsfjorden and with very comfortable rooms, most of which have a lake view.

EATING

Eating in Evje is more take-what-you-can-get than fine dining.

Stigeren Restaurant (☎ 37 93 08 28; mains Nkr119-238; 🕑 lunch & dinner) In the centre of town this place does a three-course à la carte menu with soup, meat and fish dishes, and des serts; they also do pizza from Nkr119.

Pernille Cafeteria (☎ 37 93 00 69; mains Nkr89-129; 🕑 breakfast, lunch & dinner) Located on the same street as Stigeren, this place serves a good variety of tasty traditional Norwegian offerings, fish dishes and burgers.

Dragon Inn (☎ 37 93 09 19; dishes Nkr85-149; 🕑 lunch & dinner) Near Rv9, just south of the centre the Dragon Inn serves passable Chi nese specialties.

GETTING THERE & AWAY

The daily Nor-Way Bussekspress bus be tween Kristiansand (Nkr100, one hour)

ENERGETIC IN EVJE

The **Setesdal Rafting & Activity Centre** (☎ 37 93 11 77; www.troll-mountain.no), about 7km north of Evje, and **Viking Adventures Norway** (☎ 37 93 13 03), in town, both or ganise a range of outdoor adventure activi ties, from white-water rafting (from Nkr380 per day), canoeing (around Nkr250), kayak ing, paintball, canyoning and river-board ing to rock climbing and abseiling.

The Setesdal Rafting & Activity Centre also offers hiking and nightly elk safaris (adult/child Nkr250/200), as well as mountain biking (Nkr25/250 per hour/day) and horse riding so that you can head off on your own.

---

and Haukeligrend (Nkr250, three hours) runs via Evje. It provides access to Byg landsfjord, Valle, Bykle and Hovden, and connects with services to Haugesund and Bergen at Haukeligrend.

Setesdalsmuseet

This fine collection of folk **museums** (☎ 37 93 63 03; adult/child/family Nkr20/10/40; 🕑 11am-5pm mid-end Jun & early–mid-Aug, 10am–6pm Jul) along Rv9 is a good way to break up your journey through Setesdalen.

Coming from the south, the main **Setes-dalsmuseet** (setesdalsmuseet@c2i.net; Rysstad) is a fine, refurbished exhibition space display ing period interiors and cultural artefacts. Around 10km further north is **Tveitetunet** (Valle), a wonderful log farm with a store house dating from 1645. Best of all is **Rygnes-tadtunet**, 9km north of Valle, where the farm has a unique three-storey storehouse (from 1590) and an extraordinary collection of 15th-century painted textiles. Local legend has its owner as a man known as Evil Ås mund, who served as a mercenary around Europe and who brought back looted weap ons and artwork from his travels. Staff may be dressed in traditional costume.

Bykle

A nice short stop for drivers through Setes dalen is the distinctive log-built **Bykle Kirkje** (☎ 37 93 81 01; admission Nkr20; 🕑 11am-7pm mid-Jun–mid-Aug). The church is one of the small est churches in Norway and all the more delightful because of it, with painted stalls, altar, and organ. The building and altar date from 1619; roses on the front of the galleries and traditional rose paintings on the wall were added in the 1820s, after an 1804 restoration.

There's also a lovely signpost-guided **walk** above the Otra River, 5km south of town. The route, which takes about 30 minutes, dates from at least 1770 and was once the main route through Setesdalen.

Hovden
pop 278

If you come to Hovden, set in a wild, open landscape at the very top of Setesdalen, in the summer, you may wonder what all the fuss is about: this is winter skiing territory. The **Hovdenferie** (☎ 37 93 96 30; www.hovden.com; 🕑 9am-5pm Mon-Fri, 10am-2pm Sat, noon-4pm Sun)

Tourist information about the region is dispensed here.

SIGHTS & ACTIVITIES

Hovdenferie organises **rafting** (Nkr350), **canyon walks** (Nkr450) and nightly **elk safaris** (adult/child Nkr290/190). Also available is advice on hikes in the region and route descriptions of five itineraries for those with their own vehicle.

In summer, for fine views you can reach the summit of Mt Nos (1176m) by taking the **chairlift** (adult/child Nkr80/55; 11.30am-2pm Jul, 11.30am-2pm Wed & Sat Aug). During the ski season, lift tickets cost Nkr275/495 for one/ two days or Nkr460 for a weekend pass.

For general information about skiing, contact **Hovden Skisenter** (37 93 94 00). For alpine equipment (from Nkr230/330/410 for one/two/three days) or snowboards (from Nkr265/420/525), there are three places in town: **Skiservice Hovden** (37 93 95 50); **Skibua** (37 93 81 80), which you'll find at the ski centre; and **Hovden Høyfjellsenter** (37 93 95 01). The last place is the cheapest, but the equipment tends to be older and it doesn't have a ski school.

In any season, climbers may want to practise on the 6m-high indoor climbing wall at the **G-Sport shop** (37 93 95 66). If the weather's bad, try the adventure swimming pool **Hovden Badeland** (37 93 93 93; admission 3hr for Nkr115; May-Dec).

SLEEPING & EATING

Your best bet for accommodation is Hovdenferie's **Sentralbooking** (37 93 93 75; post@ hovden.com) service which can connect you with the dozens of ski huts, flats, chalets and hotels offering good deals in summer.

Hovden Fjellstoge & Vandrerhjem (37 93 95 43; www.hovdenfjellstoge.no; Lundane; dm/s/d incl breakfast Nkr160/320/490; meals Nkr95) Accommodation at this hostel is in a traditional-style

wooden building with a grass roof. It also serves traditional Norwegian meals.

Quality Hovden Høyfjellshotell (37 93 96 00; www.choicehotels.no/hotels/no055; s/d from Nkr790/979) At the top of the town, this is Hovden's finest.

You'll find a range of meal options at the **Furumo Kafé** (37 93 97 72) and **Bamse Gatekjøkken** (37 93 91 88).

GETTING THERE & AWAY

The daily Nor-Way Bussekspress bus between Kristiansand (Nkr320, 3¾ hours) and Haukeligrend passes through Hovden; from the latter there are connections to Bergen.

SIRDAL

Sirdal, one of Norway's most important hydroelectric regions, is best known as the access route to the scenic 1000m road descent through 27 hairpin bends to Lysebotn (p207). From the well-appointed DNT hut at **Ådneram**, at the top of Sirdal, hikers can reach Lysebotn in nine hours (you need to follow the road for the last 4km). The road is closed by snow, except between mid-June and mid-September.

For tourist information and details of wilderness tours, horse riding and dogsledging, contact **Sirdalsferie** (38 37 13 90; www .sirdalsferie.com; Tjørhom).

Sinnes Fjellstue (38 37 11 21; info@sinnes-fjellstue .no; Sinnes; s/d from Nkr550/750) is a tidy mountain lodge offering accommodation at summer time.

Bus No 471 runs once daily except Sunday between Tonstad and Ådneram (Nkr68, 1¼ hours), but advance booking is required for pick-up at Ådneram. The Nor-Way Bussekspress Suleskarekspressen connects Stavanger (Nkr174, two hours) and Oslo (Nkr520, 7½ hours) via Fidjeland, 7km south of Ådneram, daily from the months of June to September.

Central Norway

143

CENTRAL NORWAY

Norway's central regions are truly special with enchanting wooden villages, exceptional snow-capped mountains and activities to satisfy even the most ardent adventurers.

No-one should come to Norway without pausing in Røros, an enchanting former mining town whose dark-log and colourful houses have been inscribed on Unesco's list of World Heritage sites. Nearby, Femundsmarka National Park promises a rare sighting of wild reindeer.

Pretty Lillehammer was transformed from one of the most popular Norwegian winter resorts to a place of world renown by the 1994 Winter Olympics. With the athletes long gone, most of the Olympic sites can now be experienced, sometimes even at Olympic speed.

From pretty villages to an altogether more clamourous world: Oppdal and Sjoa promise high-adrenaline thrills with some of the best white-water rafting in northern Europe. Whether you're a keen rafter or a beginner with kids, you'll find this one of the most exhilarating ways to see the great Norwegian outdoors.

Hikers will similarly relish Rondane and Dovrefjell-Sunndalsfjella National Parks. The latter offers wonderful bird-watching and the chance to spy the iconic musk ox. Glaciers, snow-capped peaks and access from the breathtaking Sognefjellet Rd combine to make Jotunheimen National Park one of the premier wilderness places in Europe.

Lom, the gateway to Jotunheimen, and Ringebu to the southeast add architectural interest with two scenically located stave churches.

CENTRAL NORWAY

HIGHLIGHTS

- Stepping back in time in the charming Unesco World Heritage–listed town of **Røros** (p152)

- Trekking along the extensive hiking routes through the breathtaking **Jotunheimen National Park** (p167)

- White-water rafting in **Sjoa** (p160) or **Oppdal** (p157)

- Strolling down memory lane or racing down the bobsled run at the former Olympic sites in lovely **Lillehammer** (p145)

- Going in search of the prehistoric musk oxen in **Dovrefjell-Sunndalsfjella National Park** (p163)

- Driving over the roof of Norway along **Sognefjellet Rd** (p167), one of the most scenic roads in Norway

| AREA: 63,803 SQ KM | HIGHEST ELEVATION: GALDHØPIGGEN 2469M | POPULATION: 614,300 |

Getting There & Away

Most towns in Central Norway fall within the triangle formed by Trondheim, Bergen and Oslo, ensuring ample and smooth connections. In the case of taking the Oslo–Bergen railway, a scenic transport connection is offered.

EASTERN CENTRAL NORWAY

LILLEHAMMER

pop 19,100

Lillehammer has long been a popular Norwegian ski resort, but it was thrust into the international spotlight in 1994 when the city hosted the Winter Olympics. These Olympics, overwhelmingly considered a great success, still provide the town with its most interesting and diverse sights more than a decade later. Lying at the northern end of the lake Mjøsa and surrounded by farms, forests and small settlements, it's a laid-back place with attractive and interesting architecture.

Orientation

Lillehammer's one-way streets can be confusing for motorists, but for pedestrians the centre is small and readily negotiated. Most of the Olympic sites are a 30-minute walk uphill from the centre.

The main shopping street is Storgata, just two blocks east of the Skysstasjon (the bus and train stations).

Information

Internet café (Jernbanegata 6; per hr Nkr40; 🕙 10am-5pm Mon-Fri, noon-4pm Sat) Almost opposite the train/bus station, this place offers speedy Internet connections.

Library (☎ 61 24 71 40; Wiesegate 2; 🕙 11am-3pm Mon-Wed & Fri, 11am-6pm Tue & Thu) Also offers free, but time-limited Internet access.

Lillehammer og Omland DNT (☎ 61 25 13 06; Storgata 34; 🕙 10am-3pm Tue-Thu & Sat) Sells hiking and skiing maps, dispenses mountain hut information and organises mountain hiking trips.

Lillehammer tourist office (☎ 61 28 98 00; www .lillehammerturist.no; 🕙 9am-7pm Mon-Sat & 11am-6pm Sun mid-Jun–mid-Aug, 9am-4pm Mon-Fri & 10am-2pm Sat rest-of-year) Located at the station and provides tourist information and advice.

Sights & Activities

OLYMPIC SITES

When Lillehammer won its bid for the 1994 Winter Olympics, the Norwegian government ploughed over two billion kroner into the infrastructure. Most of these amenities remain in use and visitors can tour the main Olympic sites over a large area called the **Olympiaparken** (☎ 61 25 11 40; www.olympiaparken .no; 🕙 9am-8pm Jun-Sep, shorter hours Oct-May).

Lygårdsbakkene Ski Jump

This is a very impressive complex. The main **ski jump** (K120) drops 136m with a landing-slope angle of 37.5°. The speed at takeoff is an exhilarating 91km/h with a record leap of 136.5m. During the Olympics, the site was surrounded by seating for 50,000 spectators and it was here that the opening ceremony was held; the tower for the **Olympic flame** is still standing near the foot of the jump. There's also a smaller jump (K90) alongside where you'll often see athletes honing their preparations for the next big jump.

The **ski jump chairlift** (adult/child return Nkr35/30) ascends to a panoramic view over the town. Alternatively you can walk for free as long as the prospect of 952 steps doesn't prove too daunting. The chairlift price includes entry to the **Lygårdsbakkene ski jump tower**, which costs Nkr15 on its own. Here you can stand atop the ramp and imagine the experience with all the prejump nerves.

To get close to the experience of the men's downhill race (and the Olympic bob-sledding course) without being an Olympic athlete, try the **simulator** (adult/child Nkr40/30, 5 min), which can be found at the bottom of the jump. It's a rough but exciting ride.

A combined ticket (adult/child Nkr65/45) is also available for the chairlift, tower and simulator.

Norwegian Olympic Museum

At the Håkons Hall ice-hockey venue can be found this excellent **Olympic museum** (☎ 61 25 21 00; Olympiaparken; adult/child Nkr60/30, combined ticket with Maihaugen Folk Museum Nkr120/55; 🕙 10am-6pm mid-May–mid-Sep). On the ground floor is a well-presented display covering the ancient Olympic Games as well as all Olympics of the modern era, with a focus on the exploits of Norwegian athletes.

Upstairs, you can look down on the ice-hockey arena, which is circled by corridors

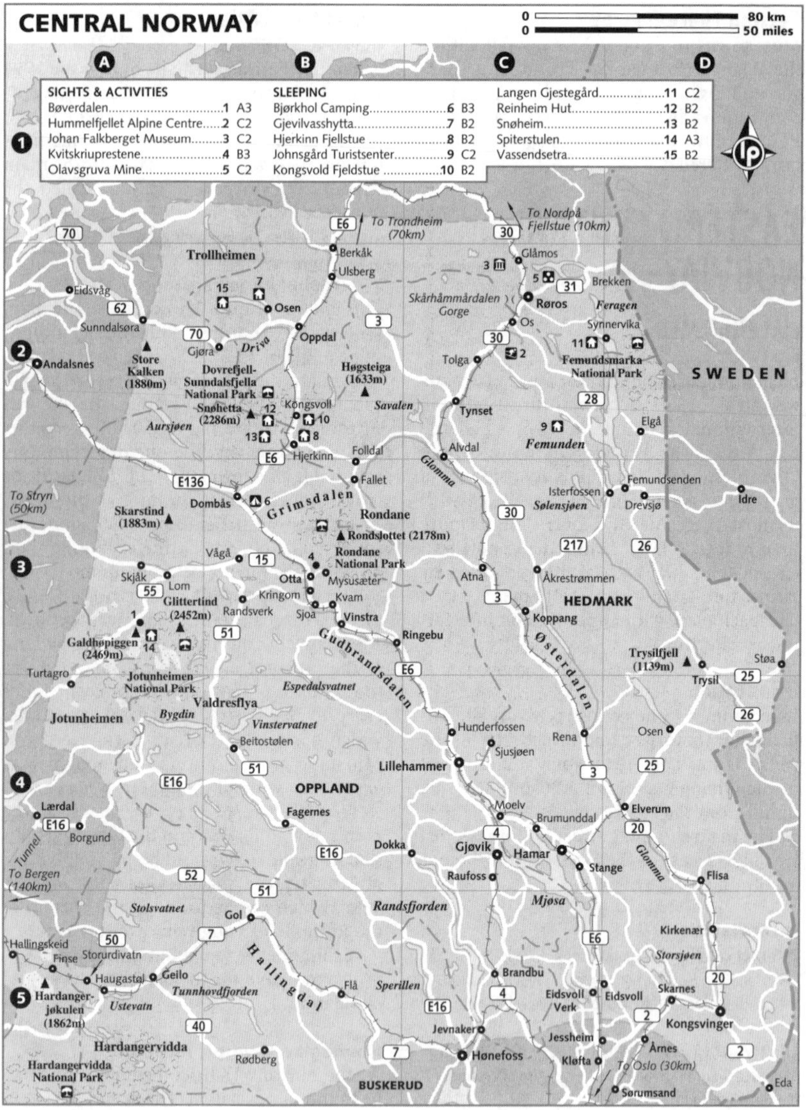

with displays and video presentations from the Lillehammer Games.

Olympic Bobsled Run

At Hunderfossen, 15km north of town, you can career down the **bobsled run** (☎ 61 27 75 50; Hunderfossen; admission to grounds Nkr15; 🕑 11am-6pm daily late Jun–mid-Aug, 11am-6pm Sat late May-late Jun, 11am-6pm Sat & Sun mid-Aug–mid-Sep, shorter hours rest-of-year) with a professional bobsled pilot. Taxibobs (the real thing at over 130km/h) run from November to Easter, take four passengers and cost Nkr850 per person for 70 seconds. Wheel bobsledding is possible the rest of the year; it's the same thing but on wheels and at a much more sedate

LILLEHAMMER

0 ▭▭▭▭▭▭ 1 km
0 ▭▭▭▭▭▭ 0.5 miles

A **B** **C** **D**

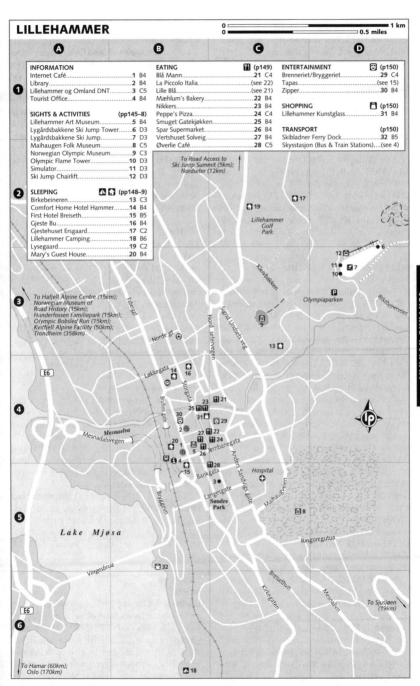

CENTRAL NORWAY

110km/h. Wheel bobs take five passengers and cost Nkr170/85 per adult/child. Bookings are advised during winter.

Ski Slopes
Lillehammer has two Olympic ski slopes. The **Hafjell Alpine Centre** (☎ 61 27 47 00; www .hafjell.no), 15km north of town, hosted the downhill events, while the **Kvitfjell Alpine Facility** (☎ 61 28 36 00), 50km north of town, was dedicated to cross-country. Both offer public skiing between late November and late April. Hafjell is accessible on the ski bus (Nkr31, 20 minutes, six or seven daily); lift tickets start from Nkr285/225 per adult/child for the first day and full equipment starts from Nkr285 (downhill or snowboard). Cross-country equipment starts from Nkr150.

MAIHAUGEN FOLK MUSEUM
Norway's finest folk museum and one of its most popular is the open-air **folk museum** (☎ 61 28 89 00; www.maihaugen.no; Maihaugveien 1; adult/child/student/senior/family Nkr90/40/70/70/200, combined ticket with Olympic Museum adult/child Nkr120/55; ☷ 10am-5pm mid-May–Sep, 11am-4pm Oct–mid-May). Rebuilt like a small village, the collection of around 180 buildings includes the transplanted Garmo stave church, traditional Gudbrandsdalen homes and shops and 27 buildings from the farm Bjørnstad. The life's work of local dentist Anders Sandvig, it also houses temporary exhibitions in the modern exhibition hall, workshop demonstrations by interpreters in period costumes, and a section featuring Norwegian homes from every decade of the 20th century. Maihaugen is a 20-minute walk from the train station; go up Jernbanegata, right on Anders Sandvig's gate and left up Maihaugveien.

LILLEHAMMER ART MUSEUM
This architecturally striking **art museum** (Lillehammer Kunstmuseum; ☎ 61 26 94 44; Stortorget 2; adult/child Nkr60/50; ☷ 11am-5pm Tue-Sun mid-Jun–mid-Aug, 11am-4pm rest-of-year) covers Norwegian visual arts from the early 19th century to the present, with emphasis on the period between 1820 and 1930. Highlights include the inspired works by some of Norway's finest artists: Johan C Dahl, Christian Krogh, Edvard Munch, Axel Revold and Erik Werenskiold.

NORWEGIAN MUSEUM OF ROAD HISTORY
Lying 15km north of Lillehammer is the impressive **Museum of Road History** (Norsk Vegmuseum; ☎ 61 28 52 50; www.vegmuseum.no; Hunderfossen; admission free; ☷ 10am-6pm mid-May–Aug, 10am-3pm Sep–mid-May). Apart from displays on road-building, construction vehicles and video presentations, don't miss the **Fjellsprengnings-museet**, up the hill and part of the same complex. This 240m-long tunnel gives you a real insight into the difficulties of building a tunnel through the Norwegian mountains. The walk, guided with lighting, models and flat-screen video commentary, takes around 30 minutes. Outside the entrance, you'll see the enormous rock-blasting machinery.

HUNDERFOSSEN FAMILIEPARK
The kids will love you for taking them to this **park** (☎ 61 27 55 60; www.hunderfossen.no; Hunderfossen; adult/child Nkr230/205; ☷ 10am-8pm mid-Jun–mid-Aug, shorter hours rest-of-year). It's one of Norway's best parks for children with water rides, 3-D presentations, fairy-tale palaces, wandering trolls and a host of kids-focused activities. In summer there are up to five buses a day from the Lillehammer Skysstasjon (adult/child Nkr27/14, 20 minutes), with less frequent departures the rest of the year.

Festivals & Events
For two weeks around the Christmas and New Year holidays, Lillehammer puts on its **Christmas Festival**. This event features sleigh rides, ski tours, Christmas-tree felling, Christmas parties, Santa visits and especially appealing winter lighting along the pedestrian shopping street. The tourist office has all the details.

There's also the four-day **Lillehammer Jazz Festival** (☎ 81 53 31 33; www.dolajazz.no) in mid-September; tickets go on sale from 1 July each year. In March there's a large women-only ski race; contact the tourist office for details.

Sleeping
BUDGET
Lillehammer Camping (☎ 61 25 33 33; www.lillehammer-camping.no; Dampsaveien 47; tent/caravan sites from Nkr120/160, 2-bed cabins Nkr350-600; ☷ year-round) Camping is available here on the lakeshore, a typical urban site with cooking and laundry facilities, water-sports equipment, children's play areas and cable TV.

Gjeste Bu (☎ /fax 61 25 43 21; gjestebu@lillehammer
.online.no; Gamleveien 110; dm Nkr100, s/d with shared
bathroom Nkr225/350, s/d apt from Nkr550/650) This
friendly guesthouse is an appealing option
with a range of accommodation. There are
shared kitchen facilities, while the small
and large apartments (which can sleep up
to 11 people) are great if you're going to be
in town for a while. Breakfast costs extra.
Highly recommended.

Mary's Guest House (☎ 61 24 87 00; www.mary
sguesthouse.no; Jernbanegata 2; dm incl breakfast Nkr225,
s/d incl breakfast Mon-Fri Nkr517/705, Sat & Sun Nkr495/
650) This good-value place, upstairs at the bus/
train terminal, has high-standard rooms
with shower and toilet.

MID-RANGE & TOP END

Birkebeineren (☎ 61 26 47 00; www.birkebeineren
.no; Birkebeinerveien 24; with shared bathroom from
Nkr365/530, s/d with private bathroom from Nkr595/890,
apt from Nkr1050) This very good place, close to
the bottom of the ski jump, offers a range
of accommodation to suit different budgets;
prices include breakfast and cost less the
longer you stay.

Gjestehuset Ersgaard (☎ 61 25 06 84; www.ersg
aard.no; Nordseterveien 201; s Nkr350-550, d Nkr590-675)
This is a great choice, in refurbished farm
buildings high on the hill overlooking town,
on the road up to the ski jump.

Lysegaard (☎ 61 26 26 63; lysgaard@c2i.net; Lyseg
aard; dm Nkr150; 2-/4-bed apt Nkr500/700) Another
converted farmhouse with loads of character up on the hill, this place also represents
great value.

Comfort Home Hotel Hammer (☎ 61 26 35 00;
hammer@comfort.choicehotels.no; Storgata 108; s/d with
half board Nkr740/940) Part of the Quality hotel
chain, this hotel offers very comfortable
rooms right in the centre of town.

First Hotel Breiseth (☎ 61 24 77 77; www.breiseth
.com; Jernbanegata 1-5; s/d Mon-Fri Nkr1019/1169, Sat &
Sun Nkr910/1060) Opposite the train station,
this stylish hotel offers top-quality rooms
and service and is just a stone's throw from
the central thoroughfare.

Eating

Despite its size, Lillehammer offers the
same culinary variety as Oslo. All places
listed here are open lunch and dinner daily
unless stated otherwise.

Smuget Gatekjøkken (☎ 61 25 92 12; Storgata 83;
burgers Nkr45-85) This place dishes up a variety
of fast food, with very good value to be had
by choosing the fish burger (Nkr40) or the
kebab with chips and salad (Nkr75).

Vertshuset Solveig (☎ 61 26 27 87; Storgata 68B;
light meals Nkr98-119, mains Nkr136-169; ☺ 10am-10pm
Mon-Sat, 1-7pm Sun) This unpretentious but
appealing restaurant has a range of lunch
specials and meat and fish dishes, as well
as nachos (Nkr98) and a children's menu
(Nkr55 to Nkr69).

One-Hand Clapping (☎ 61 25 12 22; Storgata;
☺ 9.10am-5pm Mon-Sat) This very cool little
coffee shop does superb coffee (Nkr20 to
Nkr32), as well as croissants and home-
made chocolate cake (Nkr15) to die for.
The two easy chairs on the pavement are
prime people-viewing spots if you're fortu-
nate enough to snaffle one.

Blå Mann (☎ 61 26 22 03; Lilletorvet 1; brunch
& sandwiches from Nkr79, Mexican dishes Nkr129-179,
mains Nkr63-295) This recommended spot has
a trendy menu offering everything from
baguettes to Mexican and some of the most
exotic Norwegian specialities, such as reindeer (Nkr295) and ostrich (Nkr243). The
downstairs Lille Blå is less formal, supercool
and a great place to spend a summer's afternoon writing postcards. There's great coffee
and drinks and it stays open until 2am on
weekends.

Nikkers (☎ 61 27 05 56; Elvegata 18; lunches Nkr69-
108, baguettes Nkr59, mains Nkr129-198) Known as
the place where a moose has apparently
walked through the wall (look outside on
the east wall for the full effect), it serves international cuisine and has one of the more
pleasant outdoor terraces, next to a bubbling brook. The ambience is somewhere
between English pub and Oslo café. It also
has kids' menus (Nkr45 to Nkr65).

Also recommended:

Øverlie Café (☎ 61 25 03 61; Storgata 50; meals from
Nkr39-69) Filling, inexpensive meals (eg meatballs and
mashed potatoes).

Peppe's Pizza (☎ 61 26 47 15; Storgata 69; Mon-Fri
lunch buffets from Nkr84, pizzas from Nkr138) Great, large
pizzas.

La Piccolo Italia (☎ 61 05 45 10; Storgata 73; pasta
Nkr70-85, small/large pizzas from Nkr60/120) Good Italian
place with reasonable prices.

Mæhlum's Bakery (☎ 61 25 02 06; Storgata 73;
☺ 8.30am-5pm Mon-Fri, 10am-4pm Sat, 11am-4pm Sun)
Bakery with bread, pastries and ciabatta (Nkr40).

Spar Supermarket (Cnr Jernbarnegata & Storgata;
☺ 9am-9pm Mon-Fri, 9am-6pm Sat)

CENTRAL NORWAY

Entertainment

Bars are an integral part of the Lillehammer experience, especially during the ski season. Most places are clustered around the intersection of Storgata and Elvegata, and along the river Mesnaelva. All places are open from at least 11am to 2am daily.

Nikkers (☎ 61 27 05 56; Elvegata 18) The place with the moose and his droppings is one of the most popular bars in town. It's got a young vibe that welcomes families by day and a happy crowd of young and young-at-heart drinkers by night.

Brenneriet/Bryggeriet (☎ 61 27 06 60; Elvegata 19) This pub, nightclub and disco appeals to a varied clientele from the just-legal to time-worn veterans.

Dirty Nelly (Storgata 93) Lillehammer's Irish pub is dark wood-pannelling, friendly staff and quiet until around 8pm.

Haakon's Bar (Storgata 93) During the day Haakon's Bar is the sole preserve of elbow-on-the-bar locals and very slow. After the sun sets, it kicks into action, becoming a crowded and agreeable place to drink.

Zipper (☎ 61 22 22 81; Nymosvingen 2) This student hang-out appeals to the 18-to-30 set with a pub, disco and club evenings.

Tapas (☎ 61 24 77 77; Jernbanegata 1-5; cold tapas Nkr27-103, hot tapas Nkr37-69; 5-11pm Mon-Thu, 4pm-midnight Fri & Sat) For a change of scene, try this Spanish-flavoured bar, which plays Latin music, does good tapas and has a pleasant, buzzy ambience when it's full.

Shopping

Lillehammer Kunstglass (☎ 61 25 79 80; Elvegata 17; 9am-5pm Mon-Wed & Fri, 9am-7pm Thu, 9am-3pm Sat mid-Jun–mid-Aug, shorter hours rest-of-year) You can watch the glass-blowers at work (9am to 2pm weekdays) at this glass outlet and buy the beautiful results (from Nkr100).

Getting There & Away

Lillehammer Skysstasjon (☎ 177) is the main transport terminal for buses, trains and taxis. There are Nor-Way Bussekspress services to/from Oslo (Nkr250, 3½ hours, three to four daily). To/from the Western Fjords, buses pass through Lillehammer several times daily. There's also one daily run to/from Bergen (Nkr590, 9¼ hours).

Rail services run between Oslo (Nkr282, 2¼ hours, 11 to 17 daily) and Trondheim (Nkr546, 4¼ hours, four to six daily).

For details of the *Skibladner* paddle steamer, see the boxed text, p151.

HAMAR

pop 28,600

Hamar hosted a number of Olympic events during the 1994 Lillehammer Winter Olympics, leaving behind a signature piece of modern architecture. This commercial town beside the immense lake Mjøsa also boasts a couple of excellent museums. All of which is just as well, because Hamar would never win a beauty contest. The **tourist office** (☎ 62 51 75 03; hamar-turistkontor@hoa.net; 8am-6pm Mon-Fri, 10am-6pm Sat & Sun mid-Jun–mid-Aug, 8am-4pm Mon-Fri rest-of-year) can be found at the Viking Ship Sports Arena.

Sights

VIKING SHIP SPORTS ARENA

Hamar's landmark is this **sports arena** (Vikingskipet; ☎ 62 51 75 00; www.hoa.no in Norwegian; Åkersvikaveien; adult/child Nkr30/10; 8am-6pm Mon-Fri, 10am-6pm Sat & Sun Jun–mid-Aug), a graceful structure with the lines of an upturned Viking ship. The building, which hosted the speed-skating during the Winter Olympics, holds 20,000 spectators, encompasses 9600 sq metres of ice and is 94.6m long. It has been described as a 'sports cathedral without equal'. It's still used for events (everything from antique fairs to international speed-skating). From late July to mid-August, the ice is open to the public for ice-skating (Nkr70).

NORWEGIAN RAILWAY MUSEUM

Established in 1896 in honour of Norway's railway history, this open-air **railway museum** (Norsk Jernbanemuseum; ☎ 62 51 31 60; www.norsk-jernbanemuseum.no; Strandveien 163; adult/child Nkr70/40; 10.30am-5pm daily Jul–mid-Aug, 10.30am-3.30pm daily Jun, 10.30am-3.30pm Tue-Sun rest-of-year), lies on the Mjøsa shore. In addition to lovely historic stations, engine sheds, rail coaches and the 1861 steam locomotive named *Caroline*, you'll learn about the extraordinary engineering feats required to construct the railways through Norway's rugged terrain.

HEDMARK MUSEUM & GLASS CATHEDRAL

The extensive open-air county **museum** (Hedmarkmuseet; ☎ 62 54 27 00; www.hedmarksmuseet.no; Strandveien 100; adult/child Nkr70/30; 10am-5pm daily mid-Jun–mid-Aug, 10am-4pm Tue-Sun mid-May–mid-Jun & mid-Aug–early Sep), 1.5km west of the town centre, includes 18th- and 19th-century buildings, a local folk-history exhibit featuring the creepy Devil's Finger, the ruins of the castle, and the extraordinary showcase 'glass cathedral' (Domkirkeodden). The cathedral and castle dominated Hamar until 1567, when they were sacked by the Swedes. Take bus No 6 from the town library (Nkr25, hourly).

NORWEGIAN EMIGRANT MUSEUM

Around 10km east of town, this fine open-air **museum** (Norsk Utvandrermuseum; ☎ 62 57 48 50; www.museumsnett.no/emigrantmuseum; Åkershagan; admission free; ☒ 9am-3.30pm Mon-Fri, 10am-4pm Sat, noon-4pm Sun mid-Jun–mid-Aug, closed weekends rest-of-year) focuses on exhibits and archives from Norwegian emigrants to America from the 1880s. There's also a research library open to members (Nkr150).

Festivals & Events

Hamar hosts a couple of excellent festivals. In the first week of September, the **Hamar Music Festival** (www.musicfest.no in Norwegian) attracts a growing band of international acts; concert tickets range from Nkr50 to Nkr350, while passes start from Nkr500. On the second weekend in June, Hamar hosts the Middle Ages Festival, with locals in period costume and Gregorian chants in the glass cathedral; contact the tourist office for details.

Sleeping & Eating

Vikingskipet Motell og Vandrerhjem (☎ 62 52 60 60; www.vi-sees.no; Åkersvikavegen 24; dm/s/d Nkr190/300/380, 4-bed apt Nkr750) Opposite the Viking Ship Sports Arena, this is an excellent choice with simple but very well-kept rooms and terrific self-contained, spick-and-span apartments. Breakfast costs Nkr60.

Seiersted Pensjonat (☎ 62 55 12 44; www.seierstad .no; Holsetgata 64; s/d Nkr400/750) Centrally located Seiersted Pensjonat offers a homey, pleasant atmosphere and nicely decorated rooms. Dinner is available from Nkr70. To get there go to the train station and take Vangsveien to the northwest, then St Olav's gate just before the stadium.

Quality Hotel Astoria (☎ 62 70 70 00; quality.astoria .hotel@eunet.no; Torggata 23; s/d Nkr690/890) This pleasant modern hotel in the town centre has well-appointed rooms equipped with all

---

THE WORLD'S OLDEST PADDLE STEAMER

Skibladner (☎ 61 14 40 80; www.skibladner.no), the world's oldest paddle steamer, is a wonderfully relaxing way to explore lake Mjøsa. First built in Sweden in 1856, the boat was refitted and lengthened to 165ft in 1888. From late June to early August, the *Skibladner* plies the lake between Hamar, Gjøvik and Lillehammer. Most travellers opt for the route between Hamar and Lillehammer (Nkr220, 3½ hours) on Tuesday, Thursday and Saturday, which can be done as a return day trip (from Hamar only, Nkr320). Jazz evenings aboard the steamer cost Nkr450, including food.

---

the mod-cons, although some can get a bit hot in summer.

Stallgården (☎ 62 54 31 00; cnr Bekkegata & Torggata; lunch Nkr65-79, snacks & light meals Nkr65-145, mains Nkr175-235; ☒ lunch & dinner) The downstairs café is particularly popular for its outdoor tables in summer, while the upstairs restaurant (dinner only Monday to Saturday) is more formal.

Other good choices:

Artichoke (☎ 62 53 23 33; Parkgata 21; mains from Nkr125; ☒ 11am-5pm Tue, 11am-11pm Wed-Sat; noon-5pm Sun) Chic minimalist décor and creative cooking.

Alle Tiders (1st fl, Torggata 71; snacks & light meals Nkr62-109; ☒ lunch & dinner) Great cakes, snacks and coffee (Nkr35).

Poesi (Torggata 32; ☒ 10am-5pm) Also good for coffee.

Getting There & Away

Nor-Way Bussekspress buses run to/from the Western Fjords several times daily. Frequent trains run between Oslo and Hamar (Nkr205, 1¼ hours, once or twice hourly); some services continue to Trondheim (Nkr585, five hours, four or five daily) via Lillehammer. Trains also run to Røros (Nkr425, 3¼ hours, one to three daily).

ELVERUM

pop 12,500

Set amid the vast and lush, green timberlands of southern Hedmark county (home to dense populations of moose and beaver), the nondescript town of Elverum presents a landscape more typical of Sweden or Finland than the classic image of Norway. For Norwegians, the area provides abundant timber

THE DARK DAYS OF WWII

Elverum played a proud but tragic role in the Norwegian resistance to the Nazis. When German forces invaded Norway in April 1940, King Håkon and the Norwegian government fled northwards from Oslo. They halted in Elverum and on 9 April the parliament met at the folk high school and issued the Elverum Mandate, giving the exiled government the authority to protect Norway's interests until the parliament could reconvene. When a German messenger arrived to impose the Nazis' version of 'protection' in the form of a new puppet government in Oslo, the king rejected the 'offer' before heading into exile. Two days later, Elverum became the first Norwegian town to suffer massive bombing by the Nazis and most of the town's old wooden buildings were levelled.

resources and clear streams brimming with grayling, pike, trout and whitefish. It's also home to the excellent forestry museum. The **tourist office** (☎ 62 41 31 16; www.elverum-turistinfo .com; Storgata 24; ☉ 9am-6pm mid-Jun–mid-Aug, closed weekends rest-of-year) is located right in the centre of town.

Sights

The pleasant and expansive **Norwegian Forestry Museum** (Norsk Skogmuseum; ☎ 62 40 90 00; www.skogmus.no in Norwegian; incl Glomdal Museum adult/child/student/senior Nkr80/35/60/60; ☉ 10am-6pm mid-Jun–mid-Aug, 10am-4pm rest-of-year) is located on Rv20, 1km south of central Elverum. This impressive place covers the multifarious uses and enjoyments of Norwegian forests, and boasts a number of things on offer. It includes a nature information centre, children's workshop, informative geological and meteorological exhibits, wood carvings, an aquarium, nature dioramas with all manner of stuffed native wildlife (including a mammoth) and an extensive 20,000-volume reference library.

The large open-air **Glomdal Museum** (☎ 62 41 91 00; incl Forestry Museum adult/child/student/senior Nkr80/35/60/60; ☉ 10am-4pm mid-Jun–mid-Aug) is a collection of 90 historic buildings from along the Glomma valley, including an old apothecary and doctor's surgery. The museum is accessible from the bridge from the forestry museum.

Sleeping & Eating

Elverum Camping (☎ 62 41 67 16; www.elverum camping.no; Halvdans Gransv 6; tent sites Nkr120, 4-bed cabins from Nkr500) This place is well signposted in a green setting immediately south of the Norwegian Forestry Museum.

Glommen Pensjonat (☎ 62 41 12 67; Vestheimsgata 2; s/d from Nkr350/400) This simple establishment is 500m west of the centre and a good choice for a more personal touch than the hotels.

Hotel Central (☎ 62 41 01 55; www.hotel-central .no; Storgata 22; s/d from Nkr690/825) This place doesn't win any prizes for creativity but it is in the heart of town, with modern and comfortable rooms.

Forstmann (☎ 62 41 69 10; mains from Nkr115; ☉ lunch & dinner mid-Jun–mid-Aug) The fish-and-game restaurant at the Forestry Museum is a nice leafy place with good traditional Norwegian cooking.

Getting There & Away

The Nor-Way Bussekspress 'Trysil Ekspressen' runs between Oslo (Nkr190, 2½ hours) and Trysil (Nkr98, 1¼ hours) via Elverum seven times daily.

NORTHERN CENTRAL NORWAY

RØROS
pop 3400

Charming little Røros is a gem, a fact recognised by Unesco in 1981 when it added the town to its World Heritage List. Formerly called Bergstad (mountain city), this historic copper-mining town of climbing streets lined with wooden homes manages to preserve its past without losing its community spirit. Set in a small hollow of stunted forests amid bleak and treeless fells, medieval Røros is one of the most enchanting places in Norway.

Information

Røros Internet Café (☎ 72 41 00 90; Kjerkgata 42; per hr Nkr50; ☉ noon-9pm Sun-Thu, noon-11pm Fri & Sat)
Tourist office (☎ 72 41 11 65; www.rorosinfo.com; Peder Hiortsgata 2; ☉ 9am-6pm Mon-Sat, 10am-4pm Sun mid-Jun–mid-Aug, 9am-3.30pm Mon-Fri rest-of-year) This helpful office is in a historic building just a block from the train station. It has knowledgeable staff keen to tell you what to see and do in Røros and the surrounding region.

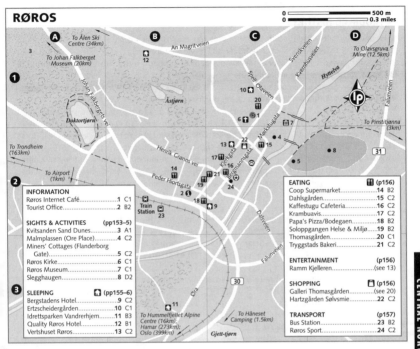

RØROS

Sights

HISTORIC DISTRICT

Røros' historic district, characterised by the striking log architecture of its 80 protected buildings, takes in the entire central town area. The two main streets, **Bergmannsgata** (its taper from southwest to northeast was intended to create an optical illusion and make the town appear larger than it was!) and **Kjerkgata**, are lined with historical homes and buildings, all under preservation orders. If you follow the river Hyttelva upstream, you'll reach the historic smelting district and its tiny turf-roofed **miners' cottages** at the mine's Flanderborg Gate, the smelter and other mine company buildings, and protected **slegghaugan** (slag heaps) and other mining detritus, which overlook rainbow-coloured earth made barren by chemical residue from the smelting process.

If it all looks a bit familiar, that may be because several films have been made here, including Røros author Johan Falkberget's classic *An-Magrit*, starring Jane Fonda. Flanderborg gate starred in some films of Astrid Lindgren's *Pippi Longstocking* classics and the district even stood in for Siberia in the film of Solzhenitsyn's *A Day in the Life of Ivan Denisovich*.

RØROS KIRKE

Røros' Lutheran **church** (Kjerkgata; tours adult/child Nkr25/free; tours 10am-5pm Mon-Sat, 1-3pm Sun mid-Jun–mid-Aug, shorter hours rest-of-year) is one of Norway's largest, with a seating capacity of 1640, and has seen many different manifestations. Constructed in 1650, it had fallen into disrepair by the mid-18th century and from 1780 to 1784 a new baroque-style church was built just behind the original at a cost of 23,000 *riksdaler* (the old currency; one *riksdaler* is the equivalent of Nkr4, and at the time miners earned about 50 *riksdaler* per year). The posh King's Gallery at the back, identified by both royal and mining company logos, has never hosted a king, as visiting royals have always opted to sit among the people. A particular oddity is the pulpit, which sits over the altarpiece (a rendition of *The Last Supper*). The organ (1742) is the oldest Norwegian-built organ still functioning.

A TROUBLED HISTORY

Like any fairy-tale village worth its salt, Røros has origins which carry a whisper of legend. In 1644 a local, Olsen Åsen, shot a reindeer at Storvola (Storwartz). The enraged creature leapt about and pawed up the ground, revealing a glint of copper ore that would secure the future of Røros. News spread quickly and in the same year Røros Kobberverk was established, followed two years later by a royal charter that granted it exclusive rights to all minerals, forest products and waterways within a 40km radius of the original discovery.

The mining company located its headquarters at Røros due to the abundant wood (fuel) and the rapids along the river Hyttelva (hydroelectric power in the 17th century). The use of fire in breaking up the rock in the mines was a perilous business and cost Røros dearly. Røros first burnt to the ground during the Gyldenløve conflict with the Swedes between 1678 and 1679, and the smelter was damaged by fire again in 1953. Smelting continued in Sweden but in 1977, after 333 years of operation, the company went bankrupt. Fortunately, by then Røros was no longer a one-industry town and managed to continue despite the initial economic hardship.

Until 1865 the building was owned by the mining company and this is reflected in most of the church art. By the altar you'll see the grizzled Hans Olsen Åsen, credited with the discovery of Røros copper, among other company dignitaries. There are also paintings of the author Johan Falkberget and the original 1650 church.

For five weeks from early July to early August, the church hosts **organ recitals** (adult/child Nkr50/free; 6pm Mon-Sat), often accompanied by renowned orchestral musicians from across Europe.

A five-year restoration began in 2004, with plans to return the church to its original state – expect some closures during this period.

RØROS MUSEUM

Housed in old smelting works, this **museum** (72 40 61 70; Malmplassen; adult/child/senior/student/family Nkr60/30/50/50/140; 10am-7pm Mon-Sat, 10am-4pm Sun mid-Jun–mid-Aug, shorter hours rest-of-year), is a town highlight. The building was reconstructed in 1988 according to the original 17th-century plan. Upstairs you'll find geological and conservation displays, while downstairs are a large balance used for weighing ore, some well-illustrated early mining statistics, and a series of brilliant working models of the mines and the water- and horse-powered smelting processes. Outside the museum entrance spreads the large open area known as the **Malmplassen** (Ore Place), where loads of ore were dumped and weighed on the large wooden scale.

In summer, your entry ticket entitles you to a free guided tour at 11am, 12.30pm,

2pm or 3.30pm; the last is in English and/or German.

OLAVSGRUVA MINE

Don't miss the **Olavsgruva mine** (72 41 11 65; Kojedalen; adult/child/senior/student/family Nkr60/ 30/50/50/140; 10am-5pm mid-Jun–mid-Aug), 13km north of Røros. The moderately interesting exhibition building is made worthwhile by **mine tours** (11am, 12.30pm, 2pm, 3.30pm and 5pm mid-June to mid-August) which pass through the historic Nyberget mine, dating from the 1650s. The modern Olavsgruva mine beyond it was begun in 1936 and operated until the 1970s. The ground can get muddy and the temperature in the mine is a steady 5°C; bring a jacket and good footwear. To get to the mine, use your own wheels or take a taxi (Nkr450 return).

JOHAN FALKBERGET MUSEUM

Røros' favourite son, author Johan Falkberget (1879–1967), grew up at Trondalen farm in the nearby Rugel valley. His works (now translated into 19 languages) cover 300 years of the region's mining history. His most famous work, *An-Magrit*, tells the story of a peasant girl who transported copper ore in the Røros mining district. The **museum** (72 41 46 27; Ratvolden; adult/child Nkr50/30; 11.30am-3pm Tue-Sun Jul–early-Aug, 11.30am-1.30pm Tue-Sun early Aug–mid-Sep) is beside the nearby lake Rugelsjø. Guided tours run at noon Tuesday to Sunday, with an extra one at 1.30pm in July. To get there, take a local train to Rugeldalen station, 20km north of Røros, where a small walking track leads to the museum.

Activities

Hiking (and, in winter, **nordic skiing**) possibilities abound across the semiforested Røros plateau. Numerous tracks head out through the hills and valleys and you can walk for anything from an hour to a week; ask the tourist office for advice. Note, however, that many areas remain snow-covered well into the summer, and on the higher fells, skiing is possible until July. **Hummelfjellet Alpine Centre** (☎ 62 49 71 00; www.hummelfjell.no in Norwegian), 16km south of Røros, has one lift and four slopes, while **Ålen Ski Centre** (☎ 72 41 55 55), 34km northwest of town, boasts two lifts and four slopes.

A 1km **walk** northwest from Røros will take you to the sand dunes of Kvitsanden, the largest in Scandinavia. Scoured, transported and deposited there by water flowing under an ancient glacier, they're more novel than beautiful.

Another kilometre to the west lies Skårhåmmårdalen, a gorge with sand-lined pools, which offers **swimming** on hot days and appears as if it might harbour trolls.

The tourist office has details of cycling trips, including one-day options and longer five-day tours (around Nkr2820 per person). It can also organise canoe hire (one/two days Nkr200/380), horse riding (per hour Nkr100, one- to three-day riding tours Nkr510 to Nkr2500), and ice-fishing (per day Nkr135) for trout at Pinstitjønna, 3km east of town.

Tours

In winter, the tourist office organises excursions by dog-sled (two to five hours Nkr600 to Nkr800) or horse-drawn sleigh (Nkr600 per hour for four people); in summer dog-cart trips offer an all-you'll-get-at-this-time-of-year substitute. You can also join a winter day trip to the Southern Sami tent camp at Pinstitjønna, 3km from town and 1km off the road, where you'll dine on reindeer and learn such unique skills as ice-fishing and axe-throwing. The three-hour tour costs around Nkr500 per person (minimum 10 people).

The tourist office runs **guided walking tours** (adult/child Nkr50/free; ☼ tours 11am Mon-Sat May–mid-Jun & mid-Aug–mid-Sep, 10am, 11.30am, 1pm, 2.30pm Mon-Sat, noon & 2pm Sun mid-Jun–mid-Aug, 11am Sat rest-of-year) of the historic district which are terrific; the summer tours at 1pm Monday to Friday and 2pm Saturday are in English and German.

Festivals & Events

The biggest winter event is Rørosmartnan (Røros Market), which began in 1644 as a rendezvous for hunters who ventured into town to sell their products to miners and buy supplies. Thanks to a royal decree issued in 1853 stipulating that a grand market be held annually from the penultimate Tuesday of February to the following Saturday, it continues today. Nowadays, it's celebrated with cultural programmes, street markets and live entertainment.

From early to mid-August every second year (2005, 2007 etc), Røros stages a nightly three-hour rock opera in Swedish entitled *Det Brinner en Eld*, or 'Fiery Call for Peace'. It recounts the invasion of Trøndelag by Swedish soldiers in 1718, covering the occupation of Røros and the subsequent death of thousands of soldiers on their frozen trek homewards to Sweden. Written in 1980 by Arnfinn Strømmevold and Bertil Reithaug, it's enacted on the slag heaps in the upper part of town. If you can manage to get there, don't miss it.

Sleeping

The tourist office keeps a list of summer cabins and guesthouses, some within walking distance of town, from around Nkr2500 to Nkr4000 per week in the high season.

Håneset Camping (☎ 72 41 06 00; fax 72 41 06 01; Osloveien; tent or caravan sites Nkr130 plus per person Nkr25, 2-/4-bed cabins Nkr320/420) Simple but well-kept cabins are available at this excellent site, with cooking and laundry facilities, a common room and TV; it's about 2km south of town.

Idrettsparken Vandrerhjem (☎ 72 41 10 89; www.idrettsparken.no; Øra 25; tent/caravan sites Nkr90/135, dm incl breakfast Nkr200, hostel s/d Nkr375/450, cabins s/d Nkr475/600, hotel s/d from Nkr650/875) The family-run Idrettsparken Vandrerhjem, 500m from the train station, serves a good breakfast and the rooms range from simple and tidy to very comfortable.

Ertzscheidergården (☎ 72 41 11 94; fax 72 41 19 60; Spell Olaveien 6; s/d Nkr590/890) This appealing 16-room guesthouse lies just a stone's throw from the church and mining museum and has rooms loaded with character and excellent home-made breakfast buffets.

Vertshuset Røros (☎ 72 41 93 50; www.vertshuset roros.no; Kjerkgata 34; s/d Nkr760/990, 2-/3-/4-bed apt per person Nkr580/485/420) Located in a historic build-ing right on the main pedestrian thorough-fare, this cosy place is another excellent choice with attractive rooms.

Bergstadens Hotel (☎ 72 40 60 80; www.bergs taden.no in Norwegian; Osloveien 2; s/d Nkr820/990 mid-Jun–mid-Aug & Sat & Sun, Nkr1235/1420 rest-of-year) The cosy and down-to-earth Bergstadens Hotel, near the train station, offers well-appointed rooms, and is very close to the centre. The piano bar is unlikely to bother you and is pleasant enough, but the nightclub can get a bit noisy on weekends.

Quality Hotel Røros (☎ 72 40 80 00; booking.roros@ qualitychoicehotels.no; An Magrit veien 10; s/d Nkr740/940 mid-Jun–mid-Aug & Sat & Sun, Nkr1195/1395 rest-of-year) The Quality Hotel Røros is at the top end of town and has extremely well-appointed rooms with a touch more char-acter than most chains. Some rooms have a commanding view. There's also a piano bar that attracts a nostalgic, older crowd although it's pretty slow-paced. There's a livelier disco which thuds into life on weekends.

Eating

Røros has some good restaurants, all of which are open for lunch and dinner daily unless stated otherwise. Most places have good value lunch-time buffets or specials on offer. Within a block of the tourist office, you'll also find a couple of bakeries and a **Coop supermarket** (P Hiortsgata 7). **Solop-pgangen Helse & Miljø** (☎ 72 41 29 55; Kjerkgata 6) sells health foods.

Vertshuset Røros (☎ 72 41 24 11; Kjerkgata 34; starters Nkr75-79, mains Nkr175-239) For formal din-ing but without a stuffy atmosphere, the finest option is probably Vertshuset Røros with its varied menu of Norwegian speciali-ties ranging from beef and freshwater fish to elk and reindeer (Nkr235).

Papa's Pizza/Bodegaen (☎ 72 40 60 20; Berg-mannsgata 1; pizzas Nkr105-170, mains Nkr85-218) Pa-pa's, at the bottom end of Bermannsgata, serves pizza, burgers, beef, fish and chicken dishes, as well as beer and wine. It also has the town's most attractive outdoor terrace in summer with views all the way up this historic street. It also does kids' menus (Nkr40 to Nkr60).

Krambuavis (☎ 72 41 05 67; Kjerkgata 28; starters Nkr39-83, mains Nkr86-199) This is an excellent choice with large servings, friendly waiters and good food, which ranges from Mexican to spare ribs and fish dishes.

Kafestuggu Cafeteria (☎ 72 41 10 33; Bergmanns-gata 18; light meals from Nkr49, mains Nkr75-165; ⏱ 8am-5pm Mon-Fri, 9am-5pm Sat & 11am-5pm Sun) This informal cafeteria offers a good range of coffee, pastries, cold snacks and light meals.

There are also many small coffee shops (some attached to crafts and souvenir shops):

Dahlsgården (☎ 72 41 19 89; Mørkstugata 5)

Galleri Thomasgården (☎ 72 41 24 70; Kjerkgata 48; cakes Nkr15-50) Good cakes and pastries.

Trygstads Bakeri (☎ 72 41 10 29; Kjerkgata 12; ⏱ 8.30am-7pm Mon-Fri, 9am-4pm Sat, noon-5pm Sun) Great coffee and pleasant outdoor tables.

Entertainment

The Bergstadens Hotel and Quality Hotel Røros (left) both feature nightclubs, discos, Elton John-favourites piano bars and oc-casional live music with dancing.

Ramm Kjelleren (☎ 72 41 24 11; Kjerkgata 34; ⏱ 7pm-late Wed, Fri & Sat) This wonderfully at-mospheric place occupies the bank vaults of a building dating from the mid-1700s. Cool bar staff, great decoration and a buzzy am-bience when full make for a great evening out. It offers (free) live music on Friday night at around 9pm. A half-litre of beer costs Nkr55, while a glass of wine goes for Nkr45. Highly recommended.

Shopping

Given its unaffected ambience, it isn't sur-prising that Røros has attracted over 40 artists and artisans. The town also has a glass-blower, a copper shop and several general handicraft shops.

Hartzgården Sølvsmie (☎ 72 41 05 50; Kjerkgata; ⏱ 10am-7pm Mon-Fri, 10am-4pm Sat, noon-5pm Sun) Of special interest is this silversmith's shop, where you'll find locally handcrafted sil-ver jewellery with an emphasis on Viking themes, as well as a small historical jewel-lery exhibit.

Galleri Thomasgården (☎ 72 41 24 70; Kjerkgata 48; ⏱ 10am-8pm Mon-Fri, 10am-4pm Sat, noon-6pm Sun) At the worthwhile Galleri Thomasgården, potter Torgeir Henriksen creates rustic stoneware and porcelain. You'll also find the wonderful nature-inspired wood carvings of Henry Solli. The player piano is one of only two in Norway and dates back to 1929.

Getting There & Away

Røros has one **Widerøe** (www.wideroe.no) flight to/from Oslo (from Nkr430) daily except Saturday. There are three daily buses between Oslo (Nkr582, six hours) and Trondheim that stop in Røros. There are several other daily services to/from Trondheim. Røros lies on the eastern railway line between Oslo (Nkr582, five hours) and Trondheim (Nkr215, 2½ hours); for Oslo, you may need to change in Hamar.

Getting Around

In winter, you can opt for a *spark*, a locally popular kick-sled that resembles a dog-sled without the dogs. For summer cycling, you can rent a mountain bike from **Røros Sport** (☎ 72 41 12 18; Bergmannsgata 13).

FEMUNDSMARKA NATIONAL PARK

The national park which surrounds Femunden, Norway's second-largest lake, was formed in 1971 to protect the lake and the forests stretching eastwards to Sweden. This has long been a source of falcons for use in the European and Asian sport of falconry and several places in the park are known as Falkfangerhøgda, or 'falcon hunters' height'. You may also see wild reindeer grazing in the heights and, in summer, a herd of around 30 musk oxen roams the area along the Røa and Mugga Rivers (in winter they migrate to the Funäsdalen area). It's thought that this group split off from an older herd in the Dovrefjell area and wandered all the way here (see the boxed text, p164).

Sleeping

The two main sleeping options are **Johnsgård Turistsenter** (☎ 62 45 99 25; fax 62 45 99 55; Sømådalen; tent sites Nkr100, 4–8-bed cabins Nkr200-550), 9km west of Buvika, and **Langen Gjestegård** (☎ 72 41 37 18; fax 72 41 37 11; Synnervika; s/d Nkr350/500), a cosy turf-roofed farmhouse near the lake.

Getting There & Away

The historic ferry M/S *Fœmund II* sails daily between mid-June and late August from Synnervika (also spelt Søndervika), on the northern shore of lake Femunden, to Elgå (continuing to Buvika Wednesday and Sunday, early July to early August). On Wednesday from mid-July to early August, it continues all the way to Femundsenden, at the lake's southern tip.

From mid-June to late August, buses run between Røros and Synnervika once or twice daily. The 8.15am departure from Røros allows you to cruise around Femunden on *Fœmund II* and return to Røros on the same day. You can reach the southern end of Femunden on the Trysil Ekspressen buses, which runs seven times daily from Hamar to Trysil, via Elverum, then change to buses for Engerdal/Drevsjø.

OPPDAL
pop 3700

Oppdal isn't the most architecturally distinguished town in central Norway, but the beauty of its surrounds more than compensates. As such, it makes a pleasant staging post en route between Lillehammer and Trondheim. Oppdal is also an activity centre *par excellence* and that's why most people come here.

Information

There are two main sources of tourist information in Oppdal. For general tourist information about Oppdal and surrounding districts, the **tourist office** (☎ 72 40 04 70; www .oppdal.com; ☺ 9am-6pm Mon-Fri, 10am-4pm Sat & Sun mid-Jun–mid-Aug) is just a block from the train and bus stations. For more activities-based information, head for **Oppdal Booking** (☎ 72 40 08 00; www.oppdal-booking.no; ☺ 8am-4pm Mon-Fri mid-Jun–mid-Aug, 8am-6pm daily mid-Jan–Easter, shorter hours rest-of-year), which operates as a central reservations service for accommodation and activities; booking fees apply.

Tours

For those with little time, **Oppdal Booking** (☎ 72 40 08 00; www.oppdal-booking.no) organises a Troll & Fjord Tour (adult/child Nkr630/ 315), a day-trip to Trondheim and Kristiansund using train, ferries and bus. It's a little rushed, but it takes the hassle out of arranging your own transport; the train departs at 6.45am and bookings must be made at least one day in advance.

Sleeping

If you're unable to find a bed, contact Oppdal Booking or the tourist office for assistance (above).

Oppdalstunet Vandrerhjem (☎ 72 42 23 11; fax 72 42 23 13; Gamle Kongsvei; dm/s/d Nkr150/370/450; ☺ May-Sep) This place, 1.5km northeast of

CENTRAL NORWAY

OUT AND ABOUT IN OPPDAL

Oppdal could just be Central Norway's capital for adventure activities.

White-water Rafting

The nearby, wild and white Driva offers several excellent rafting runs from May to October. The outdoor adventure company **Opplev Oppdal** (☎ 72 40 41 80; www.opplev-oppdal.no in Norwegian; Olav Skasliens vei 12) organises a range of worthwhile trips. The three-hour Class I–II family trip (adult/family Nkr410/1230) is designed more as a wilderness experience than an adrenaline rush, but you can also opt for half/full-day Class III–IV trips (Nkr520/760) that provide substantial thrills. The more daring can opt for a five-hour river surfing trip (Nkr760). Prices for all of these expeditions increase by Nkr50 on weekends.

The same company also offers canoe rental (Nkr295 per day), canyoning (Nkr760) and low-level rock climbing (adult/child Nkr740/490).

Musk Ox & Elk Safaris

To see the decidedly prehistoric musk ox (see the boxed text, p164), take one of the safaris organised by Oppdal Booking (see p157). They leave every morning (around 10am) from mid-June to mid-August, last for five to six hours and cost Nkr250/100 per adult/child.

The humble elk can also be tracked down by taking an elk safari, which leaves on Wednesday evenings (Nkr275, two to three hours) in summer and can be booked through the tourist office.

Hang-gliding

To get an aerial view of scenic Central Norway, a tandem hang-glide could be just what you need. To find out more, contact **Walter Brandsegg** (☎ 72 42 21 30; walter@brandsegg.no); costs start from around Nkr550 per person.

Skiing & Snowboarding

The three-part Oppdal Skisenter climbs the slopes from Hovden, Stølen and Vangslia, all within easy reach of town. The smaller Ådalen ski area nearby has two lifts. Vangslia is generally the easiest, with a couple of beginners' runs, while Stølen offers intermediate skiing and Hovden has three challenging advanced runs. Lift passes for one/two/three days cost Nkr275/475/625 and a morning/afternoon of skiing is Nkr200/260. The season varies, but generally runs from late November to late April.

---

central Oppdal, offers good hostel accommodation on a gentle rise overlooking the valley.

Quality Oppdal Hotel (☎ 72 40 07 00; post@oppdal-booking.no; Olav Skasliens vei 8; s/d from Nkr840/890) Part of the Nordisk Hotel Pass network, this comfortable hotel offers very pleasant rooms that are a touch overpriced, but easily the best in central Oppdal. There's also a popular bar on the premises.

Sletvold Apartment Hotel (☎ 72 42 23 11; booking@sletvold-stolen.no; Gamle Kongsvei; s/d from Nkr550/690) If you don't mind being on the town's northern fringe, this fine place (part of the Skan Plus hotel pass network) represents excellent value with tidy and appealing rooms, some of which come with views down over the valley.

Eating

Møllen Restaurant & Pizzeria (☎ 72 42 18 00; Dovreveien 2; pasta & kebabs Nkr83-125, small/large pizza from Nkr79/152, fish or meat mains Nkr135-179; ☯ lunch & dinner) Right in the town centre, alongside the E6, this is a good choice if you feel like a sit-down meal that's a cut above hamburgers, but with a reasonable price tag.

Café Ludvik (☎ 72 42 01 40; Inge Krokanns vei 21; mains Nkr75-145) The popular Café Ludvik is also good though with a touch less class. It serves a range of inexpensive light meals, including beef dishes, omelettes and pasta. It's 300m south of the centre.

Perrongen Steak House (☎ 72 40 07 00; starters Nkr86-99, mains Nkr112-239; ☯ lunch & dinner) This place, in the Quality Oppdal Hotel, has the best food and the most sophistication of any place in town. Reindeer steak goes for Nkr239, while the roast mountain trout with broccoli and potatoes (Nkr163) is highly recommended.

Getting There & Away

The best access to Oppdal is via the four or five daily train services between Oslo (Nkr585, 4¾ hours) and Trondheim (Nkr200, 1½ hours). Oppdal lies on the twice-daily Nor-Way Bussekspress route between Bergen (Nkr770, 12½ hours) and Trondheim (Nkr185, two hours).

TROLLHEIMEN

The small Trollheimen range, with a variety of trails through gentle mountains and lake-studded upland regions, is most readily accessed from Oppdal. You can either hitch or hike the 15km from Oppdal up the toll road (Nkr30) to **Osen**, which is the main entrance to the wilderness region. The best map to use is Statens Kartverk's *Turkart Trollheimen* (1:75,000), which costs Nkr120 at the tourist office in Oppdal.

A straightforward hiking destination in Trollheimen is the hut and historic farm at **Vassendsetra**. From Osen (the outlet of the river Gjevilvatnet), 3km north of the main road to Sunndalsøra, you can take the boat *Trollheimen II* all the way to Vassendsetra (Nkr150 return). From July to mid-August it leaves from Osen daily at noon and from Vassendsetra at 3.30pm. Alternatively, you can drive or hike 6km along the road from Osen to the Den Norske Turistforening (DNT) hut, **Gjevilvasshytta**, and follow the lakeshore trail for 12km to Vassendsetra, where you'll find the cabins called **Vassendsetra** (☎ 72 42 32 20; fax 72 42 34 30; dm for DNT members/nonmembers Nkr150/230, breakfast Nkr75/125, dinner Nkr160/200; ☒ Jul & Aug). About midway you'll pass several outstanding sandy beaches, with excellent summer swimming.

The popular three-day 'Trekanten' hut tour follows the impressive route of Gjevilvasshytta–Trollheimshytta–Jøldalshytta–Gjevilvasshytta; contact Oppdal Booking (p157) for details.

RINGEBU

pop 1300

The southernmost small community of Gudbrandsdalen, the narrow river valley which stretches for 200km between lake

Mjøsa and Dombås, Ringebu is worth a short detour for its lovely **stave church** (☎ 61 28 43 50; adult/child Nkr40/20, combined adult/child ticket to the church & vicarage Nkr60/30; ☒ 8am-8pm mid-Jun–mid-Aug, shorter hours rest-of-year). The church, 2km south of town and just off the E6, dates from around 1220, but was restored in the 17th century when the distinctive red tower was attached. Inside, there's a statue of St Laurence dating from around 1250 as well as some crude runic inscriptions. Entrance to the grounds is free. Some 300m uphill to the east, the buildings from 1743 house **Ringebu Samlingene** (☎ 61 28 27 00; adult/child Nkr40/20; ☒ 11am-5pm Tue-Sun mid-Jun–mid-Aug), which served as the vicarage until 1991.

For further information, contact the Ringebu **tourist office** (☎ 61 28 47 00; ☒ 8am-6pm Mon-Thu, 8am-8pm Fri, 10am-1pm Sat, 5-8pm Sun mid-Jun–mid-Aug).

Nor-Way Bussekspress bus routes between Oslo (Nkr305, five hours) and the Western Fjords stop in Ringebu three times daily. Trains to Oslo (Nkr394, 2¾ hours) or Trondheim (Nkr500, 3½ hours) stop in Ringebu four or five times daily.

SJOA

The small settlement of Sjoa, 8km west of Kvam, would have little to detain you were it not for the fact that this is one of the major white-water rafting centres in Norway (see the boxed text, p160).

Most rafting participants stay at **Sjoa Vandrerhjem** (☎ 61 23 62 00; sjoa-vh@online.com; dm Nkr155, 2-bed r incl breakfast Nkr320-420; ☒ mid-May–Sep), an atmospheric hillside hostel. Dinner costs Nkr100 and is served in the wonderful 1747 log-farmhouse building.

The camping ground at **Sæta Camping** (☎ 61 23 51 47; tent/caravan sites Nkr120/160, 1–5-bed huts per person from Nkr330) is down by the riverbank. It is a pleasant grassy site with a front-row seat for some of the minor rapids.

Nor-Way Bussekspress bus routes between Oslo and the Western Fjords pass through Sjoa three times daily.

OTTA

pop 1600

Set deep in Gudbrandsdalen, at the confluence of the Otta and Lågen Rivers, Otta's size makes it a great jumping-off point for hikes in Rondane National Park. The helpful **tourist office** (☎ 61 23 66 50; www.visit

---

WHITE-WATER RAFTING

Sjoa is arguably the white-water rafting capital of Norway. The season runs from the middle of May until the end of September, although it can extend into October if water levels allow. Excursions range from sedate Class I runs (ideal for families) up to thrilling Class Vs. Prices start from Nkr450 for a 3½-hour family trip; there are also half-day trips (from Nkr590) through to seven-hour day trips (from Nkr790), or even two-day expeditions (from Nkr2150) that pass through the roiling waters of the Åsengjuvet canyon.

The main players for this activity, all of whom are recommended:

- **Heidal Rafting** (☎ 61 23 60 37; www.heidalrafting.no; Sjoa) is 1km west of E6 along Rv257.

- **Sjoa Rafting** (☎ 88 00 63 90; www.sjoarafting.com; Nedre Heidal) is 7.5km upstream from Sjoa along Rv257.

- **Norwegian Wildlife & Rafting** (☎ 61 23 87 27; www.nwr.no) is 32km upstream from Sjoa in Randswerk.

- **Go Rafting** (☎ 61 23 50 00; www.gorafting.no) is 3.5km north of Sjoa along the E6.

Most of these companies also organise other activities, including river-boarding, low-level rock climbing, canyoning, caving and hiking, but their main focus remains waterborne thrills.

---

rondane.com; ☺ 8.30am-7pm Mon-Fri, 11am-6pm Sat & Sun mid-Jun–mid-Aug, shorter hours rest-of-year), at the bus/train station, provides local information, including advice on hiking in Rondane National Park. For more information on Rondane National Park, visit the **National Park Centre** (☎ 61 23 14 25; otta@nasjonalparker.org; ☺ 10am-4pm Mon-Fri, 10am-2pm Sat); it's located 50m south of Milano Restaurant.

Sights

The unusual 6m-high natural pillar formations of **Kvitskriuprestene** (White-scree Priests) resemble an assembly of priests and were formed by erosion of an ice age moraine (deposit of material transported by a glacier). Although much of the moraine material has been washed away by the elements, the pillars are protected by capstones. They can be found 4km east along the Nkr10 toll road from Sel towards Mysusæter, and a steep 20-minute hike uphill.

Sleeping

Otta Camping (☎ 61 23 03 09; fax 61 23 38 19; Ottadalen; tent or caravan sites for 2 people Nkr130, 4-bed cabins Nkr300-500) The convenient and popular riverside Otta Camping is a 1.5km walk from the train and bus stations; cross the Otta bridge from the centre, turn right and continue about 1km upstream.

Killis Overnatting (☎ 61 23 04 92; Ola Dahlsgate 35; s/d/tr with shared bathroom Nkr230/250/300) Killis Overnatting has simple rooms (showers cost Nkr5) and is overseen by a delightful woman who'll make you feel at home.

Grand Gjestegård (☎ 61 23 12 00; fax 61 23 04 62; Ola Dahlsgate; s/d smoking Nkr510/670, non-smoking Nkr560/740) Smokers of the world rejoice! You may not be able to indulge your habit in restaurants and you may be made to feel like a social leper just about everywhere else, but here you get a discount! The rooms are comfortable and it's centrally located.

Norlandia Otta Hotell (☎ 61 21 08 00; service@otta .norlandia.no; Ola Dahlsgate 7; s/d Nkr685/890) The best rooms in town are to be found here. They're nothing startling but are well appointed. There's a lively disco on Friday (free) and Saturday (cover charge Nkr50), which appeals to the 18-to-35 crowd.

Eating

There's not a bad sprinkling of restaurants in Otta, all of which are open lunch and dinner daily.

Milano Restaurant & Pizzeria (☎ 61 23 19 93; Storgata 17B; starters Nkr75-85, fish & meat mains Nkr85-175, pasta & pizza from Nkr75) This Italian-run place does the best Italian food in town. Its pizzas are mainly the Italian version, although there are a few thicker, American-style offerings. Highly recommended.

Pillarguri Kafé (☎ 61 23 01 04; Storgata 7; mains Nkr85-165) Another good choice, this place promises a varied menu, with Norwegian fare (reindeer stew costs Nkr138), as well as sushi (individual pieces Nkr35 to Nkr58,

GURI SAVES THE DAY

During the Kalmar War between Sweden and Denmark, when Norway was united with Denmark, 550 Scottish mercenaries arrived in Norway in August 1612 to aid the Swedish cause. Along their route, they had to pass through Gudbrandsdalen. Having learned of the approaching mercenaries, the local peasants armed themselves with axes, scythes and other farming implements. They stacked up rocks and branches across the track to block the route and, to set up a diversion, placed several older men across the river to fire their rifles at the column, using blanks.

As the Scots approached a narrow section of path between the river and a steep hillside at Høgkringom, 3km south of Otta, the heroic Pillarguri (Guri) dashed up the hill to announce their arrival by sounding her shepherd's birch-bark horn. This was the signal for the old farmers to fire. The Scots, confident they'd meet with little resistance, fired back across the river, then responded to Guri's music by waving their hats and playing their bagpipes, unaware of the trap.

As Guri sounded her horn again, more rocks were tumbled across the trail behind the column, blocking any hope of retreat. The farmers attacked with more rocks and their crude weapons, savagely defeating the trapped contingent and making the river flow red with blood.

Only six farmers were killed in the battle and the victors intended to take the 134 surviving Scots as prisoners to Akershus Fortress. However, during the victory celebrations at Kvam, the farmers, who had to get on with their harvest and couldn't be bothered with a tiresome march to Oslo, executed the prisoners one by one.

The ingenuity (and brutality) of the peasant 'army' is still remembered in Otta, where the local *bunad* (national costume) is a distinctly un-Norwegian tartan and there's a statue of Pillarguri near the train station. There's also a war memorial at Kringom commemorating the victory, across the river from which rises the hill Pillarguri, named in honour of the local heroine.

plate Nkr128). It also has a range of cheaper lunch specials.

Otta Kafé (☎ 61 23 03 24; Johan Nygårdsgate 10; snacks Nkr49-89, mains Nkr59-135) Unpretentious options are on offer here, including omelettes, steak, chicken and meatballs.

Self-caterers should visit the Kiwi supermarket on Storgata.

Getting There & Away

Local buses to/from Lom (normal/express Nkr73/92, two/one hours) leave up to six times daily, less often on weekends. NorWay Bussekspress has up to seven buses to/from Lillehammer daily (normal/express Nkr117/160, two hours/1¼ hours) and as many as seven buses to Oslo (express Nkr370, five hours); there are also twice-daily buses to Trondheim (Nkr320, 2½ hours). The town also lies on the Dovre rail line between Oslo (Nkr489, 3¼ hours) and Trondheim (Nkr420, three hours), with at least four services daily.

RONDANE NATIONAL PARK

Henrik Ibsen described the 572-sq-km **Rondane National Park** (Rondane Nasjonal Park; www .visitrondane.com), as 'palace piled upon palace'. It was created in 1962 as Norway's first national park to protect the fabulous Rondane massif, regarded by many as the finest alpine hiking country in Norway. Ancient reindeer-trapping sites and burial mounds provide evidence that the area has been inhabited for thousands of years. Much of the park's glaciated landscape lies above 1400m and 10 rough and stony peaks rise to over 2000m, including the highest, Rondslottet (2178m), and Storronden (2138m). Rondane's range of wildlife includes 28 mammal species – from lemmings to reindeer – and 124 bird species.

For hikers, Rondane provides ample opportunities for high-country exploration and the relatively dry climate is an added bonus. The most accessible route into the park is from the Spranghaugen car park, about 13km uphill along a good road from Otta and via the toll road (Nkr10). From there, it's a straightforward 6km (1½ hour) hike to **Rondvassbu**, where there's a popular, staffed DNT hut; there are also other DNT huts in the park.

From Rondvassbu, it's a five-hour return climb to the summit of Storronden. Alternatively, head for the spectacular view from the more difficult summit of **Vinjeronden** (2044m), then tackle the narrow ridge leading to the neighbouring peak, Rondslottet (about six hours return from Rondvassbu).

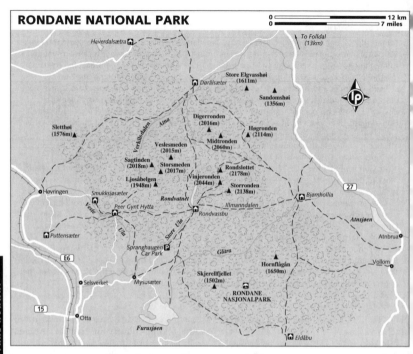

RONDANE NATIONAL PARK

The best maps to use are Statens Kartverk's *Rondane* (1:100,000; Nkr99) and *Rondane Sør* (1:50,000).

Just down the hill from the 'Bom' (toll post) gate is a small shop selling staple provisions and supplies. Camping is permitted anywhere in the national park except at Rondvassbu, where you're restricted to the designated area. **Mysusæter Fjellstue** (☎ 61 23 39 25; Mysusæter; dm Nkr220, d with shared/private bathroom Nkr550/680) promises a basic roof over your head; while the **Rondane Spa Høyfjellshotell** (☎ 61 23 39 33; hotel@rondane.no; Mysusæter; per person with full board from Nkr775) is a comfortable upmarket option with good spa facilities, including pedicures for worn-out hikers' feet.

Getting There & Around

Buses run twice daily between Otta and Mysusæter (Nkr26, 45 minutes), from where it's a further 4km to the car park.

From Rondvassbu, the ferry *Rondegubben* crosses the lake Rondvatnet to Nordvika (Nkr45, 30 minutes) three times daily from early July to late August.

DOMBÅS

pop 1200

Dombås, a popular adventure and winter-sports centre, makes a convenient break for travellers between the highland national parks and the Western Fjords. That said, there's more choice of activities to the north in Oppdal (p158), while for rafting you should head to Sjoa (p160).

Information

Dovrefjell National Park Centre (Dovrefjell Nasjonalparksenter; ☎ 61 24 14 44; dombaas@nasjonalparker .org; Sentralplassen; admission free; ☼ 9am-8pm mid-Jun–mid-Aug, shorter hours rest-of-year) Is an adjunct to the tourist office, although its exhibitions have been incorporated into the neighbouring Trollpark.

Tourist office (☎ 61 24 14 44; www.dovrenett.no; ☼ 9am-8pm mid-Jun–mid-Aug, shorter hours rest-of-year) In Dombås is in a car park in the centre of town.

Sights

The **Dovregubbens Rike Trollpark** (☎ 61 24 12 90; Sentralplassen; adult/child Nkr40/20; ☼ 10am-8pm Mon-Fri, 10am-7pm Sat & 11am-8pm Sun mid-Jun–mid-Aug, 9am-4pm Mon-Fri, 9am-2pm Sat rest-of-year) brings to life the legendary Norwegian trolls and the 'Realm of the Mountain King' (the Dovre massif), inhabited by the friendliest and most powerful troll. There's also a film explaining local natural history and various displays, from stuffed animals and prehistoric hunting techniques to the creation of the national parks in the region.

Tours

Moskus-Safari Dovrefjell (☎ 99 70 37 66; www.moskus-safari.no) offers a range of well-run, guided tours:

Elk Safari This tour (Nkr 200) departs from tourist office from mid-June to mid-August Tuesday, Wednesday and Thursday; advance booking required.

Hiking to Snøhetta This five- to seven-hour (Nkr400) guided hike to the summit of Snøhetta (2286m) takes place on Saturday from mid-June to mid-August; requires a minimum of five people and reservations are essential.

Musk Ox Safari This five-hour tour (Nkr250) departs at 9am from the tourist office from June to August and weekends in September. No advance booking is necessary.

Sleeping & Eating

Bjørkhol Camping (☎ 61 24 13 31; bjorkhol@dovrenett .no; Bjørkhol; tent/caravan sites Nkr80/110, 2-/5-bed cabins with shared bathroom Nkr350/375, 2–4-bed cabins with private bathroom Nkr450) One of Norway's best-value and probably friendliest camping grounds it's found 7km east of Dombås. The facilities are in excellent nick and a bus runs several times daily from Dombås.

Dombås Vandrerhjem Trolltun (☎ 61 24 09 60; firmapost@trolltun.no; dm/s/d incl breakfast Nkr190/ 260/350) This excellent place is about 1.5km off the sinuous E6 from the town centre and offers dinner for Nkr100. Accommodation is simple but tidy and excellent value.

Rica Dombås Hotell (☎ 61 24 10 01; www.dombas-hotel.no; s/d from Nkr445/670) With its commanding position overlooking the valleys, this upmarket choice has light and quite charming rooms and a good restaurant. Ask for a room with a view (south-facing).

Norlandia Dovrefjell Hotell (☎ 61 24 10 05; service@dovrefjell.norlandia.no; s/d from Nkr625/790) This is another fine place with attractive rooms and just far enough removed from the centre to remind you that you're on the fringe of a wilderness area. You'll find it off the E136, about 2km northwest of the centre.

The main commercial complex in the centre includes the popular **Frich's Cafeteria** (☎ 61 24 10 23; Sentralplassen), where you can get everything from sausage and chips (Nkr45) to pepper steak. In the same complex is **Senter-Grillen** (☎ 61 24 18 33; Sentralplassen), which serves pizza. Both places are open from 9am to 11pm daily.

Getting There & Away

Dombås lies on the railway line between Oslo (Nkr515, 3¾ hours) and Trondheim (Nkr350, 2½ hours). It is also the cut-off point for the spectacular Raumabanen line down Romsdalen to Åndalsnes (Nkr195, 1¼ hours), which runs two or three times daily. Åndalsnes (Nkr170, two hours) and Ålesund (Nkr335, 4¼ hours) are served nightly by bus. Nor-Way Bussekspress buses between Bergen (Nkr685, 11¼ hours) and Trondheim (Nkr295, 3¼ hours) call in twice daily in either direction.

DOVREFJELL-SUNNDALSFJELLA NATIONAL PARK

This 4367-sq-km national park, Norway's largest continuous protected area, protects the dramatic highlands around the 2286m-high Snøhetta and provides a suitably bleak habitat for Arctic foxes, reindeer, wolverines and musk oxen (see the boxed text, p164). Snøhetta can be ascended by hikers from Snøheim (allow six hours; left for details on guided hikes). The Knutshøene massif (1690m) section of the park, east of the E6, protects Europe's most diverse intact alpine ecosystem.

The **Fokstumyra marshes**, recently incorporated into the park's boundaries, are home to an astonishing array of birdlife. Approximately 75 species nest in the area and up to 40 others are occasionally observed. Among the more unusual species breeding near the water are the ruff, great snipe, Temminck's stint, whimbrel, great northern diver (loon), lapwing, lesser white-fronted goose and hen harrier. Species which breed in the surrounding hills and forests include the snow bunting, ring ouzel, field fare, purple sandpiper, great grey shrike, dipper, brambling, peregrine falcon, dotterel, short-eared owl, raven and shore lark.

Many of these species can be viewed from the 7km-long marked trail near the Dombås end of the reserve; note that from May to July, visitors are strictly restricted to this trail to prevent disturbance of nesting birds.

MUSK OX

Although a member of the Bovidae family, the musk ox *(Ovibos moschatus)* bears little resemblance to its nearest relations (sheep, goats and cattle) or indeed to any other animal. During the last ice age, it was distributed throughout much of the northern hemisphere's glaciated areas but its range is now much more restricted. Wild herds can be found in parts of Greenland, Canada, Alaska, and the Dovrefjell-Sunndalsfjella and Femundsmarka National Parks in Norway.

The musk ox, weighing between 225kg and 445kg, has incredibly high shoulders and an enormous low-slung head with two broad, flat horns that cross the forehead, curving outwards and downwards before twisting upwards and forwards. Its incredibly thick and shaggy coat, with a matted fleece of soft hair underneath, covers the whole body and hangs down like a skirt to almost reach the ground. Below this hair only the bottom part of the legs protrude, giving the animal a solid, stocky appearance reminiscent of a medieval horse dressed for a joust. This analogy is especially appropriate because, during the rutting season, when the males gather their harems, they repeatedly charge each other, butting their heads together with a crash that's often heard for miles around. This heated battle continues until one animal admits defeat and lumbers off.

Traditionally, the musk ox's main predator has been the wolf; their primary defence is to form a circle with the males on the outside and females and calves inside, trusting in the force of their collective horns to rip open attackers. This defence has proven useless against human hunters, especially the Greenlandic Inuit, and numbers have been seriously depleted. Only with restocking have they been able to thrive again.

In 1931, 10 animals were reintroduced to Dovrefjell from Greenland. Musk oxen all but vanished during WWII, but 23 were transplanted from Greenland between 1947 and 1953. The herd has now grown to around 80 animals and some have shifted eastwards into Femundsmarka National Park to form a new herd.

Musk oxen aren't inherently aggressive toward humans, but an animal that feels threatened ċan charge at speeds of up to 60km/h and woe betide anything that gets in its way. Hikers should stay at least 200m away; if an animal seems agitated or paws at the ground don't run, but back off slowly until it relaxes.

To get there, you can rent a bike from the Dombas tourist office (per hour/day Nkr25/75) or take a taxi (around Nkr170 one way).

Hikers will fare best with the Statens Kartverk map *Dovrefjell* (1:100,000). However, it doesn't include the Knutshø section; for that, you need Statens Kartverk's *Einunna 1519-I* and *Folldal 1519-II* topographic sheets.

Sleeping & Eating

The original DNT Snøheim hut was, thankfully, judged to be too near the army's Hjerkinn firing range and was replaced by the new self-service Reinheim Hut, 5km north and at 1341m, in Stroplsjødalen. DNT also maintains several other self-service huts in the adjacent Skrymtheimen region; keys are available from Dombås tourist office.

Kongsvold Fjeldstue (☎ 72 40 43 40; fax 72 40 43 41; Kongsvold; d from Nkr550) Park information, maps, meals and accommodation are available at this charming and historic place, 13km north of Hjerkinn on the E6. The intriguing early-18th-century timber buildings huddle deep in Drivdalen, 500m from tiny Kongsvold station (trains stop only on request). Breakfast, lunch and dinner are possible in the attached cafeteria.

Hjerkinn Fjellstue (☎ 61 24 29 27; fax 61 24 29 49; Hjerkinn; s/d Nkr750/950) This cosy inn is about 1.5km east of Hjerkinn on Rv29. There's also a restaurant and camping is available.

Getting There & Away

There's no public transport into the park, although tours from Dombås offer musk ox safaris (see p163). The only public transport between Dombås and Hjerkinn is by train (Nkr72, 25 minutes).

VÅGÅ

pop 1500

Vågå surprises passers-by with its wealth of old log and timber buildings. The original wooden stave church was constructed around 1150 with a single nave and stood 300m west of the present cruciform **church**

(Vågå Sentrum; adult/child Nkr30/free; ☺ 9am-7pm Mon-Sat, 11am-7pm Sun Jun-Aug, closes 8pm Jul), which was constructed between 1625 and 1630. On the wall at the entrance, you'll see carved wooden panels from the ancient church, which mostly represent animal subjects. The baptismal font also dates from the original church, and the early Gothic crucifix is from the 13th century.

For tourist information, contact the very helpful **tourist office** (☎ 61 23 82 90; Edvard Storms veg 4; www.visitvaga.no; ☺ 11am-5pm Mon-Thu, 10am-5pm Fri, 10am-4pm Sat & noon-4pm Sun mid-Jun–mid-Aug); it also has information (and sells maps) for Jotunheimen National Park. Outside summer, call ☎ 61 23 78 80 for tourist information.

WESTERN CENTRAL NORWAY

LOM

Lom, straddling the river Bøvra at the Prestfossen waterfall, is a crossroads town which stands at the junction to roads leading to Geiranger (p234) and the spectacular Jotunheimen National Park (p167). It can get pretty crowded but that's because it's a great place to base yourself for a few days. Lom also has enough of its own charms to warrant an afternoon's wander.

Information

The knowledgeable and helpful Lom **tourist office** (☎ 61 21 29 90; www.visitlom.com; ☺ 9am-9pm Mon-Fri, 10am-8pm Sat & Sun mid-Jun–mid-Aug, shorter hours rest-of-year), in the Norwegian Mountain Museum, readily dispenses advice, brochures and answers to questions you hadn't yet thought of. Visitors can purchase a Fellesbillet (adult/child Nkr80/free), which includes admission to the stave church, the Presthaugen Bygdemuseum and the Norwegian Mountain Museum.

The tourist office also provides Internet access (per minute Nkr1).

If you're around for a while, pick up the *Nature and Culture Guide for Lom* (Nkr48) written by Torgeir Garmo, which contains an exhaustive rundown on local trails and attractions. It's available at the Fossheim Steinsenter. Hiking maps are sold at the tourist office.

Sights
LOM STAVKYRKJE

This lovely 12th-century Norman-style stave **church** (☎ 61 21 73 38; adult/child Nkr40/free; ☺ 9am-8pm daily mid-Jun–mid-Aug, 10am-4pm mid-May–mid-Jun & mid-Aug–mid-Sep), in the centre of town, is one of Norway's finest, a fact enhanced by its location on a rise by the water. Still the functioning local church, it was constructed in 1170, extended in 1634 and given its current cruciform shape with the addition of two naves in 1663. Guided tours explain the interior paintings (from around 1700) and Jakop Sæterdalen's chancel arch and pulpit (from 1793). At night, the church is subtly lit to fairy-tale effect. Entry to the grounds is free.

In the adjacent souvenir shop, there's a small **museum** (admission Nkr10) about the stave church; it's open the same hours as the church and there are plans for an expanded exhibit.

FOSSHEIM STEINSENTER

Don't miss the humorous exhibit on compulsive collectors at the **Fossheim Steinsenter** (☎ 61 21 14 60; www.fossheimsteinsenter.no; admission free; ☺ 9am-8pm Mon-Sat, 9am-7pm Sun mid-Jun–mid-Aug, 9am-6pm mid-Aug–mid-Nov & mid-Mar–mid-Jun, 10am-3pm Mon-Fri rest-of-year), a rewarding and memorable place. It combines Europe's largest selection of rare and beautiful rocks, minerals, fossils, gems and jewellery for sale and on display, but it also includes a large museum of Norwegian and foreign geological specimens.

The knowledgeable owners of the centre, both avid rock collectors, travel the world in search of specimens but they're especially proud of the Norwegian national stone, thulite. It was discovered in 1820 and is now quarried in Lom; the reddish colour is derived from traces of manganese.

NORWEGIAN MOUNTAIN MUSEUM

Acting as the visitors centre for Jotunheimen National Park, this worthwhile **mountain museum** (Norsk Fjellmuseum; ☎ 61 21 16 00; adult/child Nkr60/free; ☺ 9am-9pm Mon-Fri, 10am-8pm Sat & Sun mid-Jun–mid-Aug, shorter hours rest-of-year) contains mountaineering memorabilia, as well as exhibits on natural history and cultural and industrial activity in the Norwegian mountains; the woolly mammoth is a highlight. There's also an excellent 10-minute mountain slide show, a discussion of tourism and its impact on wilderness and, upstairs, a scale model of the park.

PRESTHAUGEN OPEN-AIR MUSEUM

Behind the Mountain Museum, this **museum** (Presthaugen Bygde-museum; ☎ 61 21 19 33; Lom; adult/child Nkr20/free; ☺ noon-5pm Jul–mid-Aug, noon-4pm last week of Jun & 2nd half Aug) is a collection of 19th-century farm buildings, several *stabbur* (elevated storehouses), an old hut (it's claimed that St Olav slept here) and an example of a summer mountain dairy. Watch out particularly for the exhibition on early irrigation methods in highland Norway.

Activities

Although the serious hiking takes place in the neighbouring Jotunheimen National Park (see p167 for details), there are several **hiking trails** closer to town, including some with excellent views of Ottadalen and Bøverdalen. A popular route is the 3km return loop up Lomseggi (1289m) to the century-old stone cottage called Smithbue, once occupied by Fridjof Smith, a 19th-century German artist; the tourist office can provide maps and route descriptions.

For something a touch more fast-paced, contact **Lom Rafting** (☎ 95 80 90 90; www.lomrafting.no), which has an office adjacent to the bridge in the centre of town. Prices start from Nkr450 for family trips.

Tours

The Lom **tourist office** (☎ 61 21 29 90; www.visitlom.com) can arrange two- to three-hour guided tours of the town for groups, with an emphasis on the history and local culture.

Sleeping

Apart from the huts at Nordal Turistsenter, there is no budget accomodation, so travellers will need to continue on up the valley to Bøverdalen (p167). For everyone else, there are a handful of appealing options.

Nordal Turistsenter (☎ 61 21 93 00; www.nordalturistsenter.no; tent sites Nkr110, 4-bed hut with shared bathroom Nkr350, 8-bed cabin with private bathroom Nkr1100, s/d Nkr750/1050) It offers a range of accommodation in a good location, by the water in the heart of town.

Fossheim Turisthotell (☎ 61 21 95 00; www.fossheimhotel.no; s Nkr700-825, d Nkr850-1080, 4-bed apt Nkr1500) At the eastern end of town is this

excellent and cosy traditional-style hotel. There are simple rooms in an annexe, very pleasant, well-appointed rooms in the main building, and the apartments, featuring modern design in a former barn, are the last word in luxury and offer great views across town.

Fossberg Hotell (☎ 61 21 22 50; www.fossberg.no; s/d from Nkr695/1090) Not quite up to the same standard as the Fossheim Hotell, this is nonetheless an appealing place, smack-bang in the centre of town. The rooms come with pine furniture and there's a gymnasium for use by guests.

Eating

Fossberg Hotell (☎ 61 21 22 50; snacks & mains Nkr45-215; ☺ lunch & dinner) This cafeteria-style place is always busy, especially for its outdoor tables. The food's nothing to write home about but at least it's a pleasant place to do so.

Kræmarhuset (☎ 61 21 15 60; mains Nkr89-159; ☺ 10am-11pm) Centrally located, Kræmarhuset specialises in traditional Norwegian mountain fare, but without the flourishes of the Fossheim Turisthotell.

The Nordal Turistsenter has a popular *gatekjøkken* (a place that sells greasy fast food). The fish and chips is only Nkr35.

THE AUTHOR'S CHOICE

Humble Lom boasts one of the finest restaurants in Norway: the **Fossberg Turisthotell** (☎ 61 21 22 50; ☺ lunch & dinner). People travel from all over the country to taste the traditional Norwegian meals, which follow in the footsteps of the former owner, renowned chef Arne Brimi. His specialities include wild trout, reindeer, elk and ptarmigan. The lunch buffets are highly recommended (from Nkr225), while the evening meals consist of set menus; the standard meal costs Nkr300, while Arne Brimi's speciality menu costs Nkr485. There's also a lovely terraced garden area where cheaper (but still top-notch) dishes are available for Nkr80 to Nkr160. Opening times can be a bit erratic outside summer so ring ahead. Just across the car park is **Brimi Bue** (☎ 61 21 95 92; ☺ 9am-9pm mid-Jun–mid-Aug), where you'll find the great chef's recipe books, homeware lines and organic foods.

It's a hang-out for local youth. The affiliated **Nordalsfjoset Pub** (☎ 61 21 93 08), in an old two-storey barn, serves up pizza from Nkr135 and the usual range of alcoholic beverages.

Getting There & Away
The thrice daily Nor-Way Bussekspress service between Oslo (Nkr475, 6½ hours) and Måløy (Nkr325, 4½ hours) passes through Lom. It's also on Ottadalen Billag's summer route between Otta (Nkr85, one hour) and Sogndal (Nkr215, 3½ hours, two daily), which serves Sognefjellet Rd.

JOTUNHEIMEN NATIONAL PARK
The high peaks and glaciers of the Jotunheimen National Park (1145 sq km) are Norway's best-loved and busiest wilderness destination. Hiking routes lead from ravine-like valleys and past deep lakes, plunging waterfalls and 60 glaciers to the tops of all the peaks in Norway over 2300m, including Galdhøpiggen (the highest peak in northern Europe at 2469m), Glittertind (2452m) and Store Skagastølstind (2405m). DNT

maintains staffed huts along most of the wilderness routes and there's also a choice of private lodges by the main roads.

For park information, contact Lom **tourist office** (☎ 61 21 29 90; www.visitlom.com).

Sights & Activities
SOGNEFJELLET ROAD
Snaking through the park – and providing access to many of the trailheads – is the high and stunningly scenic Sognefjellet Rd (Rv55), billed as 'the road over the roof of Norway'. It connects Lustrafjorden with Lom and was constructed in 1939 by unemployed youth to a height of 1434m. This makes it the highest mountain road in northern Europe, thereby providing those with a vehicle a taste of some of Norway's finest mountain scenery.

Access from the southwest is via the multiple hairpin bends climbing up beyond the tree line to **Turtagrø**, with a wonderful vista of the **Skagastølstindane** mountains on your right. If you're coming from Lom, the ascent is more gradual, following beautiful **Bøverdalen**, the valley of the Bøvra river, with its

CENTRAL NORWAY

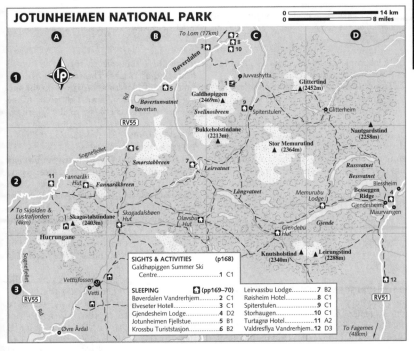

JOTUNHEIMEN NATIONAL PARK

0 ————— 14 km
0 ————— 8 miles

HIKING IN JOTUNHEIMEN

Jotunheimen's hiking possibilities are practically endless and all are spectacular. The best maps by far are Statens Kartverk's *Jotunheimen Aust* and *Jotunheimen Vest* (1:50,000; Nkr95 each). The tourist office in Lom can offer advice and some route descriptions, as well as organising guided hikes throughout the national park.

Krossbu

Krossbu, near the head of Bøverdalen, lies at the outset of a tangle of hiking routes, including a short day trip to the Smørstabbreen glacier.

Galdhøpiggen

With its tangle of dramatic cirques, arêtes and glaciers, this is a fairly tough eight-hour day hike from Spiterstulen, with 1470m of ascent. Although the trail is well marked, you'll need a map and compass.

Øvre Årdal

From Øvre Årdal you may want to head 12km northeast up the Utladalen valley to the farm Vetti, from where hiking tracks lead to Vettisfossen (275m), usually described as Norway's highest free-falling waterfall, and also to the little-visited, unstaffed hut at Stølsmaradalen. This is also an alternative access route, via upper Utladalen, to longer hikes in Jotunheimen.

The Hurrungane

The fabulous Hurrungane massif rises darkly above the westernmost end of the park. Most experienced mountaineers will be able to pick their way to some of these prominent peaks – with several even accessible to skilled scramblers.

For an amenable hiking experience, however, most people would prefer to head eastwards from Turtagrø. From the hotel, a four-hour hike will take you to Norway's highest DNT hut, Fannaråki, on the summit of Fannaråken (2069m), with fabulous views. To get started, walk about

little lakes, glacial rivers, grass-roofed huts and patches of pine forest.

The road summit on **Sognefjell** offers superb views of mountain lakes, glaciers and snowy peaks.

The snow doesn't normally melt until at least early July, and at higher elevations drivers should prepare for new snow at any time of year. The road can get very narrow, but there are plenty of places to pull over and allow cars to pass (and not to mention to admire the spectacular view). You'll also find ample camping and other accommodation options lining the road (see p169).

From mid-June to late August, Ottadalen Billag buses (Nkr215, 3½ hours, two daily) run between Otta and Sogndal via Sognefjellet Rd.

GALDHØPIGGEN SUMMER SKI CENTRE

Juvvashytta hut serves as the gateway to this **ski centre** (☎ 61 21 17 50; fax 61 21 21 72), at 1850m on the icy heights of Norway's highest mountain. From Galdesand on the Rv55,

follow the Galdhøpiggen road (Nkr70 toll) to its end at 1841m. The season runs from June to mid-November. Apart from the skiing opportunities, this road takes you to the highest point reachable by road in Norway.

SCENIC DRIVES
Turtagrø to Øvre Årdal

The toll mountain road between **Turtagrø** and the industrial town of **Øvre Årdal** is one of Norway's most scenic short drives. Open from late May to October, it leads across high, wild and treeless country. From late June to late August, the route is served by bus once daily (Nkr100, one hour). The vehicle toll of Nkr50 is collected at the pass. For tourist information, contact **Årdal Reiselivslag** (☎ 57 66 11 77).

Nor-Way Bussekspress runs once daily between Lillehammer (Nkr280, four hours) and Bergen (Nkr300, 4¾ hours) via Øvre Årdal. Local and express buses also run six to nine times daily to/from Sogndal (Nkr101, 1½ hours) and every hour or two

500m up the road and follow the track up Helgedalen. At Ekrehytta hut, a narrow track starts a steep 800m climb to the top.

You can either return the way you came or descend the eastern slope along the well-marked track to Keisarpasset and thence back to Ekrehytta. To launch into a multiday trip, you can also descend Gjertvassdalen to Skogadalsbøen hut and, once there, choose from one of many routes eastwards through Jotunheimen.

Besseggen

No discussion of hiking in Jotunheimen would be complete without a mention of Besseggen ridge, the most popular hike in Norway. Indeed, it could even be described as *too* popular, with at least 30,000 hikers in the three months a year that it's passable. If you want to avoid the crowds, choose another route, but if you don't mind sacrificing solitude for one of Norway's most spectacular trips, you probably won't regret it. Henrik Ibsen wrote of Besseggen: 'It cuts along with an edge like a scythe for miles and miles...And scars and glaciers sheer down the precipice to the glassy lakes, 1600 feet below on either side.' So daunting did it appear to him, that one of Peer Gynt's mishaps was a plunge down to the lake on the back of a reindeer.

The day hike between Gjendesheim and Memurubu Lodge takes about six hours and climbs to a high point of 1743m. From Gjendesheim hut, follow the DNT-marked track towards Glitterheim for about 30 minutes, where a left fork strikes off up the Veltløyfti gorge, which leads upward onto the level Veslefjellet plateau.

After a short descent from the plateau, the track leads you onto the Besseggen ridge, which slices between the deep-blue lake Bessvatnet and the 18km long glacier-green lake Gjende, coloured by the 20,000 tonnes of glacial silt which are dumped into it each year by the Memuru river.

Besseggen is never less than 10m wide and only from a distance does it look precarious. After passing the head of Bessvatnet, the route passes a small plateau lake, Bjørnbøltjørn, and shortly thereafter begins its descent to the modern chalet-style Memurubu Lodge.

Once there, you can decide whether to take the boat M/S *Gjende* back to Gjendesheim (Nkr67, 30 minutes, five daily in summer), continue west to Gjendebu hut, either on foot or on the boat (Nkr67, 30 minutes), or hike north to Glitterheim.

to/from Lærdal (Nkr67, one hour). Express buses to/from Oslo (Nkr410, six hours) run two or three times daily.

Randen to Fagernes

Between Randsverk and Fagernes, the Rv51 climbs through the hilly and forested Sjodalen country onto a vast wild upland with far-ranging views of peaks and glaciers. It's one of Norway's most scenic mountain routes and is used by lots of hikers heading for Jotunheimen's eastern reaches.

The first DNT hut at **Gjendesheim** was constructed in 1878, but most of the current building dates from 1935 to 1937. It's the launching point for the very popular day hike along the Besseggen ridge.

From mid-June to early September, there are two daily buses between Otta and Gol, via Vågå, Randen, Gjendesheim, Valdresflya and Fagernes. You'll have to change buses at Gjendesheim. From Otta, the trip to Gjendesheim takes two hours and costs Nkr81. Valdresflya is just 15 minutes further.

Sleeping & Eating

The following places all lie on, or are accessible from Juvvashytta hut the Sognefjellet Rd, starting from those closest to Lom.

Spiterstulen (☎ 61 21 14 80; fax 61 21 19 72; Spiterstulen; tent sites per person Nkr60, s/d with shared bathroom Nkr350/450) The private Spiterstulen lodge, at an old *sæter* (summer dairy), is convenient for access to Galdhøpiggen. The poorly maintained toll road to Spiterstulen costs Nkr60 per vehicle. On foot, you can approach on the five-hour marked route from Leirvassbu hut, further west.

Bøverdalen Vandrerhjem (☎ /fax 61 21 20 64; Bøverdalen; dm Nkr110, s/d with shared bathroom Nkr200/270, with shower Nkr390/490; ☷ Jun-Sep) This fine riverside hostel has a small café, tidy rooms and delightful surrounds to enjoy once the day-trippers have returned home.

Røisheim Hotel (☎ 61 21 20 31; www.roisheim.no; Bøverdalen; s/d from Nkr890/990) This charming place combines rustic, historical buildings with modern comforts. Quite simply, it's a wonderful place to stay.

Storhaugen (☎ /fax 61 21 20 69; Bøverdalen; self-catering house from Nkr525, cabins Nkr350-1500) A highly recommended upmarket alternative is this friendly farm run by Marit and Magner Slettede. It's a traditional-style timber farm with views of both the Jotunheimen heights and Bøverdalen. At Galdesand, turn south on the Galdhøpiggen road and continue 1.5km to the signposted right turn-off for Storhaugen.

Elvesæter Hotell (☎ 61 21 20 00; Bøverdalen; s/d Nkr750/750, dinner Nkr225) This comfortable hotel is high on novelty value, adjacent as it is to the Sagasøyla, a 32m-high carved wooden pillar tracing Norwegian history from unification in 872 to the 1814 constitution.

Leirvassbu Lodge (☎ 61 21 29 32; fax 61 21 29 21; dm DNT members/nonmembers Nkr130/140, s/d with private bathroom Nkr310/540) Leirvassbu, a typical mountain lodge at 1400m and beside lake Leirvatnet, is a good base for hiking in Jotunheimen; guided glacier walks on Smørstabbreen cost Nkr500. Despite its large capacity, it can get crowded, especially in high season. The toll on the access road is Nkr40 per car.

Jotunheimen Fjellstue (☎ 61 21 29 18; www.jotunheimen-fjellstue.no; s Nkr600-750, d Nkr1200-1500, half board per person from Nkr895) This modern mountain lodge has a lovely location, good rooms and decent food.

Krossbu Turiststasjon (☎ 61 21 29 22; fax 61 21 26 80; r Nkr400-600) At this roadside lodge, the larger rooms have attached bath and dinner is available. Guided glacier hikes and courses cost Nkr250 (four to six hours).

Turtagrø Hotel (☎ 57 68 08 00; www.turtagro.no; s/d Nkr1010/1280, tower r Nkr1275/1640, full board from Nkr1255/1810; 🖳) This historic hiking and mountaineering centre is a friendly and laid-back base for exploring Jotunheimen/Hurrungane. The main building was completely destroyed by fire in 2001, but a new building with discreet modern design has arisen in its place, with wonderful views and supremely comfortable rooms. It also conducts week-long climbing courses, guided day trips (hiking, climbing and skiing) and has laid out new hiking routes. There's also a great bar full of historic Norwegian mountaineering photos. The dining room serves excellent hearty meals (daily special Nkr89, available until late afternoon), and the library has Internet access.

Across the mountains on the eastern side of the park, you'll find the popular

Gjendesheim Lodge (☎ 61 23 89 10; fax 61 23 89 65; beds DNT members Nkr90-185, nonmembers Nkr150-235) and the quiet, well-run hostel **Valdresflya Vandrerhjem** (☎ 94 10 70 21; Valdresflya; dm/s/d Nkr130/225/280), about 15 minutes' drive south from Gjendesheim. The latter place prides itself on being the highest hostel in northern Europe, at 1389m. There's no guest kitchen but breakfast/dinner costs Nkr60/105 and there's a daytime café serving excellent waffles to passers-by.

HARDANGERVIDDA

The bleak and desolately beautiful Hardangervidda plateau, part of the 3430-sq-km Hardangervidda National Park, is home to wonderful tundra landscapes and Norway's largest herd of wild reindeer (caribou). Long a trade and travel route connecting eastern and western Norway, it's now crossed by the main railway and road routes between Oslo and Bergen.

Old snow lingers here until early August and new snow is a possibility at any time of year, but the region is best known for its hiking opportunities and altitude-stretched cross-country ski season. For details of adventure possibilities on the plateau, see the boxed text (p138) or visit the Hardangervidda National Park Centre (p136).

Hikers and skiers will find essential the Statens Kartverk maps *Hardangervidda Øst* and *Hardangervidda Vest*, both at a scale of 1:100,000.

GEILO
pop 2300

At Geilo (pronounced *Yei*-lo), midway between Oslo and Bergen, you can practically step off the train onto a ski lift. In summer, there's plenty of fine hiking in the area. A popular nearby destination is the expansive plateau-like mountain called Hallingskarvet, frosted with several small glaciers. For more information, contact the Geilo **tourist office** (☎ 32 09 59 00; turistinfo@geilo .no; 🕐 9am-9pm Mon-Fri, 9am-5pm Sat & Sun Jul–mid-Aug, shorter hours mid-Aug–Jun).

Activities
Geilo Aktiv (☎ 32 09 39 50; tore.haugen@geiloaktiv .com) offers Glacier trekking on Hardangerjøkulen (1862m) three times weekly from July

to mid-September. The standard 10-hour tour (including train to/from Finse) costs Nkr575 per person. The company also offers a variety of rafting tours (Nkr650 to Nkr800), river-boarding (Nkr700 to Nkr800) and a two-hour moose safari (Nkr375) once a week.

Sleeping & Eating
For its size, Geilo has a boggling choice of accommodation options, most of which is geared towards the outdoor-activity and adventure crowds. The tourist office has a list of full details and prices for the different accommodation types.

Some of the more reasonable options include: **Øen Turistsenter & Geilo Vandrerhjem** (☎ 32 08 70 60; geilo.hostel@vandrerhjem.no; Lienvegen 137; dm Nkr130-160, d Nkfr400-500, breakfast Nkr60); **Haugen Hotell** (☎ 32 09 06 44; fax 32 09 03 87; Gamleveien 16; s/d from Nkr500/790), one of the best-value summer hotels 500m from the centre; and **Ro Hotell & Kro** (☎ 32 09 08 99; fax 32 09 07 85; Geilovegen 55; s/d Nkr525/690, dinner mains from Nkr85).

There's also a Rimi supermarket between the tourist office and the main road through town.

Getting There & Around
The only long-distance bus service connects Geilo with Kongsberg (Nkr235, 3¼ hours) once or twice daily. Many visitors arrive on the train between Oslo (Nkr450, 3½ hours) and Bergen (Nkr390, three hours).

FINSE
Heading west from Geilo, the railway line climbs 600m through a tundra-like landscape of lakes and snowy peaks to Finse, lying at 1222m near the Hardangerjøkulen icecap. This region offers nordic skiing in winter and hiking in summer, including the popular four-hour trek to the Blåisen glacier tip of Hardangerjøkulen. The great three- or four-day Finse–Aurland trek follows Aurlandsdalen down to Aurlandsfjorden and has a series of DNT and private mountain huts a day's walk apart. The nearest is Finsehytta, 200m from Finse station. For more on this route, see p214.

Sights
FINSE NAVVIES MUSEUM
East of Finse station, this **museum** (Rallarmuseet Finse; ☎ 56 52 69 66; adult/child Nkr40/20; ⌚ 10am-

8pm Jul-Sep) documents the history of the Oslo–Bergen railway and the 15,000 people who engineered and built this hard-won line in 2.5 million worker days.

RALLARVEGEN
The Rallarvegen, or Navvies' Rd, was constructed as a supply route for Oslo–Bergen railway workers (the railway opened on 27 November 1909). Nowadays, this 80km route of asphalt and gravel extends from Haugastøl through Finse to Flåm, with a 43km branch from the Upsete end of the Gravhals tunnel and down the Raundal valley to Voss. The section from Storurdivatn to Myrdal via Finse passes through some lovely highland plateau country and is open only to bicycles and foot traffic, while sections down the Flåm and Raundal valleys are also open to vehicle traffic. The popular stretch between Vatnahalsen and Flåm descends 865m in 29km, with an initial series of hairpin bends.

Cyclists and hikers will find optimum conditions between mid-July and mid-September, after the snow has melted. Most people do the route from east to west due to the significant altitude loss.

Sleeping & Eating
Most budget travellers stay at the staffed DNT hut, **Finsehytta** (☎ 56 52 67 32; dm DNT members Nkr90-190, nonmembers Nkr160-240), while the friendly **Finse 1222** (☎ 56 52 71 00; booking@finse1222.no; full board Nkr850-1100) offers comfortable rooms in sight of the glacier, and a good three-course dinner.

Getting There & Away
Five daily trains run between Oslo (Nkr480, 4½ hours) and Bergen (Nkr310, 2¼ hours).

MYRDAL
West of Finse, Myrdal is the junction of the Oslo–Bergen railway and the spectacularly steep Flåmbanen railway, and is a famous stop on the 'Norway in a Nutshell' tour. The dramatic Flåmbanen line twists its way 20km down to Flåm on Aurlandsfjorden, an arm of Sognefjorden. It connects with ferries to Gudvangen, via the spectacular Nærøyfjorden, from where a connecting bus follows the scenic road to Voss. For more information, see p211 or p404.

172

Bergen & the Southwestern Fjords

CONTENTS

From remote farms high on the cliffs of a fjord to buzzing waterfront cafés in sophisticated cities, the argument could be made that this is Norway's finest corner.

Seemingly everywhere you look, there are astonishing, breathtaking views. Hardangerfjord, with its wonderfully green shores, almost seems manicured compared to its counterparts further north, and there are some lovely villages from which to explore, most notably Eidfjord and Ulvik. The iconic and hauntingly beautiful Lysefjord is home to the world-famous and perilous lookout points of Preikestolen (Pulpit Rock) and Kjeragbolten, which add a touch of danger to the otherwise sedate fjord experience. There's nothing sedate about Voss, a capital for Norway's extreme-sports fraternity.

The region's two largest cities, Bergen and Stavanger, serve as the gateways to the southwestern fjords, and are everything that Oslo is not – architecturally distinguished, historically fascinating and vibrantly cosmopolitan. Bergen is quite simply a gem, one of the world's most beautiful cities, with a rich history of seafaring trade and an abundant heritage of historic buildings to remind you of its past at every turn. Stavanger may be one of Norway's most underrated cities, but it's a feel-good city with a wealth of attractions and some exceptional architecture near its pretty harbour.

While the rest of the country has so much to offer, you could easily spend all of your time here and still feel like you've seen the best that Norway has to offer.

HIGHLIGHTS

- Strolling through the historic **Bryggen** (p177) trading district in Bergen, a Unesco World Heritage site
- Soaking up the clamour and great food at the renowned waterfront **Torget market** (p175)
- Climbing to **Preikestolen** (p206) or **Kjeragbolten** (p207)
- Relaxing on a slow boat up **Hardangerfjord** (p189)
- Ambling through cosmopolitan Stavanger, particularly the historic timber houses of **Old Stavanger** (p198)
- Plummeting to earth or down the rapids in the high-octane thrills of **Voss** (p189)

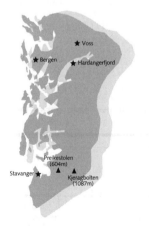

| AREA: 23,515 SQ KM | HIGHEST ELEVATION: FOLGEFONN (1654M) | POPULATION: 833,900 |

Getting There & Around

Bergen is one of the most well-connected cities in Norway, nowhere more spectacularly than on the stunning Oslo–Bergen Railway (p13). Getting around makes a nonsense of the challenging terrain with tunnels cutting through the mountains ferries always waiting to carry you across the water. Don't omit to collect your copy of *Fjord Norway Travel Guide* (free) from the Bergen tourist office (p175), or visit www.fjordnorway.com, both of which have extensive transport (and accommodation) information.

BERGEN

pop 212,600

Bergen is a wonderful, beautiful city. With the Unesco World Heritage–listed Bryggen, exceptional old houses, vibrant fish market, cable cars offering stunning views, great museums, and dynamic cultural life, Bergen amply rewards as much time as you can give it. Norway's second-largest city, Bergen also somehow manages to retain a pleasantly slow pace of life.

History

During the 12th and 13th centuries, Bergen served as Norway's capital. Despite the fact that 70% of the population was wiped out by the Black Death in 1349, by the early 17th century Bergen served as the trading hub of Scandinavia and had also become the country's most populous city, with 15,000 people.

The peninsula on which Bergen resides is surrounded by seven mountains and seven fjords, ensuring a history closely tied to the sea. It became one of the central ports of the Hanseatic League, which dominated northern European trade during the late Middle Ages and which bequeathed to Bergen its picturesque waterfront (see the boxed text, p177).

Orientation

Hilly greater Bergen has suburbs radiating out onto outlying peninsulas and islands, but the central area remains pleasantly compact and easily manageable on foot. The bus and train stations lie only a block apart on Strømgaten, a 10-minute walk southeast from the ferry terminals. Most of the restaurants, hotels, museums, tourist sites and picturesque streets and passages cluster around Vågen, the inner harbour.

Information

BOOKSHOPS

Norli (Map pp178-9; ☎ 55 90 90 40; Torgalmenningen 7; ⏱ 9am-8pm Mon-Fri, 9am-4pm Sat) Great selection of travel and English-language books.

EMERGENCIES

Ambulance (☎ 113)
Police (☎ 112)

INTERNET ACCESS

Bergen Internet Café (Map pp178-9; Kong Oscars Gate 2B; per hr Nkr45; ⏱ 9am-11pm)

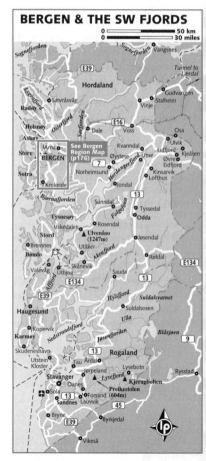

BERGEN & THE SW FJORDS

Bergen Library (Map pp178-9; ☎ 55 56 85 00; Strømgaten 6; free access; ☻ 10am-6pm Mon-Thu, 10am-4.30pm Fri, 10am-3pm Sat)
Bergen Print Shop (Map pp178-9; ☎ 55 32 72 48; Torggaten 11; per 15 min/hr Nkr15/45; ☻ 9am-4pm Mon-Fri)
Cyberhouse (Map pp178-9; Hollendergaten 3; per hr Nkr50; ☻ 9am-11pm)

LAUNDRY
Jarlens Vaskoteque (Map pp178-9; ☎ 55 32 55 04; Lille Øvregaten 17; wash/detergent/dry Nkr45/Nkr5/Nkr15; ☻ 10am-6pm Mon, Tue & Fri, 10am-8pm Wed & Thu, 10am-3pm Sat) Full service takes two hours.

LEFT LUGGAGE
Lockers at the train and bus stations station start at Nkr30.

LIBRARY
Bergen Library (Map pp178-9; ☎ 55 56 85 00; Strømgaten 6; ☻ 10am-6pm Mon-Thu, 10am-4.30pm Fri, 10am-3pm Sat) Good selection of foreign newspapers.

MEDICAL SERVICES
Legevakten Medical Clinic (Map pp178-9; ☎ 55 56 87 00; Vestre Strømkaien 19; ☻ 24hr) Handles emergencies.
Pharmacy (Map pp178-9; ☎ 55 21 83 84; Bus station; 8am-11pm Mon-Sat, 10am-11pm Sun)

MONEY
You can change money at the post office, tourist office (3% less than bank rates) or at any of the many banks (most with ATMs) dotted around the centre.

POST
Main post office (Map pp178-9; Småstrandgaten; ☻ 8am-8pm Mon-Fri, 9am-6pm Sat mid-Jun–mid-Aug, shorter hours rest-of-year)

TOURIST INFORMATION
Bergen Turlag DNT office (Map pp178-9; ☎ 55 32 22 30; fax 55 32 81 15; Tverrgaten 4; ☻ 10am-4pm Mon-Wed, 10am-6pm Thu, 10am-4pm Fri, 10am-2pm Sat) For maps and information on hiking and hut accommodation throughout the Bergen region, contact this place.
Bryggen Visitor Centre (Besøkssenter; Map pp178-9; ☎ 92 08 93 53; Bryggen 19; adult/child Nkr20/free; ☻ 9am-6pm Jun-Aug) The place to visit to find out more about Bryggen.
Tourist office (Map pp178-9; ☎ 55 55 20 00; www.visit Bergen.com; Vågsallmenningen 1; ☻ 8.30am-10pm Jun-Aug, 9am-8pm May & Sep, 9am-4pm Mon-Sat Oct-Apr) This place is, not surprisingly, one of the best and busiest in the country. The office distribute a free *Bergen Guide*

booklet which is an essential companion for exploring Bergen; it's also available at many hotels. The office is in the hall of the old Den Norske Bank (1862). While you're waiting, take a look at the three frescoed walls painted by Axel Revold between 1921 and 1923.

TRAVEL AGENCIES
Kilroy Travel (Map pp178-9; ☎ 02633; www.kilroy travels.com; Vaskerelven 16; ☻ 10am-5pm Mon-Fri, 10am-3pm Sat) Specialises in student tickets.

Dangers & Annoyances
Although Bergen is generally a safe city, pickpockets are known to operate around the fish market and Bryggen areas so keep a close watch on your belongings.

Bergen suffers a reputation as one of the wettest cities in Norway – you can reliably expect rain or showers on at least 275 days of the year; a brolly is an essential accessory.

Sights & Activities
Bergen has lots of quaint cobblestone streets lined with timber-clad houses; some of the most picturesque are the winding lanes and alleys located above the Fløibanen funicular station.

TORGET
The waterfront fish market at Torget has a happy, bustling vibe that's hard to tear

BERGEN REGION

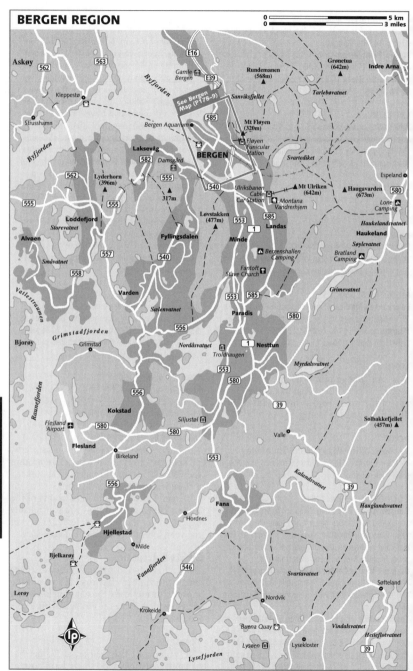

yourself away from. Here, fishy odours assault the olfactory senses, spilt effluent turns the quay into a slippery mess, and you'll find a range of tasty seafood snacks at excellent prices (see p186).

BRYGGEN

Bergen's oldest and most enchanting quarter runs along the eastern shore of Vågen Harbour. Once a major commercial centre for northern Europe (see the boxed text, below), the long parallel rows of buildings with stacked-stone foundations and reconstructed rough-plank construction run back from gabled fronts facing the wharf.

Despite strict prohibitions on the use of fire, many buildings of Bryggen were destroyed by fire at least seven times, most recently in 1955. The notable tilt of the structures in Bryggen was caused in 1944, when a Dutch munitions ship exploded in the harbour, blowing off the roofs and shifting the pilings. After the 1955 fire, archaeologists took the opportunity to excavate the area and were excited at the discovery of finding over one million artefacts, foundations of earlier buildings, and evidence of the big fires of 1170 and 1198.

In 1979, 58 of the wooden structures along the Bryggen waterfront were added to Unesco's World Heritage list.

A great place to find out more is at the Bryggen Visitor Centre (p175), which has an excellent scale model of Bryggen in 1900, cutaway sections of foundations, displays on excavations, old black-and-white photos and video displays.

HANSEATIC MUSEUM

Providing a window into the world of Hanseatic traders, is this terrific **museum** (Map pp178-9; ☎ 55 31 41 89; www.hanseatisk.museum.no; Finnegårdsgaten 1a; adult/child Nkr45/free May-Sep, Nkr25/free Oct-Apr, also valid for Schøtstuene; 🕑 9am-5pm Jun-Aug, 11am-2pm May & Sep, 11am-2pm Tue-Sat & noon-5pm Sun Oct-Apr). Housed in a rough-timber building from 1704, it starkly reveals the contrast between the austere living and working conditions of Hanseatic merchant sailors and apprentices and the lifestyles of the management. Highlights include the manager's office, quarters, private liquor cabinet and

BRYGGEN & THE HANSEATIC LEAGUE

By the 13th century, Bergen had developed into a major centre for European trade, as well as being the capital of the Norwegian monarchy. At around the same time, the city states of Germany – recently granted autonomy by royal charter and liberated from clerical rule – allied themselves into trading leagues, the most significant of which was the Hanseatic League with its centre in Lübeck. At its zenith, the league had over 150 member cities and was northern Europe's most powerful economic entity.

The sheltered harbour of Bryggen drew the Hanseatic League's traders in droves. They established their first office here around 1360, soon transforming Bryggen into one of the league's four major headquarters abroad with up to 2000 mostly German resident traders who imported grain and exported dried fish, among other products,

In the early 14th century, there were about 30 wooden buildings on Bryggen, each of which was usually shared by several *stuer* (trading firms). They rose two or three storeys above the wharf and combined business premises with living quarters and warehouses. Each building had a crane for loading and unloading ships, as well as a large assembly room, or *schøtstue*, where employees met and ate.

For over 400 years, Bryggen was dominated by a tightknit community of German merchants who weren't permitted to mix with, marry or have families with local Norwegians. By the 15th century, competition from Dutch and English shipping companies, internal disputes and, especially, the Black Death that killed a third of Europe's population ensured that the influence of the Hanseatic League fell into terminal decline (although Hamburg, Bremen and Lübeck are still known as Hanseatic cities and Hamburg and Bremen retain city-state status). By the 17th and 18th centuries, many Hanseatic traders opted to take Norwegian nationality and join the local community. Although the Hanseatic League lasted until the mid-18th century, Bryggen continued as an important maritime trade centre until 1899, when the Hanseatic League's Bergen offices finally closed.

BERGEN

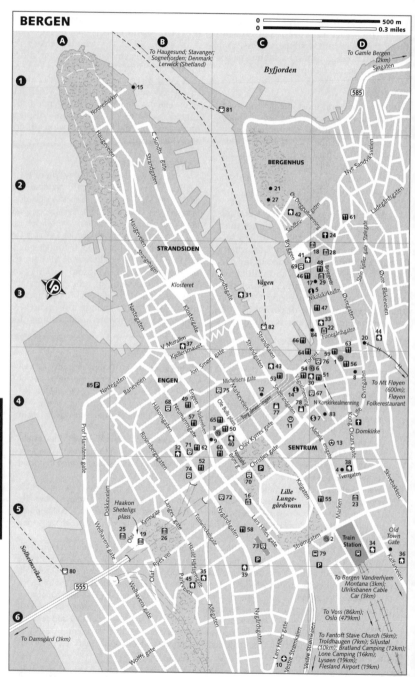

| 0 | | 500 m |
| 0 | | 0.3 miles |

Byfjorden

To Haugesund; Stavanger;
Sognefjorden; Denmark;
Lerwick (Shetland)

To Gamle Bergen
(2km)
Sjøgaten

585

BERGENHUS

Nordnesbukten

15

81

21
27

42

61

STRANDSIDEN

24

Klosteret

41
69

18
48
28

Vågen

46

17
29

31

5
Nikolaikirkeallm

82

47

33

22

66

84

Finnegårdsgaten

44

20

V Murallm
37

Kjellersmauet

64

63

59
76
77
1
56

Jon Smørs gate

43

54
6

8

Michelsens gate

53

30

51

To Mt Fløyen
(600m);
Fløyen
Folkerestauranten

85

Nøstegaten

Banevelen

ENGEN

75

12

14

78

N Korskirkeallmenning

67

68

49

Neumannsgate

57

65

Torgallmenningen

77

11

83

Håkonsgaten

3

50

9

40

60

Olav Kyrres gate

SENTRUM

13

Kong Oscars gate
Domkirke

32

71

62

Rosenbergsgaten

52

74

Christies gate

Kalfaret

38
4

Tverrgaten

Haakon
Sheteligs
plass

Prof Hansens gate

70

Lille
Lunge-
gårdsvann

Dokkeveien

25

19

72

16

55

23

26

58

Markeveien

Nygårdsgaten

Lars Hilles gate

Old
Town
Gate

80

555

73

2

Train
Station

34

36

Solheimsviken

35

39

45

79

P

Kalfarveien

To Damsgård (3km)

10

To Bergen Vandrerhjem
Montana (3km);
Ulriksbanen Cable
Car (3km)

To Voss (86km);
Oslo (479km)

To Fantoft Stave Church (5km);
Troldhaugen (7km); Siljustøl
(10km); Bratland Camping (12km);
Lone Camping (16km);
Lysøen (19km);
Flesland Airport (19km)

BERGEN & THE
SOUTHWESTERN FJORDS

summer bedroom; the apprentices' quarters where beds were shared by two men for spatial rather than sensual reasons; the fish storage room, which pressed and processed over a million pounds of fish a month; and the *fiskeskrue*, or fish press, which pressed the fish into barrels.

SCHØTSTUENE

An essential complement to the Hanseatic Museum, **Schøtstuene** (Map pp178-9; ☎ 55 31 60 20; Øvregaten 50; adult/child combined ticket with Hanseatic Museum Nkr45/free; ⏲ 10am-5pm Jun-Aug, 11am-2pm May & Sep, 11am-2pm Sun Oct-Dec & Mar-Apr) is a reconstruction of one of the original assembly halls where the fraternity of Hanseatic merchants once met for their business meetings and beer guzzling. Don't miss the interesting downstairs kitchen.

BRYGGENS MUSEUM

The archaeological **museum** (Map pp178-9; ☎ 55 58 80 10; Dreggsallmenning 3; adult/child Nkr40/free, free with Bergen Card; ⏲ 10am-5pm May-Aug, 11am-3pm Mon-Fri, noon-3pm Sat, noon-4pm Sun Sep-Apr) was built on the site of Bergen's first settlement, and the 800-year-old foundations unearthed during the construction have been incorporated into the exhibits, which include medieval tools, pottery, skulls and runes. The permanent exhibition documenting Bergen in around 1300 is particularly interesting.

THETA MUSEUM

This excellent one-room reconstruction of a clandestine Resistance headquarters, uncovered by the Nazis in 1942, is now Norway's tiniest **museum** (Map pp178-9; Enhjørningsgården; adult/child Nkr20/5; ⏲ 2-4pm Tue, Sat & Sun mid-May–mid-Sep). Appropriately enough, finding it is still a challenge – it's at the back of the Bryggen building with the unicorn figure-head; pass through the alley and up the stairs to the 3rd floor.

MARIAKIRKEN

The stone Mariakirken **church** (Map pp178-9; ☎ 55 31 59 60; Dreggen; adult/child Nkr10/free mid-May–Aug, free Sep–mid-May; ⏲ 9.30-11.30am & 1-4pm mid-May–Aug, noon-1.30pm Tue-Fri Sep–mid-May), with its Romanesque entrance and twin towers, dates from the early 12th century and is Bergen's oldest building. The interior features 15th-century frescoes and a splendid baroque pulpit donated by Hanseatic merchants in 1676.

BERGEN & THE SOUTHWESTERN FJORDS

OLE BULL

Born in Bergen in 1810, Ole Bull was a child prodigy with an affinity for the violin. He joined the Bergen Philharmonic Orchestra when only eight years old and by age 25 had already accomplished solo performances with the Paris opera. Bull travelled and performed all over the Western world for 45 years, bringing Norwegian folk music to a prominence it had never before enjoyed.

After the death of Ole Bull's French-born wife, Felicité Villeminot, Bull purchased the 70-hectare Lysøen island. Between 1872 and 1873, he and architect Conrad Fredrik von der Lippe constructed the fantasy villa 'Lysøen'. This 'Little Alhambra' took much of its extravagant inspiration from the architecture of Moorish Granada and integrated not only intricate frets and trellises, but also onion domes, romantic garden paths, Italian marble columns and a high-ceilinged music hall of Norwegian pine.

When Bull died at Lysøen in August 1880, about 10,000 mourners accompanied the funeral procession to the Assistentkirkegården near Bergen's old City Gate. In 1973, Bull's grandchild, Sylvea Bull Curtis, donated the entire property to the Foreningen til Norske Fortidsminnesmerkers Bevaring (the Norwegian Society for Historical Preservation) and, since 1984, the site has been a museum dedicated to Norway's best-loved violinist. You'll also see a statue and fountain dedicated to the virtuoso on Ole Bulls plass, in the heart of Bergen.

ROSENKRANTZ TOWER

Built in the 1560s by Bergen governor Erik Rosenkrantz, this **tower** (Rosenkrantztårnet; Map pp178-9; ☎ 55 31 43 80; Bergenhus; admission Nkr15; ⌚ 10am-4pm daily mid-May–Aug, noon-3pm Sun Sep–mid-May) was a residence and defence post. It also incorporates parts of the keep (1273) of King Magnus the Lawmender and the 1520s fortress of Jørgen Hansson. Spiral staircases lead past unadorned halls and sentry posts to a good harbour view from the summit.

HÅKONSHALLEN

This large ceremonial **hall** (Map pp178-9; ☎ 55 31 60 67; Bergenhus; adult/child Nkr25/12; ⌚ 10am-4pm daily mid-May–Aug, noon-3pm Fri-Wed, 3pm-6pm Thu Sep–mid-May), adjacent to the Rosenkrantz Tower, was constructed by King Håkon Håkonsson from 1247–61 and completed for his son's wedding and coronation. The roof was blown off in 1944 thanks to the explosion of a Dutch munitions boat, but extensive restoration has been carried out. There are hourly guided tours in summer.

BERGEN ART MUSEUM

Sitting beside the lake Lille Lungegårdsvann is this **art museum** (Bergen Kunstmuseum; Map pp178-9; ☎ 55 56 80 00; www.bergenartmuseum.no; Rasmus Meyers Allé 3 & 7; adult/child Nkr50/free; ⌚ 11am-5pm daily mid-May–mid-Sep, 11am-5pm Tue-Sun rest-of-year). It exhibits a superb collection of 18th- and 19th-century pieces by international and Norwegian artists, including works by Munch, as well as contemporary European works by Miró, Picasso, Kandinsky, Paul Klee and others.

UNIVERSITY MUSEUMS

The two main university **museums** (www.museum.uib.no; adult/child combined ticket Nkr30/free; ⌚ 10am-5pm Tue-Sat, 11am-5pm Sun Jun-Aug, 11am-2pm Tue-Sat, 11am-3pm Sep-May), at the end of Christies gate, include the **Natural History Collection** (Naturhistorisk Samlinger; Map pp178-9; ☎ 55 58 29 20; Muséplass 3) full of stuffed creatures and mineral displays; and, probably of greater interest, the **Cultural History Collection** (Kultur-historik Samlinger; Map pp178-9; ☎ 55 58 31 40; Haakon Sheteligs plass 10) with Viking weaponry, medieval altars, folk art and period furnishings. There are also sections dedicated to Inuit and Aleut cultures and displays covering everything from Henrik Ibsen to Egyptian mummies.

MARITIME MUSEUM

Such is the wealth of attractions around Bergen that this **museum** (Sjøfartsmuseet; Map pp178-9; ☎ 55 54 96 00; Haakon Sheteligs plass 15; adult/child Nkr30/free; ⌚ 11am-3pm daily Jun-Aug, 11am-2pm Sun-Fri Sep-May) tends to get missed by many people. That's a pity because it's an essential cog in fully understanding the history of this seafaring city. It features models of ships from Viking times to the present, and exhibits tracing Norway's maritime history.

GAMLE BERGEN

The open-air museum, **Old Bergen Museum** (Map pp178-9; ☎ 55 39 43 04; Elsesro, Sandviken; adult/

child Nkr60/30; ☿ hourly tours 10am-5pm daily mid-May–early Sep), is 4km north of the city centre and boasts a fine collection of 35 structures from the 18th and 19th centuries, including a number of historic commercial enterprises. It lies just within walking distance of Torget (about 30 minutes), or take a bus (No 20–23). Entrance to the grounds is free and open all year.

LEPROSY MUSEUM

For something a bit different, visit this unusual **museum** (Lepramuseet; Map pp178-9; ☎ 55 96 11 55; St George's Hospital, Kong Oscars gate 59; adult/child Nkr30/15; ☿ 11am-3pm daily mid-May–Aug). Although most of the buildings at St George's Hospital date from the 19th century, in medieval times the site served as a leprosarium. Exhibits detail Norway's contributions to leprosy research, including the work of Dr Armauer Hansen, who gave his name to Hansen's disease, the modern name for leprosy.

TROLDHAUGEN

This two-storey **home** (Map pp178-9; ☎ 55 92 29 92; www.troldhaugen.com; Hop; adult/child Nkr50/free, Nkr20 with Bergen Card; ☿ 9am-6pm daily May-Sep, shorter hours Oct-Apr), dates from 1885 and occupies an undeniably lovely setting on a lush and scenic peninsula by the coastal Nordåsvatnet Lake. Here composer Edvard Grieg (see the boxed text, below) and his wife Nina Hagerup spent every summer from 1885 until Grieg's death in 1907. Today the house and grounds are open to the public, there's a multimedia Grieg exhibition and a 200-seat concert hall. Of particular interest are the Composer's Hut, where Edvard mustered his musical inspiration; the Steinway piano, which was a gift to celebrate Edvard and Nina's 50th

---

A VERY NORWEGIAN COMPOSER

Norway's best known and most universally loved composer, Edvard Grieg, has always been inextricably tied to Bergen. He composed his first symphony in Copenhagen, but so disappointed was he with the result that he scrawled across the score that it must never be performed! Thankfully, his wishes were ignored, even if he steadfastly refused to acknowledge it as his own creation.

Grieg's early style strongly reflected his German romantic training, but he always understood the expectation that he would compose national music for his homeland, Norway. After returning to Christiania (Oslo) in 1866, Grieg became increasingly influenced by Norway's folk music and melodies. In 1868, he completed his first great, signature work, *Piano Concerto in A minor,* which has since come to represent Norway as no other work before or since.

Two years after the concerto, Grieg, encouraged by the resulting acclaim and by support from luminaries such as Ole Bull (see the boxed text, p180) and Franz Liszt, collaborated with Bjørnstjerne Bjørnson, setting the latter's poetry and writing to music. The results – *Before a Southern Convent, Bergliot* and *Sigurd Jorsalfar* – established Grieg as the musical voice of Norway. This was followed by a project with Henrik Ibsen (see the boxed text, p44), setting to music Ibsen's wonderful novel *Peer Gynt.* The score found international acclaim and became his – and Norway's – best-remembered classical work.

In 1874, a government grant allowed Grieg to return to Bergen and set his creative juices flowing; the result was his *Ballad in G minor, The Mountain Thrall,* the *Norwegian Dances for Piano* and *The Holberg Suite.* Between 1880 and 1882, he conducted an orchestra in Bergen, but resigned in order to return to his preferred work of composing. In 1885, he and his wife Nina moved into the coastal home Troldhaugen, from which he set off on numerous concert tours of Europe. At Troldhaugen he created the *Sonata for Violin and Piano in C minor,* the *Haugtussa Songs,* the *Norwegian Peasant Dances and Tunes,* and the *Four Psalms,* his last major work, based on a series of Norwegian religious melodies.

It was only after his death in Bergen on 4 September 1907, that his music garnered Europe-wide acclaim. However, perhaps the greatest praise for this most Norwegian of composers came from his first biographer, Aimer Grøvald, who noted that it was impossible to listen to Grieg without sensing a light, fresh breeze from the blue waters, a glimpse of grand glaciers and a recollection of the mountains of Western Norway's fjords.

wedding anniversary in 1892; and the couple's tombs, which are embedded in a rock face overlooking Nordåsvatnet. It's an impressive place.

In summer, **concerts** are held on Wednesday, Saturday and Sunday and during the Bergen International Festival; tickets (Nkr160 to Nkr200, less with a Bergen Card) and schedules are available at the tourist office.

Take any bus from platforms 19 to 21 to the Hopsbroen stop. From there, follow the signs to Troldhaugen; it's a 20-minute walk.

SILJUSTØL MUSEUM

Another well-known Norwegian composer's home lies 3km south of Troldhaugen. Harald and Marie Sæverud lived in **Siljustøl** (Map p176; ☎ 55 92 29 92; www.siljustol.no; Siljustøl; adult/child Nkr50/free; ⏰ noon-4pm Sun May–mid-Oct), a simple timber home. It was constructed in the 1930s of natural stone and untreated wood in an attempt to create unity with the environment. Harald Sæverud's first symphony was completed in 1920 and he endeared himself to Norwegians everywhere when, during WWII, he wrote protest music against the Nazi occupation. In 1986, he was made official composer of the Bergen International Music Festival, a position he honoured by creating a symphonic suite to the Ibsen play *Kjeser og Galilæer*. When he died in March 1992, he was given a state funeral and buried at Siljustøl, as he'd requested.

To get there, take bus No 30 from platform 20.

DAMSGÅRD

The 1770 **Damsgård manor** (Map p176; ☎ 55 33 66 33; www.vk.museum.no; Laksevåg; adult/child Nkr50/free; ⏰ 11am-5pm daily late May-Aug, hourly tours 11am-4pm), 3km west of town, may well be Norway's (if not Europe's) finest example of 18th-century rococo timber architecture. The building's superb (some may say over-the-top) highlight is the baroque garden, which includes sculptures, ponds and plant specimens which were in common use 200 years ago. To get there, take bus No 19, 70 or 71 from the centre.

LYSØEN

This beautiful **estate** (Map p176; ☎ 56 30 90 77; lysoen@online.no; Lysøen; adult/child incl guided tour Nkr50/20; ⏰ noon-4pm Mon-Sat, 11am-5pm Sun mid-May–Aug, noon-4pm Sun Sep), on the island of the same name, was constructed in 1873 as the summer residence of Norwegian violinist Ole Bull (see the boxed text, p180). Many of the musicians who flourished under Ole Bull's patronage used Lysøen as a retreat. The grounds are crisscrossed with 13km of leisurely walks and there's a small café. From the bus station, take the Lysefjorden bus (No 566 and 567) from platform 19 or 20 to Buena Quay, where there's a passenger ferry (hourly noon to 3pm, to 4pm Sun) to Lysøen. The return bus fare is Nkr110, while the ferry costs Nkr40/20 per adult/child.

FUNICULARS
Fløibanen

For an unbeatable city view, ride the 26-degree Fløibanen **funicular** (Map pp178-9; ☎ 55 33 68 00; www.floibanen.no; Vetrlidsalmenning 21; adult/child Nkr60/30 return; ⏰ 7.30am-midnight daily May-Aug, 7.30am-11pm Sun-Fri, 8am-11pm Sat Sep-Apr) to the top of Mt Fløyen (320m); the front (lower) seats offer the best views, but you'll need to sharpen your elbows to get one.

From the top, well-marked hiking tracks lead into the forest; the possibilities are mapped out on the free *Gledeskartet* or *Turløyper På Byfjellene Nord/Øst* (Nkr10) maps available from the Bergen Tourist Office. Track No 2 makes a 1.6km loop near Skomakerdiket Lake and Track No 1 offers a 5km loop over hills, through forests and past several lakes. For a delightful 40-minute walk back to the city from Fløyen, follow Track 4 clockwise and connect with Track 6, which switchbacks down to the harbour through neighbourhoods of old timber houses. There are also two other intermediate stops on the funicular on the way down, allowing you to walk the rest of the way down.

Ulriksbanen

The Ulriksbanen **cable car** (Map pp178-9; ☎ 55 20 20 20; www.ulriken.no; adult/child return Nkr80/40; ⏰ 9am-10pm daily Jun-Aug, 9am-7pm daily May & Sep, 10am-5pm daily Oct-Apr) ascends to the radio tower and café atop Mt Ulriken (642m), offering a panoramic view of the city and surrounding fjords and mountains. The 'Bergen in a Nutshell' ticket (p183) includes the cable car and a return bus from the tourist office. Otherwise, it's a 45-minute walk from the centre or a few minutes' ride on bus No 2 or 31 from the post office or bus No 50 from Bryggen.

A popular excursion is to ride up on the cable car and walk six hours north along a well-beaten track to the top of the Fløibanen funicular railway.

BERGEN AQUARIUM

At the end of the Nordnes Peninsula, this **aquarium** (Bergen Akvariet; Map p176; ☎ 55 55 71 71; www.akvariet.com; Nordnesbakken 4; adult/child Nkr100/50; ⏰ 9am-7pm May-Aug, 10am-6pm Sep-Apr) has a big outdoor tank with seals and penguins, as well as 70 indoor tanks. You'll never forget the loveable steinbit, the hideous anglerfish or the school of herring which seems to function as a single entity. There are seal and penguin feedings at noon, 3pm and 6pm from May to September; noon and 3pm from October to April.

On foot, you can get there from the Torget in 20 minutes; alternatively, take the Vågen ferry (p189).

FANTOFT STAVKIRKE

The Fantoft **stave church** (Map pp178-9; ☎ 55 28 07 10; Paradis; adult/child Nkr30/5; ⏰ 10.30am-2pm & 2.30-6pm mid-May–mid-Sep), in a lovely leafy setting (which goes by the name 'Paradise') south of Bergen, was built in Sognefjord around 1150 and moved to the southern outskirts of Bergen in 1883. It was burned down by a Satanist in 1992, but it has since been painstakingly reconstructed. The adjacent **cross**, originally from Sola in Rogaland, dates from 1050. From Bergen take any bus leaving from platform 20, get off at the Fantoft stop on Birkelundsbakken and walk uphill through the park for about five minutes.

Tours

All of the following tours can be booked through the Bergen tourist office unless otherwise stated.

AROUND BERGEN
Boat tours

Bergen Fjord Sightseeing (☎ 55 25 90 00) operates a one-hour **harbour tour** (adult/child Nkr100/ 50, 2.30pm), which offers some wonderful views of Bryggen and the surrounding hills, or a four-hour **fjord tour** (adult/child Nkr320/160; 3.30pm July to mid-August, 10am May to June and mid-August to

mid-September), which explores the fjords around Bergen. Boats depart from the waterfront next to the fish market.

Flaggruten (☎ 56 39 17 00) also operates a range of day-long veteran boat tours to the surrounding fjords. The most popular is the trip to the stunning Osterfjord aboard the M/S *Bruvik* (adult/child Nkr400/200, with Bergen Card Nkr350/175), which departs on Sundays at 9am from June to August; you'll be back in Bergen at 6.15pm.

Bus tours

A good way to reach the more outlying sights is to join one of the three-hour **Bergen Guided Tours** (☎ 55 55 44 54; each tour adult/child Nkr250/ 160, 35 ☎ discount with Bergen Card), which depart from the tourist office twice daily (10am and 2pm) every day from May to September.

An alternative offering more flexibility is the **Attractions Bus** (Nkr75 per 24hr; mid-Jun–mid-Aug), a hop-on-hop-off service that covers central Bergen, the Bergen Aquarium and as far out as Troldhaugen, but doesn't include any entry fees.

For sights within Bergen, the old **'Bergen in a Nutshell' bus** (☎ 55 20 20 20; www.bergeninnut shell.no; adult/child Nkr130/65; ⏰ every half-hour 9am-9pm May-Sep) runs from next to the fish market, along the Bryggen waterfront, to the Ulriksbanen cable car and back again. The price includes a return ticket for the cable car and free Grieg mini concerts (hourly from 3pm to 8pm June to August) up the top. Commentary is available in eight languages.

Train tours

The Bergen Express **toy train** (☎ 55 53 11 50; www.bergensexpressen.no; adult/child Nkr100/40; ⏰ half-hourly 10am-7pm daily mid-Jun–mid-Aug, shorter hours May–mid-Jun & mid-Aug–mid-Sep) trundles along the Bryggen waterfront and up into some of the more interesting back streets. The trip takes one hour.

From early June to mid-September, another popular excursion is the Sunday tour by veteran steam train between Garnes and Midtun. It begins at 9am on the historic ferry M/S *Bruvik* from the Bryggen to the **railway museum** (☎ 55 24 91 00) at Garnes and from there the 18km steam chugs to Midtun. From Midtun back to Bergen, the tour uses a historic bus. The whole trip takes four hours (Nkr225/120 adult/child). The train trip alone costs Nkr120 return.

Walking Tours

The best way to get explore Bryggen is with the (summer only) 1½-hour **guided walking tour** of Bergen's old quarter. You could do the walk on your own, but the entertaining and informative commentary includes descriptions of life during Bergen's trading heyday and is worth every kroner. The ticket (adult/child Nkr80/free) includes admission to Bryggens Museum, Schøtstuene and the Hanseatic Museum (and allows you to re-visit these museums later on the same day). Daily tours take place from June to August, with two in English (11am and 1pm), one in German (10am), one in Norwegian (noon) and (sometimes) one in French. Tours begin at the Bryggens Museum where you can also buy the ticket.

If you prefer to do it at your own pace, Bryggens Museum also has a (free) brochure entitled *Meeting Point Bryggen* which allows **self-guided tours** covering 12 stops in the old town.

AROUND NORWAY

The popular **'Norway in a Nutshell'** tour is a great way to see everything you can in just one day. The day ticket (Nkr750/375) from Bergen combines a morning train from Bergen to Flåm, a ferry up the spectacular Nærøyfjord to Gudvangen, a bus to Voss and a train back to Bergen in time for a late dinner (or you can continue on to Oslo to arrive around 10pm).

Festivals & Events

The **Bergen International Festival** (☎ 55 36 55 66; www.festspellene.no), held for 12 days at the end of May and beginning of June, is the big cultural festival of the year, with dance, music and folklore presentations, and other events throughout the city.

On the last Sunday in May, there's the Seven Peaks Hike, where all the peaks must be visited on foot. It's an arduous 30km, with 2200m of ascent, but the record time is only 4½ hours!

Other highlights on the Bergen summer calendar include the **Jazz Festival** (www.natt jazz.no) at the end of May, the **Dragon Boat Festival** (www.dragebat.no) in early June, **Seafood Festival** (www.sjomat.no) in early September and the **Food Festival** (www.matfest.no) in early to mid-September.

For a full list of events, see the website www.visitbergen.com.

Sleeping

Bergen has accommodation to suit every budget. The tourist office has a booking service (Nkr30 for walk-ins, Nkr50 for advance booking). The tourist office also books single/double rooms in private homes (without breakfast) starting at Nkr210/320, plus a booking fee of Nkr20.

BUDGET

Lone Camping (Map p176; ☎ 55 39 29 60; booking@ lonecamping.no; Hardangerveien 697, Haukeland; tent sites Nkr120 plus per person Nkr20, cabins Nkr390-875) This lakeside camping ground is about 16km from town, at a petrol station between Espeland and Haukeland. It's overpriced for what's on offer (the cheaper cabins are downright basic), but it's readily accessible by public transport. Bus No 900 runs to/from town (Nkr38, 30 minutes) every half-hour.

Bratland Camping (Map p176; ☎ 55 10 13 38; www .bratlandcamping.no; Bratlandsveien 6, Haukeland; tent sites Nkr110 plus per person Nkr20, cabins Nkr350-1200; ☯ mid-May–mid-Sep) Also accessible on Bus No 900, this well-equipped site is 4km south of Lone Camping.

Bergen Vandrerhjem YMCA (Map pp178-9; ☎ 55 60 60 55; ymca@online.no; Nedre Korskirkealmenning 4; dm Nkr125, 4–6-bed r per person Nkr160, d with private bathroom Nkr600; ☯ May–mid-Sep; ☐) This friendly 175-bed HI hostel is about as central a hostel as you'll find in Norway. There are same-sex or mixed dorms and kitchen facilities are available.

Intermission (Map pp178-9; ☎ 55 31 32 75; Kalfarveien 8; dm Nkr110; ☯ mid-Jun–mid-Aug) The hospitable Christian Student Fellowship offers some of the cheapest beds in Bergen,

---

THE AUTHOR'S CHOICE

Steens Hotell (Map p176; ☎ 55 30 88 88; www .steenshotel.no; Parkveien 22; s/d with Fjord Pass Nkr625/780, without Nkr790/990; ☐) This is a terrific choice. This lovely 19th-century building (part of the Fjord Pass network) has kept much of its original charm with period furniture, large rooms and there's also a wonderful dining room with stained-glass windows. It's a bit away from the harbour area (15-minute walk), but this leafy, residential area is well away from the tourist scrum. Highly recommended.

with use of the kitchen in a period home near the old town gate. The basic breakfast costs a bargain Nkr25.

Montana Vandrerhjem (Map pp178-9; ☎ 55 20 80 70; montvh@online.no; Johan Blyttsvei 30; dm from Nkr135, s/d with shared bathroom Nkr400/570, with private bathroom Nkr420/610; 🖳) The fine 332-bed Montana HI hostel is 5km southeast of the centre near the Ulriksbanen cable car. Take bus No 31 from city centre. Breakfast is included.

Marken Gjestehus (Map pp178-9; ☎ 55 31 44 04; markengjestehus@smisi.no; Kong Oscars gate 45; dm from Nkr165, s/d with shared bathroom Nkr355/470, with private bathroom Nkr495/610) This guesthouse is midway between the harbour and the train station. It has simple, well-kept rooms with bunk beds, a good communal kitchen and that unmistakable hostel feel. Breakfast costs Nkr60.

Skansen Pensjonat (Map pp178-9; ☎ 55 31 90 80; www.skansen-pensjonat.no; Vetrlidsalmenning 29; s/d with shared bathroom from Nkr350/550, d with balcony Nkr650, apt Nkr700) Great choice. Centrally located, light and airy rooms and some great views make for a terrific combination a stone's throw from Bryggen. Prices include breakfast.

Crowded House (Map pp178-9; ☎ 55 90 72 00; www.crowded-house.com; Håkonsgaten 27; s/d/tr with shared bathroom Nkr390/590/885, d with private bathroom Nkr690) Crowded House is a cool place to hang out. The rooms are simple, spacious and tidy, there's a laid-back downstairs coffee-shop-cum-bar called **Fusion** (✷ 9am-midnight Sun-Wed, 9am-1am Thu, 9am-2am Fri & Sat) and there are cooking and kitchen facilities.

Also recommended:

Kjellersmauet Gjestehus (Map pp178-9; ☎ 55 96 26 08; www.gjesthuset.com; Kjellersmauet 22; s/d from Nkr400/700, apt Nkr1200) Simply furnished and well equipped; prices don't include breakfast.

Nygård Apartment (Map pp178-9; ☎ 55 32 72 53; markengjestehus@smisi.no; Nygårdsgaten 31; s/d with shared bathroom Nkr365/530, with private bathroom Nkr510/650; ✷ Jun–mid-Aug) Small student rooms with access to cooking facilities.

MID-RANGE

Hotel Park Pension (Map pp178-9; ☎ 55 54 44 00; fax 55 54 44 44; Harald Hårfagresgate 35; s/d mid-Jun–mid-Aug Nkr650/900, rest-of-year Nkr880/1080; 🖳) In the same area as Steens Hotell, this family-run place is another option with loads of character, 19th-century atmosphere and lots of antiques. The rooms are spacious and very attractive.

Grand Hotel Terminus (Map pp178-9; ☎ 55 21 25 00; www.grand-hotel-terminus.no; Zander Kaaesgate 6; s/d/tr from Nkr625/890/1040; 🖳) Opposite the train station, the Grand Hotel Terminus has historically been the hotel of choice for the city's well-heeled visitors. The location is less than picturesque and some rooms are decidedly cramped. There is, however, an old-world charm about the place with elaborate décor which may not be to everyone's taste.

Clarion Hotel Admiral (Map pp178-9; ☎ 55 23 64 00; booking.admiral@clarion.choicehotels.no; C Sundts gate 9; s/d with Nordisk Hotel Pass mid-Jun–mid-Aug Nkr700/900, d with harbour view Nkr1100-1250, s/d rest-of-year from Nkr850/1050; 🖳) Okay, so you want a view of Bryggen? This is the best view to wake up to in Bergen and worth the price tag. Rooms are extremely comfortable, but book ahead to guarantee one with a harbour view. The hotel also have their own cruise boat with a cigar and cognac salon.

Also recommended:

Rainbow Hotel Bryggen Orion (Map pp178-9; ☎ 55 30 87 00; bryggenorion@rainbow-hotels.no; Bradbenken 3; s/d from Nkr650/750; 🖳) Good location, prices include light evening meal.

TOP END

Radisson SAS Hotel Norge (Map pp178-9; ☎ 55 57 30 00; bergen@radissonsas.com; Ole Bulls plass 4; d from Nkr1090; 🖳 ⌨) This centrally located place is one of the most elegant hotels in Bergen. The rooms have all the luxurious things in the right places, thoughtful decoration and a price tag that's surprisingly reasonable. This place is reluctant to give single rates, but will do so if pushed.

Also recommended:

First Hotel Marin (Map pp178-9; ☎ 53 05 15 00; booking.marin@firsthotels.no; Rosenkrantz gate 8; s/d from Nkr998/1198; 🖳) Top location, elegant rooms and some great views.

Radisson SAS Royal Hotel (Map pp178-9; ☎ 55 54 30 00; sales.bergen@radissonsas.com; Bryggen; s/d Nkr1395/1595; 🖳 ⌨) Comfortable and modern business-class hotel.

Rica Strand Hotel (Map pp178-9; ☎ 55 59 33 00; www.strandhotel.no; Strandkaien 2-4; s/d mid-Jun–mid-Aug Nkr790/1090, rest-of-year from Nkr450/690; 🖳) Reasonable rooms, some with great Bryggen and Torget views.

Eating

All of Bergen's restaurants listed are open for lunch and dinner daily unless stated otherwise.

BUDGET

Pygmalion Café (Map pp178-9; ☎ 55 32 33 60; Nedre Kors-kirkealmenning 4; light meals Nkr65-115; ☺ 11.30am-11pm Tue-Sat, 11am-5pm Sun) This is a very cool place. With contemporary art adorning its walls, a chilled ambience and top-notch organic food (salads, pancakes etc), this is a great choice at any time of the day.

Café Opera (Map pp178-9; ☎ 55 23 03 15; Engen 18; snacks Nkr23-92, mains Nkr85-115) Trendy Café Opera attracts artists and students with good, reasonably priced meals such as pastas, salads, ciabatta and grilled salmon.

Augustus Café (Map pp178-9; ☎ 55 32 35 25; Galleriet, Torgalmenningen 8; mains Nkr69-115; ☺ lunch & dinner Mon-Sat) The recommended Augustus Café serves both hot and cold dishes including lasagna (Nkr95) and quiche (Nkr89).

Lido (Map pp178-9; ☎ 55 32 59 12; Torgalmenningen 1; specials & mains from Nkr110) Lido is an inexpensive cafeteria with good traditional grub. Its budget credentials take a battering from the Nkr5 they charge to go to the toilet.

Mr Bean Coffee Shop & Dr Livingstone Travellers Café (Map pp178-9; ☎ 55 56 03 12; Kong Oscars gate 12; coffee from Nkr25, light meals Nkr65-110; ☺ noon-10pm) This travel-savvy place is understandably popular and a great place to meet other travellers. This place brews up enormous cups of coffee but, unfortunately, only late sleepers can use it as a morning kick-start.

The **Rimi supermarket** (Map pp178-9; Nygårdsgaten; ☺ 9am-11pm Mon-Sat, 11am-11pm Sun) has longer opening hours than most, while the **Sparmarket** (Map pp178-9; Nye Sandviksveien; ☺ 9am-8pm Mon-Fri, 9am-6pm Sat) has a terrific takeaway deli with whole grilled chickens for only Nkr30. **Kinsarvik Frukt** (Map pp178-9; Olav Kyrres gate 38; ☺ 9am-5pm Mon-Fri, 10am-3pm Sat) is a food shop with a health-food section. All of the above places offer loads of choice for those planning picnics.

Bakeries are also in plentiful supply. Some of our favourites:

Baker Brun (Map pp178-9; Zachariasbryggen Quay & Bergen; ☺ 8am-8pm Mon-Sat, 11am-6pm Sun) Popular for pastries, rolls and Bergen's own *shillingsboller* (local pastry speciality shaped in a ball, which translates as shilling, ie the old currency unit) buns; another branch at Bryggen.

Godt Brød (Map pp178-9; Nedre Korskirkealmenningen 12; ☺ 7am-6pm Mon-Fri, 7am-4.30pm Sat) Delicious organic breads and pastries.

Sol Brød (Map pp178-9; Cnr Vetrlidsalmenning & Kong Oscars gate; ☺ 8am-5pm Mon-Fri, 8am-5.30pm Sat, 9am-4pm Sun) Bread, pastries and sandwiches.

MID-RANGE

Stragiotti (Map pp178-9; ☎ 55 90 31 00; Vestre Torvgate 3; lunch specials Nkr49-129, mains Nkr120-280; ☺ 2-11.30pm Mon-Sat, 2-10.30pm Sun) This revamped Italian restaurant is stylish indoors, nice and breezy outside on the terrace and serves up authentic Italian food at very reasonable prices.

Bar Celona (Map pp178-9; ☎ 55 23 42 33; Vaskerelven 16-18; tapas Nkr19-89, light meals Nkr35-85; ☺ 2pm-1.30am Mon-Thu, 1pm-2.30am Fri & Sat) Another chic choice, this Spanish-inspired restaurant-bar is super stylish, friendly and has great food.

Tapas Tapas Bar (Map pp178-9; ☎ 55 96 22 10; Vetrlidsalmenning 15; vegetarian dishes Nkr45-79, other mains Nkr130-290) Near the Fløibanen terminal, Tapas Tapas Bar offers more Mediterranean flavours in a pleasant upstairs dining area.

Peppe's Pizza (Map pp178-9; ☎ 55 96 41 99; Zachariasbryggen; pizza from Nkr134; ☺ 11am-11pm Mon-Thu, 11am-midnight Fri & Sat) The ubiquitous Peppe's offers the usual large pizza that's a cut above the rest. The outdoor tables have views of the harbour and Bryggen and they also do great coffee (eg iced coffee mocha for Nkr29). The service is also consistently good and with a young vibe.

Pars (Map pp178-9; ☎ 55 56 37 22; Sigurdsgate 5; starters Nkr49-69, mains Nkr89-189; ☺ 4-11pm Tue-Thu, 4pm-midnight Fri & Sat, 3-10pm Sun) The Middle Eastern atmosphere at the Pars Persian restaurant works well in cosmopolitan Bergen. The food is excellent, including inexpensive vegetarian choices (from Nkr65), and there is a children's menu (Nkr89).

THE AUTHOR'S CHOICE

Bergen's most enjoyable eating experience awaits you at the **fish market** (Torget; Map pp178-9; ☺ 7am-5pm Sun-Fri, 7am-4pm Sat Jun-Aug, 7am-4pm Mon-Sat Sep-May). Right alongside the harbour and a stone's throw from Bryggen, here you'll find everything from strawberries and cherries to bountiful seafood salads (Nkr90), from elk burgers and reindeer sausages to English-style fish and chips (Nkr90), crab (Nkr50), open sandwiches and fish cakes. And then there are the fish stalls: cuts of salmon, whale meat and a host of other fishy wonders that stallholders are happy to make into a take-away platter or a sealed bag to take home. You may find yourself making this a regular lunch pit stop.

Ma-Ma Thai (Map pp178-9; ☎ 55 31 38 70; Kaigaten 20; lunch specials Nkr75-89, starters Nkr55-89, mains Nkr129-189) Ma-Ma Thai is a cosy and authentic Asian place that attracts university students with its good value specials and tasty seafood, beef, chicken, pork and lamb dishes.

TOP END

Enhjørningen (Map pp178-9; ☎ 55 32 79 19; Bryggen; 3-course dinner Nkr440, starters Nkr95-140, mains Nkr205-380; ☺ lunch & dinner Mon-Sat) The popular and upmarket Enhjørningen offers delicious fish and seafood. The name means 'unicorn', and above the door it appears that such a beast, clearly in a state of sexual arousal, is attempting an escape! Such diversions notwithstanding, this is one of Bryggen's finest dining experience for quality food and old-style elegance.

Bryggen Tracteursted (Map pp178-9; ☎ 55 31 59 55; Bryggen; light meals Nkr95-145, starters Nkr82-145, mains Nkr225-275; ☺ lunch & dinner May-Sep) Another great Bryggen experience, this 300-year-old Bryggen tavern is filled with crumbling character, decent food and plenty of hungry tourists.

Dickens (Map pp178-9; ☎ 55 36 31 30; Kong Olav Vs plass 4; lunch Nkr109-159, dinner mains Nkr179-231; ☺ lunch & dinner) Popular Dickens, has a sunny dining room overlooking Kong Olav Vs plass, outdoor tables in summer and generous servings to linger over.

Wesselstuen (Map pp178-9; ☎ 55 55 49 49; Ole Bulls plass 6; light meals Nkr69-135, starters Nkr69-89, mains Nkr179-225, 3-course meal Nkr335; ☺ lunch & dinner) The richly decorated Wesselstuen offers excellent value and is especially popular with postgraduate students, philosophers and intellectuals in the local 30- to 40-year-old crowd.

Also recommended:

Ole Bull (Map pp178-9; ☎ 55 57 30 00; Ole Bulls plass 5; lunch buffet Nkr225 (dinner Nkr275 ☺ lunch 11.30am-3.30pm; dinner 6-9pm) Park view and tempting buffet.

Louisiana Créole Restaurant (Map pp178-9; ☎ 55 54 66 60; Vågsalmenning 6; mains Nkr179-289) Laudable attempt at Cajun cuisine (including steak and alligator); lighter meals at the downstairs café.

Bryggeloftet & Stuene (Map pp178-9; ☎ 55 31 06 30; Bryggen 11; daily specials from Nkr89, mains Nkr89-275) Another Bryggen favourite for traditional Norwegian fare (including reindeer, venison, bacalao and catfish).

Fiskekrogen (Map pp178-9; ☎ 55 55 96 55; Zachariasbryggen; lunch from Nkr79, dinner mains Nkr245-295) Gourmet game and seafood dishes next to the harbour.

Entertainment

Bergen has something for everyone, from high culture to after-dark action.

For some concerts, folklore performances and even admission to a nightclub, the Bergen Card offers significant discounts.

CINEMA

Bergen Kino (Map pp178-9; ☎ 82 05 00 05; Neumannsgate 3; admission Nkr60-80) First-run movies are shown in their original languages at this 13-screen complex.

CONCERTS

Bergen has a busy programme of concerts throughout summer, many of them classical performances focusing on Bergen's favourite son, composer Edvard Grieg (see the boxed text, p181), and taking place at evocative open-air venues such as Troldhaugen, Lysøen, Siljustøl, atop Mt Fløyen and in the park adjacent to Håkonshallen. For details and schedules, contact the tourist office. Tickets (Nkr150 to Nkr220) are sold by **Billett Service** (☎ 81 03 31 33), the tourist office or at the gate to the venue.

The renowned **Bergen Philharmonic Orchestra** (☎ 55 21 61 50; www.harmonien.no) stages classical concerts at **Grieghallen** (Map pp178-9; ☎ 55 21 61 00; www.grieghallen.no; Edvard Griegs plass; tickets Nkr150-250), with a particularly busy season from June to August.

From mid-June to mid-August, Grieg concerts are held in one of the galleries of the wonderful old Det Norske Bank (tourist office) building. Performances usually take place from Wednesday to Saturday, start at 10pm and cost Nkr160 (Nkr120 with Bergen Card).

FOLKLORE

Fana Folklore (Map pp178-9; ☎ 55 91 52 40; Fana church/Ramsbergstunet; tickets Nkr270; ☺ Thu & Fri early Jun-late Aug) If you're finding traditional Norwegian culture elusive, this folklore show in the Fana Stave Church may start to cut through the obscurity. Yes, it's tourist-oriented, but it's well done and a healthy proportion of the spectators is likely to be Norwegian. Fana Folklore buses pick up ticket holders at Festplassen at 7pm, returning at 10.30pm; tickets can be bought at the tourist office.

Bergen Folklore (Map pp178-9; ☎ 55 55 20 06; adult/child Nkr95/free; ☺ 9pm Tue late Jun-late Jul, 9pm Sun early-mid-Jun & early-late Aug) Another group performs traditional one-hour music and dance routines. The Tuesday performances take place at Bryggens Museum, while the Sunday offerings are in the atmospheric Schøstuene. Tickets are available from the tourist office or at the door.

PUBS, CLUBS & DISCOS
Kvarteret (Map pp178-9; ☎ 55 58 99 10; Olav Kyrres gate 49; ⌚ 11.30-1am Sun-Thu, 11.30-3am Fri & Sat) If Norwegian alcohol prices have unearthed the teetotaller in you, here's the place to break the drought. Half-litre glasses (themselves a rarity these days in Norway) go for just Nkr33/42 before/after 10pm. There's also a laid-back student buzz that can be lots of fun.

Garage (Map pp178-9; ☎ 55 32 02 10; Christies gate 14; ⌚ noon-late Mon-Sat, 6pm-late Sun) Bergen's top rock music venue serves both local and Irish beer and is another terrific choice for a night out.

Rick's (Map pp178-9; ☎ 55 55 31 31; Veiten 3; ⌚ 10pm-3am Sun-Thu, 10pm-3.30am Fri & Sat, cover charge Nkr75 Fri & Sat) This complex of pubs and discos includes a rock disco with DJ, a music bar with English staff, a varied live music and dancing venue, a disco for over-25s, and the adjacent Irish-style pub **Finnegan's** (Map pp178-9; ⌚ 2pm-1am Sun-Thu, 2pm-2am Fri & Sat); at the latter, 0.45L beers cost Nkr46.

Engelen (Map pp178-9; ☎ 55 54 31 50; Bryggen; cover charge Nkr75; ⌚ 8pm-late Wed-Sat) More upbeat and attracting a younger crowd, this place offers up disco music from the 1970s and beyond and cheap drinks on Thursday.

Banco Rotto (Map pp178-9; ☎ 55 32 75 20; Vågsalmenning 16; cover charge Nkr80, free with Bergen Card; ⌚ 6pm-late daily) Make the most of your Bergen Card by coming to Banco Rotto, which attracts everyone from the ages of 30 to 60 with its weekend live music shows (contemporary/chart hits), while the attached Blue Velvet Bar puts on live jazz performances on some weekdays.

If you're in search of pleasant outdoor tables around the harbour, it's hard to beat **Scruffy Murphy** (Map pp178-9; ☎ 55 31 34 96; Torget 15; ⌚ noon-late), which is earthy and Irish, or **Pacific Bar** (Map pp178-9; Torget 15; ⌚ 4pm-late), which is considerably more stylish.

Sports-oriented bars to watch the latest sport match include the excellent **Fotballpuben** (Map pp178-9; ☎ 55 90 05 79; Vestre Torggate 9; half-litre beer Nkr35; ⌚ noon-late).

Shopping
The shops along Bryggen are mostly tourist-oriented with hideous fridge-magnets, cheese slicers and trolls a recurring theme, but there are also some worthwhile and excellent souvenirs among the kitsch on offer. Most of these shops open at 9am and close at 10.30pm in summer conveniently catered for travellers.

The broadest selection of handicrafts, wooden toys and traditional clothing is found at **Husfliden** (Map pp178-9; ☎ 55 31 78 70; Vågsalmenning 3; ⌚ 9am-4.30pm Mon-Wed & Fri, 9am-7pm Thu, 9am-3pm Sat).

Getting There & Away
Bergen is a main starting point for journeys into the Western Fjords with excellent transport.

AIR
Bergen's **airport** (Map pp178-9; ☎ 55 99 80 00) is at Flesland, about 19km southwest of the centre. **SAS Braathens** (www.sasbraathens.no; ☎ 81 52 00 00), at the airport, connects Oslo and Bergen (from Nkr739) many times daily. There are also direct flights to Trondheim (Nkr830), Kristiansand (Nkr581) and Stavanger (Nkr353). **Widerøe** (www.wideroe.no; ☎ 81 00 12 00), also at the airport, flies to Stavanger for the same price, as well as a few other smaller airports in the Western Fjords region.

There are also international flights to the following destinations: Copenhagen, Stockholm, London, Newcastle and Aberdeen; see p387 for more information.

BOAT
For destinations in Sognefjord, there are daily **Fylkesbåtane** (☎ 55 90 70 70; www.fylkesbaatane.no) express boats to Balestrand (Nkr385, four hours) and Flåm (Nkr530, 5½ hours). For Nordfjord, there are also daily ferries to/from Måløy (Nkr570, 4½ hours) and Selje (Nkr615, five hours).

HSD/Flaggruten (☎ 55 23 87 80; www.flaggruten.no) has up to four daily departures to/from Stavanger (one-way/return Nkr560/670, four hours), via Haugesund (Nkr350/440, three hours). In Bergen, all these boats use the Strandkaiterminal (Map pp178-9).

The Hurtigruten coastal ferry leaves from the Frieleneskaien (Map p398), south of the university, at 8pm daily. See p398 for details.

International ferries to/from Bergen dock at Skoltegrunnskaien (Map pp178–9), north of the Rosenkrantz tower. See p393 for details.

BUS
Nor-Way Bussekspress runs to:

Destination	Departures	Cost	Duration	
Ålesund	1 to 2 daily	Nkr595	10½hr	✔
Kristiansand (via Haukeligrand)	1 daily	Nkr610	12hr	
Odda	1 to 3 daily	Nkr275	3¼hr	
Oslo	3 daily	Nkr640	11½hr	
Stavanger	every 2hr daily	Nkr410	5¾hr	
Stryn	3 daily	Nkr415	6½hr	
Trondheim	2 daily	Nkr810	14¼hr	

TRAIN
For details of the spectacular train journey between Bergen and Oslo (Nkr670, 6½ to eight hours, five daily), see p13. Local trains run between Bergen and Voss (Nkr155, one hour) leave every hour or two; four of these trains run to/from Myrdal (Nkr215, 2¼ hours).

Getting Around
TO/FROM THE AIRPORT
The airport is in Flesland, 19km by road southwest of central Bergen. Flybussen (adult/child Nkr65/35, 45 minutes) runs at least twice hourly between the airport, the Radisson SAS Royal Hotel, the Radisson SAS Hotel Norge and the main bus terminal. Local bus No 523 also runs between the bus terminal and Flesland airport (Nkr40, one hour), with departures more or less hourly.

BICYCLE
You can hire cycles from **Sykkelbutikken** (Map pp178–9; ☎ 55 32 06 20; Østre Skostredet 5; per day from Nkr150).

BUS
City buses cost Nkr15, while fares beyond the centre are based on the distance travelled. Route information is available on ☎ 177. Free bus No 100 runs between the main post office and the bus terminal.

CAR & MOTORCYCLE
Except where there are parking meters, street parking is reserved for residents. In busy areas, metered parking is limited to 30 minutes or two hours; the parking areas at Sydnes allow up to nine hours (free at night). Less restricted are the indoor car parks; the largest and cheapest (Nkr75 per 24 hours) is the 24-hour Bygarasjen at the bus terminal. Remember also that parking is free in many places for the duration of your Bergen Card.

BOAT
From May to mid-September, the **Vågen Harbour Ferry** (Map pp178–9; ☎ 55 56 04 00; one-way/return adult Nkr30/40, child Nkr20/30) runs between the Torget fish market and Tollbodhopen at Nordnes (near the Bergen Aquarium) approximately every half-hour from 10am to 6pm.

HARDANGERFJORD

VOSS
pop 5500
The inland town of Voss is the de facto capital of the Hardangerfjord region and the place to get a big adrenaline rush – Voss is one of Norway's adventure capitals.

History
From medieval times, Voss served as an agricultural centre and staging post for trade between eastern and western Norway. In 1023, King Olav Haraldsson den Heilige (St Olav) stopped by to erect a cross in honour of Voss' conversion to Christianity. The town centre was devastated by German bombers in 1940, but was reconstructed after WWII.

Information
Nordic Ventures (☎ 56 51 00 17; ⏰ 9am-8pm mid-Apr–Sep; per 30min Nkr35) Contact this place for Internet access. It is located by the lakeside behind the Park Hotel.
Tourist office (☎ 56 52 08 00; www.visitvoss.no; Uttrågata; ⏰ 9am-7pm Mon-Sat, 2-7pm Sun Jun-Aug, 8am-3.30pm Mon-Fri Sep-May) This well-informed office is well worth a visit.

Sights
VANGSKYRKJA & ST OLAV'S CROSS
Voss' stone **church** (☎ 56 51 94 00; Uttrågata; adult/child Nkr20/free; ⏰ 10am-4pm Jun-Aug, shorter hours rest-of-year) occupies the site of an ancient pagan temple. A Gothic-style stone church

SOUTHWESTERN FJORDS BERGEN & THE

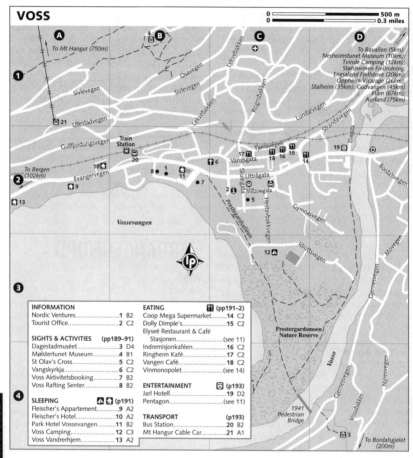

VOSS

0 _____ 500 m
0 _____ 0.3 miles

To Mt Hangur (750m)

To Bavallen (5km);
Nesheimstunet Museum (10km);
Tvinde Camping (12km);
Stølsheimen Fjellridning;
Engjaland Fjellstove (20km);
Oppheim Vicarage (26km);
Stalheim (35km); Gudvangen (45km);
Flåm (67km);
Aurland (75km)

To Bergen
(102km)

Vossevangen

Prestegardsmoen /
Nature Reserve

1941
Pedestrian
Bridge

To Bordalsgjelet
(200m)

INFORMATION	
Nordic Ventures....................**1** B2	
Tourist Office.......................**2** C2	

SIGHTS & ACTIVITIES (pp189–91)	
Dagestadmuséet...................**3** D4	
Mølstertunet Museum...........**4** B1	
St Olav's Cross....................**5** C2	
Vangskyrkja........................**6** C2	
Voss Aktivitetsbooking..........**7** B2	
Voss Rafting Senter..............**8** B2	

SLEEPING 🏠 🏠 (p191)	
Fleischer's Appartement.........**9** A2	
Fleischer's Hotel..................**10** A2	
Park Hotel Vossevangen........**11** B2	
Voss Camping.....................**12** C3	
Voss Vandrerhjem.................**13** A2	

EATING 🍴 (pp191–2)	
Coop Mega Supermarket........**14** C2	
Dolly Dimple's....................**15** C2	
Elyseé Restaurant & Café	
Stasjonen........................(see 11)	
Indremisjonkaféen...............**16** C2	
Ringheim Kafé....................**17** C2	
Vangen Café......................**18** C2	
Vinmonopolet.....................(see 14)	

ENTERTAINMENT 🎭 (p193)	
Jarl Hotell.........................**19** D2	
Pentagon..........................(see 11)	

TRANSPORT (p193)	
Bus Station........................**20** B2	
Mt Hangur Cable Car............**21** A1	

was built here in the mid-13th century, for
which the city elders received a congratula-
tory letter from King Magnus Lagabøte in
1271. Although the original stone altar and
the unique (and rather ugly) wooden spire
remain, the Lutheran Reformation of 1536
brought about the removal of many original
features. The 1923 stained-glass work commemorates the 900th anniversary of Christianity in Voss. Miraculously, the building
escaped destruction or any sort of devastation during the intense German bombing
of Voss in 1940.

In a field southeast of the church stands
a **stone cross**, erected by St Olav in 1023
to commemorate the local conversion to
Christianity.

PRESTEGARDSMOEN

The **Prestegardsmoen Recreational and Nature
Reserve**, which extends southward from
Voss Camping, offers a series of hiking
tracks and the chance to observe 140 species of plants and 124 bird species.

VOSS FOLK MUSEUM

The main portion of the Voss Folk Museum
(Voss Folkemuseum) is the **Mølstertunet Museum** (☎ 56 51 15 11; Mølstervegen 143; adult/child
Nkr40/free; ☽ 10am-5pm daily mid-May–mid-Sep, 10am-
3pm Mon-Fri, noon-3pm Sun rest-of-year), which lies
at the farm Mølster, on the hillside above
town. This collection of historic farm buildings, which date from the mid-17th to mid-
19th centuries, displays various facets of life

in earlier times from their fine hilltop location. There are guided tours (included in the admission price) on the hour, every hour.

The other two portions of the museum, the **Nesheimstunet Museum** and the old wooden **Oppheim vicarage**, lie 10km and 26km from Voss respectively, along Gudvangen Rd (E16). Although the grounds themselves are open, to see inside the buildings you'll need to ring ahead.

DAGESTADMUSÉET

This **museum** (☎ 56 51 65 33; Helgavangen 52; adult/child Nkr30/free; ☻ 11am-2pm Tue-Sun Jun–mid-Aug) was opened in 1950 by renowned local wood-carver Magnus Dagestad (1865–1957) and features his lifetime of carvings, drawings and traditional wooden furniture creations, as well as works by his wife, Helena Dagestad. It's an unusual and worthwhile exhibit. It lies about 1.5km from the town centre.

Tours

The famous 'Norway in a Nutshell' tour, normally done between Oslo and Bergen, also works as a day tour from Voss. It involves rail trips from Voss to Myrdal and Flåm, the boat to Gudvangen and the bus back to Voss (adult/child Nkr480/240, 6½ to 8½ hours). Book through the tourist office, any travel agency, or directly through **NSB** (☎ 56 52 80 07) at the train station.

The tourist office also organises 6½-hour day excursions to Ulvik (p193) and Eidfjord (p197) through a bus-ferry combination; tickets cost from Nkr250/180 per adult/child. The tourist office can also organise guided hiking tours in the surrounding hills.

Festivals

For details of Voss' **Extreme Sports Festival**, see the boxed text, p192.

On the last weekend of August, the **Voss Blues & Roots Festival** (☎ 56 51 63 03; www.vossblues .no; Fri/Sat day pass Nkr400/500, festival pass Nkr790) is one of Norway's better music festivals.

The late September **Sheep's Head Food Festival** involves exploring the culinary delights of sheep heads. It's definitely an acquired taste.

Sleeping

Voss Camping (☎ 56 51 15 97; www.vosscamping.no; Prestegardsalléen 40; tent/caravan sites Nkr110/130, cabins Nkr400) The lakeside and centrally located Voss Camping has basic facilities. It can get a bit rowdy in summer but the location's a winner.

Tvinde Camping (☎ 56 51 69 19; www.tvinde.no; Tvinde; tent sites per person from Nkr100, cabins from Nkr300) If you don't mind being a bit out of town, this scenic alternative lies beside a waterfall about 12km north of town. Without a car, access is on the Voss–Gudvangen bus (Nkr30, 20 minutes).

Voss Vandrerhjem (☎ 56 51 20 17; www.vossvan drerhjem.no; Evangervegen 68; dm/s/d incl breakfast Nkr195/420/540; ☻ year-round; P) The modern Voss hostel offers en suite rooms and fine lake views; ask for a top floor, lakeside room. Bicycles, canoes and kayaks can be hired and there's a free sauna.

Fleischer's Hotel (☎ 56 52 05 00; www.fleischers.no; Evangervegen; s/d Nkr1125/1490; 💻 P 🐾) For historic character, the enormous and beautiful Fleischer's Hotel, opened in 1888, oozes old-world charm and is the best place in town. Some rooms have lake views and special offers abound to make this even more affordable in summer.

Fleischer's Appartement (☎ 56 52 05 00; hotel@ fleischers.no; Evangervegen; 2-/4-bed apt per person Nkr495/395; 💻 P 🐾) This lakeside annexe of the Fleischer's Hotel offers small but adequate self-catering units.

Park Hotel Vossevangen (☎ 56 53 10 00; www .parkvoss.no; Uttrågata 1; s Nkr725-825, d Nkr950-1250; 💻 P) While this place lacks the elegance of Fleischer's Hotel, the modern rooms are nonetheless very comfortable and many overlook the lake Vossevangen.

Eating

Elysée (☎ 56 51 13 22; Park Hotel Vossevangen; Uttrågata 1; mains Nkr119-239; ☻ lunch & dinner) The finest restaurant option in Voss specialises in French and international cuisine and has a particularly extensive wine list. In the same hotel is the popular train-theme Café Stasjonen (dishes Nkr30 to Nkr155), where they offer snacks, light meals (including nachos for Nkr45) and heartier dishes such as oven-baked salmon with vegetables (Nkr115).

Dolly Dimple's (☎ 56 51 00 40; Vangsgata 52; pizzas from Nkr115; ☻ lunch & dinner) Dolly Dimple's serves good, large pizzas which make a meal for two.

The restaurant in the **Fleischer's Hotel** (above; ☻ lunch & dinner) is also excellent, with

EXTREME SPORTS IN VOSS

If high-energy thrills are your thing, Voss will be something of a haven from slow fjord boats. It all comes together in late June, when Voss hosts **Extremesport Week** (☎ 48 06 60 92; www.ekstrem sportveko.com), which attracts adrenaline junkies with a range of activities and competitions with most events open to public participation.

For bookings, or to get an idea of what's available, contact **Voss Aktivitetsbooking** (Voss Activity Booking; ☎ 99 47 65 75; ☺ 10am-5pm Mon-Thu & Sun, 10am-8pm Fri & Sat), opposite the Park Hotel (see p191). Alternatively, you can contact the operators directly.

Horse riding

For details on horse riding in Stølsheimen (Nkr450/750 for three hours/full day), contact the English-run **Stølsheimen Fjellridning/Engjaland Fjellstove** (☎ 56 51 91 66; www.engjaland.no; Engjaland), 20km north of Voss. In the high season, B&B accommodation in this simple lodge costs Nkr300 to Nkr375. It's also a good base for hut-to-hut hiking in the spectacular Stølsheimen mountains.

Paragliding, Parasailing & Bungee-Jumping

Nordic Ventures (☎ 56 51 00 17; www.nordicventures.com) is one of the best activity centres of its kind in Norway, offering tandem paragliding flights (Nkr1000 to Nkr1200), parasailing (Nkr450 to Nkr1500) and even bungee jumps from a parasail (Nkr1495)! Their expeditions sometimes run for a whole day and include a barbecue lunch. As their motto says: 'Be brave. Even if you're not, pretend to be. No-one can tell the difference.'

Skiing

The ski season in Voss lasts from early December until April, depending on snow conditions. The winter action focuses on the cable car route up Mt Hangur. Those with vehicles can opt for Bavallen, 5km north of the centre, which has two chairlifts and is used for international downhill competitions. Lift tickets and equipment hire are available at either slope; from mid-May until mid-August, the **cable car** (☎ 56 51 12 12; adult/child Nkr75/45 return; h11am-5pm) takes day-trippers. There's a winter ski school at Hangur. On the plateau and up the Raundalen Valley at Mjølfjell, you'll also find excellent cross-country skiing. For weather and snow conditions, call ☎ 56 51 94 88.

Watersports

If you're unable to take to the air, you don't need to be left behind. **Voss Rafting Senter** (☎ 56 51 05 25; www.vossrafting.no) has everything from white-water rafting (Nkr450 to Nkr700 or Nkr1600 per family) and canyoning (Nkr700) to waterfall abseiling (from Nkr700) and river-boarding (Nkr750). Rafters and river-boarders can choose between three very different rivers: the Stranda (Class III to IV), Raundalen (Class III to V) and Vosso (Class II). Not to be outdone in the motto stakes, theirs is: 'We guarantee to wet your pants'.

Nordic Ventures (☎ 56 51 00 17; www.nordicventures.com) also runs sea-kayaking expeditions, ranging from lake tours (four to five hours, Nkr550) to one-/two-/three-day tours (Nkr890/1495/ 2250). The longer tours take place in the vicinity of the stunning Nærøyfjord (p214).

a salad buffet (Nkr95), light meals (Nkr85 to Nkr105) and main dishes (Nkr175 to Nkr225).

For cakes, snacks and reindeer roast, try **Vangen Café** (☎ 56 51 12 05; Vangsgata 42; dishes Nkr45-102; ☺ 10am-6pm Mon-Fri, 10.30am-4pm Sat, 12.30-6pm Sun), while traditional Norwegian food is served at **Indremisjonskaféen** (☎ 51 56 14 08; Vangsgata 46; snacks & light meals Nkr35-99; ☺ 9.30am-6pm Mon-Fri, 9.30am-3pm Sat, noon-6pm Sun). You'll find a more varied menu at the **Ringheim Kafé** (☎ 56 51 13 65; Vangsgata 32; mains Nkr89-199; ☺ lunch & dinner).

The Coop Mega supermarket and Vinmonopolet are both in the same block on Strandavegen.

Entertainment

Park Hotel Vossevangen (☎ 56 53 10 00; Uttrågata 1) has a piano bar, for those who like their music light, and the somewhat more energetic and popular Pentagon weekend disco. The pub in the **Jarl Hotell** (☎ 56 51 19 33; Elvegata 9) has a cellar disco which attracts the 18-to-25 crowd with house and techno.

Getting There & Away

Buses stop at the train station, west of the centre. Frequent bus services connect Voss with Bergen (Nkr158, two hours) and Aurland (Nkr122, 1½ hours), via Gudvangen and Flåm, but only three to seven daily run between Voss and Norheimsund (Nkr130, two hours).

NSB rail services (☎ 56 52 80 00) on the renowned *Bergensbanen* to/from Bergen (Nkr155, one hour, hourly) and Oslo (Nkr575, 5½ to six hours, five daily) connect at Myrdal (Nkr85, 50 minutes) with the scenic line down to Flåm (see p213).

Getting Around

Bicycle hire is available for around Nkr200 per day from **Voss Aktivitetsbooking** (☒ 10am-5pm Mon-Thu & Sun, 10am-8pm Fri & Sat), beside the Park Hotel Vossevangen, or for Nkr150/250 per half/full day from the Voss Vandrerhjem (see p191).

STALHEIM

This gorgeous little spot high above the valley was, between 1647 and 1909, a stopping-off point for travellers on the Royal Mail route between Copenhagen, Christiania (Oslo) and Bergen. Here they rested and changed horses after climbing up the valley and through the Stalheimskleiva gorge, flanked by the Stalheim and Sivle waterfalls. What draws people these days are the breathtaking views down Nærøydalen from the **terrace** (☒ 9.30am-6pm mid-May–Sep) of the Stalheim Hotel.

The **Stalheim Folkemuseum** (☎ 56 52 01 22; Stalheim; adult/child Nkr40/free; ☒ on request), near the hotel, includes folk exhibits and 30 log buildings laid out as a traditional farm.

One place where the view makes all the difference is **Stalheim Hotel** (☎ 56 52 01 22; www.stalheim.com; s/d Nkr890/1290; ☒ mid-May–Sep) so make sure you ask when making a booking. The hotel once featured in *Conde Nast's* 'best rooms-with-a-view'. The rooms are spacious and comfortable, but you'll scarcely be able to tear yourself away from the window to notice. Lunch/dinner buffets cost Nkr210/335, but lighter meals are available.

To reach Stalheim from Voss (Nkr56, one hour, four to 11 daily), take any bus towards the towns of Gudvangen/Aurland, but you may have to hike 1.3km up from the main road unless you can persuade the bus driver to make the short detour to the lovely town.

NORHEIMSUND & ØYSTESE

pop 3700

Quiet little Norheimsund is a gateway to Hardangerfjord and a terminal for ferries to the inner reaches of one of Norway's finest stretches of inland water.

For details of cruises and tourist offices, see the boxed text, p194.

Just 1km west of Norheimsund along Rv7 is the picturesque **Steinsdalsfossen waterfall**. It may be a far cry from Norway's highest, but it does offer the chance to walk behind the water. Another attraction in town is the unusual **Hardanger Boat-building Museum** (Hardanger Fartøyvernsenter; ☎ 56 55 33 50; www.fartoyvern.no; adult/child Nkr50/25; ☒ 10am-5pm daily end May–end Aug), where you'll find old wooden boats, restoration procedures, rope making and exhibitions; they sometimes also offer two-hour cruises on the breathtaking fjord in a restored cutter.

Sleeping & Eating

Sandven Hotel (☎ 56 55 20 88; www.sandvenhotel .no; Norheimsund; s/d from Nkr700/1040; ☐ ℗) Located right on the waterfront in the centre of Norheimsund, the atmospheric Sandven Hotel dates from 1857 and has loads of charm, expansive balconies and excellent views. You may also want to try the Crown Prince suite (Nkr2000) – this is where the future king of Norway stayed.

Hardangerfjord Hotell (☎ 56 55 63 00; www.hardangerfjord-hotell.no; s/d from Nkr700/1010; ☐ ℗ ☒) Another good choice, this modern hotel offers pleasant rooms and a fjord-side location in Øystese.

Campers are well catered-for at either **Mo Camping** (☎ 56 55 17 27; tent sites Nkr110, cabins from Nkr400), 1km west of town off Rv7, or **Oddland Camping** (☎ 56 55 16 86; odaksnes@online.no; tent sites Nkr110, cabins from Nkr400) in Øystese.

EXPLORING HARDANGERFJORD

To get the best of Hardangerfjord takes careful planning.

From Norheimsund, Eidfjord & Lofthus

Norheimsund is one of the easiest place to start your exploration. The routes most geared towards tourists are the **Hardanger Fjord Cruises** (☎ 55 23 87 80; www.hsd.no; May–mid-Sep). The most popular route is from Norheimsund to the delightful Eidfjord (adult/child Nkr304/190 return) and back again. Departures are at 8.55am (arrival in Eidfjord 11.40am), while the return journey leaves from Eidfjord at 2.40pm (1.05pm on Saturday) making it back to Norheimsund at 5.25pm (3.55pm Saturday). Tickets can be purchased from the **Norheimsund tourist office** (☎ 56 55 19 88; k-reise@online.no; h9am-6pm Mon-Fri, 10am-4pm Sat mid-Jun–mid-Aug), in **Øystese tourist office** (☎ 56 55 59 10; www.kvam-reiselivskontor.no; h9am-7pm Mon-Fri, 9am-6pm Sat, 3-8pm Sun mid-Jun–mid-Aug, 9am-3.30pm Mon-Fri rest-of-year), or on board the boat. From mid-June to mid-August, there are sightseeing tours (adult/child Nkr165/95) in Eidfjord. The boats also connect with buses to/from Bergen.

A shorter alternative route, runs between Norheimsund and Lofthus (adult/child Nkr240/150 return), leaving Norheimsund at 8.55am (arrival in Lofthus at 10.05am), and returning at 4.15pm (2.40pm Saturday) to arrive in Norheimsund at 5.25pm (3.55pm Saturdays).

Another possibility is to join the four-hour scenic cruise on Fyksesund, a narrow arm of the fjord just east of Øystese. These generally run from Norheimsund (adult/child Nkr200/100) on Mondays in summer only at 11am. Remember that sailing times can change so contact the Norheimsund tourist office to confirm sailing times.

From Ulvik

The **Ulvik tourist office** (☎ 56 52 63 60; ulvikturist@ulvik.org) sells tickets to a range of self-guided excursions which take in much of Hardangerfjord by boat, ferry and express boat from June to August. These are:

- Eidfjord (adult/child Nkr190/96 return; Monday–Saturday) – via Bruravik and Brimnes; allows two hours each at Hardangervidda Nature Centre and Eidfjord; departs Ulvik 8.55am and arrives back at 3.10pm
- Eidfjord & Vøringfossen Waterfall (adult/child boat only Nkr160/80, with tour of nature centre and waterfall Nkr355/275; Monday–Saturday) – departs 11.10am and arrives back at 3.10pm
- Kinsarvik and Utne (Nkr205/102; Monday–Friday) – via Bruravik, Brimnes, Kvanndal and Granvin; departs Ulvik at 8.55am and arrives back 4.40pm
- Hardanger Grand Tour (Nkr310/155; Monday–Friday) – same as previous tour but also stops in Odda

From Bergen

There are numerous summer possibilities for day-trips to Hardangerfjord from Bergen using bus and ferries. Lasting for up to 12 hours with stops of two to six hours to allow you explore the towns and surrounds, possible destinations include Rosendal (adult/child Nkr350/250), Lofthus (Nkr450/275), Ulvik (Nkr595/320), Utne and Kinsarvik (Nkr450/275) and Eidfjord (Nkr610/415 plus Nkr195/110 sightseeing in Eidfjord). Tickets can be purchased at **NSB** (Norwegian State Railways; ☎ 55 96 69 00) in Bergen or the **Bergen tourist office** (☎ 55 55 20 00).

Getting There & Away

Three to seven daily buses run between Voss and Norheimsund (Nkr130, two hours) via Øystese. Six to 12 daily buses run from Øystese to Bergen (Nkr137, 1¾ hours) via Norheimsund.

ULVIK & OSA

pop 682

There's something special about Ulvik, in the heart of Norway's apple-growing territory. Framed by hills and mountains and with wonderful views up the fjord, Ulvik is a place to surround yourself with tranquil silence.

The Ulvik **tourist office** (☎ 56 52 63 60; www .visitulvik.com; ☻ 8.30am-5pm Mon-Sat, 1-5pm Sun mid-May–mid-Sep, 8.30am-1.30pm Mon-Fri rest-of-year) hires bicycles for Nkr35/80/150 per hour/ half-day/day, and they also organise **fruit -farm visits** (Nkr125; open from Monday to Friday from mid-June to mid-August).

At the **Stream Nest complex** (☎ 56 52 69 90; Osa; adult/child Nkr30/free; ☻ 10am-4pm mid-May–mid-Aug), 10km east of Ulvik, highlights include the ecological herb garden, several artworks including Allan Christensen's *Rambukk* (pile driver), and the odd eponymous log sculpture, *Stream Nest*, originally conceived by Japanese artist Takamasa Kuniyasu for the 1994 Winter Olympics in Lillehammer. The sculpture resounds with the tuba music of Geir Løvold, just as it did during the Games.

Sleeping & Eating

Ulvik Fjordcamping (☎ 56 52 61 70; camping@ulvik .org; Ulvik; tent or caravan sites Nkr110, huts from s/d Nkr200/300) This convenient place, 500m from the centre of town, is small and right by the water's edge.

Uppheim Gård (☎ 56 52 62 93; www.uppheim-farm .com; Ulvik; s/d Nkr650/750) This lovely old farmhouse, 2km uphill and north of the village, has lovely accommodation and great views.

Ulvik Fjord Pensjonat (☎ 56 52 61 70; www.ulvik-fjordpensjonat.no; Ulvik; s/d from Nkr550/780) Another excellent choice, this well-run guesthouse offers very comfortable rooms. It's across the road from the water, but some rooms have balconies terraces overlooking a bubbling stream.

Rica Brakanes Hotel (☎ 56 52 61 05; www.braknes-hotel.no; Ulvik; s/d from Nkr710/990; buffet dinner Nkr325, mains from Nkr139; ⌨ P ⌨) This huge modern hotel has a front-row seat to some of the best views in Hardangerfjord, although you pay an extra Nkr100 per person for a fjord view. The hotel also organises 15-minute helicopter sightseeing flights (per person Nkr550).

You'll find a supermarket and kiosk for snacks located a few doors west of the tourist office.

Getting There & Around

Between Voss and Ulvik (Nkr75, 1¼ hours), buses run two to six times daily. For ferry services, see the boxed text, p194.

ODDA

pop 5500

Industrial, iron-smelting Odda is the ugly cousin of beautiful Hardangerfjord. Frequently cited as Norway's ugliest town – it fights hard for the honour with some pretty dire places in Finnmark – its reputation is redeemed by the fact that offers a front-row view of one of Norway's finest landscapes: the innermost reaches of Hardangerfjord with a riotous waterfall and the icy heights of the fabulous Folgefonn glacier. Just try not to breathe in while you're admiring the view. The Odda **tourist office** (☎ 53 64 12 97; www.visitodda.com; ☻ 9am-6pm Mon-Fri, 9am-5pm Sat, 11am-5pm Sun Jun-Aug, 8.30am-4pm Sep-May) is near the Sørfjorden shore and has Internet access (per 15 minutes Nkr15). It also offers advice on exploring Folgefonn and surrounds. If you're in town on a Thursday or Friday in summer, they can also point you in the direction of restored workers' cottages in town and which date from 1910, as well as some good hiking trails nearby.

Sights

FOLGEFONN

Folgefonn, mainland Norway's third-largest icefield, offers summer skiing, snowboarding and sledding from mid-June to October. Short tours to the ski centre leave from Jondal Quay at 10.30am from mid-June to mid-August and return at 3.30pm, connecting with ferries and buses to/from Norheimsund. From Odda, weekend glacier trips run to Odda Turlag's Holmaskjær mountain hut; contact the tourist office for details.

Anyone in good physical condition with warm clothing and sturdy footwear can take a guided one-hour hike up the lovely Buer valley followed by a glacier walk on the Buer arm of Folgefonn (minimum three persons, Nkr350/person, including crampons and ice axes). Transport to the starting point, at Buer, 9km west of Odda, isn't included. You can also walk to the glacier face on your own (24km return from Odda).

TYSSESTRENGENE WATERFALL

About 5km east of town, in Skjeggedal, the 960m, 42-degree **Mågelibanen Funicular** runs on Wednesday and Friday for Nkr100/50 adult/child return. Hikers can head for the top of the **Tyssestrengene waterfall** (646m) and the outrageous **Trolltunga rock feature**, from either Skjeggedal (eight to 10 hours return) or the upper funicular station (six to eight hours return). Contact the tourist office for further details.

Sleeping & Eating

Odda Camping (☎ 41 32 16 10; Odda; tent/caravan sites Nkr130; ☺ mid-May–Aug) The most convenient camping is on the shores of the lake Sandvinvatnet, a 20-minute uphill walk south of the town centre.

Hardanger Hotel & Restaurant (☎ 53 65 14 00; post@hardangerhotel.no; Eitrheimsveien 17; s/d Nkr890/110, lunch Nkr59-139, dinner mains Nkr195-258, specials Nkr85-105) The upmarket Hardanger Hotel offers comfortable rooms with modern facilities and a reasonable restaurant/cafeteria.

Tyssedal Hotel (☎ 53 64 69 07; tyssohot@online .no; Tyssedal; s/d from Nkr850/950, 3-course menu Nkr325, mains Nkr89-289) The recommended Icelandic-run Tyssedal Hotel has great en suite rooms for those who don't believe in ghosts (the hotel is reputedly haunted). There's also an extraordinary gallery of fantastic fairy-tale and Hardangerfjord landscape paintings by Eidfjord artist Nils Bergslien and an Icelandic chef, who rustles up delicacies like *skyr* (Icelandic yoghurt) and fruit (Nkr85).

Getting There & Away

Between Odda and Jondal (Nkr135, 2½ hours), local buses operate one to three times daily. One to three daily Nor-Way Bussekspress buses run to/from Bergen (Nkr275, 3¾ hours) and Oslo (Nkr490, 7¼ hours).

ROSENDAL & AROUND

pop 955

Just west of Folgefonn, scenic Rosendal can now be reached by an 11km-long road **tunnel** (car Nkr60; ☺ 6am-10pm) under the icefield from Odda. The **tourist office** (☎ 53 48 42 80; ☺ 9am-6pm Mon-Fri, 10am-5pm Sat, 11am-5pm Sun May-Sep) is by Rosendal Quay.

At Sunndal, 4km west of the tunnel, take the road up the Sunndal valley (drivable for 1km), then walk 2km on a good track to lake Bondhusvatnet, where there's a wonderful view of the glacier **Bondhusbreen**. In Uskedalen, 14km west of Rosendal, there's an extraordinary rock-slab mountain, Ulvenåso (1247m), offering some of the best **rock climbing** in Norway; contact the tourist office in Rosendal for details.

The 1665 **Baroniet Rosendal** (☎ 53 48 29 99; Rosendal; adult/child Nkr75/10; ☺ variable hours daily May-Aug, hourly guided tours), Norway's only baronial mansion, features period interiors, a Renaissance rose garden, concerts and art exhibitions.

In Sunndal, there's the reasonable **Sundal Camping** (☎ 53 48 41 86; fax 53 48 18 20, Sunndal; tent sites Nkr100, cabins Nkr300-500).

The ornate **Rosendal Gjestgiveri** (☎ /fax 53 47 36 66; Skålagato 17; Rosendal; s/d with shared bathroom Nkr550/750, mains Nkr89-179) dates from 1887 and offers an atmospheric B&B. The restaurant is probably the best in the area and there's a decent pub in the basement.

Buses run three to seven times daily between Rosendal and Odda via Sunndal. There are also up to seven daily runs between the Løfallstrand ferry quay (4km north of Rosendal) and Uskedalen, via Rosendal, and two daily connections to Bergen via Løfallstrand.

UTNE, LOFTHUS & KINSARVIK

pop 3200

At the picturesque fruit-growing village of Utne, you'll find the excellent open-air **Hardanger Folk Museum** (☎ 53 67 00 40; www.har danger.museum.no; adult/child Nkr40/free; ☺ 10am-4pm daily May-Jun, 10am-5pm daily Jul-Aug, 10am-3pm Mon-Fri Sep-Apr), which comprises a collection of historic homes, boats, shops, outhouses and a school, plus exhibitions on Hardanger women, weddings, fiddle-making, fishing, music and dance, orchard crops and the woodcarvings of local artist Lars Kinsarvik; they also bake delicious local cakes on Tuesdays (noon to 3pm) in July.

At Kinsarvik, a ferry ride (per person/vehicle Nkr28/70; 30 minutes) across Sørfjorden, you'll see one of Norway's first **stone churches** (admission free; ☺ 10am-7pm May-Aug). First built in around 1250, it was restored in 1880 and 1961. Chalk paintings on the walls depict the weighing of souls by Michael the Archangel.

Kinsarvik offers an appealing access trail past the cooling **Husedalen waterfalls** and onto the network of tracks through the wild forest of **Hardangervidda National Park** (p136). Nearby Lofthus has **Grieg's Hut** (Lofthus; admission free; ☺ always open), the one-time retreat of Norwegian composer Edvard Grieg (see p181) located in the garden of Hotel Ullensvang.

For information on hiking in the national park, contact the **Kinsarvik tourist office** (☎ 53 66 31 12; www.kinsarvik.com; ☾ 9am-7pm mid-Jun–mid-Aug, shorter hours rest-of-year) or **Lofthus tourist office** (☎ 53 66 11 90; turistinfo@lofthus.no; ☾ 9am-7pm mid-Jun–mid-Aug, shorter hours rest-of-year).

Sleeping

Bråvoll Camping (☎ 53 66 35 10; Kinsarvik; tent/caravan sites Nkr120 plus Nkr20 electricity, s/d huts Nkr270/330) This simple, friendly place is right by the water's edge and has a water slide for kids and the young-at-heart.

Hardanger Gjestegård (☎ 53 66 67 10; post@ hardanger-gjestegard.no; Alsåker; s/d Nkr600/650) This atmospheric guesthouse, 10km west of Utne on Fv550, is in a pretty 1898 building with character-filled rooms.

Utne Hotel (☎ 53 66 64 00; utnehot@online.no; Utne; s/d with shared bathroom Nkr350/550, with private bathroom Nkr790/1250; ☐ ℗) The historic wooden Utne Hotel was built in 1722 after the Great Nordic War; it has been in business ever since and was restored in 2003. The hotel's fabulous décor makes it worth a look even if you're not staying.

Hotel Ullensvang (☎ 53 67 00 00; www.hotel -ullensvang.no; Lofthus; s/d from Nkr715/1070, fjord view extra Nkr100 per r; buffet dinner Nkr375; ☐ ℗ 🏊) This enormous, luxurious place has exceptional views, supremely comfortable rooms and a good restaurant.

Getting There & Away

Nor-Way Bussekspress buses run between Bergen (Nkr210, 2½ hours), and Oslo (Nkr535, 8¼ to nine hours) via Odda (Nkr77, one hour), and pass through Utne once or twice daily.

For ferries around Hardangerfjord, see the boxed text on p194.

EIDFJORD & AROUND

pop 580

At the innermost reaches of Hardangerfjorden you'll find sheer mountains, huge cascading waterfalls, spiral tunnels and charming farms perched on mountain ledges with great views. The town of Eidfjord has a stunning location and is an excellent base from which to explore the region. The **tourist office** (☎ 53 67 34 00; www.eid fjordinfo.com; ☾ 9am-6pm Mon-Fri, noon-6pm Sat & Sun mid-Jun–mid-Aug, shorter hours rest-of-year) is helpful with advice on local sights.

Sights

Apart from the view from the water's edge, there are some wonderful sights in the Eidfjord vicinity. The **Kjeåsen Farm**, 6km northeast of Eidfjord, above all others should not be missed. One of Norway's top scenic locations, the wonderfully remote farm buildings are still inhabited by an old woman who sometimes shows visitors around from 9am to 5pm daily. It's possible to climb up on foot (four hours return), but it's steep and quite perilous involving at least one rope-bridge; ask the tourist office for details and directions. The road goes through a one-way tunnel – driving up on the hour, down on the half-hour; ignore the signs that list the last time as 5.30pm as the road is open 24 hours.

At the foot of the road leading up to the farm, the **Sima Power Plant** (☎ 53 67 34 00; adult/child Nkr50/40; guided tours at noon, 2pm daily mid-Jun–mid-Aug) runs guided tours (one hour).

The excellent **Hardangervidda Natursenter** (☎ 53 66 59 00; www.hardangervidda.org; Øvre Eidfjord; adult/child Nkr80/40; ☾ 9am-8pm daily Jun-Aug, 10am-6pm Apr-May & Sep-Oct) is a terrific introduction to one of Norway's most beautiful national parks. The centre shows a must-see 19-minute movie, interactive displays and interesting natural history and geology exhibits.

Another spectacular spot is the 145m-high **Vøringfoss waterfall**, 18km southeast of Eidfjord along Rv7. Although there are good views from along the road, the best views are from the car park (Nkr20) of the Fossli Hotel.

Sleeping & Eating

Sæbø Camping (☎ 53 66 59 27; scampi@online.no; Øvre Eidfjord; tent sites Nkr100, cabins Nkr250-550) This good camping ground combines well-kept facilities with a pretty location just 500m from the Hardangervidda Natursenter.

Quality Hotel Vøringfoss (☎ 53 67 41 00; voring foss@quality.choicehotels.no; s/d mid-Jun–mid-Aug from Nkr890/990, Sat & Sun mid-Aug–Dec Nkr790/890) This swish hotel opened in 2001 and offers extraordinary views from its fjord-facing rooms. Even if you're staying in cheaper places elsewhere, this is a great place for a splurge to wake up to an exceptional vista. It also has a café which serves light meals and snacks (Nkr35 to Nkr145, kids' menu Nkr45); the wild boar burger with curry mayonnaise (Nkr120) makes a change from Norwegian kiosk food.

Vik Pensjonat (☎ 53 66 51 62; www.vikpensjonat .com; Eidfjord; s/d/tr with shared bathroom incl breakfast from Nkr350/450/650, d with private bathroom & kitchen incl breakfast Nkr850, cabins from Nkr650) This appealing place just behind the tourist office in the centre of town is set in a lovely, renovated old home, offers a range of good accommodation and has a small café.

Ingrid's Appartement (☎ 53 66 54 85; fax 53 66 57 10; Eidfjord; d Nkr600, 4-bed f Nkr750) This recommended, family-run place has well-kept apartments with bathroom and kitchen and some have good views.

Eidfjord Hotel (☎ 53 66 52 64; eidfjordhotel@produkt nett.no; Eidfjord; s/d with Fjordpass from Nkr675/780; mains Nkr75-159) This modern hotel offers comfortable, if simple and uninspiring rooms, some of which have partial views of the fjord. The garden terrace is a good place to chill and the restaurant is reasonable.

Getting There & Away
Buses run between Geilo and Odda via Vøringfoss, Øvre Eidfjord and Eidfjord once or twice daily, plus several extra runs daily except Sunday between Øvre Eidfjord, Eidfjord and Odda. See the boxed text on p194 for details of ferries.

STAVANGER

pop 171,300

Stavanger, Norway's fourth-largest city, is one of our favourite cities in Norway, a lively, cosmopolitan place which has never lost its small-town feel. Home to a well-preserved timbered old town, a historic harbour and some of Norway's more interesting museums, Stavanger well deserves its prize as the designated 2008 European Capital of Culture. The town is also the ideal base for exploring the extraordinary beauty of Lysefjord (p206) and its eyrie-like vantage point Preikestolen (p206).

Orientation
The bus and train stations are located alongside each other on the southwestern shore of the lake Breiavann, about 10 minutes' walk from the harbour. Most sites of interest are within easy walking distance of the attractive harbour.

Information
Most major banks are represented along Olav V's gate and Håkon VII's gate. Den Norske Bank and the adjacent post office offer competitive rates.

C@fe.com (☎ 51 55 41 20; Sølvberggata 15; 🕐 11am-9pm Mon-Sat, noon-9pm Sun; per hr Nkr55) For Internet access visit this place.

Fisketorget laundry services (Rosenkildetorget; wash-and-dry Nkr35; 🕐 24hr)

Public library (Kulturhus) Time-limited but free Internet access.

Stavanger Turistforening DNT (☎ 51 84 02 00; off Musegata; 🕐 10am-4pm Mon-Fri, 10am-6pm Sat, 10am-2pm Sun) This office has information on hiking and mountain huts.

Tourist office (☎ 51 85 92 00; www.visitstavanger .com; Rosenkildetorget 1; 🕐 9am-8pm daily Jun-Aug, 9am-4pm Mon-Fri, 9am-2pm Sat Sep-May) The Stavanger office is a rich source of local information, including details on Lysefjord and Preikestolen.

Sights
At last count, Stavanger had 23 museums; the tourist office has a full list.

OLD STAVANGER
Gamle (Old) Stavanger is a delight. The old town's cobblestone walkways pass between rows of 173 well-preserved late-18th-century whitewashed wooden houses, all immaculately kept and adorned with cheerful, well-tended flowerboxes, all scarcely a stone's throw from the buzzing harbour area. Now home to all sorts of artists' studios selling paintings, ceramics, weavings, hand-crafted jewellery and other items, it well rewards an hour or two's ambling.

NORWEGIAN EMIGRATION CENTRE
This **centre** (☎ 51 53 88 60; www.emigrationcenter .com; Strandkaien 31; 🕐 9am-3pm Mon & Wed-Fri; 9am-7pm Tue) helps foreigners of Norwegian descent trace their roots. In mid-June it stages a popular Emigration Festival.

STAVANGER CATHEDRAL
This partly Gothic, partly Anglo Norman-style **cathedral** (Stavanger Domkirke; Haakon VIIs gate; admission free; 🕐 11am-7pm daily Jun-Aug, shorter hours Sep-May) is an impressive, but understated, medieval stone cathedral dating from approximately 1125; it was extensively renovated following a fire in 1272. Despite once containing an arm of St Swithun (!) and a

STAVANGER

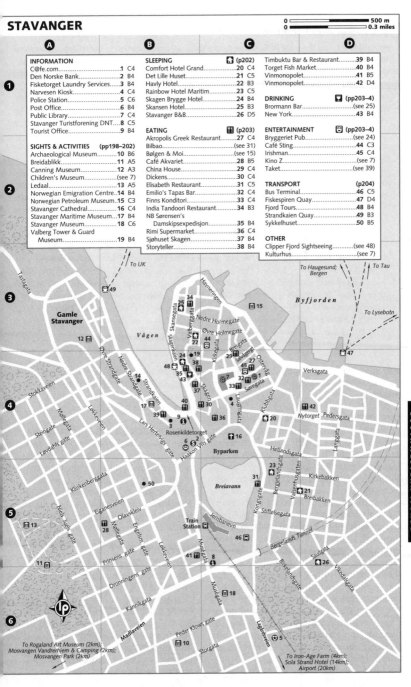

THE LOWLY SARDINE & THE CULT OF IDDIS

Around Stavanger the word *iddis*, derived from the local pronunciation of *etikett* (label), has come to apply to the colourfully artistic labels which appear on Norwegian sardine tins measuring precisely 75mm by 105mm. The first of Stavanger's original canneries, Stavanger Preserving, appeared in 1873 and initially produced tinned meat; by the turn of the century, however, the company's attentions had turned to brisling sardines, which had become a mainstay of the local economy. As Stavanger grew into Norway's sardine canning centre, more enterprises took interest and, by 1922, the city's canneries provided 50% of the town's employment. Each cannery had its own label, ranging from depictions of royalty, wild animals, polar explorers and seafaring scenes to architectural features, zeppelins, sports events and leisure activities. No-one knows exactly how many designs were actually used, but some estimates place the figure at up to 40,000.

These sardine tin labels created a stir in the local community, which recognised their artistry and collectability. Workers had access to the labels but other collectors had to await a *sjeining*, in which bundles of labels were cast to the wind to be gathered up by the general populace. In fact, these *iddis* became a form of currency for children, and were traded much the same as pokemon cards are today.

Perhaps the most popular and sought-after designs are the Christian Bjelland & Co *Man with a Fish* by Kittelsen, and the Skippers' sea captain, which depicts Scotsman William Duncan Anderson dressed in oilskins. The latter was designed by the Scottish artist Angus Watson, who came up with the name 'Skippers'. He purchased the copyright on a photo of Anderson, which he'd selected as the *iddis* for his brand, and commissioned an artist to come up with a likeness for the label. Unfortunately for poor William Duncan Anderson, the label turned him into a laughing stock and made it impossible for him to secure serious work with any fishing fleet. As a result, he was placed on the Skippers payroll for the rest of his days, and continued to work as an artists' model.

fine altar, these and other icons and relics went missing in the years following the Reformation.

NORWEGIAN PETROLEUM MUSEUM

This state-of-the-art **museum** (Norsk Oljemuseum; ☎ 51 93 93 00; www.norskolje.museum.no; Kjeringholmen; adult/child Nkr75/35; ☒ 10am-7pm daily Jun-Aug, 10am-4pm Mon-Sat, 10am-6pm Sun Sep-May) is one of Norway's best museums. Loaded with high-tech interactive displays, gigantic models and authentic reconstructions, its many highlights include the 3-D video covering the history of Earth, the extraordinary model of 'Ekofisk city' and the avant-garde 'petrodome' movie feature. Tracing the history of oil formation and exploration in the North Sea from discovery in 1969 until the present, the museum nicely balances the technical side of oil exploration and extraction with archive footage and newspapers of significant moments in the history of Norwegian oil. Not least among these are coverage of the Alexander L Kielland tragedy in 1980, when 123 oil workers were killed, and the 1950s declaration

by a Norwegian government commission that there was no prospect of finding oil in Norwegian waters! The museum also has a range of summer activities for kids.

VALBERG TOWER & GUARD MUSEUM

The historic **tower** Valbergtårnet was constructed as a guards' lookout in 1850 and now contains this interesting **museum** (Vekter-museet; ☎ 90 72 63 94, Valbergjet 2; over/under 5 years Nkr20/free; ☒ 10am-4pm Mon-Wed & Fri, 10am-6pm Thu 10am-2pm Sat). From behind the west side of the tower at ground level there are some reasonable views over the city.

STAVANGER MUSEUM

The large **five-part museum** (☎ 51 84 27 00; www.stavanger.museum.no; combined ticket adult/family Nkr40/90; ☒ 11am-4pm daily mid-Jun–mid-Aug 11am-4pm Sun only rest-of-year; Stavanger, Maritime & Canning museums also 11am-3pm Tue-Fri 1-14 Jun & 16 Aug-10 Sep), with its sites scattered around Stavanger, could easily fill a sightseeing day but you'd have to keep up a brisk pace to fit them all in. If you start early you should be able to see them all.

Stavanger Museum
The main **museum** (☎ 51 84 27 00; Muségata 16) reveals nearly 900 years of Stavanger's history, 'From Ancient Landscape to Oil Town'. Features include evidence of Stone Age habitation, the medieval bishopric, the herring years and the development of the city into a modern oil capital. The Stavanger of the 1880s is described in a series of tableaus focusing on local author Alexander L Kielland.

Canning Museum
Don't miss out on this **museum** (Hermetikkmuseet; ☎ 51 52 65 91; Øvre Strandgate 88-90); housed in an old cannery, it's one of Stavanger's most appealing museums. Here you'll get the lowdown on Stavanger's main industry from the 1890s to 1960 – canning brisling and fish balls. Before oil there were sardines – Stavanger was once home to more than half of Norway's canning factories. The exhibits take you through the whole 12-stage process from salting, through to threading, smoking, decapitating and packing. There are no labels but there's a handy brochure available at the entrance and guides are always on hand to answer your questions or crank up some of the old machines. Upstairs, there's an eclectic and fascinating display of historical sardine can labels, while an adjoining building houses a café and a restored workers' cottages furnished in 1920s and 1960s style. On the first Sunday of every month (and Tuesday and Thursday from mid-June to mid-August), the fires are lit and you can sample smoked sardines straight from the ovens.

Ledaal
The recently restored empire-style **Ledaal** (Eiganesveien 45) was constructed between 1799 and 1803 for wealthy merchant ship owner Gabriel Schanche Kielland, and now serves as the local royal residence and summer home. You'll see the king's 250-year-old four-poster bed, unusual antique furniture and a pendulum clock from 1680.

Breidablikk
The excellent Breidablikk **manor** (Eiganesveien 40A) was also constructed for a merchant ship owner, Lars Berentsen. These days, it allows you to see the opulent lifestyles of the rich and famous in late-19th-century

Norway, displaying old farming implements, books and knick-knacks.

Stavanger Maritime Museum
This extensive and worthwhile **museum** (Sjø Fartsmuseet; Nedre Strandgata 17-19) covers 200 years of Stavanger's maritime history spread over two warehouses dating from around 1800. There's also a large collection of model boats, sailing vessels, a noisy wind-up foghorn, a reconstruction of a late-19th-century sailmaker's workshop, a shipowner's office and an excellent general store, as well as the merchant's living quarters. The museum also owns two historic sailing vessels, the 1848 *Anna of Sand* and the 1896 *Wyvern*, both on display.

ARCHEOLOGICAL MUSEUM
This well-presented **museum** (☎ 51 84 60 00; www.ark.museum.no; Peder Klows gate 30A; adult/child Nkr20/10; ☼ 11am-8pm Tue, 11am-3pm Wed-Sat & 11am-4pm Sun Jun-Aug, shorter hours rest-of-year), traces 11,000 years of human history including the Viking Age. Exhibits include skeletons, tools, a runestone and a description of the symbiosis between prehistoric humans and their environment. There's also a full programme of activities for kids (eg treasure hunts) in summer.

IRON-AGE FARM
The reconstruction of a 1500-year-old **Iron-Age Farm** (Jernaldergarden; ☎ 51 80 70 00; www.for historiskeopplevelser.no; Ullandhaugvn 3, Ullandhaug; adult/child Nkr30/10; ☼ 11am-4pm daily Jun–mid-Aug, 11am-4pm Sun only May-Oct), 4km south of the centre, features various activities, staff in period dress and food preparation on Sunday. Take bus No 25 or 26 towards Sandnes to Ullandhaug (Nkr24, 15 minutes).

ROGALAND ART MUSEUM
This **museum** (Rogaland Kunstmuseum; ☎ 51 53 09 00; Henrik Ibsensgate 55; adult/child Nkr50/30; ☼ 11am-4pm Tue-Sun) displays in its collection Norwegian art from the 18th century to the present, including the haunting *Gamle Furutrær* and other landscape paintings by Stavanger's own Lars Hertervig (1830–1902). A nine-sided annexe houses the Halvdan Hafsten Collection, the largest assemblage of mid-20th-century Norwegian art, including work by Harald Dal, Kai Fjell, Arne Ekeland and others.

BERGEN & THE SOUTHWESTERN FJORDS

CHILDREN'S MUSEUM

A great place to take the kids is this **museum** (Norsk Barnemuseum; ☎ 51 91 23 93; www.norsk barnemuseum.no; Arneageren; adult/child Nkr65/35; 11am-3.30pm Mon-Sat, noon-4.30pm Sun), which has a range of activity-based exhibits (eg old toys, a labyrinth) centred around the themes of landscape, labyrinth, curiosity and theatre.

MOSVANGEN

The large forest **park** at Mosvangen is a popular destination for local recreation, but it's also a remarkable wildlife refuge. The lake and its small attached lagoon, which are encircled by footpaths, attract large numbers of nesting and breeding ducks, geese, and sea birds, as well as songbirds. It's a pleasant 3km walk from the centre or 10 minutes on bus No 130 (Nkr20).

Tours

Clipper Fjord Sightseeing (☎ 51 89 52 70; www .rodne.no) offers 1½-hour cruises (adult/child Nkr100/50) around the waters surrounding Stavanger. Departing from the Gjestehavn (Guest Harbour) along Skansegata at 7pm Thursday to Saturday, they're a good chance to get a fantastic seaborne perspective on Stavanger.

For details of tours to Lysefjord, see the boxed text on p207.

Sleeping

Accommodation in Stavanger is always snapped up well in advance during July; book as far ahead as possible. Ask the tourist office for the *'Bed & Breakfast Circle'* leaflet.

For the hostel or camping ground, take bus No 78 or 79 (Nkr21) from opposite the cathedral to Ullandhaugveien.

Mosvangen Vandrerhjem (☎ 51 87 29 00; fax 51 87 06 30; Henrik Ibsensgate 21; dm/d Nkr175/350, mid-May–mid-Sep) The pleasant and well-equipped lakeside hostel, 3km southwest of the city centre, charges Nkr60 for breakfast.

Mosvangen Camping (☎ 51 53 29 71; fax 51 87 20 55; Tjensvoll 1b; tent sites without/with car Nkr85/120, with caravan or camper Nkr130, 2-/4-person huts Nkr 275/375, mid-May–mid-Sep) During nesting season around Mosvangen lake, campers are treated to almost incessant birdsong amid the green and thoroughly agreeable surroundings.

Stavanger B&B (☎ 51 56 25 00; www.stavangerbed andbreakfast.no; Vikedalsgata 1a; s/d/tr with shared toilet Nkr540/640/740) This quiet but popular place comes highly recommended by readers and it's not hard to see why. The simple rooms are tidy and come with satellite TV, shower and a smile from the friendly owners. Packed lunches are available for a bargain Nkr25, and at 9pm nightly, free coffee, tea and waffles are served.

Skansen Hotel (☎ 51 93 85 00; www.skansenhotel .no; Skansegt 7; s/d/f from Nkr445/598/928 mid-Jun–mid-Aug, from Nkr560/645 rest-of-year) This centrally located place, opposite the old Customs House, has a cool vibe and the friendly young owners who have recently taken over are slowly turning this place (where the rooms are simple but with increasingly nice touches) into a pleasant, comfortable and intimate hotel.

Skagen Brygge Hotel (☎ 51 85 00 00; www.skagen bryggehotell.no; Skagenkaien 30; s/d Nkr700/850 Jul & Sat & Sun, Nkr1350/1450 rest-of-year) This large and opulent hotel offers good weekend value and it is a superb location right on the water. There are a range of rooms to choose from, but your best bet is to ask for a room with a pretty harbour view.

Rainbow Hotel Maritim (☎ 51 85 05 00; maritime@ rainbow-hotels.no; Kongsgate 32; s/d from Nkr550/690) Part of the consistently comfortable Rainbow chain of hotels, this modern hotel keeps up the standard with excellent value (by Norwegian standards) for spacious, well-appointed rooms, some of which overlook the lake Breiavatnet.

Sola Strand Hotel (☎ 51 94 30 00; www.solastrand hotel.no; s/d from Nkr650/775) The recommended historic Sola Strand Hotel, by a quiet sandy beach 14km southwest of Stavanger, has large rooms and a great breakfast. It also contains an entire lounge from a former cruise ship.

Also recommended:

Det Lille Huset (☎ 51 89 40 89; Vaisenhusgaten 40; s/d Nkr350/550) A 1869 home, with family atmosphere and kitchen facilities.

Havly Hotell (☎ 51 89 67 00; www.havly-hotell.no; Valberggt 1; s/d Nkr590/660 mid-Jun–mid-Aug, Nkr580/ 710 Sat & Sun, Nkr935/1080 rest-of-year) Central and well-run.

Comfort Hotel Grand (☎ 51 89 58 00; booking .stavanger@comfort.choicehotels.no; Klubbgata 3; s/d Nkr640/690 mid-Jun–mid-Aug & Sat & Sun, Nkr1250/1450 rest-of-year) Modern and comfortable.

BERGEN & THE SOUTHWESTERN FJORDS

Eating

As you'd expect of an oil capital, Stavanger has a welter of eating establishments offering a range of international menus, but prices in some places are aimed at highly paid oil executives. Watch out for the Stavanger food festival in late July, when the restaurants of Stavanger set up stalls along the harbour. Unless otherwise stated all places listed here are open for lunch and dinner daily.

SNACKS

Café Akvariet (☎ 51 56 44 44; Olavskleiv 16; snacks around Nkr50) For those of you not on an oil-industry salary, this students' cultural hangout has an inexpensive bar serving coffee, beer and basic snacks.

For mouth-watering pastries, sandwiches and ice cream, try **Finns Konditori** (Arneageren; ☻ 9am-5pm Mon-Fri, 9am-2pm Sat, 9am-6pm Sun), across from the entrance to the Kulturhus.

Fresh fish is sold at the Torget fish market and you'll find wine and liquor at the Vinmonopolet outlets on Olav V's gate and Nytorget. For self-caterers there always the **Rimi Supermarket** (Skagen; ☻ 9am-8pm Mon-Fri, 9am-6pm Sat).

FISH RESTAURANTS

NB Sørensen's Damskipsexpedisjon (☎ 51 84 38 20; Skagen 26; specials Nkr85-125, mains Nkr125-275) The recommended seafood spot in Stavanger, this place serves gourmet-quality food with harbourside tables in summer and an atmospheric dining area for when the weather turns.

Sjøhuset Skagen (☎ 51 89 51 80; Skagenkaien 16; specials Nkr59-89, mains Nkr105-255) Almost as good as NB Sørensen's Damskipsexpedisjon (some locals claim that the balance of power has already shifted), this place also has a prime waterside location, great fish dishes and loads of character in a restored warehouse on the wharf.

Bølgen & Moi (☎ 51 93 93 51; Norsk Oljemuseum, Kjerringholmen; mains Nkr115-295) The imaginative menus in this stylish restaurant include monkfish, lamb and veal. The desserts are highly recommended.

Timbuktu Bar & Restaurant (☎ 51 84 38 00; Nedre Strandgate 15; mains from Nkr235; ☻ 6pm-midnight Mon-Wed, 6pm-2am Thu-Sat) This hip place attracts a young-and-trendy crowd for its excellent fish dishes; lighter, less expensive meals are also available.

INTERNATIONAL

Akropolis Greek Restaurant (☎ 51 89 14 54; Solvberggata 14; specials Nkr59-129, mains from Nkr110) This very popular place serves authentic Greek food at reasonable prices for those in search of great salads, grilled meats and moussaka. It also does a Sunday lunch buffet (Nkr129).

Emilio's Tapas Bar (☎ 51 89 64 00; Solvberggata 13; tapas Nkr45-120, mains from Nkr77; ☻ Mon-Sat) Opposite the Akropolis and continuing on the Mediterranean theme, this pleasant Spanish tapas bar serves good Iberian food.

Elisabeth Restaurant (☎ 51 53 33 00; Kongsgate 41; 2-/3-/4-course meals Nkr365/425/485) Upstairs and overlooking the lake Breiavatnet, this elegant restaurant serves high-quality Basque cuisine from a thoughtful menu which changes weekly, while downstairs the same owners run **Bilbao** (starters Nkr 78-119, mains Nkr160-215, tapas buffet (minimum 2 people) Nkr295), a waterside restaurant-cum-bar.

Also recommended:

Storyteller (☎ 51 89 44 11; Skagen 27; specials Nkr99, mains Nkr179-269) Cajun cooking for oil workers missing the Gulf of Mexico.

China House (☎ 51 89 18 38; Salvågergata 3; specials from Nkr99, mains Nkr115-179, Mongolian grill buffet Nkr149) Good Chinese fare in no-frills setting.

India Tandoori Restaurant (☎ 51 89 39 35; Valberggata 14; mains Nkr109-209; ☻ from 4pm) Reasonably priced and extensive menu.

Dickens (☎ 51 89 59 70; Skagenkaien 6; pizza buffet Nkr89; mains Nkr69-176) Rustic pub atmosphere and decent pizzas.

Drinking & Entertainment

One thing to remember about drinking late in Stavanger is that since 1 July 2004, all places serving spirits are required by law to close at 1am.

Most of the livelier bars are right on the waterfront and cater to a younger crowd with a penchant for loud, energetic music. **New York** (☎ 51 89 95 50; Skagenkaien 24; ☻ Wed-Sat) is one of the busier such places with an infectious energy, while **Taket** (☎ 51 84 37 20; Nedre Strandgate 15; ☻ until 3.30am) attracts a slightly older, more crowd although the latter wears off as the night wears on.

Up the hill but not so far away, **Café Sting** (☎ 51 89 38 78; Valbergjet 3; ☻ 11am-midnight Mon-Thu & Sun, 11-3.30am Fri & Sat) is a great café by day (the pistachio milk shake at Nkr36 is a highlight). By night, it transforms into a pulsating nightclub after dark with the DJ spinning rock and other disco classics. This place also have occasional live performances.

For something a little more sedate, try **Bryggeriet Pub** (☎ 51 85 00 00; Skagen 28) where you'll get good jazz (admission Nkr20) on most summer nights. **Irishman** (☎ 51 89 41 81; Hølebergsgata 9; ☺ until 1am) is Stavanger's friendly Irish pub with (free) live Irish folk music in summer on Thursday (around 9.30pm) and Saturday (3pm).

For one of the coolest bars where you can actually hear the conversation, **Brormann Bar** (☎ 51 93 85 00; Skansegt 7; ☺ 5pm-1am) is an intimate place which has great bar staff, attracts a discerning over-30s crowd and serves great-value half-litre beers (Nkr57) and cocktails (from Nkr75). This place is highly recommended.

For cinema features (some in English), try the eight-screen **Kino Z** (☎ 82 05 11 00; adult/child Nkr65/35) in the Kulturhus.

Getting There & Away
AIR
The **airport** (☎ 51 65 80 00) is at Sola, 14km south of the city centre. **SAS Braathens** (☎ 81 52 00 00; www.sasbraathens.no) fly between Stavanger and Oslo (from Nkr739) and Bergen (Nkr353) at least once daily, and **Widerøe** (☎ 81 00 12 00; www.wideroe.no) offers similar prices to/from Bergen. Stavanger is also served by SAS-Braathens to/from London or Newcastle and SAS-Braathens and Widerøe to/from Aberdeen, in Scotland, several times daily; see p387 for more information on international flights.

BOAT
From Fiskepiren, **Flaggruten's** (☎ 51 86 87 80; www.flaggruten.no) express boats to Bergen (Nkr560, four hours) via Haugesund (Nkr230, 1½ hours) leave up to four times daily. Also from here, there are ferries to Tau (car/person Nkr112/33, 40 minutes), while those travelling by road to Haugesund will need to first drive to Mortavika (tolls Nkr140) for the ferry to Arsvågen (Nkr97/50, 30 minutes).

For ferries to Lysefjord, see the boxed text on p207.

For ferries between Stavanger's Strandkaien Quay and England, see p394.

BUS
Nor-Way Bussekspress runs to:

Destination	Departures	Cost	Duration
Bergen	every 2hr daily	Nkr410	5¾hr
Haugesund	every 2hr daily	Nkr195	2¼hr
Kristiansand	2-4 daily	Nkr350	4½hr
Oslo	up to 5 daily *	Nkr720	9½hr

* some services change at Kristiansand

TRAIN
Trains run from Stavanger to Egersund (Nkr128, one hour, 10 daily) and Oslo (Nkr783, eight hours, up to five daily), via Kristiansand (Nkr379, three hours, up to three daily), including an overnight service.

Getting Around
TO/FROM THE AIRPORT
Between early morning and mid- to late evening, **Flybussen airport buses** (☎ 51 52 26 00) run up to four times hourly between the city centre and the airport at Sola (Nkr55, 30 minutes). Alternatively, take city bus No 143 (Nkr36, 35 minutes), which runs approximately every half-hour between early morning and midnight.

A taxi from the city centre to the airport costs roughly Nkr180 to Nkr220.

BICYCLE
You can hire mountain bikes at **Sykkelhuset** (☎ 51 53 99 10; Løkkeveien 33; per day/week Nkr60/250).

BUS
Local buses (from Nkr15) frequently crisscross the centre of town.

HAUGELANDET & RYFYLKE

North and east of Stavanger lies a region of mountains, extensive fjords and relatively flat coastal islands that don't see many tourists.

HAUGESUND
pop 40,300
The North Sea port of Haugesund lies well off the beaten routes and is rarely visited by travellers, which is a shame because it's

a pretty place with a vibrancy that belies its size, particularly during its increasingly popular jazz and film festivals. The Haugesund **tourist office** (☎ 52 74 33 53; www.haugesund.no; Smedasundet 77; ☺ 10am-6pm Mon-Fri, 10am-4pm Sat Jun-Aug, 10am-2pm Mon-Fri Sep-May) certainly has its act together, even though it doesn't get a lot of tourists. The office has comprehensive brochures and friendly staff.

Sights

Haugesund's has retained many of its historical buildings, with the highlights including the **Rådhus** (town hall). About 75m south is the **Krosshaugen** mound and stone cross, erected in celebration of Christian gatherings around 1000.

About 5km south of central Haugesund, King Håkon Håkonsson's huge **stone church** (☎ 52 83 84 00; Avaldsnes; admission free; ☺ 10am-5pm Mon-Sat, noon-5pm Sun Jun-Aug) was dedicated to St Olav in 1250. The adjacent 6.5m spire, known as the **Virgin Mary's Needle**, leans towards the church wall and legend suggests that when it actually falls against the wall, the Day of Judgement is at hand; it was still standing when we were there. Near the church, at the reconstructed **Viking farm** (☎ 52 83 84 00; www.vikinggarden.no; Avaldsnes; adult/child Nkr30/10; ☺ 10am-6pm Mon-Fri noon-6pm Sun mid-Jun–mid-Aug), you'll be guided by staff in period dress.

Wonderful **Skudeneshavn**, 37km south of Haugesund (on Karmøy), has many traditional wooden buildings and an extensive museum, **Mælandsgården** (☎ 52 84 54 60; Skudeneshavn; adult/child Nkr40/10; ☺ 11am-5pm Mon-Fri, noon-6pm Sun mid-May–mid-Aug) with excellent collections of household articles, rooms with period furnishings, and agricultural and nautical exhibits.

Sleeping & Eating

Norneshuset (☎ 52 82 72 62; pnornes@online.no; Nordnes 7, Skudeneshavn; s/d from Nkr480/580) One of the most atmospheric and friendly B&Bs in Norway, Norneshuset is located in a former warehouse that was shipped from Riga, Latvia, in the 1830s.

Strandgaten Gjestgiveri (☎ 52 71 52 55; post@gjestegiveri.net; Strandgate 81; s/d with shared bathroom Nkr500/650) On offer at Strandgaten Gjestgiveri, you'll get simple, tidy rooms that are a touch overpriced but fine for a overnight stay or two.

HAUGESUND'S QUIRKY HISTORY

The area around Haugesund carries huge historical significance for Norwegians. It was in the nearby Hafrsfjord that the decisive battle took place and Norway was first unified. **Haraldshaugen**, the burial site of Viking King Harald Hårfagre (p22), who died of plague at Avaldsnes on nearby Karmøy, is 1.5km north of Haugesund. The obelisk, erected in 1872, commemorates the decisive 872 battle.

But Haugesund's history ranges much further than nearby fjords. Locals are inordinately proud that copper from the mine at Visnes – now the **Visnes Mining Museum** (☎ 52 83 84 00; www.karmoy.kommune.no; Visnes; adult/child Nkr40/10; ☺ 11am-5pm Mon-Fri, noon-6pm Sun mid-May–mid-Aug) – 4km west of Avaldsnes, was used to build the Statue of Liberty in New York.

Finally, to add a touch of celebrity, Haugesund also claims to be the ancestral home of Marilyn Monroe, whose father, a local baker, emigrated to the USA. A monument on the quay commemorates the 30th anniversary of her death.

Comfort Hotel Amanda (☎ 52 80 82 00; booking.amanda@comfort.choicehotels.no; Smedasundet 93; s/d from790/850; 🖳) This waterfront hotel in the centre of town offers attractive, very well-appointed rooms in a wonderful early-20th-century building.

Lothes Mat & Vinhus (☎ 52 71 22 01; Skippergata 4; snacks from Nkr45, specials Nkr149; mains Nkr145-258; ☺ lunch & dinner) Lothes is possibly the smartest and trendiest restaurant in Haugesund.

Peppe's Pizza (☎ 22 22 55 55; Smedsundet 90; pizzas from Nkr134; ☺ lunch & dinner) This nationwide chain serves the usual creative pizzas.

Getting There & Away

The easiest approach with the Flaggruten ferry between Bergen (Nkr350, three hours) and Stavanger (Nkr230, 1½ hours) up to four times daily.

Nor-Way Bussekspress buses connect Haugesund with Oslo (Nkr585, 8½ hours, one daily), Stavanger (Nkr195, 2¼ hours, every two hours) and Bergen (Nkr275, 3½ hours).

SAS Braathens (☎ 81 52 00 00; www.sasbraathens.no) has up to five daily flights between

BERGEN & THE SOUTHWESTERN FJORDS

Haugesund Airport (☎ 52 85 79 00) and Oslo (Nkr739), while **Coast Air** (☎ 52 84 85 00; www .coastair.no) operates international flights as well as a few domestic services.

The **Fjord Line ferry** (☎ 81 53 35 00; www .fjordline.com) between Bergen and Newcastle (England) also calls in (see p394).

LYSEFJORD

All along the 42km-long Lysefjord (light fjord), the granite rock glows with an ethereal, almost ambient light, even on dull days, all offset by perpetually luminous mist. This is many visitors' favourite fjord, and there's no doubt that it possesses a quite captivating beauty. Whether you cruise from Stavanger, hike up to Preikestolen (604m), or drive the treacherous road down to Lysebotn, it's one of Norway's must-sees.

Information

Lysefjordsenteret (☎ 51 70 36 60; www.ryfylke.com; Oanes; adult/child Nkr50/25; ☿ 11am-8pm Jun-Aug, 11am-5pm Sep-May), in a fabulous setting north of the ferry terminal at Oanes, provides tourist information and presents Lysefjord in audiovisual displays. There are also geological and folk history exhibits.

At the trailhead, both the Preikestolhytta Vandrerhjem (right) and the **kiosk** (☎ 97 16 55 51; ☿ 9.30am-8.45pm May–mid-Sep) at the entrance to the car park dispense information about Preikestolen and can sell walking guides of the region's various trails.

For details on base jumping contact the **Stavanger Base Club** (☎ 51 88 12 10; vibknuts@online .no; Nedre Lyngnes veien 62, 4018 Stavanger) or the **Lysebotn Tourist Center** (☎ 51 70 36 71; midsoe@ online.no).

Preikestolen (Pulpit Rock)

The sight of awestruck visitors scrambling without fear to the edge of this extraordinary granite rock formation is one of Norway's signature images. Preikestolen, with astonishingly uniform cliffs on three sides plunging 604m to the fjord below, is a freak of nature which, despite the alarming crack where it joins the mountains, is likely to be around for a few more centuries. While looking down can be a bit daunting, you won't regret the magical view directly up Lysefjord. It's quite simply a remarkable place, a vantage point unrivalled anywhere else in the world.

There are no fences and those with vertigo will find themselves unable to go right to the edge (even watching the death-defying antics of people dangling limbs over the abyss can make the heart skip a beat). However, the local authorities assured us that there have been no reported cases of anyone accidentally falling off (even the French daredevil who balanced on the edge atop three chairs!). That said, please take all due care even if other people don't. Rocky trails also lead up the mountains behind, offering more wonderful views.

The two-hour, 3.8km trail up to Preikestolen leaves from Preikestolhytta Vandrerhjem (below). It begins along a steep but well-marked route, then climbs past a series of alternating steep and boggy sections to the final climb across granite slabs and along some windy and exposed cliffs to Preikestolen itself. The steepest sections are at the beginning and in the middle parts of the trail and can be challenging for those of low fitness.

The area also offers several other fabulous walks – the **Vatnerindane ridge circuit** (two hours), **Ulvaskog** (three hours), the **Refsvatnet circuit** (three hours) and summit of **Moslifjellet** (three hours) – all of which are accessible from the Preikestolhytta car park.

SLEEPING & EATING

Preikestolhytta Vandrerhjem (☎ 97 16 55 51; www .preikestolhytta.no; Jørpeland; dm incl breakfast Nkr200, d incl breakfast Nkr545-620) The fine turf-roofed hostel by a lakeside is adjacent to the start of the Preikestolen walking track. It's a well-run place with a café (dishes Nkr35 to Nkr145) in an ideal location. It also rents out rowing boats.

Preikestolen Camping (☎ 51 74 97 25; Jørpeland; tent sites without/with car Nkr90/130 plus per person Nkr20; ☿ Apr-Oct) The closest camping ground to Preikestolen (5km, or 1km off the Rv13) isn't anything to write home about but proximity is everything. Kitchen facilities are available, but you can also eat at the attached shop/restaurant.

Just down the road in Oanes (16km south of the Preikestolen turn-off along the Rv13) you'll find **Lysefjord Hyttegrend** (☎ 51 70 38 74; www.lysefjord-hyttegrend.no; 4–6-person cabins Nkr410-600). Also in Oanes, **Lysefjordsenteret** (☎ 51 70 31 23; mains Nkr59-129, Sun buffet Nkr175) is a restaurant serving good, reasonably priced traditional meals.

Lysebotn

The ferry ride from Stavanger takes you to the fjord head at Lysebotn, where a narrow and much-photographed road corkscrews spectacularly 1000m up towards Sirdal in 27 hairpin bends.

ACTIVITIES

After Preikestolen, the most popular Lysefjord walk leads to **Kjeragbolten**, an enormous oval-shaped boulder, or 'chockstone', lodged between two rock faces about 2m apart. The 10km return hike involves a strenuous 700m ascent from the Øygardsstølen Café car park (parking Nkr30), near the highest hairpin bend above Lysebotn.

The route trudges up and over three ridges and, in places, steep muddy slopes can make the going quite rough. Once you're at Kjeragbolten, actually reaching the boulder requires some tricky manoeuvring, including traversing an exposed ledge on a 1000m-high vertical cliff! From there, you can step (or crawl) directly onto the boulder for one of Norway's most astonishing views. The photo of you perched on the rock is sure to impress your friends.

VISITING LYSEFJORD

Ferry, Car & Walking

If you've your own vehicle, you can take the car ferry from Stavanger's Fiskespiren Quay to Tau (car and driver Nkr112, 40 minutes, up to 24 departures daily). From the pier in Tau, a well-signed road (Rv13) leads to Preikestolhytta Vandrerhjem, 19km away (take the signed turn-off after 13km). It costs Nkr50/25 per car/motorcycle to park here. From the car park, the two-hour trail leads up to Preikestolen.

An alternative route from Stavanger involves driving to Lauvik (via Sandnes along Rv13) from where a ferry crosses to Oanes (car and driver/adult foot passenger Nkr60/19, 10 minutes, departures almost every half hour).

Either way, the trip between Stavanger and the trailhead takes around 1½ hours.

Ferry, Bus & Walking

The ferry from Stavanger to Tau costs Nkr33/16 for adult/child foot passengers. Almost all ferries (though less often on Sundays) are met by a bus (Nkr50) which runs between the Tau pier and the Preikestolhytta Vandrerhjem, at the foot of the walking trail to Preikestolen. The last bus from Preikestolhytta to Tau leaves at 4.25pm.

Ferry to Lysbotn

The daily **Veteran Fjord Cruise** (☎ 51 86 87 80; car/motorcycle & driver Nkr340/250, adult/child & senior foot passenger Nkr150/75) departs Stavanger's Fiskespiren Quay at 10am daily mid-June to late August (Friday to Sunday only first two weeks of June and last week of August). The journey takes four hours (the return from Lysebotn departs at 3pm), there's a café on board and endearingly idiosyncratic commentary to accompany you. There are stops for photos. Those travelling with a car need to make a booking *at least* two days in advance. From Lysebotn, the road twists up the mountain from where you can continue on into the Setesdalen region (p139) and Oslo.

Tours

At least two tour companies in Stavanger offer guided boat tours part of the way up Lysefjord, including the view of Preikestolen from below. Both depart from along Skagenkaien in Stavanger's harbour, and tickets are usually sold on the quay up to half an hour before departure.

FjordTours (☎ 51 53 73 40; www.fjordpanorama.no; adult/senior/student/child Nkr270/210/210/135) offers 3½-hour cruises every day from mid-May to the end of August, which depart at noon.

Clipper Fjord Sightseeing (☎ 51 89 52 70; www.rodne.no; adult/senior/student/child Nkr290/220/220/150) departs five times weekly (noon) in May, daily (noon) in June, twice daily (10.30am and 4.30pm) from July to mid-August and daily (noon) from mid-August to mid-September.

SLEEPING & EATING
Lysebotn Tourist Center (☎ 51 70 34 90; fax 51 70 34 03; Lysebotn; tent/caravan sites Nkr120/140, apt Nkr350-800) If you can't face the daunting road up the mountain or, more likely, you can't bear to leave, Lysebotn Turistsenter occupies an incredible setting at the head of the fjord. It's a lovely quiet spot to be after the ferry has left for the day.

Øygardsstølen Café (☎ 38 37 74 00; Lysebotn; snacks & light meals Nkr45-120; ☷ 10am-6pm mid-Jun–mid-Sep) For views, you can't beat the 'eagle's nest', perched atop the cliff overlooking the hairpin twists down to Lysebotn. There's a viewing deck for those who don't wish to eat.

AROUND RYFYLKE
The Rv13 road through the wild and lightly populated country north of Lysefjord has been proposed as a national scenic road. It's definitely the slow route between Stavanger and Bergen, but it's worth it if you have the time. The finest scenery is around **Årdal**, **Jøsenfjorden**, **Suldalsosen** and **Suldalsvatnet**.

Sauda Turistsenter (☎ 52 78 59 00; post@sauda -turistsenter.no; Saudasjøen; tent sites Nkr120, cabins Nkr350/625) is a camping ground located 3km west of the town centre. It has a fast-food outlet, a supermarket and decent facilities.

For considerably more comfort and charm, grand old **Sauda Fjord Hotel** (☎ 52 78 12 11; sauda@online.no; Saudasjøen; s/d from Nkr600/800, mains Nkr75-239) offers fine accommodation and good meals at reasonable prices.

The best public transport is the ferry between Stavanger and Sauda (Nkr288, 2¼ hours, two or three daily). Rv13 is best followed by private car.

The Western Fjords

In 2004, *National Geographic* selected the Norwegian fjords as the world's best travel destination, ahead of other dream lands such as the Alps, the Galapagos Islands and Australia's Great Barrier Reef. The prestigious travel magazine also placed Norway's fjords ahead of other comparable natural wonders such as the fretted coastlines of Chile and New Zealand. It's easy to see why.

Scoured and gouged by glaciers, of which a few vestigial traces still groan and creak, these formidable, deep, sea-drowned valleys are pincered by almost impossibly rugged terrain. Amazingly, this hasn't deterred Norwegians from settling and farming their slopes and heights for thousands of years. You'll find a confounding number of things to see and do, in the water, up the mountains or just on the level. The topography is so convoluted that just sorting out an itinerary is a challenge in itself.

Ferries are fun. When planning your trip, bear in mind that these reliable work horses don't just lop off huge detours around a fjord by cutting straight across; they're also an enjoyable part of the journey in their own right, offering great and otherwise inaccessible panoramas of the coastline before and behind you.

Although you'll be hard pressed to find more than a few flat patches, the Western Fjords also make for great hiking country, whether in a guided group over one of the glaciers that are such a feature of the region or on one of the signed trails. The Western Fjords slit deeply into the two administrative regions of Sogn og Fjordane and, to its north, Møre og Romsdal.

And if, after so much fresh air and wide open space, you begin to crave a little small-town sophistication, drop into the charming coastal settlement of Ålesund.

HIGHLIGHTS

- Cruising between Geiranger and Hellesylt past the daunting cliffs of **Geirangerfjord** (p234)
- Riding the dramatic **Flåmsbana railway** (p213) between wild Hardangervidda and gentle Aurlandsfjorden
- Bucking over the spectacular **Trollstigen route** (p231) between Åndalsnes and Valldal
- Getting your boots damp on but a tiny tongue of the vast **Jostedalsbreen icecap** (p220)
- Savouring Art Nouveau in the charming town of **Ålesund** (p237)
- Jazzing it up at the **Molde Jazz Festival** (p243)

| AREA: 32,460 SQ KM | HIGHEST ELEVATION: LODALSKÅPA (2083M) | POPULATION: 351,800 |

THE WESTERN FJORDS

SOGNEFJORDEN

Sognefjorden, Norway's longest (204km) and deepest (1308m) fjord, cuts a deep slash across the map of western Norway. In places, sheer walls rise more than 1000m above the water while elsewhere a gentler shoreline supports farms, orchards and small towns. The broad, main waterway is impressive but by cruising into its narrower arms, such as the deep and lovely Nærøyfjorden to Gudvangen, you'll see idyllic views of abrupt cliff faces and cascading waterfalls.

Getting There & Away
From May to September, **Fylkesbaatane** (☎ 55 90 70 70; www.fylkesbaatane.no) operates a daily express boat between Bergen and Flåm, near the head of the Sognefjorden, stopping at 10 small towns along the way. It leaves Bergen at 8am daily and arrives in Flåm (Nkr530) at 1.25pm. Stops en route include Vik (Nkr365, 3½ hours) and Balestrand (Nkr385, 3¾ hours). The return boat leaves Flåm at 3.30pm, arriving in Bergen at 8.40pm. Students and Inter-Rail pass holders get a 50% discount. Numerous local ferries also link Sognefjord towns, and there's an extensive (if infrequent) bus network.

FLÅM
pop 600
Tiny Flåm, at the head of Aurlandsfjord, occupies a spectacular setting and, as a stop on the popular 'Norway in a Nutshell' tour, it probably sees more foreign tourists than any other village of its size in Norway. The **tourist office** (☺ 8.30am-3pm & 3.30-8pm Jun-Aug, 8.30am-4pm May & Sep) is located within the train station, where you'll also find four Internet points (per hour Nkr8) for convenient and easy access.

Sights & Activities
NORWAY IN A NUTSHELL
Although most visitors do 'Norway in a Nutshell' from either Oslo or Bergen (see p404), you can do a mini version (adult/child Nkr480/240). This circular route – boat to Gudvangen, bus to Voss, rail to Myrdal, then train again down the spectacular Flåmsbana railway to Flåm – is truly

the kernel within the nutshell and takes in all the most dramatic elements.

TRAIN RIDE
If you didn't come into Flåm by train, plan to leave that way, by the spectacular Flåmsbana railway (see p213), or enjoy this magnificent 20km run as an out-and-back day trip.

BOATING & CANOEING
To get out and about on the fjord, pass by Heimly Pensjonat (below), which hires out rowing boats and canoes (per hour/day Nkr50/250), small motor boats (Nkr150/500 plus fuel) and throatier ones (up to six passengers; Nkr200/700).

Njord (☎ 91 32 66 28; www.fjordpaddlenorway.com) does a variety of sea-kayak trips from Flåm ranging from a two-hour induction to a two-day excursion to Gudvangen.

CYCLING
To potter along the shoreline, rent a bike from the tourist office (per hour/day Nkr30/175) or Heimly Pensjonat (per hour/day Nkr50/200).

Sleeping & Eating
Fretheim Hotel (☎ 57 63 63 00; www.fretheim-hotel.no; s/d Nkr1125/1450; ☺ Apr-Nov; P ▯) With a haunt of the English aristocracy in the 19th century (they came for the fishin'), the vast, yet at the same time intimate and welcoming Fretheim is as much sports and social centre as hotel. It has its own fishing reach (you can hire equipment during the salmon and sea trout run in July and August) and will arrange and advise on walking and bike trips. Exertions over, the pub is a pleasant place to relax and sometimes has live entertainment, while the restaurant dishes up fine fare.

Heimly Pensjonat (☎ 57 63 23 00; www.heimly.no; s/d incl breakfast from Nkr685/890) At water level on the fringe of the village and away from all the port hubbub, this place has straightforward rooms with a magnificent view along the fjord.

Flåm Camping & Youth Hostel (☎ 57 63 21 21; flaam.hostel@vandrerhjem.no; camping sites Nkr75-130, hostel dm Nkr120, s/d from Nkr200/380, cabins Nkr450-700; ☺ May-Sep) This friendly camping ground and hostel has good facilities and is only a few minutes' walk from the station.

THE WESTERN FJORDS

0 ━━━━━━━━━━ 50 km
0 ━━━━━━━━━━ 30 miles

A   **B**   **C**   **D**

1

ATLANTIC
OCEAN

Dyrnesvågen
Smøla
Grip
Aure
Leina
Kristiansund
Bremsnes
19
Frei
E39
Halsanaustan
Skei
Atlanterhavsveien
16
E39
Vevang
Averøya
5
Gjemnes
Bud
11
Sylte
E39
Ona
Aukra
Driva
River
Aukra
Molde
Hollingsholmen
Harøy
Olrøy

2

Langfjorden
Sunndalsøra
Romsdalfjorden
MØRE OG ROMSDAL
Lepsøy
Isfjorden
Åndalsnes
Eikesdalsvatnet
Mardals-
fossen
Blindheim Vigra
E136
Trollvegen Romsdalshorn
▲(1550m)
Valderøy
Giske
E39
Godøy
Ålesund 22
Spjelkavik
Runde
Sykkylven Stordal
RV63
Ulsteinvik
Stranda Valldal 15
Gurskøy
E39
Eldsdal
Tafjord
Ørsta
60 10
Zakariasdammen
Øye 6
Volda 665
Urasætra
Ørnevegen
Geiranger
Hellesylt 13 Dalsnibba
▲(1496m)
Grotli

3

Stadhavet
Bjorli
To Dombås
(28km)
E316
Railway
OPPLAND
To Otta
(54km)
Skjåk
Lom

4

Kråkenes
Lighthouse
Selje
8
Kråkenes
Kannesteinen
Måløy
Bremanger
Smørhamn
Frøya
Kalvåg
Svelgen
Hoven
Batalden
Florø
Kinn
Askrova
Tansøy
Svanøy
Askvoll

Nordfjord
Nordfjordeid
Lote
Anda
Vingen
Petroglyphs
Ålfotbreen
Sunndalen
Norddal
2
Naustdal
RV611
Førde
Jølstra River

Hornindal
Stryn
Videsæter
9
Geirangerfjorden
Jostedalsbreen
National Park Centre
Olden Loen
Sandane
Byrkjelo
SOGN OG
FJORDANE
E39
Stardal
River
Jostedalsbreen
National Park
Skei
Fjærland
Gaupne

Gamle
Strynefjellsvegen
15
Styggevatnet
Bøverdal
RV55
7
Gjerde
Krossbu
Skjolden 21
Fortun
Lustrafjorden
Lusterfjorden
Memurubu

1
See Jostedalsbreen NP Map p221

5

Dale
Sande
E39 Høyanger
Fjærlandsfjorden
RV13
Dragsvik
Balestrand
Leikanger
5
Sogndal 12
Solvorn
Kaupanger
Øvre Ardal
Lærdal
3

Larvik
Oppedal
Vangsnes
Vik
Aurlandsfjorden
Borgund
Tunnel
(24.5km)
E16

Ytre
Sula

6

Matre
Austrheim
E39
Vinje
E16
Nærøyfjord
RV13
Undredal
Aurland
18
Gudvangen Flåm
Myrdal
23
20
Geiteryggen
14
To Bergen
(75km)
Voss

THE WESTERN FJORDS

Furukroa (☎ 57 63 23 25; mains Nkr60-86) This large, rustic-looking café-plus at the ferry dock has a range of self-service dishes, from snacks to full meals, while the separate restaurant offers a buffet lunch (Nkr175).

Togrestauranten (☎ 57 63 21 55; mains Nkr85-115) This novel restaurant – housed in a pair of old wooden rail cars – offers a couple of traditional Norwegian dishes and leafy salads.

Getting There & Away

BOAT

From Flåm, boats head out to towns around Sognefjorden. The most scenic trip from Flåm is the ferry up Nærøyfjorden to Gudvangen (Nkr185/228 single/return) via Aurland (Nkr60, 15 minutes), which leaves at 3pm daily year-round and also at 9am and 1.25pm mid-June to mid-August. At Gudvangen, a connecting bus takes you on to Voss, where you can pick up the train for Bergen or Oslo. The tourist office sells all ferry tickets, plus the ferry-bus combination from Flåm to Voss (Nkr261).

There's at least one daily express boat between Flåm and Bergen (Nkr530, 5½ hours) via Balestrand (Nkr185, 1½ hours).

BUS

Two to five (six to nine, mid-June to mid-September) daily buses connect Flåm, Gudvangen (Nkr36, 20 minutes), Aurland (Nkr28, 10 minutes) and Lærdal (Nkr68, 1¼ hours) but you won't see much of the spectacular scenery; most of these routes are inside particularly long tunnels. Regular buses connect Flåm with Songdal (Nkr75, 1½ hours) and Bergen (Nkr235, three hours).

TRAIN

Flåm is the only Sognefjorden village with a rail link. The 20km **Flåmsbana railway** (☎ 57 63 21 00; www.flaamsbana.no; adult/child single Nkr150/75, return Nkr250/150) is a highlight in its own right. This engineering wonder descends 865m at a gradient of 1:18 from Myrdal on the bleak and treeless Hardangervidda plateau, past thundering waterfalls (there's a photo stop at awesome Kjosfossen), to the relatively lush and tranquil Aurlandsfjord. It runs up to 12 times daily in summer, with connections to Oslo–Bergen services at Myrdal and to the Gudvangen ferry and the Sognefjorden ferries from Flåm.

UNDREDAL

pop human 120, goats 500

Undredal, midway between Flåm and Gudvangen, is a truly lovely little village, its pleasures enhanced – and its traditional quality sustained – because you need to make that bit of extra effort to get there.

The tiny, barrel-vaulted **village church** (adult/child Nkr30/free; ⊙ core hours noon-5pm mid-May–mid-Sep), originally built as a stave church in 1147 and seating 40, is the smallest still-operational house of worship in mainland Scandinavia. Look up at the roof with its charmingly naive roof paintings of angels, Christ on the cross and other biblical figures, surrounded by stylised stars.

Undredal's other claim to fame is its cheeses. Or not exactly fame, as you'll only find them in a few specialised cheese shops and delicatessens within Norway. Around 500 goats freely roam the surrounding grassy slopes and between them provide the milk for around 10 tonnes of cheese per year (work it out; that's a hugely impressive yield per nipple). The village's two remaining dairies – once there were 10 – still produce the firm yellow Undredal cheese and its brown, slightly sweet variant, made from the boiled and concentrated whey. You can pick up a hunk of each at the village shop; it's the light blue building beside the shore.

The lone white building perched precariously just along the coast is the farm **Stigen** dating from 1603; the access path is so steep that you needed a *stige* (ladder) to reach it (it was deftly removed whenever tax collectors were about). The farmer will collect you in his boat or you can do a deal for the short trip with one of the local boat owners.

Undredal is 6.5km north of the E16. The narrow road (single track but with passing bays) threads steeply downhill beside a hurtling torrent. If travelling by bus from Flåm or Gudvangen, get off at the eastern end of the 11km tunnel that leads to Gudvangen. By ferry, ask the captain to make the optional stop at Undredal's harbour. Best of all, take the bus out, walk down the spectacular valley along the lightly trafficked road and return by boat (press the switch beside the yellow blinking lamp on the café wall beside the jetty to alert the next passing ferry).

GUDVANGEN & NÆRØYFJORDEN
pop 100

Nærøyfjorden lies west of Flåm and provides a vision of archetypal Norway: a deep blue fjord (only 250m across at its narrowest point), towering 1200m-high cliffs, isolated farms, and waterfalls plummeting from the heights. It can easily be visited as a day excursion from Flåm.

Kjelsfossen waterfall, one of the 10 longest in the world, descends from the southern wall of Nærøydalen valley, above Gudvangen village. Notice too the avalanche protection scheme above Gudvangen. The powerful avalanches here typically provide a force of 12 tonnes per sq metre, move at 50m per second and, local legend reckons, can bowl a herd of goats right across the fjord!

In high summer, **Nordic Ventures** (☎ 56 51 00 17; www.nordicventures.com) do sea-kayak hire (Nkr375 per day) and full day guided kayak tours (Nkr890).

Rooms in the wing building of **Gudvangen Fjordtell** (☎ 57 63 39 29; www.gudvangen.com; s/d from Nkr590/790, cafeteria mains Nkr82-112; ☯ May-Sep; Ⓟ) overlooking the pleasant port are attractive and comfortable. For a real treat, go for one of the 12 Viking rooms (s/d Nkr680/980); each, with wooden swords and shields for wall decoration and pelts as bed covers, teeters just the right side of

naff. The restaurant is worth visiting for its gorgeous view down the fjord though the food, while quite acceptable, is nothing to write postcards home about.

There are a pair of camping grounds on either side of the road, 1.25km from the ferry point. **Gudvangen Camping** (☎ 57 63 39 34; tent & 1-3 campers Nkr50, with 4-6 persons Nkr80, 4-person cabins Nkr320; ☯ May-Oct) and **Vang Camping** (☎ /fax 57 63 39 26; person/site Nkr15/70, cabins Nkr200-375; ☯ mid-May–mid-Sep) each beautifully situated at the base of sheer cliffs down which the waterfalls tumble

Ferries between Gudvangen and Flåm (Nkr185/228 one-way/return) via Aurland run three to five times daily. The car ferry to/from Kaupanger costs Nkr167/406 per adult/car. Buses run to Flåm (Nkr36, 20 minutes), Aurland (Nkr48, 30 minutes) and Voss (Nkr72, 50 minutes).

AURLAND
pop 590

Aurland is known as the end of the popular and spectacular Aurlandsdalen hiking route (see p215). These days it's even more renowned as one end of the world's longest road tunnel called Lærdalstunnel (over 7km longer than Switzerland's St Gotthard tunnel, its nearest rival). An essential link in the E16 highway that connects Oslo and Bergen, is the 24.5km link between Aurland and Lærdal. It provides a fast alternative to the beautiful but sinuous and seasonal 45km-long **Snøvegen** (Snow Rd; ☯ Jun–mid-Oct), which climbs from sea level, twisting precipitously to the high plateau (1309m) that separates the two towns. Tunnel vision, speed and convenience set against a sometimes hair-raising ascent that offers inspirational views all the way...

Between Flåm and Aurland and high above the fjord, the restored hamlet of **Otternes** (adult/child Nkr30/free; ☯ 10am-6pm mid-Jun–mid-Aug) well merits a brief detour. This complex of 27 buildings, the earliest dating from the 17th century, offers rural activities such as spinning, weaving, baking – and beer brewing. To get full value from the visit, follow the one-hour guided tour (Nkr50; available in English).

The Aurland **tourist office** (☎ 57 63 33 13; www.alr.no; ☯ 9am-7pm Mon-Fri, 10am-5pm Sat Jun-Aug, 8am-3.30pm Mon-Fri Sep-May) is beside the village church.

MODERN DAY VIKINGS   *Miles Roddis*

'Actually, I'm a professional Viking,' said the lady with the flowing red hair before her husband arrived sporting, confusingly, a furry Cossack hat (just back from an international Viking fair, he'd been doing a bit of bartering, he explained). Freyja and Ragnar (I never learnt their original names) both moved here from Bournemouth in the UK, having eschewed the easy life. In their second season of camp outside the Gudvangen Fjordtell, they were living in a pair of felt tents strewn with Viking artefacts and implements, most of which they'd crafted themselves. With their Norwegian partner, Georg, they'd laid the keel of a Viking ship and were planning to construct a village of some 20 dwellings – before, perhaps, sailing away and emulating their adopted ancestors.

Activities
WALKING
The famous trek down Aurlandsdalen from Geiteryggen to Aurland gives you the chance to follow a stream from source to sea while following one of the oldest trading routes between eastern and western Norway. In summer, you can start this four-day walk in Finse, on the Oslo–Bergen rail line, with overnight stops at Geiterygghytta, Steinbergdalen and Østerbø. But many walkers select only the most scenic section, from Østerbø to Vassbygdi, which can be done as a day hike (allow six to seven hours).

From the rambling Østerbø complex, the route heads down-valley to Tirtesva, where it splits. The best option (a short cut of sorts) climbs to Bjørnstigen, at 1000m, then soon descends steeply. An hour later, however, the drop grows gentler and heads for the river far below; from there to the Vassbygdi power station, the track follows the river, passing waterfalls and sections blasted from sheer rock.

The lower sections of this route are usually open between early June and late September. From Vassbygdi (Nkr25, 15 minutes) and Østerbø (Nkr52, one hour), buses run to Aurland three times daily.

Sleeping & Eating
Aurland Fjordhotell (☎ 57 63 35 05; www.aurland-fjord hotel.com; s/d from Nkr735/1070 mid-Jun–Aug, Nkr625/850 rest-of-year, mains Nkr70-120, buffet dinner Nkr175; **P**) At this friendly hotel the majority of the comfortable, well-furnished rooms have fjord views and there's a solarium, steam bath and sauna.

Vangsgaarden (☎ 57 63 35 80; www.vangsgaarden .no; s/d with shower Nkr375/575, d with bathroom Nkr775, cabins Nkr800-1000; **P**) The complex embraces a couple of 18th-century buildings, six cabins down at sea level and the Duehuset (Dovecot) Café & Pub. Rooms are furnished in antique style; the dining room, for example, could be your grandmother's parlour.

Lunde Gard & Camping (☎ 57 63 34 12; tent/caravan sites Nkr60/80 plus per person Nkr15, cabins Nkr300-700; May-Sep) This welcoming camping ground nestles beside the river, 1.4km up the valley.

Getting There & Away
Buses run two to 11 times daily (fewer at weekends) between Aurland and Flåm (Nkr28, 10 minutes) and one to three times daily between Aurland and Lærdal (Nkr56, 30 minutes). Buses to/from Bergen (Nkr235, 3¼ hours) run two to eight times daily.

Watch out for the speed cameras in Lærdalstunnelen; they'll certainly have their eye on you...

LÆRDAL & BORGUND
pop 2250
Since the opening of Lærdalstunnelen, visitor numbers have increased, with more people than ever heading for the Borgund Stave Church, about 30km up the valley from Lærdal. Lærdalsøyri, at the fjord end of town, makes for pleasant strolling beside 18th- and 19th-century timber homes. The **tourist office** (☎ 57 64 12 07; Øyra plassen 7; 9am-7pm mid-Jun–Jul, 9am-4pm early Jun & Aug) has a free town map that describes the best of them and sets out a walking route.

Sights & Activities
WILD SALMON CENTRE
To learn all you'd ever want to know about Atlantic salmon and their unique migration and breeding habits, visit this **museum** (Norsk Villaks Senter; ☎ 57 66 67 71; www.norsk-villakssenter.no; adult/child Nkr70/35; 10am-5pm, 6pm or 7pm May-Jun & Aug-Sep, to 10pm Jul). You can watch wild salmon and sea trout through viewing windows, see an excellent 20-minute film about the salmon's life cycle and learn to tie flies to increase the odds of you hooking one or your own.

BORGUND STAVE CHURCH
Some 30km southeast of Lærdal, this 12th-century **church** (adult/child Nkr50/25; 8am-8pm Jun–mid-Aug, 10am-5pm May & mid-Aug–Sep) was raised beside one of the major trade routes between eastern and western Norway. The Borgund Stave Church is and dedicated to St Andrew. It's one of the best-known, most-photographed and best-preserved of Norway's stave churches and well deserves the detour. Build in time to undertake the two-hour circular hike on ancient paths and tracks that starts and ends at the church, passing through Sverrestigen and Vindhella.

FISHING
There's free fishing in the fjord and the upper reaches of the Lærdal river are good

for trout. For licences and for the low-down on when the salmon are running, contact the tourist office.

Sleeping & Eating
Lærdal Ferie og Fritidspark (☎ 57 66 66 95; www .laerdalferiepark.com; camp sites Nkr120, s/d with bathroom Nkr475/495, 2-/3-/4-bed cabins with bathroom Nkr550/625/695) This pretty camping ground, almost at the water's edge, has sweeping views of the fjord and is very good value.

Lindstrøm Hotell (☎ 57 66 62 02; hotlin@sr.telia .no; s incl breakfast Nkr650-785, d incl breakfast Nkr785-1050; ☽ May-Sep; **P** ☐) The most charming house of this five-unit complex, these days a protected building, is, alas, no longer used for accommodation. Ask for a room in the gabled building just behind it, constructed in 1899, renovated with all modern conveniences and a great second best.

Borlaug Vandrerhjem (☎ 57 66 87 80; borlaug.hos tel@vandrerhjem.no; dm/s/d Nkr125/200/290) This friendly roadside hostel, 10km east of Borgund, serves good meals and is popular with hikers.

Getting There & Away
Heading south, you have the choice between the world's longest road tunnel linking Aurland and Lærdal or, in summer, climbing up and over, following the Snøvegen. For details, see p214. Buses run to/from Bergen (Nkr275, 3¾ hours) two to six times daily.

Four daily ferries run to/from Gudvangen (adult single/return Nkr178/238, child Nkr60/120, three hours).

VANGSNES
pop 200
The sole claim to fame of the farming community of Vangsnes, across the fjord from Balestrand, is the 12m-high hilltop statue of saga hero Fridtjof the Intrepid, erected in 1913 by Kaiser Wilhelm of Germany, that broods above it. The statue – and a pretty good view of Sognefjord – lies 1.5km uphill along the road from the ferry landing. Legend has it that Fridtjof is buried nearby.

VIK
pop 1100
Vik's **tourist office** (☎ 57 69 56 86; ☽ 10am-7pm Mon-Fri, 10am-3pm Sat & Sun mid-Jun–mid-Aug; 10am-4pm Mon-Fri, 10am-3pm Sat May–mid-Jun & mid-Aug–Sep) is beside the express boat docking point.

The factory village of Vik boasts the splendid **Hopperstad stave church** (Hopperstad; adult/child Nkr40/free; ☽ 10am-5pm mid-May–mid-Sep, 9am-7pm mid-Jun–mid-Aug), about 1km south of the centre. Built in 1130, it escaped demolition by a whisker in the late 19th century. For an additional Nkr10, you can use the same ticket for the near-contemporaneous Hove stone church, 1km away.

The small **Kristianhaus Båtmotor Museum** (☽ 10am-4pm Jul–mid-Aug) has a collection of boats and boat engines.

Frequent local buses run to and from Vangsnes (Nkr25, 15 minutes). Buses also run once or twice daily to Sogndal (Nkr72, 1½ hours) and Bergen (Nkr235, 3¼ hours).

BALESTRAND
pop 800
Balestrand, the main Sognefjorden resort destination, enjoys a mountain backdrop and a genteel, low-key atmosphere. The **tourist office** (☎ 57 69 12 55; www.sognefjord.no; ☽ 7.30am-6pm daily mid-Jun–mid-Aug, 9am-5.30pm Mon-Fri May, early Jun & mid-Aug–Sep) is near the ferry quay, behind the Spar supermarket. It has Internet access (per 15 minutes Nkr25) and, for Nkr25, will book accommodation.

Sights & Activities
The road running south along the fjord, bordered by apple orchards and farmsteads, sees little motor traffic. Beside it, the **Church of St Olav** (1897) was constructed in the style of a traditional stave church at the instigation of English expatriate Margaret Green, who married Norwegian mountaineer and hotel-owner Knut Kvikne. Should you find it closed, the owner of Midtnes Pensjonat (see p217) has the key.

Less than 1km south along the fjord, excavation of two **Viking-age burial mounds** revealed remnants of a boat, two skeletons, jewellery and several weapons. One mound is topped by a statue of legendary **King Bele**, erected by Germany's Kaiser Wilhelm II, who was obsessed with Nordic mythology and regularly spent his holidays here prior to WWI (a similar monument honouring Fridtjof, the lover of King Bele's daughter, rises across the fjord in Vangsnes).

Near the ferry dock is the **Sognefjord Aquarium** (☎ 57 69 13 03; adult/child Nkr60/30, incl a free hour of canoe or rowing boat; ☽ 9am-10pm mid-Jun–mid-Aug; 10am-5pm mid-Apr–mid-Jun & mid-Aug–Oct), which has a good audiovisual presentation and plenty of tanks in which saltwater creatures lurk.

WALKING

The 1km **Granlia forest nature trail** is a signed loop, beginning just above the Rv55 tunnel.

For a longer hike, take the small passenger ferry from the jetty across Esefjord to the Dragsvik side, where an abandoned country road forms the first leg of an 8km walk back to Balestrand.

For more ideas about walks, long and short, in the area, buy *Balestrand Turkart* (Nkr70), a good walking map at 1:50,000 with trails marked up.

Sleeping & Eating

Kvikne's Hotel (☎ 57 69 42 00; www.kviknes.no; s Nkr745-1460, d Nkr880-1910, extra per person for fjord view in the annexe/main building Nkr100/200; ✍ Easter-Oct; Ⓟ ⬜) The pale-yellow, timber-built Kvikne's Hotel, right on the point near the ferry landing, offers more than a taste of mid-19th-century luxury. Guests have use of the Jacuzzi, billiards room, fitness room and sauna, as well as a boat and fishing gear. The newer building – whose rooms are comfortable to a fault – is a grotesque concrete pile by comparison. The hotel's Balholm Bar og Bistro is a reliable place for snacks and light meals (Nkr45 to Nkr170). For the gastronomic works, you can't do better than invest Nkr375 in their superb dinner buffet, groaning with fish galore and seafood and weighed down by gooey, creamy desserts (save a cranny, though, for the equally impressive cheeseboard). Magnificent value and totally diet-defying...

Midtnes Pensjonat (☎ 57 69 11 33; www.midtnes .no; s incl breakfast Nkr575-610, d incl breakfast Nkr680-825; ✍ year-round; Ⓟ ⬜) Beside St Olav's church, this family-run place has a place to eat breakfast with great views of the water, an attractive terrace and a lawn that extends down to a jetty, where a rowing boat, free for guests, is moored. It's worth paying top whack for a room with a balcony overlooking the fjord.

Balestrand Hotell (☎ 57 69 11 38; www.balestrand .com; s incl breakfast Nkr565-615, d incl breakfast Nkr790-890; ✍ Jun-Aug; Ⓟ ⬜) This summertime-only hotel, also family-run, is a friendly, jolly, intimate place that eschews the tour groups who fill so many beds elsewhere in town. Here too, it's well worth paying that little extra for inspirational views down over the fjord.

Vandrerhjem Kringsjå (☎ 57 69 13 03; www.kring sja.no; dm incl breakfast Nkr190, d incl breakfast with bathroom Nkr280; ✍ mid-Jun–mid-Aug) Balestrand's HI-affiliated hostel, an outdoor activities centre during the school year, is a fine lodge-style place.

Sjøtun Camping (☎ 57 69 12 23; www.camping.sjo tun.com; adult/child Nkr20/10 plus per tent/caravan Nkr60, 4-/6-bed cabins Nkr225/310; ✍ Jun-Aug) At Sjøtun Camping, a 15-minute walk south along the fjord, you can pitch a tent on the camping grounds amid the green apple trees or rent a rustic cabin.

Café Galleri (salads Nkr50-70, snacks & sandwiches Nkr32-40) This place is located next door to the tourist office. It is a quaint little place with an art gallery beside it. Outside, the tables of its pleasant terrace are adorned with fresh cut flowers.

Getting There & Away

Buses link Balestrand and Sogndal (Nkr90, 1¼ hours, three to five daily).

Express boats to/from Bergen (Nkr385, four hours) hurtle off twice daily, Monday to Saturday, and to/from Sogndal (Nkr120, 45 minutes) once daily.

Between May and September, a popular local car and passenger ferry departs at 8.15am and noon and follows the narrow Fjærlandsfjorden to Fjærland (Nkr147/220 one-way/return, 1¼ hours), gateway to the glacial wonderlands of Jostedalsbreen. For a great day trip, Nkr395/197 per adult/child will get you a return on the ferry, bus to the glacier museum, museum admission and bus to the glacier.

The scenic Gaularfjellsvegen (Rv13) is an exciting drive to Førde, on Førdefjord, negotiating hairpin bends and skirting Norway's greatest concentration of roadside waterfalls.

Getting Around

The tourist office hires out bicycles with rental rates starting at Nkr80/150 per half/full day.

SOGNDAL

pop 2900

The modern regional centre of Sogndal, though not the area's prettiest place, has a couple of good museums in and around town.

Information

Its **tourist office** (☎ 57 67 30 83; www.sogne fjorden.no; Gravensteinsgata; ⏰ 8.30am-8pm Mon-Fri, 9am-3pm Sat, 3-8pm Sun mid-Jun–mid-Aug, 8am-3.30pm Mon-Fri rest-of-year), a five-minute walk east of the bus station, can book cabins, chalets and rooms in private homes. To stretch your legs, ask for its booklet of local hill walks. Upstairs, the town library has Internet access. Outside summer, the tourist office works within the **Spare Bank** (Gravenstein-sgata 19), just across the road.

Sights & Activities

At the extensive **Sogn Folkmuseum** (☎ 57 67 82 06; Vestreim; adult/child Nkr50/25 incl guiding in English; ⏰ 10am-5pm Jun-Aug, 10am-3pm May & Sep) over 40 buildings cover 600 years of local history and there's an informative exhibition.

Fjord People (☎ 99 39 88 95; www.fjordpeople .com), based 250m before the bridge, rents canoes and kayaks (per half/full day from Nkr150/250) and offers a variety of guided kayak tours.

In summer, **NorCopter AS** (☎ 88 00 14 14; www .norcopter.com in Norwegian) offers exhilarating, seat-of-your-pants 15-minute spins over the glaciers (per person Nkr600).

In nearby **Kaupanger**, about 12km southeast along the Rv5, the **Sogn Fjordmuseum** (admission free with Sogn Folkmuseum ticket, otherwise adult/child Nkr25/10; ⏰ 10am-5pm Jun-Aug) has a collection of 19th- and 20th-century fishing boats and equipment. From here, you can also hire a motor boat (per half/full day Nkr350/500) and chug around the sound.

Kaupanger's main claim for your attention is its impressive **stave church** (adult/child Nkr30/20; ⏰ 9.30am-5.30pm Jun–mid-Aug). Constructed in 1184, its wonderfully ornate interior is shaped like an upturned Viking ship. The wall paintings feature musical annotation and the Celtic-style chancel arch is unique.

Sleeping & Eating

Hofslund Fjord Hotel (☎ 57 67 10 22; www.hofslund -hotel.no; s/d/tr Nkr710/910/1110; P ☒) This venerable hotel has been run by the same family for four generations, since its inception. Service is courteous and friendly and it enjoys a wonderful location. Most

rooms have a balcony and view of the fjord, a neatly cropped lawn sweeps down to the water, the pool's heated – and there are a couple of rowing boats and fishing gear, free on loan to guests.

Loftesnes Pensjonat (☎ 57 67 15 77; Fjøravegen; s/d/tr Nkr360/580/660) This small place, above the China House restaurant, is great value. Nine of its 12 rooms have full bathroom and there are self-catering facilities and a roof-top terrace. If no-one's around, take any room that has its key in the lock and sign the guest register. If no-one has turned up before you leave, pay the restaurant staff below.

Sogndal Vandrerhjem (☎ 57 67 20 33; sogndal .hostel@vandrerhjem.no; Helgheimsvegen 10; dm/s/d Nkr100/175/250, d with bathroom Nkr400; ⏰ mid-Jun–mid-Aug) This well-equipped, summertimeonly HI-affiliated hostel, near the bridge that carries the Rv5, functions as a boarding school during the rest of the year.

Quality Hotel Sogndal (☎ 57 62 77 00; www .sogndal-hotel.no; Gravensteinsgata 5; s Nkr780-1300, d 990-1400; P ☒) Though short on character, this is a more than acceptable top-end alternative. Its three restaurants also offer about the best eating option in a town where gastronomic pleasures are limited.

Kjørnes Camping (☎ 57 67 45 80; www.kjornes.no; camping Nkr80 plus per person Nkr25; cabins Nkr250-500, apt Nkr650; ⏰ May-Sep) This camping ground is well positioned above the lake, 2km from town off the Rv5.

Dr Hagen Café (mains Nkr80 to Nkr195) has a short à la carte list while its main restaurant, Compagniet, does a copious dinner buffet (Nkr270).

There's a cheap but unexceptional cafeteria located in the Domus supermarket on Gravensteinsgata.

Getting There & Away

Sogndal has Sognefjord's only **airport** (☎ 57 67 26 16) officially called Haukåsen, with one to two daily Widerøe flights to/from Bergen and three to five to/from Oslo.

Local buses run between Sogndal and Kaupanger (Nkr25, 20 minutes, four Monday to Friday), Fjærland (Nkr56, 45 minutes, four to six daily) and Balestrand (Nkr90, 1¼ hours, three to five daily). Twice daily buses (mid-June to late August) head northeast past Jotunheimen National Park to Lom (Nkr220, 3¼ hours) and Otta (Nkr295, 4¼ hours).

STAVE CHURCHES

Most of Norway's 31 stave churches date from the 12th and 13th centuries. Construction began by laying down horizontal sills above ground level on a raised stone foundation, on which the vertical plank walls rested. At each corner is an upright stave post – hence the name of the style – which ties together the sill below and a wall plate above.

Most stave church interiors are little more than a small nave and a narrow chancel. In some, the nave and chancel are combined into a single rectangular space, divided only by a chancel screen. The most elaborate stave church still standing, at Borgund, also has a semicircular apse at the eastern end.

Typically, the roof of the nave is supported by freestanding posts spaced about 2m apart and standing about 1m from the walls, although smaller churches had just one central post. All remaining stave churches are surrounded by outer walls, creating external galleries or protective passageways that, together with the use of tar on the roofs as a preservative, have helped them to survive.

Interior walls are often painted in elaborate designs, including *rosemaling,* or traditional rose paintings, and the complex roof lines are frequently enhanced by scalloped wooden shingles and Viking-age dragon head finials, rather like those of Thai monasteries. Often, the most intricate decoration comes from the wooden carvings on the support posts, door frames and outer walls (especially at Urnes), representing tendrils of stems, vines and leaves. Often, these are entwined with serpents, dragons and other fantasy creatures, thus meshing Norway's proud pagan past with newer Christian themes.

Boats connect Sogndal with Balestrand (Nkr120, 45 minutes, once or twice daily) and Bergen (Nkr460, 4¾ hours, once daily).

SKJOLDEN

pop 600

Skjolden, on Lustrafjorden at the inner end of Sognefjorden, is a charming little village. In Fjordstova, you'll find a lot of things tucked under one roof: the **tourist office** (☎ 57 68 67 44; ☻ 11am-7pm, mid-Jun–mid-Aug; 2-7pm early Jun & late Aug), which has Internet access (per 30 minutes Nkr25), a café, a swimming pool and even a climbing wall. The bit of industrial-looking junk on display outside is a turbine from the Norsk hydropower station.

About 2km east of Skjolden is the lovely turquoise glacial lake Eidsvatnet. The valley Mørkridsdalen, which runs north of the village is good for hiking.

Further up the valley towards Fortun and 3km from Skjolden, **Vassbakken Kro & Camping** (☎ 57 68 61 88; vassbakken@skjolden.com in Norwegian; tent/caravan sites Nkr80 plus per adult/child Nkr20/10, 2-/4-bed cabins Nkr350/450, with bathroom Nkr600) is a smallish camping ground with a lovely setting.

Bus No 155 connects Skjolden with Sogndal (Nkr84, 1¼ hours) and Fortun (Nkr24,

10 minutes) up to six times daily. Skjolden is also on the twice-daily summer bus route between Otta and Sogndal (see p218).

If you're heading north on Rv55, check your fuel gauge; Skjolden's petrol stations are the last for 77km.

URNES

pop 40

Norwegian poet Paal-Helge Hauge wrote of Urnes stave church:

Someone came here, shouldering a man's load of visions and spread them out over the walls and pillars; gaping beasts, angels' wings, dragons out under the knife, the hand, the brush; tendrils of ochre, red, grey, white, a sinuous short way from paradise to damnation...

For its unique and elaborate wooden ornamentation, described in similar exuberant vein by Hauge, the **stave church** (adult/child Nkr40/25; ☻ 10.30am-5.30pm early Jun-Aug) at Urnes features on Unesco's World Heritage List.

This lovely structure overlooking Lusterfjord was probably built between 1130 and 1150, making it one of the oldest stave churches in Norway. There have been several alterations through the ages and it's likely that the unique and elaborate carvings that cover its gables, pillars, door frames and several strips on the outer wall were transferred from an 11th-century building that previously stood here.

The *Urnes* car and passenger ferry shuttles hourly between Solvorn and Urnes (adult/child/car Nkr24/12/65, 20 minutes); many drivers prefer to leave their vehicles on the Solvorn bank. Bus No 155 calls by the Solvorn ferry terminal on its frequent runs between Sogndal (Nkr35, 25 minutes) and Skjolden (Nkr60, 1¼ hours). From the Urnes ferry landing, it's a 1km uphill walk to the stave church.

JOSTEDALSBREEN

With an area of 487 sq km, the many-tongued Jostedalsbreen dominates the highlands of Sogn og Fjordane county and is mainland Europe's largest icecap, in places 400m thick. The main icecap and several nearby outliers are protected as the Jostedalsbreen National Park (for details of the park information centre, see p225).

The best hiking map for the region is Statens Kartverk's *Jostedalsbreen Turkart* (Nkr110) at a scale of 1:100,000. The *Jostedalsbreen Glacier Walks* brochure, available at tourist offices and many other venues, gives a comprehensive list of glacier walks, walking companies and fees.

For more details on the gateway towns of Skei, Stryn, Olden and Loen, see p224.

FJÆRLAND
pop 300
The farming village of Fjærland (also called Mundal), at the head of scenic Fjærlandsfjorden, lies near two particularly accessible glacial tongues, Supphellebreen and Bøyabreen – and so pulls in as many as 300,000 visitors each year. This tiny place, known as the 'Book Town' of Norway (www.bokbyen.no), is a bibliophile's nirvana, with a dozen shops selling a wide range of used books, mostly in Norwegian but with lots in English and other European languages. Its annual book fair, held on the Saturday nearest 23 June, pulls in booksellers and antiquarians from around the country. The village leaps to life in early May, when the ferry starts to run, and it virtually hibernates

from October onwards. The **tourist office** (☎ 57 69 32 33; www.fjaerland.org; ☼ 10am-6pm May-Sep) located within the Bok & Bilde bookshop on the main street, 300m from the ferry point. It displays a full list of accommodation options, together with prices, on the main door.

Sights & Activities
SUPPHELLEBREEN & BØYABREEN
You can drive to within 300m of the Supphellebreen glacier, then walk right up and touch the ice. Ice blocks from here were used as podiums at the 1994 Winter Olympics in Lillehammer.

Counter to the global norm these days, glaciers in Norway are actually advancing – and the creaking blue Bøyabreen, more spectacular than Supphellebreen, its brother over the hill, presses forward faster than most. You might be lucky enough to see glacial calving as a hunk tumbles into the meltwater lagoon beneath the glacier tongue.

NORWEGIAN GLACIER MUSEUM
For the story on flowing ice and how it has sculpted the Norwegian landscape, visit this superbly executed **museum** (Norsk Bremuseum; ☎ 57 69 32 88; adult/child Nkr80/40; ☼ 9am-7pm Jun-Aug, 10am-4pm Apr-May & Sep-Oct).

The hands-on exhibits will delight children. You can learn how fjords are formed, see an excellent 20-minute multiscreen audio-visual presentation on Jostedalsbreen, wind your way through a tunnel that penetrates the mock-ice and even see the tusk of a Siberian woolly mammoth, which met an icy demise 30,000 years ago. There's also an exhibit on the 5000-year-old 'Ice Man' corpse, which was found on the Austrian–Italian border in 1991.

HIKING
The tourist office has a free leaflet, *Escape the Asphalt*, that lists 11 major hiking routes around the region. Supplement this with the map *Turkart Fjærland* (Nkr70), at a scale of 1:50,000, which comes complete with route descriptions and trails indicated, pull on your boots and you're away. Most walks follow routes the local shepherds used until quite recently to lead their flocks to higher summer pastures. After you complete five, the local sports association will register your

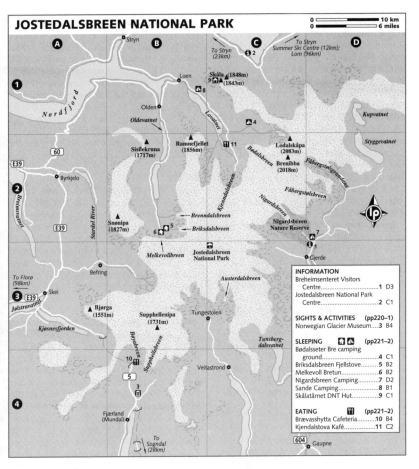

JOSTEDALSBREEN NATIONAL PARK

0 ———— 10 km
0 ———— 6 miles

INFORMATION
Breheimsenteret Visitors
Centre.....................................1 D3
Jostedalsbreen National Park
Centre.....................................2 C1

SIGHTS & ACTIVITIES (pp220–1)
Norwegian Glacier Museum....3 B4

SLEEPING (pp221–2)
Bødalsseter Bre camping
ground.....................................4 C1
Briksdalsbreen Fjellstove..........5 B2
Melkevoll Bretun......................6 B2
Nigardsbreen Camping.............7 D2
Sande Camping.........................8 B1
Skålatårnet DNT Hut................9 C1

EATING (pp221–2)
Brævasshytta Cafeteria............10 B4
Kjendalstova Kafé...................11 C2

achievement and issue a diploma, available through the tourist office!

Tours

A bus meets the twice-daily ferry from Balestrand, leaving the quayside at 9.40am (Nkr120) and 1.15pm (Nkr90). Both tours stop en route to allow visits to the interactive Glacier Museum (free with tour) and Bøyabreen glacier. The earlier tour also takes in the Supphellebreen glacier and leaves plenty of bookshop browsing time at the Bok & Bilde bookshop before you catch the ferry back to Balestrand. Alternatively, a taxi from the Fjærland dock to Bøyabreen, with waiting time, costs about Nkr400 return.

Sleeping & Eating

Hotel Mundal (☎ 57 69 31 01; hotelmundal@fjordinfo .no; s/d from Nkr860/1280; ☺ May-Sep) This excellent option, built in 1891 and run by the same family ever since, features a welcoming lounge and a lovely round tower (invest Nkr1950 and you can sleep the night in its one room with wraparound views). The dining room (look for the evocative 1898 map of Sognefjorden) serves truly wonderful traditional four-course Norwegian dinners (Nkr415). Because the food comes fresh, non-residents need to book by 6pm at the latest.

Fjærland Fjordstue Hotell (☎ 57 69 32 00; www .fjaerland.no; s/d incl breakast from Nkr590/700; ☺ May-Sep; Ⓟ) The majority of this charming small

THE WESTERN FJORDS

hotel's 16 rooms overlook the fjord where, with a smattering of luck, you might see porpoises playing. Its restaurant (lunch mains Nkr130 to Nkr145, dinner buffet Nkr290), a favourite with campers who drift down the road from Bøyum Camping, offers stunning views and does pizzas and salads, as well as full meals.

Ms Haugen's Rooms (☎ 57 69 32 43, 97 63 78 70; d Nkr350-400; ☼ year-round) In the white building behind the village church, Ms Alma Haugen rents just a couple of rooms that share a common kitchen and brand new bathroom ('Nkr92,000, this cost us,' said a proud Ms Haugen!) and represent outstanding value. The bigger double rooms cost slightly more.

Bøyum Camping (☎ 57 69 32 52; kfodne@frisurf .no; dm mattress Nkr125, tent & car sites Nkr115, basic d Nkr250-300, 6-bed cabins Nkr530-630; ☼ Jun-early Sep) Conveniently situated beside the Glacier Museum, Bøyum Camping has something for all pockets and sleeping preferences. Cabins have both bathroom and kitchen.

Brævasshytta Cafeteria (☎ 57 69 32 96; rolls Nkr18-36, snacks Nkr58-89, mains Nkr98-115; ☼ May-Sep) Do visit the Brævasshytta, built into the moraine of the glacier's latest major advance, even if it's only for a cup of coffee. With the glacier right there and in your face, it's like eating in an IMAX cinema, but for real.

There's also a good cafeteria at the Glacier Museum.

Getting There & Away

Four to six daily buses run to/from Sogndal (Nkr56, 45 minutes), Florø (Nkr185, 2¾ hours) via Skei (Nkr44, 30 minutes) and Stryn (Nkr159, two hours).

Ferries run twice daily between Balestrand and Fjærland (Nkr147/220 one-way/return, 1¼ hours) between May and September. The 9.40am departure connects in Balestrand with the boat to Flåm and the 3.40pm links with the Bergen-bound ferry.

Drivers may need to stock up at an ATM before visiting Fjærland. The long tunnels on either side of the village cost Nkr400 million to burrow and there's a punitive toll of Nkr150 to travel to/from Sogndal; by contrast, roll in from the Skei side and it's free.

Getting Around

The tourist office rents bikes (per hour/day Nkr25/125).

NIGARDSBREEN

Among the Jostedalsbreen glacier tongues visible from below, Nigardsbreen ranks among the most dramatic and easily visited, so it's a very popular visitor destination. If you find it all too touristy and have wheels, nip further up the road past the braided glacial streams at Fåbergstølsgrandane to the dam that creates the big glacial lake Styggevatnet. Along the way you'll find several scenic glacial tongues and valleys offering excellent wild hiking.

Sights

Inside the **Breheimsenteret visitors centre** (☎ 57 68 32 50; www.jostedal.com; adult/child Nkr50/35; ☼ 9am-7pm mid-Jul–mid-Aug, 10am-5pm May–mid-Jul & mid-Aug–Sep) at Jostedal, displays tell the story of the formation and movement of glaciers and how they sculpt the landscape. There's also a 20-minute film on the area and an exhibit on the girl Jostedalsrypa, the only villager to survive the Black Death.

Activities

Jostedalen Breførarlag (☎ 57 68 31 11; www.bfl.no) does several guided glacier tours. Easiest is the family walk to the glacier snout and briefly along its tongue (around one hour on the ice, adult/child Nkr140/70). Fees for the two-hour (Nkr310) and three-hour (Nkr390) walks on the ice both include the brief boat trip across the Nigardsvatnet.

For a truly original glacial perspective, sign on for a guided kayak outing with **Ice Troll** (☎ 57 68 32 50; www.icetroll.com). Tours of around six hours (Nkr600), suitable for first-timers as well as the more experienced, take you where those without paddles never get. They also do overnight sorties (Nkr1100) and, when the weather's murky, shorter trips on tamer Nigardsbrevatnet (per hour Nkr125).

The Breheimsenteret takes bookings for both outfits.

Sleeping & Eating

Jostedal Hotel (☎ 57 68 31 19; www.jostedalhotel.no; Girde, Jostedal; s/d incl breakfast Nkr600/800) Five kilometres down the road from Breheimsenteret, in Gjerde village, this newly renovated place brims with character and makes a good, away-from-it-all stop.

Nigardsbreen Camping (☎ 57 68 31 35; Jostedal; tent/caravan sites Nkr90/120, cabins Nkr300; ☼ late

May-Sep) Camping and cabins are available by the entrance to the toll road, 400m from Breheimsenteret.

The Breheimsenteret has a small café, where the rather steep prices are compensated for by the great view.

Getting There & Around

From late June to August, bus No 159 connects Sogndal and Jostedal Breheimsenteret (Nkr96, 1½ hours) one to three times daily. For much of the way from the Rv55 at Gaupne, the road to the glacier follows the brilliant turquoise-blue Jostedalselva. Watch also for the splashes of bright red lichen on the rocks beside the route.

From Breheimsenteret, a 6km-long toll road (per vehicle Nkr22) or a pleasant hike leads to the car park at Nigardsvatnet, the lagoon at the glacial snout. Between mid-June and early September, a ferry shuttles over the lagoon to the glacier face (Nkr30 return).

BRIKSDALSBREEN

From the small town of Olden at the eastern end of Nordfjord, a scenic road leads 23km up Oldedalen to the twin glacial tongues of Melkevollbreen and Briksdalsbreen. The more easily accessible, Briksdalsbreen, attracts hordes of tour buses; whenever a tourist pony cart crosses the strategically placed bridge over the river that flows from beneath the ice, the dominant sound is the click of camera shutters. In 1997, the tongue of Briksdalsbreen licked to its furthest point for around 70 years but has subsequently retreated by around 150m.

Activities

Two companies offer a range of outdoor activities and identical prices.

Briksdal Breføring (☎ 57 87 68 00; www.briksdals bre.no) is at Briksdalsbre Fjellstove, the end of the blacktop road, while **Olden Activ** (☎ 57 87 38 88; www.briksdalsbreen.com), which operates from the Melkevoll Bretun camping ground, is a five-minute walk down the hill. Both organise a good range of glacier hikes and climbs that don't demand previous experience.

You can choose between a three-hour trip (Nkr250) with an hour on the ice; or a four-hour trip (Nkr300 to Nkr350) with two hours on the ice. Walks depart from either Briksdalsbre Fjellstove or Melkevoll Bretun five times daily, mid-May to September.

Olden Activ will lay on introductions to mountaineering, bouldering and rock climbing (book in advance). It also offers four hours of ice-climbing instruction and practice (Nkr400). Briksdal Breføring, specialising in high mountain walking, can draw up tailored trekking programmes.

It's about a 5km-return walk to the glacier face, either up the steepish path or along the longer, more gentle cart track. **Oldedalen Skysslag** (☎ 57 87 68 05) runs pony-cart rides (per adult Nkr260) and contraptions like giant golfing carts (Nkr160), but you'll still have a 15-minute hike on a rough path to see the ice. Advance booking for both is essential.

The recently erected activity tower opposite Briksdalsbre Fjellstove offers a range of climbing activities for all ages.

Sleeping & Eating

Briksdalsbre Fjellstove (☎ 57 87 68 00; www.briksdals bre.no; s/d Nkr400/800) This cosy mountain lodge, run by Briksdal Breføring (left), has six comfortable rooms, a café/restaurant (mains Nkr63 to Nkr150, including trout and reindeer dishes) and a souvenir shop.

Getting There & Away

Between June and August, a bus leaves Stryn for Briksdalsbre (Nkr64, one hour) at

---

AUTHOR'S CHOICE

Melkevoll Bretun (☎ 57 87 38 64; www.mel kevoll.no; basic cabins Nkr270-370, fully equipped 6-bed cabins Nkr570-690) This place has accommodation for all pockets and gorgeous views whichever way you turn. Look south and the Melkevollbreen glacier is sticking its tongue out towards you, spin west and the long, slim Volefossen waterfall cascades, turn south and the long reach of the Lake Oldevatnet shimmers, while eastwards, the Briksdalbreen glacier blocks the horizon. There's a gorgeous green camping ground with stacks of space between pitches. The larger cabins (Nkr570 to Nkr690), sleeping six, are fully equipped and well furnished and there are simpler, more basic cabins (Nkr270 to Nkr370). For budget sleeping with attitude, spread your sleeping bag in the 'stone-age cave' (Nkr90) or wigwam (Nkr50).

THE WESTERN FJORDS

9.30am, calling by Loen and Olden. The return bus leaves Briksdal at 1.40pm. There's also a second departure at 3.45pm on weekdays from Stryn to Melkevoll Bretun.

If you park for the day at Melkevoll Bretun (Nkr40), there's a free sauna thrown in after your hike.

KJENNDALSBREEN & BØDALSBREEN

Lovely Kjenndalsbreen is 17km by road from the Nordfjord village of Loen. Probably the least visited of the four best-known glacial tongues, it vies with Nigardsbreen for the most beautiful approach as you run parallel to the glacial lake of Lovatnet. Bødalsbreen, in a nearby side valley, provides good hiking possibilities.

Tours

Both **Briksdal Breføring** (☎ 57 87 68 00; www.briks dal.no) and **Stryn Fjell og Breførarlag** (☎ 57 87 68 00; www.strynglaciertours.no) offer six-hour guided glacier walks on Bødalsbreen (Nkr350) and considerably more demanding 12-hour Saturday treks (Nkr500) to the 2083m-high nunatak Lodalskåpa. Tours set out from the Bødalsseter Bre camping ground.

Sleeping

Sande Camping (☎ 57 87 45 90; www.sande-camping .no;Loen; tent/caravans Nkr80, 2-/4-bed cabins Nkr250/375, 4-/6-bed apt Nkr475/770) Popular Sande Camping, near the northern end of Lovatnet, offers scenic lakeside tent and caravan camping, as well as an exhaustive range of cabins and apartments.

Getting There & Away

A wonderful way to approach Kjenndalsbreen is on the *Kjendal* that chugs up Lovatnet from Sande (adult/under 10 return Nkr160/free), a trip that includes a return bus between Kjendalstova Café, at the end of the lake, and the glacier car park. From here, it's a 2km walk to the glacier face. From June to August, the boat leaves Sande at 10.30am and Kjendalstova at 1.30pm. You can book the boat trip through **Hotel Alexandra** (☎ 57 87 50 50) in Loen.

While you're sailing along, watch out for the huge blocks of stone that dislodged from Ramnefjell and crashed down into the lake in 1905, 1936 and 1950 and prepare to duck; the first wave killed 63 people and deposited the lake steamer 400m inland, the

second killed 72, while the third just left a bigger scar on the mountain.

If you're driving, take care where the toll road (Nkr30) running above Lovatnet narrows to a single track.

STRYN SUMMER SKI CENTRE

Nowhere near the town of Stryn, despite its name, this **ski centre** (Sommerskisenter; ☎ 92 25 83 33; www.strynefjellet.com; Videdalen; ☣ 10am-4pm Jun-Aug) is in fact on the Tystigen outlier of Jostedalsbreen, at its northernmost point. Here is Norway's most extensive and best known summer skiing, and most of those photos of bikini-clad skiers you see around were snapped here. The longest Alpine run extends for 2100m with a drop of 520m and there is also 10km of cross-country ski tracks.

A ski bus runs from Stryn (Nkr70 one-way, one hour) at 9am and returns from the ski centre at 4pm, roughly between mid-June and mid-July, depending upon snow conditions. Drivers will enjoy the scenic Gamle Strynefjellsvegen, the old road that connects Grotli with Videsæter. Pick up a free leaflet at Stryn tourist office.

SOGNEFJORDEN TO NORDFJORD

For most travellers the 100km-long Nordfjord is but a stepping stone between Sognefjorden and Geirangerfjorden. These two popular fjords are linked by a road that winds around the head of Nordfjord past the villages of Byrkjelo, Olden and Loen to the larger town of Stryn.

SKEI

pop 390

The inland village of Skei lies near the head of lake Jølstravatnet. The worthwhile **Astruptunet museum** (☎ 57 72 67 82; adult/child Nkr40/free; ☣ 10am-6pm Jul, 11am-5pm late May-Jun & Aug, 11am-4pm Sep), 15km west of the village on the south side of the lake, is the former home of artist Nicolai Astrup (1880–1928) and includes a gallery plus open-air exhibits.

Jølster Rafting (☎ 90 06 70 70; www.jolster-rafting .no in Norwegian) does white-water rafting on the Stardal and Jølstra rivers. Shorter trips range from Nkr550 to Nkr750 while one- and two-day excursions are both Nkr1190.

At the junction of Rv5 and the E39 is this sporty hotel **Skei Hotel** (☎ 57 72 78 00; www.skei hotel.no; s/d from Nkr975/1130; P ⬚). It has a swimming pool, sauna, Jacuzzi, solarium, rowing boat, cycles – and even a tennis court. Unappealing from the outside, it's much more attractive within and has a cosy bar and decent restaurant.

For good value meals and snacks, drop into this cafeteria **Audhild Vikens Vevstove** (☎ 57 72 81 25; pizza Nkr48, mains around Nkr100; ☾ 8.30am-10pm Jul-Aug, core hours 10am-6.30pm Sep-Jun) of Norway's largest tax-free shop. Christmas products are sold year-round at this friendly place, less than 100m from the road junction.

Many long-distance buses connect at Skei, including services to Fjærland (Nkr44, 30 minutes, four to six daily), Sogndal (Nkr96, one hour, three to seven daily), Stryn (Nkr120, 1½ hours, three daily), Ålesund (Nkr225, 4¾ hours, two to four daily), Florø (Nkr155, 2¼ hours, two to four daily) and Bergen (Nkr285, 4½ hours, three to four daily).

STRYN
pop 2100
The small town of Stryn is the de facto capital of upper Nordfjord. Because it lies on several long-distance transport routes, many visitors break their journey here. The helpful **tourist office** (☎ 57 87 40 40; www.nordfjord .no; ☾ 8.30am-8pm Jul, 8.30am-6pm Jun & 1-15 Aug, 8.30am-3.30pm Mon-Fri mid-Aug–May) is two blocks south of Tonningsgata, the main drag. For a fee of Nkr30, it will arrange accommodation, charges Nkr1 per minute for Internet access and rents mountain bikes (per hour/ day Nkr50/190). Its free booklet, *Guide for Stryn*, includes local hikes, while *På Sykkel i Stryn*, also free, outlines cycling routes. For more detail, invest Nkr30 in *Kart over Fjall-turar I Stryn*, on which a whole holiday's worth of biking and hiking trails feature.

Sights & Activities
Oppstryn, 15km east of Stryn is home to **Jostedalsbreen National Park Centre** (Jostedalsbreen Nasjonalparksenter; ☎ 57 87 72 00; www.jostedalsbre.no; adult/child Nkr60/30; ☾ 10am-4pm or 6pm May-Aug). It has glacier-oriented exhibits, a unique garden with 325 species of endemic vegetation and a lively audiovisual presentation. For good measure, it also covers avalanches,

local minerals and meteorites and has a section on the Lovatnet disasters (see p224).

Sleeping & Eating
Stryn Vandrerhjem (☎ 57 87 11 06; stryn.hostel@vand rerhjem.no; dm incl breakfast Nkr185, basic s/d incl break-fast Nkr250/400, d with bathroom incl breakfast Nkr500; ☾ Jun-Aug) This excellent, friendly HI-affiliated hostel, on the hillside and 2km by road from town, was once a German military barracks.

Stryn Hotel (☎ 57 87 07 00; www.strynhotel.no; Vis-nesvegen; s/d Nkr895/1095; P ⬚) It's no more expensive to take a room overlooking the fjord at this modern hotel, just over the bridge from the centre. The lunch buffet (Nkr150) and dinner equivalent (Nkr215) are among the best deals in town and there is also a dinner à la carte menu (mains Nkr100 to Nkr188).

Stryn Camping (☎ 57 87 11 36; www.stryn-camping .no in Norwegian; Bøavegen; tent/caravan sites Nkr130/160, cabins Nkr350, 6-bed cabins with bathroom Nkr850-950; ☾ Jun-Aug) There are good facilities at well-kept Stryn Camping, located just two blocks uphill from the main drag at the eastern end of town.

Restaurant Tonningstova (☎ 57 87 77 30; Ton-ningsgata 33) On the main street, Restaurant Tonningstova, recently under new management, has an open air streetside terrace and cosy interior, complete with dart board. It does a range of salads and staples from around the world – Italy, Spain, Mexico and further afield.

For wholesome local food with a Norwegian slant, eat at the cafeteria of the **Coop supermarket** (crn Tonningsgata & Tinggata) or at **Kafe Hjorten** (Tinggata), the café attached to the town cultural centre.

Drinking & Entertainment
Base Camp (☎ 57 87 23 83; Tonningsgata 31) This is a popular bar and disco.

Scala disco (☎ 57 87 07 00; Visnesvegen; ☾ to 2.30am Wed & Fri-Sun) Rock bands and other live music features here at the club in Stryn Hotel, mainly for the 18- to 21-year-old set.

Getting There & Away
Stryn lies on the Nor-Way Bussekspress routes between Oslo (Nkr615, 8½ hours, three daily) and Måløy (Nkr145, two hours); Ålesund (Nkr220, 3½ hours, two to three daily) and Bergen (Nkr393, six hours, four

to six daily); and Bergen and Trondheim (Nkr510, 7½ hours, twice daily). Bergenbound buses call in at Loen (Nkr25, 10 minutes) and Olden (Nkr32, 15 minutes). The Ålesund route passes Hellesylt (Nkr80, one hour), where there are boat connections to Geiranger.

OLDEN
pop 540
Olden serves as a Jostedalsbreen gateway and has a seasonal **tourist office** (☎ 57 87 31 26; ☽ 10am-6pm mid-Jun–mid-Aug).

Singersamlinga (☎ 57 87 31 06; adult/child Nkr20/10; ☽ by appointment) displays the artwork of William Henry Singer, American millionaire and local philanthropist. From 1913 to his death in 1943, he and his wife spent their summers in Olden and his paintings bear witness to the affinity he felt for the landscapes of western Norway.

If you fancy a little fishing, the **Isabella** (☎ 91 35 10 42 or book via Olden or Stryn Tourist Office) does two- to three-hour trips (per person including gear Nkr150), leaving Olden marina at 4pm and 7.30pm, Monday to Friday.

Sleeping & Eating
There are around 10 camping grounds in the area, most along the route to Briksdalsbreen and several in stunningly pretty sites.

Olden Fjordhotel (☎ 57 87 34 00; www.olden-hotel .no; s incl breakfast Nkr900-1050, d incl breakfast Nkr1200-1500; ☽ May-Sep) The automatic swing doors that purr open when you're still a couple of metres from the threshold are symptomatic of the warm welcome the Fjordhotel imparts. All of its comfortable rooms have views of the fjord, nearly all have balconies and the hotel does a fine Norwegian buffet dinner (Nkr350).

Alda Camping (☎ 57 87 31 38; persaget@online.no; sites without/with car Nkr35/60, 4-bed cabins Nkr240-300; ☽ mid-May–Aug) On the fringe of Olden, this friendly, no-frills camping ground extends each side of the Rv60, just before the road bridge.

LOEN
pop 420
Loen, a great touristy place located at the mouth of dramatic Lodalen, is another gateway to Jostedalsbreen and its icecap, providing bus and boat connections along

Lovatnet to the spectacular Bødalen and Kjenndalen glacial tongues.

A great, though strenuous five- to six-hour hike from Loen leads to the Skålatårnet tower (now a self-service Den Norske Turistforening hut), near the 1848m-high summit of Skåla. The route begins near Tjugen farm, north of the river and immediately east of Loen.

Sleeping & Eating
Hotel Alexandra (☎ 57 87 50 00; www.alexandra.no; s/d incl breakfast from Nkr960/1480; P ☐) Loen's undisputed centre of action is as much holiday centre as hotel and dominates tourism in the valley. It offers restaurants, bars, nightclub, swimming pool, spa and fitness centre, tennis court, marina, and boat and bicycle hire. Although run as a family hotel since 1884, its current architecture approaches the eyesore level. From the hotel you can book the Lovatnet boat and other Jostedalsbreen excursions.

Hotel Loenfjord (☎ 57 87 50 00; www.loenfjord .no in Norwegian; s/d incl breakfast Nkr800/1200; P) Under the same ownership as the Alexandra, the Loenfjord offers waterside accommodation that's a little less expensive and altogether gentler on the eye. Less crowded, it too offers boat and bicycle hire so you can really get away.

Lo-Vik Camping (☎ 57 87 76 19; fax 57 87 78 11; tent sites without/with car Nkr70/90 plus per person Nkr20, 4-bed cabins Nkr350, with bathroom Nkr650-850; ☽ mid-May–mid-Sep) This establishment enjoys a green site overlooking the water.

NORDFJORDEID
Above the village of Nordfjordeid, midway between Stryn and Måløy, are the stables of the **Norsk Fjordhestsenter** (☎ 57 86 48 00), which specialises in the rearing of the stocky, handsome Norwegian Fjord ponies with their bristle-stiff, Mohican manes and creamy-caramel hides. To book a ride (Nkr250 for the first hour, Nkr100 for subsequent hours), do reserve since the ponies are often in demand for school groups and summer camps.

FLORØ
pop 8100
Florø, Norway's westernmost town, is a pleasant little place whose coat of arms features, appropriately, three herrings rampant.

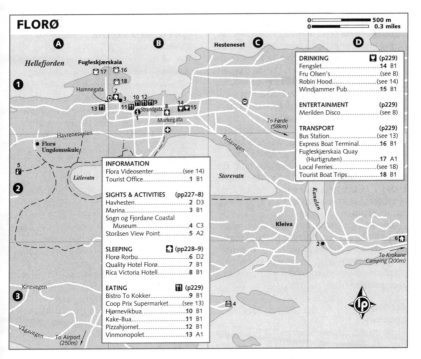

FLORØ

0 — 500 m
0 — 0.3 miles

DRINKING	(p229)
Fengslet.............................14 B1
Fru Olsen's..........................(see 8)
Robin Hood..........................(see 14)
Windjammer Pub..................15 B1

ENTERTAINMENT	(p229)
Merilden Disco.....................(see 8)

TRANSPORT	(p229)
Bus Station..........................(see 13)
Express Boat Terminal............16 B1
Fugleskjærskaia Quay
(Hurtigruten)....................17 A1
Local Ferries........................(see 18)
Tourist Boat Trips................18 B1

INFORMATION	
Flora Videosenter................(see 14)
Tourist Office.......................1 B1

SIGHTS & ACTIVITIES	(pp227–8)
Havhesten...........................2 D3
Marina................................3 B1
Sogn og Fjordane Coastal
Museum..........................4 C3
Storåsen View Point..............5 A2

SLEEPING	(pp228–9)
Florø Rorbu.........................6 D2
Quality Hotel Florø...............7 B1
Rica Victoria Hotell...............8 B1

EATING	(p229)
Bistro To Kokker...................9 B1
Coop Prix Supermarket........(see 13)
Hjørnevikbua.......................10 B1
Kake-Bua............................11 B1
Pizzahjornet........................12 B1
Vinmonopolet......................13 A1

The town was founded on 'fishy silver' in 1860 as a herring port, but is now sustained by fish farming, ship building and the black gold of the oil industry. As one of the southernmost ports on the Hurtigruten coastal ferry route, it sees lots of fleeting visitors but merits at least a day of exploring and relaxing. For a scenic overview, it's an easy 10-minute climb up the Storåsen hill from the Florø Ungdomsskule on Havrenesveien.

Information

Flora Videosenter (Strandgata 56; 1-10pm; per hr Nkr20) You can access the Internet here.

Laundrette At the Marina.

Tourist office (57 74 75 05; www.vestkysten.no; Strandgata 30; 8am-6pm Mon-Fri, 10am-4pm Sat, noon-4pm Sun mid-Jun–mid-Aug; 9am-3.30pm Mon-Fri rest-of-year)

Sights

SOGN OG FJORDANE COASTAL MUSEUM

The two main buildings at this **museum** (57 74 22 33; Brendøyvegen; adult/child Nkr35/15; 11am-6pm Mon-Fri, noon-4pm Sat & Sun mid-Jun–mid-Aug, 10am-3pm Mon-Fri, noon-3pm Sun, closed Sat Sep–mid-Jun) are chock-full of fishing exhibits and

there's a model 1900 fishing family's home too. Also within the complex are several old warehouse buildings, moved from Florø and Måløy, and an old herring salthouse with a display that pays homage to the fish that made Florø.

On a more contemporary theme, the Snorreankeret oil platform displays the history, exploration and exploitation of the North Sea oil and gas fields.

THE OLD QUARTER

On and around Strandgata, the main street, the most interesting of the mainly 19th-century timbered houses are well signed and documented in both Norwegian and English.

OFFSHORE ISLANDS

Ferries connect the mainland to the islands of Kinn, Svanøy, Batalden, Askrova and Tansøy from Fugleskjærskaia Quay. The schedules are intermittent and complicated; check for current information with the tourist office, which can also advise on island accommodation.

THE WESTERN FJORDS

Kinn has a beautifully restored 12th-century **church** (🕐 11am-12.30pm Mon, Wed, Fri, Jul–mid-Aug), believed to have been built by British Celts sheltering from religious persecution. In late June, it's the site of the Kinnespelet pageant, which celebrates the church history on the island. Climbers and hikers also savour the dramatic landscapes, particularly the Kinnaklova cleft.

On **Svanøy**, you can hike, visit the **deer centre** (☎ 57 75 21 80; guided tours Tue & Thu mid-Jun–mid-Aug) or go **horse riding** (☎ 57 74 70 10).

On **Batalden**, check out the gallery at the pleasant **Batalden Havbu fishing cottages** (☎ 57 74 54 22), where you can overnight in their sensitively restored **cottages** (per person Nkr400-450; 🕐 Apr-Oct).

Askrova has a prehistoric Troll Cave, whose deepest depths have never been explored and adjoining **Tansøy**, connected to it by a bridge, rises to 233m, from where you have great panoramic views over the surrounding archipelago.

Activities

BOATING
Florø Rorbu (right) hires motor boats (per day Nkr200 to Nkr400) and sea-kayaks (per day Nkr200), while Krokane Camping (right) rents out rowing boats (per three hours/day Nkr50/100) and motor boats (Nkr200/300).

HIKING & BIKING
The tourist office sells two useful booklets: *Cycling in Flora* (Nkr20) and *On Foot in Flora* (Nkr50).

SWIMMING
If the fjord's too chilly, plunge into one of the three indoor heated pools at **Havhesten** (☎ 57 75 67 20) or get all aglow in the sauna.

Tours
From late June to mid-August, the tourist office runs a number of tempting tours. At 10am on Friday, there's a glorious day tour by boat (adult/child Nkr350/175) to the offshore lighthouses at Stabben, Kvanhovden and the remote Ytterøyane (no landing at Ytterøyane). It's very popular, so do book in advance.

Other good options include its guided tours of Kinn (adult/child Nkr160/75, Wednesday and Friday), departing at 10am

> ### THE WORLD'S LONGEST HERRING TABLE
>
> OK, so the competition may not be all that extensive but a herring table 400m long is an impressive achievement in its own right. Each year, Florø and Haugesund, further down the coast, used to vie with each other for the year's largest and longest spread but, now that Haugesund has retired, there's no longer the same north–south rivalry and Florø has the field to itself.
>
> Every third weekend in June, the table is erected in the heart of Florø. Just try to imagine a standard 400m running track, straightened out and laden with plates of herring, potatoes, bread and drinks, all free of charge, and you've got the scene.

and returning at 3.30pm and its visits to Svanøy (adult/child Nkr225/115, Tuesday and Thursday), with a visit to a 17th-century manor farm and the deer centre. Bring your own lunch.

Sleeping
The tourist office can book holiday cabins in secluded waterside locations.

Florø Rorbu (☎ 57 74 81 00; www.florbu.com; Krokane Kai; 4-bed apt Nkr400-550, 6-bed apt Nkr500-760) These excellent, family-owned, fully furnished flats are right beside the water and have their own moorings (you can hire a boat and putter around the fjord to celebrate sunset).

Quality Hotel Florø (☎ 57 75 75 75; www.florahotel.no; Hamnegata 7; s/d Nkr790/890; 🅿 💻) On the quayside and right beside the marina, this hotel has rooms – including a couple with 'boat beds' – that represent excellent value. It also runs an elegant restaurant, Bryggekanten (mains Nkr195 to Nkr225), that warrants a visit in its own right.

Rica Victoria Hotell (☎ 57 74 10 00; www.victoriahotell.no; Markegata 43; s/d from Nkr750/900) Set back in town, this is another reasonable choice that very much speaks of the 1970s. It too runs a good restaurant and has one disabled-equipped room, a sauna and mini-gym.

Krokane Camping (☎ 57 75 22 50; camp sites Nkr100, cabins with bathroom 2-4 persons Nkr340-450, 5-6 persons Nkr500-700; 🕐 year-round) Friendly

Krokane Camping occupies a pleasantly wooded site on a peninsula 2.5km east of town. From the centre, buses run at least hourly from Monday to Saturday; get off at Solheim.

Eating

Hjørnevikbua (☎ 57 74 01 22; Strandgata 23; lunch Nkr65-125) The 2nd floor of the Hjørnevikbua pub and restaurant, with its ship-like interior, serves lunches including some mean fish soups (Nkr85). You can also eat outdoors, on their barge that's moored to the quay.

Pizzahjornet (☎ 57 42 23 18; Strandgata 25; pizzas Nkr150-170) Pizzahjornet serves up decent pizzas, fish and chips, and kebabs.

Kake-Bua (☎ 57 75 01 60; Strandgata 21; salads & snacks around Nkr70; mains around Nkr120; ⊙ Mon-Sat) This place has something for all tastes and appetites. It combines a pastry shop, pub, café and restaurant, both self-service and à la carte, crammed with nautical artefacts. Upstairs, there's a pleasant terrace overlooking the fjord.

Bistro To Kokker (☎ 57 75 22 33; Strandgata 33; dishes Nkr50-120) For light lunches, fast food and seafood dinners, this place 50m east of the tourist office does squid, salmon, monkfish and other seafood. For more pedestrian palates, it has fish and chips (Nkr45), burgers (Nkr55 to Nkr100), and good salads (Nkr70) too.

Vinmonopolet is in the same block as the Coop Prix supermarket, next to the bus station.

Drinking & Entertainment

Windjammer Pub (☎ 57 74 29 88; Strandgata 58) On weekends, this place is divided into an animated pub with live music (Thursday to Saturday) and a disco for patrons aged 18 to 22. The rest of the week, it's just a drinking den.

Fru Olsen's (☎ 57 74 10 00; Markegata 43) A pub, located at the Rica Victoria Hotell. It is a quiet drinking spot.

Bar Blue Nightclub (cover charge Nkr50 after 11pm) Also in the Rica Victoria Hotell, this place attracts all ages, all types of crowds and people for a fun night out.

Fengslet (2nd flr, Strandgata 56) attracts a young crowd while the **Robin Hood** (☎ 57 74 38 70; 2nd fl, Strandgata 56), on the same floor, tends to attract a slightly older crowd.

Getting There & Away

AIR
DAT (www.dat.dk) offers budget flights two to four times daily to/from Oslo from **Florø airport** (☎ 57 74 67 00).

BOAT
The town is also a stop on the Hurtigruten coastal ferry between Bergen (Nkr510, 6¼ hours) and Kirkenes. Northbound, it calls by at 2.15am (4.45am mid-September to mid-April) and southbound at 8.15am. Stops further north include Måløy (Nkr162, 2¼ hours), Ålesund (Nkr475, 6½ hours) and Trondheim (Nkr1155, 30 hours).

Express boats run twice daily between Bergen (Nkr450, 3½ hours) and Måløy (Nkr160, one hour), stopping in Florø en route.

BUS
Florø lies at the end of the Nor-Way Bussekspress route from Oslo (Nkr679, 10½ hours, twice daily).

CAR & MOTORCYCLE
The most scenic way to Måløy by road is via Bremanger Island.

Getting Around
The town runs an excellent Sykkelbyen scheme, where you can rent a one-speed city bike for only Nkr30 per day at the tourist office, Quality Hotel Florø or Krokane Camping. The tourist office also hires out more versatile mountain bikes.

AROUND FLORØ
Vingen Petroglyphs
The 1500 early Stone Age petroglyphs at Vingen, facing the sea from the slopes of Vingenfjellet, are northern Europe's largest concentration. They're thought to be the work of early Stone Age hunters, chipped into the rock between 6000 and 4000 BC. There's no road to the paintings, which are protected, but the Florø tourist office organises a biweekly boat (Nkr270/150), departing from Florø and/or Bremanger between 1 July and mid-August.

Ausevik Rock Carvings
These excellent rock carvings, featuring deer and other motifs from around 1000 BC, are more accessible and a mere five-minute

THE WESTERN FJORDS

KALVÅG

If you're travelling from Florø to Måløy via Bremanger island, do make the 5km detour from the ferry landing point at Smørhamn to the sensitively preserved fishing village of Kalvåg (population 370). Nowadays it's picture-postcard pretty and there's just one giant fish-processing factory on its outskirts. But at its peak Kalvåg had over 50 herring salt houses that employed a seasonal workforce of around 10,000. You can still visit one or two of them; ask at the friendly quayside **tourist office** (☎ 57 79 22 69; ☼ 10am-4pm or 5pm Mon-Sat, noon-4pm Sun Jul–mid-Aug; 10am-4pm Thu-Fri, noon-4pm Sat & Sun May; 10am-4pm Sat-Thu Jun), itself once a salthouse.

---

walk from the Fv611 (about 40 minutes' drive south of Florø).

MÅLØY
pop 3100

The little fishing town of Måløy, at the mouth of Nordfjord, lies on Vågsøy island. Nestling beneath a pair of rounded hills, for all the world like a pair of giant breasts, it's linked to the mainland by the graceful S-curve Måløybrua bridge.

There's little of major interest in the town itself but the island is laced with sea-view hiking routes (pick up the 1:50,000 walking map *Friluftskart* for Nkr75 at the tourist office). Two places are well worth a visit: the bizarre seaside rock, **Kannesteinen**, about 10km from town, rising from the sea like a giant stone mushroom, and the **Kråkenes Lighthouse**, perched precariously on a rock shoulder. Sunny or stormy, it's a romantic spot with stunning views where you can have a meal, and you can enjoy coffee and home-made cakes – even spend the night (right).

Måløy's **tourist office** (☎ 57 85 08 50; Gate 1 No 53; ☼ 10am-6pm Mon-Fri, 10am-4pm Sat & Sun Jul, 10am-4pm Mon-Sat mid-end Jun & early Aug) is on the main street. It has an Internet point (per hour Nkr50).

Sleeping & Eating
Norlandia Måløy Hotel (☎ 57 84 94 00; www.norland ia.no in Norwegian; Gate 1 No 25; s/d from Nkr685/890) This large glass-fronted hotel is the centre of most tourist activity in town. Its recommended Aquarius restaurant offers a three-course dinner (Nkr235) and a good à la carte selection.

Steinvik Camping (☎ 57 85 10 70; oddbnyg@online .no; person/pitch Nkr10/80, 2-bed cabins with toilet Nkr350, 4-bed cabins with bathroom Nkr500, 4-bed self-catering flats Nkr450-600) The nearest camping ground to Måløy has spectacular views over the fjord. To get there cross the bridge to the east bank, turn right after 2km beside a school and follow the track downhill for 1.2km. Take any eastbound bus as far as the school.

Galeåsen Pub (☎ 57 85 22 40; Sjøgata) It's vast and a bit like eating in a station waiting room but this covered pub at the harbour opposite the Norlandia Måløy hotel lays on decent food and often has dancing on weekend evenings.

Havfruen Fiskeutsalg (☎ 57 85 23 36) The Mermaid, beside the express boat jetty, is both a wet fish shop ('Born to fish, forced to work', says the plaque on the wall) and small café, serving rich fish soups (Nkr50 to Nkr60), salmon sandwiches (Nkr25) and other fishy dishes.

Getting There & Away
Nor-Way Bussekspress runs three times daily to/from Oslo (Nkr735, 11 hours), via Stryn (Nkr136, 2¼ hours, six buses daily).

The express boat from Bergen to Selje goes via Florø and Måløy (Nkr570, 4½ hours from Bergen). The northbound Hurtigruten coastal ferry passes daily at 4.30am (7.30am mid-September to mid-April); the southbound at 5.45am.

AUTHOR'S CHOICE

Kråkenes Lighthouse (☎ /fax 57 85 55 27; Kråkenes; beds Nkr300, 6-bed ste Nkr650; ☼ Apr-Sep) Here's a delightful, truly original over-nighting option, run to a high standard by the enterprising German couple who have made this wild coastline their home. You can either stay in the former lighthouse keeper's house (rooms for two to four people) with self-catering facilities and external bathroom or enjoy the splendid top-floor suite, with bathroom, in the lighthouse itself. Meals are also available, if you order in advance.

SELJE & SELJA ISLAND
pop 715

Few visitors traipse all the way out to Selje, which is one of the northernmost outposts of Sogn og Fjordane county on the western edge of Norway, but those who do find a very pleasant small town and one of the finest beaches in the country. You may also want to make the trek out to Vestkapp, 32km by road from Selje. Despite the name, it isn't in fact Norway's westernmost point but it still provides superb sea views.

Selje's **tourist office** (☎ 57 85 66 06; sunniva1@ start.no; ☿ 9am-7pm Jul, 10am-4pm Jun & Aug, 8am-3pm Mon-Fri Sep & Apr-May, Mon-Tue Oct-Mar), at the harbour, keeps lists of cabins and apartments in the area.

The lovely ruins of **Selje monastery** and the **church of St Sunniva** on Selja island date from the 11th and 12th centuries, respectively. You can climb the 40m-high tower for a splendid panorama. Between 20 June and end-August, there are daily guided tours (adult/child Nkr120/60 including return boat trip, two hours). The small ferry makes the 15-minute crossing to the island from Selje at 10am daily and there are two additional daily departures in July. Pay at the tourist office, with whom it's prudent to reserve in advance.

The **Selje Hotel** (☎ 57 85 88 80; www.seljehotel .no; s/d from Nkr815/1060), a sumptuous affair right beside the beach, is the village's only hotel. Within it is Spa Thalasso, a health centre with pool, Jacuzzi and a range of relaxing activities and treatments to tone you up, something you might welcome if you've stayed up late to enjoy the hotel's live music (daily in summer except Sunday).

Buses run between Måløy and Selje (Nkr72, one hour) two to three times daily on weekdays (catch the 8.45am from Måløy if you intend to take the guided tour of the island). Selje is also the end of the once or twice daily Nordfjord express-boat route from Bergen (Nkr615, five hours).

THE NORTHERN FJORDS

Yet more crinkly coastline, yet more deeply incised fjords await the visitor who pushes further northwards into the region of Møre og Romsdal. Geirangerfjord, a must on most tours and a favourite anchorage for cruise ships, weathers the summer influx. This watery mecca apart, you'll find the waterways and roads less crowded and the scenery almost as spectacular. The pleasant coastal towns of Ålesund and Kristiansund each deserve an overnight stop – and the spectacular drive over the Trollstigen pass will linger in the memory.

The region's official website, www.visit mr.com, although only in Norwegian, has a host of useful links.

ÅNDALSNES
pop 2000

There are two spectacular ways to approach Åndalsnes; by road through the Trollstigen pass or via the spectacularly scenic Raumabanen, the rail route from Dombås, as it ploughs through a deeply cut glacial valley flanked by sheer walls and plummeting waterfalls. Badly bombed during WWII, the modern town is rather nondescript, but the surrounding landscapes are top-notch.The **tourist office** (☎ 71 22 16 22; www.visitandalsnes .com; ☿ 9am-6pm Mon-Fri, 10am-6pm Sat, noon-6pm Sun mid-Jun–mid-Aug; 9am-3.30pm Mon-Fri rest-of-year) is located at the train station. It has Internet access (per 15 minutes Nkr20).

Sights
TROLLVEGGEN

Approaching from Dombås, the road and rail lines follow the dramatic 1800m-high Trollveggen, or Troll Wall, first conquered in 1965 by a joint Norwegian and English team. The highest vertical mountain wall in Europe, its ragged and often cloud-shrouded summit is considered the ultimate challenge among mountaineers.

TROLLSTIGEN

The Trollstigen (Troll's Ladder), south of Åndalsnes, is a thriller of a road, completed in 1936 after eight years of labour, with 11 hairpin bends and a 1:12 gradient. To add an extra daredevil element, it's one lane practically all the way. On request, bus passengers get a photo stop at the thundering 180m-high Stigfossen waterfall, and a quick halt at the top for a dizzy view down the valley. If you have wheels and a camera, make sure you pause for photos of the dramatic peaks of Karitind, Dronningen, Kongen and Bispen – as well as Norway's only 'Troll Crossing' road sign.

More energetically, you can also take it at a slower pace and puff your way up and over the old horse trail, narrow and blazed with white spots, that was previously the only communication between the two valleys. Both routes are closed in winter.

The small **Vegmuseum** (☎ 99 29 20 00; Trollstigen; admission Nkr15; ⏱ 11am-3.30pm late Jun–mid-Aug) at the pass tells the engineering history of this awesome road.

Activities
RAUMABANEN RAILWAY
Diesel trains run daily year-round along this spectacular route (www.raumabanen .com). For real nostalgia, take a trip on the steam train (adult/child/family return Nkr295/70/660) that chugs from the lakeside station up to Bjorli, at 600m, two or three times weekly from late June to early August.

HIKING
The tourist office has around 20 leaflets (Nkr5 each) describing a range of excellent signed hiking trails around the Romsdalen Alps. You'll need to supplement them with the map *Romsdals-alpene* at 1:80,000, which it sells for Nkr98.

An excellent day hike, signed by red markers, begins in town, 50m north of the roundabout before the Esso petrol station, and climbs to the summit of Nesaksla (715m), the prominent peak that rises above Åndalsnes. At the top, the payoff for a steep ascent is the magnificent panorama. In fine weather, the view extends down Romsdalsfjord, up Romsdalen and into Isterdalen, rivalling any in Norway.

From the shelter at the top, you can retrace your steps or undertake the straightforward ascent to the summit of Høgnosa (991m) and trek on to Åkesfjellet (1215m). In summer, the ascent can be hot in the midday sun, so get an early start and carry water. Alternatively, you can traverse along the marked route 5km eastward and descend to Isfjorden village, at the head of the Isfjord.

CLIMBING
The best local climbs are the 1500m-long rock route on Trollveggen and the 1550m-high Romsdalshorn, but there are heaps more. Serious climbers should buy from the tourist office *Klatring i Romsdal* (Nkr280),

which includes rock and ice climbing info in both Norwegian and English.

Mountaineers may enjoy **Norsk Tindemuseum** (☎ 71 22 16 22; adult/child Nkr50/10; ⏱ 6-9pm late Jun–mid-Aug), 1.5km from town on the road to Åndalsnes Camping, with exhibits on the expeditions of renowned mountaineer Arne Randers Heen.

FISHING
Four-hour fishing tours on Romsdalsfjorden, running three times daily in summer, are available through the tourist office for Nkr300 per person, including rod hire.

CANOEING
Trollstigen Hytteutleie (see p233) organises guided canoe trips, as well as mountain walks.

Festivals & Events
If climbing's your passion, visit Åndalsnes in early July and take in the five-day **Norsk Fjellfestivalen**, a jamboree for mountaineers. The town's other big moot is **Rauma Rock** (www.raumarock.com), central Norway's largest pop gathering, held over two days in early August.

Sleeping & Eating
The tourist office keeps a list of a few private homes offering accommodation for around Nkr400.

Hotel Aak (☎ 71 22 71 71; www.hotelaak.no; s/d Nkr495/790 mid-Jun–mid-Aug, Nkr920/1440 rest-of-year; ℗) This charming place, the oldest tourist hotel in Norway, offers exceptional value in summer. It's beside the E136, direction Dombås, about 5km from town. Each of the 13 comfortable bedrooms is named after a mountain (ask for Blånabba, the largest), which you can see from the bedroom window (though in one or two you may have to poke your head out a little!). Its **restaurant** (mains Nkr150-190; ⏱ dinner only), in the oldest part of the building, is equally impressive and offers excellent traditional cuisine. Since it's so small, do reserve in advance.

Åndalsnes Vandrerhjem Setnes (☎ 71 22 13 82; aandalsnes.hostel@wandrerhjem.no; dm/s/d incl breakfast Nkr200/350/500 mid-May–mid-Sep, dm only Nkr150 mid-Sep–mid-May) This welcoming HI-affiliated, sod-roofed hostel is 1.5km from the train station on the E136. It's worth staying here for the pancakes-and-pickled-herring bumper breakfast alone. The Ålesund bus that meets the train passes right by.

Grand Hotel Bellevue (☎ 71 22 75 00; www.grand hotel.no; Åndalgata 5; s/d Nkr795/995 Jun-Aug, Nkr695/795 Sep-May; **P** 🖳) This large, whitewashed tour-group favourite caps a hillock in the centre of town. Most rooms have fine views, particularly those facing the rear. There's a public swimming pool only 100m away and the hotel hires bikes and canoes (both per hour/day Nkr50/150). The nightclub has live music on Friday and Saturday nights. It's **restaurant** (mains Nkr165-215; ✕ dinner only) offers the town's most formal dining, but you can always nibble on a lighter dish for around Nkr100.

Trollstigen Hytteutleie (☎ 71 22 68 99; www.troll stigen-hytteutleie.no; tent with car/motorhome/cara-van Nkr100/110/125, 4-/5-bed cabins from Nkr400/500) This well-organised and well-kept camping ground also has a scenic location about 1.5km along the Rv63 highway towards Geiranger. See also p232.

Åndalsnes Camping (☎ 71 22 22 79; www.andal snescamp.no; car/caravan sites Nkr100, 6-7 bed cabins with bathroom Nkr750; ✕ May–mid-Sep; 🖳) Less than 2km from town, it enjoys a dramatic setting beside the River Rauma and has Internet access (per hour Nkr60).

Buona Sera (☎ 71 22 60 75; Romsdalsveien 6; dishes from Nkr80) The Italian-oriented Buona Sera predictably specialises in pizza, yet has much more character than most Norwegian pizza joints. All wood, with intimate crannies and friendly staff, it also does crispy salads (Nkr90) and juicy meat mains (Nkr165 to Nkr175).

For sandwiches, sweet treats and all things delicious, follow the locals to the **Måndalen Bakeri** (Havnegate 5), on the waterfront near the train station.

Getting There & Away
BUS
Buses along the 'Golden Route' to Geiranger (Nkr146, three hours), via Trollstigen, the Linge–Eidsdal ferry and the scenic Ørnevegen, operate between mid-June and August. The Trollstigen pass is cleared and opens by at least 1 June, and early in the season it's an impressive trip through a popular cross-country ski field, between high walls of snow. Buses leave Åndalsnes at 8.30am and 5.30pm daily, and from Geiranger at 1pm and 6.10pm.

There are also services to Molde (Nkr88, 1½ hours, six to nine daily) and Ålesund (Nkr175, 2½ hours, twice daily).

TRAIN
Trains to/from Dombås (Nkr179, 1½ hours) run one to three times daily, in synchronisation with Oslo–Trondheim trains (for details of the summer steam train, see p232). Trains connect in Åndalsnes twice daily with Togbuss services to Ålesund (Nkr182, 2¼ hours, two daily) and Molde.

VALLDAL & AROUND
Valldal
In season, people pour through Valldal, having driven over the famous Trollstigen pass from Åndalsnes or savoured the exquisitely beautiful ferry journey from Geiranger. It's an attractive little town, perched in a nick of Norddalsfjord, whose agricultural surrounds lay claim to be Europe's northernmost orchards. Here apples, pears and even cherries thrive – and also strawberries in profusion, commemorated in an annual Strawberry Festival on the last weekend in July.

The **tourist office** (☎ 70 25 77 67; www.visitnord dal.com; ✕ 10am-7pm daily mid-Jun–mid-Aug, 10am-5pm Mon-Fri rest-of-year) rents bikes (per day Nkr200) and can also arrange motorboat hire (per hour/day Nkr85/400). Ask for its free guide sheets of walks in the area.

From Valldal, you can join a four-hour white-water rush down the Valldøla river (Nkr490, 11am daily May to September). Contact **Valldal Naturopplevingar** (☎ 90 01 40 35), whose headquarters is 200m from the tourist office.

SLEEPING & EATING
There's no shortage of camping grounds, many overpopulated with caravans, parked semi-permanently. For somewhere with more character, push on to **Gudbrandsjuvet Camping** (☎ 70 25 86 31; fax 70 25 70 44; tent/cara-van sites Nkr100/130, 4-bed cabins Nkr300; ✕ Jun-Aug), 15km towards Åndalsnes up the Rv63, where the stream races through a tight gorge.

Fjellro Turisthotell (☎ 70 25 75 13; www.fjellro.no in Norwegian; Valldal; s/d incl breakfast Nkr650/850) At charming 'Mountain Peace', just behind (northeast of) Valldal's church, the welcome is warm and rooms are well appointed.

There's a café and upstairs restaurant (mains Nkr75 to Nkr200) and a pub on the ground floor that has live music most weekends. And at the rear is a tranquil garden with a small children's playground.

Muritunet/Lupinen Café (☎ 70 25 84 10; mains Nkr50-88) This café serves pizza, beef and fish dishes and puts on an inexpensive buffet (Nkr155).

Jordbærstova (☎ 70 25 76 58; May-Sep) About 6km up the Åndalsnes road, Jord-bærstova honours the valley's mighty strawberry. Stop in for a fat slice of their gooey, creamy strawberry cake (Nkr40) or the local pancake speciality known as *svele*, served with strawberries and cream. They also do light meals and dinner and a Sun-day buffet lunch (Nkr175).

GETTING THERE & AWAY
Valldal lies on the 'Golden Route' bus ser-vice that runs from mid-June to August between Åndalsnes (Nkr88, 1¾ hours) and Geiranger (Nkr75, 1¼ hours), up and over the spectacular Trollstigen pass. If you're driving, pause too at Gudbrandsjuvet, 15km up the valley from Valldal, where the river slots through a 5m-wide, 20m-deep canyon.

Equally scenic is the spectacular ferry cruise (adult/child single Nkr130/65, return trip Nkr195/95, 2¼ hours) that runs twice daily between Valldal and Geiranger from mid-June to mid-August.

Tafjord
In 1934 a devasting accident took place. An enormous chunk of rock 400m high and 22m long – a total eight million cu metres – broke loose from the hillside and crashed into Korsnæsfjord, creating a 64m tidal wave that washed 700m inland and claimed 40 lives in Fjørra and Tafjord.

The **Tafjord Power Museum** (Kraftverkmuseum; ☎ 70 17 56 00; admission free; noon-5pm mid-Jun–mid-Aug), within a now-defunct power sta-tion, shows how the advent of hydroelectric power changed the valley. The road that climbs from the village up to the Zakarias reservoir passes through a bizarre cork-screw tunnel and, a couple of kilometres higher up, a short walking route drops to the crumbling bridge at the dam's nar-row base, where you feel at close range the stresses the structure has to tolerate.

Stordal
If you're travelling between Valldal and Ålesund on the Rv650, do make a short stop at Stordal's **Rose Church** (Rosekyrkya; adult/child Nkr30/free; 11am-4pm mid-Jun–mid-Aug). Unassuming from the outside, it was con-structed in 1789 on the site of an earlier stave church, elements of which were re-tained. Inside comes the surprise; the roof, walls and every last pillar are sumptuously painted in an engagingly naive interpreta-tion of high baroque.

GEIRANGER
pop 210
Scattered cliffside farms, most long aban-doned, still cling along the towering walls of twisting, 20km-long emerald-green Gei-rangerfjord, and breathtaking waterfalls – De Syv Søstre (Seven Sisters), Friaren (The Suitor) and Brudesløret (Bridal Veil) – sluice and tumble. The one-hour ferry trip along its length between Geiranger and Hellesylt is as much mini-cruise as means of transport.

If you arrive from Hellesylt, Geiranger itself, at the head of the fjord, comes as a bit of a disappointment despite its fabu-lous site, as you mingle with the hordes of sightseers whose tours pass through. Every year, Geiranger wilts under the presence of over 600,000 visitors and over 150 cruise ships (last time we visited, the *QE2*, less than regal, was there, polluting the pure air with dark fumes from its smokestack, while its bumboats belched diesel vapours at the jetty).

By contrast, if you drop from the north along the Rv63 from Åndalsnes and Valldal (called Ørnevegen, the Eagle's Way), you can't fail but gasp as it twists down the al-most sheer slope in 11 hairpin bends, each one affording a yet more impressive view along the narrow fjord. And however you're coming or going, in the evening, once the last cruise ship and tour bus has pulled out, serenity returns to this tiny port.

The **tourist office** (☎ 70 26 30 99; www.geiranger .no; 9am-7pm mid-Jun–mid-Aug, 9am-5pm mid-May–mid-Jun & mid-Aug–mid-Sep) is beside the pier.

Sights & Activities
NORWEGIAN FJORD CENTRE
Bringing together a collection of old arte-facts, this **museum** (Norsk Fjordsenter; ☎ 70 26 18 00;

www.fjordsenter.info; adult/child Nkr75/35; 10am-7pm mid-Jun–mid-Aug; 10am-5pm May–mid-Jun & mid-Aug–Sep) has tools and even whole buildings that have been uprooted and brought here, illustrating the essential themes – the mail packet, avalanches, the building of early roads, the rise of tourism – which have shaped the land and its people.

FLYDALSJUVET

You've probably seen that classic photo, beloved of brochures, of the overhanging rock Flydalsjuvet, usually with a figure gazing down at a cruise ship in Geirangerfjord? The car park, signposted Flydalsjuvet, about 5km uphill from Geiranger on the Stryn road, offers a great view of the fjord and the green river valley, but doesn't provide exactly the postcard view. For that, you'll have to drop about 150m down the hill, then descend a slippery and rather indistinct track to the edge. Your intrepid photo subject will have to gingerly scramble down to the overhang about 50m further along...

WALKING

All around Geiranger you'll find great hiking routes to abandoned farmsteads, waterfalls and vista points. The tourist office map features 13 such short walks from the village.

A popular longer hike begins with a ride on the fjord sightseeing boat (below). On the way back, the boat stops (on request) at the start of the walking route. Climb from the landing for 45 minutes to the precariously perched hillside farm known as Skageflå. From there, it's a gradual two- to three-hour hike back to Geiranger.

Another recommended hike follows a normally muddy path to the Storseter waterfall, where the track actually passes behind the cascading water. Allow about 45 minutes each way from the starting point at the Vesterås farm.

BOAT TOURS

Geiranger Fjordservice (70 26 30 07; www.geiranger fjord.no) does 1½-hour sightseeing **boat tours** (adult/child Nkr75/35; sailings 5 or 6 times daily, Jun-Aug). You can get tickets at the tourist office.

CANOEING

Coastal Odyssey (95 11 80 62; www.coastalodyssey .com) rents sea-kayaks (per hour/half-day/

day Nkr150/300/500) and does daily hiking and canoeing trips to one of the high mountain farms overlooking the fjord (Nkr500, five to seven hours), departing at 11.30am.

Sleeping & Eating

Around the village, you'll find plenty of *rom* signs, indicating private rooms and cabins for rent (singles/doubles around Nkr300/500). Hotels are often booked out by package tours, but a dozen or so camping possibilities skirt the fjord and hillsides.

Below the Grande Ford Hotel are a couple of friendly, tranquil camping grounds in unbeatable locations. Even if you're carrying a weighty pack, it's well worth the 2km walk northwestward to get there. Both rent rowing and motor boats and have Internet access (per hour Nkr60).

Grande Fjord Hotel (70 26 94 90; www.grande fjordhotel.com; d Nkr980, with fjord view Nkr1080; P) This warmly recommended 48-room hotel does great buffet breakfasts and dinners. It's well worth paying the extra Nkr100 for a room with balcony and magnificent view over the fjord. Take the shoreside Rv63, direction Åndalsnes, for 2km to find yourself half a world away from the ferry terminal bustle.

Union Hotel (70 26 83 00; www.union-hotel.no; d without/with fjord views Nkr745/895; Feb–mid-Dec; P) The large, spectacularly situated Union Hotel is high on the hill above town. It has a couple of pools (one indoor and heated) and its two lounges overlook the fjord – as does the bar, which has live music every evening. Even if you're not staying here, head up the hill, then roll back down after tucking into their gargantuan dinner buffet (Nkr365), which has a minimum of 65 dishes on offer. The restaurant also offers à la carte (mains Nkr225 to Nkr325) and a two-course lunch (Nkr205).

Geiranger Camping (/fax 70 26 31 20; person/pitch Nkr15/95; mid-May–mid-Sep;) A short walk from the ferry terminal, Geiranger Camping, though short on shade, is pleasant and handy for an early morning ferry getaway.

Grande Hytteutleige og Camping (70 26 30 68; www.grande-hytteutleige.no; person/pitch Nkr15/90; basic 4-bed cabins 200-360, with bathroom Nkr320-680, 5-/6-bed Nkr390-830; May-Sep;) Take the smaller, northernmost of its two grounds for the best views up the fjord.

Geirangerfjorden Feriesenter (☎ 95 10 75 27; www.geirangerfjorden.net; person/pitch Nkr20/90, 4-bed cabins Nkr400-660, 5-bed cabins Nkr500-840; ☺ May–mid-Sep; 🖳) Nearby, this is another excellent camping option.

Laixas (☎ 70 26 07 20; ☺ 10am-10pm mid-Apr–Sep) At the ferry terminal, just beside the tourist office, the young team at this airy, welcoming place put on a handful of tasty hot dishes, good salads (Nkr80 to Nkr90) and snackier items such as focaccia, wraps and sandwiches.

Getting There & Away
The popular, hugely recommended ferry between Geiranger and Hellesylt (passengers/cars Nkr90/180, one hour), quite the most spectacular scheduled ferry route in Norway, shuttles up and down the fjord. It has four to 10 sailings daily between May and late September (every 90 minutes, mid-June to mid-August).

From mid-April to mid-September, the Hurtigruten coastal ferry makes a detour from Ålesund to Geiranger (departs 1.30pm) on its northbound run only.

BUS
In summer, daily buses to Åndalsnes leave Geiranger (Nkr146, three hours) at 1pm and 6.10pm. The morning bus from Åndalsnes and Valldal continues from Geiranger to Langvatn and, en route back to Geiranger, does a 10km return tourist run to the 1496m summit of Dalsnibba. From Geiranger, the return trip is Nkr105. If you're driving, the toll road up Dalsnibba costs Nkr55 per car.

For Molde, change buses in Åndalsnes; for Ålesund, change at Linge.

HELLESYLT
pop 250
The old Viking port of Hellesylt, through which a roaring waterfall cascades, is altogether calmer, if a mite less breathtaking, than Geiranger.

The **tourist office** (☎ 70 26 38 80; ☺ 11am-7pm Jun-Aug) shares premises with **Peer Gynt Galleriet** (adult/child Nkr50/free; ☺ 11am-7pm Jun-Aug), a collection of fairly kitsch bas-relief wood carvings illustrating the Peer Gynt legend and fashioned by local chippy, Oddvin Parr. You may find the food at the complex's cafeteria more to your taste.

Both Hellesylt Camping and the Union Hotel rent rowing boats.

Sleeping & Eating
Grand Hotel (☎ 70 26 51 00; www.grandhotel-hellesylt .no; s/d from Nkr560/760; ☺ May-Sep; 🅿) Highlights of the rustic old 1875 Grand Hotel building are its great pub and the dining room, which does good breakfasts (Nkr65), a three-course dinner menu (Nkr265) and imaginative mains (Nkr170 to Nkr185). (If you're staying at the hostel, it's a short walk away.) All the bedrooms, overlooking the fjord and most with balcony, are in a motel-type block down beside the waterfront.

Hellesylt Vandrerhjem (☎ /fax 70 26 51 28; helle sylt.hostel@wandrerhjem.no; dm Nkr125, 4-bed cabins Nkr300; ☺ Jun-Aug) The HI-affiliated hostel, perched on the hillside overlooking Hellesylt, is on the road towards Stranda, about 200m from the junction. Go for one of the cabins with stunning fjord views if you're in a group.

Hellesylt Camping (☎ 90 20 68 65; person/pitch Nkr15/95) The absence of shade is more than compensated for by its fjord-side location and proximity to the ferry pier.

Getting There & Away
The spectacular ferry ride to/from Geiranger (passengers/cars, Nkr90/180, one hour, every 90 minutes mid-June to mid-August) runs four to 10 times daily in the summer.

Some of these services connect with buses to/from Stryn (Nkr80, one hour) and Ålesund (Nkr140, 2¾ hours). The once or twice daily Nor-Way Bussekspress buses between Bergen (Nkr473, 8¼ hours) and Ålesund also pass through Hellesylt.

NORANGSDALEN
pop 100
One of the most inspiring yet little visited crannies of the Northern Fjords is Norangsdalen, the hidden valley that connects Hellesylt with the Leknes–Sæbø ferry, or the scenic Hjørundfjorden, via the village of Øye.

The scenery gradually unfolds past towering snowy peaks, ruined farmsteads and haunting mountain lakes. In the upper part of the valley at Urasætra, beside a dark mountain lake, are the ruins of several stone crofters' huts. Further on, you can still see the foundations of one-time farmhouses beneath the surface of the pea-green lake Langstøylvatnet, created in 1908 when a rockslide crashed down the slopes of Keipen.

Hikers and climbers will find plenty of scope in the dramatic peaks of the adjacent Sunnmørsalpane, including the lung-searingly steep scrambling ascent of Slogen (1564m) from Øye and the superb Råna (1586m), a long, tough scramble from Urke.

Beside the road 2km south of Øye, there's a monument to one CW Patchell, an English mountaineer who lost his heart to the valley.

The historic 1891 **Hotel Union** (☎ 70 06 21 00; www.unionoye.no; Øye; s/d Nkr740/1480, lunch mains Nkr175-195, 4-course dinner Nkr410; ☯ May-Sep) has attracted mountaineers, writers, artists and royalty for over a century. Decorated with period artwork and original and collected furnishings, panelled in wood and speaking old-world charm, it's a delight. Rooms are named after celebrities who have slept in them: Sir Arthur Conan Doyle, Karen Blixen, Kaiser Wilhelm, Edvard Grieg, Roald Amundsen, Henrik Ibsen, a host of kings and queens – and even Coco Chanel.

RUNDE
pop 160
The island of Runde, 67km southwest of Ålesund, plays host to half a million sea birds of 230 to 240 species, including 100,000 pairs of migrating puffins that arrive in May and stick around until late July. You'll also see colonies of kittiwakes, gannets, fulmars, storm petrels, razor-billed auks, shags and guillemots, plus about 70 other species that nest here. You'll see the best bird-watching sites – as well as offshore seal colonies – on a 2½-hour boat tour (adult/child Nkr150/100; sailings 11am, 1pm and 4pm May to August). Buy your ticket from the shop at the camping ground (below) – and ring to reserve in the high summer season.

The island **tourist office** (☎ 70 01 37 90) is in Ulsteinvik.

Sleeping
Runde Camping & Vandrerhjem (☎ 70 08 59 16; www.runde.no; per person/site Nkr15/60, dm Nkr120, s/d cabins Nkr240/300) This HI-affiliated hostel and small camping ground are attractively sited, almost at the water's edge.

Getting There & Away
Runde is connected by bridge to the mainland. You can take quite a pleasurable catamaran-bus-taxi combination day trip to the island (total cost Nkr266 return) on weekdays from mid-June to mid-September. The catamaran sails at 8.30am from Ålesund's Skateflukaien quay to Hareid, where it connects with a bus to Fosnavåg. Here a taxi connection picks you up and drops you off in Runde at 11am.

To return to Ålesund the same day, the taxi leaves Runde at 5.05pm and the catamaran gets back to port at 8pm. It sounds complicated but the connections are reliable and, with but a little initiative, you'll have a great day out where few other independent travellers manage to go.

ÅLESUND
pop 44,000
The agreeable coastal town of Ålesund is, many consider, as beautiful as Bergen, if on a much smaller scale, and it's certainly far less touristy.

After the sweeping fire of 23 January 1904, which left 10,000 residents homeless, the German emperor Kaiser Wilhelm II sent shiploads of provisions and building materials and Ålesund was rebuilt in record style in characteristic Art Nouveau (Jugendstil) style as teams of young, committed Norwegian architects, trained for the most part in Germany, brought to the movement traditional local motifs and ornamentation. Buildings graced with turrets, spires and gargoyles sprout throughout town, with the best examples along Apotekergata, Kirkegata, Øwregata, Løvenvoldgata and, especially, Kongensgata.

Ålesund is crowded onto a narrow, fishhook-shaped sea-bound peninsula. So tightly packed is the town centre that expansion would be impossible; today most of the town's people live scattered across nearby islands and peninsulas.

Information
Laundrette (Guest Marina) There's a laundrette below the kiosk in the Guest Marina service building. It's signed only *Gueste Toalett*, but just breeze in and you'll find the machine.

ÅLESUND

0 |————————| 300 m
0 |————————| 0.2 miles

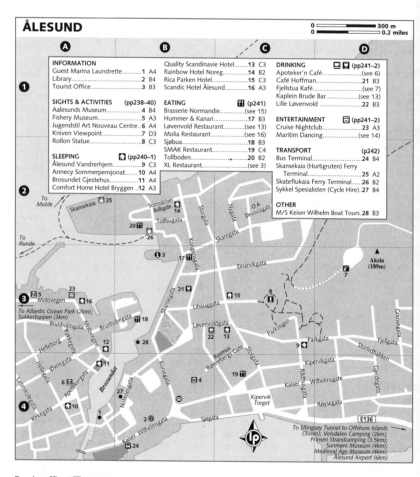

Tourist office (☎ 70 15 76 00; www.visitalesund.com; Skaregata 1; ⏰ 8.30am-7pm Mon-Fri, 9am-5pm Sat, 11am-5pm Sun Jun-Aug, 8.30am-4pm Mon-Fri Sep–May) Located in a new quayside premises. Its free booklet *On Foot in Ålesund* details the town's architectural highlights in a walking tour. It has two Internet points (per hr Nkr60) or you can log on for free at the library in the town hall.

Sights & Activities

SUNNMØRE MUSEUM

This is Ålesund's celebrated **museum** (☎ 70 17 40 00; Borgundgavlen; adult/child Nkr60/15; ⏰ 11am-5pm Mon-Sat, noon-5pm Sun late Jun-Aug, 11am-3pm Mon-Tue & Fri, noon-4pm Sun Sep–mid-Jun) and is at the site of the old Borgundkaupangen trading centre, located 4km east of the centre. There are 55 old buildings, visiting displays

on traditional crafts and textiles and for ship-lovers a collection of 30 historic boats, including replicas of Viking-era ships and a commercial trading vessel which dates from around AD 1000. To get there take bus No 13 or 24.

Nearby is the **Medieval Age Museum** (☎ 70 17 40 00; Borgundgavlen; admission included in Sunnmøre Museum entry; ⏰ noon-3pm Tue, Thu & Sun mid-Jun–mid-Aug), with archaeological excavations, an on-site reproduction of the 10th-century town of Borgundkaupangen and exhibitions about the trade, art, crafts and religion of the west Norwegian coastal folk who lived there in the 10th century. There is also information regarding their hunting and fishing cultures in medieval times.

ATLANTIC OCEAN PARK

At the peninsula's western extreme, 3km from the centre, the **Atlantic Ocean Park** (Atlanterhavsparken; ☎ 70 10 70 60; Tueneset; adult/child Nkr90/55; ☺ 10am-7pm Sun-Fri & 10am-4pm Sat Jun-Aug; 11am-4pm Tue-Sun Sep-May) can merit a whole day of your life. It introduces visitors to the North Atlantic's undersea world with glimpses of the astonishing richness of coastal and fjord submarine life. Children will wow at the 'snails, seashells and weird marine animals' section, while the whole family will gasp at the enormous four-million-litre aquarium. Be there at 1pm when the largest ocean fish thrash and swirl as they're fed by human divers.

There's also a sanctuary for orphaned seals and the grounds offer superb coastal scenery, bathing beaches and walking trails. Bus No 18 passes by, mid-June to August.

ART NOUVEAU CENTRE

Everyone from serious aesthetes to kids out for fun will get pleasure from this **art centre** (Jugendstil Senteret; ☎ 47 70 10 49 70; www.ju gendstilsenteret.no; Apotekergata 16; adult/child Nkr50/25; ☺ 10am-7pm Mon-Fri, 10am-5pm Sat, noon-5pm Sun Jun-Aug, 11am-5pm Tue-Fri, 11am-4pm Sat, noon-4pm Sun Sep-May). The introductory Time Machine capsule presents 'From Ashes to Art Nouveau', a high-tech, very visual story of the rebuilding of Ålesund after the great fire, while the displays offer carefully selected textiles, ceramics and furniture of the genre. It's in and above a renovated chemist's shop (look for the large *Apothek* sign above the entrance), which has retained its magnificent corkscrew staircase and 1st floor dining room.

AALESUNDS MUSEUM

The **town museum** (☎ 70 12 31 70; Rasmus Rønnebergs Gate 16; adult/child Nkr30/10; ☺ 11am-4pm Mon-Fri, noon-3pm Sat & Sun mid-Jun–mid-Aug; 11am-3pm Mon-Sat, noon-3pm Sun Feb–mid-Jun & mid-Aug–Dec, 11am-4pm Mon-Fri only Mar) concentrates on the history of sealing, fishing, shipping and industry in the Sunnmøre region, the fire of 1904, the German WWII occupation and the town's distinctive Art Nouveau architecture. There's also a collection of boats and ships, including the *Uræd* lifeboat (piloted across the Atlantic in 1904 by Ole Brude), and an 1812 barn, converted into an old-time grocery.

The affiliated, much smaller and less frequently open **Fishery Museum** (Ålesund Fiskerimuseet; ☎ 70 10 00 84; Molovegen 10; adult/child Nkr20/10; ☺ noon-3pm Sun Jun; noon-2pm & 6-8pm Wed-Fri Jul–mid-Aug), in the 1861 Holmbua warehouse (one of the few to survive the 1904 fire), contains exhibits on fishing through the ages and a special section on drying stockfish and the processing of cod liver oil.

HARBOUR BOAT TOUR

For a different perspective of the town, take the **M/S Keiser Wilhelm** (☎ 70 19 29 91; adult/child Nkr100/50; sailings noon & 2pm – also 4pm & 6pm Jun-Aug), which does 1¼-hour tours of the harbour and nearby skerries.

For a more exotic sail, hop aboard the Borgundknarren, a replica Viking trading ship that leaves Sunnmøre Museum for a one-hour cruise (adult/child Nkr50/free) every Wednesday, late June to mid-August.

AKSLA

The 418 steps up Aksla lead to the splendid **Kniven viewpoint** over Ålesund and the surrounding mountains and islands. Follow Lihauggata from the pedestrian shopping street Kongensgata to the start of the 20-minute puff to the top of the hill. There's also a road to the top; take Røysegata east from the centre, then follow the Fjellstua signposts up the hill.

Up top, the **Fjellstua Kafé** (☎ 70 10 74 00; ☺ mid-May–Aug) is a good place to recover your breath while enjoying a drink with a view.

SUKKERTOPPEN

A more challenging hike leading to an even wider ranging view leads to the summit of Sukkertoppen (314m). It begins on the street Sukkertoppvegen, on the hook of Ålesund's peninsula. The track follows the easiest route, right up the east-pointing ridgeline. Take bus No 13 from town.

MARDALSFOSSEN

It's about a two-hour drive up Langfjorden and past the dramatic lake, Eikesdalsvatnet, to Mardalsfossen – once the fifth highest waterfall in the world. How did it lose this status? Well, in the 1970s, this two-level 655m waterfall (the greatest single drop is 297m) was extinguished by a hydroelectric project.

Although environmentalists chained themselves together to prevent the construction, it went ahead and Mardalsfossen now flows strictly for the tourists, from late June to mid-August.

For mountain thrills, take the bucking single-track mountain road Aursjøvegen (Nkr50 toll), open between late June and September and linking Mardalsfossen and Sunndalsøra.

OFFSHORE ISLANDS
The offshore islands of Valderøy, Vigra, Giske and Godøy make pleasant day trips from Ålesund. Bus No 64 runs to Valderøy (Nkr40, 20 minutes), Giske (Nkr46, 30 minutes) and Godøy (Nkr48, 45 minutes).

Giske is the historic seat of the Viking-age ruling family, Arnungane, which ruled feudally from 990 to 1582. The island was also the home of Gange-Rolv (known as Rollon in France; he's also claimed by Vigra), the Viking warrior who besieged Paris, subsequently founded the Duchy of Normandy in 911 and was an ancestor of England's William the Conqueror. In 1911, when Normandy celebrated its millennium, a copy of the Rollon statue in Rouen was presented to Ålesund, where it now stands in Byparken. Giske's ornate 12th-century **marble church** (adult/child Nkr20/10; 10am-5pm Mon-Sat, 1-7pm Sun Jun-late Aug) was restored in 1756 and the Makkevika marshes are a prime spot for bird-watching.

Worthwhile sites on other islands include the **Skjonghellaren caves** on northwestern **Valderøy** and the **Blindheimssanden** (also called Blimsand) white-sand beach on northwest **Vigra**. At the northern tip of **Godøy**, the picturesque 1876 **lighthouse** (70 18 51 96; adult/child Nkr20/10; noon-6pm Jun-Aug) in the fishing station of **Alnes** has a small exhibition. Both Valderøy and Godøy offer excellent short mountain walks.

Tours
To really delve into Ålesund's Art Nouveau heritage, sign on for the tourist office's excellent 1½- to two-hour **guided town walk** (adult/child Nkr60/free; mid-Jun–mid-Aug), which sets off from the office at noon.

Festivals & Events
Ålesund knows how to party. In the second half of May, there's the **Big Band Festival**.

Yachties will be in seventh heaven at the **Ålesund Boat Festival**, a week of watery pleasures in the first half of July, while the **Norwegian Food Festival** in the last week of August is a treat for all gourmets and gourmands.

Sleeping
The tourist office keeps a list of private rooms that start at around Nkr250 per person. It will also book accommodation of whatever kind for a fee of Nkr30.

Brosundet Gjestehus (70 12 10 00; www.brosundet.no; Apotekergata 5; s/d incl breakfast from Nkr550/750 mid-Jun–mid-Aug, Nkr750/990 Sun-Thu, Nkr630/830 Fri & Sat rest-of-year; P) There's a sauna, kitchen and washing machine/dryer for guest use at this friendly, excellent value, family-owned hotel, right on the waterfront, where harbour views cost no extra. An ex-warehouse and listed building, it was converted in the 1990s (just look at the wonderful old beams they've preserved and feel the way the floors list and slope).

Comfort Home Hotel Bryggen (70 12 64 00; www.choicehotels.no; Apotekergata 1-3; s/d Nkr690/920 mid-Jun–mid-Aug, Nkr1250/1560 Sun-Thu, Nkr720/980 Fri & Sat rest-of-year;) This wonderful 130-room waterfront option is another converted fish warehouse, artfully decorated with former tools and equipment. Rates include a light evening meal and there's a sauna, free to guests.

Quality Scandinavie Hotel (70 15 78 00; www.choicehotels.no; Løvenvoldgata 8; s/d from Nkr605/790 mid-Jun–mid-Aug, Nkr1090/1390 Sun-Thu, Nkr690/990 Fri & Sat rest-of-year; P) This fine place, by contrast, was built as a hotel – Ålesund's oldest and the first to be constructed after the fire of 1904. With touches and flourishes of Art Nouveau (the furniture is original and in keeping and even the lobby flat-screen television seems to blend in), it exudes style and confidence. Not least of its charms is the excellent Løvenvold restaurant (see p241).

Scandic Hotel Ålesund (21 61 45 00; www.scandic-hotels.com; Molovegen 6; d incl breakfast Nkr790 mid-Jun–mid-Aug, s/d incl breakfast from Nkr945/1395 Sun-Thu, Nkr740/840 Fri & Sat rest-of-year; P) The Scandic has a lot going for it. Around 30% of the rooms, all of which have parquet flooring, overlook the harbour, there's a free sauna and three rooms are equipped for the disabled. Guests – and droppers in – also eat well; choices at the buffet breakfast are truly substantial and the dinner buffet (Nkr155) at its restaurant, the Molia, is a bargain. Families will welcome the separate children's buffet and dining room play area.

Rica Parken Hotel (☎ 70 12 50 50; www.rica.no; Storgata 16; s/d Nkr755/940 Sun-Thu mid-Jun–mid-Aug & Fri & Sat year-round, Nkr1040/1250 Sun-Thu rest-of-year; P 🖳) Equipped to the usual high Rica chain standards, some of its attractive modern rooms have views of the town park. Its Brasserie Normande (right) is another quality eating option.

Annecy Sommerpensjonat (☎ 70 12 96 30; Kirkegata 1b; basic s/d Nkr340/360, d with bathroom Nkr470; mid-Jun–mid-Aug) The simple Annecy Sommerpensjonat is an excellent budget choice, letting out self-contained student rooms in summer.

Rainbow Hotel Noreg (☎ 70 12 29 38; www .rainbow-hotels.no; Kongensgata 27; s/d from Nkr630/790; P 🖳) Though much less rich in character, Hotel Noreg is a reliable place, offering good breakfasts and comfortable en suite rooms with parquet flooring.

Ålesund Vandrerhjem (☎ 70 11 58 30; aalesund .hostel@wandrerhjem.no; Parkgata 14; dm/s/d incl breakfast Nkr200/390/510; May-Sep) This central HI-affiliated hostel has self-catering facilities.

Volsdalen Camping (☎ 70 12 58 90; fax 70 12 14 94; Volsdalsberga; tent/caravan Nkr100/150, 2-/4-bed cabins Nkr300/450, with bathroom Nkr750; May–mid-Sep) Above the shore about 2km east of the centre, this is the friendliest camping option and also the nearest to town. Take bus No 13, 14, 18 or 24.

Eating

XL Restaurant (☎ 70 12 42 53; Skaregata 1; dishes from Nkr100; dinner only) This small, 1st-floor place overlooking the harbour is another excellent choice, whether you're searching for a café, restaurant or simply a bar.

Sjøbua (☎ 70 12 71 00; Brunholmgata 1a; mains Nkr250-360; Mon-Sat) In yet another converted wharfside building, stylish Sjøbua is one of northern Norway's finest fish restaurants, where you can choose your crustacean from the lobster tank.

Tollboden (☎ 70 12 86 70; Tollbugata 1; pasta dishes Nkr115-135, other mains Nkr115-226) A solid upper-range place with a great harbourside location near the Hurtigruten quay, Tollboden has an eclectically international menu on offer and also does a lip smacking fish stew (Nkr220).

AUTHOR'S CHOICE

Hummer & Kanari (☎ 70 12 80 08; Kongensgata 19; mains Nkr100-275; Mon-Sat) This place is the perfect hybrid. Downstairs, the bistro serves up ample portions of pasta (Nkr90 to Nkr120) and pizza (Nkr100). Behind the bar sit row upon row of liqueur and spirit bottles for mixers and shakers and on it are three different draft beers. But the greatest pleasure lies in wait upstairs, in their restaurant. To save the decision making, simply sit back, put yourself in the cook's capable hands and go for the best the sea can offer that day, the quaintly glossed 'Hummer & Kanari's composition of available delicacies of the sea' (Nkr265).

Løvenvold Restaurant (☎ 70 15 78 00; Løvenvoldgata 8; mains Nkr120-230, dinner buffet Nkr170) This restaurant, in the Quality Scandinavie Hotel, serves fine Mediterranean dishes beneath its lovely gilded ceiling.

Brasserie Normande (☎ 70 13 23 00; mains Nkr250-270) This brasserie, the main eating option at the Rica Parken Hotel, runs a short but impressive menu of local and international dishes.

SMAK Restaurant (☎ 70 12 62 62; Kipervikgata 5; lunch Nkr70, dinner Nkr100) The minimalist-style SMAK Restaurant, a cafeteria by day, turns into a restaurant and animated pub by night.

Along the harbour front beside Skansegata, you can buy fresh shrimps directly from the fishing boats.

Drinking & Entertainment

Café Hoffmann (☎ 70 12 37 97; Kongensgata 11; mains Nkr85-120) Take a table upstairs at this café with its fine harbour views.

Lille Løvenvold (☎ 70 12 54 00; Løvenvoldgata 2; 11am-midnight Mon-Thu, 11am-3am Fri & Sat) This intimate place is great for a coffee in relaxing surroundings.

Apoteker'n Café (☎ 70 10 49 70) Within the Art Nouveau Centre (see p239), this stylish little place rustles up good snacks, tempting cakes and great coffee.

Cruise Nightclub (☎ 70 12 84 80; Molovegen) Immediately west of the centre, this club has a weekend disco as well as an Irish-style pub.

Maritim Dancing (Fri & Sat) Located in the Hotel Noreg, this place attracts a slightly older crowd and features a DJ at weekends.

Kaplein Brude Bar (☎ 70 15 78 00; Løvenvoldgata 8) Savvy locals tend to gravitate to this place at Quality Scandinavie Hotel.

Getting There & Away
AIR
From Ålesund's **airport** (☎ 70 11 48 00), SAS Braathens has two to three daily flights to/ from Bergen and six to eight to/from Oslo. The budget airline Norwegian also flies once/twice daily to/from the capital.

BOAT
An express boat links Ålesund with Molde (Nkr177, 2¼ hours) from Skateflukaia ferry terminal twice daily on weekdays in July only. Hurtigruten coastal ferries arrive/depart at 8.45am/6.45pm northbound and depart at 12.45am southbound; on its northbound run, there's a popular detour, mid-April to mid-September, via Geiranger (hence the large gap between arrival and departure times).

BUS
The bus terminal is diagonally opposite the tourist office. Nor-Way Bussekspress buses run to/from Hellesylt (Nkr140, 2¾ hours, one to four daily), Stryn (Nkr220, 3½ hours, two to three daily) and Bergen (Nkr558, 11½ hours, twice daily). There's also an express bus once or twice daily between Ålesund, Molde (Nkr136, two hours) and Trondheim (Nkr494, 7¾ hours) and a twice daily service to/from Oslo (Nkr710, 10 hours). Local buses run to/from Åndalsnes (Nkr175, 2½ hours, twice daily).

Getting Around
Ålesund's airport is on Vigra island, connected to the town by the undersea tunnels to Ellingsøy (3.6km) and Valderøy (4.2km). **Flybuss** (☎ 70 14 47 70) departs from Skateflukaia (Nkr67, 25 minutes) and the bus station one hour before the departure of domestic flights.

Drivers to the airport and the offshore islands pay tunnel tolls totalling Nkr60 each way for a car and driver plus Nkr19 per additional passenger.

Sykkel Spesialisten (☎ 70 12 28 20; Notenesgata 3) rents bicycles (per day Nkr140).

MOLDE
pop 18,500
Molde, hugging the shoreline at the wide mouth of Romsdalsfjorden, is known as the 'Town of Roses' because of its fertile soil, rich vegetation and mild climate (this said, it chucked it down unremittingly last time we were there). The town's chief claim to fame is its annual July jazz festival.

Modern Molde, though architecturally unexciting, is a friendly, pleasantly compact little place whose coastal landscapes recall New Zealand or Seattle's Puget Sound. To test the comparison, drive or trek up to the Varden overlook, 400m above the town.

Information
Dockside Pub (Torget) For Internet access.
Laundrette (Guest Marina)
Library (Kirkebakken 1-3) Opposite the Tourist office.
Tourist office (☎ 71 25 71 33; www.visitmolde.com; Storgata 31; ⏰ 9am-6pm Mon-Fri, 9am-3pm Sat & noon-5pm Sun mid-Jun–mid-Aug, 8.30am-3.30pm Mon-Fri rest-of-year) Sells *Molde Fraena* (Nkr95, 1:50,000), the best walking map of the area. Also offers free Internet access.

Sights
ROMSDALEN FOLK MUSEUM
Sprawling across a large open area within this open-air **museum** (Romsdalsmuseet; ☎ 71 20 24 60; Per Amdamsveg 4; admission free; ⏰ 8am-10pm) are close on 50 old buildings, shifted here from around the Romsdal region. Highlights include Bygata (an early-20th-century town street) and a 'composite church', assembled from elements of now-demolished local stave churches. There are very worthwhile **guided tours** (adult/child Nkr45/ free; ⏰ 11am-6pm Mon-Sat, noon-6pm Sun Jul, 11am-5pm Mon-Sat, noon-3pm Sun 15-30 Jun & 1-15 Aug) in English on request.

FISHERY MUSEUM
This **museum** (Fiskerimuseet; ☎ 71 20 24 60; Hjertøya; adult/child Nkr45/free; ⏰ noon-5pm mid-Jun–early Aug) is a short ferry ride from the Torget terminal. Also open-air, it brings to life the coastal fishing cultures around the mouth of Romsdalfjorden from the mid-19th-century until now. When it's open, **ferries** (☎ 99 54 98 94) run daily from Molde at 11am, noon, 2pm and 4pm and from Hjertøya at 12.45pm, 1.45pm, 3.45pm and 5.45pm.

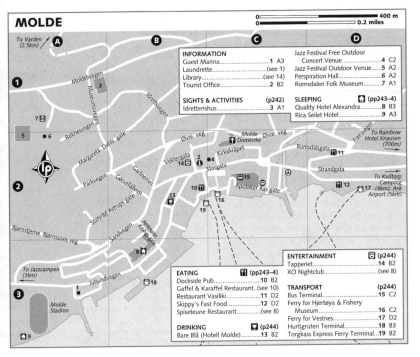

MOLDE

INFORMATION
Guest Marina.............................1 A3
Laundrette..............................(see 1)
Library..................................(see 14)
Tourist Office.........................2 B2

SIGHTS & ACTIVITIES   (p242)
Idrettenshus..........................3 A1

Jazz Festival Free Outdoor
  Concert Venue.....................4 C2
Jazz Festival Outdoor Venue......5 A2
Perspiration Hall......................6 A2
Romsdalen Folk Museum..........7 A1

SLEEPING   (pp243–4)
Quality Hotel Alexandra...........8 B3
Rica Seilet Hotel......................9 A3

ENTERTAINMENT   (p244)
Tapperiet................................14 B2
XO Nightclub........................(see 8)

TRANSPORT   (p244)
Bus Terminal..........................15 C2
Ferry for Hjertøya & Fishery
  Museum.............................16 C2
Ferry for Vestnes...................17 D2
Hurtigruten Terminal..............18 B3
Torgkaia Express Ferry Terminal..19 B2

EATING   (pp243–4)
Dockside Pub........................10 B2
Gaffel & Karaffel Restaurant..(see 10)
Restaurant Vasiliki.................11 D2
Skippy's Fast Food.................12 D2
Spiseteune Restaurant.........(see 8)

DRINKING   (p244)
Bare Blå (Hotell Molde)..........13 B2

Festivals & Events

The renowned Molde International Jazz Festival is a magnet for jazz fiends from all over Norway and wider afield.

Sleeping & Eating

The tourist office will book accommodation free of charge. It has a number of private homes on its books, most with kitchen facilities and costing from Nkr150 to Nkr200 per person. During the Molde Jazz Festival, many local households also offer private accommodation, and a large temporary camping ground, **Jazzcampen** (per person Nkr60-100), is set up 3km west of the centre.

Rica Seilet Hotel (☎ 71 11 40 00; www.rica.no; Gideonvegen 2; s/d Nkr545/846 mid-Jun–mid-Aug, Nk1395/1495 Mon-Fri, Nkr895/995 Sat & Sun rest-of-year; P 🖥) This architecturally stunning hotel, Molde's newest, juts out into the sound like a huge silver sail and represents outstanding summertime value. It has two rooms equipped for the handicapped and facilities include an exercise centre and sauna. There are bedrooms up to the 14th floor, each with large picture windows and magnificent views and the room price is constant, however high you roost.

Quality Hotel Alexandra (☎ 71 20 37 50; www.choicehotels.no; Storgata 1-7; s/d Nkr640/790 mid-Jun–mid-Aug, Nk1245/1395 Mon-Thu, Nkr795/945 Fri-Sun rest-of-year; P 🖥 🖳) Most rooms have a balcony and offer great views. There's a sauna and mini-gym, free to guests, a good restaurant, the Spiseteune, and, for an aperitif, the cosy Getz Bar, named after the immortal saxophonist. The hotel's high point (literally: it's up on the top floor) is its indoor heated pool, open all year, even when the snow's around.

Kviltorp Camping (☎ 71 21 17 42; www.kviltorp camping.no in Norwegian; Fannestrandveien 142; tent/caravan sites Nkr100/115 plus per person Nkr10, 2-bed cabins Nkr350, 4-bed cabins with shower Nkr650) This fjordside camping ground occupies a potentially noisy spot at the end of the airport runway but fortunately there's little air traffic. Cabins are available year-round. Bus No 214 and the Flybuss pass right by.

Dockside Pub/Gaffel & Karafel Restaurant (☎ 71 21 93 90; Torget; soup Nkr45, mains Nkr150-190, salads Nkr82-99) This hybrid place, recently

MOLDEJAZZ

Every year, Moldejazz pulls in up to 100,000 fans and host of stars, mainly Scandinavian but with a sprinkling of the internationally famous (in 2004, for example, Stevie Wonder topped the bill and Ladysmith Black Mambazo, the boo-be-doers behind Paul Simon's Graceland, also zapped the crowds).

The town rocks all the way from Monday to Saturday in the middle of July. Of over 100 concerts, a good third are free, while big events are very reasonably priced at Nkr100 to Nkr280.

Trad jazz sweats it out in Perspiration Hall, the big draws perform outdoors near the Romsdalsmuseet, indoor concerts take place at the Idrettenshus (sports hall) and there are free events (including a daily street parade) from noon onwards in front of the Rådhus.

For the low-down on this year's events, dial ☎ 71 20 31 50 or log onto www.molde jazz.no. You can book by credit card for a Nkr10 surcharge through **BillettService** (☎ 81 53 31 33).

revamped, well merits a visit. Upstairs is Gaffel & Karafel, mainly restaurant but also serving drinks with meals. Downstairs, there's a more than decent pub, which also serves meals, while on the open-air quayside terrace, you can get both.

Skippy's Fast Food (☎ 71 25 22 30; Fergeterminalen; meals around Nkr100) Between two ferry terminals, Skippy's offers no more and no less than what its name claims, except, bizarrely, for its exotic Hawaiian pork special (Nkr96).

Restaurant Vasiliki (☎ 71 25 31 00; Romsdalsgata 20) The tempting part of Vasiliki's menu is its great selection of Greek appetizers and mains, but it also dishes up pizzas and pastas.

Drinking

Bare Blå (☎ 71 21 58 88; Storgata 19), located in Hotell Molde, is a popular pub on the main drag. Down by the quayside, Dockside Pub (see p243) is another good watering hole that sometimes puts on live performances and shows.

Entertainment

Tapperiet (☎ 71 24 13 50; Kirkebakken 1-3) Tapperiet, run by the student association, is a great place to meet young Norwegians. Cover charges apply only when there's live music.

XO Nightclub (☎ 71 20 37 50; Storgata 1-7; cover charge around Nkr80) This place, in the Quality Hotel Alexandra, has live music and DJs at weekends and appeals to a slightly older crowd.

Getting There & Away

AIR

Molde's **Årø airport** (☎ 71 21 47 80) stretches beside the shore 5km east of the city centre. The Flybuss (Nkr30, 10 minutes) meets and greets all flights. SAS Braathens has three to five flights daily to/from Oslo and two daily to/from both Trondheim and Bergen.

BOAT

The express ferry between Ålesund and Molde's Torgkaia terminal (Nkr177, 2¼ hours) sails twice daily on weekdays in July only. Northbound, the Hurtigruten coastal ferry leaves Storkaia in Molde at 10pm (6.30pm mid-September to mid-April); southbound, at 9.30pm.

BUS

Buses run three to nine times daily to/from Kristiansund (Nkr140, 1½ hours), Åndalsnes (Nkr88, 1½ hours) and Ålesund (Nkr136, two hours). Most buses to Ålesund first require taking the ferry from Molde to Vestnes.

CAR & MOTORCYCLE

If you're driving towards Åndalsnes, a car and driver pays Nkr65 to pass through the Fannefjorden tunnel, plus Nkr23 per passenger. Travelling northwards on the Rv64, the Tussentunnelen short cut (Nkr15) avoids a dog leg and lops off a good 15 minutes.

AROUND MOLDE
Ona

The beautiful outer island of Ona, with its bare rocky landscapes and picturesque lighthouse, is home to an offshore fishing community. Small and unobtrusive, its one major event was the enormous tidal wave that washed over it back in 1670. It makes a popular day trip from Molde. En

HMS GLASGOW

The Rica Seilet Hotel's Glasgow bar commemorates an event at the end of April 1940, when Molde was briefly the residence of King Håkon and capital of Norway. As German forces bombarded the town, HMS *Glasgow* slipped into port and bore the king away into exile, together with 36 tonnes of gold from the state reserves.

The last of his country that the king saw before heading for exile in Britain was the collapsing spire of the burning church. On a happier note, one local hero saved the old altarpiece painting, Axel Ender's *Resurrection*, by ripping it out with a knife as the bombs fell.

route, WWII buffs may want to stop off at **Gossen Krigsminnesamling** (☎ 71 17 15 77; Gossen; adult/child Nkr30/15; ⊗ noon-5pm Tue-Sun late Jun-early Aug), a former Nazi wartime airstrip built by Russian POWs on the low island of Gossen. The abandoned summer-house village of Bjørnsund, where a café and shop operate, June to August, also warrants a brief stop on the way to the island.

Bud

The Rv63 coastal route between Molde and Kristiansund makes a pleasant alternative to the faster, ferry-less E89. En route lies the rustic little fishing village of Bud, huddled around its compact little harbour. In the 16th and 17th centuries, it was the greatest trading centre between Bergen and Trondheim, but is better known for its role in more recent history.

Serving as a WWII museum and memorial, **Ergan Coastal Fort** (Ergan Kystfort; ☎ 71 26 15 18; adult/child Nkr50/30; ⊗ 10am-6pm Jun-Aug) was hastily erected by Nazi forces in May 1940. Various armaments and a network of bunkers and soldiers' quarters are dispersed around the hill with the sick bay and store sunk deep inside the mountain.

The camping ground of **Bud Camping** (☎ 71 26 10 23; www.budcamping.no in Norwegian; car/caravan sites Nkr130, 4-bed cabins Nkr300, 8-bed with bathroom Nkr800) lies beside a small marina, where you can hire canoes, rowing boats and motor boats for Nkr50/100/300 per day.

There is a rustic old fish restaurant called **Sjøbua Mat og Vinhus** (☎ 71 26 14 00; Vikaveien; mains Nkr160-195; ⊗ daily mid-May–mid-Sep, Fri-Sun mid-Sep–mid-May), which serves up the local catch in a harbourfront warehouse with wooden floorboards and a boat in the middle of the room. Fish soup costs Nkr90 and main courses include whale.

On weekdays, bus No 253 runs between Molde and Bud (Nkr68, 50 minutes) one to four times daily except Sunday.

Trollkirka

If you're heading towards Bud and Atlanterhavsveien, it's worth making a short side trip to the mystical cave Trollkirka, the 'Trolls' Church'. This series of three white marble grottoes is connected by subterranean streams, and one contains a fabulous 14m waterfall. The entrance is a steep uphill walk (2.5km; allow two to three hours for the return trip) from the signed car park. You'll need a torch and good boots to explore the caves fully. From Molde, bus No 241 passes the car park two to seven times daily.

Atlanterhavsveien & Averøya

The eight storm-lashed bridges of Atlanterhavsveien between Vevang and the island of Averøya connect 17 islands. On calm days, you may wonder what the big deal is, but in a storm, you'll experience nature's wrath at its most dramatic. Look out for whales and seals offshore along the route and perhaps make a short detour north of the main road to the dramatically exposed **Hestskjæret Fyr** lighthouse. Rock fans can check out the bizarre Steinbiten stone exhibition, at the Statoil petrol station in Bremsnes.

Well worth the detour is the **Kvernes stave church** (adult/child Nkr30/free; ⊗ 10am-5pm daily mid-Jun–mid-Aug, Sun only mid-May–mid-Sep) on Averøya, which dates from around 1300 but was rebuilt in 1633. Inside are a large 300-year-old votive ship and a 15th-century Catholic-Lutheran hybrid altar screen. There's also a small open-air museum and a gallery/handicrafts outlet nearby.

A strongly recommended, hyperfriendly place is **Skjerneset Bryggecamping** (☎ 71 51 18 94; www.skjerneset.com in Norwegian; Sveggevika; camp sites Nkr90, cabins with bathroom Nkr500-600, rorbuer r d Nkr350, tr with bathroom Nkr500). It's located right beside the sea, 1km along a dirt road at Sveggevika on Ekkilsøya, west of Bremsnes. The owners, themselves former commercial fisherfolk, organise deep-sea trips in their own boat or you can hire a motor boat and sling your own line. Rooms are in a former fish warehouse, which houses a fascinating family museum on the top floor.

Håholmen Havstuer (☎ 71 51 72 50; www.hahol men.no; Håholmen; s/d Nkr640/980) is a novel place, as it's a former fishing station on an offshore islet north of the middle of the archipelago. It is run by explorer Ragnar Thorseth and his wife, Kari, who also run a great fish restaurant (mains Nkr135 to NKr240). It's the final resting place of the *Saga Siglar*, a replica of a Viking vessel that looped the globe between 1983 and 1986. A small boat shuttles hourly, leaving the roadside car park on the hour, between 11am to 9pm, late June to mid-August.

Buses run between Molde and Bremsnes (Nkr118, 1¾ hours) two to four times daily. Buses run from Bremsnes to Kvernes (Nkr30, 15 minutes) three to seven times daily except Sunday. From Bremsnes, there are frequent ferry connections to Kristiansund.

KRISTIANSUND
pop 16,900

The historic cod-fishing and drying town of Kristiansund ranges over three islands. It still looks very much out to sea even though the waters are no longer so bountiful, the huge hauls of yesteryear now the source of tales as tall as any angler's. Its best restaurants serve dishes from the deep, fishing boats, large and small, still moor alongside its quays and Mellemværftet, unkempt and chaotic, hangs on as a working boatyard.

Information

Ark bookshop (☎ 71 57 09 60; cnr Kaibakken & Nedre Enggate) Also good for maps.

Laundrette (Guest Marina)

Onkel og Vennene (☎ 71 67 58 10; Kaibakken 1) This place offers Internet access.

Tourist office (☎ 71 58 54 54; www.visitkristiansund .com; Kongens plass 1; ⊗ 9am-6pm Mon-Fri, 10am-3pm Sat, 11am-4pm Sun mid-Jun–mid-Aug; 9am-4pm Mon-Fri rest-of-year) Free Internet access.

Sights

Kristiansund's **Gamle Byen**, or old town, occupies part of Innlandet island, where you'll find clapboard buildings dating from as early as the 17th century. The opulent **Lossiusgården**, at the eastern end of the historic district, was the distinguished home of an 18th-century merchant. The venerable 300-year-old **Dødeladen Café** – where you can still get a decent meal and a drink – hosts cultural and musical events, including a festival in early July (contact the tourist office for details). The best access from the centre is on the Sundbåt ferry (see p249) from Piren.

In the town centre, the monumental 1914 **Festiviteten**, plain enough from outside, has an attractive Art Nouveau interior and is used for theatre and opera. Beside the Piren ferry point, the **Klippfiskkjerringa statue** by Tore Bjørn Skjøsvik represents a fishwife carrying cod to the drying racks.

MELLEMVÆRFTET

Something of a nautical junkyard, **Mellemværftet**, free and accessible any time, is best approached on foot along the quayside from the Smia Restaurant. It's difficult to make out what's what amid the agreeable clutter but it includes the remnants of Kristiansund's 19th-century shipyard, a forge and workshop, and workers' quarters.

MUSEUMS

Kristiansund has several museums housed, for the most part, in historic buildings whose exteriors alone warrant a visit. Happily so, since some have severely reduced opening hours – or none at all except by appointment. We detail here the situation as it was when we last visited and trust that things may have improved when you visit. The helpful tourist office will be au fait. Otherwise, try your luck on ☎ 71 58 70 00, the central phone number for all museums, or www.nordmore.museum.no.

The dust of time certainly hasn't settled on **Handelshuset** (Freiveien; admission free; ⊗ noon-8pm Tue-Sun mid-Jun–Aug, Sun only Sep–mid-Jun). Here at this functioning café, you can tuck into traditional Norwegian dishes such as *svele* (a rich pancake, speciality of the Romsdal area), *rømmegrot* (a delicious sour cream variant upon porridge, traditionally served at Christmas) and *bacalao* (fish dish using cod), browse among old posters and signs, learn something of Kristiansund's commercial history and drink the freshest coffee, roasted on Norway's oldest operational coffee roaster. It may be difficult to drag older guests away from the magnificent vintage jukebox with its old 45rpm hits by Presley,

KRISTIANSUND

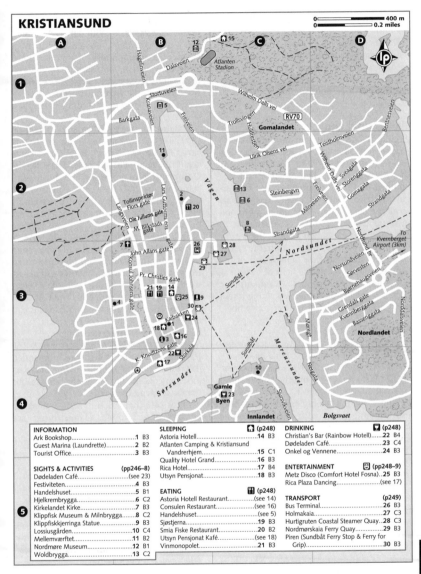

INFORMATION	
Ark Bookshop	1 B3
Guest Marina (Laundrette)	2 B2
Tourist Office	3 B3

SIGHTS & ACTIVITIES	(pp246–8)
Dødeladen Café	(see 23)
Festiviteten	4 B3
Handelshuset	5 B1
Hjelkrembrygga	6 C2
Kirkelandet Kirke	7 B3
Klippfisk Museum & Milnbrygga	8 C2
Klippfiskkjerringa Statue	9 B3
Lossiusgården	10 C4
Mellemværftet	11 B3
Nordmøre Museum	12 B1
Woldbrygga	13 C2

SLEEPING	(p248)
Astoria Hotell	14 B3
Atlanten Camping & Kristiansund Vandrerhjem	15 C1
Quality Hotel Grand	16 B3
Rica Hotel	17 B4
Utsyn Pensjonat	18 B3

EATING	(p248)
Astoria Hotell Restaurant	(see 14)
Consulen Restaurant	(see 16)
Handelshuset	(see 5)
Sjøstjerna	19 B3
Smia Fiske Restaurant	20 B2
Utsyn Pensjonat Kafé	(see 18)
Vinmonopolet	21 B3

DRINKING	(p248)
Christian's Bar (Rainbow Hotell)	22 B4
Dødeladen Café	23 C4
Onkel og Vennene	24 B3

ENTERTAINMENT	(pp248–9)
Metz Disco (Comfort Hotel Fosna)	25 B3
Rica Plaza Dancing	(see 17)

TRANSPORT	(p249)
Bus Terminal	26 B3
Holmakaia	27 C3
Hurtigruten Coastal Steamer Quay	28 C3
Nordmørskaia Ferry Quay	29 B3
Piren (Sundbåt Ferry Stop & Ferry for Grip)	30 B3

the Stones, the Beach Boys and other distant icons.

The **Norwegian Klippfish museum** (Norsk Klippfiskmuseet; ☎ 71 67 15 78; adult/child Nkr50/free; ☼ noon-5pm Mon-Sat, 1-4pm Sun mid-Jun–mid-Aug) is in the 1749 **Milnbrygga warehouse** on the Gomalandet peninsula. It presents the 300-year history of the dried-cod export industry in Kristiansund and the fishy setting is as intriguing as the subject matter. To get there from the town centre, take the Sundbåt ferry and ask to be dropped at the Klippfish Museum.

Just north of this museum are **Hjelkrembrygga**, a former klippfish warehouse dating from 1835, and neighbouring **Woldbrygga**, a barrel factory constructed in 1875. Both are open only by appointment.

Nordmøre Museum (Dalaveien; adult/child Nkr50/free; ⊗ by appointment) includes regional archaeological artefacts from as early as 7000 BC, as well as an old *stabbur* (raised storehouse), a historic smokehouse and an early waterwheel.

KIRKELANDET CHURCH

Architect Odd Østby's inspirational **church** (Langveien; ⊗ 10am-6pm May-Aug, 10am-2pm Sep-Apr) was built in 1964 to replace the one that burned down when Kristiansund was bombed by the Germans in 1940. The angular exterior, with its clean lines and alternating copper and concrete is sobre and measured. Inside all lines direct the eye to the 320 panes of stained glass at the rear of the chancel. Moving upward from the earthy colours at the base, they lighten and, at the top, replicate the 'celestial light of heaven'.

Behind the church lies Vanndammene Park with plenty of greenery, walking tracks and the fine Varden watchtower viewpoint.

Sleeping & Eating

Quality Hotel Grand (☎ 71 57 13 00; www.choicehotels.no; Bernstorffstredet 1; s/d Nkr790/890 mid-Jun–mid-Aug, Nkr1205/1415 Sun-Thu, Nkr785/945 Fri & Sat rest-of-year; P ⬚) With its 109 rooms, the Hotel Grand is Kristiansund's largest. Six rooms are equipped for the handicapped and 30 take into account guests with allergies. Rooms are comfortable and attractively furnished and there's no need to cast around for a decent dinner; the hotel's own Consulen Restaurant has an à la carte menu that's as good as anywhere in town.

Astoria Hotell (☎ 71 67 84 37; www.astoriahotell.no in Norwegian; Skolegata 2; s/d/tr Nkr695/795/895) The recently opened Astoria is Kristiansund's only family-run hotel. Rooms are generally on the small side but there are one or two larger ones, which cost no more. It also runs a decent restaurant (mains Nkr135 to Nkr165) and, if you've worked up a thirst, you can slake it at the next-door bar.

Rica Hotel (☎ 71 67 64 11; www.rica.no; Storgata 41; s/d Nkr790/960 mid-Jun–mid-Aug, Nkr1260/1460 Sun-Thu, Nkr860/960 Fri & Sat rest-of-year; P ⬚) Rooms overlooking the water at this fjord-edge hotel carry no supplement and the view gets better, the higher you rise. There's a free sauna and mini-gym for guest use.

Utsyn Pensjonat (☎ 71 56 69 70; fax 71 56 69 90; Kongens plass 4; s/d 450/570) With only eight rooms, the Utsyn is a quiet, uncomplicated, bog-standard boarding house. More exceptional is its café, which, in addition to the run of the mill pastas and pizzas, does wraps, wok dishes and a recommended Norwegian daily special (Nkr85 including coffee and dessert).

Atlanten Camping & Kristiansund Vandrerhjem (☎ 71 67 11 04; www.atlanten.no; Dalaveien 22; tent/caravan sites Nkr100/120, cabins Nkr330-450, with bathroom Nkr550, hostel s/d/tr with bathroom Nkr350/400/450) Occupying joint premises, this hostel and camping ground lies within reasonable walking distance of the centre. It's a friendly place and the well-equipped hostel kitchen boasts 17 fridges!

Smia Fiskerestaurant (☎ 71 67 11 70; Fosnagata 30; mains Nkr140-220) The much garlanded Smia fish restaurant is in an old forge, adorned from wall to ceiling with bellows and blacksmith's tools – plus a couple of whale vertebrae and a hanging split cod. The fish soup (Nkr80) makes a great starter, or you can also have it as a main course (Nkr120). A highly regarded fish restaurant.

Sjøstjerna (☎ 71 67 87 78; Skolegata 8; mains Nkr170-235) This place, another highly recommended fish restaurant, has a similar menu and marine-theme interior to Smia, plus an outdoor terrace on pedestrianised Skolegata.

For a café that's rich in atmosphere, go out of your way to visit Handelshuset (see p246).

Vinmonopolet (crn Langveien & Helsingsgata) is the place to visit for all your alcoholic beverage requirements.

Drinking

Onkel og Vennene (☎ 71 67 58 10; Kaibakken 1) This pub/café has a pleasant atmosphere and is a good place for an evening beer or snack. Upstairs is more fun for a drink, while whenever the sun shines, the streetside terrace is even better.

Christian's Bar (☎ 71 57 03 00; Storgata 17) In Rainbow Hotell Kristiansund, Christian's Bar is an attractive pub for over-25s.

Entertainment

Metz Disco (☎ 71 67 40 11; Haugata 16), within Comfort Hotel Fosna, is where you'll find the town's younger movers and shakers, while **Rica Plaza Dancing** (☎ 71 67 64 11; Storgata

41), open Saturday night only, is more for slow waltzers.

Getting There & Away
AIR
The town's Kvernberget **airport** (☎ 71 68 30 50) is on Nordlandet island. SAS Braathens has three to four flights daily to/from Oslo and two to three to/from Bergen. Coast Air flies to/from Trondheim once Monday to Friday and to/from Bergen, two to three times daily.

BOAT
For day trips to the eastern end of the Atlanterhavsveien and the Kvernes stave church, take the Bremsnes ferry (Nkr21, 25 minutes, every 20 to 30 minutes) from Holmakaia Quay.

Express boats connect Kristiansund with Trondheim (Nkr415, 3½ hours, three daily from Nordmørskaia). The Hurtigruten coastal ferry also calls in daily at Holmakaia. The southbound ferry departs at 5pm, northbound at 1.45am (11pm mid-September to mid-April).

BUS
The main bus terminal lies immediately north of Nordmørskaia ferry quay. Services include Molde (Nkr140, 1½ hours, three to eight daily) and Trondheim (Nkr360, 3¼ hours, one to three daily).

Bussekspress runs between Kristiansund and Oppdal (Nkr260, 3¾ hours, two to six daily) via Sunndalsøra (Nkr170, 2½ hours), connecting with trains to/from Oslo and Trondheim.

Getting Around
Town buses cost Nkr17 per ride. Flybuss services run to Kvernberget airport (Nkr35, 20 minutes, three to seven daily).

The **Sundbåt ferry** (single journey adult/child Nkr15/8, day ticket Nkr40/20) is well worth the ride for its own sake and for the special perspective it gives of the harbour. It links the town centre and the islands of Innlandet, Nordlandet and Gomelandet, running every half hour, 7am to 5.15pm Monday to Friday, 10.15am to 3.45pm on Saturday. The full circuit takes 20 minutes.

AROUND KRISTIANSUND
Grip
Crowded onto a tiny rocky island, the colourful village of Grip with its pastel painted houses sits amid an archipelago of 80 islets and skerries. In the early 19th century, a drop in cod hauls and two powerful storms left the village crushed and practically abandoned. It eventually bounced back and was for years Norway's smallest municipality before being appended to Kristiansund in 1964.

The island's **stave church**, much restored, was originally constructed in the late 15th century and has an interesting, manifestly Catholic altar cabinet. It is open according to the ferry's arrival. On an offshore skerry the lofty, 47m tall Bratthårskollen lighthouse, built in 1888, prods skywards and stands out among the skerries.

From mid-May to late August, the **M/S Gripskyss** (☎ 92 28 65 63) plies the 14km between Kristiansund and Grip (Nkr170 return, 30 minutes) one to three times daily.

Trøndelag

Far and away the major draw of the Trøndelag is the attractive city of Trondheim, Norway's third-largest and something of a magnet for the whole region. It's the most northerly place in Norway that merits the title 'city'. You can find fulfilment simply wandering the medieval streets and quays of this attractive university town with its buzzing student life, pretty wharf-side restaurants and bars. Highlights include Nidaros Cathedral, Scandinavia's largest medieval structure, and the open-air Sverresborg Trøondelaog Folk Museum, on an equally grand scale.

The area also marks a couple of beginnings, one historical, the other contemporary. Stiklestad, site of the martyrdom of King Olav (St Olav) is at the heart of every Norwegian's sense of national identity and marks the transition from Viking to medieval times. With its lovely little church, impressive visitors centre and open-air museum, it well deserves the minor detour from the Arctic Highway. The town of Steinkjer, for its part, marks the start of the ultra scenic Kystriksveien. Also called, more prosaically, the Rv17 (Steinkjer's tourist office, conveniently located in a kiosk right beside the E6, is well endowed with information about this tempting alternative), this coastal route continues as far as Bodø, Nordland, and offers a stimulating alternative to the Arctic Highway for those who can spare the time – and cash – for the extra ferry fares. Even if the chronometer or a krone shortfall precludes your following all of the Kystriksveien, you can get the flavour of the coastal alternative by diverting to the little coastal settlement of Namsos, then cutting back eastwards to rejoin the E6 at Grong.

HIGHLIGHTS

- Browsing **Nidaros Cathedral** (p252), Trondheim, Norway's most sacred building
- Working your way through Trondheim Microbryggeri's range of **great draught beers** (p261)
- Trundling a trolley along the no-longer-active **Namsos–Grong railway line** (p265)
- Prowling the medieval battlefield at **Stiklestad** (p263), where St Olav met his untimely fate
- Telling the folks back home you've been to **Hell** (p263) and back on holiday
- Hiking in the wilderness of **Bymarka** (p258), right in the city's backyard

- Namsos–Grong Railway Line
- Stiklestad
- Bymarka ★★ ★ Hell
- Trondheim

| AREA: 38,615 SQ KM | HIGHEST ELEVATION: KRÅKVASSTIND (1699M) | POPULATION: 398,300 |

TRONDHEIM

pop 145,700
Trondheim is Norway's original capital and third-largest city after Oslo and Bergen. With its wide streets and partly pedestrianised heart, it's a simply lovely city with a long history. Fuelled by a large student population, it buzzes with life. Cycles zip everywhere, it has some good cafés and restaurants, and it's rich in museums. It will almost have you reeling if you arrive from the sparsely populated north of Norway. You *can* absorb it in one busy day, but it merits more if you're to slip into its lifestyle.

History
In 997, the Christian King Olav Tryggvason selected a broad sandbank at the river Nid estuary to moor his longboat. The natural harbour and strategic position made Nidaros (meaning 'mouth of the River Nid'), as the settlement was then called, especially useful for defence against the warlike pagan chiefs of Lade, who were a perceived threat to Christianity – and to stability – in the region. It is believed that Leifur Eiríksson visited the king's farm two years later and was converted to Christianity before setting sail for Iceland and Greenland and possibly becoming the first European to set foot in North America.

In 1030 another, now more famous, King Olav (Haraldsson) was martyred in battle at Stiklestad (see p263), about 90km to the northeast, and canonised the following year. Nidaros became a centre for pilgrims from all over Europe. When Norway became a bishopric in 1153, Nidaros emerged as the ecumenical centre for Norway, Orkney, the Isle of Man, the Faroe Islands, Iceland and Greenland. It served as the capital of Norway until 1217, ruling an empire that extended from what is now western Russia to, possibly, the shores of Newfoundland. The cult of St Olav continued until the Reformation in 1537, when Norway was placed under the Lutheran bishopric of Denmark.

After a fire razed most of the city in 1681, Trondheim was redesigned with wide streets and Renaissance flair by General Caspar de Cicignon.

Trondheim's location became key once again in WWII, when German naval forces made it their base for northern Norway but the city avoided major damage.

Orientation
Central Trondheim forms a triangular peninsula bordered by the river Nidelva to the southwest and east and Trondheimsfjorden to the north. The combined train station/bus terminal (Trondheim Sentralstasjon) and boat quays are squeezed between the canal immediately north of the centre and Trondheimsfjorden.

The epicentre of town is Torvet, the central square (also spelt 'Torget'), with a small daily fruit and veg market, well-framed views of Nidaros Cathedral and a statue of King Olav Tryggvason atop a column.

Just east of the centre, across the Gamle Bybro (Old Town Bridge), is the Bakklandet neighbourhood, where, within old warehouses and workers' housing, recently renovated, are some of the city's most colourful places to eat and drink. The small Solsiden, even more recently restored, is where you'll find Trondheim's trendiest cafés and wharf-side restaurants.

Information
ATMs abound in the heart of town.

Ark Bruns Bokhandel (☎ 73 51 00 22; Kongens gate 10) Carries a good selection of novels in English.

Bell Internett Café (☎ 73 80 85 42; Kongens gate 34; per 30min Nkr20; ☽ 11am-10pm Mon-Sat, 2-10pm Sun)

Elefanten Vaskeri (☎ 73 51 29 89; Mellomveien 20; ☽ 10am-6pm Mon-Fri, 11am-4pm Sat) Enjoy the free coffee at this congenial place, Norway's northernmost laundrette.

Main post office (Dronningens gate 10)

Spacebar (☎ 73 51 53 50; Kongens gate 19; per hr Nkr40; ☽ 10-2am Sun-Thu, 24hr Fri & Sat) This Internet café can be entered from Prinsens gate.

Tourist office (☎ 73 80 76 60; www.visit-trondheim .com; Torvet; ☽ 8.30am-6pm Mon-Fri, 10am-4pm Sat & Sun mid-May–Jun, 8.30am-10pm Mon-Fri, 10am-6pm Sat & Sun Jul-Aug, 9am-4pm Mon-Fri, 10am-2pm Sat & Sun Sep–mid-May)

Sights
NIDAROS CATHEDRAL & ARCHBISHOP'S PALACE
Trondheim's dominant landmark and Scandinavia's largest medieval building, constructed in the late 11th century, is **Nidaros Cathedral** (Nidaros Domkirke; Kongsgårdsgata; adult/child Nkr40/20 incl Archbishop's Palace; ☽ 9am-3pm Mon-Fri,

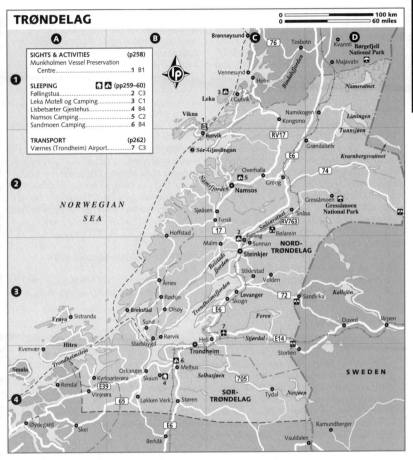

TRØNDELAG

0   100 km
0   60 miles

A   B   C   D

SIGHTS & ACTIVITIES   (p258)
Munkholmen Vessel Preservation
   Centre.................................1 B1

SLEEPING   (pp259–60)
Føllingstua...............................2 C3
Leka Motell og Camping...........3 C1
Lisbetsæter Gjestehus...............4 B4
Namsos Camping......................5 C2
Sandmoen Camping..................6 B4

TRANSPORT   (p262)
Værnes (Trondheim) Airport......7 C3

Brønnøysund   Tosbotn   Kvannli   Børgefjell
National Park
Majavatn

Vennesund   Holm   Namsvatnet

Leka   Gulvik   Namskogen   Limingen
Kongsmo

Vikna   RV17   Grøndalselv   Tunnsjøen

Rørvik   E6   Kvarnbergsvattnet

Sør-Gjæslingan   Overhalla   74
5   Grong   Gressåmoen
Namsfjorden   Namsos   Gressåmoen
National Park

NORWEGIAN
SEA   Sjøåsen   Fossli   Snåsa

Hoffstad   17   Snåsavatnet   RV763
Bølarein
Malm   Sunnan   NORD-
Beitstad   Steinkjer   TRØNDELAG
Fjorden

Ärnes   Stiklestad
Rødsjø   Volden   Kallsjön
Brekstad   Olsøy   Levanger   72   Sandvika
Frøya   Sistranda   Trondheimsfjorden   Skogn
Sund   E6   Feren   Duved   Järpen
Rørvik   Heli
Kvenvær   Stadsbygd   Stjørdal   E14
Hitra   Trondheim   Storlien
Trondheimsleia   6   Melhus   SWEDEN
Smøla   Orkanger   Skaun   Selbusjøen   705
Rendal   Kyrksæterøra   4   SØR-
E39   TRØNDELAG   Tydal   Nesjøen
Vinjeøra   65   Løkken Verk   Støren
Øydegard   Skei   Ramundberger
   E6
Berkåk   Vauldalen

9am-2pm Sat, 1-4pm Sun May–mid-Jun & mid-Aug–mid-Sep; 9am-6pm Mon-Fri, 9am-2pm Sat, 1-4pm Sun mid-Jun–mid-Aug; noon-3.30pm Mon-Fri, 11.30am-2pm Sat, 1-3pm Sun mid-Sep–Apr). Outside, the wonderful ornately embellished west wall is nearly top to bottom statues of biblical characters and Norwegian bishops and kings. Within, the cathedral is subtly lit (just see how the vibrantly coloured, modern stained glass glows, especially in the rose window at the west end), so let your eyes attune to the gloom.

The altar was placed over the original grave of St Olav, the Viking king who replaced the Nordic pagan religion with Christianity. When Norway became a separate archbishopric in 1153, a larger cathedral was built. The current transept and chapter house were constructed between 1130 and 1180 and reveal Anglo-Norman influences (many of the craftsmen were English), while the Gothic choir and ambulatory were completed around the early 14th century. The nave, repeatedly ravaged by fire across the centuries, is mostly a faithful 19th-century reconstruction.

Down in the crypt is a display of mostly medieval carved tombstones (the majority restored from fragments since many marble headstones were broken up and carted away to be recycled in domestic buildings). Look for one inscribed in English and dedicated to one William Miller, Shipmaster, of Dundee, Scotland, who met his end near Trondheim in the 18th century.

You can wander around freely but it's worthwhile joining a tour (a 15-minute canter or a more detailed 45-minute visit). Times vary but there are up to four in English (usually at 11am, noon, 1.30pm and 4pm). Music lovers may want to time their visit to take in a **recital** (admission free; ☼ 1pm Mon-Sat mid-Jun–mid-Aug) on the church's magnificent organ.

From mid-June to mid-August, you can climb the cathedral's **tower** for a great view over the city. There are ascents every half hour from its base in the south transept. The crown jewels, temporarily out of commission, will again be displayed in 2006, centenary of the last full royal coronation in the cathedral.

Admission to the cathedral also includes the complex of the adjacent 12th-century **Archbishop's Palace** (Erkebispegården; ☎ 73 53 91 60; Kongsgårdsgata; ☼ 10am-5pm Mon-Sat, noon-5pm Sun Jun-Aug, 11am-3pm Tue-Sat & noon-4pm Sun rest-of-year). It was commissioned around 1160, making it the oldest secular building in Scandinavia.

Of greater interest is the modern **museum** in the same compound. After visiting the well-displayed statues, gargoyles and carvings from the cathedral, drop to the lower level, where only a selection of the myriad artefacts revealed during the museum's construction in the late 1990s are on show. Take in too its enjoyable 15-minute audiovisual programme.

The adjoining **National Military Museum** (☎ 73 99 52 80; Rustkammeret; admission free; ☼ 9am-3pm Mon-Fri, 11am-4pm Sat & Sun Jun-Aug only), in the same courtyard, is full of antique swords, armour and cannons and recounts the days from 1700 to 1900, when the Archbishop's Palace served as a Danish military installation. On the top floor is the **Hjemmesfront** (Home Front) museum, describing Trondheim's role in the WWII resistance.

SVERRESBORG TRØNDELAG FOLK MUSEUM

West of the centre, the **Folk Museum** (☎ 73 89 01 00; Sverresborg Allé; adult/child/family Nkr70/25/185;

THE PILGRIMS' WAY

Nidaros Cathedral was built on the site of the grave of St Olav, canonised and declared a martyr after his death at the battle of Stiklestad on 29 July 1030. The cult of St Olav quickly grew in popularity and 340 churches were dedicated to the saint in Scandinavia, Britain, Russia, the Baltic States, Poland, Germany and the Netherlands. Pilgrims from all over Europe journeyed to his grave at Nidaros, making it the most popular pilgrimage site in northern Europe. Historically, both rich and poor journeyed from Oslo for up to 25 days, while others braved longer sea voyages from Iceland, Greenland, Orkney and the Faroe Islands. St Olav's grave became the northern compass point for European pilgrims; the other spiritual cornerstones were Rome in the south, Jerusalem in the east, and Santiago de Compostela in the west.

As pilgrims travelled from village to village, their routes became arteries for the spread of the cult of St Olav. During medieval times, the journey itself was considered an exercise in unity with God, and early routes, with wild mountains, forests and rivers to cross, certainly gave plenty of opportunity to reflect upon the hardships of life's journey towards eternity. Most pilgrims travelled on foot, while the better off journeyed on horseback. Those without means relied on local hospitality along the way; in Norway, travelling pilgrims were held in high esteem and openly welcomed.

In 1997, the Pilgrims' Way – 926km in all, counting alternative sections – was inaugurated, reviving the ancient pilgrimage route between Oslo and Trondheim. The rugged route – mainly mountain tracks and gravelled roads – has been blazed (look for the logo – the cross of St Olav intertwined with that quatrefoil knot indicating a tourist attraction that you see everywhere). It follows, wherever practicable, ancient, documented trails. Along the trail are signs indicating place names and monuments linked to the life and works of St Olav, as well as ancient burial mounds and other historic monuments.

For further information, contact the **Pilgrims Office** (Pilegrimskontoret; ☎ 22 33 03 11; www.pilegrim .no; Kirkegata 34a, N-0153 Oslo) or consult its website.

The Pilgrim Road to Nidaros by Alison Raju, published by Cicerone Press, is an indispensable guide if you're thinking of taking on a stretch.

11am-6pm daily Jun-Aug, 11am-3pm Mon-Fri, noon-4pm Sat & Sun Sep-May) is one of the best of its kind in Norway. The indoor exhibition, Livsbilder (Images of Life) in the main building, displays artefacts from clothing to school supplies to bicycles, from the mid-19th century to today and has a short multimedia presentation. English tours are conducted nearly hourly.

The rest of the museum, with over 60 period buildings, is open-air, adjoining the ruins of King Sverre's castle and giving fine hill-top views of the city. In the urban section, houses, the post office, the dentist's and other shops splay around the central market square. There are farm buildings from rural Trøndelag, the small Haltdalen stave church (1170) and a couple of small museums devoted to telecommunications (some great old phones) and skiing (with elaborately carved wooden skis).

The museum's restaurant, Vertshuset Tavern (see p260), is a great place to try Norwegian specialities. Take bus No 8 (direction Stavset or Byåsen Heimdal) from Dronningens gate.

OTHER MUSEUMS

The **Ringve Museum** (☎ 73 87 02 80; Lade Allé 60; adult/child/family Nkr70/25/140; 11am-3pm Mon-Fri, 11am-4pm Sun mid-Apr–mid-May, 11am-3pm mid-May–mid-Jun & early Aug–mid-Sep, 11am-5pm mid-Jun–early Aug, 11am-4pm Sun only mid-Sep–mid-Apr) is Norway's national museum for music and musical instruments. The Russian-born owner was a devoted collector of rare and antique musical instruments, which music students demonstrate on tours of the main house. You can also browse the old barn with its rich collection of instruments from around the world. The botanical gardens, set within the surrounding 18th-century estate are a quiet green setting for a stroll. Take bus No 3 or 4 and walk up the hill.

The intimate **Trondheim Maritime Museum** (Trondheims Sjøfartsmuseum; ☎ 73 89 01 00; Fjordgata 6a; adult/concession Nkr25/15; 10am-4pm Jun-Aug), housed in an old prison, is an appealing little place full of relics, from 18th-century whaling ships and frigates to navigational instruments and models, paintings and photos of historic sailing ships.

The **Museum of Natural History & Archaeology** (Vitenskapsmuseet NTNU; ☎ 73 59 21 45; Erling Skakkes gate 47; adult/child/family Nkr25/10/50; 9am-4pm Mon-Fri, 11am-4pm Sat & Sun May–mid-Sep, 9am-2pm Tue-Fri & noon-4pm rest-of-year), a museum of natural history and archaeology, belongs to NTNU, the Norwegian University of Science & Technology. There's a hotchpotch of exhibits on the natural and human history of the Trondheim area: streetscapes and homes, ecclesiastical history, archaeological excavations and Southern Sami culture. More ordered is the small, alluring section in a side building devoted to church history and the fascinating everyday artefacts in the medieval section, covering Trondheim's history up to the great fire of 1681.

The eclectic **National Museum of Decorative Arts** (Nordenfjeldske Kunstindustrimuseum; ☎ 73 80 89 50; Munkegata 5; adult/child Nkr50/25; 10am-5pm Mon-Sat, noon-5pm Sun Jun-late Aug, 10am-3pm Tue-Sat, noon-4pm Sun rest-of-year) exhibits a fine collection of contemporary arts and crafts, including creations by Norway's highly acclaimed tapestry artist, Hannah Ryggen.

The **Trondheim Art Museum** (Trondheim Kunstmuseum; ☎ 73 53 81 80; Bispegata 7b; adult/child/family Nkr40/20/10; 10am-5pm Tue-Sun Jun-Aug, 11am-4pm Tue-Sun May-Sep) houses a collection of modern Norwegian and Danish art from 1800 onwards, including a hallway of Munch lithographs.

STIFTSGÅRDEN

Scandinavia's largest late baroque–style wooden **palace** (☎ 73 84 28 80; Munkegata; adult/child/family Nkr50/25/100; 10am-4pm Mon-Sat, noon-4pm Sun Jun-late Aug, closed during royal visits) was constructed between 1774 and 1778. It is now the official royal residence in Trondheim. Admission is by tour only, every hour on the hour.

HISTORIC NEIGHBOURHOODS

The picturesque **Gamle Bybro** (Old Town Bridge) was originally constructed in 1681, but the current structure dates from 1861. From it, there's a superb view of the **Bryggen**, a line-up of 18th- and 19th-century riverfront warehouses reminiscent of their better known counterparts in Bergen. To the east, the revived working-class neighbourhoods of **Møllenberg** and **Bakklandet** now house trendy shops, bars and cafés.

The cobblestone streets immediately west of the centre are lined with mid-19th-century wooden buildings, notably the octagonal 1705 timber church, **Hospitalskirken**

TRONDHEIM

A | **B** | **C** | **D**

INFORMATION
Ark Bruns Bokhandel.............................**1** C6
Bell Internett Café................................**2** E3
Hospital..**3** E6
Library...(see 17)
Main Post Office..................................**4** C5
Police Station.......................................**5** D4
Spacebar..**6** B6
Tourist Office.......................................**7** B6
Trondhjems Turistforenig DNT Office..**8** D3

SIGHTS & ACTIVITIES   (pp252–8)
Archbishop's Palace
  (Erkebispegården)..............................**9** F5
Gregorius Kirke Ruins
  (Sparebanken)...................................**10** C6
Hospitalkirken......................................**11** D3
King Olav Tryggvason Statue...............**12** B6
Kristiansten Fort (Festning)..................**13** G4
National Military Museum (Ruskammeret)
  & Home Front (Hjemmesfront)
  Museum..**14** F5
National Museum of Decorative Arts
  (Nordenfjeldske
  Kunstindustrimuseum)......................**15** F4
Nidaros Cathedral (Domkirke)..............**16** F4
Olavskirken Ruins................................**17** C6
Pirbadet Water Park & Pools................**18** F1
Science Centre (Vitensenteret).............**19** C6
Stiftsgården..**20** B5
Sverresborg Trøndelag Folk
  Museum..**21** A6
Synagogue & Jewish Museum.............**22** E5
Trondheim Art Museum
  (Trondheim Kunstmuseum)..............**23** E4
Trondheim Maritime Museum
  (Trondheims Sjøfartsmuseum)..........**24** D4
Vitenskapsmuseet NTNU (Natural History
  & Archaeology)................................**25** D4

SLEEPING   (pp259–60)
Britannia Hotel....................................**26** C5
Chesterfield Hotel................................**27** C4
Clarion Hotel Grand Olav....................**28** D4
Munken Hotel......................................**29** E3
Pensjonat Jarlen..................................**30** E3
Radisson SAS Royal Garden Hotel......**31** D4
Rainbow Gildevangen Hotel................**32** C4
Rainbow Trondheim Hotell..................**33** B6
Trondheim InterRail Centre.................**34** F6

EATING   (pp260–1)
Abelone Mat & Vinkjeller.....................**35** B5
Akropolis..**36** C4
Bakklandet Skydsstasjon......................**37** G4
Benitos..**38** C6
Café Erichsen......................................**39** C5
Café ni Muser......................................**40** E4
Chablis...**41** G4
Credo..**42** B4
Dromedar...**43** G4
Dromedar...**44** C6
Edgar Café..(see 34)
Egon..**45** C5
Fruit & Vegetable Market...................(see 12)
Grenaderen..**46** E5
Grønn Pepper.......................................**47** C4
Havfruen Fiskerestaurant.....................**48** F4
Palmehaven Restaurant.....................(see 26)
Ravnkloa Fish Market..........................**49** B4
Sushi Bar...**50** B4
Vertshuset...**51** A6
Zia Teresa..(see 38)

DRINKING   (pp261–2)
Bare Blåbær...**52** H2
Café 3-B..**53** C4
Druen..**54** H2
Luna..**55** H2
Macbeth...**56** C4
Metro...**57** F4
Studentersamfundet.........................(see 34)
Trondheim Microbryggeri.....................**58** B5

ENTERTAINMENT   (p262)
Frakken...**59** C5
Nova Kinosenter..................................**60** C5
Olavshallen.......................................(see 28)
Prinsen Kino..**61** E4
Rio..**62** C4
Trøndelag Teater..................................**63** E4

TRANSPORT   (pp262–3)
Bike Lift...**64** D4
City Bus Terminal (Rutebilstasjon)....**65** F2
Express Boats to Kristiansund..........(see 67)
Ferries to Munkholmen........................**66** B4
Pirterminalen Quay..............................**67** F1
St Olavsgata Tram Station...................**68** E3
Team Trafikk (Bus) Central Transit
  Point..**69** B5
Tripps Estuary Cruises.......................(see 66)

OTHER
Vinmonopolet......................................**70** B6

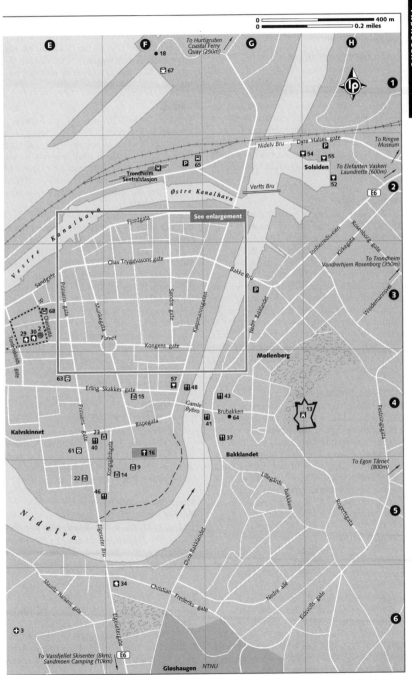

0 ——————————— 400 m
0 ——————————— 0.2 miles

E   **F**   **G**   **H**

● 18

To Hurtigruten
Coastal Ferry
Quay (250m)

1

67

Nidelv Bru   Dyre Halses gate   To Ringve
Museum

54   55

Solsiden   To Elefanten Vaskeri
Laundrette (600m)

65   **Trondheim
Sentralstasjon**

Verfts Bru   52

E6

2

Østre Kanalhavn

Vestre Kanalhavn   Fjordgata

See enlargement

Olav Tryggvasons gate   Bakke Bru   Innherredsveien   Rosenborg gate   Kirkegata   To Trondheim
Vandrerhjem Rosenborg (350m)

Sandgate   Prinsens gate   Munkegata   Søndre gate   Kjøpmannsgaten   Nedre Bakklandet

68   2   Torvet   Kongens gate   **Møllenberg**   Weidemannsvei

29   30   @

Tornebakkolds gate

3

63   Erling Skakkes gate   57   48   43   13

15   Gamle
Bybro   Brubakken
● 64   Festningsgata

Kalvskinnet   Prinsens gate   Bispegata   41   37

23   To Egon Tårnet
(800m)

61   40   **Bakklandet**

16   Lillegårds bakken   Rogertsgata

22   9   14

46

4

5

N i d e l v a

Elgeseter Bru   Øvre Bakklandet   Nedre allé   Eidsvolls gate

34   Christian Frederiks gate

Mauritz Hansens gate   Elgesetergate

✛ 3

To Vassfjellet Skisenter (8km);
Sandmoen Camping (10km)   E6

Gløshaugen   NTNU

6

(Hospitalsløkka 2-4), in the hospital grounds (although it's not generally open).

KRISTIANSTEN FESTNING

For a bird's-eye view of the city, climb 10 minutes from the Gamle Bybro to **Kristiansten Fort** (☎ 73 99 58 31; Festningsgaten; admission free; 🕑 10am-3pm Mon-Fri, 11am-4pm Sat & Sun Jun-Aug), built after Trondheim's great fire of 1681. During WWII, the Nazis used it as a prison and execution ground for members of the Norwegian Resistance. The **grounds** (admission free) are open year-round, whenever the flag is raised.

MUNKHOLMEN

In Trondheim's early years, the islet of Munkholmen – the Monks' Island – was the town execution ground. That distinction notwithstanding, in the early 11th century it became the site of a Benedictine monastery, which stood until the mid-17th century when the island became a prison, then a fort and finally a customs house. Today, it's a popular picnicking and sunbathing venue. From late May to late August, ferries (Nkr50 return) leave at least hourly between 10am and 6pm from beside the Ravnkloa fish market. Guided tours of the island (Nkr25, 30 minutes) are available.

MEDIEVAL CHURCH RUINS

During excavations for the library, archaeologists found ruins thought to be part of the 12th-century church, **Olavskirken**, now visible in the municipal library courtyard, together with a pair of skeletons and a supplementary skull. In the basement of the nearby bank Sparebanken (Søndre gate 4) are the ruins of the medieval **Gregorius Kirke**, also discovered during excavations. There's free access to both during regular business hours.

OTHER SIGHTS

Trondheim's **Synagogue** (☎ 73 52 20 30; Arkitekt Christies gate 1B; 🕑 10am-2pm Mon-Thu, noon-3pm Sun) claims to be the world's northernmost. It was restored in 2001 and contains a small museum of the history of the local Jewish community (halved by the Holocaust).

Children will enjoy the hands-on experiments at the **Science Centre** (Vitensenteret; ☎ 73 59 61 23; Kongens gate 1; adult/concession/family Nkr60/35/120; 🕑 10am-5pm Mon-Fri, 11am-5pm Sat & Sun mid-Jun–mid-Aug, to 4pm rest-of-year).

Activities

The free map, *Friluftsliv i Trondheimsregionen* (Outdoor Life in the Trondheim Region; text in Norwegian), available at the tourist office, shows all nearby outdoor recreation areas and walking trails.

HIKING

West of Trondheim spreads the Bymarka, a gorgeous green woodland area laced with wilderness footpaths and ski trails. Take the Gråkalbanen tram, in itself a lovely scenic ride through the leafy suburbs, from St Olavsgata station to **Lian**; it too has excellent views over the city and a good swimming lake, Kyvannet.

For more serious two-legged stuff, contact the local DNT office, **Trondhjems Turistforenig** (☎ 73 92 42 00; Sand gate 30).

SKIING

The Vassfjellet mountains, south of town, offer both downhill and cross-country skiing. In season, a daily ski bus runs directly from Munkegata to the Vassfjellet Skisenter, only 8km beyond the city limits. The Bymarka also offers excellent cross-country skiing, as does the Trondheim Skisenter Granåsen, where the brave or foolhardy can launch themselves from the world's largest plastic-surfaced ski jump.

BOAT TRIPS

Tripps (☎ 73 52 87 15; adult/child Nkr120/50; 🕑 Tue-Sun late Jun–mid-Aug) run a pleasant 1½-hour cruise along the estuary of the River Nid and out into the fjord, sailing at 2pm for sure with possible additional departures at 4pm and 6.30pm. Buy your ticket on the boat.

PIRBADET WATER PARK

Pirbadet (☎ 73 83 18 00; adult/child Mon-Fri Nkr95-60, Sat & Sun Nkr115/70; 🕑 10am-9pm Mon-Sat, 10am-7pm Sun), on the Pirterminalen quay, is Norway's largest indoor water park with a wealth of liquid pleasures including a wave pool, sauna and 100m water slide.

Tours

Between late May and August, **Trondheim Aktivum** gives a good overview of the city by running a two-hour guided city bus tour (adult/child Nkr180/75), departing daily at noon from the tourist office, where you can reserve.

Festivals & Events

Olavsfestdagene (www.olavsfestdagene.no in Norwegian), a major cultural festival in celebration of St Olav, takes place during the week around 29 July. There's a procession, a medieval market and a rich programme of classical music, jazz and pop.

Every other year in October and November, Trondheim's 25,000 university students stage the three-week **UKA** (www.uka.no in Norwegian) celebration, Norway's largest cultural festival. It's a continuous party with concerts, plays, and other festivities based at the round and red Studentersamfundet (Student Centre), next due to take the city by storm between 6 and 30 October 2005.

In February or March every second year, students put on **ISFiT** (www.isfit.org), an international student gathering with participants from over 100 countries. It's altogether more serious in tone and intent, but with plenty of concerts and events to occupy the leisure hours. The next moot is scheduled for February-March in 2007.

Sleeping

For a fee of Nkr20, the tourist office will book a room in a private house (singles approximately Nkr250 to Nkr330, doubles Nkr400 to Nkr450).

Trondheim InterRail Centre (☎ 73 89 95 38; Elgesetergate 1; dm incl breakfast Nkr115; ☼ late Jun–mid-Aug) OK, so you're on a cot bed in a dorm with between 15 and 40 sweating, snoring others but the advantages outweigh the downside at this convivial, informal, excellent-value place, run by the Studentersamfundet. There's free Internet access, a big-screen sports bar for major events, frequent live music and curfew's an ugly word. Its Edgar Café serves inexpensive meals and beer (Backpacker Evening, 9pm to 11pm every Tuesday and Friday with beers only Nkr25). Should you hear strange shufflings after the nightly partying subsides, it's just the ghost of one S Møller, a student who mysteriously disappeared in the 1930s.

Trondheim Vandrerhjem Rosenborg (☎ 73 87 44 50; trondheim.hostel@wandrerhjem.no; Weidemannsvei 41; dm incl breakfast Nkr210, s/d incl breakfast Nkr395/445, with bathroom Nkr500/570) On a hillside 2km east of the train station, this more conventional hostel, HI-affiliated, offers various options from simple dorms to a luxury suite for four (Nkr1200). It has an Internet point.

Britannia Hotel (☎ 73 in Norwegian; Dronningens gate Nkr750/900, Sun-Thu rest-of-year Sat Nkr825/990; P ☐) This m with its nearly 250 room most venerable, constructe . . . . Service is attentive and the pla fairly exudes old-world grace from the mellow, wooden panelling in public areas to the magnificent oval Palmehaven restaurant with its central fountain – but one of three places to eat – which does a great dinner buffet spread (Nkr275).

Clarion Hotel Grand Olav (☎ 73 80 80 80; www .choicehotels.no; Kjøpmannsgata 48; s/d mid-Jun–mid-Aug & Fri & Sat year-round from Nkr750/970, r Sun-Thu rest-of-year from Nkr1150) The Clarion offers sleek luxury above an airy shopping complex and the Olavshallen concert hall. It has 27 different styles among its over 100 rooms, so no guest can complain of lack of choice.

Chesterfield Hotel (☎ 73 50 37 50; www.bestwestern .no; Søndre gate 26; s/d mid-Jun–mid-Aug & Fri & Sat year-round Nkr670/895, Sun-Thu rest-of-year Nkr995/1095; ☐) Is it the mantelpiece and high-backed leather armchairs in the public lounge or the trouser press in each room that adds that 'touch (sic) of England' the brochure lays claim to? Whatever, all its 43 rooms are well furnished and spacious, the best of all being those on the 7th (top) floor, which have huge skylights giving broad city views. In summer, rates are a particular bargain (singles/doubles Nkr595/695) if you have a rail ticket, even if it's only for the next station down the line.

Radisson SAS Royal Garden Hotel (☎ 73 80 30 00; www.radissonsas.com; Kjøpmannsgata 73; s/d mid-Jun–mid-Aug Nkr950/1050, Sun-Thu rest-of-year Nkr1275/1525, Fri & Sat Nkr900/1000; P ☐ ☎) This first-class, contemporary river-side hotel (you can fish from your window in some rooms) has Trondheim's only hotel pool and fitness room. It's open, light and airy – and particularly family-friendly; children are accommodated for free and there's a playroom and separate kid's buffet breakfast.

Munken Hotel (☎ 73 53 45 40; www.munken.no; Kongens gate 44; s/d mid-Jun–mid-Aug & Fri & Sat year-round Nkr495/590, with bathroom Nkr595/790, Sun-Thu rest-of-year Nkr550/690, with bathroom Nkr650/890) Request a room with kitchen for no extra charge at this simple, central place that's friendliness itself. There's a large public car park just across the road.

AUTHOR'S CHOICE

Lisbetsæter Gjestehus (☎ 72 86 42 10; www
.lisbetseter.no, Skaun; s/d incl breakfast Nkr700/950;
🕑 mid-May–early Oct) In the mid-19th century, Dr Eyvind Kraft became personal physician to the king of Hawaii, but when one of
the princesses fell in love with him the
king paid Kraft a large sum to go home. In
1890, Kraft used the windfall to build a sanatorium and hydrotherapy spa on a medieval
mountain dairy farm, 25 miles southwest of
Trondheim. Perched on a hillock and surrounded by deep forest, this lovely, deep-
balconied wooden building makes a great
hideaway.

Rainbow Trondheim Hotell (☎ 73 88 47 88; www
.rainbow-hotels.no; Kongens gate 15; s/d mid-Jun–mid-Aug
Nkr630/790, Sun-Thu rest-of-year Nkr995/1245, Fri & Sat
Nkr680/880) Pleasant, up-to-date accommodation and complementary light evening
meals are offered in this central Rainbow
hotel. Inside is more appealing than its
plain, boxy exterior, the side wall's much
in need of a lick of paint.

Rainbow Gildevangen Hotell (☎ 73 87 01 30;
www.rainbow-hotels.no; Søndre gate 22b; s/d mid-Jun–
mid-Aug Nkr630/790, Sun-Thu rest-of-year Nkr995/1245,
Fri & Sat Nkr680/880; ℗) Also in the Rainbow
chain, this hotel offers the same amenities
and is only a couple of minutes' walk from
the train station.

Pensjonat Jarlen (☎ 73 51 32 18; www.jarlen.st.no
in Norwegian; Kongens gate 40; s/d Nkr400/500) There's
nothing fancy about this central spot but it
does have price on its side. All rooms have
full bathroom and nearly all are furnished
with bunk beds.

Sandmoen Camping (☎ 72 88 61 35; www.sand
moen.no; car/caravan sites Nkr130/175, cabins Nkr450,
with bathroom from Nkr650; 🕑 May–mid-Oct) About
12km south of the city, this is the handiest
camping ground if you're travelling the E6.
It has an affiliated motel about 1km away.

Eating
RESTAURANTS

Vertshuset (☎ 73 87 80 70; Sverresborg Allé 11; meals
Nkr110-250) Once in the heart of Trondheim,
this historic (1739) eating choice was lifted
and transported, every plank of it, to sit
with its near-contemporaries at the Trøndelag Folk Museum. Locals and visitors alike

flock here to enjoy the special atmosphere
of its low-beamed rooms, tuck into its rotating specials of traditional Norwegian fare
or just peck at waffles with coffee.

Abelone Mat & Vinkjeller (☎ 73 53 24 70; Dronningens gate 15; mains Nkr156-200) At this elegant
restaurant, staff bustle around in crisp
white shirts and bow ties. But, deep within a
vaulted cellar, dating from 1842, it's actually
fairly informal and you're sure to dine well.

Credo (☎ 73 53 03 88; Ørjaveita 4; 3-/5-course menus
Nkr420/510) There's no need for a formal à la
carte menu at this adventurous Spanish-
influenced world-cuisine spot – the chef
chooses the day's best items and serves
them in fine style. There's also a trendy bar
upstairs.

Grenaderen (☎ 73 51 66 80; Kongsgårda 1; mains
Nkr164-270) A more central historic place to
dine, Grenaderen, just behind the Archbishop's Palace was originally a smithy,
built in 1790. It too offers local cuisine,
served in the intimate, candle-lit interior
or on the outdoor terrace. It has a decent
summer lunch-time salad buffet (Nkr130).

Havfruen Fiskerestaurant (☎ 73 87 40 70; Kjøpmannsgata 7; mains Nkr210-285; 🕑 Mon-Sat) This
fancy river-side venue serves oysters, lobsters and fresh fish. The quality, reflected in
the prices, is excellent, as are their accompanying wines.

Grønn Pepper (☎ 73 51 66 44; Fjordgata 7; mains
Nkr165-210) Bright Mexican blankets and –
'fraid so – sombreros add colour and life
to the Pepper's architecturally staid interior. The food's Tex-Mex and you can slam
down a tequila or two. Monday's special is
four tacos with rice and salad (Nkr90).

Benitos/Zia Teresa (☎ 73 52 64 22; Vår Frue gate 4;
mains from Nkr90) At these two related restaurants – fancy Italian trattoria and informal
pizza and pasta joint – the gregarious, ex-
trovert owner bears a striking resemblance
to Luciano Pavarotti and may well provide
operatic accompaniment.

Akropolis (☎ 73 51 67 51; Fjordgata 19; mains
Nkr130-200) This Greek place does good
combination plates, including a vegetarian
mixed platter (Nkr108).

Sushi Bar (☎ 73 52 10 20; Munkegata 39; mains
Nkr175-240) It also serves quality meat and fish
dishes but the name says it all; the house
speciality is sushi in multifarious forms.
To savour the flavours, go for the 16-item
sushi selection (Nkr200).

Egon (☎ 73 51 79 75; Thomas Angellsgata 8; mains Nkr160-200) Trondheim's most visited restaurant is a huge complex on several floors with a menu almost as tall that has something for everyone. If you're out to fill yourself up, tuck into the all-you-can-eat pizza and salad buffet, served until 6pm, Monday to Saturday.

Egon Tårnet (☎ 73 87 35 00; Otto Nielsens veg 4) Egon's sister restaurant serves the same menu while rotating 74m up a telecommunications tower east of town. Take bus No 20 or 60 from the centre.

CAFÉS
Trondheim has a number of lovely cafés for coffee and cakes. Some stay open at night and turn into lively pubs.

Café Erichsen (☎ 73 87 45 50; Nørdre gate 8; light meals around Nkr100) Established in 1856, this is a charming place for a coffee, snack or something more substantial, whether in the stylish interior or – you'll be lucky to find a spare chair on a sunny day – on the terrace alongside traffic-free Nørdre Gate. It's self-service so throughput is swift.

Dromedar (☎ 73 50 25 02; Nedre Bakklandet 3) Also self-service, this is another long-standing local favourite that serves light dishes such as focaccia and bagels, and very good coffee indeed, in all sizes, squeezes and strengths. Inside is cramped so, if the weather permits, relax on the exterior terrace bordering the cobbled street. There's a second **branch** (☎ 73 53 00 60; Nørdre gate 2), similar in style, also with a pavement/sidewalk terrace and serving equally aromatic coffee.

Café ni Muser (☎ 73 53 25 50; Bispegata 9; light dishes Nkr60-100) For inexpensive light meals and an arty crowd, go to the café of the Trondheim Art Museum. On sunny afternoons, the outdoor terrace turns into a beer garden.

Baklandet Skydsstasjon (☎ 73 92 10 44; Øvre Bakklandet 33; mains Nkr115-170) Within are several cosy rooms and a heated patio where you can tuck into their tasty mains or renowned *bacalao* (fish dish using cod) while always leaving a cranny for one of their huge range of cakes (Nkr40 to Nkr55).

SELF-CATERING
For self-caterers, there's a grand little open-air fruit and veg market on Torvet each morning and you can munch on inexpensive fish cakes or other finny fare at the Ravnkloa fish market.

Drinking
As a student town, Trondheim offers heaps of nightlife, though venues change frequently. The free papers, *Natt & Dag* and *Plan B*, have listings, mostly in Norwegian.

Trondheim Microbryggeri (☎ 73 51 75 15; Prinsens gate 39) This splendid home-brew pub deserves a pilgrimage as reverential as anything accorded to St Olav from all committed *øl* (beer) quaffers. With up to eight of its own brews on top and good light meals coming from the kitchen, it's a place to linger and tipple in good company.

Macbeth (☎ 73 50 35 63; Søndregate 22b) Homesick Scots will feel at home, Geordies with nostalgia can weep into their draught Newcastle Brown and the rest of us can watch big-screen football or racing (don't get yourself into the corner where the committed racegoers sit, though, or you'll be persona-really-non-grata). And absolutely everyone can enjoy a dram or two of their more than 20 single malt whiskies…

Studentersamfundet (Student Centre; ☎ 73 89 95 38; Elgesetergate 1) This place has several lively bars, a cinema and frequent live music. During the academic year the main party night is Friday, while in summer it's mostly a travellers' crash pad (see p259).

Café 3-B (☎ 73 53 15 50; Brattørgata 3b) A place where loud music for rockers is played, people in black and self-professed alternative types frequent.

Metro (☎ 73 52 05 52; Kjøpmannsgata 12; 🕙 10pm-2am Wed, Fri & Sat) At the time of writing this was Trondheim's only gay bar, and also pub, lounge and disco and a meeting place for

AUTHOR'S CHOICE
Chablis (☎ 73 87 42 50; mains 160-210) The Chablis is beside the river – indeed part of it's on the water; reserve a table on their floating pontoon, linked to the restaurant by a footbridge. Alternatively, the interior of this brasserie-style place is light and appealing. And from the kitchen come the most delightful dishes, both Norwegian and international with more than a hint of the Mediterranean.

both boys and girls. You could also take a peek at www.gaytrondheim.com, though the information there is sparse in the extreme.

With the construction of a new footbridge, the attractively named Solsiden (Sunnyside), a wharf-side of bars and restaurants, has become Trondheim's trendiest leisure zone. Informed local sources reckon that Bare Blåbær is the place to be seen. Luna dishes up tapas and its neighbour Druen also has a deep terrace overlooking the one-time dock.

Entertainment

Frakken (☎ 73 52 24 42; Dronningens gate 12) is a multistorey nightclub and piano bar that features both Norwegian and foreign musicians. **Rio** (☎ 73 52 70 20, Nordregate 23; ☺ Tue-Sun) is the current 'it' dance club; it's almost too crowded on weekends.

The main concert hall, **Olavshallen** (☎ 73 99 40 50; Kjøpmannsgata 44), at the Olavskvartalet cultural centre, is the home base of the Trondheim Symphony Orchestra. It also puts on international rock and jazz concerts, mostly between September and May.

The handsomely refurbished **Trøndelag Teater** (☎ 73 80 51 00; Prinsens gate) stages large-scale dance and musical performances.

The town's two main cinemas are **Nova Kinosenter** (☎ 82 05 43 33; Olav Tryggvasons gate 5) and **Prinsen Kino** (☎ 82 05 43 33; Prinsens gate 2b).

Getting There & Away

AIR

Værnes airport, 32km east of Trondheim, is connected by SAS Braathens to all major Norwegian cities, as well as Copenhagen. Widerøe flies between Værnes and Sandefjord (near Oslo, one hour and five minutes),

Namsos (35 minutes), Rørvik (35 minutes), Brønnøysund (45 minutes) and all of northern Norway. These smaller aircraft provide the most scenic flights in the country.

Of Norway's burgeoning budget airlines, Coast Air flies to/from Kristiansund once daily, Monday to Friday, while Norwegian Air flies between Trondheim and Oslo five to eight times daily, Bergen five times weekly and Tromsø, likewise.

BOAT

The Hurtigruten coastal ferry stops in Trondheim leaving at noon (northbound) and 6.30am (southbound). Express passenger boats between Trondheim and Kristiansund (Nkr415, 3½ hours) depart from the Pirterminalen quay.

BUS

The city bus terminal (Rutebilstasjon) adjoins the Trondheim Sentralstasjon (train station, also known as Trondheim S).

As the main link between southern and northern Norway, Trondheim is a bus transport crossroads. Nor-Way Bussekspress services run at least daily to Ålesund (Nkr494, 7¾ hours), Bergen (Nkr803, 16½ hours), Namsos (Nkr285, 3¾ hours) and Oslo (Nkr610, 8½ hours). If you're travelling by public transport to Narvik and points north, it's quicker – all is relative – to take the train to Fauske or Bodø (the end of the line), then continue by bus.

CAR & MOTORCYCLE

There's an E6 bypass that avoids Trondheim – but why would you want to take it? The main route ploughs through the heart

---

TROND-*WHAT*?

Listen to Trondheimers talk about their city, and you may wonder whether they're all referring to the same place.

Since the late Middle Ages, the city was called Trondhjem, pronounced 'Trond-yem' and meaning, roughly, 'home of the good life'. But, in the early 20th century, the fledgling national government was bent on making Norwegian city names more historically Norwegian; just as Christiania reverted to its ancient name of Oslo, on 1 January 1930 Trondhjem was changed back to Nidaros.

Some 20,000 locals, perhaps upset at losing the good life without even moving, took to the streets in protest, and by 6 March the government relented – sort of. The compromise was 'Trondheim,' the etymologically Danish '*hj*' having been duly exorcised.

Nowadays, the official pronunciation is 'Trond-haym', but many locals still say 'Trond-yem'. Thanks to the vagaries of the local dialect, still others call it 'Trond-yahm'. Typical of this tolerant city, any of these pronunciations is acceptable, as is the 'Trond-hime' uttered by most English speakers.

of the city. Between 6am and 6pm Monday to Friday, drivers entering this central zone must pay a toll of Nkr15 (the motorway toll into town also covers the city toll, so keep your receipt). Use the 'Manuell' lane and pay up or you risk a steep fine.

Among car-hire options are **Avis** (☎ 73 84 17 90; Kjøpmannsgata 34), **Europcar** (☎ 73 82 88 50; Thonning Owesens gate 36) and **National** (☎ 73 50 94 40; Ladeveien 24). All also have kiosks at the airport.

TRAIN
For train information, phone ☎ 81 50 08 88. There are three to four daily trains to Oslo (Nkr748, 6½ hours) and two to Bodø (Nkr861, 10¾ hours) via Mosjøen (Nkr582, 4¼ hours), Mo i Rana (Nkr690, 6½ hours) and Fauske (Nkr830, 10 hours). You can also train it to Steinkjer (Nkr196, two hours, hourly).

Getting Around
TO/FROM THE AIRPORT
Flybussen (☎ 73 82 25 00; Nkr60), the airport bus, runs from 5am to 8pm, every 15 minutes (less frequently on weekends). The journey takes about 40 minutes and stops at major landmarks such as the Studentersamfundet, Trondheim Hotell in Torvet, Britannia Hotel and the train station.

Trains too run frequently between Trondheim Sentralstasjon and the Værnes airport station (Nkr60, 35 minutes).

BICYCLE
Trondheim has around 200 green bicycles available free of charge for use on the central peninsula and stored in bicycle racks around the centre. This said, we never saw a single one since – sad indictment of human nature – they're gradually being stolen, wrecked or simply not returned. If you're lucky enough to come across one, keep the news to yourself, insert a Nkr20 coin and ride off with it smartly. Your money will be returned when you re-lock the bike to any of the official bike racks.

Cyclists heading from the Gamle Bybro up the Brubakken hill to Kristiansten Fort (and not just them; it's worth going out of your way simply to enjoy the brief experience) can hitch themselves to Trampe, the world's only bike lift. Lift cards are available for a Nkr100 refundable deposit at the tourist office or Dromedar Café in Bakklandet.

CAR & MOTORCYCLE
Parking garages throughout town offer better rates and greater convenience than the krone-gobbling street-side meters.

PUBLIC TRANSPORT
The city bus service, **Team Trafikk** (☎ 73 50 28 70), has its central transit point on the corner of Munkegata and Dronningens gate; all lines stop here. Bus and tram cost Nkr22 per ride (Nkr65 for a 24-hour ticket). Exact change is required.

Trondheim's tram line, the Gråkalbanen, runs west from St Olavsgata to Lian, in the heart of the Bymarka. Antique trolleys run along this route on Saturdays in summer. Transfers are available from city buses.

TAXI
To call a taxi, ring ☎ 07373 or ☎ 08000.

THE ROUTE NORTH

HELL
Hell has little to offer but its name, which roughly translates as 'prosperity' in Norwegian. All the same, lots of travellers stop here for a cheap chuckle or at least to snap a photo of the sign at the train station. And forever after, whenever someone suggests you go here, you can honestly say you've already been and it wasn't all that bad.

STIKLESTAD
The site of Stiklestad commemorates what in terms of numbers was a small skirmish but which, in its impact, is at the heart of Norwegians' sense of national identity. They flock here by the thousand, some as pilgrims, to visit the church associated with St Olav, most to picnic and enjoy the fresh air, open space and associated exhibitions.

On 29 July 1030, a force of barely 100 men led by the Christian King Olav Haraldsson was defeated in Stiklestad by the larger and better-equipped forces under the command of local feudal chieftains. King Olav had been forced from the Norwegian throne by King Knut (Canute) of Denmark and England. He briefly escaped to Russia and, on his return, met resistance from local chiefs, disaffected by his destroying pagan shrines and executing anyone who persisted with heathen practices.

The Battle of Stiklestad is considered Norway's passage between the Viking and medieval periods, between prehistory and modern times. Although Olav was killed in action, the battle is generally lauded as a victory for Christianity in Norway and the slain hero recalled as a martyr and saint.

St Olav developed a following all over northern Europe and his grave in Trondheim's Nidaros Cathedral became a destination of pilgrims from across the continent. The site, around most of which you can wander for free, is laid out rather like a sprawling theme park, with exhibits on the Battle of Stiklestad, an outdoor folk museum and, predating all, the 12th-century Stiklestad church.

Sights & Activities

Within the **Stiklestad Cultural Centre** (Stiklestad Kulturhus; ☎ 74 04 42 00; www.stiklestad.no; adult/child mid-Jun–mid-Aug Nkr95/50, rest-of-year Nkr40/30; ☺ 9am-8pm mid-Jun–mid-Aug, 11am-5.30pm rest-of-year) is a well-executed exhibit about St Olav and an evocative walk-through **Stiklestad 1030** exhibition about the battle, plus a small resistance museum.

In the grounds is an **open-air museum** (admission free), a collection of over 30 historical buildings from humble crofts and artisan's workshops to the Molåna, a much grander farmhouse and, within it, a small, summer-time café.

Across the road, you can visit the lovely Stiklestad **church**, built from 1150 to 1180 above the stone where the dying St Olav reputedly leaned. The original stone was believed to have healing powers, but it was removed during the Reformation and hasn't been seen since.

It's well worth enlisting the services of a guide (adult/child Nkr40/30) to take you around both the open-air museum and the church. Alternatively, the booklet *Stiklestad Yesterday & Today*, on sale at the Centre, gives a succinct background to the site and its significance for Norwegians.

Festivals & Events

Every year during the week leading up to St Olav's Day (29 July) Stiklestad hosts the **St Olav Festival** with a medieval market, lots of wannabee Vikings in costume and a host of other folksy activities. The high point of the festival is an outdoor pageant, held over

the last four days, which enjoyed its 50th anniversary in 2004. Some of Norway's top actors and actresses – including recently, Liv Ullman – traditionally take the major roles while locals play minor parts and swell the crowd scenes. The text by Olav Gullvåt and music by Paul Okkenhaug conjure up the conflicts between the King and local farmers and chieftains.

Sleeping

Stiklestad Camping (☎ 74 04 12 94; www.stiklestad camping.no; E757; tent/caravan sites Nkr70/100, cabins Nkr290-670; ☺ Jun-Aug) About 3km from the cultural centre and near the River Verdal, this place has decent cabins in a grassy location.

STEINKJER & NORTH
pop 11,200

Steinkjer was mentioned in medieval sagas as a major trading centre and continues to be a crossroads, requiring a decision from northbound travellers; to opt for the fabulous Kystriksveien coastal route (Rv17) to Bodø or to continue northwards on the E6 (Arctic Highway). The **tourist office** (☎ 74 16 36 17; www.steinkjer-turist.com; Namdalsvegen 11; ☺ 9am-8pm Mon-Fri, 10am-8pm Sat, noon-8pm Sun late Jun-early Aug, 9am-4pm Mon-Fri rest-of-year) is located beside the E6. To get there from the train station, take the foot tunnel. Doubling as the Kystriksveien Info-Center, it can book accommodation for free in town and along the coastal route, rents bikes (Nkr30/100 per hour/day) and has Internet access (per hour Nkr60).

Sights & Activities

Steinkjer's main attraction is **Egge Museum** (☎ 74 16 31 10; Fylkesmannsgården; adult/child Nkr40/free; ☺ 10am-3.30pm Tue-Fri, noon-4pm Sun mid-Jun–mid-Aug), an open-air farm complex 2.5km north of town furnished with period furniture and tools. On the same hill-top site are several Viking burial mounds and stone circles.

North of Steinkjer, the E6 follows the north shore of the 45km-long, needle-thin lake **Snåsavatnet**, bordered by majestic evergreen forests. However, you may want to take the Rv763 along the quieter southern shore to see the **Bølarein**, a 5000- to 6000-year-old rock carving of a reindeer and several other images, with more still being discovered – the most recent (a man in a boat) in July 2001. Pass by the **Bølabua**

CHRISTOPHER WOOD

Breathtaking view of a fjord near Flåm (p211)

ANDERS BLOMQVIST

Ice climbers at Jostedal glacier (p222)

Waterfront buildings in the coastal town of Ålesund (p237)

DEANNA SWANEY

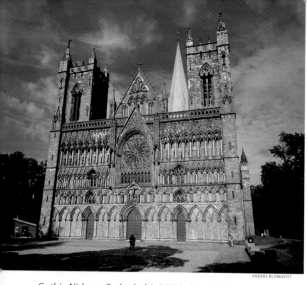

ANDERS BLOMQVIST

Gothic Nidaros Cathedral (p252) in Trondheim

DEANNA

Arctic tern mid-flight
over Bymarka (p258)

Waterfront warehouses in Trondheim (p252)

NE

restaurant & gift shop (☎ 45 42 65 88; ☺ late Jun–early Aug), a short walk from the carving, for information.

To see real antlered creatures, Arnfinn Vesterhus offers a four-hour **elk safari** (adult/child Nkr350/150; Mon-Fri mid-Jun–mid-Aug) and elk-meat barbecue. Reserve at the tourist office, from where tour minibuses leave.

Sleeping & Eating

Føllingstua (☎ 74 14 71 90; www.follingstua.com; E6, Følling; tent/caravan sites Nkr100/120, cabins Nkr630, 3–4-bed rooms with shared bathroom Nkr450) Beside the E6 14km north of Steinkjer, near the lake's southwestern end, this lovely, welcoming camping ground may tempt you to linger for a day or two, fish in the lake or rent one of their boats and canoes.

Guldbergaunet Sommerhotel & Camping (☎ 74 16 20 45; g-book@online.no; Elvenget 34; tent/caravan sites Nkr140/150, s/d Nkr490/590, d with bathroom Nkr690, cabins Nkr330-450; ☺ hotel mid-Jun–mid-Aug, cabins year-round) Normally student accommodation, this camping ground and summer hotel is located 2.25km from town amid a grassy area. A small river, ideal for paddling and bathing, flows right by.

Rainbow Hotel Tingvold Park (☎ 74 14 11 00; www.tingvoldhotel.no in Norwegian; Gamle Kongeveien 47; s/d mid-Jun–mid-Aug & Fri & Sat year-round Nkr660/840, Sun-Thu rest-of-year Nkr1070/1370; P ☐) Beside an old Viking burial site, this tranquil, good-value option overlooking Steinkjer has a pleasant lawn and garden.

Brod & Cirkus (☎ 74 16 21 00; Kongensgate 40; ☺ Mon-Sat) This bright, modern, attractively designed restaurant, on the main street 150m from the train station, bakes its own bread daily and offers a range of tempting à la carte dishes. They'll even knock you up a six-tier wedding cake, if you've a happy event on the horizon…

NAMSOS
pop 8900

Namsos, the first scenic port town on the northbound coastal route between Trondheim and Bodø, makes a pleasant overnight stop and has a couple of interesting diversions.

It has the dubious distinction of having Norway's shortest toll road, not even 500m long, which will set you back Nkr15 if you pass along it between 6am and 8pm on a weekday.

The **tourist office** (☎ 95 98 81 48; www.namsosinfo .no; Damskipskaia; ☺ 9am-6pm Mon-Fri, 10am-4pm Sat, noon-4pm Sun mid-Jun–mid-Aug, 9am-3.30pm rest-of-year) is at the quayside, co-located with the local bus and ferry companies. It rents cycles (per half/full day Nkr80/150) and also provides information about the Kystriksveien.

Cumberland Café (☎ 74 28 74 55; Kirkegata 11; per hr Nkr40; ☺ noon-10pm Mon-Sat, 3-10pm Sun) has several Internet terminals.

Sights & Activities

A scenic and easy 20-minute walk up Kirkegata from the centre will take you to the lookout atop the prominent loaf-shaped rock **Bjørumsklumpen** (114m) with good views over Namsfjorden, the town and its environs. About a third of the way up, a sign identifies a track leading to some impressive WWII-era German bunkers hewn from solid rock.

For some novel exercise for both the body and in nostalgia, you can hire a trolley (single Nkr200, up to four riders Nkr300) from Namsos Camping (see p266) and trundle it for 15km along the disused railway line between Namsos and Grong as it follows the gentle River Nansen.

If you're interested in wood chopping and chipping, check out the **Norsk Sagbruksmuseum** (☎ 74 27 13 00; Spillumsvika; admission Nkr30; ☺ 9am-5pm Tue-Sat, May-Aug, tours 10am, noon, 2pm & 4pm mid-Jun–mid-Aug), over the bridge 4km east of town, which commemorates Norway's first steam-powered sawmill (1853).

The **Namdal Museum** (Namdalsmuseet; ☎ 74 27 40 72; Kjærlighetstien 1; adult/child Nkr30/free; ☺ 11am-3pm Tue-Sun late Jun–mid-Aug) has displays on local history, including the typical wooden sailing boats of the area, and is – hold on to your hat – 'Norway's only museum featuring exhibits of hospital equipment presented in chronological order'.

For an active break, drop by the novel **Oasen swimming hall** (☎ 74 21 90 40; Jarle Hildrums veg; adult/child/family Nkr70/35/170; ☺ 10am-8pm Mon-Fri, 10am-4pm Sat & Sun). About 1km east of town, it has three heated pools and a 37m water slide built deep inside the mountain – quite an engineering feat.

The **Namsos Candle Foundry** (Lysstøperiet; ☎ 74 21 29 01; Lokstallen) makes and sells amazingly lifelike sculpted candles (such as tropical flowers and – incongruously – ice), in a former train shed.

TRØNDELAG

Sleeping & Eating

Namsos Camping (☎ 74 27 53 44; namsoscamp@online
.no; tent/caravan Nkr120/160, 4-bed cabins Nkr300-400,
with bathroom Nkr750-800) This superior camping ground has a large kitchen and dining
room, playground and mini golf. Basic
cabins are a bargain and the more expensive ones are well equipped. It's beside the
water – and also at the end of the airport
runway. Fortunately, planes are few and
light. Take Rv17, direction Grong, then
follow airport signs.

Borstad Gjestgiveri (☎ 74 27 21 31; gjestgive@on
line.no; Carl Gubransons gate 19; s/d Sun-Thu mid-Jun–mid-
Aug & Fri & Sat year-round Nkr670/890, Sun-Thu rest-of-
year from Nkr800/1040; (P)) Opposite the post
office, the bright, friendly Borstad has
large sunny rooms and a pleasant outdoor
garden. There's a cosy lounge, complete
with piano, and the huge oak dining table
at which breakfast is served was once used
for company board meetings. One room
is equipped for disabled guests (eg bars to
hold, big handles to grab).

Tino's Hotell (☎ 74 21 80 00; Verftsgata 5; s/d
Jul–mid-Aug from Nkr700/800, Sun-Thu rest-of-year from
Nkr900/1100, Fri & Sat Nkr700/900) Rooms are large
and comfortable at this hotel, just a stone's
throw from the waterside. Tino, the owner,
Italian as they come despite many years in
Norway, runs a great little restaurant where
you can enjoy both international food and
fine Italian cuisine, a continent away from
Norway's usual pizza and pasta joints.

Cumberland Café (☎ 74 28 74 55; Kirkegata 11;
🕑 noon-10pm Mon-Sat, 3-10pm Sun) Although it
wouldn't claim to be in the same league as
Tino's, it does offer good burgers in three
sizes, ciabattas and grills, all at very reasonable prices (Nkr48 to Nkr115).

Aakervik (☎ 74 27 20 90; Herlaugs gate 16) A
great little place for salmon and other fish,
game and other meats, either to pack for
your picnic or nibble at the wooden tables
outside. The interior is a mini-menagerie of
stuffed animals and birds eyeing you glass-
ily from all angles; pay your respects to the
amiable brown bear.

Getting There & Away

Nor-Way Bussekspress runs twice daily Between Namsos and Trondheim (Nkr285,
3¾ hours). Buses also run between Namsos
and Brønnøysund (Nkr273, six hours), further up the Kystriksveien.

RØRVIK

Although it's too far off the beaten track
for most visitors, tiny Rørvik buzzes when
both the northbound and southbound Hurtigruten coastal ferries call in each day at the
same time (9.15pm). What gets passengers
up early from the dinner table is the **Norveg
Centre for Coastal Culture & Industries** (Senter for
Kystkultur og Kystnæring; ☎ 74 39 00 41; Woxengs Samlinger; adult/child/family Nkr80/40/220; 🕑 10am-10pm mid-
Jun–Aug, 10am-5pm Sep–mid-Jun & when the Hurtigruten's
in port). Looking like a giant sailing ship from
a distance and the right angle, this brand
new centre recounts 10,000 years of coastal
history through a variety of media, including
an accompanying audioguide in English.

The museum also operates the **Munkholmen Vessel Preservation Centre**, on the islet
of Munkholmen 1km from town, and the
Sør-Gjæslingan fishing village on an island
35 minutes away by ferry.

Buses between Rørvik and Namsos
(Nkr184, three hours) run several times daily.
You can get to/from Namsos via express passenger boats (Nkr143, 1¾ hours) several
times weekly, or via frequent daily car ferries
between the ports of Hofles and Lund (per-
son/car-and-driver Nkr27/77, 25 minutes).

LEKA

pop 645

You won't regret a short side-trip to the wild
and beautiful red serpentine island of Leka;
for hikers, the desert-like Wild West landscape is particularly enchanting. This prime
habitat for the white-tailed sea eagle (hold on
to the little ones; in 1932, a three-year-old girl
was snatched away by a particularly cheeky
specimen) also has several Viking Age burial
mounds and Stone Age rock paintings.

Bed down at **Leka Motell og Camping** (☎ 74
39 98 23; www.leka-camp.no; tent/caravan sites Nkr80/
120, cabins Nkr250-700, d/q with bathroom & kitchen
Nkr600/700). In June 2004 this highly regarded
complex was graced with a visit by the
King and Queen. For comfort, reserve one
of their well-equipped, reasonably priced
motel rooms. For something different and
more spartan, hire a sod-roofed stone hut
(Nkr350), sleeping up to four in bunk beds.

Leka is accessed by ferry from Gutvik (per
person/car-and-driver Nkr23/60, 20 minutes), which lies about 20 minutes off the
Rv17 coast road. Buses run from Rørvik to
Gutvik (Nkr102, 2¾ hours) on weekdays.

Nordland

There's a difficult choice to make as you head north: is it to be the spectacular Kystriksveien Coastal Route, ferry hopping and perhaps detouring to take in a glacier or two? Or the almost as stunning inland Arctic Highway, faster, more direct but still lightly trafficked?

Whichever you choose, try to build in time to cross the waters and take in the Lofoten, a necklace of offshore islands with razor-sharp peaks and Caribbean-coloured bays. Here, cod is still king, as manifested in the small fishing museums, *rorbuer* (fisherfolks' cabins), and rickety drying-frames. Connected to the mainland by bridges and with reasonable public transport, the islands are easy to hop around. Then again, you may want to linger longer and hire a bike or pull on your boots; it's cycling for softies and the hiking's as gentle or as tough as you care to make it. Push further north to Andenes, at the northern tip of Andøya, a continuation of the Lofoten archipelago, and you'll enjoy the best whale-watching in all Norway.

As you move northwards through the long, narrow Nordland region, the crossing of the Arctic Circle is almost palpable; fields give way to lakes and forests, vistas open up, summits sharpen and the tree line descends ever lower on the mountainsides. In summer, this is where northbound travellers get their first taste of the midnight sun; in winter, the northern lights slash the night sky.

In addition to Nordland county, this chapter also includes the northeastern section of Vesterålen, a continuation of the Lofoten archipelago that belongs administratively to the county of Troms.

HIGHLIGHTS

- Ferry hopping and hugging the splendid **Kystriksveien coastal route** (p282)

- Being a wide-eyed kid again at the **Norwegian Aviation Museum** (p284) in Bodø

- Lingering in the tiny, preserved fishing village of **Å** (p299) in Lofoten

- Hiking the coastal Queen's Route to **Stø** (p305), in Vesterålen

- Taking the easy way up from Narvik to the Swedish border by the **Ofotbanen mountain train** (p281), then trekking downhill towards the fjord

- Taking time out to explore **Mosjøen's** (p269) historic Sjøgata, its galleries, museum and cafés

- Getting cold feet on one of the glaciers in **Saltfjellet-Svartisen National Park** (p274)

| AREA: 36,300 SQ KM | HIGHEST ELEVATION: OKSSKOLTEN (1916M) | POPULATION: 237,100 |

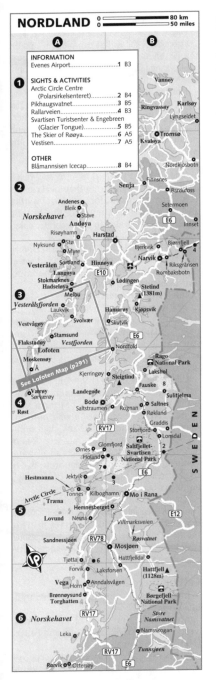

NORDLAND

0 ___ 80 km
0 ___ 50 miles

INFORMATION
Evenes Airport............................1 B3

SIGHTS & ACTIVITIES
Arctic Circle Centre
  (Polarsirkelsenteret)..............2 B4
Pikhaugsvatnet.........................3 B5
Rallarveien..............................4 B3
Svartisen Turistsenter & Engebreen
  (Glacier Tongue)....................5 B5
The Skier of Røøya....................6 A5
Vestisen.................................7 A5

OTHER
Blåmannsisen Icecap..................8 B4

See Lofoten Map (p291)

Getting Around

Travel through Nordland is extremely rewarding, but the maze of schedules and operators of buses and, particularly, coastal route ferries can be daunting. Still, any challenges are eminently surmountable with a little planning.

Local tourist offices are best at navigating the region, and the *Kystriksveien* (Coastal Route) booklet is a wonderful resource produced by the **Kystriksveien Info-Centre** (☎ 74 16 36 17; www.rv17.no) in Steinkjer. The Nordland travel information line (☎ 177) is also helpful, although it tends to be sketchy on smaller locales. For general travel info for the region, contact **Nordland Reiseliv** (☎ 75 54 52 00; www.nordlandreiseliv.no; Bodø).

THE ARCTIC HIGHWAY

MOSJØEN
pop 9600

Arriving in Mosjøen (pronounced *moo-sher-en*) along the E6, you may be put off by the industrial face of this aluminium-producing town. Don't be. About 1km south, along the lake-like Vefsnfjorden, historic Sjøgata and a street or two nearby are among the most charming in northern Norway and well merit a browse.

The town has a strong historical connection with the UK; in the mid-19th century, five Englishmen imported technically advanced steam engines and sawmill machinery and established the North of Europe Land & Mining Company Ltd to provide timber for Britain's burgeoning industrial towns and cities. What was a tiny coastal settlement quickly became the region's first registered town. The **tourist office** (☎ 75 11 12 40; www.visithelgeland .com; ⏱ 9am-6pm Mon-Fri mid-end Jun & early Aug, 9am-7pm Mon-Fri, 11am-4pm Sat & Sun Jul, 9am-3.30pm Mon-Fri early Aug–mid-Jun) is located at Sjøgata's southern end. It has Internet access (per 15 minutes Nkr20) and readily dispenses advice about the best local hiking routes and fishing possibilities on the river Vefsna.

Sights & Activities
SJØGATA

A stroll around the Sjøgata area, with over 100 listed buildings, takes you past galleries, coffee shops, restaurants and private homes in attractively renovated former warehouses, workshops and boatsheds. *The History of a Town* (Nkr25), on sale at the museum, is an excellent small booklet that brings Mosjøen's history to life.

VEFSN MUSEUM
Mosjøen's **museum** (☎ 75 17 23 95; Austerbrygdveien 2; combined ticket Nkr20; ☺ 10am-3.30pm Mon-Fri, 11am-3pm Sun) is in two parts.

In Sjøgata, the **Jakobsensbrygga warehouse** (Sjøgata 31B; ☺ 10am-9pm Mon-Fri, to 2pm Sat Jul, 10am-3.30pm Mon-Fri, to 2pm Sat Aug-Jun) is an excellent small museum that portrays, via some particularly evocative photo blow-ups, the history of Mosjøen from the early 19th century onwards. There's an English guide-pamphlet for each section.

Northeast of the centre, the **rural building collection** (Bygdesamlinga) features 12 farmhouses, shops and the like from the 18th and 19th centuries, which you can view from the exterior. It too has a pamphlet in English. Adjacent is the **Dolstad Kirke** (☺ 8am-3.30pm Mon-Fri mid-Jun–mid-Aug), which dates from 1735 and is built on the site of a medieval church dedicated to St Michael. If it's closed, ask for the key at the museum.

LAKSFORSEN
About 30km south of Mosjøen and a 600m detour from the E6, the roaring 17m-high Laksforsen **waterfall** has leaping salmon in season and makes a pleasant picnic spot, although it's a bit of a struggle to reach the shore below the torrent. The café, a churlish place with its 'no photo' and 'guests only beyond this point' notices, is one to avoid.

Sleeping & Eating
Fru Haugans Hotel (☎ 75 11 41 00; www.fruhaugans .no; Strandgata 39; s/d mid-Jun–mid-Aug from Nkr570/780, rest-of-year Sun-Thu from Nkr1125/1175, Fri & Sat Nkr625/850) Don't be deterred by the bland main façade that somehow slipped past the planning authorities; it's quite out of keeping with the rest of this appealing lodging. The hotel, northern Norway's oldest, occupies several buildings and has grown organically over the years, dating in part from 1794, while its lovely green garden gives panoramic views directly onto the fjord. The annexe has a few cheaper rooms (s/d Nkr425/650) with shared facilities and bags of character.

Mosjøen Camping (☎ 75 17 79 00; www.mosjoen camping.no; Mathias Bruuns gata 24; tent/caravan sites Nkr90/130, cabins Nkr350-480) At this camping ground off the E6, about 500m southeast of the centre, cabins range from basic to considerably more plush, and there's a bowling alley.

Mosjøen Hotell (☎ 75 17 11 55; www.mosjoencamp ing.no; Vollanveien 5; s/d Nkr350/450, with bathroom from Nkr490/750; P ⌨) Under the same ownership as the camping ground, about 100m north of the train station, this run of the mill roadhouse offers cosy, good value but unexceptional rooms.

Heimebakeriet (☎ 75 17 20 90; cnr Jurgensens & CM Havings gates) Pop into another local classic, very different in tone, for a couple of waffles and to savour the intimacy of this historic bakery (1842) that also does coffee, cakes and light dishes.

Oksen Ferdinand (☎ 75 11 99 91; Sjøgata 23; mains Nkr180-290) You can eat very well indeed at this steakhouse, also a historic building, that does tasty fish dishes too.

Café Kulturverkstedet (☎ 75 17 27 60; Sjøgata 22-24) Run by the local heritage society, this delightful café enjoys, appropriately, one of Sjøgata's largest and most appealing renovated buildings. There are books in plenty to leaf through and it also hosts temporary art exhibitions.

Lille Torget (☎ 75 17 04 14; Strandgate 24; ☺ Mon-Sat) With its pub interior (admire the gorgeous Art Nouveau maiden bearing a lamp at its heart) and a terrace giving onto the main square, this one-time bank, then clothing store and now a pub, has seen lots of action over the years. It attracts all ages and you're guaranteed an excellent brew; five of its staff reached the 2003 finals of Norway's annual coffee-making championship.

There are two superb restaurants at Fru Haugans (see left): **Ellenstuen** (mains Nkr200-240) is an intimate place that preserves many of the hotel's original fittings, while **Hagestuen** (mains Nkr155-245), altogether larger and tapestry-bedecked, is an Arctic Menu place.

Getting There & Away
Widerøe flies to/from Mo i Rana (25 minutes) twice daily.

Mosjøen lies on the rail line between Trondheim (Nkr582, 5¼ hours) and Fauske (Nkr439, 3½ hours).

Buses run once or twice daily except Saturday between Mosjøen and Brønnøysund

(Nkr195, 3½ hours); there are also onward connections via Sandnessjøen (Nkr102, 1½ hours, two to three daily).

For drivers, a lovely detour follows the wild and scenic Villmarksveien route, which runs parallel to the E6 east of Mosjøen and approaches the bizarre 1128m peak, Hatten (or Hattfjell); from the road's end, the hike to the top takes about two hours. However, taking this route does cut out Mosjøen itself.

MO I RANA

pop 17,900

Said to be Norway's friendliest town, Mo i Rana (just plain Mo to those who know her) is the third largest city in the north and gateway to the spruce forests, caves and glaciers of the Arctic Circle region, one of Europe's largest wilderness areas. Its friendly reputation is often attributed to its rapid expansion due to the construction of a steel plant; nearly everyone here knows how it once felt to be a stranger in town.

Although Mo's predominant architectural style is boxy, the town is becoming lighter in tone as its heavy industry gives way to a tech-based economy. The **tourist office** (☎ 75 13 92 00; www.arctic-circle.no; Ole Tobias Olsens Gate 3; ⏰ 9am-8pm Mon-Fri, to 4pm Sat, to 7pm Sun mid-Jun–mid-Aug, 9am-4pm Mon-Fri rest-of-year) is exceptionally helpful. It also gives advice about and can make reservations for activities around the region and help in the organisation of a shared taxi to get you there and back.

Sights & Activities

A combined ticket (Nkr20) gives entry to both of Mo's **museums** (⏰ 10am-3pm Tue-Fri year-round & 6-9pm Thu, 10am-2pm Sat mid-Jun–Aug) listed in the details below.

The **Rana Museum of Natural History** (☎ 75 14 61 80; Moholmen) concentrates on the geology, ecology, flora and wildlife of the Arctic Circle region and features several hands-on exhibits that will engage children. Its sister museum, **Rana Museum of Cultural History** (☎ 75 14 61 70; Fridtjof Nansensgata 22) concentrates on the local southern Sami culture and the history of Nordic settlement in southern Nordland.

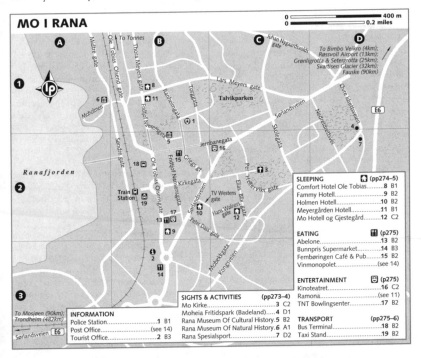

At the **indoor water park** (Moheia Fritidspark; ☎ 75 14 60 60; Øvre Idrettsveien 1; adult/child Nkr75/50; ⏰ noon-8pm Mon-Fri, noon-6pm Sat & Sun), also called Badeland, you can sample the four pools and three saunas – and zoom down its 42m-long water slide.

The oldest building in town, Mo's original **church** (Mo Kirke; ⏰ free guided tours 7.30-9.30pm Mon-Fri mid-Jun–mid-Aug) was constructed in 1724 and renovated later that century. With its steeply pitched roof and onion dome, it deserves to be open to visitors during more than the current brief hours only. In the graveyard is a monument to Russian prisoners who died in captivity and the gravestones of eight British soldiers, killed in commando raids in May 1940.

CAVES

The limestone and marble country northwest of Mo i Rana is riddled with caves and sinkholes, formed when river water dissolved marble between layers of mica schist. Thanks to mineral deposits, the glacial water that runs into ponds and rivers as you approach the caves can change colour from green to grey to blue.

The most accessible and most visited cave is **Grønligrotta** (☎ 75 13 25 06; Grønli; adult/child Nkr85/40; ⏰ tours hourly 10am-7pm mid-Jun–Aug), in business for nearly a century and 25km north of Mo. There's electric lighting (it's the only illuminated tourist cave in Scandinavia) and the 30-minute tour takes you along an underground river, through a rock maze and past a granite block torn off by a glacier and deposited in the cave by the brute force of moving water.

About 1km closer to town, the two-hour trip through **Setergrotta** (☎ 75 16 23 50; Røvassdalen; Nkr175; ⏰ tours 11.30am & 3pm early Jun-late Aug) is considerably more adventurous. Highlights include a couple of extremely tight squeezes and a thrilling shuffle between rock walls while straddling a 15m gorge. The operators provide headlamps, hardhats, gumboots and overalls.

OUTDOOR ACTIVITIES

Two local operators, **Rana Spesialsport** (☎ 90 95 11 08, 75 12 70 88; www.spesialsport.no; Øvre Idrettsveien 35) and **Arctic Viking** (☎ 75 19 38 00; www.arctic-viking.no), offer a range of activities including kayaking, guided hikes and glacier trekking.

Tours

Mo i Rana is also the most convenient base for exploring the **fjords** to the west (although still some 110km away). From the port of Konsvikosen, near Tonnes, **Polarsirkel Maritime** (☎ 75 09 47 90; www.polarsirkel-maritime.no in Norwegian) offers visits to local fjords and a short raft trip (Nkr100 return, operating April to September) to Vikingen (aka Polarsirkeløya), a small island with a globe marking the Arctic Circle. Ferry passengers only get to ride past it as the boats cross the magic line, blasting a celebratory toot. Trips to Hestmanna (Horseman) island (see the boxed text, p33) can also be arranged.

For tours to the **Svartisen glacier**, see p274. There's no public transport from Mo but you can hire a bike from the tourist office (see p274) and pedal the 32km each way to the ferry point beside Svartisen lake.

The tourist office does a pair of daily **guided walks** (Nkr50; ⏰ Jul-late Aug), each leaving its premises at 8pm. You can choose either the one-hour town walk or, for spectacular views, the 90-minute mountain walk (don't be put off by the term; it won't overtax you). Sign up by 4pm on the day.

Sleeping

Fammy Hotell (☎ 75 15 19 99; www.fammy.no in Norwegian; Ole Tobias Olsens Gate 4; s/d/tr Nkr595/695/895) Flats are bright and have minikitchens at this excellent-value, central spot. Ground floor rooms (Nkr100 extra) are particularly large and split level, with the sleeping area upstairs. You might want to choose a rear-facing room as the street can be noisy until the traffic dies down. Guests get a 15% discount at Abelone (see p273), right next door.

Mo Hotell og Gjestegård (☎ 75 15 22 11; fax 75 15 23 38; Elias Blix gate 3; s/d incl breakfast Nkr500/600) Up the hill, this pleasant 15-room guesthouse is in a quiet location and has a small garden where you can sit out and relax.

Meyergården Hotell (☎ 75 13 40 00; www.meyergarden.no; 28 Fridtjof Nansens gate 28; s/d mid-Jun–mid-Aug Nkr670/840, rest-of-year Sun-Thu Nkr1150/1350, Fri & Sat Nkr615/790; **P** 🖥) An affiliate of the Rica chain, Mo's longest-established hotel is full of character with fine rooms, the Romona nightclub and a highly regarded Arctic Menu restaurant. If price is a factor, go for one of the six economical rooms with shared facilities in the original – and much more atmospheric – late-19th-century wing. Reception is genial if a trifle dizzy.

Holmen Hotell (☎ 75 15 14 44; www.rainbow-hotels .no; TV Westens gate 2; s/d mid-Jun–mid-Aug Nkr685/890, rest-of-year Sun-Thu Nkr925/1025, Fri & Sat Nkr650/790; P) The welcome is friendly and rooms are quite plush here, despite the drab exterior.

Comfort Hotel Ole Tobias (☎ 75 15 77 77; www.ole -tobias.no; Thora Meyersgate 2; s/d incl breakfast mid-Jun–mid-Aug Nkr740/1040, rest-of-year Sun-Thu Nkr1125/1295, Fri & Sat Nkr690/850) This railway-themed hotel – the corridor carpets simulate a railway track and each room has the name of a station – commemorates the local teacher and priest who convinced the government to build the Nordlandsbanen railway connecting Trondheim with Fauske and Bodø. As well as breakfast, tariffs include a light evening meal.

Eating

Abelone (☎ 75 15 38 88; Ole Tobias Olsens Gate 6; mains Nkr174-194) Abelone looks unprepossessing from the street but inside the simulated log cabin makes for a very congenial dining environment. The emphasis is on quality meat dishes, especially beef.

Bimbo Veikro (☎ 75 15 10 01; Saltfjelletveien 34; mains Nkr65-190) North of town, this roadhouse has something for everyone. It serves up the usual sandwiches, pizzas and grills, for bimbos, himbos and the rest of us (the 'truck drivers' special' is eggs, bacon, beans and potatoes for Nkr80). And it's also an Arctic Menu restaurant, offering altogether more subtle fare. 'Bimbo' alludes to a nearby elephant-shaped rock formation, not the classy waitresses.

For liquid picnics, both Bunnpris supermarket and Vinmonopolet are just south of the tourist office.

Drinking

Penetrate the narrow doorway and climb the stairs to the first floor to **Fembøringen Café & Pub** (☎ 75 15 09 77; Jernbanegata 12), a cosy, casual pub that would have been blue with smoke in the good ol' days before tobacco prohibition.

Entertainment

Ramona (☎ 75 13 40 00; Fridtjof Nansensgata 28) Within the Meyergården Hotell, this spot – here comes another superlative – claims to be the largest nightclub in northern Norway.

ARCTIC MENU

To guarantee yourself a good meal in northern Norway, visit a restaurant affiliated to the Arctic Menu scheme. Members, who range from small, family-owned concerns to the restaurants of chain hotels, undertake to use the region's natural ingredients. It may be a sauce, simmered with local berries, an Arctic char, pulled from the icy waters, reindeer, seal, whale or, of course, cod – every last bit of it from the rich flesh to local delicacies such as the cheek, roe, liver, stomach or tongue.

You'll find such restaurants indicated within a town's Eating section. The scheme's website (www.arktiskmeny.no) has a full list of its 30 or so participants and most tourist offices carry its booklet. This comes complete with a few recipes so you can try a dish or two out back home – if, that is, you can get those fresh, northern Norway ingredients...

Kinoteatret (☎ 75 14 60 50; Rådhusplass 1) Mo i Rana's cinema is at the top of Jernbanegata.

TNT Bowlingsenter (☎ 75 15 78 00; Fridtjof Nansensgata 1) You can go bowling here for Nkr50 per round at peak times.

Getting There & Away

Widerøe flies from Mo i Rana's Røssvoll airport, 14km from town, to/from Bodø (two to four times daily), Mosjøen (twice daily) and Trondheim (once daily). Every flight is fabulous, unless it's misty down below, with excellent views of the Svartisen icecaps.

By bus, your options are fairly limited. There are services daily except Saturday between Mo i Rana and Sandnessjøen (Nkr153, 3¼ hours). From Sunday to Friday there's at least one daily Ranaekspressen bus to and from Mosjøen (Nkr98, two hours). For information about journeys to/from Umeå in Sweden, see p392.

Most visitors arrive at Mo i Rana's attractive octagonal **train station** (☎ 75 15 01 77) on the two or three daily trains from Trondheim (Nkr690, 6½ hours) or Fauske (Nkr270, 2¼ hours).

Getting Around

Flytaxi (☎ 90 16 21 57) does an airport run for all flights, calling by major hotels.

If you're driving, pick up a free visitors' parking permit, valid for four hours, from the tourist office, which also hires bicycles (per hour/day Nkr40/150).

Call ☎ 7550 for a taxi.

SALTFJELLET-SVARTISEN NATIONAL PARK

The 2105-sq-km Saltfjellet-Svartisen National Park combines the Svartisen icecap (Norway's second largest icefield, with its rugged peaks, a combined area of 369 sq km); and the high and rolling moor lands of the Salfjellet massif near the Swedish border.

Information

The best map to use is Statens Kartverk's *Turkart Saltfjellet*, at a scale of 1:100,000.
Bodø og Omegn Turistforening DNT office (☎ 75 52 14 13; Storgata 17) Visit this place for information about western Svartisen. For the eastern side, your best bet is the Mo i Rana tourist office.

Statskog-Helgeland National Foresty Authority (in Mo i Rana ☎ 75 15 79 50, in Fauske ☎ 75 64 59 66) This place has national park information.

Svartisen

The two Svartisen icecaps, separated by the valley Vesterdalen, straddle the Arctic Circle between Mo i Rana and the Meløy peninsula. At its highest, the icecap averages about 1500m altitude but some of its tongues lick into the valleys to become the lowest-lying glaciers in Europe outside of Iceland and Svalbard. Svartisen can be visited from either the east or west, but to travel between the two main access points requires a major technical expedition on foot and a one- or two-day detour in a car. Most visitors to the glacier just make a quick hop by boat, but hikers will find more joy approaching from the east.

VESTISEN

The estranged Vestisen icecap probably attracts more visitors than any other part of the park. Travellers along the Kystriks-veien will catch glimpses of the Svartisen icecap from the Kilboghamn–Jektvik and Ågskardet–Forøy ferries, and there are good views from the highway along Holandsfjorden. From Holand, **ferries** (☎ 94 86 55 16; adult/child return Nkr60/30) shuttle at least four times daily across Holandsfjorden to the tip

of the Engebreen glacial tongue. **Polarsirkel Maritime** (☎ 75 09 47 90; www.polarsirkel-maritime.no in Norwegian) also runs journeys to the glacier from the port of Tonnes, if you reserve in advance.

A 15-minute walk from the ferry landing takes you to the **Svartisen Turistsenter** (☎ 75 75 00 11; www.svartisen.no; ☼ Jun–mid-Aug) with its café and shop. It does guided five-hour glacier walks (Nkr500 including gear) from the end of Engabrevatnet lake. Reserve in advance. Independent hikers can slog up the steep route along the glacier's edge to the Tåkeheimen hut, near the summit of Helgelandsbukken (1454m).

Northbound travellers on the Hurti-gruten coastal ferry can visit the Svartisen glacier as an optional add-on to their journey. You can also get there by boat/bus combination from Bodø (check with the tourist office for schedules).

ØSTISEN

From the end of the Svartisdalen road, 20km up the valley from Røssvoll (the airport for Mo i Rana), **ferries** (☎ 75 16 23 79; adult/child Nkr80/40 return; ☼ mid-Jun–Aug) cross Svartisen lake (Svartisvatnet) at least four times daily. It takes 20 minutes. From the ferry landing at the western end of the lake, it's a 3km hike to the beginning of the Auster-dalsisen glacier tongue, which has receded about 1km in the past two decades. There's a kiosk and camping ground at the lake.

From the end of the road you can also trek up to the hut on the shore of the mountain lake Pikhaugsvatnet, surrounded by peaks and ice. This is an excellent base for day hikes up the Glomdal valley or to the Flatisen glacier. Experienced technical climbers will find excellent challenges on Nordre Kamplitinden (1532m) and Skiptinden (1591m).

Saltfjellet

The landscape along the Arctic Circle is characterised by the broad upland plateaus of the Saltfjellet massif, connecting the peaks surrounding the Svartisen icecap and the Swedish border. Dotted around this relatively inhospitable wilderness are numerous fences and sacrificial sites attributed to the Sami people; some sites date from as early as the 9th century and evidence suggests reindeer-herding as early as the 16th century.

A 15km walk to the east leads to Graddis, near the Swedish border, and the venerable **Graddis Fjellstue og Camping** (☎ 75 69 43 41; fax 75 69 43 88; s Nkr400, d 520-620; ☯ mid-Jun–mid-Aug). This cosy little guesthouse, run by the same family since its establishment in 1867; is an excellent base to launch yourself into one of Norway's least tramped hiking areas. Camping is also available. (Have a look at Methuselah, the 1000-year-old pine tree, which is 200m from the hostel.)

One of the area's best short hikes leads through the wildly twisting Junkerdalsura gorge, a rich botanical reserve. From Storfjord, where the E6 and Rv77 intersect, head east and cross the swinging bridge over the Junkerdal river. After 200m, you'll reach an information notice board. From there, a hiking path follows an old cart track for 4km up the gorge to the Junkerdalen bridge, near the village of Solvågli.

Getting There & Away
Rail travellers can disembark at Lønsdal en route between Fauske and Trondheim, but you may have to request a stop. By car, access to Saltfjellet is either along the E6 or the Rv77, which follows the southern slope of the Junkerdalen valley.

ARCTIC CIRCLE CENTRE
Precisely 66°33' N latitude marks the southernmost extent of the midnight sun on the summer solstice and the ragged edge of the polar night on the winter solstice. As the Arctic Highway between Mo i Rana and Fauske cuts across this imaginary line, it should be a magical moment.

However, the **Polarsirkelsenteret** (☎ 75 12 96 96; E6, Rognan; optional exhibition adult/child/family Nkr50/20/100; ☯ 8am or 10am-10pm mid-May–mid-Sep), beside the E6 and surrounded by the bleak moors adjoining Saltfjellet-Svartisen National Park, is a bit of a tourist trap. There's an exhibition of stuffed wildlife and an audiovisual presentation on the Arctic regions, but the place exists mostly to stamp postcards with a special Arctic Circle postmark and sell certificates (Nkr50) for visitors to authenticate crossing the line. There's also boreal kitsch – miniature polar bears, trolls and other fluffy, furry things – by the basket load. More sober and serious are the memorials to the forced Slav labourers who, during WWII, constructed

the Arctic Highway for the occupying German forces.

Northbound travellers will feel spirits rising again as they descend into a relatively lush, green environment, more typical of northern Norway.

FAUSKE
pop 6000
Fauske is known mainly for marble quarrying and its 'Norwegian Rose' stone features in many a monumental building, including the Oslo Rådhus, the UN headquarters in New York and the Emperor's palace in Tokyo. It's also the jumping-off point for Sulitjelma and the Rago National Park. From here, northbound rail passengers must hop on a bus to continue to Tromsø.

Unless you're pressed for time, it's well worth making a detour west to Bodø, the northern end of the Kystriksveien Coastal Route, interesting in its own right and port for a popular ferry route to southern Lofoten. The **tourist office** (☎ 75 64 33 03; www .saltenreiseliv.no; Sjøgata 86; ☯ 9am-6pm Mon-Fri, 10am-5pm Sat & Sun mid-Jun–mid-Aug, 8.30am-3pm Mon-Fri rest-of-year) provides information on the surrounding natural areas. It sells samples and various artefacts, from pocket-sized to seriously chunky, tooled in the streaky salmon-coloured Fauske marble. During July, it can arrange a guided tour (adult/child Nkr100/50) of the largest of the local quarries.

Sights
Sights in town include the marble-themed **town square**, and the park-like collection of historic buildings of the **Fauske Bygdetun museum** (☎ 75 64 46 98; Sjøgata; adult/child/family Nkr30/15/50; ☯ 10am-6pm Mon-Fri, to 6pm Sat & Sun late Jun-late Aug, 7.30am-3pm Mon-Fri late Aug-late Jun), which makes a lovely spot for a picnic.

Sleeping & Eating
Lundhøgda Camp & Café (☎ 75 64 39 66; lunghogda@ c2i.net; Lundveien; sites Nkr100, 4-bed cabins Nkr250-550) This complex, situated 3km west of town, has superb views of the fjord and surrounding peaks.

Seljestua (☎ 90 73 46 96; seljestua@hotmail.com; Seljeveien 2; s/d Nkr350/400; ☯ late Jun–mid-Aug) This student residence, 500m from the train station, functions as a summer hostel and can offer family rooms with bathroom.

NORDLAND

Fauske Hotell (☎ 75 60 20 00; www.rica.no; Storgata 82; s/d Nkr700/850 midJun–mid-Aug, rest-of-year Sun-Thu Nk875/1380, rest-of-year Fri & Sat Nkr832/1059; 🖳) Fauske's only year-round upmarket choice has renovated, cheerful rooms although common areas feel decidedly dated. The restaurant does an Arctic Menu.

Brygga Hotell (☎ 75 64 63 45; s/d Nkr700/850; 🕙 mid-Jun–Jul) This less monolithic 30-room annexe of the Fauske Hotell, right beside the fjord, is an attractive alternative, should you pass through town during the brief window when it's open.

Huset (☎ 75 64 41 01; Storgata 74) This attractive eating choice on the main street does prime cuts of meat with garnishing, sold by weight, and other meaty mains (Nkr150 to Nkr210). It also has an imaginative range of snacks and salads (Nkr78 to Nkr90), plus the inevitable pizza.

Getting There & Away
BUS
The popular Nord-Norgeekspressen between Bodø (Nkr99, 1¼ hours) and Narvik (Nkr381, 5½ hours) passes through Fauske twice daily and on the especially scenic Narvik route allows substantial discounts for holders of ScanRail, Inter-Rail and Eurail passes. You can also travel directly to Lofoten on the Fauske–Lofoten Ekspressen, which crosses to Sortland (Nkr367, 5¼ hours, twice daily); one bus daily continues to Svolvær (Nkr517, 8½ hours).

To/from Harstad, on the Vesterålen island of Hinnøya, you can take the daily Togbussen (Nkr343, 5½ hours). The Saltens Bilruter local bus between Fauske and Bodø (Nkr90, 1¼ hours) runs at least three times daily.

TRAIN
Trains ply the Nordlandsbanen between Trondheim (Nkr830, 10 hours) and Bodø (Nkr92, 45 minutes), via Fauske, at least twice daily and there are additional trains (up to five daily) between Fauske and Bodø.

AROUND FAUSKE
Saltdal & Blood Road Museums
Saltdal Historical Village (☎ 75 68 22 90; Saltdal; adult/child/family Nkr30/15/50; 🕙 11am-6pm Mon-Fri, 1-4pm Sat, 1-6pm Sun, 20 Jun-20 Aug), just off the E6 near Saltnes, is a collection of rural

and fishing-related buildings. Within the grounds is the **Blood Road Museum.** In an old German barracks, it reveals conditions for Allied prisoners of war who died building the highway between Saltnes and Saksenvik. The prisoners' cemetery (some 7000 souls) is about 3km north, in Botn.

Sulitjelma
As an interpretive panel just north of Fauske will confirm, you're exactly half way along the E6 and it's an appropriate moment to break free from the Arctic Highway for a short while.

It's a gorgeous 40km run along the Rv830, up scenic Langvassdalen to the tiny community of Sulitjelma. It wasn't always such a backwater; in 1860, a Sami herder discovered copper ore in the forested country north of Langvatnet and suddenly the Sulitjelma region was attracting all sorts of opportunists from southern Norway. Large ore deposits were discovered and the Sulitjelma Gruber mining company was founded in 1891. By 1928, the wood-fuelled smelter had taken its toll on the surrounding birch forests, as did high concentrations of CO_2, a by-product of the smelting process. Nowadays, with the furnaces long since cold, the environment is well on its way to recovery.

SIGHTS & ACTIVITIES
A one-hour guided tour of the **Sulitjelma Show Mine** (Besøksgruve; ☎ 75 64 06 95; adult/child Nkr125/50; 🕙 1pm mid-May–early Aug) includes a 1.5km rail ride deep into the mountain.

Beside the fjord, the **Sulitjelma Mining Museum** (Gruvemuseum; ☎ 75 64 02 40; adult/child/family Nkr20/10/50; 🕙 10am-6pm Sun-Fri, noon-3pm Sat mid-Jun–early Aug) records the area's 100 years of mining history and displays some awesome, rusting equipment.

The country east and south of Sulitjelma enjoys especially scenic glacial surroundings and there are ample **hiking** opportunities. Trekkers can choose from several routes past nine major huts – pick up a DNT key from Fauske's tourist office.

For technical climbers, favoured destinations are the three *nunataks* (mountain peaks protruding through a glacier or icecap), Vardetoppen (1722m), Stortoppen (1830m) and Sulistoppen (1930m), all in the Sulitjelmasisen icecap. The 123-sq-km

Blåmannsisen icecap (1571m), further north, is also extremely popular and is associated with a rather famous saga (see the boxed text, p33).

The topo sheets to use are *Låmivatnet* (sheet 2229-III), *Sulitjelma* (sheet 2129-II) and *Balvatnet* (sheet 2128-I), all at 1:50,000.

SLEEPING

Jakobsbakken Fjellsenter (☎ 75 64 02 90; dm Nkr110, apt with bathroom & kitchen Nkr550; ✌ Mar-Dec) This hilltop, church-run facility, in a one-time mining community at the end of the road, has great views of the surrounding valleys and makes an excellent, economical base for enticing day-walks. Dorms range from two to six beds.

Sulitjelma Turistsenter (☎ /fax 75 64 04 33; scamfri@online.no; Daja; tent/caravan sites Nkr100/120, cabins with bathroom Nkr500) It's a 3.5km drive beyond the mining museum, the last 750m or so on dirt road, to this attractively sited camping ground with a small lake just below. Run by a taciturn couple, it's open year-round and you can rent a rowing boat or canoe (per hour Nkr30). There's great walking hereabouts too, with one signed trail leading directly from the site.

Rago National Park

The small (167 sq km), scarcely visited **Rago National Park** is a rugged chunk of forested granite mountains and moor lands, riven with deep glacial cracks and capped by great icefields. Rago, together with the large adjoining Swedish parks, Pakjelanta, Sarek and Stora Sjöfjallet, belongs to a protected area of 5500 sq km. Wildlife includes not only beavers in the deep Laksåga (aka Nordfjord) river valley, but also wolverines in the higher areas.

Rago is best known, however, for the series of foaming cascades and spectacular waterfalls in the relatively lush Storskogdalen valley; from bottom to top, they include Værivassfoss (200m), Trollfoss (43m) and Storskogsfoss (18m).

For serious hikers hoping to escape the crowds, hotel-like huts and highway-like tracks typical of the most popular Norwegian national parks, Rago is the place to go. From the main trailhead at Lakshol, it's a three-hour, 7km walk up the valley to the free Storskogvasshytta and Ragohytta huts, then a stiff climb up and over the ridge into Sweden to connect with the well-established trail system over the border.

Maps to use for the park are *Sisovatnet* (sheet 2129-I), at a scale of 1:50,000, or *Sørfold*, at 1:75,000. To reach Lakshol, turn east off the E6 at the Trengsel bridge and continue about 6km to the end of the road.

Several daily buses (No 2 and 841) run from Fauske (Nkr40, one hour). Ask the driver to stop at Trengsel bru, and mention that you are going to Rago National Park.

NARVIK

pop 14,200

Narvik was established in 1902 as an ice-free port for the rich Kiruna iron mines in Swedish Lapland. Recently it's begun to capitalise on the unique sporting and sightseeing activities available in its majestic, wild and historic surroundings, including the spectacular Ofotbanen Railway to Sweden.

History

The Narvik region was inhabited as early as the Stone Age, as evidenced by the distinct rock carving of a moose found at Vassvik, northwest of the centre.

During WWII, control of this strategic port was essential to the Nazi war machine, intent upon halting iron supplies to the Allies and usurping the bounty. In April 1940, 10 German destroyers ploughed through a blizzard to enter the port and sink two Norwegian battleships. Next day five British destroyers arrived and a fierce naval battle resulted in the loss of two ships on each side. In May, British, Norwegian, French and Polish troops disembarked and took back the town.

But the Germans didn't retreat and the town was decimated, as evidenced by the remains of soldiers in the cemeteries and 34 ships of five nations (Norway, Britain, France, the Netherlands and Germany) in the harbour. On 8 June 1940 the Allies surrendered Narvik, which remained under German control until 8 May 1945.

Although the town was admirably rebuilt, downtown Narvik is less than prepossessing (some would say it's ugly). Still, the surrounding fjord, forest and mountain country borders on the spectacular in all directions, and the trans-shipment facility bisecting the city still loads ore from rail cars onto ships and is fascinating in a big-machinery sort of way.

NORDLAND

NARVIK

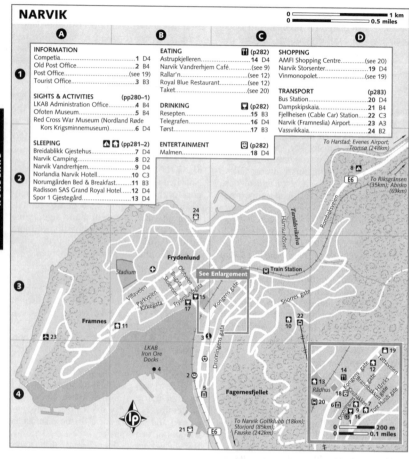

INFORMATION
Competia..............................1 D4
Old Post Office....................2 B4
Post Office.......................(see 19)
Tourist Office......................3 B3

SIGHTS & ACTIVITIES (pp280-1)
LKAB Administration Office.........4 B4
Ofoten Museum.....................5 B4
Red Cross War Museum (Nordland Røde
   Kors Krigsminnemuseum)...........6 D4

SLEEPING (pp281-2)
Breidablikk Gjestehus...............7 D4
Narvik Camping.....................8 D2
Narvik Vandrerhjem.................9 D4
Norlandia Narvik Hotell.............10 C3
Norumgården Bed & Breakfast......11 B3
Radisson SAS Grand Royal Hotel.....12 D4
Spor 1 Gjestegård.................13 D4

EATING (p282)
Astrupkjelleren....................14 D4
Narvik Vandrerhjem Café.........(see 9)
Rallar'n........................(see 12)
Royal Blue Restaurant...........(see 12)
Taket..........................(see 20)

DRINKING (p282)
Resepten.........................15 B3
Telegrafen.......................16 D4
Tørst............................17 B3

ENTERTAINMENT (p282)
Malmen...........................18 D4

SHOPPING
AMFI Shopping Centre............(see 20)
Narvik Storsenter.................19 D4
Vinmonopolet...................(see 19)

TRANSPORT (p283)
Bus Station.......................20 D4
Dampskipskaia....................21 B4
Fjellheisen (Cable Car) Station.....22 C3
Narvik (Framneslia) Airport.........23 A3
Vassvikkaia.......................24 B2

Orientation

Straddling a valley that contains the huge iron ore docks, Narvik is surrounded by islands to the west and mountains in every other direction, while spectacular fjords stretch north and south. The E6 (Kongens gate) slices through the heart of town. The train station is at the north end of town and the bus station, just beside the AMFI shopping centre.

Information

Competia (☎ 76 97 72 22; 52 Dronningens gate; per min Nkr1; ☿ 9am-4pm Mon-Fri) For Internet access.

Tourist office (☎ 76 94 33 09; www.destinationnarvik .com; Kongens gate 26; ☿ 9am-5pm Mon-Fri, 10am-2pm Sat, 11am-2pm Sun early Jun, 9am-7pm Mon-Fri,

10am-5pm Sat, 11am-5pm Sun mid-Jun–mid-Aug, 9am-5pm Mon-Fri, 10am-3pm Sat late Aug, 8.30am-3.30pm Mon-Fri Sep-May) Has a particularly good website. Holds DNT cabin keys.

Sights

Narvik's **Red Cross War Museum** (Nordland Røde Kors Krigsminnemuseum; ☎ 76 94 44 26; Kongens gate; adult/child Nkr50/25; ☿ 10am-10pm Mon-Sat, noon-6pm Sun mid-Jun–mid-Aug, 11am-3pm daily rest-of-year) admirably illustrates the military campaigns fought hereabouts in the early years of WWII. The presentation may not be flash but it will still stun you.

The unique **Ofoten Museum** (☎ 76 96 00 50; Administrasjonsveien 3; adult/child Nkr30/15; ☿ 10am-3pm Mon-Fri, noon-3pm Sat & Sun late Jun-early Aug, 10am-3pm

Mon-Fri early Aug-late Jun) occupies a wonderfully colourful early-20th-century building and tells of Narvik's farming, railway building and ore trans-shipment heritage. Most interesting is the collection of historic photos, contrasted with modern photos taken from the same angles.

In the park just up the road is the restored building that served as the **post office** from 1888 to 1898.

The vast **LKAB iron ore trans-shipment complex**, an impressive tangle of rusty industrial machinery, conveyors, ovens, railways and heaps of iron pellets, has a strange intimidating appeal and says it all about Narvik's *raison d'être*. An average tanker-load of ore weighs in at 125,000 to 175,000 tonnes and takes an entire day to load. Tours (adult/child Nkr40/20, minimum six participants) leave from the LKAB administration offices at 3pm from mid-June to mid-August. Times may vary so do check with the tourist office.

Above the town, the **Fjellheisen cable car** (☎ 76 94 16 05; Mårveien; adult/child Nkr100/60 return; 1-9pm early Jun & Aug, 10-1am mid-Jun–Jul) climbs 656m for breathtaking views over the surrounding peaks and fjords, weather permitting. Several marked walking trails radiate from its top station.

Activities

For **hiking** inspiration, pick up a copy of *Seven Easy Walking Tours in the Fringe of Urban Narvik* (Nkr20) from the tourist office, which has a similar illustrated guide to mountain bike routes in preparation. **Narvik og Omegns Turistforening** (www.narvikfjell.no) is an excellent source of information about hiking and hikers' cabins.

A popular hike that parallels the **Ofotbanen railway** (☎ 76 92 32 50) is along the old navvy trail, the **Rallarveien**. Few people actually walk the entire way between Sweden's Abisko National Park and the sea, opting instead for all or part of the descent from Riksgränsen or Bjørnfell (in Norway) to Rombaksbotn at the head of the fjord, the location of the main camp when the railway was being built (it's since returned to nature). The E10 also runs roughly parallel and you can catch a boat from Rombaksbotn back to Narvik. The tourist office sells, *Hikes Along the Navvy Road* (Nkr45), a booklet that includes a good map of the

route from Abisko to Rombaksbotn. For more information about the Ofotbanen railway, see p281.

From late autumn until June, Fjellheisen cable car above town will take you some 1000m up for trail and off-piste **skiing** (☎ 76 96 04 94; ski@narvikinfo.no) with outstanding views as a bonus. You can also ski at Riksgränsen, just across the Swedish border (see p281).

Narvik Dyk & Aventyr (☎ 99 51 22 05) and **Narvik Wreck Diving** (☎ 76 94 41 44) can set you up with diving equipment to check out the local waters, chock-a-block with sunken ships from WWII.

The fjord-side journey to the **Narvik Golfklubb** (☎ 76 95 12 01; full round Nkr350, club rental Nkr100) at Skjomendalen is wondrous (follow the signs to Skjomdal just before the Skjomen bridge on the E6, about 18km south of town). Sheer, treacherous faces will leave you guessing how there could possibly be a golf course here. Yet nature works wonders, and there's a valley hidden amid the peaks. Not a golfer? There's also worthwhile hiking nearby.

Tours

Boat tours of the fjord (adult/child/family Nkr180/110/450 return) leave Narvik's Vassvikkaia quay to Rombaksbotn at 5pm on Saturday and Sunday from early July to mid-August, returning from Rombaksbotn at 6pm. Buy your ticket at the train station.

Festivals & Events

Each year in March, Narvik holds its **Vinterfestuka**, an action-packed winter week of events, partly in commemoration of the navvies who built the railway.

On the last Saturday in June, some 2000 walkers take the train to various stops along the Rallarveien and hike back to party at Rombaksbotn. Off-road cyclists, by contrast, should plan to be around in late June for the annual **Scandinavian Free Ride** (www.freeridefestival.com), a whole week of mountain bike events.

Sleeping

Spor 1 Gjestegård (☎ 76 94 60 20; post@spor1.no; Brugata 2a; dm Nkr160-200, s/d 450/500) The welcome at 'Trail 1' begins with the pots of fresh flowers flanking the entrance. In former rail cabins by the tracks, it has a sauna,

---

AUTHOR'S CHOICE ✓

Norumgården Bed & Breakfast (☎ 76 94 48 57; http://norumgaarden.narviknett.no; Framnesveien 127; s/d Nkr350/500, d with kitchen Nkr600; ☺ late Jan-Nov) This little treasure of a place (it has only four rooms so reservations are essential) is very special and offers excellent value. Used as a German officer's mess in WWII (the owner will proudly show you a 1940 bottle of Coca Cola, made under licence in Hamburg), it nowadays brims with antiques and character. Choose the Heidi room (it's the only one without a shower but the little balcony more than compensates) and you'll be sleeping in the bed once occupied by King Olav.

---

kitchen and great pub with outdoor terrace. You're guaranteed a good chat; its enthusiastic hosts are themselves experienced backpackers.

Breidablikk Gjestehus (☎ 76 94 14 18; www.breidablikk.no in Norwegian; Tore Hunds gate 41; dm/s/d Nkr185/425/550; P 🖳) The higher rooms in this pleasant hillside *pension* have sweeping views over town. It's a cheerful place with a cosy communal lounge and serves a delicious buffet breakfast. Dorms have four beds.

Narvik Camping (☎ 76 94 58 10; Rombaksveien 75; tent/caravan sites Nkr100/180; 4-/6-bed cabins with bathroom Nkr550/650) This camping ground, overlooking the fjord and main road, is 2km northeast of the centre. A reader reports that tent sights, near the E6, can be noisy.

Narvik Vandrerhjem (☎ 76 96 22 00; narvik.hostel@wandrerhjem.no; Dronningens gate 58; dm Nkr140-170, s/d 350/450; P) Narvik's youth hostel has recently moved to smart new premises in a former hotel. Its 30 beds are quickly snapped up in summer so do reserve.

Norlandia Narvik Hotell (☎ 76 96 48 00; www.norlandia.no; Skistuaveien 8; s/d from Nkr625/790) Located at the base of the cable car, you'll find a rustic atmosphere, comfy rooms and friendly staff.

Raddison SAS Grand Royal Hotel (☎ 76 97 70 00; www.radissonsas.com; Kongens gate 64; s/d mid-Jun–mid-Aug Nkr770/980, Fri & Sat year-round, Sun-Thu rest-of-year Nkr1090/1230; P 🖳) Narvik's top-of-the-line hotel, although something of a monolith from the exterior, makes an attractive stopover. There's a free sauna for guests,

a beauty salon and a few handicapped-equipped rooms.

Eating

Grand Royal Hotel (www.radissonsas.com; Kongens gate 64) This hotel has a pair of great dining options. Its **Royal Blue Restaurant** (☎ 97 70 76) does a tempting three-course Arctic Menu. If your stomach's really flapping, tuck into their hugely varied buffet dinner. For lighter fare **Rallar'n** (☎ 76 97 70 77), its pub, has pizza, pasta and creative mains (Nkr160 to Nkr220), such as pan-fried char fillet (Nkr160).

Astrupkjelleren (☎ 76 94 04 02; Kinobakken 1; mains Nkr160-235) Established in 1903, the year after Narvik itself, Astrupkjelleren, with its thick stone walls, dim lighting and intimate corners, has an almost conspiratorial air about it. Strong on fish dishes and popular for its off-menu fillet of reindeer (Nkr295), it also offers huge servings of pasta, steak and other local specialities.

Narvik Vandrerhjem (☎ 76 96 22 00; narvik.hostel@wandrerhjem.no; Dronningens gate 58; dinner Nkr14) This light, pleasant, self-service café serves food between 11am and 5.30pm.

Taket (☎ 76 96 34 30; AFMI shopping centre; mains Nkr69-168) In addition to the usual snack and sandwich fare, Taket does a range of wraps and stir-fried noodles. Pick a window seat for great city views.

Narvik's Vinmonopolet is on the 3rd floor of the Narvik Storsenter.

Drinking & Entertainment

Telegrafen (☎ 76 95 43 00; Dronningens gate 56) This popular hang-out attracts the 20-to-35-crowd. It shows sport on wide-screen TV and has occasional live bands (with cover charge).

Taket (☎ 76 96 34 30; AFMI shopping centre) A daytime café that gets gussied up at 8pm prompt, dusts down its long bar and becomes a lively pub. There's a disco on Wednesday, Friday and Saturday.

In winter, the bar at the **Norlandia Narvik Hotell** (☎ 76 96 48 00; www.norlandia.no; Skistuaveien 8) is Narvik's leading après-ski venue.

Over the bridge from the centre are a couple of good pubs. **Resepten** (☎ 76 94 26 38; Industriveien 5) has an intimate atmosphere, while **Tørst** (☎ 76 95 51 50; Brugata 3) is more your down-to-earth neighbourhood drop-in.

The weekend disco at **Malmen** (☎ 76 94 20 00; Kongens gate 44) attracts mostly students.

Getting There & Away

AIR
There are two to five daily flights to/from Bodø (40 minutes) from Narvik's small Framneslia airport, on the Framnes peninsula about 3km west of the centre. All other flights leave from Evenes airport, 1¼ hours away, which Narvik shares with Harstad.

BOAT
The Arctic Fjord Express sails once daily, June to September (twice a week in winter) to/from Svolvær (Nkr310, 3½ hours) from the Dampskipskaia dock on Havnegata, 1km south of the centre along Kongens gate.

BUS
Nor-Way Bussekspress runs twice daily between Narvik and Bodø (Nkr467, 6½ hours) via Fauske (Nkr381, 4½ hours). The Narvik–Lofoten Ekspressen runs once daily between Narvik and Leknes (Nkr501, 6¼ hours) via Sortland (Nkr297, 3¼ hours) and Svolvær (Nkr436, 5¾ hours).

Nord-Norgeekspressen buses between Narvik and Tromsø (Nkr320, 4¼ hours) ply at least three times daily.

TRAIN
Heading for Sweden, there are at least two daily services between Narvik and Bjørnfjell (50 minutes), continuing to Riksgränsen (one hour) and Kiruna (three hours). Trains continue to Boden (six hours), from where you can pick up connections to Stockholm (20½ hours) and Gothenburg (25¼ hours).

The route takes you up the spectacular Ofotbanen Railway and, in Sweden, past Abisko National Park, which offers excellent hiking and lovely Arctic scenery.

Getting Around
Narvik's Framneslia airport is 3km from the centre. Flybussen buses between Narvik and Harstad's Evenes airport run six to 10 times daily (Nkr95, 1¼ hours). For a taxi, phone ☎ 07550.

OFOTBANEN RAILWAY & RALLARVEIEN
The mountain-hugging **Ofotbanen railway** (☎ 76 92 32 50) spans a range of landscapes – fjord-side cliffs, birch forests and rocky plateaus – all within 55 minutes between

SVARTABJØRN
No one knows for sure whether there actually was a comely cook nicknamed Svartabjørn (Black Bear) who dished up meals for the navvies that built the railway of the Ofoten line. But her name certainly lives on in legend and in fiction. In his Malm trilogy, published in 1914, novelist Ernst Didring recounts some of the stories the navvies passed on to him.

It's said that this dark, beautiful girl, although still too young to be away from home, got on well with the rail workers and was a great little cook into the bargain. But she fell in love with the same man that another woman coveted and was beaten to death with a laundry paddle.

The navvies arranged for her burial at the Tornehamn cemetery. Today, the grave bears the name Anna Norge, but the date of death has been changed at least three times to fit different women who at different times have been assumed to be the true Svartabjørn.

Narvik and the Swedish border. It was constructed by migrant labourers (navvies) at the end of the 19th century to connect Narvik with the iron ore mines at Kiruna, in Sweden's far north, and was opened by King Oscar II in 1903. Currently it transports 14 to 16 million tonnes of iron ore annually and is also a major magnet for visitors.

The train route from Narvik train station to Riksgränsen, the ski resort just inside Sweden (one hour, adult Nkr100 each way, including up to two children), features some 50 tunnels and snowsheds. You'll also see the impressive Norddal trestle, used from 1902 to 1988 when the line was shifted to the north. It was built to last by a German engineering firm, MAN, and the Nazis, ironically, were unable to destroy it in WWII. Towards the Narvik end of the rail line, you can also see the wreck of the German ship *Georg Thiele* at the edge of the fjord.

You can run the line as a day or half-day trip, leaving Narvik at 11.10am and returning from Svenskegrensen, the border station, at 12.50pm or 5.20pm.

The big summer attraction at Riksgränsen is an **exhibition** (☎ 46-0980 431 11 in

Sweden; Riksgränsen; exhibition & slide show Nkr60) of stunning nature photographs of the region by Sven Hörnell, the Swedish photographer who live here for half a century until his death in 1992. Although the narration of the accompanying slide show is usually in Swedish, the photos and music speak for themselves.

Riksgränsen has a big ski hotel, the **Riksgränsen Turiststation hotel** (☎ 46-0980 400 80 in Sweden; www.riksgransen.nu; Riksgränsen; s/d from Nkr630/950; ☯ mid-Feb–Sep). The ski season normally runs mid-February to midsummer.

In Sweden, several long-distance trails radiate out from the railway, including the connecting route with Øvre Dividal National Park, in the Norwegian county of Troms, and the world-renowned Kungsleden, which heads south from Abisko into the heart of Sweden.

KYSTRIKSVEIEN – THE COASTAL ROUTE

At Steinkjer in Trøndelag, road travellers must choose: the Arctic Highway to Narvik, or the slower, less-frequented, more expensive – but incredibly beautiful – E17, the 650km-long Kystriksveien (Coastal Route) with Bodø at its northern end. There's magic (and a photo opportunity) around every bend here, and if you have a vehicle and enough cash for the ferries – or enough time to take the buses – you won't want to miss it. Many Norwegians agree that this is the best of mainland Norway – or very close to it.

Be sure to see the note on p269. That free *Kystriksveien* booklet, distributed by tourist offices and many lodgings along the way, is a mini-Bible and the Coastal Route's website, www.rv17.no, gives even more detail. For information on the southern Kystriksveien, see p264.

BRØNNØYSUND
pop 4300
Brønnøysund is surrounded on one side by an archipelago of islets in a tropical-looking sea and on the other by lovely farm country. Its **tourist office** (☎ 75 01 80 00; www.visithelgeland .com; ☯ 9am-7pm Mon-Fri, 10am-6pm Sat, noon-6pm Sun mid-Jun–mid-Aug, 9am-4pm rest-of-year) rents bicycles (Nkr30/100 per hour/day). It sells tickets for a popular daily mini-cruise (adult/child Nkr303/152, 7½ hours) on the Hurtigruten. The trip from Brønnøysund passes Torghatten (see below) on its way south to Rørvik in Trøndelag, and returns the same day.

Sights & Activities
A collection of 400 types of herbs, 100 varieties of roses and around 1000 species of cacti make this **herb farm** (Hildur's Urterarium; ☎ 75 02 52 12; Tilrem estate, Rv17, Tilrem; adult/child Nkr30/free; ☯ 10am-5pm mid-Jun–mid-Aug) a worthwhile stop, about 6km north of town. There are some rustic old farm buildings, a small art gallery and the shop carries locally grown products. The garden also makes a lovely spot for a lunch stop, dishes seasoned with locally grown herbs, of course.

Some 15km south of Brønnøysund, **Torghatten** on Torget island is one of the most bizarre rock formations in Norway, and a significant local landmark. The peak is pierced by a hole, 160m long, 35m high and 20m wide, and is accessed by a good 20-minute walking track from the base. You can reach the island via a bridge from town, but the hole is best seen from the southbound Hurtigruten coastal ferry as it rounds the island. For information on the legend of Torghatten, see the boxed text, p33.

Sleeping & Eating
The Brønnøysund tourist office can book private farm cabins and *rorbuer* (fishing cabins; Nkr500 to Nkr800), accommodating four to eight people.

Torghatten Hotell (☎ 75 00 89 00; www.torghatten hotell.no in Norwegian; Valveien 11; s/d mid-Jun–mid-Aug Nkr775/900, rest-of-year Sun-Thu Nk1160/1360, Fri & Sat Nkr850/950) Despite its dull shell, this is Brønnøysund's top lodging, with plush rooms. Its lovely restaurant, Schrøders Stue (mains Nkr175 to Nkr280) serves whale, monkfish, game and more conventional fare.

Torghatten Camping (☎ 75 02 54 95; pkha@online .no; Torghatten; tent/caravan sites Nkr80/120, 4–6-bed cabins with bathroom Nkr750) This lovely option with its small beach beside a man-made lake is great for children and only 15 minutes' walk from the Torghatten peak. You can hire a bike (per day Nkr60) or motor boats (Nkr450 to Nkr550) and even take the plunge and sign on for a dive.

Galeasen Hotell (☎ 75 00 85 50; www.galeasen.no in Norwegian; Havnegata 32-36; s/d daily mid-Jun–mid-Aug

NORDLAND

& Fri & Sat year-round Nkr725/925, Sun-Thu rest-of-year Nkr1060/1250) The small, attractive 22-room Galeasen has a convenient location, right by the docks, and runs a pleasant restaurant.

Getting There & Away
Widerøe (☎ 75 01 81 20) serves Brønnøysund from Sandnessjøen and Trondheim; the approach route passes right over Torghatten and azure seas.

Helgeland Trafikkselskap buses link Brønnøysund and Sandnessjøen (Nkr170, three hours). Brønnøysund is also a port for the Hurtigruten coastal ferry.

TRÆNA & LOVUND
If you have time for just one offshore visit along the Kystriksveien, Træna is a good bet. It's an archipelago of over 1000 small, flat skerries, five of which are inhabited.

Ferries from the mainland dock on the island of Husøy, which has most of Træna's population and lodgings, but the main sights are on the adjacent island of Sanna. Sanna is just over 1km long and a miniature mountain range runs along its spine, culminating at the northern end in the 318m spire, Trænstaven.

Near Sanna's southern end, archaeologists discovered a cemetery and artefacts (now at the Tromsø Museum) a good 9000 years old inside the cathedral-like **Kirkehelleren Cave.**

Husøy's only attraction is the jewel-box **Petter Dass Chapel** (donation Nkr20), dating from 1996, with paintings by Bodø artist Karl-Erik Harr. The hill outside the chapel provides your best views of Sanna. Local lodgings have keys.

The steep-sided island of Lovund, where prolific bird colonies and 240 humans roost, rises 623m above the sea. Every 14 April the island celebrates Lundkommerdag, the day 200,000 puffins return to the island to nest until mid-August.

Sleeping
Lovund Rorbuhotell (☎ 75 09 45 32; rorbu@lovund .net; Lovund; s/d from Nkr700/900, 2-/4-bed cabins with bathroom Nkr800/1000) This hotel is your only option on Lovund but it's a good one. Rooms are spruce and you can almost dangle your feet in the water from the cosy cabins. It has a restaurant and – amazingly for such a small place – a couple of bars. Even more

unexpected is its squash court, surely a contender for the world's northernmost.

Træna Gjestegård (☎ 75 09 52 28; fax 75 09 52 29; Husøy; s/d incl breakfast Nkr550/700) This place has simple rooms with shared facilities. It runs a small restaurant and will arrange for transport to/from the boat dock.

Getting There & Away
Helgelandske (☎ 75 06 41 00) runs express catamarans connecting Sandnessjøen and Træna (Nkr168, 2½ hours, Monday to Saturday) and car ferries three times per week (six hours).

SANDNESSJØEN
pop 5700
Sandnessjøen, the main commercial centre of Nordland's southern coast, has as its backdrop the imposing Syv Søstre (Seven Sisters; 1072m) range. Hardy hikers can reach all seven summits without technical equipment and every several years there's a competition taking in all the peaks. Don't bust a gut, however, trying to crack the record of three hours, 54 minutes...

Central Sandnessjøen's backbone is pedestrianised Torolv Kveldulvsons gate, one block from the harbour. The **tourist office** (☎ 75 04 25 80; www.helgelandskysten.com in Norwegian; ✆ 9am-6pm Mon-Fri, 10am-4pm Sat, 11am-3pm Sun mid-Jun–mid-Aug, 9am-3pm Mon-Fri rest-of-year) is by the docks and hires bicycles (per hour/day Nkr30/100).

Day Trips
The tourist office can suggest walks in the Syv Søstre range, reached most conveniently via the Rv17 at Breimo, located about 1km from town. From there it's a couple of kilometres' walk to the foot of the sheer mountains.

From the port of Tjøtta (40km south of Sandnessjøen), you can catch a ferry to the island of Tro and try to make out the **Skier of Røøya** rock carving, somewhere between 3000 and 4000 years old, which was also the symbol used for the 1994 Lillehammer Winter Olympics. Request the driver for a stop and pick-up when you board the ferry.

Sleeping & Eating
Rica Hotel Sandnessjøen (☎ 75 06 50 00; www.rica.no; Torolv Kveldulvsons gate 16; s/d mid-Jun–mid-Aug

NORDLAND

Nkr715/880, Sun-Thu rest-of-year Nk1142/1270, Fri & Sat Nkr695/850) Sandnessjøen's top-end choice, this large hotel offers all the comfort you'd expect from a member of the Rica chain.

Buri's Bistro (☎ 75 04 40 40; Torolv Kveldulvsons gate 71; mains Nkr120-235) This country-style option on the same street is a great place to dine.

Getting There & Away
Buses run daily except Sunday between Sandnessjøen and Brønnøysund (Nkr165, three hours). Sandnessjøen is also a stop for the Hurtigruten coastal ferry.

ØRNES
pop 1500

Ørnes, one of the smallest ports of call for the Hurtigruten coastal ferry, is a pretty little town amid very pleasant surroundings that offers plenty of nearby hiking opportunities near the Svartisen glacier (see p274).

This small pier-side hotel, **Ørnes Hotell** (☎ 75 75 45 99; fax 75 75 47 69; Havneveien 12; s/d mid-Jun–mid-Aug Nkr700/850, rest-of-year Nkr 890/995) is a little bit blocky, but its 24 rooms are well tended.

Several times daily, buses connect Bodø with Ørnes (Nkr176, 2½ hours), and most of these continue on to the Engebreen ferry terminal at Holand (Nkr72, one hour).

BODØ
pop 33,500

Bodø, Nordland's largest town, anchors an area of diverse attractions. Founded in 1816 as a trade centre, it turned to fishing in 1860 during an especially lucrative herring boom. The town centre, almost completely levelled by WWII bombing and rebuilt, is unexciting architecturally – and in summer it can reek of the fish that sustain it – but it's open, tidy and facing the sea with a pleasant refurbished marina. The city's charm also lies in its open backdrop of distant rugged peaks and vast skies, while dramatic islands that support the world's densest concentration of sea eagles – not for nothing is Bodø known as the Sea Eagle Capital – dot the seas to the north.

Many holiday-makers give it a miss in their rush to reach the far north or leap on a ferry to Lofoten. However, it's a great place to spend a day or two (it's only 63km west of Fauske on the Arctic Highway and is the northern terminus of the Nordlandsbanen railway) and the hinterlands too hold some top-notch attractions.

Orientation
Central Bodø slopes down a gradual hill towards the shoreline. The two main streets, Sjøgata and largely pedestrianised Storgata run in parallel, punctuated by the huge Glasshuset shopping mall. The tourist office, bus station and express boat terminal are all conveniently co-located, a couple blocks west of the Glasshuset.

Information
Ludvig's Bruktbokhandel (☎ 75 52 02 99; Dronningens gate 42) Good selection of used books in English plus old LPs, comics and videos. A treasure trove for all addicted browsers.

Sundem Libris (Glasshuset) Reasonable selection of books in English.

Tourist office (☎ 75 54 80 00; www.visitbodo.com; Sjøgata 3; 9am-8pm Mon-Fri, 10am-6pm Sat, noon-8pm Sun mid-May–Aug, 9am-4pm Mon-Fri, 10am-3pm Sat Sep–mid-May) Publishes the excellent free Bodø Guide brochure. Has two Internet terminals (per hr Nkr60).

Sights & Activities
NORWEGIAN AVIATION MUSEUM
This **museum** (Norsk Luftfartsmuseum; ☎ 75 50 78 50; Olav V gata; adult/concession/child/family Nkr75/50/40/180; 10am-7pm Sun-Fri, 10am-5pm Sat mid-Jun–mid-Aug, 10am-4pm Mon-Fri, 11am-5pm Sat & Sun rest-of-year) is huge fun to ramble around if you have even a passing interest in flight and aviation history. Allow at least half a day in your itinerary to see it all.

Exhibits include a complete control tower and hands-on demonstrations. The affiliated Norwegian Air Force Museum has plenty of examples of historic military and civilian aircraft from the Tiger Moth to the U2 spy plane (the ill-fated US plane that was shot down over the Soviet Union in 1960, creating a major diplomatic incident, was en route from Peshawar in Pakistan to Bodø). Children and kids at heart will thrill and shudder at the small simulator, which, for an extra charge, takes you on some pretty harrowing virtual flights, including a fighter jet.

If you're flying into Bodø for real, you'll see that, from above, the striking modern grey and smoked glass main museum building has the shape of an aeroplane propeller.

NORDLAND MUSEUM

This small **museum** (Nordlandmuseet; ☎ 75 52 16 40; Prinsens gate 116; adult/child Nkr30/15; ☼ 9am-3pm Tue-Fri, noon-3pm Sat & Sun) has a droll 20-minute film on the history of Bodø with English subtitles. Highlights of the collection are a number of silver articles from Viking times. Other exhibits cover Sami culture, the history of women in northern Norway, regional fishing culture and natural history.

The museum has an open-air component, the **Bodøsjøen Friluftsmuseum**, 3km from town near Bodøsjøen Camping. Here you'll find 4 hectares of historic homes, farm buildings, boat sheds, WWII German bunkers and the square-rigged sloop *Anna Karoline af Hopen*. You can wander the grounds for free but admission to the buildings is by appointment. The museum is also the start of a long-distance **walking track** up the river Bodøgårdselva, which eventually leads to the wild, scenic Bodømarka woods.

BODIN KIRKE

This charming little onion-domed **stone church** (☎ 75 56 54 20; Gamle riksvei 68; ☼ 10am-7pm mid-Jun–mid-Aug) dates from around 1240. The Lutheran Reformation brought about substantial changes to the exterior, including the addition of a tower, and a host of lively 17th- and 18th-century baroque elements grace the interior.

WALKING

Bodø og Omegns Turistforening (BOT; ☎ 75 52 14 13; bot@online.no; 2nd fl, Storgata 17; ☼ noon-3pm Tue, Wed, Fri, 11am-5pm Thu) holds DNT cabin keys. **Intersport Bodø** (☎ 75 54 98 50; 4th fl, Glasshuset) produces an excellent local walking guide and also holds keys for DNT cabins.

BOAT TRIPS

From July to mid-August, you can take a delightful three-hour cruise (Nkr390), leaving at 11am for the outer skerries and including a light lunch at Landego lighthouse. The equivalent evening sailing (Nkr440) sets out at 7.30pm. Reserve at the tourist office.

Festivals & Events

The **Nordlands Music Festival** in the first half of August is a full 10 days of music in its widest definition with symphony orchestras, jazz, rock and folk – all types of music are covered.

Sleeping

Norrøna Hotell (☎ 75 5? Storgata 4b; s/d Nkr490/6? 690, d Nkr860 mid-Aug–n Bodø's oldest hot place, full of character. . fortable and good value – partic. you're travelling alone – although it can get booked with large groups.

Bodø Gjestegård (☎ 75 52 04 02; johansst@online .no; Storgata 90; s/d Nkr370/470, d with bathroom Nkr570) There's something for everyone in this complex. At its heart is the B&B, a charmingly renovated house. In a neighbouring building, there are fully furnished apartments (Nkr890 to Nkr980).

Bodø Vandrerheim (bodo.hostel@wandrerhjem .no; dm/s/d Nkr150/250/350) Since mid-2004, the Gjestegård has managed this HI-affiliated hostel, which occupies the large red building next door. They share the one reception in the Gjestegård.

Rainbow Hotel Nordlys (☎ 75 53 19 00; www.rain bow-hotels.no; Moloveien 14; s/d mid-Jun–mid-Aug & Fri & Sat year-round Nkr630/790, Sun-Thu rest-of-year Nk1115/1145) Bodø's newest and most stylish hotel, with Scandinavian design touches throughout, also overlooks the marina and runs the Egon, a good restaurant choice with picture windows.

Rica Hotel Bodø (☎ 75 54 70 00; www.rica.no; Sjøgata 23; s/d mid-Jun–mid-Aug Nkr625/790, Sun-Thu rest-of-year Nkr1175/1440, Fri & Sat Nkr625/825) Thoroughly renovated and upgraded in 2002, this welcoming, well-managed new addition to the Rica chain has especially large rooms. You needn't even leave the building to visit Blix restaurant, Bodø's finest dining choice (see p286), with which it interconnects.

Opsahl Gjestegård (☎ 75 52 07 04; post@opsahl -gjestegaard.no; Prinsens gate 131; s/d Nkr430/600) The room décor at this comfortable 15-room guesthouse, similar in character to the Bodø Gjestegård, ranges from flowery to less florid.

Comfort Hotel Grand (☎ 75 54 61 00; www.choice hotels.no; Storgata 3; s/d mid-Jun–mid-Aug Nkr590/790, rest-of-year Sun-Thu Nk1170/1470, Fri & Sat Nkr620/820; ℗ 💻) With the resources of the Glasshuset shopping centre right beside it and but a stroll from the quayside, the Grand, with its comfortable rooms is well positioned. Room rates include both breakfast and light buffet dinner and there's a sauna and steam bath, both free to guests.

NORDLAND

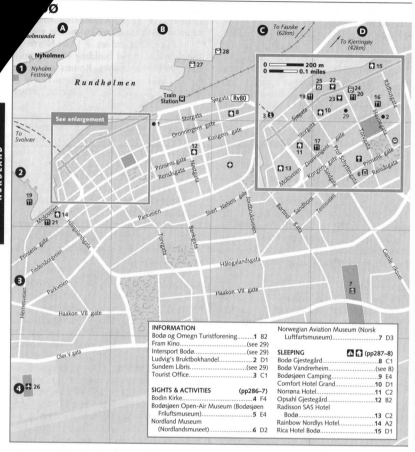

INFORMATION

Bodø og Omegn Turistforening.........**1** B2
Fram Kino.................................(see 29)
Intersport Bodø........................(see 29)
Ludvig's Bruktbokhandel...............**2** D1
Sundem Libris..........................(see 29)
Tourist Office.........................**3** C1

SIGHTS & ACTIVITIES   (pp286–7)
Bodin Kirke............................**4** F4
Bodøsjøen Open-Air Museum (Bodøsjøen
    Friluftsmuseum).....................**5** E4
Nordland Museum
    (Nordlandsmuseet)....................**6** D2

Norwegian Aviation Museum (Norsk
    Luftfartsmuseum)......................**7** D3

SLEEPING   (pp287–8)
Bodø Gjestegård..........................**8** C1
Bodø Vandrerheim......................(see 8)
Bodøsjøen Camping.......................**9** E4
Comfort Hotel Grand....................**10** D1
Norrøna Hotel..........................**11** C2
Opsahl Gjestegård......................**12** B2
Radisson SAS Hotel
    Bodø..................................**13** C2
Rainbow Nordlys Hotel..................**14** A2
Rica Hotel Bodø........................**15** D1

Bodøsjøen Camping (☎ 75 56 36 80; fax 75 56 46 89; Kvernhusveien 1; tent sites Nkr100 plus per person Nkr30, caravan/motor home sites Nkr190, cabins Nkr250-500, with bathroom Nkr600-950) This waterside camping ground is 3km from the centre. It has a grassy area with picnic tables exclusively for tent campers. Bus No 12 and 23 stop 250m away.

Radisson SAS Hotel Bodø (☎ 75 51 90 00; www.radis sonsas.com; Storgata 2; s/d mid-Jun–mid-Aug Nkr650/820, r Sun-Thu rest-of-year Nkr950-1250, Fri & Sat Nkr695/890; ☐ ☐) This contemporary hotel has bright rooms and a top-floor bar to better view the harbour and mountains. Breakfast is held at Sjøsiden restaurant with its picture windows, while its Pizzakjeller'n (see p287) is one of Bodø's most popular eateries.

Eating

Blix (☎ 75 54 70 99; Sjøgata 25; mains around Nkr200) A favourite among Bodø's discerning diners, the Blix has a justified reputation for fine cuisine and keeps a select wine list. Reserve a window table for great harbour views.

Molostua (☎ 75 52 05 30; Moloveien 9; mains Nkr85-210) This dockside restaurant is another upmarket choice that specialises in fish and regional cooking – and offers even better views!

Paviljongen (☎ 75 52 01 11; Torget; mains Nkr90-130) This great outdoor spot in the main square is the place to down a coffee or light, inexpensive lunch while watching the world pass (see how people adapt their pace to the rhythm of the buskers who strum and play nearby).

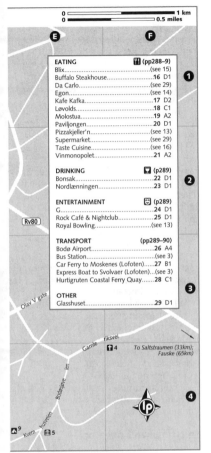

snacks, pizza and burger fare. It partly occupies the sealed bridge above the shopping mall's main alley so you can snoop upon the shoppers.

Buffalo Steakhouse (☎ 75 52 15 40; Havnegata 1; mains Nkr99-340) A place for committed carnivores, it's well worth a visit if you're craving large hunks of juicy, well-prepared, cowboy-style beef.

Taste Cuisine (☎ 75 51 90 26; Havnegata 1; mains Nkr135-225) Downstairs from Buffalo and changing both continents and cuisine, you'll find highly regarded Pan-Asian specialities in an artistic setting.

Kafé Kafka (☎ 75 52 35 50; Sandgata 5b; mains Nkr58-118) This contemporary café and coffee bar serves burgers, Mexican dishes and salads. There's one Internet terminal, free to clients. Some Saturdays, it turns into a club with DJs.

At the docks, you can buy inexpensive fresh shrimp; the Vinmonopolet is just a couple of blocks farther west. Inside the Glasshuset shopping centre you'll find a supermarket and several quick-service choices.

Drinking & Entertainment

Rock Café & Nightclub (☎ 75 50 46 33; Tollbugata 13b) This, the town's largest disco, also puts on concerts.

Bonsak (☎ 75 52 29 90; Sjøgata 17) A few doors away from Rock Café & Nightclub, you get fine keyboard playing and a cosy intimate atmosphere for drinking and chatting.

G (☎ 75 56 17 00; Sjøgata; ☻ 9pm-3am Fri & Sat) With its cave-like entrance on Sjøgata, below the main square, Bodø's newest *discoteka* packs in the over-25s.

Nordlænningen (☎ 75 52 06 00; Storgata 16) This low-key basement pub beside the main square has occasional live music.

Fram Kino (Storgata 8) Bodø's cinema, near the entrance to the Glasshuset, has several showings daily and a downstairs pub.

You can knock some pins down at **Royal Bowling** (☎ 75 52 28 80; Storgata 2), on the ground floor of the Radisson SAS Hotel.

Getting There & Away
AIR

From Bodø's airport, southwest of the city centre, SAS Braathens has four to seven daily flights to Oslo, two to seven to Trondheim and four to six to Tromsø. Widerøe

Løvold's (☎ 75 52 02 61; Tollbugata 9; dishes Nkr25-98) This popular historic quayside cafeteria, Bodø's oldest eating choice, offers sandwiches, grills and hearty Norwegian fare with good quayside views thrown in.

Pizzakjeller'n (☎ 75 51 90 00) The Radisson SAS Hotel's popular informal basement eatery is something of a misnomer. Yes, it serves up a long list of pizzas and other snacky and more substantial items, but for something more original, go for the daily special (Nkr100), which indeed changes daily, or its weekly equivalent (Nkr160).

Da Carlo (☎ 75 50 46 05; 2nd fl, Glasshuset) A pleasant place, with lots of greenery. Its popular with Bodø's younger movers and shakers, where you can down the usual

flies directly to a number of destinations in northern Norway, including Leknes (three to six times daily), Harstad (two to four) and Mo i Rana (four).

Norwegian has one/two daily flights to/from Oslo.

BOAT

Bodø is a stop on the Hurtigruten coastal ferry. The Hurtigruten quay and adjacent Lofoten car ferry docks are a five-minute walk north of the train station. Hurtigbåt express catamaran boats dock beside the bus station.

OVDS (☎ 76 96 76 00) car ferries sail five to six times daily in summer (less frequently during the rest of the year) between Bødo and Moskenes in Lofoten (person/car-and-driver Nkr132/477, 3½ hours). Most days at least one calls in at the southern Lofoten islands of Røst and Værøy, either before or after landing in Moskenes. If you're taking a car, it's extremely wise to book in advance (an additional Nkr150 in summer). There's also a summertime express passenger ferry between Bodø and Svolvær (Nkr290, 3½ hours, Sunday to Friday).

BUS

The Nor-Way Bussekspress bus to/from Narvik (Nkr467, 6½ hours), via Fauske (Nkr99, 1¼ hours) runs twice daily. Along the Kystriksveien, there are three buses daily between Bodø and Ørnes (Nkr176, 2½ hours).

TRAIN

From Bodø it's a straight shot by train to Fauske (Nkr92, 45 minutes, three to seven daily), Mo I Rana (Nkr374, three hours, two to four daily) and Trondheim (Nkr861, 10¾ hours, two daily).

Getting Around

Local buses cost Nkr22 per ride. The tourist office rents bikes from Nkr70 per day.

AROUND BODØ
Kjerringøy

It's easy to see why this sleepy peninsula, washed by luminescent turquoise seas and with a backdrop of soaring granite peaks, is a regular location for Norwegian film makers. Some 40km north of Bodø, its principal man-made feature is the 19th-century trading station Kjerringøy. Here, the entrepreneurial – some would say exploitative – Erasmus Zahl family established an important trading post, providing local fishing families with supplies in exchange for their catches, and after making their fortune, expanded into mining, banking and steam transport concerns.

Most of the timber-built historic district has been preserved as an **open-air museum** (☎ 75 51 12 57; Kjerringøy; adult/concession Nkr40/20; ⏱ 11am-5pm late May–mid-Aug), where the spartan quarters and kitchens of the fishing families contrast with the sumptuous décor and living standards of the merchants. There's also a slide presentation, included in the museum price. Admission to the main building (adult/child Nkr25/15) is by guided tour.

Several buses connect Bodø and Kjerringøy daily (Nkr86, 1½ hours) and in summer it's possible to do a return trip on the same day. Check at Bodø's tourist office for the current timetable.

Whether by bus or car, the trip involves the ferry crossing between Festvåg and Misten. It runs frequently, Monday to Friday, with fewer weekend runs. Along the way, you pass the distinctive profile of **Landegode island** (see the boxed text, p33), the white sandy beaches at **Mjelle** (whose car park is some 20 minutes' walk away) and the dramatic peak **Steigtind**, which rises a few kilometres south of Festvåg.

Saltstraumen Maelstrom

It really is worth planning your day to take in this natural phenomenon, guaranteed to occur four times every day. At the 3km-long, 150m-wide Saltstraumen Strait, the tides cause one fjord to drain into another, creating the equivalent of a waterfall at sea. The result is a churning, 20-knot watery chaos that shifts over 400 million cu metres of water one way, then the other, every six hours. It's an ideal environment for plankton, which in turn attracts an abundance of both fish and anglers. In spring, you can also see the squawking colonies of gulls that nest on the midstream island of Storholmen.

This maelstrom, claimed to be the world's largest, is actually a kinetic series of smaller whirlpools that form, surge, coalesce, then disperse. The experience is more immediate from the shoreline but for the best views, stand on the north side of the arching Salt-straumbrua bridge over the strait at its apex and watch as the waters swirl like emerald nebulae.

Nearby on the northern shore, the **Salt-straumen Opplevelsessenter** (☎ 75 56 06 55; adult/child/family Nkr80/45/225; ⊙ 11am-8pm May-Aug) presents a 15-minute multimedia show that gives an introduction to tidal currents, as well as the local history and nature but it's hard put to match the original.

The tourist office in Bodø and the Opplevelsessenter keep tide tables and can tell you exactly when to expect the best shows.

LOFOTEN

From a distance, the 'Lofoten Wall' of unearthly glacier-carved peaks appears as an unbroken mass, but once you get in closer, you'll see why Lofoten is a place of incredible and, yes, intimate charm – the soul of Northern Norway.

The main islands, Austvågøy, Vestvågøy, Flakstadøy and Moskenesøy, are separated from the mainland by the Vestfjorden. On each are sheltered bays, sheep pastures and picturesque villages, where the looming craggy backdrops might be mistaken for painted Hollywood film sets. This overwhelming scenery and the special quality of the Arctic light have long attracted artists, who are represented in galleries throughout the islands.

But Lofoten is also very much a place of business. Each winter the meeting of the Gulf Stream and the icy Arctic Ocean draws spawning Arctic cod from the Barents Sea. For centuries, this in turn drew migrating north coast farmer-fishermen who found open landscapes and rich soils to complement their seafaring work. Although cod stocks have dwindled dramatically in recent years, fishing still vies with tourism as Lofoten's largest industry, as evidenced by the wooden drying racks which lattice nearly every village on the islands.

Both www.lofoten-tourist.no and www.lofoten.info take you to the same useful website, rich in information about the whole archipelago.

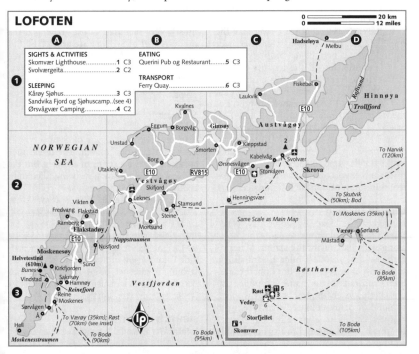

LOFOTEN

SIGHTS & ACTIVITIES		EATING	
Skomvær Lighthouse................1 C3		Querini Pub og Restaurant.......5 C3	
Svolværgeita............................2 C2			
		TRANSPORT	
SLEEPING		Ferry Quay.............................6 C3	
Kårøy Sjøhus...........................3 C3			
Sandvika Fjord og Sjøhuscamp..(see 4)			
Ørsvågvær Camping................4 C2			

Getting around isn't too difficult as the four main islands are linked by bridge or tunnel and buses run the entire E10 from the Fiskebøl–Melbu ferry in the north to Å at road's end in the southwest.

History

The history of Lofoten is essentially that of its fishing industry. Numerous battles have been fought over these seas, which became exceptionally rich in spawning cod after the glaciers retreated about 10,000 years ago. In 1120, King Øystein set up the first church and built a number of *rorbuer* (literally 'rowers' dwellings'), 4m by 4m wooden cabins for the fishermen with a fireplace, earthen floor and small porch area. In so doing, he took control of the local economy and ensured rich tax pickings for himself.

In the 13th century, traders of the German Hanseatic League moved in and usurped power, and despite an increase in exports, the general populace were left in abject poverty. By 1750, however, the trade monopoly lost its grip and locals, supplemented by opportunists from southern Norway again, took control and power of their own economic ventures.

In the early 19th century, power over the trade fell to local *nessekonger*, or 'merchant squires' who'd bought up property. These new landlords forced the tenants of their *rorbuer* to deliver their entire catch at a price set by the landlords themselves. The Lofoten Act of 1857 greatly diminished the power of the *nessekonger* but not until the Raw Fish Sales Act of 1936 did they lose the power to set prices. By the end of WWII, trade was again freed up and Lofoten fishing families could finally conduct their own trade, set prices and export their resources with a relative minimum of outside interference.

Lofoten Lodging

King Øystein's legacy lives on today, as Lofoten's lodging of choice remains the *rorbu*, along with its cousin, the *sjøhus*. Whereas *rorbu* (plural *rorbuer*) once meant dingy, tiny red-painted fishing huts on the harbours, nowadays the name is applied increasingly loosely to just about any wooden oxblood or ochre-coloured structure, from historic cabins to simple holiday homes to plush, two-storey, multiroom, fully equipped self-catering units. There are few real bargain *rorbuer* around nowadays but lots are rich in character and it's worth spending at least a night in one of the more traditional ones.

A *sjøhus* (literally 'sea house') is normally a bunkhouse-style building on the docks where fishery workers processed the catch and, for convenience, also ate and slept. While some of the *sjøhus* retain this traditional feel, others have been converted into summer tourist lodges and apartments, usually of the simpler, more economical kind. There are also higher end hotels and some wonderfully situated camping grounds.

While summer prices tend to be lower in the rest of Norway, the opposite obtains in Lofoten; in hotels you can expect to pay Nkr250-plus per room above the rest of the year prices although the difference is less pronounced in *rorbuer* and *sjøhus*. To book you can ring them up or make contact via the website, if they have one.

AUSTVÅGØY

pop 9250

Many visitors make their acquaintance with Lofoten on Austvågøy, the northernmost island in the group and the one with the most visitor facilities. Those arriving at the modern port of Svolvær are greeted by Lofoten's finest hotels and restaurants while if you arrive by ferry from Melbu, in Vesterålen, you're first confronted by wild, craggy peaks.

Svolvær

pop 4150

The modern port town of Svolvær is as busy as it gets on Lofoten. The town once sprawled across a series of skerries, but the in-between spaces are now being filled in to create a reclaimed peninsula.

The **tourist office** (☎ 76 06 98 00; www.lofoten .info; ⊙ 9am-4pm Mon-Fri, 10am-2pm Sat late May–mid-Jun & Aug, 9am-4pm & 5-9.30pm Mon-Fri, to 8pm Sat, 10am-9.30pm Sun mid-Jun–Jul, 9am-4pm Mon-Fri Sep-late May), right beside the ferry quays, can provide information on the entire archipelago. It has an Internet point (per 15 minutes Nkr20) and you can also log on at the **library** (Vestfjordgate; ⊙ 11am-3pm Mon-Fri, to 7pm Wed).

SIGHTS & ACTIVITIES

Lofoten War Memorial Museum (Krigsminne-museum; ☎ 76 07 00 49; Fiskergata 12; adult/child Nkr50/20;

GLORY BE TO COD

For centuries, catching and drying cod has been a way of life in Lofoten and by far its biggest industry.

Although cod populations have been depleted by over-fishing, the overall catch is still substantial, 50,000 tonnes annually (30,000 tonnes without the heads). The fishing season peaks from January to April when the fish come to Vestfjorden to spawn. Around the end of March each year the unofficial World Cod Fishing Championship is held in Svolvær, attracting up to 300 entrants.

There are two ways to preserve cod. For *saltfish*, it's filleted, salted and dried for about three weeks. For *klipfish*, the saltfish is cleaned, resalted and dried, originally on cliffs (*klip* in Norwegian) and nowadays in large heated plants.

However, Lofoten is all about *stockfish*. In this ancient method, 15,000 tonnes of fish are decapitated each year, paired by size, then tied together and hung to dry over the huge wooden A-frames you see everywhere on the islands. The fish lose about 80% of their weight, and most are exported to Italy, with some to Spain and Portugal.

Stockfish stays edible for years, and it's often eaten raw (a trifle chewy but goes well with beer), salted or reconstituted with water. It's concentrated goodness; 1kg of stockfish has the same nutritional value as 5kg of fresh fish.

Even before drying, very little of a cod goes to waste: cod tongue is a local delicacy – children extract the tongues and are paid by the piece – and the roe is salted in enormous German wine vats. The heads are sent to Nigeria to form the basis for a popular spicy dish.

Then there is the liver, which produces the vitamin D–rich oil that has long been known to prevent rickets and assuage the depression brought on by the long, dark Arctic winters. In 1854, Lofoten pharmacist Peter Møller decided to introduce this magic-in-a-bottle to the world and constructed a cauldron for steam-boiling the livers. The oil he skimmed received honours at trade fairs in Europe and abroad. Even after skimming, the livers were steamed in large oak barrels and then pressed to yield every last, profitable drop. Every summer, thousands of barrels of it were shipped to Europe, and the smell pervaded the village of Å, whose inhabitants liked to comment that it was the scent of money.

And what of cod-liver oil's notorious taste? Locals will tell you that it tastes bad only when it becomes rancid. Fresh cod-liver oil can be quite nice, like salad oil with a slightly fishy bouquet.

Modern Norwegian fishing folk are vociferously protective of this asset, in certain northern districts as many as 90% of votes were against EU membership. For if Norway joined the EU, the Spanish fishing fleet and others would have access to Norway's inshore waters – a potential modern-day Armada that Norway's fisher folk are determined to repel. There have even been skirmishes with Icelandic trawlers over territorial fishing rights.

Fun cod fact: one in 20,000 cod is a king cod; the distinctive lump on its forehead is said to indicate intelligence and bring good luck to the fishing family that catches it. King cod are often dried and hung on a string from the ceiling; as the string expands and contracts with humidity, the fish rotates like a barometer, hence the nickname 'weather cod'.

The latest news from the world of cod involves the fishes' mating calls; it seems that the grunts they use to attract mates can be loud enough to block submarines' sonar devices, making underwater navigation almost impossible!

Mark Kurlansky's book *Cod* (1999) is an excellent, thoroughly entertaining study of this piscatorial powerhouse.

NORDLAND

10am-4pm & 6.30-10pm Jun-Sep, 6.30-10pm May & early Oct) is one of the best such museums in Norway with a large collection of original military uniforms and largely unpublished WWII-era photos.

The **Lofoten Theme Gallery** (Lofoten Temagalleri; 76 07 03 36; adult/child Nkr50/25; 10am-3pm & 6-9pm year-round) is very much the creation of one man, Geir Nøtnes, himself from a long fishing background. One room is devoted to cod fishing, another to whaling and there's a 25-minute film with English commentary.

The *Sykkelguide* booklet (Nkr120), available around town and at the tourist office, describes with full maps 10 bike routes around Lofoten, each between 20km and 50km.

SVOLVÆR

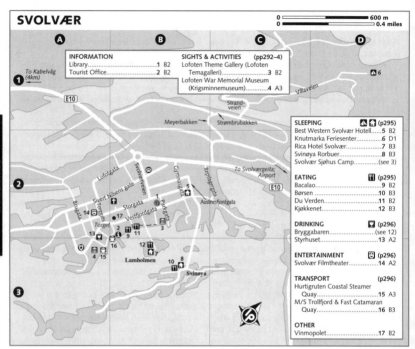

Svolværgeita, the Svolvær Goat and one of the symbols of Lofoten, is a distinctive two-pronged peak towering above town. Daredevils like to scale the peak then jump from one 'horn' to the other, and although it's been listed as one of Norway's greatest adrenaline rushes, don't try leaping alone. Nearly anyone can get to the base of Svolværgeita, but reaching the horns, Storhornet and Lillehornet, requires a 40m technical climb before you make the 1.5m jump between them. The North Norwegian Climbing School (see p295) runs almost daily trips with a guide and full equipment.

The island of **Skrova** is a fun day trip from Svolvær and offers a couple of short walks. The ferry from Svolvær (Nkr28, 30 minutes) runs four times daily in summer then continues on to Skutvik, on the mainland (see p294), to connect with buses to Bodø.

TOURS

One of the highlights of the Hurtigruten route is the narrow Raftsund channel, which separates Austvågøy and the Vesterålen island of Hinnøya. The short side trip into Trollfjord, 2km long but spectacularly steep and narrowing to only 100m, is particularly memorable as the steamer practically scrapes the rock walls before doing a three-point (Y) turn and heading off.

You can combine the two as a great day trip from Svolvær like this:
- 12.30pm: take the bus to Stokmarknes in Vesterålen;
- 2.15pm: arrive Stokmarknes;
- 3.15pm: Hurtigruten departs for Svolvær via Trollfjord;
- 6.15: arrive back in Svolvær.

The tourist office sells tickets (per person/couple Nkr300/430).

If you're not on the Hurtigruten, smaller boats (around Nkr300 per person) sail daily in summer from Svolvær into Trollfjord's constricted confines.

Between mid-May and August, **Trollfjord I** and its sister boat, **Trollfjord II** (☎ 76 07 17 90, 92 23 13 23), organise four-hour trips, including the chance to do a little spot of fishing, offered twice daily. Alternatively, three-hour cruises without fishing run up to six times

KING OF CAFFEINE

No, it's not yet another 'northernmost' but it's still a pretty impressive statistic: the friendly staff of Præstenbrygga swear that a New Zealander perched himself on their terrace one sunny day. And sat and read and sat and read... And swilled down 54 cups of coffee before bidding them goodbye as if he'd just popped in for a morning shot.

above the E10 north of town. Built to minister to the influx of seasonal fisher folk, its seating capacity of 1200 far surpasses Kabelvåg's current population.

SLEEPING & EATING

Two inlets and 3km west of Kabelvåg, there are a couple of great camping grounds, the one beside the other.

Kabelvåg Hotell (☎ 76 07 88 00; kabelvaag@dvgl. no; Kong Øysteinsgate 4; s/d Nkr675/950; ☼ mid-May–mid-Aug) In the centre of Kabelvåg, this hotel was rebuilt in 1995 in its original Art Deco style. Popular with bus tours, it's also home to the Krambua restaurant (mains Nkr185 to Nkr210), specialising in fish.

Nyvågar Rorbuhotell (☎ 76 06 97 00; booking@ nyvagar.dvgl.no; Storvåganveien 22; 4-bed rorbuer incl breakfast from Nkr1400) At Storvågan, below the museum complex, this snazzy, modern seaside place owes nothing to history, but its *rorbuer* are attractive and fully equipped. Its acclaimed restaurant (mains Nkr185 to Nkr210) serves primarily local specialities.

Kabelvåg Vandrerhjem & Sommerhotell (☎ 76 06 98 98; kabelvag.hostel@wandrerhjem.no; Finnesveien 24; dm/s/d incl breakfast Nkr200/380/560; ☼ Jun–mid-Aug) Less than 1km north of the centre, the Vågan Folkehøgskole school houses this popular hostel outside the teaching year. There's a kitchen and Internet terminal (Nkr10 per 30 minutes) for guest use. Dorms have two, four and 10 beds.

Sandvika Fjord og Sjøhuscamp (☎ 76 07 81 45; www.sandvika-camping.no; bike/car or caravan sites Nkr80/ 130; cabins Nkr350-500, with bathroom from Nkr650, sea house apt Nkr700) This beautifully located camping area, next door to Ørsvågvær Camping, has its own beach and motorboats for rent (per hour Nkr110).

Ørsvågvær Camping (☎ 76 07 81 80; www.orsvag .no in Norwegian; bike/car/caravan sites Nkr50/100/130; 4-bed cabins Nkr390, 7-bed sea house apt Nkr790-940;

☼ mid-May–mid-Aug) While their cabins are basic, the *rorbuer* have full facilities and offer splendid views. There's a sauna and you can rent a motorboat (per hour/day Nkr170/500).

Præstenbrygga (☎ 76 07 80 60; Torget) In central Kabelvåg, the fish, sandwich and pizza pub has character, history and worthwhile mains (Nkr35 to Nkr150). There's often live music, and for Nkr20, you can drink coffee all day with free refills on the lively patio.

GETTING THERE & AWAY

From Svolvær you can walk the 5km to Kabelvåg, or take the town bus (Nkr26, 15 minutes) which leaves more or less hourly. Connections are difficult on weekends.

Henningsvær

It's a delightful 8km shore-side drive southwards to the still active fishing village of Henningsvær, perched at the end of a thin promontory. Its nickname 'the Venice of Lofoten' may be a tad overblown but it's certainly the lightest, brightest and trendiest place in the archipelago. While it's the region's largest and most active fishing port, these days the harbour bustles with as many pleasure craft as fishing boats. The outdoor seating at the waterside bars and restaurants makes a great perch for observing the lively scene.

SIGHTS & ACTIVITIES

The **Lofoten Hus Gallery** (☎ 76 07 15 73; Hjellskjæret; adult/concession/child Nkr60/50/25; ☼ 10am-6pm late May-early Sep, 9am-7pm mid-Jun–mid-Aug), in a former fish-processing house, displays a fine collection of paintings from what is known as the Golden Age of Norwegian painting, between 1870 and 1930. Admission includes an 18-minute slide show of photos by Frank Jenssen, shown on the hour. Revealing the people and landscapes of Lofoten throughout the seasons, it's marred only by the trite, syrupy background music.

The **North Norwegian Climbing School** (Nord Norsk Klatreskole; ☎ 90 57 42 08; www.nordnorskklatre skole.no in Norwegian; Misværveien 10; ☼ Mar-late Sep) offers a wide range of technical climbing and skiing courses all around northern Norway and even as far away as the Himalayas. To tackle Svolværgeita (see p292) or any other Lofoten peak, climbing with an experienced guide, including equipment,

costs Nkr1500 for up to four people; book
at least one day in advance. For ideas, check
out the 320-page *Climbing in the Magic
Islands*, by Ed Webster, the last word on
climbing in Lofoten and sold at the attached
mountaineering shop.

Engelskmannsbrygga (☎ 76 07 52 85; Dreyersgate
1; admission free; ☺ 10am-8pm mid-Jun–early Aug, noon-
5pm Tue-Fri, to 4pm Sat & Sun, early Aug–mid-Jun), or
'Englishman's Wharf', is the open studio
and gallery of three artists: a glass-blower,
photographer and ceramic artist, whose
works you can browse and buy.

Festvåg (☎ 91 65 55 00; www.festvag.no), 2km
north of town beside a large humpback
bridge, offers sea-kayak hire (from Nkr200)
and guided three-hour outings (adult/child
Nkr300/150), canoeing, deep-sea fishing
and a range of land-based sporty activities.
The minibus (Nkr100 per person return)
will pick you up from your lodging, whether
in Henningsvær, Kabelvåg or Svolvær.

SLEEPING & EATING
You'll find signs advertising rooms for rent
all over town.

Nord Norsk Klatreskole (☎ 90 57 42 08; www.nord
norskklatreskole.no in Norwegian; Misværveien 10; ☺ Mar-
late Sep; dm Nkr175) The climbing school's café
and hostel (reservation recommended) face
each other down a side alley, friendly, informal places both, they cross a Lofoten
rorbu with an English pub and a Himalayan
trekkers' lodge. Beds are in a dorm or quad-
rooms and its Klatrekafeen serves up snacks
and a small selection of good value home-
made dishes (Nkr75 to Nkr130).

Henningsvær Bryggehotel (☎ 76 07 47 50;
Hjellskjæret; s/d from Nkr1025/1190; ☺ mid-Jan–Nov)
Overlooking the harbour, this attractive
hotel is Henningsvær's finest choice. It's
modern, with comfortable rooms furnished
in contemporary design, yet constructed in
a traditional style that blends harmoniously
with its neighbours. Its Arctic Menu restaurant (mains Nkr165 to Nkr230) is equally
stylish.

Johs H Giæver Sjøhus og Rorbuer (☎ 76 07 47
19; www.giaever-rorbuer.no; Hellandsgata 790; rorbuer
Nkr400-900, sea house r Nkr350-550) In summer,
workers' accommodation in a modern sea
house belonging to the local fish plant is
hired out to visitors. Spruce rooms have
shared facilities, including a large kitchen
and dining area, and are good value. The

company also has three *rorbuer* that are
equally well priced and more central.

Fiskekrogen (☎ 76 07 46 52; Dreyersgate 29; mains
Nkr195-245) At the end of a slipway overlooking the harbour, this dockside Arctic Menu
place, a favourite of the Norwegian royal
family, is Henningsvær's culinary claim
to fame. Try, in particular, the outstanding
fish soup (Nkr115).

GETTING THERE & AWAY
Bus No 510 shuttles between Svolvær
(Nkr40, 35 minutes), Kabelvåg (Nkr38,
30 minutes) and Henningsvær at least four
times daily.

VESTVÅGØY
pop 10,750
The E10 snakes its way through the heart
of Vestvågøy island, whose only big-name
attraction is the Lofotr Viking Museum. A
more attractive route follows the alternative, less travelled and only slightly longer
Rv815, which runs initially eastwards from
Leknes beside quite stunning coastal and
mountain scenery.

The lacklustre town of Leknes is where
you'll find the tourist office inside the Rådhus. It rents cycles for Nkr150 per day.

Most lodgings are on the south coast,
near Stamsund.

Sights & Activities
LOFOTR VIKING MUSEUM
In 1981 at Borg, near the centre of Vestvågøy,
a local farmer inadvertently ploughed up the
ruins of the 83m-long dwelling of a powerful Viking chieftain, the largest building of
its era ever discovered in Scandinavia.

The **Lofotr Viking Museum** (☎ 76 08 49 00; www
.lofotr.no in Norwegian; Borg; adult/child/family incl guided
tour Nkr90/45/225; ☺ 10am-7pm late May-31 Aug),
14km north of Leknes, offers a glimpse of
life in Viking times. Horses graze nearby as
you walk the 1.5km of trails on open hilltops from the replica of the chieftain's hall
(the main building, shaped like an upside-
down boat) to the Viking ship replica on
the water. Costumed guides conduct multilingual tours and, inside the chieftain's hall,
artisans explain their trades. You can row
the Viking ship as a member of the crew at
2pm daily, paying Nkr20 for the privilege.

In summer, visitors can try a bowl of lamb
broth (Nkr60) accompanied by thick slabs

DEANNA SWANEY

Mountain on the shore of the fjord waters along the Kystriksveien Coastal Route (p282)

Fish drying racks in the harbour of Svolvær on Austvågøy Island (p290)

CHRISTIAN ASLUND

A youth hostel in the town of Å (p299)

NED FRIARY

DAVID

Reindeer crossing a road in Arctic Norway (p324) in the winter

CHRISTIAN ASLUND

Skiing under a midnight sun in Tromsø (p314), a unique experience

INGRID RODDIS

Arctic Cathedral (p316)

A tourist-laden boat lands at Magdalenefjord (p366), northern Spitsbergen

DEANNA SWANEY

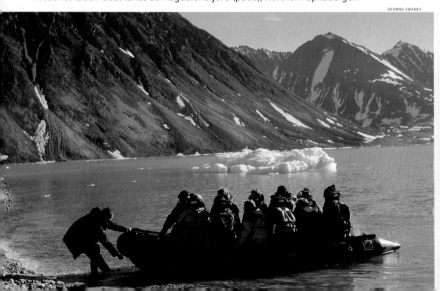

AUTHOR'S CHOICE

Justad Rorbuer og Vandrerhjem (☎ 76 08 93 34; fax 76 08 97 39; Stamsund; dm/s/d Nkr90/250/300, 4-bed cabins Nkr450-700; ☺ mid-Dec–mid-Oct) The island's HI-affiliated youth hostel, a 1.2km walk from the Hurtigruten quay, has its regular clientele who come back year after year – one particularly loyal guest has stayed here over 50 times – so be sure to reserve. You can see what draws folk back; it's right beside the water in an old fishing complex, there's a laundry and self-catering facilities and the friendly manager dispenses information about local hiking routes, rents bicycles (Nkr80 to Nkr100 per day) and lends rowing boats and fishing lines for free.

of peasant bread or a glass of mead (Nkr45). The café serves more contemporary dishes.

The Svolvær–Leknes bus passes the museum's entrance.

UNSTAD TO EGGUM HIKE

A favourite hike connects these two tiny villages on the island's west coast. A 9km coastal track winds past several headlands, a solitary lighthouse and superb seascapes. Eggum is known for its views of the midnight sun and Vesterålen and for the ruins of a fortress by the ocean, while Unstad has the area's only accommodation (see right).

Take care after rain as the trail, particularly around Unstad, can be slick with mud plus, if you're very unlucky and as one reader attests, sheep dip. Eggum and Unstad are both about 9km from the main road and served infrequently by buses.

Sleeping & Eating

Statles Rorbusenter (☎ 76 05 50 60; www.statles.no; Mortsund; 2–8-bed cabins Nkr500-2400) To really get off the beaten track, head down a quiet road to its end at the scenic hamlet of Mortsund, where this friendly facility of 40 pleasant cabins sprawls across a rocky promontory. The restaurant serves both local dishes and light meals. Bicycle and boat hire are available, as is nearby hiking.

Brustranda Sjøcamping (☎ 76 08 71 00; bl-tjoen@ online.no; Rolvsfjord; tents with bike/car Nkr60/100, caravan sites/cabins Nkr120/350, cabins with bathroom Nkr600-1000) This well-tended, beautifully situated seaside place, 14km northeast of Stamsund

along the Rv 815, also has an art gallery and café.

Also recommended:

Unstad Camping (☎ 97 06 12 01; www.lofot-ferie. com in Norwegian; Unstad; tent/caravan sites/cabins Nkr100/130/750; ☺ May–mid-Sep)

Getting There & Away

Leknes airport connects the island with Bodø. Leknes is also the island's transport hub, with bus connections to Å (Nkr95, 1½ hours, four to five daily), Stamsund (Nkr35, 25 minutes, two to five daily except Sunday) and Svolvær (Nkr98, 1½ hours, four to six daily). Stamsund is the island's port for the Hurtigruten coastal ferry.

FLAKSTADØY
pop 1540

Most of Flakstadøy's residents live along its flat north shore, around the town of Ramberg, but the craggy south side provides the most dramatic scenery. Many visitors just zip across it but it's worth stopping to sun yourself (sandy beaches are the exception in Lofoten) and perhaps to build in a detour to the arty village of Nusfjord.

The excellent, free *Flakstad & Moskenes Guide* is widely available.

Sights
NUSFJORD

This secluded village, around a constricted little south-coast harbour, makes a superb day trip. In addition to a delightfully picturesque waterfront and a lovely restored general store, you'll find a selection of *rorbuer*. Many artists consider it to be the essence of Lofoten but be warned: so do tour operators.

RAMBERG & FLAKSTAD

Imagine an arch of tropical white sand fronting a sparkling blue-green bay with a backdrop of snow-capped Arctic peaks. That's pretty much **Ramberg** and **Flakstad** beaches, on the north coast, when the sun shines kindly on them. Should you hit such a day, no-one back home will believe that your holiday snaps of this place were taken north of the Arctic Circle, but you'll know it if you stick a toe in the water.

Set back from Flakstad beach and bypassed these days by the E10, the red onion-domed **Flakstad Kirke** (admission Nkr20;

FISHY MEDICINE

Remember the breakfast tantrums, the spoon being forced into your mouth and that strong fishy flavour, overcoming the nutty taste of corn flakes, as your parents forced the fluid down your throat to stave off winter colds?

It wasn't always so. *Tran*, cod-liver oil, was originally used as fuel for lamps or in the tanning process for skins and nobody would have dreamed of imbibing it. But gradually its medicinal properties were understood and, in an early example of deliberate – and highly successful – marketing, cod-liver oil became the preventative of choice throughout Europe. It's a bit like olive oil; the first pressing, the virgin oil, is considered the purest while steam cooking – a technological advance that reduced production costs and enhanced yield – enables much more of the oil to be used.

Early hunch is nowadays backed up by objective medical evidence. Cod-liver oil, rich in vitamins A and D, plus omega-3 fatty acids, is good for your heart and blood circulation, eyesight, skin, bone development and brain.

So take a breath, pinch your nostrils, join one in three of all Norwegians and take your medicine like a man/woman…

(🕑 11am-3pm late Jun-early Aug) was built in 1780 but has been extensively restored. Most of the original wood was ripped out of the ground by the Arctic-bound rivers of Siberia and washed up here as driftwood.

GLASSHYTTA

You can make a 4km side trip to Vikten to visit the **gallery** (☎ 76 09 44 42; 🕑 10am-7pm May-Aug) of glassblower Åsvar Tangrand, designer of the Lofoten Rune, the region's seven-pronged logo, which evokes a longboat. His glass and ceramic creations range from around Nkr400 to Nkr3500.

SUND FISKERIMUSEUM

This **fishery museum** (☎ 76 09 36 29; Sund; adult/child Nkr40/10; 🕑 10am-4pm or 6pm May-Aug), near the bridge to Moskenesøy, has a collection of shacks containing displays on fishing, the blacksmith's trade and boat propulsion. The resident blacksmith, who has his gallery on-site, has gained a reputation for his iron cormorant sculptures.

Sleeping & Eating

Ramberg Gjestegård (☎ 76 09 35 00; www.ramberg-gjestegard.no; E10; tent with bike/car Nkr90/110, caravan Nkr120, 2-/4-bed cabins with bathroom Nkr700/900) This friendly camping ground, right on the beach, is a great place to drop anchor and spend a day or two. You can rent a kayak or rowing boat (per hour/day Nkr25/100), upgrade to a motorboat (Nkr100/350) or explore the island by bike (Nkr25/100). There's a justifiably popular Arctic Menu restaurant (mains Nkr160 to Nkr200) that

does a range of creative fish dishes and offers cheaper but still very tasty lunch specials (Nkr80 to Nkr100).

MOSKENESØY

pop 1270

The 34km-long glaciated island of Moskenesøy, a spiky pinnacled igneous ridge rising directly from the sea and split by deep lakes and fjords, could almost be from the imagination of Tolkien. While these formations are mainly a paradise for mountaineers, there are also a few places where non-technical hikers can gain the upper reaches of this tortured island, including its highest point, Hermannsdalstind (1029m).

ORIENTATION & INFORMATION

The E10 runs along the island's south coast, past the communities of Hamnøy, Sakrisøy and Reine (once voted the most scenic place in Norway) before reaching the functional village of Moskenes and its ferry terminal. The route ends at the museum-like village of Å (population 100). Mountains occupy the rest of the island.

The **tourist office** (☎ 76 09 15 99; www.lofoten-info.no; 🕑 10am-6pm daily Jul, 10am-5pm Mon-Fri Jun & Aug, 10am-2pm Mon-Fri Jan-May Sep-Dec) at Moskenes harbour covers the islands of Moskenesøy and Flakstadøy. It publishes the free and informative *Flakstad & Moskenes Guide*, has an Internet point (per hour Nkr60) and provides information on and makes reservations for a variety of tours. The *Flakstad & Moskenes Guide* has several hiking suggestions and the youth hostel in Å carries a free information sheet describing six walks on the island of between two and seven hours. You can deep-sea fish for a day (Nkr300) on tours from several Moskenesøy ports, using the traditional long lines. At sea, there's good bird-watching and the possibility of whale sightings. Options include fishing the Reinefjord, off Nusfjord or near the maelstrom off Å.

'Sjøhus' signs all along the E10 indicate private rooms.

GETTING THERE & AWAY

Four to five buses connect Leknes and Å (Nkr95, 1½ hours) daily in summer, stopping in all major villages along the E10.

OVDS (☎ 76 96 76 00) car ferries sail five to six times daily in summer (less frequently during the rest of the year) between Bødo and Moskenes (person/car and driver Nkr132/477, 3½ hours). Most days, at least one calls in at the southern Lofoten islands of Røst and Værøy, either before or after landing in Moskenes.

NORDLAND BOATS

You're bound to come across the uniquely shaped Nordland boat. Taking its inspiration from early Viking ships, it has served local fishing communities from the earliest days of settlement in this region. These boats have come to symbolise the earthy, self-sufficient lifestyles of the hardy coastal folk, here up north. Today, they're still in use from Namsos, in Nord Trøndelag, right up to the Kola Peninsula in Arctic Russia, but the greatest concentrations are found in Lofoten.

The smallest versions are known as *færing*, measuring up to 5m, while larger ones are called *hundromsfæring* (6m), *seksring* (7m), *halvfjerderomning* (7.5m), *firroing* (8m), *halvfemterømming* (9m), *åttring* (10m to 11m) and *femboring* (11m to 13m).

Traditionally, the larger the boat, the greater was the status of its captain, or *høvedmann*. Whatever the size, Nordland boats are excellent for both rowing and sailing, even in rough northern seas. Until quite recently, sailing competitions, pitting fishing communities against each other, were one of the great social events of the year.

A good place to see museum-quality examples is in the harbour at Å i Lofoten.

Å

At the tail-end of Moskenesøy, the bijou village of Å (appropriately, the last letter of the Norwegian alphabet!), often referred to as Å i Lofoten, is truly a living museum – a preserved fishing village with a shoreline of red *rorbuer*, cod drying racks and picture-postcard scenes at almost every turn. It's an almost feudal place, carved up between two families, now living very much from tourism but in its time a significant fishing port (upwards of 700,000 cod would be hung out to dry right up to WWII).

It's pedestrianised in principle so do leave your vehicle at the car park up the hill beyond a short tunnel and walk down.

SIGHTS

Fourteen of Å's 19th-century boathouses, storehouses, fishing cottages, farmhouses and commercial buildings constitute the **Norwegian Fishing Village Museum** (Norsk Fiskeværs Museum; ☎ 76 09 14 88; adult/child Nkr45/25; ☺ 10am-5.30pm mid-Jun–mid-Aug, 11am-3pm Mon-Fri rest-of-year). Highlights of the guided tour (included in admission) are Europe's oldest cod-liver oil factory, where you'll be treated to a taste of the wares and can pick up a bottle (Nkr40) to stave off those winter sniffles; the smithy, who still makes cod-liver oil lamps; the still-functioning bakery from 1844; the old *rorbuer* with period furnishings; and a couple of traditional Lofoten fishing boats.

In a former fish warehouse nearby, the **Lofoten Stockfish Museum** (Lofoten Tørrfiskmuseum; ☎ 91 15 05 60; adult/concession/child Nkr40/25/free; ☺ 11am-5.30pm late Jun–mid-Aug, 11am-4pm Mon-Fri rest of Jun & Aug) devotes itself to Lofoten's traditional mainstay: the catching and drying of cod for export, particularly to Italy. Displays take you through the process, from hauling the fish out of the sea through drying, grading and sorting to despatch. The enthusiasm of the museum's proprietor-curator may well have you considering a simpler life and a change of career!

Beyond the camping ground just south of Å, there's an excellent hillside view of Værøy island, across the Moskenesstraumen strait. The mighty **maelstroms** created by tidal flows between the two islands were first described 2000 years ago by Pytheas and later appeared as fearsome adversaries on fanciful early sea charts. They also inspired tales of maritime peril by Jules Verne

NORDLAND

and Edgar Allen Poe and are still said to be among the world's most dangerous waters. This formidable expanse is exceptionally rich in fish and attracts large numbers of sea birds and marine mammals.

SLEEPING & EATING

Moskenesstraumen Camping (☎ /fax 76 09 11 48; camping for 1/2/3 persons Nkr70/90/100, caravans Nkr100, 2-/4-bed cabins Nkr300/400, with bathroom Nkr400/600; ☽ Jun-Aug) This wonderful cliff-top camping ground, just south of the village, has flat, grassy sites between the rocks, just big enough for your bivouac. Cabins too have great views, as far as the mainland on clear days.

Å Vandrerhjem og Rorbuer (☎ 76 09 11 21; aa .hostel@wandrerhjem.no; www.lofoten-rorbu.com; hostel dm Nkr130, d/tr in sea house per person Nkr225; rorbuer Nkr800-1350) There's accommodation for all budgets, dispersed throughout Å's historic buildings, the more expensive ones fully equipped and furnished with antiques. Very much the hub of the village, the office provides general tourist information and also rents bikes (per hour/day Nkr30/150). It also rents *rorbuer* in the nearby and more tranquil hamlet of Tind, 1km to the north.

Å-Hamna Rorbuer & Hennumgården (☎ 76 09 12 11; www.lofotenferie.com; 2-4-bed r per person Nkr100, 4-8-bed rorbuer Nkr600-950) In summer you can stay here in restored fishing huts or the hostel-style Hennumgasjøhus. Prices drop significantly outside high summer.

Brygga restaurant (☎ 76 09 11 21; mains around Nkr200; ☽ Jun-Sep) This excellent eating place, hovering above the water, is Å's one decent dining choice. The menu, as is right and proper in a village with such a strong fishing tradition, is mainly of things with fins, imaginatively prepared. But they also do a daily vegetarian special (Nkr110) and a tempting lemon fried chicken with apple butter (Nkr190). It's also a great little spot simply for a drink as the water sloshes below your feet.

Sørvågen

Beside the E10 in Sørvågen, south of Moskenes, the **Norwegian Telecommunications Museum** (☎ 76 09 14 88; adult/child Nkr30/20; ☽ core hr noon-4pm late Jun–mid-Aug) presents itself as a study in 'cod and communications'. Granted, it's not an immediately winning combo, but in fact this small museum com-

memorates a huge advance in fishing techniques. In 1906, what was Norway's second wireless telephone station was established in this tiny hamlet. From that day on, weather warnings could be speedily passed on, and fishing vessels could communicate with each other, pass on news about where the shoals were moving and call up the bait boats.

Moskenes

The Moskenes **tourist office** (☎ 76 09 15 99; www .lofoten-info.no; ☽ 10am-6pm daily Jul, 10am-5pm Mon-Fri Jun & Aug, 10am-2pm Mon-Fri Jan-May Sep-Dec) can provide information on and make reservations for a variety of tours on the island. It publishes the *Flakstad & Moskenes Guide* and has Internet access (per hour Nkr60).

Despite great waterside views, **Moskenes Camping** (☎ 76 09 13 44; Moskenes; tent/caravan sites Nkr70/110; ☽ May-Sep), in a gravel-surfaced spot, is pretty spartan, although there's a grassy area for lightweight campers. It's convenient for an early getaway from the ferry terminal, only 400m away.

Lofoten Sykkelutleie (☎ 92 23 13 24) has a summertime base beside the ferry exit where you can rents bikes (per day Nkr175).

Reine

Reine is a rather characterless place but gosh, it looks great from above, beside its placid lagoon backed by pinnacled peaks. You already get a great view from the road that drops to the village from the E10 but for a truly exceptional panorama of the lagoon and islands, **hike** up the precipitous track to the summit of Reinebringen (670m). The track starts at the tunnel entrance about 1.2km south of the Reine turnoff from the E10, and climbs very steeply to the ridge (448m). Experienced hikers who want to keep going can continue to the peak for spectacular views of the freshwater lake below, then drop steeply down a very exposed route to the col of Navaren and on to Navaren's 730m summit.

From Reine, you can choose among several worthwhile boat tours between June and August. The most popular is a six-hour midnight sun excursion (adult/child Nkr600/300) via the Maelstrom to the cave **Refsvikhula**, a 115m-long, 50m-high natural rock cathedral. Around midsummer, the midnight sun shines directly into the mouth of the cave and illuminates a panel

NORDLAND

AUTHOR'S CHOICE

Hamnøy Mat og Vinbu (☎ 76 09 21 45; Hamnøy; mains Nkr140-165; ☻ May-Sep) This welcoming restaurant, run by two generations of the same family, is well regarded for local specialities, including *bacalao* and cod tongues. Mother takes care of the traditional dishes – just try her fish cakes – while her son is the main chef. Their fish is of the freshest, bought daily from the harbour, barely 100m away.

---

of Stone Age stick figures marching across the walls and thought to have been painted at least 3000 years ago.

Alternatively, you can take a three-hour bird- and marine mammal-watching safari (adult/child Nkr500/250) into the wild and fish-rich **Moskenesstraumen** maelstrom.

Adventure Rafting Lofoten (☎ 76 09 20 00) also offers bird cliff tours to Værøy (Nkr900, six hours), as well as Refsvikshula and the Moskstraumen, both sailings departing from Reine.

Around Reine

In summer, ferries run between Reine and **Vindstad** (Nkr64 return, 30 minutes) through the scenic Reinefjord. From Vindstad, it's a one-hour hike across the ridge to the abandoned beachside settlement of **Bunes**, where there's a very basic camping ground in the shadow of the amazing 610m Helvetestind rock slab.

Another, more demanding, route takes you via the regular fjord ferry to **Forsfjord** (you must request a stop) and follows the concrete pipeline towards Tennesvatnet Lake. At around 450m above sea level, follow the path to descend between Tennesvatnet and the Fjerdalsvann Lake to the DNT's Munkebu Cabin (the grocery shops Å Dagligvarer, Sørvågen Handel and Reine Handel all hold keys). This should take about four hours. If you'd prefer to continue directly to Soågen near Moskenes, a moderate cairned walk takes you through the Djupfjordheia moor (about five hours).

Sakrisøy

In Sakrisøy, a local woman has collected some 2500 dolls, antique teddy bears and historic toys into **Dagmar's Museum of Dolls &**

Toys (Dagmars Dukke og Legetøy Museum; ☎ 76 09 21 43; adult/concession/child Nkr40/35/20; ☻ 10am-6pm or 8pm Jun-Aug, noon-5pm Sat & Sun May). There's also an affiliated antique shop upstairs.

Reserve at the Doll Museum for a place to stay at **Sakrisøy Rorbuer** (☎ 76 09 21 43; sakrisoy@lofoten-info.no; Sakrisøy; rorbuer Nkr650-1150), a relatively authentic complex of ochre-coloured cottages hovering above the water. You can also hire motor boats (per day Nkr400 to Nkr550).

For self-catering, the fish stall **Sjømat** (☎ 90 06 15 66; Sakrisøy), across the street from the Doll Museum, is famous for smoked salmon, prawns, whale steaks and – go on, be adventurous – seagulls' eggs.

Hamnøy

Eliassan Rorbuer (☎ 76 09 23 05; rorbuer@online .no; Hamnøy; 2-/4-bed rorbuer Nkr550/750) The pretty little fishing village of Hamnøy doesn't have much action, but this spot is so close to the water that it almost feels as though you could walk across to the towering mountains on the other side.

SOUTHERN ISLANDS

Lofoten's remote southern islands of Værøy and Røst have the best bird-watching in Norway. Most people come for the little puffins but, as a result of dwindling herring stocks, their numbers have dropped by more than 50% in the past decade. Although Værøy is mainly high and rugged and Røst is flat as a pancake, both islands offer good hiking. Both offer a rare measure of relative solitude in well-touristed Lofoten.

Værøy

pop 780

Craggy Værøy, with its 780 residents hugely outnumbered by over 100,000 nesting sea birds – fulmars, gannets, Arctic terns, guillemots, gulls, sea eagles, puffins, kittiwakes, cormorants, eiders petrels, and a host of others – makes for a laid-back getaway. White sand beaches, soaring ridges, tiny, isolated villages, granite-gneiss bird cliffs and sparkling seas combine to make it one of Norway's finest gems.

The **tourist office** (☎ 76 09 52 10; ☻ 10am-3pm Mon-Sat mid-Jun–mid-Aug) is about 200m north of the ferry landing at Sørland, the main town on the east side. It's open additional hours whenever the car ferry is in port.

SIGHTS & ACTIVITIES

A great way to get around Værøy is on foot, and hiking routes lead to most of the larger sea-bird rookeries. The most scenic and popular trail begins at the end of the road around the north of the island, about 6km from Sørland and 300m beyond the former airstrip. It heads southward along the west coast, over the Eidet isthmus to the mostly abandoned fishing village of Måstad, on the east coast, where meat and eggs from the puffin colonies once supported 150 people. The route is pretty exposed in places so don't set out if bad weather threatens.

Fit hikers who relish a challenge may also want to attempt the steep climb from Måstad to the peak of Måhornet (431m), which takes about an hour each way.

Alternatively, from the quay at Sørland you can follow the road (or perhaps the more interesting ridge scramble) up to the NATO installation at Håen (438m).

SLEEPING & EATING

Gamle Prestegård (Old Vicarage; ☎ 76 09 54 11; www .prestegaarden.no in Norwegian; Nordland; s/d incl breakfast Nkr350/580, with bathroom Nkr450/640) Værøy's smartest lodging and dining is on the island's north side. There's no sign, but it's the large house with a flagpole in the garden, beside (left of) the church, just where you'd expect the vicar to have lived.

Langodden Rorbucamp og Vandrerhjem (☎ 76 09 52 25; www.langodden.com; Sørland; dm Nkr125; per person Nkr125; ☺ May-Aug) This place, in the hands of the same family for five generations, offers some of the most authentic *rorbu* accommodation (each containing five to 15 beds) in Lofoten – including occasional fish smells outside! – and has a kitchen for self-catering guests. About an hour's walk north of the ferry landing, it rents out bicycles and can arrange boat trips.

Kornelius Kro (☎ 76 09 52 99; korn-kro@online.no; Sørland; s/d Nkr300/450) The island's only nightlife option (there's live music on Saturdays) has a pub, restaurant (mains Nkr70 to Nkr170) and a few simple but clean cabins at the rear. It's known for parties around the wood-fired seawater hot tub.

GETTING THERE & AWAY

There's a summertime helicopter service to/from Bodø. The rest of us must travel by **OVDS ferry** (☎ 76 96 76 00) from Bodø or Moskenes. The ferry also provides access to Røst.

Røst

pop 655

The 356 islands and skerries of Røst form Lofoten's ragged southern edge. Røst stands in sharp contrast to its rugged neighbours to the north, and were it not for a small pimple in the middle, the main pond-studded island of Røstlandet would be dead flat. Thanks to its location in the heart of the Gulf Stream, this cluster of islets basks in one of the mildest climates in Norway and attracts 2.5 million nesting sea birds to some serious rookeries on the cliffs of the outer islands.

An unusual view of medieval life on the island is provided in the accounts of a shipwrecked merchant of Venice, one Pietro Querini, who washed up on Sandøy in 1432 and reputedly introduced stockfish to Italy. The **tourist office** (☎ 76 09 64 11; ☺ mid-Jun–mid-Aug), a short walk from the ferry dock, has a sheet outlining the tale.

TOURS

From June to mid-August, the **Kårøy Sjøhus** (☎ 76 09 62 38; rt-finni@online.no) arranges five-hour boat tours (Nkr250), which cruise past several bird cliffs, hoping to show you a seal or two and, if you're very lucky, an orca. The boat makes a stop for a short walk to the 1887 Skomvær lighthouse, once inhabited by artist Theodor Kittelsen, or, if you prefer, you can stay on the jetty and try a little fishing (lines provided). It also visits the Vedøy kittiwake colonies. Upon completion of this tour, you'll have exhausted Røst's organised activities and will be on your own until the ferry leaves.

SLEEPING & EATING

Kårøy Sjøhus (☎ 76 09 62 38; rt-finni@online.no; dm Nkr125; ☺ May-Aug) These three sea houses, divided into rooms accommodating two, four or six, are a great budget choice.

Røst Bryggehotel (☎ 76 05 08 00; www.rostbrygge hotell.no in Norwegian) This modern development in traditional style is right on the quay side. It has 16 comfortable doubles and can arrange fishing or bird-watching boat trips.

Querini Pub og Restaurant (☎ 76 09 64 80) Your best choice for meals is named after the shipwrecked merchant from Venice.

GETTING THERE & AWAY

Røst, like Værøy, is served by the **OVDS ferry** (☎ 76 96 76 00) that runs between Bodø and Moskenes.

VESTERÅLEN

pop 33,500

Administratively, the islands of Vesterålen, the northern continuation of the archipelago that includes Lofoten, are divided between the counties of Nordland and Troms but, for convenience, we cover the entire area in this chapter. Although the landscapes here aren't as dramatic as those in Lofoten, they tend to be much wilder and the forested mountainous regions of the island of Hinnøya are a unique corner of Norway's largely treeless northern coast.

The central **tourist office** (☎ 76 11 14 80; www .visitvesteralen.com; Kjøpmannsgata 2; ⊙ 9am-6pm Mon-Fri, 10am-4pm Sat, noon-6pm Sun Jun-Aug, 8am-4pm Mon-Fri Sep-May) is in the main city of Sortland. The website covers the whole region. Another good source of information in English is the book *An Encounter with Vesterålen – Culture, Nature & History* (Nkr170), outlining the history, sites and walking routes in the region and sold at tourist offices.

HADSELØYA
pop 8050

Vesterålen's link to Lofoten is the southernmost island of Hadseløya, connected by ferry from the port of Melbu to Fiskebøl on Austvågøy. Melbu has a fish museum that merits a detour and an increasingly famous summer music festival. The other main town, Stokmarknes, is a quiet market community best known as the birthplace of the Hurtigruten coastal ferry.

The island's **tourist office** (☎ 76 16 46 60; ⊙ 10am-5pm Mon-Sat, 11am-4pm Sat & Sun, mid-Jun–mid-Aug only) is on the waterfront in Stokmarknes.

Sights & Activities

The Hurtigruten coastal ferry was founded in Stokmarknes in 1893 by Richard Bernhard, with a single ship, the S/S *Vesterålen*. It called on nine ports between Trondheim and Hammerfest, carrying post, passengers and vital supplies. Now the line boasts 11 ships, carries half a million passengers

annually, serves 35 towns and villages and is a vital link for Norway, providing transport for locals and a scenic cruise-like experience for tourists.

Its history is commemorated in the **Hurtigruten Museum** (Hurtigrutemuseet; ☎ 76 11 81 90; Markedsgata 1; museum admission adult/child Nkr60/30, M/S Finnmarken Nkr40/20, combined admission Nkr80/30; ⊙ noon-4pm mid-May–mid-Jun & mid-Aug–mid-Sep, 10am-6pm mid-Jun–mid-Aug, 2-4pm Mon-Fri, noon-4pm Sat mid-Sep–mid-May). You can see the history of the line in all its glory, but if you haven't arrived by Hurtigruten, you'll be just as interested in the retired ship, M/S *Finnmarken*, claimed to be the world's largest museum piece, which plied the coastal route between 1956 and 1993.

In an abandoned herring oil factory (romantically named Neptune despite its stark functionality) in Melbu the **National Fishing Industry Museum** (Norsk Fiskerindustrimuseum; ☎ 76 15 98 25; Neptunveien; adult/child Nkr50/20; ⊙ 9am-3pm Mon-Fri) traces the life of a fish from the deep sea to the kitchen table. There's also a children's exhibition about the goings-on on the sea floor. Across the harbour from the ferry pier, it's 750m from the E10 along a pocked causeway. There are guided visits, included with the admission fee, in summer.

Festivals & Events

The **Summer–Melbu festival**, held each July, is one of northern Norway's liveliest cultural festivals with lots of thing happening: seminars, lectures, concerts, theatrical performances and art exhibitions.

Sleeping

There are a few lodgings in Stokmarknes.

Hurtigrutenhus (☎ 76 15 29 99; Markedsgata 1; s/d Nkr995/1190) Rooms within this luxury hotel, conference and arts complex represent good value for your krone. In the same complex as the museum, it's one of the few places where it's more fun to be alone than accompanied; single rooms are furnished to resemble ship's cabins.

Hurtigrutenshus Turistsenter (☎ 76 15 29 99; tent/caravans Nkr50/120) Over the bridge, cabins and rooms are overpriced at this friendly extension to the Hurtigruten complex. Camping, by contrast, is a bargain.

Rødbrygge Pub (☎ 76 15 26 66; Markedgata 6a; mains Nkr60-190) Ahoy, this popular pub across from the Hurtigruten Museum does good grills, seafood and pizzas at more modest prices and is a pleasant all-wood place for a refreshing drink.

Getting There & Around

Of course, the Hurtigruten coastal ferry still makes a detour stop in its home port of Stokmarknes...

Buses between Melbu and Stokmarknes (Nkr45, 45 minutes) run several times daily on weekdays and twice daily at weekends. A slower but more fulfilling way to cover the distance is by following the relatively low 22km hiking route between Melbu and Trolldalen, near Stokmarknes. The Ørnheihytta hut makes a good lunch stop and offers a superb view of northern Lofoten. Strong hikers can complete the trip in about six hours.

LANGØYA
pop 14,500

The high points, both literally and figuratively, of Langøya, Vesterålen's central island, are the historic, little-visited fishing villages at its northern tip. Should you be passing through Sortland around bedtime, you'll find some decent lodging options that also offer good dining.

FESTIVALS & EVENTS

The annual 170km **Arctic Sea Kayak Race** (www .askr.no) is one of the ultimate challenges in competitive sea-kayaking, but lesser beings can also opt for a shorter option or an introductory course in sea-kayaking to get geared up for the race the following year. You can register on-line.

Sortland Jazz is a long fun-filled weekend of snappy jazz music and tunes that the town hosts in September.

GETTING THERE & AWAY

In summer, two to four daily buses connect Sortland with Risøyhamn (Nkr78, one hour) and Andenes (Nkr126, two hours).

Buses to/from Harstad (Nkr125, 2¼ hours) run one to three times daily. You can also take the express bus, which passes once or twice daily, to Narvik (Nkr297, 3¾ hours) on the mainland or to Svolvær (Nkr150, 2¼ hours). The Fauske–Lofoten express bus between Fauske (Nkr367, 5¼ hours) and Svolvær runs daily too.

Sortland is also a stop on the Hurtigruten coastal ferry.

GETTING AROUND

You'll find buses between Sortland and Myre (Nkr56, 50 minutes) three to five times daily; some continue on to Stø (Nkr29, 20 minutes).

There's no public transport to Nyksund, and it's a narrow and occasionally shabby dirt road from Myre. Otherwise, the Queen's Route (p305) from Stø is a lovely hike.

Sortland
pop 4600

Sortland, Vesterålen's commercial centre and transit hub, occupies a niche in the island's east coast. Although its typical architecture is large and square (they're trying to liven it up by painting buildings a soothing sea-blue), it has most of the island's lodgings and restaurants. Here too is the helpful tourist office for Vesterålen (see p303).

Sortland Camping og Motell (☎ 76 71 03 00; www .sortland-camping.no; Vestervegen 51; tent sites Nkr75/100, caravan sites Nkr150, cabins Nkr250-400, for 5/7 persons with bathroom Nkr750/850) This family camping ground, Sortland's only option, is 1.25km from the centre. Even if you're staying elsewhere, it's well worth a visit to enjoy the home cooking, strong on northern Norway cuisine. It produces a useful information sheet about the area and can also arrange sightseeing expeditions.

SjøhusSenteret (☎ 76 12 37 40; sjoehus@online.no; Ånstadsjøen; d/tr Nkr550/625, 3-/5-bed cabins Nkr925/1175) Near the bridge, this place has both comfortable rooms and lovely waterside cabins. It too deserves a visit for its Arctic Menu restaurant, where the Danish chef produces a delightful range of à la carte dishes.

Strand Hotell (☎ 76 11 00 80; www.strandhotell .no in Norwegian; Strandgata 34; s Nkr625-840, d 840-1000

mid-Jun–mid-Aug, s Nk795-940, d Nkr965/1110 rest-of-year;
(P 🖵) The waterside, family-run Strand is
that rarity for the offshore islands – a hotel
that's less expensive in summer than during the rest of the year. With its 37 cheery,
upscale rooms, it also has a nightclub, where
there's live music at weekends. **Spisestua**
(☎ 76 12 28 78), its Arctic Menu restaurant, is
equally impressive.

Davida (☎ 76 12 77 00; Strandgata 9; mains Nkr130-
245) The town's newest and most elegant
restaurant serves an excellent selection of
lamb and fish dishes.

Nyksund

This long-abandoned fishing village has
been reborn as an artists' colony. From the
crumbling old structures to the faithfully
renovated commercial buildings, it's pic-
ture-perfect, and the lively summertime atmosphere belies the fact that Nyksund was
a ghost town until only recently.

In 1874, this struggling fishing community improved its harbour and built a mole
to protect ships and buildings from the
open seas. A church was built in 1880, and
Nyksund soon boasted a telegraph station,
bakery, selection of shops and a steamboat.
But in 1934, a fire destroyed the harbour
side; the government determined that it was
too expensive to rebuild and the harbour
proved too small for the new motorised
fishing vessels.

Many residents left but after WWII those
who stayed rebuilt much of the town in
stone and enlarged the harbour. However,
the bakery and post office shut up shop in
the 1960s and nearly everyone else left in
1975 after a storm destroyed the mole. The
last inhabitant, blacksmith Olav Larsen,
packed his bags in 1977.

Sheep and vandals ruled the site until
1984, when an international project imported youth from around Europe to reno-
vate Nyksund. The team rebuilt homes and
installed electricity, and prospective residents began envisioning utopia. In 1995,
a café and guesthouse started up, along
with artists' studios and relaxing hang-
outs. Modern Nyksund boasts a summer
population of 30 to 40 people and about a
half-dozen hardy souls remain throughout
the harsh winters.

To find out what it's like to live in
Nyksund full time, ask the enthusiastic

German owner of this cosy, historic building **Holmvik Brygge** (☎ 76 13 47 96; www.nyksund
.com; r per person Nkr225; ☺ year-round) that now
functions as a guesthouse. You can either
cater for yourself or enjoy a snack (from
Nkr55), a drink or a filling dinner (Nkr120)
at the Kai Café.

Stø

At the northernmost tip of Langøya clings
the small, distinctive fishing village of Stø.
From June to August, **Whale Tours** (☎ 76 13
44 99; www.whaletours.no) offers daily seven-
hour whale-watching cruises (adult/child
Nkr675/425), leaving at 11am. On the way to
the sperm whales' feeding grounds, they also
pause to view sea birds and seal colonies.

To get in closer, **Vesterålen Nature Events**
(☎ 91 80 32 21; www.vesteraalen-nature-events.no),
bookable through Whale Tours, put on
two-hour seal and bird-watching trips
(adult/child Nkr350/200) by raft and also
do fishing outings (Nkr450/250), with departures from both Stø and Nyksund.

The walk over the headland between
Nyksund and Stø is fabulously scenic. Most
people do the outward leg of this five-hour
circular trek via the 517m Sørkulen and
return via the considerably easier sea level
route. Called *The Queen's Route*, its name
derives from a hike taken by Queen Sonja
in 1994. Free maps detailing sites of interest along the way should be available in
Nyksund, Stø and Sortland. It's waymarked
with red Ts.

Drop down the coast to Alsvåg and this
attractive waterside place, **Tøftenes Sjøhus-
camping** (☎ 76 13 14 55; tofta@online.no; Alsvåg; tent
sites Nkr90 plus per person Nkr10, caravan sites Nkr160,
4-bed cabins with bathroom Nkr550, r Nkr500) is based
in a former trading station. It also has a
well-regarded restaurant with a small
menu of local specialities (mains Nkr135
to Nkr160).

This small waterside facility **Stø Bobilcamp**
(☎ 76 13 25 30; loleinan@frisurf.no; tent sites with bike/
car Nkr100/120, caravan sites Nkr120; ☺ mid-May–mid-
Aug) is stark indeed but it does run a neat,
unpretentious little restaurant, serving primarily fish.

ANDØYA
pop 5900

The 1000m-deep, dark, cold waters of Andøya's northwestern shore attract abundant

stocks of squid, including some very large specimens indeed, and these in turn attract the squid-loving sperm whales. The result is a fairly reliable whale-watching venue and a good share of the region's tourist trade, centred on the town of Andenes.

ORIENTATION & INFORMATION

Andøya, long, narrow and flat except for mountains on its western flank, is atypical of Vesterålen. At its northern end is Andenes, the only place of any size and a departure point for whale-watching boat trips. Other nature safaris depart from the tiny ports of Bleik and Stave, about 10km and 25km southwest of Andenes.

In the southeast corner of the island, Risøyhamn is quiet and under-touristed despite being the island's only Hurtigruten stop.

GETTING THERE & AROUND

The Widerøe route between Andenes and Tromsø is a contender for the world's most scenic flight, and Widerøe flights from Narvik or Bodø are close rivals with spectacular aerial views of the landscapes, seas and agricultural patterns.

By bus, you can reach Andenes from Sortland (Nkr126, two hours, two to four daily) via Risøyhamn (Nkr70, 1¼ hours), from where services are more frequent (a bus to/from Andenes also meets and greets the Hurtigruten in Risøyhamn). As you approach Andenes along the Rv82, you'll cross a vast, soggy moorland that contrasts sharply with the panoramas of distant ragged peaks.

From June to August, a **car ferry** (☎ 77 64 81 00; www.senjafergene.no) connects Andenes with the port of Gryllefjord (adult/car Nkr110/ 630, two hours, two to three daily) on the island of Senja (see p322), passing what must rank as the most magnificent coastal scenery in Norway south of Svalbard.

In Andenes, **Andøy Cycling** (☎ 76 14 12 22), yet another subsidiary of Norlandia, hires bikes between mid-May and mid-September.

Andenes
pop 2800

This straggling village has a rich fishing history and is northern Norway's main base for whale-watching. The harbour front is a charming jumble of wooden boat sheds and general nautical detritus.

The **tourist office** (☎ 76 14 18 10; www.andoyturist .no; Hamnegata 1, Andenes; ☼ 10am-6pm mid-Jun– mid-Aug, 9am-4pm Mon-Fri rest-of-year) covers the whole island and shares premises with the Hisnakul Natural History Centre. It produces a leaflet in English, *Andanes Vær* (Nkr25), that outlines a walking tour of the old town. There's Internet access (per hour Nkr60) on the 1st floor.

SIGHTS & ACTIVITIES

The tourist office sells a combined ticket (adult/child Nkr100/50) that give access to all sights below except the Whale Centre.

The **Hisnakul Natural History Centre** (☎ 76 14 12 03; Hamnegata 1; adult/concession Nkr50/25; ☼ 10am- 6pm mid-Jun–Aug, 9am-4pm Sep–mid-Jun) shares a restored wooden warehouse with the tourist office. It displays the natural history of northern Norway, including sea birds, topography, marine mammals, farming, fisheries and local cultures.

Next door to Hisnakul, the **Northern Lights Centre** (adult/child Nkr40/20; ☼ noon-4pm late Jun-late Aug) is an impressive high-tech Aurora Borealis exhibition featured at the 1994 Winter Olympics in Lillehammer.

The **Whale Centre** (Hvalsenter; ☎ 76 11 56 00; Havnegate 1; adult/child Nkr60/30; ☼ 8am-4pm late May–mid-Jun & mid-Aug–mid-Sep 8am-7.30pm mid-Jun– mid-Aug) provides a perspective for whale-watchers, with displays on whale research, whaling and whale life cycles. Most people visit here in conjunction with a whale-watching tour (see below).

The quaint Arctic-themed **Polar Museum** (☎ 76 14 20 88; Havnegate; adult/child Nkr35/20; ☼ 10am-6pm mid-Jun–Aug) includes displays on local hunting and fishing traditions. There's extensive coverage of the 38 winter hunting expeditions in Svalbard undertaken by Hilmar Nøis, who also collected most of the exhibits.

The town's landmark red **Andenes Fyr** (lighthouse) opened in 1859. It's been automated for many years now but still presents a classic form. **Guided visits** (adult/child Nkr25/15; ☼ late Jun-Aug), which require a climb up 40m and 148 steps, take place hourly, on the hour between noon and 4pm.

TOURS

The island's biggest outfit, **Whale Safari** (☎ 76 11 56 00; www.whalesafari.no), operating from the Whale Centre, runs popular cruises (adult/concession/child Nkr695/450/350) between late May and mid-September. The tour begins with a guided tour of the Centre and slide show, followed by a three to five-hour boat trip, with guaranteed sightings of sperm whales or your next trip is free. There's also a chance of spotting minke, pilot and humpback whales and, towards the end of the season, killer whales (orca). Trips depart at least once daily (at 10.30am) and more frequently in high summer – and staff pass around the seasickness pills, just like airline boiled sweets before take-off! A tip: weather and high seas only rarely prevent a sailing but try to build in an extra day on the island, just in case you're unlucky.

SLEEPING & EATING
The tourist office can reserve rooms for around Nkr200/300 per single/double with shared bathrooms in private houses. This service apart, the Norlandia hotel chain also seems to have a lock on Andøya's food, lodging and bike hire.

Den Gamle Fyrmesterbolig (☎ 76 14 10 27; Richard Withs gate 11; r Nkr400) In the shadow of Andenes's resplendent red lighthouse, this charming non-Norlandia option is in what was once the lighthouse keepers' cottage. Warmly recommended by readers, it has only four rooms so do reserve in advance. They also have a fully furnished apartment (Nkr600) in a separate building.

Sjøgata Gjestehus (☎ 76 14 16 37; tovekhan@online .no; Sjøgata 4; s/d/tr Nkr350/400/450) This simple but attractive wooden house has a few rooms without private facilities and represents reasonable value. There's a kitchen available for guest use.

Norlandia Andrikken Hotell (☎ 76 14 12 22; www .norlandia.no/andrikken in Norwegian; Storgata 53; s/d mid-Jun–mid-Aug from Nkr420/840, Sun-Thu rest-of-year Nkr950/1295, Fri & Sat Nkr805/1005; P) Norlandia's house-brand lodging is boxy from the outside but the rooms are comfortable and modern. It also runs a decent restaurant (mains Nkr110 to Nkr200).

Andenes Camping (☎ 76 14 12 22; fax 76 14 19 33; tent/caravans Nkr90/120) Run by Norlandia, this fairly basic camping ground, 3.5km from town, is on a seaside meadow.

Andenes Vandrerhjem (☎ 76 14 28 50; fax 76 14 28 55; Havnegata 31; dm/d per person Nkr150; ☺ Jun-Aug) This seasonal HI-affiliated hostel is in an attractive timber-built house. Near

the harbour, it's also part of the Norlandia empire.

Lysthuset (☎ 76 14 14 99; Storgata 51; mains Nkr100-225) This flexible restaurant does everything from pizzas and other speedy stuff to great salads and mains. Go with the first-class fish specialities.

Around Andenes
TOURS
Northern Wildlife Safari (☎ 76 14 28 50) leads two- to three-hour boat tours (adult/child Nkr390/190, from late May to mid-August) from Stave. These sail close to Norway's largest common seal colony before chugging on to a bird sanctuary where auks, puffins and other gulls teem.

Puffin Safari (☎ 76 14 57 75; www.puffinsafari.no), based in Bleik, also does sea bird–watching boat safaris (adult/child Nkr300/150), sailing at 1pm and 3pm, May to mid-August, and also deep-sea fishing trips (adult/child Nkr400/200).

SLEEPING
Havhusene Bleik (☎ 76 14 57 40; fax 76 14 55 51, Fiskeværsveien, Bleik; q Nkr995) With lovely sea houses over the quiet harbour of Bleik, this is a very comfortable way to rough it. Naturally, you can also book through Norlandia...

HINNØYA
Administratively, Hinnøya, the largest island off mainland Norway, splits between the two counties of Troms and Nordland. Contrasting with the islands to the south, it's mostly forested green upland punctuated by snow-caps and deeply indented by stunning fjords. Off Hinnøya's west coast, Vesterålen is divided from Lofoten by the narrow Raftsund strait and even narrower, hugely scenic Trollfjorden with its sheer walls plunging to the water and dwarfing all below.

Harstad
pop 19,500
On a hillside near the northern end of Hinnøya, Harstad is the largest and most active place in the Vesterålen region, even though it's technically in Troms county. It's a small industrial and defence-oriented town full of docks, tanks and warehouses and, in contrast to the laid back tourism-'n'-fishing

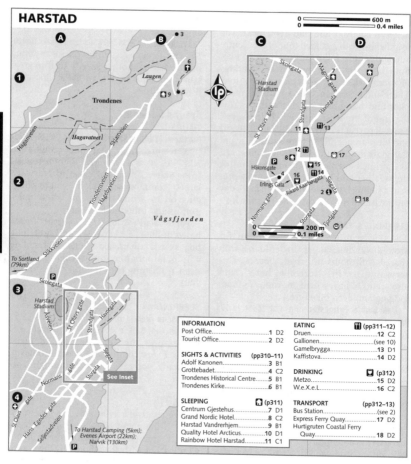

HARSTAD

INFORMATION
Post Office.....................................1 D2
Tourist Office................................2 D2

SIGHTS & ACTIVITIES (pp310–11)
Adolf Kanonen..............................3 B1
Grottebadet...................................4 C2
Trondenes Historical Centre......5 B1
Trondenes Kirke...........................6 B1

SLEEPING (p311)
Centrum Gjestehus......................7 D2
Grand Nordic Hotel.....................8 C2
Harstad Vandrerhjem..................9 B1
Quality Hotel Arcticus..............10 D1
Rainbow Hotel Harstad............11 C1

EATING (pp311–12)
Druen..12 C2
Gallionen...............................(see 10)
Gamelbrygga.............................13 D1
Kaffistova...................................14 D2

DRINKING (p312)
Metzo..15 D2
W.e.X.e.L....................................16 C2

TRANSPORT (pp312–13)
Bus Station...........................(see 2)
Express Ferry Quay...................17 D2
Hurtigruten Coastal Ferry
 Quay...18 D2

towns to the south, pulsates with a certain purposeful bustle. The **tourist office** (☎ 77 01 89 89; www.destinationharstad.no; ☺ 8am-5pm Mon-Fri, 10am-3pm Sat, 11am-2pm Sun Jun–mid-Aug, 8am-3.30pm mid-Aug–May) shares premises with the bus station.

SIGHTS & ACTIVITIES
Most sights are on the Trondenes Peninsula, north of town. For bus services, see p311.

The **Trondenes Historical Centre** (Trondenes Historiske Senter; ☎ 77 01 83 80; Trondenesveien 122; adult/concession/child Nkr70/50/25; ☺ 11am-5pm Mon-Fri, noon-5pm Sat & Sun early Jun–mid-Aug, 11am-4pm Sun only mid-Aug–early Jun) is a must for anyone remotely interested in Scandinavian medieval history. It tells the Viking history of

Hinnøya and nearby Bjarkøy, from where chieftains controlled most of Troms and Vesterålen. It also outlines the transition between the Viking and Christian ages and the bloody battles that marked it.

Trondenes Church (Trondenes Kirke), next door, was built by King Øystein around 1150, after Viking chieftains lost the battle against the unification of Norway under a Christian regime. For ages it was the northernmost church in Christendom – and still lays claim to be the northernmost *stone* church in Norway. Originally of wood, the current stone structure replaced it around 1250 and quickly came to double as a fortification against Russian aggression. Its jewels are the three finely wrought altars at the east end, all venerating Mary. Most interesting is the central one of the Virgin surrounded by her extended family with infants in arms and children tugging at skirts on all sides. Glance up too at the pair of trumpet-wielding cherubs precariously perched atop the main pillars of the rood screen. From June to early August, there are guided tours in English (adult/child Nkr25/10, 2pm and 4pm) at least twice daily except Saturday. Entry is free between tour visits.

Here's another biggest/furthest claim for Harstad: the formidable WWII weapon known as the **Adolf Kanonen** is cited as the world's largest land-based big gun, with a calibre of 40.6cm and a recoil force of 635 tonnes. Because it lies in a military area, you're obliged to take a **guided tour** (Nkr55; 11am, 1pm, 3pm & 5pm Jun–mid-Aug) of the site and to have your own vehicle. Just turn up 10 minutes before departure. The bunker also contains a collection of artillery, military equipment and instruments used by German coastal batteries during WWII.

Grottebadet (☎ 77 04 17 70; Håkonsgate 7; adult/child/family Nkr130/85/360; ☼ 10am-8pm Mon-Fri, 11am-6pm Sat & Sun), a heated indoor complex built into the hillside, has pools, rapids, slides, flume rides, steam rooms and other watery activities. Huge fun for all the family – but steel yourself to resist the kids' pleas for a *grottyburger* (Nkr100)!

SLEEPING
Centrum Gjestehus (☎ 77 06 29 38; www.centrum gjestehus.no; Magnusgata 5; s/d Nkr340/440, with bathroom Nkr390/490) Rooms are fairly basic at this exceptionally friendly, informal place, but represent great value. There are a couple of kitchens for guest use.

Quality Hotel Arcticus (☎ 77 04 08 00; www.choice hotels.no; Havnegata 3; s/d mid-Jun–mid-Aug Nkr640/840, Sun-Thu rest-of-year Nk1250/1460, Fri & Sat Nkr600/800; P) In a harmonious modern building that it shares with Harstad's cultural centre, this hotel, a short, pleasant jetty walk from the centre, has particularly large rooms. It's Nkr150 extra to be sure of reserving a waterside room with splendid views over the fjord to the mountains beyond. This said, you stand a good chance of striking lucky if you just turn up, unless a couple of tour groups have invaded.

Harstad Vandrerhjem (☎ 77 04 00 78; harstad .hostel@wandrerhjem.no; Trondenesveien 110; s/d/tr incl breakfast Nkr290/480/570) A school for the rest of the year, this summer hostel has captivating harbour views. Take bus No 117 from town.

Grand Nordic Hotel (☎ 77 00 30 00; www.rica.no; Strandgata 9; s/d mid-Jun–mid-Aug Nkr590/690, Sun-Thu rest-of-year Nk1250/1460, Fri & Sat Nkr590/790; P ▯) This is the grande dame of Harstad hotels. Request one of the larger, nicer rooms in the newer section.

Rainbow Hotel Harstad (☎ 77 00 08 00; www .rainbow-hotels.no; Sjøgaten 11; s/d mid-Jun–mid-Aug Nkr630/790, Sun-Thu rest-of-year Nk1190/1490, Fri & Sat Nkr650/790) All 141 rooms at this decent chain hotel, Harstad's newest, have attractive parquet flooring and most have views over the fjord, albeit from one block back.

Harstad Camping (☎ 77 07 36 62; www.harstad -camping.no; Nesseveien 55; 4-bed cabins Nkr330, with bathroom Nkr700-800; tent or caravan sites Nkr140; ☼ year-round) Follow the Rv83 towards Narvik for 4km, then take a dirt, potholed road to reach this small waterside site, where you can rent rowing boats (per hour/day Nkr80/230) and motor boats (Nkr140/550).

EATING
Gamelbrygga (☎ 77 00 10 20, Havnegata 23b; mains Nkr210-245; ☼ Mon-Sat) Within a former dockside warehouse, this attractive little restaurant is sandwiched between the ground-floor piano bar, from which the music wafts upwards, and a nightclub (with weekend disco) above. It's a welcoming place with a congenial atmosphere. The cuisine is refined and the presentation, quite impeccable. Lording over all is the quaint photo-portrait of a couple in formal 19th-century dress, toasting each other and – their eyes can't fail to engage your own – their fellow diners.

Gallionen (☎ 77 04 08 00; mains Nkr245-265) The restaurant of the Quality Hotel Arcticus is an Arctic Menu establishment that also does a tempting daily special (Nkr130 to Nkr150). Fish dishes are its forte, particularly the grilled fillet of wolf-fish (Nkr245). Views, whether through the dining room's picture windows or from the quayside deck, will have you gasping.

Kaffistova (☎ 77 06 12 57; Rikard Kaarbøsgata 6; dishes Nkr40-135) You'll eat well enough at this amenable spot, established in 1913. Down by the port, it opens for lunch, dinner and afternoon coffee and snacks.

NORDLAND

JAN MAYEN ISLAND

The island of Jan Mayen, which belongs to Norway, lies 600km north of Iceland, 500km east of Greenland and a full 1000km west of the Norwegian mainland. It sits squarely on the northern end of the mid-Atlantic ridge and at its northern end, known as Nord-Jan, rises Norway's only active volcano, Beerenberg (2277m). The island measures 54km long by up to 16km wide, and covers 380 sq km. This includes a 3.5-sq-km out-cropping called Nylandet, created by an eruption of Beerenburg in September 1970.

In 1614, English captain John Clarke stumbled upon the island and called it Isabella, but the name didn't stick. Later the same year, the Dutch captain Jan Jakobs May van Schellinkhout arrived in a fog so dense that he couldn't even see the length of his own ship; the island only gave itself away by the sound of the waves breaking on its barren shores. He realised he'd discovered an uncharted island, and his first mate did some mapping and ingratiatingly named the place after his captain.

Around 1633, the Dutch began whaling in the area and sent seven sailors to overwinter and thereby establish a Dutch presence and a place to boil down the blubber, but the entire mission died of scurvy. That didn't stop the whaling; however, the Greenland right whale became nearly extinct in these waters, and commercial whaling ended in 1640.

The island was then used as a staging point for polar expeditions and a meteorological post. During WWII, it was operated by Norwegian forces in exile. In 1943, the Americans established a radio installation called Atlantic City and, after the war, Norway and the USA set up a joint Loran (long-range navigation) station. Nowadays, all that remains is a small Norwegian meteorological post.

A dispute between Norway and Denmark regarding the fishing exclusion zone between Jan Mayen and Greenland was settled in 1988, granting the greater area of sovereignty to Denmark. Jan Mayen is administered nowadays by the county of Nordland, from Bodø.

Visiting Jan Mayen

Independent travel to Jan Mayen is all but nonexistent, and even organised visits are extremely rare, for understandable reasons: there's no port; safe sailing weather can never be assured; and, for each landing, ships must apply for permission from the Norwegian government, with no assurance of it being granted. Still, a handful of expeditions to or from Iceland, Greenland and Scotland list Jan Mayen in their itineraries – although do look at the small print to check whether they land or just peek offshore. One operator that includes Jan Mayen among its Arctic region tours is **Arcturus Expeditions** (www.arcturusexpeditions.co.uk).

Druen (☎ 77 07 50 75; Strandgata 14b; mains Nkr140-260) This handsome steakhouse does reliable transatlantic dishes such as Texas Ranger, Mexican Hot and – even hotter – Pepper-biff, all based on prime quality beef.

DRINKING

Metzo (☎ 77 07 58 58; Strandgata 12) This cool coffee house-cum-pub with its stylish décor serves the usual snack fare until 9pm. In bar mode, it can shake 'n' mix a huge range of cocktails, shooters, slammers and long drinks.

W.e.X.e.L (☎ 77 07 50 00; Rikard Kaarbøsgata 17; ☽ to 11pm Mon-Fri, to 4am Sat & Sun) This flexible place operates as a daytime café and evening drinks bar with a discotheque every Saturday night and live music now and again. At

weekends, the hard drinkers head for the downstairs bar.

GETTING THERE & AWAY

The Harstad–Narvik airport, at Evenes, one hour east of town by bus, has direct flights to Oslo, Bodø, Tromsø and Trondheim.

If you're heading for Tromsø, the easiest and most scenic option is by boat. There are two to three **TFDS** (☎ 77 64 81 00) express passenger ferries daily between Harstad and Tromso (Nkr430, 2¼ hours), via Finnsnes (Nkr235, 1½ hours).

TFDS also runs year-round daily express passenger ferries between Harstad and Skrolsvik (Nkr100, 1¼ hours), at the southern end of Senja island, where you'll find bus connections to Finnsnes and thence on to Tromsø. Between mid-June and mid-August, a **car ferry** (www.senjafergene .no) also runs to/from Skrolsvik (adult/car Nkr100/575, 1½ hours, two to four daily). Harstad is also a stop on the Hurtigruten coastal ferry.

Buses to/from Sortland (Nkr125, 2¼ hours) run one to three times daily. The bus to/from Narvik (Nkr142, 2½ hours), via Evenes airport (Nkr65, one hour), operates two or three times daily. There is a daily service between Harstad and Fauske (Nkr393, 5¾ hours).

GETTING AROUND

Flybussen (one way/return Nkr110/170, 50 minutes) shuttles between the town centre and Evenes airport several times daily.

Centrum Gjestehus (☎ 77 06 29 38; www.centrum gjestehus.no; Magnusgata 5; per day Nkr70-100) rents bicycles.

Buses (Nkr22, 10 minutes, hourly, Monday to Friday only) connect Trondenes with the central bus station.

Parking may not be easy to find but – God bless the good burghers of Harstad – it's free in public car parks for vehicles with non-Norwegian licence plates.

For a taxi, call ☎ 77 04 10 00.

Lødingen

The pretty coastal village of Lødingen is a major crossroads, and while it's no tourist hot spot, it's a pleasant place to cool one's jets. Its only museum, the **Lødingen Pilots' Museum & Norwegian Telecom Museum** (☎ 76 98 66 00; Ringveien 5; adult/child Nkr30/10; 4-7pm Wed, noon-3pm Thu-Sat Jun-Aug), chronicles 130 years of communications and the work of northern Norway's ship pilots.

The **Lødingen tourist office** (☎ 76 93 23 12), by the bus and taxi stand, opens mid-June to mid-August.

A friendly, immaculate guesthouse, **Centrum Overnatting** (☎ 76 93 12 94; fax 76 93 15 45; Signalveien; dm/d Nkr150/400), located across from the water, has most of its rooms and apartments with private bathrooms. Dorms are four-bed rooms. There's also a barbecue hut outside.

The express ferry M/S *Børtind*, running between Svolvær (Nkr176, two hours) and Narvik (Nkr146, 1¼ hours), calls in daily except Saturday. Lødingen is also a stop on most of the bus routes between Narvik (Nkr176, three hours) or Fauske (Nkr229, four hours) and Harstad (Nkr97, 1¼ hours), Sortland (Nkr82, one hour) and Svolvær (Nkr201, 3¾ hours).

NORDLAND

The Far North

Norway's northern counties of Troms and Finnmark arc across the top of Europe and represent Europe's last mainland frontier. This undervisited land of broad horizons alternates with dense forest and part of the thrill is the sheer effort of getting where few others go.

Tromsø, the area's only town of any size, well merits a couple of days to catch your breath before pushing deeper into the sparsely inhabited lands to the north and east. It's an animated, self-confident place; its museums will orient you for the Arctic lands beyond and, should you choose to linger longer, it makes a great base for winter sports and summer hiking – or a diversion to the dramatic island of Senja.

The goal of so many travellers is Nordkapp, North Cape, nearer to the North Pole than to Oslo and the European mainland's most northerly point. Or very nearly so; to reach the real point of no return, pack your boots and enjoy an 18km round-trek across the tundra.

The plateaus of Inner Finnmark and the wild northeastern coast are the Norwegian heartland of the Sami people, whose territory, traditionally known as Lapland, straddles the frontiers with Sweden, Finland and Russia. If you're travelling to or from Finland, build in a stop at Karasjok, the Sami 'capital', to visit its Sápmi Park, the most tasteful theme park you're ever likely to visit, the more academic Sami National Museum and the architecturally stunning, all-wood Sami Parliament.

Well worth the detour too is tiny Kirkenes, last port of call of the Hurtigruten coastal ferry. With all the feel of a frontier town, its signs are in both Norwegian and Cyrillic script and you'll hear almost as much Russian as Norwegian on the streets.

THE FAR NORTH

HIGHLIGHTS

- Reaching dramatic **Nordkapp** (p330) after the long haul northwards, then leaving the crowds behind to hike to **Knivskjelodden** (p331), continental Europe's northernmost point

- Learning about the unique Sami culture in **Karasjok** (p349) and **Kautokeino** (p346)

- Exploring **Alta's Stone-Age rock carvings** (p325), a Unesco World Heritage site, and learning more at its award-winning museum

- Dog-mushing through the snow and bruise-blue winter light near **Karasjok** (p350)

- Driving through haunting lunar terrain past reindeer herds to tiny **Hamningberg** (p341), near Vardø

- Listening to an organ recital as the midnight sun peeks through the windows of **Tromsø's Arctic Ocean Cathedral** (p316) before heading off to savour the town's summer nightlife

Nordkapp & Knivskjelodden ★
Hamningberg ★
★ Alta   ★ Karasjok
★ Tromsø
★ Kautokeino

| AREA: 71,025 SQ KM | HIGHEST ELEVATION: NJUNES (1713M) | POPULATION: 225,800 |

TROMS

This section covers the northern two-thirds of Troms county; the Troms portion of the island of Hinnøya features in the Nordland chapter.

TROMSØ

pop 52,100

Simply put, Tromsø parties. The main town of Troms county – by far the largest in northern Norway – is lively with cultural bashes, buskers, an animated street scene, a midnight sun marathon, the hallowed Mack brewery – and more pubs per capita than any other Norwegian town. Its corona of snow-topped peaks provides arresting scenery, excellent hiking in summer and great skiing and dog-sledding in winter.

Many Tromsø landmarks claim northernmost titles, including the university, Protestant cathedral, brewery (not technically – but read on), botanical garden, and even the most boreal Burger King. The city lies just off the Arctic Ocean at nearly latitude 70°N – almost 400km north of the Arctic Circle – but the climate is pleasantly moderated by the Gulf Stream, and the long winter darkness is offset by round-the-clock activity through the perpetually bright days of summer.

Tromsø received its municipal charter in 1794 when the city was developing as a trading centre, but its history goes back to the 13th century, when the first local church was built. In more recent times, the city became a launching point for polar expeditions, and thanks to that distinction, it's nicknamed 'Gateway to the Arctic' (more appropriate than 'Paris of the North', as suggested by an apparently myopic German visitor in the early 1900s).

Orientation

Tromsø's centre is on the east shore of the island of Tromsøya (Map p316), separated by hills from the west shore and airport. The lively, central port area runs from the Skansen docks, past the Stortorget (main square) and Hurtigruten coastal ferry pier to the Mack Brewery and waterfront Polaria

THE FAR NORTH

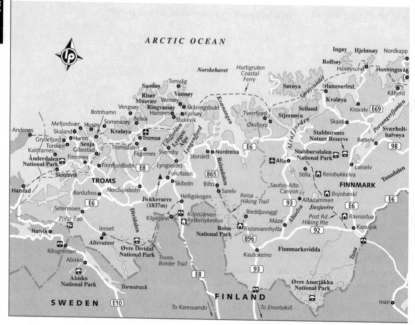

museum. The city also spills across a channel to Tromsdalen on the mainland, with suburbs on Kvaløya island to the west. Two gracefully arching bridges link the sections.

Information

Centrum Libris (Map p317; ☎ 77 66 72 00; Sjøgata 31/33) Centrally located bookstore.

Dark Light (Map p317; ☎ 77 68 74 44; 1st fl, Stotorget 1; per hr Nkr60; 🕑 3-11pm Mon-Fri, noon-11pm Sat, 6-11pm Sun) The Internet can be accessed here.

Main post office (Strandgata 41)

Tourist office (Map p317; ☎ 77 61 00 00; www .destinasjontromso.no; Storgata 61-63; 🕑 8.30am-6pm Mon-Fri, 10am-5pm Sat, 10.30am-5pm Sun Jun–mid-Aug, 8.30am-4pm Mon-Fri, 10.30am-2pm Sat & Sun mid-Aug–May, closed Sun mid-Sep–mid-May) Exceptionally well informed. Pick up its comprehensive *Infoguide* booklet.

Troms Turlag DNT office (Map p317; ☎ 77 68 51 75; www.turistforeningen.no; Grønnegata 32; 🕑 10am-2pm Tue-Wed & Fri, 10am-6pm Thu) For walking maps, books and cabin reservation.

Tromsø Bruktbokhandel (Map p317; ☎ 77 68 39 40; behind Kirkegata 6) For used books.

Via Ferieverden (Map p317; ☎ 77 64 80 02; Storgata 48) Can organise tailor-made trips to Svalbard.

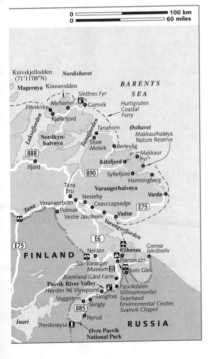

Sights & Activities

TROMSØ MUSEUM

This **museum** (Map p316; ☎ 77 64 50 00; Lars Thøringsvei 10; adult/child Nkr30/15; 🕑 9am-8pm mid-Jun–mid-Aug, 9am-6pm mid-May–mid-Jun & mid-Aug–mid-Sep, 9am-3.30pm Mon-Fri, 11am-5pm Sat & Sun mid-Sep–mid-May), near the southern end of Tromsøya, is northern Norway's largest museum. It has well-presented displays on Arctic animals, church architecture, Sami culture and regional history, and runs a short video that gives you a view of the northern lights. Catch bus No 28 from Torget.

POLARIA

This is Tromsø's daringly designed **museum** (Map p317; ☎ 77 75 01 00; Hjalmar Johansens gate 12; adult/child Nkr80/40; 🕑 10am-7pm mid-May–mid-Aug, noon-5pm mid-Aug–mid-May) of the Arctic. A panoramic film takes you to Svalbard, the cluster of islands around latitude 80°N – see left, if you become inspired). This museum has imaginative aquaria house Arctic fish and – the big draw – a quintet of energetic bearded seals. Other exhibits explore nature and human habitation at both poles. Just try to leave without a polar bear mask from the gift shop.

POLAR MUSEUM

This harbourside **museum** (Map p317; Polarmuseet; ☎ 77 68 43 73; Søndre Tollbugata 11; adult/child/family Nkr45/10/90; 🕑 10am-7pm mid-Jun–mid-Aug, 11am-3pm or 5pm rest-of-year), housed in a restored customs house near the colourful Skansen docks, focuses on polar research and exploration – and Roald Amundsen in particular. It also ventures into less universally agreeable issues such as the hunting and trapping of fuzzy Arctic creatures.

CABLE CAR

You get a fine view of the city and the midnight sun by taking the **Storsteinen Fjellheis** (Map p316; ☎ 77 63 87 37; adult/child return trip Nkr70/30; 🕑 10am-1am late May–mid-Aug, 10am-5pm Apr-late May & mid-Aug–Sep) 420m up Mt Storsteinen. There's a restaurant at the top, from where a network of hiking routes radiates. Take bus No 26 and you can get a combination bus/cable car ticket (adult/child Nkr80/40).

MACK BREWERY

Okay, this **brewery** (Map p317; Mack Ølbryggeri; ☎ 77 62 45 80; Storgata 5) isn't really the world's

THE FAR NORTH

northernmost – a recently opened microbrewery in Honningsvåg near **Nordkapp** (p330) takes that title – but it's an institution nonetheless that merits a pilgrimage. Established in 1877, it nowadays produces 16 kinds of beer, including the very quaffable Macks Pilsner, Isbjørn, Haakon and several dark beers. At 1pm year-round – plus 3.30pm, June to August – tours (Nkr100, including a beer stein, pin and pint) leave from the brewery's own **Ølhallen Pub** (Map p317; 9am-5.30pm Mon-Sat Jun-Aug, 9am-5.30pm Mon-Thu, 9am-6pm Fri, 9am-3pm Sat Sep-May). Perhaps the world's only, never mind most northerly, watering hole to be closed in the evening, it carries eight varieties on draught.

GLASS-BLOWING

Blast (Map p317; ☎ 47 77 68 34 60; Peder Hansens Gate; admission free; 10am-5pm Mon-Fri, 10am-3pm Sat) is the most northerly glass-blowing workshop in the world, well worth passing by to see the young team puffing their cheeks and perhaps to pick up an item or two.

CHURCHES

The **Arctic Cathedral** (Ishavskatedralen; Map p316; ☎ 77 64 76 11; Hans Nilsensvei 41; adult/child Nkr22/free; 10am-8pm Mon-Sat, 1-8pm Sun Jun–mid-Aug), as the Tromsdalen Kirke is styled, was strikingly designed by Jan Inge Hovig in 1964, its 11 arching triangles suggesting glacial crevasses and auroral curtains. Most striking of all is the wonderful, glowing stained-glass window that occupies almost the whole of the east end. Designed and executed by Victor Sparre almost a decade later (since for many, the church, as designed, was altogether too stark), it depicts Christ redescending to earth. Look back toward the west end and the contemporary organ, a work of steely art in itself, and up high to take in the lamps of Czech crystal, hanging in space like icicles. **Concerts** (Nkr70; Jun–mid-Aug) take place nightly at 11.30pm. The swelling organ and the light of the midnight sun streaming through the huge west window can be one of the great sensory moments of your trip.

In the city centre is the Protestant **Tromsø Domkirke** (Map p317; Storgata 25; 10am-4pm Tue-Sat, noon-4pm Sun Jun-Aug, 10am-2pm Tue-Sat, noon-4pm Sun Sep-May), one of Norway's largest wooden churches, and the **Catholic Church** (Map p317; Storgata 94; 9am-7.30pm). Both were built in 1861 and each lays claim to be – here

comes yet another superlative – 'the world's northernmost bishopric' of its kind.

HISTORIC BUILDINGS

The booklet *Town Walks*, available from the tourist office (Nkr60), is quite a well-illustrated, exhaustive rundown of Tromsø's historic buildings.

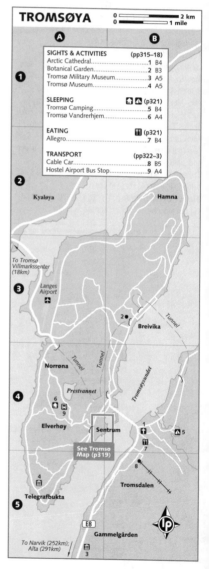

TROMSØYA

0 — 2 km
0 — 1 mile

	A	B

SIGHTS & ACTIVITIES (pp315–18)
Arctic Cathedral.....................1 B4
Botanical Garden....................2 B3
Tromsø Military Museum.........3 A5
Tromsø Museum.....................4 A5

SLEEPING (p321)
Tromsø Camping....................5 B4
Tromsø Vandrerhjem..............6 A4

EATING (p321)
Allegro................................7 B4

TRANSPORT (pp322–3)
Cable Car............................8 B5
Hostel Airport Bus Stop.........9 A4

Kvaløya   Hamna

To Tromsø
Villmarkssenter
(18km)

Langnes
Airport

2 ● Breivika

Tunnel

Norrøna

Tunnel Tunnel

Tromsøysundet

6
9
Prestvannet

Elverhøy   Sentrum   1

5

See Tromsø
Map (p319)

7

8

4
Telegrafbukta   Tromsdalen

E8   Gammelgården

To Narvik (252km);
Alta (291km)   3

TROMSØ

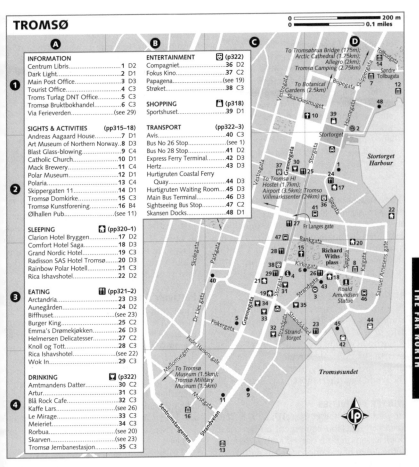

0 — 200 m
0 — 0.1 miles

THE FAR NORTH

You'll find lots of early-19th-century timber buildings around the centre. At Søndre Tollbugate 1, **Andreas Aagaard House**, built in 1838, was the first building in town to be electrically lit (in 1898). You'll also see a line-up of 1830s shops and merchants' homes along Sjøgata, a block south of the Stortorget. At Skippergaten 11, an 1833 home adjoins Tromsø's only remaining **town garden.**

ART MUSEUM OF NORTHERN NORWAY
This **art museum** (Nordnorsk Kunstmuseum; Map p317; ☎ 77 64 70 20; Sjøgata 1; adult/child/family Nkr30/20/70; ☻ 10am-5pm Tue-Fri, noon-5pm Sat & Sun) exhibits mainly 19th- to 21st-century sculpture, photography, painting and handicrafts by artists from northern Norway. It also runs

an active and full programme of temporary exhibitions.

TROMSØ KUNSTFORENING
The Tromsø branch of this national contemporary **art foundation** (Map p317; ☎ 77 65 58 27; Muségata 2; adult/concession/child Nkr30/15/free; ☻ noon-5pm Tue-Sun) makes the most of its late-19th-century premises and promotes rotating exhibitions of contemporary art.

TROMSØ MILITARY MUSEUM
The southern end of Tromsø's mainland was first developed by the Germans in 1940 as a coastal artillery battery, complete with six big guns. The cannons have been restored as the basis of the **military museum**

THE TROMSØ PALM

In and around Tromsø, you're bound to encounter the ubiquitous *Heracleum laciniatum*, which is known elsewhere by the pedestrian name of 'cow parsnip' and hereabouts by the euphemistic moniker, the 'Tromsø palm'. Although it bears a striking resemblance to edible angelica, don't mistake this poisonous beast for that tasty treat, or you're sure to regret it!

This plant, which has yellow-green flowers arranged in broad 'starburst' clusters, arrived from Asia via Britain in 1850, when it was introduced as an ornamental plant in the mining community of Kåfjord. The climate there proved too dry, however, and the seeds were transferred to Tromsø, where the plant took root, thrived and quickly spread across the island. Eventually, it took root all over northern Norway, and its enormous 2m- to 3m-high clusters have proven impossible to eradicate. What's more, because they're toxic, not even cows will eat them, and people who touch them may suffer an itchy rash.

(Tromsø Forsvarsmuseum; Map p316; ☎ 77 62 88 36; Solstrandveien; adult/child Nkr30/15; ☼ noon-5pm Wed-Sun Jun-Aug, Sun only May & Sep), which also includes a restored commando bunker and an exhibition on the 52,600-tonne German battleship *Tirpitz*, sunk by the Royal Air Force (RAF) at Tromsø on 12 November 1944.

BOTANICAL GARDENS
At around 2 hectares, the Arctic and alpine landscapes of the **Tromsø's Botanisk Hage** (Map p316; ☎ 77 64 50 00; Breivika; admission free; ☼ 24hr) make up in the quality of their flora from all over the world's colder regions, for the relatively small area they occupy. And yes, it's the world's northernmost...take bus No 20.

WINTER ACTIVITIES
In winter, **Sportshuset** (Map p317; ☎ 77 66 11 00; Storgata 87) rents ski equipment and you can book lessons in both cross-country (there are some 70km of groomed trails) and downhill skiing (including that very Norwegian variant, Telemark) at the tourist office.

Tromso Villmarkssenter (Map p316; ☎ 77 69 60 02; www.villmarkssenter.no; Kvaløysletta), warmly recommended by a couple of readers, offers dog-sled excursions, ranging from a short spin to a four-day trek with overnight camping. It's 24km south of town on Kvaløy island. (The Centre also offers a range of summer activities such as trekking and sea-kayaking.)

Tours
A **sightseeing bus** (Map p317; adult/child Nkr210/105; ☼ Jun-Aug) sets out at 3pm from opposite the Protestant cathedral for a 2½-hour tour with an English-speaking guide. It includes visits to the Tromsø Museum and Arctic Cathedral.

Three-hour **fishing trips** (adult/child Nkr275/175; ☼ mid-Jun–mid-Aug) leave from the small quay just southwest of the express ferry terminal at 6pm. Most people pay on the boat but places are much in demand; be smart and make your reservation in advance at the tourist office.

Festivals & Events
The classic **Midnight Sun Marathon** (☎ 77 67 33 63; www.msm.no) has something for all levels of fitness. The 'full monty' 42km marathon is the most northerly in the world to be recognised by AIMS (Association of International Marathons and Road Races) and there's also a half-marathon, a 10km race, a very minimarathon at 4.2km and a children's race. The particular Saturday on which the events are held varies from year to year. For information and to sign up, ring or visit the website.

Altogether more sybaritic is Tromsø's three-day **Øl-Festival** (beer festival) in August (here too the date is flexible so check with the tourist office).

Sleeping
For a fee of Nkr45, the tourist office can book accommodation, including rooms in private homes, where singles/doubles average around Nkr300/500.

Clarion Hotel Bryggen (Map p317; ☎ 77 78 11 00; www.choicehotels.no; Sjøgata 19/21; s Nkr840-1395, d Nkr980-1595; Ⓟ �🖳) This stylish, waterside hotel is architecturally exciting, with its odd angles, aluminium trim, images on the ceilings, sauna – and a top-floor Jacuzzi where you can savour the picturesque harbour and mountain views as you bubble and boil in the hot-tub.

Comfort Hotel Saga (Map p317; ☎ 77 60 70 00; www
.sagahotel.no; Richard Withs plass 2; s/d Nkr775/795 mid-
Jun–mid-Aug, Nkr1050/1350 Sun-Thu, Nkr775/795 Fri & Sat
rest-of-year; P ⌨) The Comfort lives up to its
name with up-to-date rooms, breakfast buffet, light dinner buffet and – when did you
last come across this particular feature? –
a trouser press in every room.

Grand Nordic Hotel (Map p317; ☎ 77 75 37 77;
www.nordic.no in Norwegian; Storgata 44; s/d 750/890 mid-
Jun–mid-Aug, s Nkr800-1200, d Nkr1000-1500 rest-of-year;
⌨) Prices outside summer include a light
dinner. The Grand Nordic is a welcoming
place. Tromsø's oldest hotel, it recently celebrated its centenary. There's little that's antique inside, however, since the place burnt
to the ground twice, the last conflagration
being in 1969.

Radisson SAS Hotel Tromsø (Map p317; ☎ 77 60 00
00; www.radissonsas.com; Sjøgata 7; s/d Nkr795-945 mid-
Jun–mid-Aug, Nk1330/1530 Sun-Thu, Nkr895/1095 Fri & Sat
rest-of-year) You couldn't call this high-rise,
planted plumb in the heart of town, pretty,
but rooms are the last word in comfort and
it has a reputation for professional service
(this said, we found the reception staff fairly
uninformed and offhand on our last visit)
and runs a decent pub, the Rorbua.

Rica Ishavshotel (Map p317; ☎ 77 66 64 00; www.rica
.no; Fredrik Langes gate 2; s/d Nkr1400/1536; ⌨) Down
by the quayside, this hotel, the largest in
town with its 180 rooms, tends to be clogged
up with tour groups. Rooms are attractive,
mostly with superb views of the sound,
but you may find its public areas cavern-
ous and characterless and reception tight-
lipped. The **restaurant** (mains Nkr186-Nkr280), by
contrast, is excellent. Try, for example, the
reindeer with puréed carrot and blueberry
sauce (Nkr280).

Rainbow Polar Hotell (Map p317; ☎ 77 75 17
00; www.rainbow-hotels.no/polar; Grønnegata 45; s/d
Nkr630/790 Jun–mid–Aug, Nkr925/1025 mid-Aug–May,
incl breakfast; P) This relatively simple hotel
has modern rooms and a cheery breakfast
area with city views. Summer tariffs represent great value – and whatever the season,
you'll be staying in the Rainbow chain's
northernmost hotel!

Tromsø Camping (Map p316; ☎ 77 63 80 37; www
.tromsocamping.no; Tromsdalen; tent/caravan sites Nkr150/
170, 2-bed cabins Nkr400, 4-bed Nkr500-600, 4-/5-bed
with bathroom Nkr700) This attractive camping
ground, the only one around Tromsø, has
leafy green pitches, a slow-moving stream

running through it and a cafeteria. Take
bus No 24.

Tromsø Vandrerhjem (Map p316; ☎ 77 65 76 28;
tromso.hostel@vandrerhjem.no; Åsgårdveien 9; dm/s/d
Nkr150/290/380; ☷ mid-Jun–mid-Aug) This summertime HI-affliliated hostel occupies the
university student residences some 1.5km
west of the town centre. Bus No 26 takes
you nearby.

Eating

In Tromsø, the line is blurry between restaurants, cafés and pubs and many places
function in all three modes, simultaneously
or at different times of the day.

Emma's Drømekjøkken & Kaffe Lars (Map p317;
☎ 77 63 77 30; Kirkegata 8; mains Nkr260-298; ☷ Mon-
Sat) This stylish place is the perfect example
of Tromsø flexibility. Kaffe Lars, a cosy café
and coffee place by day, metamorphoses
wondrously into an intimate pub on the
dot of 6pm. But what pulls in discriminat-
ing diners is the highly regarded **Emma's
Drømekjøkken** (☷ 6-10pm Mon-Sat), the upstairs
restaurant, with its imaginative cuisine.

Knoll og Tott (Map p317; ☎ 77 66 68 80; Storgata
62; ☷ Mon-Sat) Run by a cheerful young team,
this popular upstairs-downstairs place with
its fresh salads (Nkr90), crisp baguettes
(Nkr50) and house pies (Nkr90) is ideal
for a filling midday snack.

Wok In (Map p317; ☎ 77 69 65 46; Storgata; ☷ 11am-
midnight Sun-Tue, 11am-2am or 4am Wed-Sat) Just along
the road near Knoll og Tett, this self-service
place hits the spot if you're in need of some
late-night – or indeed any time of day –
spicy rice or noodle sustenance.

Allegro (Map p316; ☎ 77 68 80 71; Turistveien 19;
pizzas Nkr60-240) This pizza option, between
the Arctic Cathedral and the cable car,
bakes Italian-style pies in a birch-fired oven
and also knocks up salads (Nkr85), steaks
(Nkr180) and a Mexican dish or two.

Arctandria (Map p317; ☎ 77 60 07 25; Strandtorget
1; fish mains Nkr195-240) Upstairs and upscale,
Arctandria serves filling ocean catches including some, such as whale steak and the
seal starter (Nkr85), that more sensitive
readers might prefer not to see on a menu.
Less contentious and quite delicious is the
special menu (Nkr340) of goat paté, followed
by monkfish baudroie and crème brulée with
cloudberries. Note that there is one common
entrance to Arctandria, Biffhuset and the
much more pubby Skarven (see p320).

THE FAR NORTH

Biffhuset (Map p317; ☎ 77 60 07 28; Strandtorget 1; mains Nkr110-160) On two floors, wood-panelled and low-beamed, the Beef House is a seriously meaty place. Just tick/check your menu card, indicating size, cut and accompanying sauce and hand it to the server.

Helmersen Delikatesser (Map p317; ☎ 77 65 40 50; Storgata 66) For the day's sandwich fillings, this great little delicatessen carries a good range of cheeses, cold meats and salady items.

If none of the above tickle your palate, you could always simply settle for the world's northernmost **Burger King** (Map p317; ☎ 77 65 89 55; Storgata 84).

You can buy fresh boiled shrimp from fishing boats at the Stortorget waterfront.

Drinking

Tromsø has plenty of thriving nightspots. On Friday and Saturday, most stay open until 4am and many also serve light meals.

Pride of place must go to Ølhallen Pub (see p316), where you can sample Mack Brewery's ales smack bang where they are produced.

Blå Rock Café (Map p317; ☎ 77 61 00 20; Strangata 14/16) This bustling, youthful venue is a favourite rock club, with theme evenings, 75 types of beer, occasional live concerts and weekend disco music.

Le Mirage (Map p317; ☎ 77 68 52 34; Storgata 42) A less rowdy crowd gathers at Le Mirage, which offers reasonably priced sandwiches, salads, pastas and casseroles.

Meieriet (Map p317; ☎ 77 61 36 39; Grønnegata 37/39; ⏰ noon to 2am, to 3.30am Fri & Sat) This busy café/pub has billiards and a menu including burgers, Mexican and Chinese dishes.

Skarven (Map p317; ☎ 77 60 07 43; Strandtorget 1) This waterfront venue, popular mainly with the over-25s, offers fine bar meals (including selections from the restaurants Arctandria and Biffhuset).

Tromsø Jernbanestasjon (Map p317; ☎ 77 61 23 48; Strandgata 33) This railway-themed pub is typical local humour – Tromsø only *wishes* it had a railway station.

Rorbua (Map p317; ☎ 77 75 90 86; Sjøgata 7) Within the Radisson SAS, the Rorbua bills itself as Norway's most famous pub (a TV show was shot here) and has regular live music.

Amtmandens Datter (Map p317; ☎ 77 68 49 06; Grønnegata 81) This more sedate pub – the name is derived from an 1830s novel by Camille Collett – caters to an arty 25-to-35 crowd. Clients can use its newspapers, books, board games and free yet unreliable Internet access.

Artur (Map p317; ☎ 77 64 79 85; Storgata 57) This easygoing, friendly place has been nicely renovated.

Entertainment

Compagniet (Map p317; ☎ 77 65 42 22; Sjøgate 12) is a popular choice for dancing.

Tromsø's main meat market is **Strøket** (Map p317; ☎ 77 68 44 00; Storgata 52), while **Papagena** (Map p317; Storgata 44), at the Grand Nordic Hotel, is good-naturedly referred to as a 'second-hand meat market', with a crowd that starts at about age 35. There's no specific gay venue, but locals will proudly tell you that gays and lesbians are welcome everywhere.

Fokus Kino (Map p317; ☎ 77 75 30 95; Grønnegata 94) is the main cinema, located in a distinctive parabolic building.

Getting There & Away

AIR

Tromsø's **Langnes Airport** (Map p316; ☎ 77 64 84 00), the main airport for the far north, is served by SAS Braathens, Widerøe and Norwegian. Destinations with direct flights include Oslo, Harstad (Evenes), Bodø, Trondheim, Alta, Hammerfest, Kirkenes and Longyearbyen.

BOAT

TFDS (☎ 77 64 81 00) express ferries connect Tromsø and Harstad (Nkr430, 2¾ hours), via Finnsnes (Nkr195, 1½ hours), at least twice daily. Tromsø is also a stop on the Hurtigruten coastal ferry route.

BUS

The main bus terminal (sometimes called Prostneset) is on Kaigata. Nor-Way Bussekspress has at least two daily express buses to and from Narvik (Nkr340, 4¼ hours) and at least one to/from Alta (Nkr380, 6¼ hours), where you can pick up a bus for Honnningsvåg, and from there, on to the Nordkapp.

CAR & MOTORCYCLE

A two- or four-wheeled vehicle is the best way to negotiate Norway's far northern reaches. Car hire isn't cheap but it's available at **Avis** (Map p317; ☎ 77 61 58 50; Strandskillet 5),

Europcar ☎ 77 67 56 00; Alkeveien 5), **Hertz** (Map p317; ☎ 77 62 44 00; Richard Withs plass 4) and **Budget** (☎ 77 65 19 00; Vestregate 2). All also have kiosks at the airport.

Getting Around
TO/FROM THE AIRPORT
Tromsø's airport is about 5km from the centre, on the western side of Tromsøy island. The **Flybuss** (☎ 77 67 75 00; adult/child Nkr45/22) service runs between the airport and the Radisson SAS Hotel (Nkr35, 15 minutes). It connects with arriving and departing flights and stops by other major hotels along the way. Alternatively, take city bus No 42 (Nkr20); arriving air passengers can wait for it on the road opposite the airport entrance.

Taxis between the airport and the centre charge between Nkr100 and Nkr150.

BICYCLE
You can hire town bikes from **Sportshuset** (Map p317; ☎ 77 66 11 00; Storgata 87; per day Nkr175).

BUS
Local buses cost Nkr20 per ride, and Nkr60 for a 24-hour pass.

CAR & MOTORCYCLE
Tromsø has ample parking in the centre. There's also the huge Trygg underground car park, tunnelled into the hill, with its entrance on Vestregata (closed to trailers and caravans).

TAXI
Call ☎ 77 60 30 00.

AROUND TROMSØ
Belvik Ferry
This excellent bus and ferry tour by public transport will take you amid the little islands and communities to the west. The trip begins with a journey by bus No 3 from Tromsø to Belvik (Nkr52, 45 minutes), where you board the ferry for the out-and-back cruise (4½ hours), just in time to connect with a bus back to Tromsø.

Although the ferry runs every day, connections mean that you can do the entire trip on public transport only on Monday, Wednesday, Friday and Sunday from late June to mid-August, leaving the main bus terminal in Tromsø at 4.10pm and returning to Tromsø around 10pm. The Tromsø tourist office sells a combination bus/ferry/bus return ticket for Nkr180.

Sommarøy
pop 265
There's a beautiful beach, popular with Tromsø people, on the small island of Sommarøy, west of Kvaløya, where lots of locals also have holiday cottages.

For a pleasant overnight escape, **Sommarøy Kurs & Feriesenter** (☎ 77 66 40 00; www.sommaroy.no in Norwegian; Hillesøy; s/d/tr Nkr690/890/990, cabins Nkr690-1500) is a relaxing option with both hotel and cabin accommodation built in traditional style.

To reach Sommarøy, take the Hillesøy bus (Nkr94, 1½ hours, once or twice daily) from the main bus terminal in Tromsø.

Sommarøy's port of Brensholmen is also a convenient gateway for Senja (see p322).

Karlsøy
pop 2400
Here's an island with a unique and encouraging recent history. After WWII, the population of this historic fishing community began to decline until by 1970 there remained only 45 people, mostly elderly.

The trend switched dramatically when an emergent counterculture recognised the appeal of this remote island. Over the next decade, young people from elsewhere in Norway and abroad began moving to the island to create a sort of Arctic utopia, complete with communes, 'flower power', an artists' colony, the cultivation of soft drugs and generally anarchistic tendencies. New farmland was cultivated and a new economy emerged, based on the arts, tourism and the production of goats' milk. It's still a unique community and makes an interesting visit.

For the full story on Karlsøy, see the booklet *Among Church Cottages & Goats in Alfred Eriksen's Kingdom* (Nkr60), available at the tourist office in Tromsø.

Bus No 6 connects the main terminal in Tromsø with the Hansnes ferry quay (Nkr105, 1¼ hours, once or twice daily) on Ringvassøy island, from where a ferry runs to Karlsøy.

While you're in the area, you may also want to visit nearby Vannøy Island, with its sandy beaches, classic lighthouse and wild coastline. You can reach the port of Skån-ingsbukt by car ferry daily from Hansnes (Nkr40, 40 minutes) and several times weekly from Karlsøy.

Lyngen Alps

Some of the most rugged alpine peaks in all of Norway form the spine of the heavily glaciated Lyngen Peninsula, east of Tromsø; you get the best views of them from the eastern shore of 150km-long Lyngenfjord. The peaks, the highest of which is Jiekkevarre (1837m), offer plenty of opportunities for mountaineers; the challenging glacial terrain is suitable only for the experienced.

The most accessible and popular hiking area is the Lyngsdalen Valley, above the industrial village of Furuflaten. The usual route begins at the football pitch south of the bridge over the Lyngdalselva and climbs up the valley to the tip of the glacier Syd-breen, 500m above sea level (don't approach the ice as it's rotten and meltwater has created dangerous patches of quicksand).

The map to use for hiking is Statens Karverk's *M711 Storfjord*, sheet 1633IV. For information, contact the tourist office in **Furuflaten** (☎ 77 71 06 92; fax 77 71 02 08; ☑ 10am-2pm late Jun-Aug) or **Svensby** (☎ 77 71 22 25; ☑ 8.30am-8pm Jun-Aug).

SLEEPING

Svensby Tursenter (☎ 77 71 22 25; svensby.tursenter@ c2i.net, Svensby; cabins with bathroom Nkr750) This place, a short jaunt from the ferry landing, can organise outdoor activities, including fishing, wilderness evenings, glacier-hiking, mountaineering and dog-sledding.

GETTING THERE & AWAY

The Nor-Way Bussekspress bus between Tromsø (Nkr78, 1¼ hours, one to three daily) and Alta passes through Svensby. If you're driving, the easiest route involves a ferry from Breivikeidet (east of Tromsø) to Svensby.

SENJA

pop 14,000

Norway's second-largest island, Senja rivals Lofoten for natural beauty yet attracts a fraction of its visitors. The Innersida, the eastern coast facing the mainland, features a broad agricultural plain, while vast virgin forests cloak the interior. Along the western

coast, the Yttersida, a convoluted series of knife-ridged peaks rises directly from the Arctic Ocean. Colourful, isolated fishing villages such as Gryllefjord, Hamn, Ska-land, Mefjordvær, Husøy and Botnhamn are accessible via tiny back roads, making for remote getaways. The road to Mefjord-vær is particularly dramatic. The **tourist office** (☎ 77 85 07 30; www.midtitroms.no; Ringveien) has information on Senja and the surrounding region. Contact the Midt i Troms in the nondescript town of Finnsnes, on the mainland across the bridge from Senja. Its helpful *Infoguide Midt i Troms* contains suggested itineraries.

Sleeping

Fjordbotn Camping (☎ 77 84 93 10; fax 77 84 94 80; Botnhamn; car/caravan sites Nkr70/120, 4-bed cabins Nkr350, 5-/7-bed with bathroom Nkr650/750; ☑ year-round) This modest but friendly spot has a pretty water-side setting on Senja's north coast.

Hamn i Senja (☎ 77 85 98 80; www.hamnisenja.no; Hamn; apt Nkr1175) This is a restored fishing village with a new building or two grafted on, and a great get-away-from-it-all place. You can cater for yourself or eat at their restaurant, Storbrygga Spiseri (open from mid-June to mid-August), in what used to be the fishing station's gutting room. Nearby is the small dam that held back the waters for what is claimed to be the world's first hydroelectric plant, established in 1882.

Finnsnes Hotell Rica (☎ 77 87 07 77; www.rica.no; Strandveien 2, Finnsnes; s/d mid-Jun–mid-Aug Nkr696/892) In Finnsnes centre and but a couple of minutes' walk from the Hurtigruten coastal ferry dock, its boringly boxy exterior belies the comfort within. Take a room on one of the upper floors for fine views.

Getting There & Away

Buses run from Finnsnes' **bus station** (☎ 77 85 35 09) to Tromsø (Nkr185, 2¾ hours) and Narvik (Nkr220, 3½ hours).

TFDS (☎ 77 64 81 00) express ferries connect Finnsnes with Tromsø (Nkr195, 1½ hours) and Harstad (Nkr235, 1¼ hours) two to three times daily. A summertime car ferry connects Skrolsvik, on Senja's south coast, to Harstad (adult/car-and-driver Nkr100/575, 1½ hours, two to four times daily) and another makes convenient connections between Botnhamn on Senja's north coast and Brensholmen, west of Tromsø (adult/

car-and-driver Nkr50/240, 45 minutes, four to seven daily).

In summer, buses connect Finnsnes and the Senja villages of Skaland, Hamn, Botnhamn, Gryllefjord, Skrolsvik, Torsken and Mefjordvær, but not necessarily every day.

Finnsnes is also a stop for the Hurtigruten coastal ferry.

BARDU

The wooded town of Setermoen is the commercial centre for the Bardu district and a staging point for visits to Øvre Dividal National Park.

Setermoen's **tourist office** (☎ 77 18 53 00) is in the town hall. The town is best known to Norwegians as a military training centre.

Sights

Setermoen's church (☼ 10am-5pm Mon-Sat late-Jun– early Aug) was built between 1825 and 1829, and also has a bell dating from 1698. The ingenious heating system, with wood stoves and hot-water pipes beneath the pews, must encourage attendance during even the longest sermons.

The **Polar Zoo** (☎ 77 18 66 30; Bardu; adult/child/ family Nkr135/70/340; ☼ 9am-6pm Jun & Aug, 9am-8pm Jul, 9am-4pm May & Sep) features wildlife of the boreal *taiga* (marshy forest) in spacious enclosures that, but for the metal fencing, are virtually indistinguishable from the surrounding birch forests. Here you can watch and photograph those elusive faces that peer out from postcards all over Norway, including moose, brown bears, deer, musk oxen, reindeer, wolves, lynx, wolverines, badgers and foxes. The zoo is 3.5km east of the E6 and the turn-offs 23km southwest of Setermoen. Follow the keeper around at feeding time (2pm late June to September, noon Monday to Friday, 2pm Saturday and Sunday early June).

Those who are aroused by war games will have fun at the **Troms Defence Museum** (Forsvarsmuseum; adult/child Nkr30/free; ☼ 10am-6pm Mon-Fri, noon-4pm Sat & Sun mid-Jun–mid-Aug, 10am-3pm daily rest-of-year).

Sleeping

Most lodgings are in Setermoen.

Bardu Hotell (☎ 77 18 59 40; barduhotell@bardu.online.no; Toftakerlia 1; s/d Nkr650/800 mid-Jun–mid-Aug, Nkr950/1200 Sun-Thu, Nkr800/950 Fri & Sat rest-of-year; P 💻 🛏) The lobby of this hotel, with pelts splayed across the walls, has a hunting-lodge feel while rooms are decorated in a variety of often twee themes such as spring and summer, Adam and Eve. It's a fair option if you don't want to push on to Tromsø, though you may find reception overly casual. There's a sauna, Jacuzzi and year-round heated pool.

Bardu Camping (☎ 77 18 15 58; fax 77 18 15 98; tent sites Nkr100 plus per person Nkr10, 2-/3-/4-bed cabins Nkr260/360/460, with bathroom Nkr600; ☼ Jun-Aug) At the foot of the mountains off the E6, this camping ground has mini golf and river fishing.

Getting There & Away

The Setermoen bus terminal occupies a car park just east of the E6/Altevannsveien junction. The express bus between Narvik (Nkr131, 1½ hours) and Tromsø (Nkr220, 2¾ hours) calls in three to four times daily and passes within 2km of the Polar Zoo.

ØVRE DIVIDAL NATIONAL PARK

Between Setermoen and the Swedish and Finnish borders lies the wild, roadless, lake-studded Øvre Dividal National Park. While it lacks the spectacular steep-walled scenery of coastal Norway, this remote, semi-forested, 750-sq-km upland wilderness still enjoys lots of alpine peaks and views.

Activities

The most popular hike is the eight-day **Troms Border Trail**, lacing seven unstaffed DNT huts. The route begins along the northern shore of the artificial lake, Altevatnet, about 3km east of the settlement of Innset, and twists northeastwards, curling in and out of Sweden before winding up near the point where Sweden, Finland and Norway meet. At the easternmost hut, Galdahytta, the track splits. Here, you can head for either Helligskogen in Norway or better-equipped Kilpisjärvi in Finland. Many hikers also use the trail between the western end of Altevatn, in Øvre Dividal, and Abisko National Park, in northern Sweden, where you'll find the start of Sweden's renowned Kungsleden hiking route.

The map to use for the Troms Border Trail and the Abisko Link is Statens Kartverk's *Turkart Indre Troms*, at a scale of 1:100,000. In summer, the mosquitoes will drive you to distraction; use a head net, smear yourself liberally with repellent and swat every single last buzzing bastard you can, in the interests of those who follow your footsteps.

Tours

Winter visitors can join a dog-sled trip through Arctic Norway led by renowned and resourceful musher **Bjørn Klauer** (☎ 77 18 45 03; www.huskyfarm.de). In addition to tours through the national park, he runs expeditions deeper into Finnmark. Typical all-inclusive costs are Nkr14,500 for eight days and Nkr24,100 for 13 days.

In summer, he and his team organise cycle and canoe tours or you can do your own thing and hike the several signed trails that pass near. His farm is also a delightful place to stay (see below).

Sleeping

Seven unstaffed DNT huts run the length of the main hiking route through Øvre Dividal: Gaskashytta, Vuomahytta, Dividalshytta, Dærtahytta, Rostahytta, Gappohytta and Galdahytta. Keys and bookings are available from the Troms Turlag DNT office in Tromsø (see p315).

Klauerhytta (☎ 77 18 45 03; www.huskyfarm.de; per person Nkr190) Dog-musher Bjørn Klauer runs this lovely, rustic hut for hikers and other travellers plus a cabin, accommodating up to six (Nkr660). There's a well-equipped kitchen for guest use and you can be active and hire bikes and canoes (both per day from Nkr70).

Helligskogen Fjellstua (☎ 77 71 54 60; helligskogen .hostel@vandrerhjem.no; dm Nkr120; ☱ late Jun–mid-Aug) Near the eastern end of the park on the E8, 30km east of Skibotn, this hostel is surrounded by wild open highlands. It's handy for travel between Norway and Finland, and serves hikers finishing the Troms Border Trail. Follow the 'Vandrerhjem' signs.

Kilpisjärven Retkeilykeskus (☎ 358-16 537 771; www.kilpisjarvi.info in Finnish; Kilpisjärvi, Finland; d/q Nkr522/630, 4-bed cabins Nkr522; ☱ Mar-Sep) Just over the Finnish border, this friendly, inexpensive place anchors the eastern end of the Troms Border Trail. It has simple rooms, a good-value café and cooking facilities for guest use. You can arrange boat trips across Lake Kilpisjärvi and take a choice of scenic hikes through Finland's highest mountains.

WESTERN FINNMARK

Norway's northernmost mainland county, Finnmark has been inhabited for up to 12,000 years, first by the Komsa hunters of the coastal region and later by Sami fishing cultures and reindeer pastoralists, who settled on the coast and in the vast interior, respectively.

The county enjoys a distinctly dual landscape. Its wild northern coast, dotted with fishing villages, is deeply indented by grand fjords, while the relatively expansive interior is dominated by the broad Finnmarksvidda plateau, a stark wilderness with only two major settlements, Karasjok and Kautokeino.

Virtually every Finnmark town was decimated at the end of WWII by retreating Nazi troops, whose scorched-earth policy intended to delay advancing Soviets. Towns were soon rebuilt but, unfortunately, the most efficient architectural style was boxy. So in contrast to the spectacular natural surroundings, most present-day Finnmark towns are architecturally uninspiring.

Dangers & Annoyances

They're not dangerous and they're more charming than annoying but they might slow your progress and bring you to a very abrupt halt if you hit one at speed. Do keep an eye out for reindeer on the road. Sometimes in small groups, now and again in vast flocks, they might not be fazed by your inanimate car. If they refuse to budge, just get out, walk towards them and they'll amble away.

ALTA

pop 12,000

Although the fishing and slate quarrying town of Alta lies at 70°N latitude, it enjoys a relatively mild climate and, it's claimed, less precipitation than the Sahara. The Alta Museum, with its ancient petroglyphs, is a must-see and the lush green Sautso-Alta Canyon, a quick hop away, is simply breathtaking and houses some unique attractions (see p327).

The river Altaelva, which runs to the east of town, was once a Sami fishery and a popular haunt of sporting 19th-century English aristocrats. Not long ago, it became one of the most contested waterways in northern

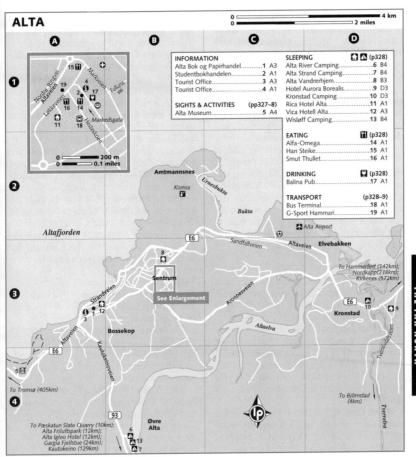

ALTA

| 0 | 4 km |
| 0 | 2 miles |

INFORMATION
Alta Bok og Papirhandel..............1 A3
Studentbokhandelen..................2 A1
Tourist Office...............................3 A3
Tourist Office...............................4 A1

SIGHTS & ACTIVITIES   (pp327–8)
Alta Museum.................................5 A4

SLEEPING   (p328)
Alta River Camping.....................6 B4
Alta Strand Camping....................7 B4
Alta Vandrerhjem..........................8 B3
Hotel Aurora Borealis..................9 D3
Kronstad Camping.....................10 D3
Rica Hotel Alta...........................11 A1
Vica Hotell Alta..........................12 A3
Wisløff Camping.........................13 B4

EATING   (p328)
Alfa-Omega.................................14 A1
Han Steike..................................15 A1
Smut Thullet...............................16 A1

DRINKING   (p328)
Balina Pub..................................17 A1

TRANSPORT   (p328–9)
Bus Terminal..............................18 A1
G-Sport Hammari.......................19 A1

THE FAR NORTH

Europe when, in the late 1970s and in the face of strong local and national opposition, a 100m-high dam, the Altadammen, was built to exploit this rich salmon-spawning stream for hydroelectric power.

Orientation

Alta has a large footprint, occupying some 15km of coastline. Its two main centres are about 2km apart: hilly Bossekop to the west, and Sentrum in – well, just that – which is office-park-like, although the traffic-free nucleus is pleasant enough.

Information

Alta Bok og Papirhandel (☎ 78 43 46 22; Altaveien 99) Maps and books can be purchased here.

Studentbokhandelen (☎ 78 43 58 77; Sentrumsparken 2) Books and maps are sold at this place.

Tourist office (☎ 78 44 50 50; Parksentret building, Sentrum; ⏲ 8.30am-4.30pm Mon-Fri, 10am-4pm year-round)

Tourist office (☎ 78 44 95 55; www.altatours.no; Sorekskriverveien, Bossekop; ⏲ 10am-8pm Mon-Fri, 10am-5pm Sat, noon-6pm Sun Jun-Aug) Has Internet access (per 10 minutes Nrk15).

Sights

Upon the cliffs, which are a Unesco World Heritage site, are around 5000 late Stone-Age carvings, estimated to date from 6000 to 2000 years ago. As the sea level decreased after the last ice age, carvings were made at progressively lower heights. Themes include hunting scenes, fertility symbols, bears, moose, reindeer and crowded boats. The works have been highlighted with red-ochre paint (thought to have been the original colour) and are connected by 3km of boardwalks which start at the main building. The short loop (1.2km; allow around 45 minutes, including viewing time) is the most visited. You can also graft on a second loop (total distance 2.1km), a pleasant seaside walk that takes in more sites.

In Hjemmeluft at the western end of town is **Alta Museum** (☎ 78 45 63 30; Altaveien 19; adult/child Nkr75/free; ⏰ 8am-9pm daily Jun-Aug, 9am-6pm daily May & Sep, 9am-3pm Mon-Fri, 11am-4pm Sat & Sun Oct-Apr). Inside, it features exhibits and displays on Sami culture, Finnmark military history, the Alta hydroelectric project and observations of the mesmerising Aurora Borealis (northern lights).

Sleeping

You'll find three outstanding riverside camping grounds, each open year-round, in Øvre Alta, 3.5km south of the E6 along the Rv93, in the direction of Kautokeino.

Alta River Camping (☎ 78 43 43 53; www.alta-river-camping.no; person/pitch Nkr20/80, cabins Nkr350-500, with bathroom for up to 6 persons Nkr1000) Special features are its sauna, from which you can plunge straight into the river and a couple of cute little barbecue huts, furnished with skins.

Wisløff Camping (☎ 78 43 43 03; www.wisloeff.no in Norwegian; person/pitch Nkr10/110, cabins Nkr290-400, with bathroom Nkr500-750) Declared Norwegian Camping Club 'campground of the year' in 2000, it still well deserves the accolade.

Alta Strand Camping (☎ 78 43 40 22; fax 78 43 42 40; site for 2/4 persons Nkr140/180, cabins Nkr260-560, with bathroom Nkr) Just down the road from Wisløff, this camping ground has mountain views.

Kronstad Camping (☎ 78 43 03 60; fax 78 43 11 55; Altaveien 375; tent/caravan sites Nkr70/100, 4-bed cabins Nkr350-450, 6-bed with bathroom Nkr600) If you're without wheels, Kronstad Camping, beside the E6 just east of Alta, isn't so prettily situated but will save you quite a walk.

Vica Hotell (☎ 78 43 47 11; www.vica.no; Fogdebakken 6; s/d Nkr1010/1190; P 💻) In a timber-built former farmhouse, the Vica, from the stuffed brown bear that greets you at the door onwards, is a welcoming place. It has a free sauna, steaming outdoor Jacuzzi (wonderful in winter when all around is snowcapped) and a lovely little family museum that the friendly owners will happily show you.

Hotel Aurora Borealis (☎ 78 45 78 00; www.hotelaurora.no; Saga; s/d Nkr750/910; P 💻) Cosy and secluded, just east of town and 200m from the E6, this renovated, art-filled hotel also has a fine restaurant.

Rica Hotel Alta (☎ 78 48 27 00; www.rica.no; Løkkeveien 61; s/d Nkr730/875 mid-Jun–mid-Aug, Nkr1250/1395 Sun-Thu, Nkr715/890 Fri & Sat rest-of-year; P) Modern, open and pleasant, the Rica is square and has parking-lot views, making it a fitting emblem for Sentrum. It also boasts a fine Arctic Menu restaurant.

Alta Vandrerhjem (☎ 78 43 44 09; alta.hostel@vandrerhjem.no; Midtbakken 52; dm/s/d Nkr140/255/285; ⏰ mid-Jun–mid-Aug) Alta's youth hostel is in a wooded residential neighbourhood, 10 minutes' walk from the Sentrum bus stop. Reservations are recommended.

Eating

Apart from hotel restaurants (the Rica, Vica and Aurora Borealis are all well regarded), pickings are slim.

Alfa-Omega (☎ 78 44 54 00; Hestekoen 22/24; mains Nkr85-120) As its name suggests, this place has two parts: a pleasant, casual bar and a contemporary café with salads, sandwiches, pastas and nice cakes.

Smut Thullet (☎ 78 44 05 11; Løkkeveien 35; mains Nkr55-210) This popular lunch and dinner option offers pastas, salads, light fare, a pretty, contemporary setting and a nightclub for after hours entertainment.

Han Steike (☎ 78 44 08 88; Løkkeveien 2) This recently opened steakhouse is the place if you're after something red and raw.

Drinking

Balina Pub (Parksentret building, Sentrum) This is a chic, sassy little place that serves great coffee and good beer and exotic cocktails. You may be tempted by the *Blow Job* (sic; Nkr63).

Getting There & Away

Alta's **airport** (☎ 78 44 95 55 for flight information) is 4km northeast of Sentrum at Elvebakken. SAS Braathens or Widerøe fly directly to/from Oslo, Tromsø, Hammerfest and Vadsø. Norwegian flies daily except Sunday to/from Oslo.

Nor-Way Bussekspress has a daily run from the bus terminal in Sentrum to/from

Tromsø (Nkr370, 6¼ hours). **FFR** (Finnmark Fylkesrederi og Ruteselkap; www.ffr.no) buses run to/from Kautokeino (Nkr193, 2¼ hours, four days per week), Hammerfest (Nkr205, 2¾ hours, three daily), and Honningsvåg (Nkr292, four hours, one to two daily).

Getting Around
Fortunately, this sprawling town has a local bus to connect its dispersed ends. On weekdays, buses run more or less hourly among the major districts and airport. Services are less frequent on Saturday and don't run at all on Sunday.

Taxis (☎ 78 43 53 53) cost about Nkr80 from the airport to town; there is a substantial pick-up charge from hotels.

You can hire bicycles from **G-Sport Hammari** (☎ 78 43 61 33; Løkkeveien 10, Sentrum; per day Nkr100).

AROUND ALTA
Not far from Alta are a couple of interesting sites, some good trekking and a decidedly different hotel.

Sights
SAUTSO-ALTA CANYON
The Altaelva hydroelectric project has had very little effect on the most scenic stretch of river, which slides through 400m-deep Sautso, northern Europe's grandest canyon. The easiest way for you to see this impressive forested gorge is to take the four-hour tour (Nkr350) that the tourist office organises daily in July, leaving at 4pm, numbers permitting (minimum five people). In addition to spectacular views of the Sauto-Alta canyon, the tour also includes a pass through the Alta Power Station dam and a snack of coffee, Sami *máze* cake and dried reindeer meat in a traditional Sami tent, or *lavvo*.

PÆSKATUN SLATE QUARRY
Located some 13km south of town, the **Alta Skiferprodukter** (☎ 78 43 33 45; Pæskatun; adult/child Nkr40/free; ☒ 11am-3pm Mon & Thu, 11am-1pm Fri) is one of Alta's economic mainstays. You can visit the quarry and historical exhibits, enjoy a fine view over the canyon – and have a little hands-on experience with the impressive and sharp slate cutting tools. It also sells a range of Finnmark minerals and souvenirs made of slate products.

Activities
TREKKING
Plenty of long-distance hiking trails trace historic routes across the Finnmarksvidda plateau to the south. Among them is the five-day, 120km, post-road hike between Alta and Karasjok, which begins at Bjørnstad in the Tverrelvdalen valley, climbs to 500m and passes through upland birch forests to wind up at Assebakti, on Rv92, 14km west of Karasjok. The Alta og Omegn Turlag (it doesn't have an office but the tourist office can put you in touch with the current club leaders), maintains self-service mountain huts at the Reinbukkelva river and Bojobæski, 16km apart. About 35km farther south is another hut, the **Ravnastua mountain lodge** (☎ 94 80 06 88), which lies just four hours from the trail's end. You'll need a tent for the third night of the route. You can buy hiking maps of the forest region in Alta at Alta Bok og Papirhandel or Studentbokhandelen (see p325).

BOAT TRIPS
From **Alta Friluftspark** (☎ 78 43 33 78; www.alta -friluftspark.no), beside the Altaelva 16km south of town, you can choose from several riverboat rides, which last from 20 minutes to three hours and cost from Nkr115 to Nkr350 per person. They leave at 1pm and 3pm daily from June to August. From 15 July to 15 August, you can also join organised half-day and full-day sea-kayaking trips on Altafjord with **AKU Finnmark** (☎ 78 43 48 40; ulf@thomassen.priv.no). All of this assumes sufficient water levels.

Sleeping & Eating
Alta Igloo Hotel (☎ 78 43 33 78; www.alta-friluftspark .no; Storelvdalen; per person with breakfast & morning sauna Nkr1295, with dinner too Nkr1595; ☒ mid-Jan– mid-Apr) This wintertime hotel, a 20-minute drive from Alta along the Kautokeino road, is Norway's first lodging made entirely of snow and ice, down to the drinking glasses!

Gargia Fjellstue (☎ 78 43 33 51; www.gargia-fjellstue .no in Norwegian & German; s/d Nkr680/850, cabins Nkr500, with bathroom Nkr800) Around 25km south of Alta, in the direction of Kautokeino, this mountain lodge offers a forest getaway and a whole range of outdoor activities including the best foot-access to the Sautso-Alta Canyon.

THE FAR NORTH

HAMMERFEST

pop 6700

Hammerfest was inhabited as early as 1620 and officially designated as a town in 1789. Because of its strategic location and excellent harbour, it has long been an important way-station for shipping, fishing and Arctic hunting. In its heyday, Hammerfest ladies wore the finest Paris fashions and the town had Europe's first electrical street lighting (1890). Nowadays it proudly claims to be the world's northernmost town. (Other Norwegian communities, while further north, are they argue, too small to qualify as towns!)

Neither man nor nature have been kind to Hammerfest: it was decimated in a gale in 1856, burned in 1890, then burned again by the Nazis in 1944. But its fortunes may firmly have turned in a way that will have huge impact upon the town. The world's longest undersea pipeline runs for 143km from huge natural gas fields in the Barents Sea to the small island of Melkøya out in the bay. With estimated reserves of 193 billion (yes, *billion*) cu metres, the pumps are due to start sucking in 2006 and are expected to pound for 25 to 30 years.

If you're arriving on the Hurtigruten coastal ferry, you'll have only a couple of hours to pace around, pick up an Arctic souvenir and scoff some fresh shrimp at the harbour, and for many people that will suffice.

Information

Bibliotek (Library; Sjøgata; free Internet access)

Linux Café (Nissen Senter, Sjøgata 6; per hr Nkr40) Enjoy 10 free minutes if you buy a cup of the excellent coffee. It's just inside the main entrance of the shopping centre.

Tourist office (☎ 78 41 31 00; www.hammerfest-turist .no; Hamnegata 3; ☽ 9am-5pm daily Jun–mid-Aug, 11am-4pm Mon-Fri, 10.30am-1.30pm Sat & Sun mid-Aug–May) Can reserve accommodation for walk-in visitors.

Sights

ROYAL & ANCIENT POLAR BEAR SOCIETY

Dedicated to preserving Hammerfest culture, the **Royal & Ancient Polar Bear Society** (☎ 78 41 31 00; Hamnegata 3; adult/child Nkr20/free; ☽ 9am-5pm daily Jun–mid-Aug, 11am-4pm Mon-Fri, 10.30am-1.30pm Sat & Sun mid-Aug–May) features exhibits on Arctic hunting and local history. It was due to move to new premises, to be shared with the tourist office, shortly after our last visit; we trust that the pair of silver bears outside, who have posed for photos with

generations of keen boreal tourists, will also safely make the short transfer.

The place is, it must be said, a bit of a come-on but the cause is good and any visitor can become a life member (Nkr150) and get a certificate, ID card, sticker and pin. For Nkr185, you also receive a champagne – well, sparkling wine – toast and, as the demure young receptionist will explain without blanching, get dubbed with the bone from a walrus's penis. It's well worth that extra Nkr35 for the conversation this unique honour will generate down the pub, once you're home.

GJENREISNINGSMUSEET

Hammerfest's **Reconstruction Museum** (☎ 78 42 26 30; Kirkegata 21; adult/child Nkr40/15; ☽ 9am-5pm mid-Jun–mid-Aug, 11am-2pm rest-of-year) commemorates the period that followed the decimation of the town after the German bombings of 1944 and reveals the hardships that the town's people endured through the following winter.

It also discusses the 'Norwegianisation' of the indigenous Sami culture in northern Norway. Although the exhibits are quite fine, virtually all the signage is in Norwegian; the free English audio guide does not do them justice.

OPEN-AIR MUSEUM

At the end of the Fuglenes Peninsula stand a **boathouse and wooden cabin**, furnished in the style of the period, one of hundreds that were shipped in, prefabricated, at the end of WWII to provide emergency housing. Both were removed from Melkøya Island and re-erected here when the gas industry heavies moved in. On the peninsula too are the foundations of the **Skansen Fortress**, which dates from the Napoleonic Wars, when the British briefly held and plundered the town, and the **Meridianstøtta**, a marble column commemorating the first survey (1816–52) to determine the arc of the global meridian and thereby calculate the size and shape of the earth. Admission is free if you've purchased entry to the Reconstruction Museum and the complex is open noon to 3pm, Monday to Friday.

HAMMERFEST KIRKE

It's worth dropping into Hammerfest's contemporary **church** (Kirkegata 33; ☽ 8am-3pm

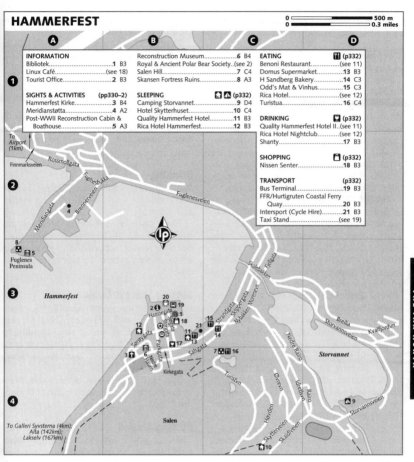

HAMMERFEST

0 — 500 m
0 — 0.3 miles

INFORMATION		
Bibliotek	1	B3
Linux Café	(see 18)	
Tourist Office	2	B3

SIGHTS & ACTIVITIES	(pp330–2)	
Hammerfest Kirke	3	B4
Meridianstøtta	4	A2
Post-WWII Reconstruction Cabin & Boathouse	5	A3

Reconstruction Museum	6	B4
Royal & Ancient Polar Bear Society	(see 2)	
Salen Hill	7	C4
Skansen Fortress Ruins	8	A3

SLEEPING	(p332)	
Camping Storvannet	9	D4
Hotel Skytterhuset	10	C4
Quality Hammerfest Hotel	11	B3
Rica Hotel Hammerfest	12	B3

EATING	(p332)	
Benoni Restaurant	(see 11)	
Domus Supermarket	13	B3
H Sandberg Bakery	14	C3
Odd's Mat & Vinhus	15	C3
Rica Hotel	(see 12)	
Turistua	16	C4

DRINKING	(p332)	
Quality Hammerfest Hotel II	(see 11)	
Rica Hotel Nightclub	(see 12)	
Shanty	17	B3

SHOPPING	(p332)	
Nissen Senter	18	B3

TRANSPORT	(p332)	
Bus Terminal	19	B3
FFR/Hurtigruten Coastal Ferry Quay	20	B3
Intersport (Cycle Hire)	21	B3
Taxi Stand	(see 19)	

To Airport (1km)
Finnmarksveien
Rossmollgata
Fuglenesbukta
Meridiangata
Brennsveien
Fuglenesveien
8
5
Fuglenes Peninsula
Hammerfest
20
19
2
12
18
21
15
11
17
3
7
16
Hamnegata
Sørøygata
Parkgata
Nedre Haurn
Sjøgata
Strandgata
Skolebakken
Storvannsveien
Felgata
Njbakken Nverevn
Nedre Raino
Øvevn
Idrebsvn
Raino
Hovden
Skjærveien
Skådiveien
Turistvn
Kirkegata
Storvannet
Breila
Kvalfjordvn
Salen
To Galleri Syvsterna (4km);
Alta (142km);
Lakselv (167km)
9
10

Mon-Fri, 11am-3pm Sat, noon-1pm mid-Jun–mid-Aug), consecrated in 1961, which has a fine stained-glass window behind the altar. The wooden frieze along the organ gallery, the work of local woodcarver Knut Arnesen, depicts highlights of the town's history. You may find reindeer grazing in the churchyard, and the chapel (1933), across the street through the cemetery, is the only building in town to survive WWII.

SALEN

For panoramic views over the town, coast and mountains (there's a free pair of binoculars for you to sweep the bay), climb **Salen Hill** (86m), topped by the Turistua restaurant (see p330) and a couple of Sami

turf huts. The 10-minute trail begins at the small park uphill behind the Rådhus.

GALLERI SYVSTERNA

If you've ever wondered what a Nobel Peace Prize looks like, local artist Eva Arnesen has a replica of the 1997 award she designed, which went to Jody Williams and the campaign to ban land mines. Her **gallery** (78 41 01 60; Fjordaveien 27; Mon-Fri) is about 4km south of town, opposite the Statoil petrol station. Arnesen's paintings evoke the colours of the region from the Northern Lights to the bright summer palette. Don't expect her to design another Nobel, though – it's a one-time honour. Her husband, woodcarver Knut, created many carvings around town

(Polar Bear Society, Hammerfest Kirke) and at Walt Disney World, in Florida, USA.

Sleeping

Quality Hammerfest Hotel (☎ 78 42 96 00; www .hammerfesthotel.no in Norwegian; Strandgata 2-4; s/d from Nkr1170/1370; P ⌨) Perfectly positioned, overlooking the fjord and only a stone's throw from the cruise ship jetty, this hotel has bags of character, three bars, a tempting restaurant and free sauna and solarium. Rooms overlooking the fjord come at no extra cost. Those in the newer wing replicate a ship's cabins, complete with bunk beds, dark woodwork and nautical décor.

Rica Hotel Hammerfest (☎ 78 41 13 33; www.rica .no; Sørøygata 15; s/d Nkr770/970 Sun-Thu mid-Jun–mid-Aug, Nkr1195/1395 Sun-Thu rest-of-year, Nkr750/950 Fri & Sat year-round; P) Constructed in agreeable mellow brick, the Rica too has harbour views, an attractive bar and lounge and well furnished rooms. Both sauna and mini-gym are free for guests.

Hotel Skytterhuset (☎ 78 41 15 11; www.skytter huset.no; Skytterveien 24; s/d Nkr675/875; P ⌨) The three spurs of this secluded hotel, up the hill from and overlooking town, look decidedly barrack-like from the outside and with good reason; it was originally built as living quarters for summertime fishwives from Finland who worked in the large Findus processing factory. Long ago converted to a friendly, cosy hotel (reindeer frequently hop over the fence to browse the garden and seek a stretch of shade), it's a good medium price option – by Norwegian standards – with free sauna and paying solarium.

Camping Storvannet (☎ 78 41 10 10; Storvannsveien; tent/caravan sites Nkr110/120, cabins Nkr350; ☽ late May-late Sep) Beside a lake and overlooked by a giant apartment complex, this site is small and Hammerfest's only decent camping option so do book in advance.

Eating

Both the restaurant at the Rica Hotel and Quality's Benoni restaurant offer fine fare in a nice setting.

Odd's Mat & Vinhus (☎ 78 41 37 66; Strandgata 24; mains Nkr200-325; ☽ Mon-Sat) Odd's place is Hammerfest's gourmet option for game, fish and seafood meals. With swathes of rope billowing from the ceiling, tiled floor and wooden seating, it pursues a resolutely

rustic and maritime theme. Reservations are all but essential.

Turistua (☎ 78 42 96 00; Salen; mains Nkr135-178) From atop Salen hill, Turistua offers great views over the town and sound. That off-putting name is actually for a lady named Turi, although 'turist' buses often make this a lunch-stop here too.

H Sandberg Bakery (☎ 78 41 18 08; Strandgata 19) is a decent place to pick up snacks, while **Domus Supermarket** (Strandgata 14/18) has an inexpensive cafeteria.

Drinking

Shanty (☎ 78 41 49 00; Storgata 27) is the place for beer, billiards – and a nightclub on Friday and Saturday.

There's also a weekend nightclub at the Rica Hotel and, of Quality's three bars, their open-air terrace is particularly pleasant for a sundowner, even if the sun refuses to go down.

Getting There & Away

Buses run to/from Alta (Nkr205, 2¾ hours, three daily) and Karasjok (Nkr283, 4¼ hours, twice daily), one service extending to Kirkenes (Nkr740, 10 to 12 hours) via Tana Bru (Nkr552, 7½ to 10 hours) on Monday, Wednesday and Friday.

The Hurtigruten coastal ferry also stops in lovely Hammerfest for 1½ hours in each direction.

Getting Around

The only possibility for cycle hire is **Intersport** (Strandgata 16), which rents precisely one bicycle at Nkr50 per day.

To call a taxi, ring ☎ 78 41 12 34.

NORDKAPP & MAGERØYA

pop 3470

What the Eiffel Tower is to Paris, Nordkapp is to northern Norway – the one attraction everyone seems to visit even if it is a tourist trap. Nordkapp bills itself as the northernmost point in continental Europe, and most of its island, Magerøya, seems devoted to funneling visitors there by the busload, some 200,000 each summer.

Nordkapp, nearer to the North Pole than to Oslo, sits at latitude 71° 10' 21"N, where the sun doesn't drop below the horizon from mid-May to the end of July. Long before other Europeans took an interest, the

AROUND NORDKAPP

0 ⊢───────⊣ 10 km
0 ⊢───────⊣ 6 miles

ARCTIC OCEAN
BARENTS SEA
Knivskjelodden
Knivskjelodden Track
Nordkapp
Nordkapphallen
Storstappen
P
Vestfjorden
Gjesværstappan
Skarsvåg
Gjesvær
Tufjorden
E69
Kamøyfjorden
Kamøyvær
Magerøya
Skipsfjord
Skipsfjorden
Vannfjorden
Honningsvåg
Magerøysundet
Nordkapptunnelen
Lafjorden
Fatima Rd
Kåfjord
Porsangerfjorden
Skuottanjarga
E69
Jernøya
Repvåg

Sami people regarded it as a power centre and sacrifice site. Richard Chancellor, the English explorer who drifted here in 1553 in search of the Northeast Passage, first gave it the name North Cape and much later, after a highly publicised visit by King Oscar II in 1873, Nordkapp became a pilgrimage spot for Norwegians. It's also, bizarrely, a pilgrimage place for Thais, of all people, thanks to a visit by King Chulalongkorn in 1907. Today this spot is marked by the Nordkapphallen, a hulking (and royally expensive) tourist centre.

Now here's a secret: Nordkapp isn't continental Europe's northernmost point. That award belongs to Knivskjelodden, an 18km round trip hike away, less dramatic, inaccessible by vehicle – and all the more to be treasured for that.

Orientation & Information

Working clockwise around Magerøya from Nordkapp, you'll find the villages of Skarsvåg, Kamøyvær, Skipsfjord and Honningsvåg – by far the island's largest settlement with some 2900 inhabitants – on the east

coast and Gjesvær on the west. The **tourist office** (☎ 78 47 70 30; www.northcape.no; Fiskeriveien 4B; ⏰ 8.30am-8pm Mon-Fri, noon-8pm Sat & Sun mid-Jun–mid-Aug, 8.30am-4pm Mon-Fri rest-of-year) is located beside the harbour in Honningsvåg. The island's helpful office has one Internet point (per 15 minutes Nkr23). Staff at Nordkapphallen's front desk also provide information.

Sights & Activities
NORDKAPPHALLEN
So you've finally made it to Europe's northernmost rip-off – an opinion shared by the regular letters we receive from readers who've felt exploited. To reach the tip of the continent, by car, by bike, on a bus or walking in, you have to pay a **toll** (adult/child/family Nkr190/55/380). It allows you unlimited entry over two days but this is small compensation for the vast majority who roll in, look around, register the achievement and roll out.

Atop Nordkapp, **Nordkapphallen** (☎ 78 47 68 60; ⏰ 9am-2am mid-Jun–Jul, noon-1am mid-May–mid-Jun, noon-midnight Aug, noon-4pm early May & Sep–mid-Oct, 12.30-2pm mid-Oct–Apr) is a love/hate kind of place. Within are small exhibits about the region and its nature and history, a cafeteria, a restaurant, the striking Grotten bar, a one-room Thai museum, the trippy St Johannes chapel ('the world's northernmost ecumenical chapel'), a post office (for that all-important Nordkapp postmark) and a souvenir shop. A five-screen, 180-degree theatre runs an enjoyable panoramic film.

But it's the view that thrills the most. In fair weather – which, counter to popular preconception, is a lot of the time – you can gaze down at the wild surf 307m below, watch the mist roll in, pay tribute to Knivskjelodden on a tiny spit to your left – and perhaps even dream of Svalbard, far away to the north.

KNIVSKJELODDEN
The continent's real northernmost point, Knivskjelodden, is mercifully inaccessible to vehicles and devoid of tat. You can hike to its lovely promontory from a marked car park 6km south of the Nordkapp toll booth. The 9km track isn't difficult despite some ups and downs, but best to wear hiking boots since it can be mucky after precipitation. When you get to latitude

71° 11' 08"N, at sea level, you can sign a guest book. Should you wish, note down your reference number from the book and you can buy – nothing but the hike comes free on this island – a certificate (Nkr50) authenticating your achievement from Nordkapp Camping or the tourist office. The journey takes about five hours return.

NORDKAPP MUSEUM

Honningsvåg's small **museum** (☎ 78 47 72 00; Fiskeriveien 4; adult/child Nkr30/5; ☷ 10am-7pm Mon-Sat, noon-7pm Sun mid-Jun–mid-Aug, noon-4pm rest-of-year), colocated with the tourist office, concentrates on Arctic fishing culture. Many find the exhibits here as good as the Nordkapphallen's, with infinitely less fray.

HONNINGSVÅG KIRKE

Honningsvåg's 19th-century **church** (Kirkegata; ☷ 8am-10pm Jun-early Sep) was the only local structure to survive the Nazis' scorched-earth retreat in 1944 and was, for a time, the villagers' communal dwelling until the first new houses were hastily erected.

BIRD-WATCHING

From the remote fishing village of **Gjesvær**, 34km northwest of Honningsvåg, the **MV Havsula** (adult/child 12-15/child under 12 Nkr400/200/free) sails two to three times daily, early June to late August, to the fabulous offshore **bird colony** on the island group of Gjesværstappan with its estimated three *million* nesting birds, including colonies of puffins, skuas, razorbills, cormorants and gannets, as well as seals. Reserve at the Honningsvåg tourist office. A reader reports very positively on the cabins of the **Gjesvær Turistsenter** (☎ 78 47 57 73; olat@birdsafari.com; Nkr500, with bathroom Nkr700; ☷ Jun-Aug), right beside the pier.

Sleeping

Astoundingly, you can spend the night in your motorhome or caravan at Nordkapp itself (fill up on water and electricity though, because you won't find any there for the taking).

Nordkapp Camping (☎ 78 47 33 77; www.nordkapp camping.no; E69, Skipsfjorden; person/site Nk25/90, dm Nkr175, 4-bed cabins Nkr460, with bathroom Nkr500-840; ☷ mid-May–mid-Sep) The friendly service and variety of lodging options more than compensate for the stark location of this place, north of Skipsfjord.

Kirkeporten Camping (☎ 78 47 52 33; www.kirkepor ten.no; Storvannsveien 2, Skarsvåg; person/site Nkr25/100, cabins Nkr400-500, 4-bed with bathroom Nkr550-750, 6-bed Nkr575-950) This is another friendly camping ground, a favourite of British adventure tour groups. Its claim to be the 'world's northernmost camping' stands up; there's a spartan affair beside the airport perimeter on Svalbard but it's without cabins and has few facilities. The cosy café does a fresh-fish dish daily (Nkr115 to Nkr145) and reindeer (Nkr115).

Honningsvåg Brygge (☎ 78 47 64 64; www.hvg .brygge.no; Vågen 1a; s/d Nkr950/1150; ☷ year-round) Of Honningsvåg's sleeping possibilities, this former fishing warehouse, recently renovated, is the most original choice and has unbeatable views from its pier location.

Eating

In Honningsvåg, there's **Corner** (☎ 78 47 63 40; Fiskerveien 1; mains Nkr100-170), which has a café serving seafood and pizza, a bar, sometimes a weekend disco and an inviting outdoor terrace overlooking the water, and on the pier, **Sjøhuset** (☎ 78 47 36 16; Vågen 1; mains Nkr170-225; ⊙ dinner only), the town's most elegant establishment, serves ample portions.

Drinking

Here too, Honningsvåg is your place.

Bryggerie (☎ 78 47 26 00; Nordkappgate 1) The splendid Mack Brewery in Tromsø has been supplanted as the world's northernmost by Honningsvåg's microbrewery. A favourite brew, now-and-again on offer, is called 'Sårry Makk', as in 'Sorry, Mack, but actually *we're* further north'.

Nøden Pub (☎ 78 47 27 11; Larsjorda 1) This local favourite near the Rica Hotel often has live music.

Ice Bar (☎ 78 47 15 00; Sjøgata 1; ⊙ 9am-9pm) This is cited as 'the northernmost ice bar in the world'. Ring to check months, cost and what is included.

During the midnight sun, the **Grotten Bar** (Nordkapphallen) is a happening place.

Getting There & Away

BOAT

The Hurtigruten coastal ferry calls at Honningsvåg. The 3½-hour northbound stop allows a quick buzz up to Nordkapp; the Hurtigruten coastal ferry offers passengers a tour (Nkr580).

BUS

An express bus connects Honningsvåg with Alta (Nkr292, four hours, one to two daily) and there's also a run to/from Hammerfest (Nkr251, three hours, twice daily except Saturday).

CAR & MOTORCYCLE

The road approach from the E6 is via Olderfjord, where the E69 branches northwards. The toll for the 6.8km long Nordkapptunnelen is a swingeing Nkr140 for a saloon car and driver plus Nkr46/23 per adult/child passenger.

Getting Around

BICYCLE

The tourist office rents bicycles for Nkr150/250 per half/full day or Nkr600 for three days. It can be a very breezy ride along the bleak, open road leading to the cape, so pack a windbreaker vest.

BUS

From mid-June to around 20 August, a local bus (adult/child Nkr80/40, 45 minutes) runs daily at 10.45am and 8.30pm between Honningsvåg and Nordkapp, setting off back from the Cape at 1.15pm and 12.15am (so that you can take in the midnight sun at midnight). If you're on a budget, scan carefully the terms of any inclusive tours, which probably charge considerably more for similar services. And bear in mind that even if you arrive by bus, you still get dunned for that Nkr190 entry fee.

Throughout the rest of the year, unless snow conditions forbid, a bus leaves Honningsvåg's pier for Nordkapp at noon and sets off back from the cape at 2.15pm. Reserve by 4pm the preceding day by ringing either the tourist office or the **FFR bus company** (☎ 78 47 58 44).

CAR & MOTORCYCLE

Until the blacktop road to Nordkapp was constructed in the mid-1950s, all access to Nordkapp was by boat. Nowadays, the route winds across a rocky plateau, past herds of grazing reindeer. Depending upon snow conditions, its open to private traffic from April to mid-October. In fringe months, ring the tourist office if the weather looks dicey.

A taxi to/from Nordkapp from Honningsvåg costs Nkr900 – plus that Nkr190 admission charge per passenger, including an hour of waiting at the cape.

In Honningsvåg **Avis** (☎ 78 47 62 62) has a special five-hour deal on car hire for Nkr725, including petrol and insurance. If that seems a bit steep, you've never hired a car or bought petrol in Norway!

LAKSELV & AROUND

pop 2200

The small, plain fishing village of Lakselv, located at the head of the great Porsangerfjord, has little to detain you as a traveller. The name means 'salmon stream', which reflects its main appeal for Norwegian holi-day-makers.

Information

Lakselv has the usual stopover amenities: restaurants, supermarkets, lodging and pet-rol. The **tourist office** (☎ 78 46 07 00; www.visitarctic norway.no; ☉ 9am-5pm Mon-Fri, 10am-5pm Sat & Sun early Jun–mid-Aug) is located in the lugubrious Porsanger Vesthus hotel.

Sights

NORTH CAPE WINE

Its products may not be from the juice of the grape but **North Cape Wine** (☎ 78 46 23 73; Meieriveien 11) is the world's northernmost winery, making its own special vintages – and very tasty they are too – from Arctic berries. Ring the winery or tourist office for a tour and tasting (Nkr95) or pick up a bot-tle at the Vinmonopolet in the Torgsenteret shopping centre.

STABBURSNES NATURE RESERVE

The Stabbursnes Nature Reserve occupies an expanse of wetlands and mudflats north of Lakselv on the Porsangerfjord's western shore. It's especially popular with bird-watchers, who come to observe many species of ducks, geese, divers and sandpipers that rest in the area while migrating between the Arctic and more temperate zones. Among the more exotic species are the lesser white-fronted goose, the bar-tailed godwit and the knot. Coastal marshes are closed to visitors during the nesting season (May and June).

The **visitors centre and museum** (☎ 78 46 47 65; adult/child Nkr40/10; ☉ 9am-8pm Jul, 11am-6pm Jun & Aug, noon-3pm Tue-Thu Sep-May) are in Stabbursnes, 15km north of Lakselv on the E6. They sell field guides and topographic maps and the museum houses Sami exhibits and a slide show.

STABBURSDALEN NATIONAL PARK

Compact (98 sq km) and undervisited, Stabbursdalen National Park offers a spectacular glacial canyon and excellent hiking in the world's most northerly pine forest. Hikers are accommodated in two mountain huts, Rurkulphytta and Ivarstua, as well as a turf hut. For trails, consult the Stabbursnes visitors centre, which also carries the relevant walking maps: Statens Kartverk's sheets 1935II and 2035III, at 1:50,000.

AUTHOR'S CHOICE

Bungalåven Vertshus (☎ 78 46 48 01; www .bungalaaven.tk; Børselv; basic s/d Nkr250/450) Located northeast of Lakselv and some 40km up the Rv98 and take a signed turning after a bridge over a sideshoot of the Porsangen fjord after 2km to reach this place. Popular with fisherfolk, this convivial converted farmhouse serves dinner with traditional food for a bargain Nkr125 while breakfast, with local salmon, costs Nkr100. The lounge is a cosy haven, the owner plays a mean squeezebox and you may find yourself up and dancing. There are also a couple of simple cabins (Nkr200) and a big one with bathroom and mini-kitchen (Nkr700) that can accommodate up to six persons.

Sleeping & Eating

Lakselv Vandrerhjem (☎ 78 46 14 76; lakselv.hos tel@vandrerhjem.no; dm Nkr200, cabins with bathroom & kitchen Nkr500-600; ☉ Jun-Aug) This HI-affiliated hostel, in a secluded wooded site, couldn't be more peaceful. Surrounded by small lakes, it's a great base for gentle strolls and has self-catering facilities. To get there, follow the E6 southwards from Lakselv for 6km, then take a dirt road to the left to its conclusion after 2km.

Lakselv Hotell (☎ 78 46 54 00; www.finnmarkhotell forening.no; Karasjokveien; s/d Nkr735/835 mid-Jun–mid-Aug, Nkr875/1075 rest-of-year; P 🖳) Lakselv's high-end alternative is 2km south of town, just off the E6. It has cosy rooms, hilltop fjord views, a sauna that's free for guests and a restaurant that does a good summer-time dinner buffet.

Solstad Camping (☎ 78 46 14 04; fax 78 46 12 14; tent/caravan sites Nkr140/160, cabins Nkr300-450, with bathroom Nkr500-900) This convenient camping ground is 2km east of town beside the Rv98.

Don't expect anything fancy to eat in Lakselv itself. Your best of few options is **Åstedet Café & Bistro** (☎ 78 46 13 77), beside Porsanger Vesthus and the tourist office. Both pub and café-restaurant, it serves a range of decent meaty mains (Nkr115 to Nkr145) plus the usual burgers, pizzas and salads.

Getting There & Away

Lakselv's North Cape Airport, an important link for central Finnmark, has daily Widerøe flights to/from Tromsø. Finnair operates a summer only flight to/from Helsinki and Rovaniemi.

Buses run to/from Alta (Nkr247, 3½ hours) and Karasjok (Nkr110, 1¼ hours) twice daily except Saturday. They also link Lakselv with Honningsvåg (Nkr238, 3¼ hours), once or twice daily except Saturday). In summer, a daily bus running between Nordkapp and Rovaniemi via Ivalo (both in Finland) calls by.

EASTERN FINNMARK

Though relatively little visited, Eastern Finnmark has a distinctly coastal feel, some charming villages and a unique history that embraces Finns, witches, explorers and wartime destruction. It's also the centre of the Eastern Sami culture.

NORDKYN PENINSULA
pop 2650
The church-shaped rock formation known as the **Finnkirke** marks the entrance to the village of Kjøllefjord and provides a majestic introduction to this remote corner of Finnmark, a treasure trove for collectors of 'northernmosts'.

Across the peninsula, the tiny coastal village of Gamvik, claims the world's northernmost museum, the **Latitude 71 Museum** (☎ 78 49 79 49; Strandveien 94; Gamvik; adult/concession Nkr50/25; ♥ 9am-4pm daily mid-Jun–mid-Aug, 9am-4.30pm Mon-Fri rest-of-year), revealing the fishing cultures of these far-flung environs. Nearby, a bird-watchers' trail runs through the **Slettnes Nature Reserve**, frequented by nesting and migrating ducks and wading birds (accessible only on foot or by private vehicle), and **Slettnes Fyr** is the world's northernmost mainland lighthouse.

In the centre are **Kinnarodden**, the northernmost point of mainland Europe (Knivskjelodden, near Nordkapp, is on an island) and the town of Mehamn, unremarkable except as the site of one of Norway's earliest environmental movements. In 1903, troops were brought in to subdue local fishermen, who protested that whaling was exterminating the whales that had historically made fishing easy by driving cod towards the shore.

Gamvik Gjestehus (☎ 78 49 62 12; vassvik@start.no; Strandveien 78, Gamvik; s/d Nkr450/550) Alone beside

the seashore, this recently renovated fishermen's cabin has a good, no-frills restaurant.

Hotel Nordkyn (☎ 78 49 81 51; nordkyn@online.no; Strandveien 136, Kjøllefjord; s/d Nkr675/850) This modest hotel has sweeping views of the Y-shaped Kjøllefjord and a popular pub/restaurant.

Buses connect Mehamn with Lakselv (Nkr207, 4½ hours, daily), Gamvik (Nkr36, 30 minutes, Monday to Friday) and Kjølleford (Nkr44, 40 minutes, Monday to Friday). Kjøllefjord and Mehamn are also brief stops on the Hurtigruten coastal ferry.

BERLEVÅG
pop 1100
This pint-sized fishing village has produced one big thing, the **Berlevåg Mannsangforening**, a male voice choir that was the subject of Knut Erik Jensen's 2001 documentary *Heftig og Begeistret* (Cool and Crazy). Something of a Nordic *Buena Vista Social Club*, the film caused a national sensation when it was released and earned international respect. You're likely to see their CDs for sale all over the north; one cover features the bright-eyed older fellows in their trademark fishermen's caps, gazing hopefully skyward.

Sights & Activities
In town the **Harbour Museum** (Havne-museum; ☎ 78 98 08 97; Havnegate; adult/child Nkr30/10; ♥ 10am-6pm Mon-Fri & 1-6pm Sat & Sun mid-Jun–mid-Aug, noon-3pm Mon-Fri rest-of-year) has the usual maritime displays, as well as an unusual old expedition dory, the *Berlevåg II*.

About 12km away is a **Sami sacrificial site** atop the 269m Tanahorn, with a wonderful view over the Arctic Ocean. The 8km return walk begins 8km west of town, along the gravel road towards the equally interesting abandoned fishing village of Store Malvik (20km west of Berlevåg).

Sleeping
Berlevåg Camping og Appartement (☎ 78 98 16 10; berlevag.camping@online.no; Havnegate 8b; tent/caravan sites Nkr85 plus per person Nkr10, s/d Nkr350/425) This friendly, well-kept complex also houses the tourist office. Between them, they can arrange a visit to a fish farm, scuba diving and fishing excursions and you can rent a bike.

Ishavshotellet (☎ 78 98 14 15; fax 78 98 16 63; Storgata 30) This place is essentially two adjacent hotels, each different in character. The newer

OPORINIA AUTUMNATA

Throughout Finnmark and over the border in Finland too, you'll come across desolate forests of birch, leafless, their trunks blackened as though fire had swept through. But the culprit is something smaller, slower, more insidious and just as destructive.

The *Oporinia autumnata* moth is dowdy and looks harmless; the caterpillars come bright green, up to 2cm long and hungry as hell, devouring the leaves and swinging on gossamer threads to their next chlorophyll meal.

Eventually, they'll eat themselves out of house and home and numbers will drop but until that time, their impact can be devastating for fragile *taiga* forest. What's needed for them to be eradicated is at least two consecutive days of temperatures below -35°C. But, while winters are harsh up here, years can go by before it gets *that* bitter.

building (singles/doubles Nkr800/1050) has rooms offering every comfort, while its older neighbour has budget accommodation (singles/doubles Nkr350/550) with corridor bathrooms.

Getting There & Away

Buses run from Tana Bru (Nkr193, 2½ hours) and Båtsfjord (Nkr131, 1¾ hours) at least once a day, Sunday to Friday. Berlevåg is also a stop on the Hurtigruten coastal ferry route.

BÅTSFJORD

pop 2300

If Berlevåg is rustic, its neighbour Båtsfjord, the largest fishing port in the Nordic countries, has a much more bustling, industrial feel to it.

There is also a town **tourist office** (☎ 78 98 55 20; www.baatsfjordnett.no; Hindberggate 16; ☻ 8am-3.30pm Mon-Fri).

Sights & Activities

BÅTSFJORD KIRKE

The main site in town is the **church** (☎ 78 98 33 33; ☻ mid-Jun–mid-Aug). Constructed in 1971, its mundane exterior contrasts sharply with the view from within of its glowing 85 sq metres of stained-glass.

MAKKAUR

A 25km hike eastward along the fjord's southern shore leads to Makkaur, an **abandoned fishing village** that dates from medieval times and escaped bombing during WWII. There's all sorts of interesting junk left over, including the remains of a German POW camp. The only permanent resident is the attendant at the 1928 lighthouse, one of the very few in Norway that isn't fully automated.

The 113-sq-km **Makkaurhalvøya Nature Reserve** immediately to the east was established in 1983 to protect the 4km-long and 200m-high Syltefjordstauren bird cliffs. In summer, it attracts around 250 breeding pairs of gannets, as well as sea eagles, cormorants, razorbills, puffins, both common and Brunnichs guillemots, and 150,000 breeding pairs of kittiwakes. You also stand a good chance of spotting seals. The tourist office can arrange boat tours.

Sleeping

Havly Fiskarheim (☎ 78 98 42 05; fax 78 98 34 81; Havnegata 31; s/d Nkr400/600) Båtsfjord's cheapest and most affordable accommodation is this simple seamen's mission with an attached cafeteria. Of its 13 rooms, six are en suite. Since it's a church establishment, alcohol isn't allowed, and like everywhere else in Norway, you can't smoke. Makes you wonder what the Russian fishermen get up to in the special social room that's reserved just for them...

Polar Hotell (☎ 78 98 31 00; polarhotell@c2e.net; s/d Nkr895/11455) Under new management, this hotel has recently had a fundamental facelift. There's also limited **camping** (car/caravan sites Nkr150) beside the hotel with access to its facilities. Its pub offers a short menu. Unlike most hotels in Norway, its main business is in winter, so if you're planning to pass by in summer, do ring in advance to ensure it's open.

Getting There & Away

The airport, 5km from town, is served by Widerøe. Direct flights run only to Mehamn and Vadsø, offering excellent views of the arctic landscapes, complete with grazing reindeer.

Buses connect Båtsfjord with Tana Bru (Nkr152, two hours). Båtsfjord is also a stop on the Hurtigruten coastal ferry.

THE FAR NORTH

TANA BRU

pop 590

Tiny Tana Bru takes its name from the picturesque bridge on the great Tana River, and no wonder. This is one of Europe's best salmon streams, where the locals use the technique of constructing barrages to obstruct the upstream progress of the fish; the natural barrage at Storfossen falls, about 30km upstream, is one of the finest fishing spots around. Test its waters, though you'll need singular good luck to pull out anything to compare with the record 36kg specimen that was once played ashore.

Sights & Activities

Stop by for a browse at **Tana Gull og Sølvsmie** (☎ 78 92 80 06; www.tanagullogsolv.com). Established over 25 years ago as eastern Finnmark's first gold- and silversmith, it creates some very fine gold and silver jewellery, inspired by traditional Sami designs.

Sleeping

Comfort Hotel Tana (☎ 78 92 81 98; www.choicehotels .no; tent/caravan sites Nkr50/150 plus per person Nkr25, s/d Nkr740/940 mid-Jun–mid-Aug, Nk995/1230 Sun-Thu, Nkr740/790 Fri & Sat rest-of-year; **P**) You'll find camping, comfortable rooms, a restaurant, bar and the tourist office at this convenient staging post where the Rv98 meets the E6/E75.

Polmakmoen Gjestegård (☎ 78 92 89 90; Polmak; s/d Nkr650/1000) Stay in a comfortable Samistyle *gamma* (turf hut) with en suite bathroom at this complex, 20km upstream from Tana Bru. It has an outside wooden hot tub and a sauna that a Finnish reader and connoisseur of the genre qualifies as one of Norway's best. It also does riverboat cruises (Nkr100, 1½ hour).

Getting There & Away

The express bus between Hammerfest (Nkr552, 7¼ hours) and Kirkenes (Nkr201, 2½ hours), running three times weekly on Monday, Wednesday and Friday, crosses the bridge at Tana Bru. Local buses run to/from Berlevåg (Nkr193, 2½ hours), Båtsfjord (Nkr152, two hours at least once daily) and to/from Vadsø (Nkr98, 1¼ hours, two to four times daily except Saturday).

If you're travelling toward Båtsfjord or Berlavåg, you'll pass by the spectacular and colourful folded sedimentary layers in the Gamasfjellet cliffs, along the eastern shore of Tanafjord.

SAMI MUSEUMS

Between Tana Bru and Vadsø are two Sami treasures, each well worth visiting.

At Varangerbotn, the excellent, strongly recommended **Varanger Sami Museum** (Várjjat Sámi Musea; ☎ 78 95 99 20; Varangerbotn; adult/child Nkr49/20; ☼ 10am-6pm mid-Jun–mid-Aug, 10am-3pm Mon-Fri rest-of-year) covers the history, religion and traditions of the coastal Sami through a variety of media, and also presents exhibitions by contemporary Sami artists.

On the E75, about 15km toward Vadsø, is an affiliated site: the **Ceavccageadge** (Fish Oil Stone; ☎ 78 95 99 20; Mortensnes; admission free; ☼ noon-6pm mid-Jun–late Aug), where you can stroll amid remnants of 10,000 years of Sami culture. Some 8km of tracks wind up to the hills and down to the sea. At the west end, past burial sites, home ruins and a reconstructed turf hut, is the namesake *ceavccageadge*, a pillar standing near the water, which was smeared with cod-liver oil to ensure luck while fishing. On a hill to the east is the Bjørnstein (bear rock), resembling a bear and revered by early Sami inhabitants. You can wander around for free but won't get much out of it unless you pick up a useful book for self-guiding (Nkr50) at the Varanger Sami Museum or reserve a guided visit (adult/child Nkr50/25) at the museum.

VADSØ

pop 5200

The administrative centre of Finnmark, Vadsø was the site of large-scale immigration from Finland; in the mid-19th century the town's population was 50% Kven, as the Fins were known. A 1977 monument at the north end of Tollbugata commemorates this cultural heritage. Vadsø is also renowned as a site for polar exploration, several expeditions having started or ended here, including some that ended in disaster.

The cemetery on Vadsø island, across a short bridge from the mainland, provides evidence of the Pomors, Russian traders and fisherfolk from the White Sea area, who prospered here in the 17th century. There are numerous ruins of protected prehistoric turf huts. If visiting in early summer, watch for the rare Stellar's duck, which nests here.

Like other Finnmark towns, it was badly mauled, by both Russian bombers and retreating German troops, in WWII. The **tourist office** (☎ 78 94 04 44; www.vadso.no; ◷ 10am-6pm Mon-Fri, 10am-4pm Sat & Sun mid-Jun–mid-Aug) is located at Kierkegate 15.

Sights

The **Vadsø Museum** (☎ 78 94 28 90; adult/child Nkr20/30; ◷ 10am-6pm Mon-Fri, 10am-4pm Sat & Sun mid-Jun–mid-Aug, 10am-2pm Mon-Fri rest-of-year) is in three sections. The **Tuomainengården** (Tuomainen estate, Slettengate 21) is a mid-19th-century Finnish farmhouse, together with its bakery, sauna and blacksmith. From the same era, **Esbensengården** (Esbensen estate, Hvistendalsgata) is an altogether more opulent merchant's house, complete with stable and servants' quarters. Admission to each costs Nkr20 (Nkr30 for both sites) and children are free.

The third element, the **Kjeldsen Fish Plant** (adult/child Nkr20/free; ◷ noon-6pm mid-Jun–mid-Aug) is at Ekkerøy, 15km east of town. It retains its old stores and lodgings, a mass of arcane fishing equipment, the old shrimp processing and bottling room and – to make you wince at childhood memories – a vast black vat and boiler for extracting cod-liver oil. Plan to arrive when hunger is beginning to bite and you can enjoy an excellent fish meal in the **Havhesten Restaurant** (☎ 90 50 60 80; mains Nkr120-180; ◷ Tue-Sun), housed in one of the outbuildings. Its maritime artefacts could be an extension of the museum, and if the wind isn't whipping, you can dine on the jetty with the sea sloshing beneath you.

On Vadsø island, the oil-rig-shaped **Luftskipsmasta** (airship mast) was built in the mid-1920s as an anchor and launch site for airborne expeditions to the polar regions. The expedition of Roald Amundsen, Umberto Nobile and Lincoln Ellsworth, which flew via the North Pole to Alaska in the airship *Norge N-1*, first used it in April 1926. Two years later it was the launch site for Nobile's airship, *Italia*, which attempted to repeat the journey but crashed on Spitsbergen. Amundsen – together with 12 steamships, 13 planes and 1500 men – joined the rescue expedition and disappeared in the attempt, becoming a national martyr as well as a hero. It's well worth the breezy 600m stroll across the grass flats with a rich variety of aquatic birds that quack and croak in the small lake just beyond it.

Beside the dock, there's a tiny belt-and-braces exhibition about the airship era – plus, incongruously, a few mounted Web pages about the *Nautilus*, the first submarine to reach the North Pole from below. It opens in summer from 8am to 9am, when the Hurtigruten coastal ferry's in dock.

As so often happens in these small Finnmark communities, the **church** (Amtmannsgate 1B; ◷ 9am-2pm Mon-Fri mid-Jun–mid-Aug) is the most interesting structure architecturally – and all too often the only building to have survived the devastation wreaked by retreating German forces. Vadsø's didn't. Built in 1958, it's simple enough yet rich in symbolism and cultural reference. The twin peaks are intended to recall an iceberg floating in the Arctic Ocean, the altarpiece looks metaphorically over the frontier and is Orthodox-inspired, while the rich stained-glass depicts the divinity of water and the seasons.

Sleeping & Eating

Rica Hotel Vadsø (☎ 78 95 16 81; www.rica.no; Oscarsgate 4; s/d Nkr611/796 mid-Jun–mid-Aug, Nk1195/1395 Mon-Thu, Nkr745/945 Fri & Sat rest-of-year; P ⌨) Plumb in the centre, the friendly Rica has nicely renovated rooms with parquet flooring and represents Vadsø's best choice, with free sauna and minigym. Its Oscar Mat og Vinhus restaurant is also the town's finest, offering a great buffet breakfast and a daily fish and meat special (Nkr130).

Nobile Hotell (☎ 78 95 33 35; www.nobilehotell.no; Brugata 2, Vadsøya island; s/d Nkr400/800 Jun-Jul, Nkr795/1195 Sun-Thu, Nkr695/895 Fri & Sat rest-of-year; P ⌨) Named after the eponymous Arctic explorer, whose blown-up photo and those of his contemporaries gaze down at you from the walls, the Nobile has recently changed hands and the young owners are gradually turning around what was a rather threadbare institution. It's a short stroll away from the Hurtigruten coastal ferry dock, has great views of the sound and its rates include a light evening meal in addition to breakfast. Ask for room No 217, slightly larger than the rest and with good views over the town and sound.

Vadsø Apartments (☎ 78 95 44 00, 92 06 80 30; Tibergveien 3; s/d Nkr400/500) The town's only mid-range choice is three blocks from the harbour. It's a good deal (all rooms have bathroom and mini-kitchen) but capacity is limited so do book in advance.

Vestre Jakobselv (☎ 78 95 60 64; ungd.senteret@c2i
.net; Lilledalsveien; tent/caravan sites Nkr75/90 plus per person Nkr10, 4-/6-bed cabins Nkr300/400) This is Vadsø's nearest camping ground, 17km west
of town.

Påls Matoppleveiser (☎ 78 95 33 84; Hvistendalsgata 6b; ☒ 9am-5pm Mon-Fri, 10am-3pm Sat)
Pål dishes up tasty sandwiches (Nkr25),
baguettes (Nkr30 to Nkr50) and salads
(Nkr90), to eat in or take away.

Indigo (☎ 78 95 16 81; Tollbugata 12; mains Nkr145-
245; ☒ Tue-Sat) It makes no such claim but
surely the long-established Indigo, with a
daily special menu at Nkr175, must rank as
Europe's, if not the world's northernmost
Indian restaurant.

FRIDTJOF NANSEN

Anyone seeking a modern hero need look no further than Fridtjof Nansen (1861–1930), the Norwegian explorer, then diplomat, who pushed the frontiers of human endurance and human compassion.

Nansen grew up in rural Store Frøen outside Oslo, enjoying a privileged childhood. He was an excellent athlete, winning a dozen or so national nordic skiing championships and breaking the world record for the one-mile skating course. Studies in zoology at the University of Christiania led to a voyage aboard the sealing ship *Viking* to study ocean currents, ice movements and wildlife. Offshore, he gained tantalising glimpses of Greenland that planted the dream of journeying across its central icecap.

That dream of his came true. In 1888, Nansen, then a mere 27, headed a six-man expedition. He wintered over in Greenland and his detailed observations of the Inuit (Eskimo) people formed the backbone of his 1891 book, *Eskimo Life*.

In June 1893, aboard the 400-tonne, oak-hulled, steel-reinforced ship *Fram,* Nansen's next expedition left Christiania for the Arctic with provisions for six whole years. Nansen left behind his wife Eva and six-month-old daughter Liv, not knowing when, if ever, he'd return.

On 14 March 1895, he and Hjalmar Johansen set out in the *Fram* for the North Pole and journeyed for five months, including 550km on foot over the ice, before holing up for nine winter months in a tiny stone hut they'd built on an island. On heading south, they encountered lone British explorer Frederick Jackson (for whom Nansen later, magnanimously, named the island where they'd spent the winter). Having given up on reaching the Pole, all three headed back to Vardø.

In 1905, a political crisis arose as Norway sought independence from Sweden. Nansen, by then a national hero, was dispatched to Copenhagen and Britain to represent the Norwegian cause.

Upon independence, Nansen was offered the job of prime minister but declined in order to pursue science, exploration and a planned expedition to the South Pole (he's also rumoured to have turned down offers to be king or president). He did, however, accept King Håkon's offer to serve as ambassador to Britain. In 1907, after the sudden death of his wife, he allowed fellow Norwegian explorer Roald Amundsen to take over the *Fram* for an expedition north of Siberia, thus abandoning his own South Pole dreams.

After WWI, Nansen took on large-scale humanitarian efforts: the new League of Nations; repatriating a half-million German soldiers imprisoned in the Soviet Union; and an International Red Cross programme against famine and pestilence in Russia. When some two million Russians and Ukrainians became stateless after fleeing the 1917 Bolshevik revolution, 'Nansen Passports' enabled thousands of them to settle elsewhere.

Probably Nansen's greatest diplomatic achievement, however, was the resettlement of several hundred thousand Greeks and Turks in the wake of the turbulence following WWI.

In 1922 Nansen, surely one of its most worthy winners, was awarded the Nobel Peace Prize – then gave it all away to international relief efforts. After 1925, he concentrated on disarmament and lobbying for a non-Soviet homeland for Armenian refugees. Although this project failed, he is still revered among Armenians worldwide.

On 13 May 1930, Nansen died quietly at his home in Polhøgda, near Oslo, and was buried in a garden nearby.

To learn more about this extraordinary man, read the biography *Nansen*, by Roland Huntford, published in the UK in 1997, or EE Reynolds' book of the same title, first published in 1932.

THE FAR NORTH

Getting There & Away

Vadsø is a stop only on the northbound Hurtigruten coastal ferry, which steams out for Kirkenes at 8.15am. There are two to four buses daily to/from Tana Bru (Nkr98, 1¼ hours) and Vardø (Nkr110, 1½ hours).

A daily bus also runs to Rovaniemi (Nkr615) via Ivalo (Nkr325) in Finland.

VARDØ
pop 2100

Vardø qualifies as Norway's easternmost town. Although this butterfly-shaped island is connected to the mainland by the 2.9km-long Ishavstunnelen (Arctic Ocean tunnel), locals maintain that theirs is the only 'mainland' Norwegian town lying within the Arctic climatic zone (its average temperature is below 10°C). Once a stronghold of trade with the Russian Pomors, it's now a major fishing port and home to many Russian and Sri Lankan immigrants.

The **tourist office** (☎ 78 98 69 07; kontact@var dovekst.no; ⊙ 10am-7pm Mon-Fri, noon-7pm Sat & Sun mid-Jun–Aug) is scheduled to move to new premises beside the harbour in 2005.

Sights & Activities

The tourist office organises short boat trips (Nkr175) to see the island of **Hornøya**, Norway's rival easternmost point with its picturesque lighthouse and teeming bird cliffs, a twitcher's paradise.

The star-shaped **Vardøhus Festning** (fortress; ☎ 78 98 85 02; Festningsgate 20; admission Nkr30; ⊙ 10am-9pm mid-Apr–mid-Sep, 10am-6pm rest-of-year) – yes, of course it's the world's most northerly – was constructed in 1737 by King Christian VI. For a fortress, it's painted in gentle fairy-tale colours, and on a nice, sunny day it's pleasant to stroll around its flower-festooned bastions, past turf-roofed buildings and Russian cannons captured by the Germans during WWII. You pay the admission fee either at the guard office or by dropping it into the WWII sea mine that guards the entrance.

Between 1621 and 1692, around 90 Vardø women were accused of witchcraft and burned; a sign and flag at Kristian IV gate 24 commemorate the site. On the 156m hill, **Domen**, about 2km south of town on the mainland, is the cave where they were supposed to have held their satanic rites and secret rendezvous with the devil.

In the centre, the **Pomor Museum** (Kaigata) recalls the historic trade between Russia and Norway, which lasted until the Bolshevik Revolution in 1917. It's due to open in 2005 in the red building behind the bronze statue of fishermen hauling in nets.

If you drop in to the 1958 **Vardø Kirke** (Kirkegaten; admission free; ⊙ 10am-1pm Mon-Thu & when the southbound Hurtigruten coastal ferry is in port), an earnest guide may show you around.

And those huge spheres on Vardø's hilltops? The official version is that they're space-tracking equipment.

Tours

Hexeria (☎ 78 98 84 05; www.hexeria.no; Kaigata 12) organises bird-watching and fishing trips and also rents boats and bikes. In a similar vein and from mid-July to end of August, **Arctic Nature Adventure** (☎ 47 64 74 59; www.ana.no) offers four-hour photosafaris to Hamningberg (Nkr750), lake fishing (Nkr850) – and a king crab safari (Nkr650) in search of these crustacean monsters whose span can reach 2m.

Sleeping & Eating

Options aren't too appealing.

Svartnes Camping (☎ 78 98 71 60; Svartnes) Vardø's only budget option is a bleak place, 2km along the Hamningberg road. Drab and with barrack-like rooms, it's strictly for if you're stuck. Campers are better off seeking a spot in the hills or along the beach.

Vardø Hotell (☎ 78 98 77 61; fax 78 98 83 97; Kaigata 8; s/d Nkr450/500 mid-Jun–mid-Aug, Nk910/990 Mon-Thu, Nkr700/800 Fri & Sat rest-of-year) The staff are willing and cheerful at this place, which could be called with equal accuracy 'Vardø's Only Hotell'. However, rooms and corridors are decidedly threadbare and passé. On the plus side, summer prices are very reasonable, many rooms overlook the harbour and a couple are handicapped-equipped.

During the summer vacation, Hexeria (above) rents student rooms in a couple of hostels (s/d Nkr275/450; open from June to August) with corridor bathrooms and self-catering facilities and also has apartments (Nkr600 to Nkr1000) on its books.

Naustet (☎ 78 98 74 74; Strandgata 8) This appealing place, part bar and part restaurant, does a daily package of main course and dessert for Nkr100. Also recommended is their platter with three different varieties of fish (Nkr95), perhaps helped down with

HAMNINGBERG

A 72km round trip northwards from Vardø along the coast brings you to the tiny, semi-abandoned, timber-built settlement of Hamningberg. The end of the road, it may seem too like the end of the world, but locals maintain it's where Norway begins.

Along the narrow road you pass some of northern Norway's most fascinating geology: lichen-covered forests of eroded stone pillars, the remnants of sedimentary layers turned on end. If the lunar terrain looks familiar, you may have seen it in the James Bond film *Moonraker*. En route, you'll pass reindeer herds and several sandy beaches. Save the bucket-and-spading until the return journey when, 7.25km south of Hamningberg, you can walk to the broadest beach through the small nature reserve of **Sandfjordneset,** with its protected sand dunes set back from the shoreline.

What makes the village special is that, being so remote, it was saved from the general destruction of the German retreat in WWII. Only one house was destroyed – and that by a Russian bomber. The rest, abandoned in the 1960s except for summer visitors, still stand as living reminders of what was once one of eastern Finnmark's largest fishing villages.

Svein Harald (☎ 97 71 65 78), a local teacher, is renovating one of the old itinerant fishermen's cabins, which will offer four double rooms with shared facilities. Planned for 2005, there's lots to be done so do ring to confirm it's open. What's already up and running is an excellent-value apartment (Nkr700) with bathroom and kitchen that sleeps three. There's also a small **café** (☾ noon-8pm Jun-Aug) that serves coffee and snacks, including – definitely an acquired taste, this – dried reindeer's heart.

During Vardø's Pomordagene (Pomor days) festival in early August, throngs of people set out to walk the scenic 37km from Vardø to Hamningberg, and those who make it are treated to a barbecue at the church. Visitors are welcome to join in.

their two choices of Mack beer. It also does sandwiches, light meals and pizzas.

No, Nordpol Kro (Northpole Pub), isn't another 'northernmost' but with its wooden boards and antique bric-a-brac, it does lay a good claim to be northern Norway's oldest.

Getting There & Away

Vardø is a stop on the Hurtigruten coastal ferry route, but otherwise, it's well off the beaten track for all but the most die-hard travellers. Buses do the scenic seaside run between Vadsø and Vardø (Nkr110, 1½ hours) two to four times daily.

KIRKENES

pop 3300

This is it: you're as far east as Cairo or Istanbul and it's the end of the line for the Hurtigruten coastal ferry. But after the rest of coastal Finnmark, remote Kirkenes seems almost like the Big City. Its rocky, forested surroundings are lush and welcoming, particularly the wild Pasvik River valley with its special microclimate. Kirkenes is also a starting point for trips into Arctic Russia, just over the border, but you do need to start the visa chase well in advance; the Iron Curtain may have fallen but up here

there's no 'just slipping' over the border for a quick taste.

Some tourist facilities and the camping ground are in the nearby small village of Hesseng.

History

The district of Sør-Varanger, with Kirkenes as its main town, was jointly occupied by Norway and Russia until 1926, when the Russian, Finnish and Norwegian borders were set (nowadays in a historical hark back, the number of Russian migrants in town is rising and Kirkenes is the only town in Norway where major streets are signed in both Western and Cyrillic script).

In 1906, iron ore was discovered nearby and Kirkenes became a major supplier of raw materials for artillery during WWI. Early in WWII, the Nazis recognised its resources and strategic position near the free Russian port of Murmansk, occupied the town and posted 100,000 troops there. As a result, tiny Kirkenes was, after Malta, the second-most bombed place during WWII, with at least 320 devastating Soviet raids. Kirkenes was also an internment site for Norwegians from all over the country who did not cooperate with the occupiers.

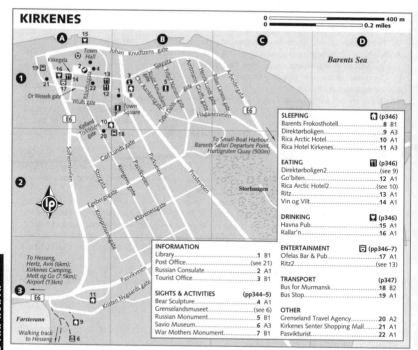

KIRKENES

0 ———————— 400 m
0 ———————— 0.2 miles

Barents Sea

SLEEPING	🏠 (p346)
Barents Frokosthotell	8 B1
Direktørboligen	9 A3
Rica Arctic Hotel	10 A3
Rica Hotel Kirkenes	11 A3

EATING	🍴 (p346)
Direktørboligen2	(see 9)
Go'biten	12 A1
Rica Arctic Hotel2	(see 10)
Ritz	13 A1
Vin og Vilt	14 A1

DRINKING	🍷 (p346)
Havna Pub	15 A1
Rallar'n	16 A1

INFORMATION	
Library	1 B1
Post Office	(see 21)
Russian Consulate	2 A1
Tourist Office	3 B1

SIGHTS & ACTIVITIES	(pp344–5)
Bear Sculpture	4 A1
Grenselandsmuseet	(see 6)
Russian Monument	5 B1
Savio Museum	6 A3
War Mothers Monument	7 B1

ENTERTAINMENT	🎭 (pp346–7)
Ofelas Bar & Pub	17 A1
Ritz2	(see 13)

TRANSPORT	(p347)
Bus for Murmansk	18 B2
Bus Stop	19 A1

OTHER	
Grenseland Travel Agency	20 A1
Kirkenes Senter Shopping Mall	21 A1
Pasvikturist	22 A1

THE FAR NORTH

Kirkenes was liberated by Soviet troops in October 1944, and as everywhere in Finnmark, the retreating Germans burned to the ground what was left. Although it was subsequently rebuilt less than glamorously, and continued to supply iron ore to much of Europe, costs were too high to sustain the industry and in 1996 the mines closed down.

Information

Library (Bibliotek; ☎ 78 99 32 51; Town Sq; ✆ core hours 11am–3pm Mon–Fri)

Tourist office (☎ 78 99 25 44; www.kirkenesinfo.no in Norwegian & German; Presteveien 1; ✆ 8.30am–5.30pm Mon–Fri, 10am–5.30pm Sat & Sun mid-Jun–mid-Aug, 8.30am–4pm Mon–Fri rest-of-year plus 10am–1pm Sat & Sun early May–mid-Jun & late Aug)

Dangers & Annoyances

The Russian border is within several kilometres of Kirkenes but don't even think about zipping across for a photo. Nowadays, in addition to vestiges of old Cold War neuroses on both sides, Norway, as a Schengen Agreement country, is vigilant in keeping illegal immigrants from enter-

ing. Both Norwegian and Russian sentries are equipped with surveillance equipment and the fine for any illegal crossings, even momentary ones, starts at a whopping Nkr5000. Greeting people on the other side, tossing anything across, using telephoto or zoom lenses or even a tripod all qualify as violations and can result in fines, so be extremely careful. As the guidance document sternly warns: 'any attempts at violations will be punished as if they had been carried out.'

Sights & Activities
GRENSELANDSMUSEET

About 1km from the centre, this well-presented **frontier museum** (☎ 78 99 48 80; Førstevannslia; adult/child Nkr40/30; ✆ 10am–6pm early Jun–mid-Aug, 10am-3.30pm rest-of-year) presents the geography and culture of the border region with special displays on WWII and the mining industry.

Within it is the **Savio collection**, a display of the distinctive Sami-inspired woodblock prints produced by local artist John A Savio (1902–38).

MONUMENTS & SCULPTURES

Up a short hill, the **Russian Monument** is dedicated to the Red Army troops who liberated the town in 1944. The **War Mothers Monument** in the town square commemorates women's efforts during the war and there's an engaging little **sculpture** of a bear mounting – in every sense of the word, it would appear – a lamppost outside the Russian consulate.

RUSSIAN MARKET

On the last Thursday of most months, Russian merchants set up shop around the town centre, selling everything from crafts and knitted tablecloths to binoculars. Prices aren't as cheap as in Russia, but they're still a bargain for Norway.

Tours

For such a small town, Kirkenes offers an impressive range of visits and activities, summer and winter alike, all of which can be booked at the tourist office or via the tour operators.

Grenseland Travel Agency (see p344) does daily one hour guided town walks (Nkr100), leaving the Rica Arctic Hotel at 1.30pm.

Barents Safari (☎ 90 19 05 94; www.barentssafari .no) runs a three-hour boat trip (adult/child Nkr740/400; at least twice daily from June to September) from Kirkenes' small-boat harbour along the Pasvik River to the Russian border at the historic town of Boris Gleb (Borisoglebsk in Russian). Afternoon sailings include a salmon meal in a Sami-style hut at the border.

If diving for giant crab in the Arctic Ocean gives you a frisson, **Arctic Dive Adventure Resort** (☎ 95 15 07 55; www.arctic-dive.no; Jarfjordbotn; ☼ Mar-Oct), based around 25km from Kirkenes, offers two dives plus one night's accommodation in a seaside cabin, from Nkr750 per day, including gear. The largest crab caught here was some 170cm across so watch your back! It also offers sea rafting and day cruises aboard a wooden fishing boat (adult/child Nkr990/450).

For adventures in the Pasvik wilderness, see p345.

Visiting Russia

Kirkenes' location and history make it a natural jumping-off point for Russia, particularly to the port of Murmansk, which is

---

THE FRENCHMAN WHO KEPT HIS SENSE OF HUMOUR

They tell the tale in the Kirkenes tourist office of the Frenchman who came in with a smile on his face, asking for help in translation. He'd been up to the frontier for a lookaround and had poked a toe over the border. Immediately, Norwegian frontier guards appeared, detained him, typed out a four-page report detailing his every movement from getting out of his car to committing the heinous offence, then slapped a Nkr5000 fine on him.

He left, poorer, still cheerful, and with every intention of framing the incriminating document, once home.

---

just exotic and inexpensive enough to make it worthwhile. But up here the bureaucracy's still decidedly chilly, despite the end of the Cold War. So decide whether it's worth *your* while since the visa chase is lengthy and expensive, requiring 14 days and an official invitation to visit Russia. Without that invitation, don't expect any help from the Russian consulate in Kirkenes (☎ 78 99 37 37). Some nationalities may be issued visas at the Russian consulate in Oslo, but if you're contemplating this paperchase, contact them even further in advance.

Despite the hurdles, cross-frontier traffic has increased substantially; in 1990, there were only around 10,000 border crossings each year, whereas 2002 saw some 135,000, mostly for trade and commercial purposes.

Fortunately, Kirkenes has two services that specialise in Russia, travel and handle invitations and visas for individuals or package tours. Even from outside Norway, you can send your passport in advance by certified mail for processing and return.

Government-set visa fees are based on country of citizenship: for example, a one-day visa costs from Nkr100 for Japanese to Nkr550 for Americans and fees escalate according to length of stay (a UK passport holder, for instance, pays Nkr450/625/775 for a one-/three-/14-day visa). Processing fees are an additional Nkr450 per person (Nkr1200 to Nkr1525 for same-day service). Your passport must be valid for at least six months and you have to specify which places you intend to visit.

For a brief taste of industrial Russia, **Grenseland Travel Agency** (☎ 78 99 25 01; www
.grenseland.no; Kongensgate 1-3) organises day trips to Nikel and Zapolyarny (Nkr690 plus visa), including lunch and guide. Its two night/three day trip to Murmansk ('Don't believe what you have heard about mafia and nuclear pollution,' its publicity defensively enjoins) costs from Nkr925 plus visa.

Pasvikturist (☎ 78 99 50 80; www.pasvikturist.no; Dr Wessels gate 9), the other main player, also offers a weekend trip to Murmansk (from Nkr1750) and trans-frontier day tours, including one to the Litza valley battlefield (Nkr1200), a key event in the WWII Arctic Front campaign which pitched Soviet and German forces against each other.

Both travel agencies can also offer programmes within Norway.

Independent travellers armed with a visa can hop aboard the Grenseland travel agency public bus to Murmansk (Nkr350/590 one way/return, five hours). It leaves Kirkenes daily (2pm Monday to Friday, 4pm Saturday and Sunday) from the Rica Arctic Hotel and returns from the Hotel Polyarnie Zory in Murmansk at 8am (noon on Sunday). For further information on independent travel, see Lonely Planet's *Russia & Belarus*.

Sleeping

Direktørboligen (☎ 78 99 18 09; www.dirboligen.no; Kristen Nygaardsgate 37; s/d Nkr800/975 mid-Jun–late Aug Nkr1040/1240 rest-of-year; P) Occupying what was formerly the residence of the directors of the Kirkenes iron industry, this bijou hotel has only six spacious rooms, so reservations are essential. It's a peaceful, comfortable, intimate place with picture windows, planted on a rise at the heart of a large garden. There's a free sauna for guests.

Rica Arctic Hotel (☎ 78 99 29 29; www.rica.no; Kongensgate 1-3; s/d Nkr766/966 mid-Jun–mid-Aug, Nkr1195/1325 Sun-Thu, Nkr750/895 Fri & Sat rest-of-year; P ⌨ 🏊) The Rica Arctic, a pleasing modern block, boasts Norway's most easterly swimming pool, heated and open year-round. Its other special attribute, its restaurant, is the best in town.

Barents Frokosthotell (☎ 78 99 32 99; fax 78 99 30 96; Presteveien 3; basic s/d Nkr500/700, with bathroom Nkr650/800) En suite rooms at this place without pretensions have been renovated. Oddly, it's the only hotel among all those

we visited in Norway where staff spoke not a word of English.

Kirkenes Camping (☎ 78 99 80 28; Maggadalen, Hesseng; tent/caravan sites Nkr90/120 plus per person Nkr15, 4-bed cabins Nkr350-700; 🕒 early Jun-Aug) This kindly but slightly run-down place, 8km west of town on the E6, is the only option for campers.

Rica Hotel Kirkenes (☎ 78 99 14 91; www.rica.no; Pasvikveien 63; s/d Nkr756/956; 🕒 Jun-Sep) This Rica really does feel like an overspill hotel, similarly priced to the Rica Arctic yet with none of the latter's charm. All the same, it's comfortable enough, and being above town, there are panoramic views from the restaurant and many bedrooms.

Eating

Ritz (☎ 78 99 34 81; Dr Wessels gate 17; mains Nkr60-220) Kirkenes' pizza place has an all-you-can-eat dinner taco buffet (Nkr98) on Wednesday and pizza buffet (Nkr95) each Friday. Attached is **Go'biten** (☎ 78 99 34 80), a neat little café with a good selection of sandwiches and cakes. It's equally pleasant inside or, the wind willing, outdoors on the terrace flanking pedestrianised Dr Wessels gate.

Vin og Vilt (☎ 78 99 38 11; Kierkegata 5; mains Nkr170-360) This gourmet choice, its décor simulating an elegant hunting lodge, has an enticing à la carte menu, where reindeer, grouse (in season) and Arctic char all feature.

Direktørboligen (☎ 78 99 18 09; Kristen Nygaardsgate 37; mains Nkr255 to Nkr325) The Mediterranean-based cuisine at this place – the chef lived in Italy for several years – is as sophisticated as the hotel itself. Again, it's essential to reserve.

Near the camping ground, the Mett og Go cafeteria with its small food shop is your lifeline.

Drinking

Havna Pub (☎ 78 99 30 10; Johan Knudtzens gate 1) This sailors' hang-out, overlooking the harbour and a rusting Russian hulk, is a great place to play pool or darts.

Rallar'n (☎ 78 99 18 73; Solheimsveien 1) Located up in town, while by no means snooty, it is less rough-and-ready than Havna.

Entertainment

Ritz (☎ 78 99 34 81; Dr Wessels gate 17) Kirkenes' most popular hang-out, its disco and pub attracting a mainly younger crowd.

Ofelas Bar & Pub (☎ 78 99 21 68; Dr Wessels gate 3) This venue pulls in a slightly older clientele and puts on live bands almost nightly.

Getting There & Away
SAS Braathens, Widerøe and Norwegian fly into **Kirkenes airport** (☎ 78 97 35 20), which has direct flights to Oslo, Tromsø, Lakselv, Vadsø and Vardø. Savvy locals save a bundle by flying in/out of Ivalo, Finland, in summer, when a daily bus (see below) runs the 250km betweeen Kirkenes and Ivalo's airport.

Buses serve Karasjok (Nkr452, 5½ hours), Hammerfest (Nkr740, 10 to 12 hours) and Alta (Nkr780, 12¾ hours) and many points in between. From July to mid-August, **Lapin Linjat** (www.eskelisen-lapinjat.com) runs to Ivalo town and airport (Nkr310, 3¼ hours, once daily except Sunday).

Kirkenes is the terminus of the Hurtigruten coastal ferry. A bus meets the boat and runs into town (Nkr22) and on to the airport (Nkr64).

Getting Around
The airport, about 15km southwest of town, is served by the Flybuss (25 minutes, Nkr64), which connects the bus terminal, the two Rica hotels and Hesseng (12 minutes, Nkr23) with all arriving and departing flights. Buses run between the centre and Hesseng (15 minutes, Nkr16) every hour or two on weekdays, at least five times on Saturday and once on Sunday. There's also a pleasant walking route, around 6km, to Hesseng, which follows the lakeshore part of the way.

Car rental agencies include **Hertz** (☎ 78 99 39 73) and **Avis** (☎ 78 97 37 05), which are both in Hesseng and prepared to deliver a car to your hotel.

PASVIK RIVER VALLEY
Even when diabolical mosquito swarms make life hell for warm-blooded creatures, the remote lakes, wet tundra bogs and Norway's largest stand of virgin *taiga* forest lend a strange appeal to odd little Øvre Pasvik National Park, in the far reaches of the Pasvik River valley. Some 100km from Kirkenes, this is the last corner of Norway where wolves, wolverines, lynx and brown bears still roam freely. It seems more like Finland, Siberia or Alaska than anywhere else in Norway. The park is also home to

moose and a host of relatively rare birds, which bird-watches will enjoy. Some of the birds including the Siberian jay, pine grosbeak, cedar waxwing, black-throated diver, red-breasted merganser, capercaillie, rough-legged buzzard, spotted redshank, hawk owl, great grey owl and even osprey.

The Stone-Age Komsa hunting culture left its mark here in the form of hunters' pitfall traps around the lake Ødevann and elsewhere in the region; some date from as early as 4000 BC.

Information
You'll find information at the **Pasvikdalen Villmarkssenter** (☎ 78 99 50 01), beside the Svanhøvd Environmental Centre, surrounded by its lovely garden, about 40km south of Kirkenes. It has exhibits on the region's natural sites, and offers dog- and reindeer-sledding and snowmobile safaris. You can also pick up the pamphlet *Bears in Pasvik*, which outlines etiquette on what to do should you encounter a testy bruin.

Sights & Activities
It's worth a stop at the Strand branch of the **Sør-Varanger Museum** (☎ 78 99 48 80; ◷ Jul–mid-Aug), which preserves Norway's oldest public boarding school, reveals the region's ethnic mix and also includes the timber-built **Svanvik chapel**, dating from 1934; and the 19th-century **Bjørklund Gård farm**.

The lookout tower **Høyden 96** (Nkr20) offers a view eastward to the Russian mining town of Nikel.

TREKKING
Hikers should douse themselves liberally in mosquito repellent before heading off into the wilds. The most accessible route is the poor road that turns southwest 1.5km south of Vaggetem and ends 9km later at the car park near the northeastern end of Lake Sortbrysttjørna. There, a marked track leads southwestwards for 5km, passing several scenic lakes, marshes and bogs to end at the Ellenvannskoia hikers' hut, beside the large lake, Ellenvatn. To extend the hike by two days, you can walk all the way around the lake, but there are no marked tracks.

Also from the Ødevasskoia car park, it's about an 8km walk due south to Krokfjell (145m) and the **Treriksrøysa**, the monument marking the spot where Norway, Finland

and Russia meet. Although you can approach it and take photos, you may not walk around the monument, which would amount to an illicit border crossing!

The topographic sheet to use is Statens Kartverk's *Krokfjellet 2333-I*, which conveniently covers the entire park at 1:25,000.

Sleeping & Eating

There are several hunting and fishing huts scattered around the park but the only one that's practical for casual hikers is Ellenvannskoia, which is free. With a licence, you can also fish in the lake, which contains perch, grayling and pike.

Øvre Pasvik Café & Camping (☎ 78 99 55 30; ordre@pasvik-cafe.no; Vaggetem; cabins Nkr250/500) This place rents canoes and bicycles, and provides infomation on local wilderness and attractions.

Pasvikdalen Villmarksenter (☎ 78 99 50 01; post@ pasvikdalen.no, Svanhøvd; r with shower & kitchen from Nkr450) Near Høyden 96 and the Svanhovd Environmental Centre, the centre has some 40 rooms and its owner has endless enthusiasm for the area and its attractions that the environs offer.

Pasvik Taiga Restaurant (☎ 78 99 54 44; www .pasvik-taiga.no; Skogfoss; s/d Nkr500/1000 incl breakfast, 3-4 course dinner Nkr500) This highly acclaimed place presents a range of gourmet fish and game dishes prepared using local herbs and berries. There are only seven rooms so it's essential to reserve in advance – this goes for the restaurant too since all food is freshly prepared on the day.

Getting There & Away

A bus leaves Kirkenes for Vaggetem (Nkr135, 2½ hours) four times per week, stopping at most sites along the way, including Skogfoss (Nkr86, 1½ hours).

GRENSE JAKOBSELV

The first settlement at Grense Jakobselv probably appeared around 8000 years ago, when the sea level was 60m lower than it is today. Only a small stream separates Norway and Russia here, and along the road you can see the border obelisks on both sides. The only real attraction – apart from the chance to gaze over the magic line – is the 1869 stone church. It was constructed within sight of the sea to cement Norway's territorial claims after local people

complained to the authorities that Russian fishing boats were illegally trespassing into Norwegian waters; it was thought that the intruders would respect a church and change their ways. When King Oskar II visited in 1873, he gave the church his name.

During school holidays, you can make a return trip between Kirkenes and Grense Jakobselv (Nkr90, 1½ hours) on Monday, Wednesday and Friday; the bus leaves at 9am and returns at 11.30am, allowing an hour in the village.

INNER FINNMARK

Nestled against the Finnish border, Norway's 'big sky country' is a place of lush greenery and epicentre of the semi-political entity known as Sápmi, the 'land of the Sami'. Kautokeino, a one street town if ever there was one, is the traditional heart of the region, although Karasjok is altogether more lively and has more Sami institutions.

KAUTOKEINO
pop 3000

While Karasjok has made concessions to Norwegian culture, Kautokeino, the traditional winter base of the reindeer (as opposed to coastal Sami), remains more emphatically Sami; some 85% of the townspeople have Sami as their first language and it's not uncommon to see a few non-tourist-industry locals in traditional costume. It is, frankly, dull in summer, the only hotel recently burnt down and so many of its people up and away with the reindeer in their warm weather pastures. What makes a visit well worthwhile is Juhls' Silver Gallery, just out of town and a magnificent repository of the best of Scandinavian jewellery design.

Settlement in the area can be traced back to the last ice age, 5000 years ago. From as early as 1553, during the gradual transition between nomadic and sedentary lifestyles, records reveal evidence of permanent settlement. Christianity took hold early on and the first church was built in 1641. The **tourist office** (☎ 78 48 79 00; destinasjonkautokeino@trolinet .no; ☉ 9am-6pm mid-Jun–mid-Aug) is located on the ground floor of the all-purpose complex beside the main road that also houses a bank and the town post office. It's a friendly place but none too well in-

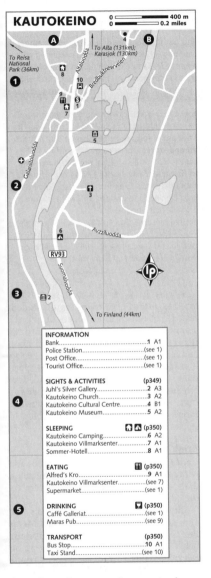

KAUTOKEINO

0 _____ 400 m
0 _____ 0.2 miles

To Reisa National Park (36km)

To Alta (131km); Karasjok (130km)

To Finland (44km)

RV93

INFORMATION	
Bank	1 A1
Police Station	(see 1)
Post Office	(see 1)
Tourist Office	(see 1)

SIGHTS & ACTIVITIES	(p349)
Juhl's Silver Gallery	2 A3
Kautokeino Church	3 A2
Kautokeino Cultural Centre	4 B1
Kautokeino Museum	5 A2

SLEEPING	(p350)
Kautokeino Camping	6 A2
Kautokeino Villmarksenter	7 A1
Sommer-Hotell	8 A1

EATING	(p350)
Alfred's Kro	9 A1
Kautokeino Villmarksenter	(see 7)
Supermarket	(see 1)

DRINKING	(p350)
Caffé Galleriat	(see 1)
Maras Pub	(see 9)

TRANSPORT	(p350)
Bus Stop	10 A1
Taxi Stand	(see 10)

formed. Readers report that opening hours may be 'unduly flexible'.

Sights & Activities

JUHLS' SILVER GALLERY

Juhls' Solvsmie is a wonderful building, all slopes and soft angles, designed and built by owners Regine and Frank Juhls, who first began working with the Sami nearly half a century ago. Their highly acclaimed **gallery** (☎ 78 48 61 89; www.juhls.no; Galaniitoluodda; admission free; ☼ 8.30am-9pm mid-Jun–mid-Aug, 9am-6pm rest-of-year) creates traditional and modern silver jewellery and handicrafts and displays the best of Scandinavian design. One wing – the building grew organically from their original simple wooden cabin – has a fine collection of oriental carpets and artefacts, reminders of their work in support of Afghan refugees during that blighted country's Soviet occupation. Staff happily show you around and you're welcome to buy items.

KAUTOKEINO CULTURAL CENTRE

If you're interested in fine modern architecture, make a similar small detour to the outskirts of town and the **Kautokeino Cultural Centre** (Bredbuktnesveien 50), winner of several awards. It's the base for the Nordic Sami Institute and also Beaivváš, the world's only professional Sami theatre company that tours throughout the region.

KAUTOKEINO MUSEUM

Outside, this charming little **museum** (☎ 78 48 71 00; Boaronjárga 23; adult/child Nkr20/free; ☼ 9am-7pm Mon-Sat, noon-7pm Sun mid-Jun–mid-Aug, 9am-3pm Mon-Fri rest-of-year) presents a traditional Sami settlement, complete with an early home, temporary dwellings and outbuildings such as the kitchen, sauna, and huts for storing fish, potatoes and lichen (also called 'rein-deer moss' and prime reindeer fodder). Inside are Sami handicrafts, farming and reindeer-herding implements, religious icons and artefacts, and winter transport gear are all on display.

KAUTOKEINO KIRKE

The timbered Kautokeino **church** (Suomalvodda; ☼ 9am-10pm Jun–mid-Aug), which dates from 1958, is one of Norway's most used, particularly at Easter. Its cheery interior, alive with bright Sami colours has some fixtures salvaged from the earlier (1701) church that was torched in WWII.

CANOEING

Between June and August, you can hire canoes (per day Nkr250) to potter around on the river. Ask at Alfred's Kro or call ☎ 95 96 49 01.

SAMI CULTURE & TRADITIONS

Sami life was originally based on hunting and fishing but at sometime during the 16th century the majority of reindeer were domesticated and the hunting economy transformed into a nomadic herding economy. While reindeer still figure prominently in Sami life, only about 16% of Sami people are still directly involved in reindeer herding and transport by reindeer sledge, and only a handful of traditionalists continue to lead a truly nomadic lifestyle. The majority these days fish or are engaged in tourist-related activities.

A major identifying element of Sami culture is the *joik* (or *yoik*), a rhythmic poem composed for a specific person to describe their innate nature and considered to be owned by the person it describes (p38). Other traditional elements include the use of folk medicine, Shamanism, artistic pursuits (especially woodcarving and silversmithing) and striving for ecological harmony.

The Sami national dress is the only genuine folk dress that's still in casual use in Norway, and you might see it on the streets of Kautokeino and Karasjok. Each district has its own distinct features, but all include a highly decorated and embroidered combination of red and blue felt shirts or frocks, trousers or skirts, and boots and hats. On special occasions, the women's dress is topped off with a crown of pearls and a garland of silk hair ribbons.

To learn more, look out for *The Sami People* published by Davvi Girji (1990) or *The Sami: Indigenous People of the Arctic* by Odd Mathis Hælta, both available in English translation. *The Magic of Sami Yoik* by Dejoda is one of several CDs devoted to this special genre, while the tracks on *Eight Seasons* by Mari Boine, a Karasjok singer, offer a greater variety of Sami music.

Festivals & Events

Easter is a time for weddings and an excuse for a big gathering to mark the end of the dark season, before folk and flocks disperse to the summer grazing. It's celebrated with panache: the reindeer racing world championships, the Sami Grand Prix – no, not a souped-up snowmobile race but the premier *yoik* contest – and other traditional Sami and religious events. Check out www.saami-easterfestival.org for more details and programme information.

Sleeping & Eating

Kautokeino Camping (☎ 78 48 54 00; samicamp@start .no; Suomaluodda 16; tent/caravan sites Nkr130, cabins Nkr300, with bathroom Nkr650-800, motel r Nkr500) Campers and cabin-dwellers have access to a communal kitchen at this friendly place. It has a large Sami *lavvo*, a warm and cosy spot to relax by a wood fire and sip the steaming coffee laid on nightly at 9pm. If you ask, the small café will also rustle up *bidos*, the traditional reindeer meat stew served at Sami weddings and other rites of passage.

Kautokeino Villmarksenter (☎ 78 48 76 02; isak mathis@hotmail.com; Hannoluohkka 2; s/d Nkr500/700, 4-bed cabins Nkr400) The only other reliable option is set above the main road. Opened recently and functioning year-round, it also runs a decent café-restaurant (mains Nkr85 to Nkr140) with an attractive open-air deck.

Sommer-Hotell (☎ 41 84 87 03, 90 83 99 39; r Nkr290, apt Nkr450) Follow signs for this student hostel that's open to allcomers during the summer vacation. Just off the main drag, it's staffed – in principle – between noon and 6pm.

Alfred's Kro (☎ 78 48 61 18; Hannoluohkka 4) Open daily, it has Mack on draught and does burgers (Nkr65 to Nkr90). In summer and more enterprisingly, it also does a whole range of traditional Sami dishes (Nkr115 to Nkr135).

Drinking

Caffé Galleriat, above the tourist office and with its principal entrance on the main drag, is a convivial little place for a relaxing coffee.

Altogether heartier, below Alfred's Kro and under separate management, Maras Pub is more intimate than its upstairs neighbour. Once the ale starts flowing on weekend nights, patrons are known to quite likely to spontaneously break into a *yoik* or two.

Getting There & Away

Buses connect Kautokeino with Alta (Nkr193, 2¼ hours, four times per week). From June to mid-August, you can also travel on the Lapin Linjat bus between Kautokeino and Rovaniemi, in Finland (Nkr280, 7¼ hours).

REISA NATIONAL PARK

Although it's technically in Troms county, Reisa National Park is most readily accessible by road from Kautokeino. For hikers, the 50km route through this remote Finnmarksvidda country is one of Norway's wildest and physically demanding challenges. The northern trailhead at Sarelv is accessible on the Rv865, 47km south of Storslett, and the southern end is reached on the gravel route to Reisevannhytta, 4km west of Bieddjuvaggi on the Rv896, heading northwest from Kautokeino.

Most people walk from north to south. From Bilto or Sarelv, you can either walk the track up the western side of the cleft that channels the Reisaelva river or hire a riverboat for the three-hour 27km trip upstream to Nedrefoss, where there's a DNT hut. En route, notice the 269m Mollesfossen waterfall, east of the track on the tributary stream Molleselva. From Nedrefoss, the walking route continues for 35km south to the Reisavannhytta hut on the lake Reisajávri, near the southern trailhead.

KARASJOK

pop 2900

It's a lovely drive between Kautokeino and Karasjok, following, for the most spectacular stretch, the River Jiešjokka.

Kautokeino may have more Sami residents, but Karasjok (Kárášjohka in Sami) is Sami Norway's indisputable capital. It's home to the Sami Parliament and Library, NRK Sami Radio, a wonderful Sami Museum and an impressive Sami theme park. Karasjok is also the site of Finnmark's oldest timber church, **Gamlekirke**, which dates from 1807 and was the only Karasjok building to survive the WWII bombings and fires. Only 18km from the border with Finland, it pulls in coaches, caravans and cars by the hundred, all heading for Nordkapp.

The **tourist office** (☎ 78 46 88 10; www.koas.no; ⏰ 9am-7pm Jun–mid-Aug, 9am-4pm Mon-Fri Aug–May) is situated in Sápmi Park, near the junction of the E6 and the Rv92. It will change money if you're stuck with euros after crossing the border from Finland.

Sights & Activities

SÁPMI PARK

Sami culture is big business here, and it was only a matter of time before it

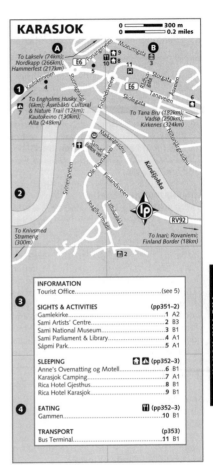

KARASJOK

0 ———— 300 m
0 ———— 0.2 miles

INFORMATION	
Tourist Office	(see 5)

SIGHTS & ACTIVITIES	(pp351–2)
Gamlekirke	1 A2
Sami Artists' Centre	2 B3
Sami National Museum	3 B1
Sami Parliament & Library	4 A1
Sápmi Park	5 A1

SLEEPING	🏠 🛖 (pp352–3)
Anne's Overnatting og Motell	6 B1
Karasjok Camping	7 A1
Rica Hotel Gjesthus	8 B1
Rica Hotel Karasjok	9 B1

EATING	🍴 (pp352–3)
Gammen	10 B1

TRANSPORT	(p353)
Bus Terminal	11 B1

consolidated into a **theme park** (☎ 78 46 88 00; Porsangerveien; adult/child Nkr95/60; ⏰ 9am-7pm Jun–mid-Aug, 9am-4pm Mon-Fri mid-Aug–May). There's a wistful, high-tech multimedia introduction to the Sami in the 'Magic Theatre', plus Sami winter and summer camps and other dwellings in the grounds, and of course, a gift shop and café. It's actually very good and presents the Sami as the normal fellow human beings they are rather than as exotic anachronisms. If you want more substance, the smaller Sami museums in Karasjok and Kautokeino are less flash and more academic.

SAMI PARLIAMENT

This **parliament** (Sámediggi; ☎ 78 47 40 00; Kautokeinoveien 50; admission free) came into being in

1989 and in 2000 moved into a glorious new building, encased in mellow Siberian wood, with a birch, pine and oak interior. The main assembly hall is shaped like a Sami *gamma* tent, and the Sami library, lit with tiny lights like stars, houses over 35,000 volumes, plus other media. In summer, there are 30-minute tours leaving hourly between 8.30am and 2.30pm (except 11.30am), Monday to Saturday. The rest of the year, tours are at 1.30pm on weekdays. There are similar Sami parliaments in Finland and Sweden.

SAMI NATIONAL MUSEUM

This **museum** (Sámiid Vuorká Dávvirat; ☎ 78 46 99 50; Museumsgata 17; adult/child Nkr25/5; ☘ 9am-6pm Mon-Sat, 10am-6pm Sun early Jun-late Aug, 9am-3pm Mon-Fri, 10am or noon-3pm Sat & Sun rest-of-year) is also called the Sami Collection. Smaller and more serious, it's been rather upstaged by the genial razzamatazz down the road. Devoted to Sami history and culture, it has displays of colourful, traditional Sami clothing, a bewildering array of tools and artefacts and works by contemporary Sami artists. Outdoors, a homestead reveals the simplicity of traditional Sami life. Signing is only in Norwegian and Sami and the English guide sheet is difficult to follow.

SAMI ARTISTS' CENTRE

This dynamic **gallery** (☎ 78 46 90 02; Jeagilvármádii 54; ☘ 10am-3pm Mon-Fri, noon-5pm Sun) mounts temporary exhibitions by contemporary Sami artists and is well worth the short journey to the limits of town.

ÁSSEBÁKTI CULTURAL & NATURE TRAIL

On the Rv92, 12km south of Karasjok heading for Kautokeino, this 3.5km trail (signed 'Kulturminner' on the highway) is well worth undertaking for a taste of the forest even though, despite its name, it doesn't actually have much that's cultural. This said, around 25 minutes out (allow two hours for the full out and back route), there are traces of trappers' pits, store mounds and, across the river, turf huts.

Tours

Engholm's Husky (see the boxed text, right) offers winter dog-sled and cross-country skiing tours, as well as summer walking tours with a dog to carry your pack – or

at least some of it – and horse riding. All-inclusive expeditions range from one-day dog-sled tours (per person Nkr1000) to eight-day Arctic safaris (Nkr9500). Consult the website, www.engholm.no, for the full range of activities.

Sleeping & Eating

Karasjok Camping (☎ 78 46 61 35; halonen@online.no; Kautokeinoveien; person/site Nkr10/100, dm Nkr130, cabins Nkr250-410, with bathroom Nkr550-850) Friendly Karasjok Camping occupies a hillside with river views and a range of cabins. Lay back on reindeer skins to the crackle of the nightly birch wood fire in the cosy *lavvo* or cook your own thing in the equally relaxing barbecue hut.

Anne's Overnatting og Motell (☎ /fax 78 46 64 32; Tanaveien 40; 2-/4-bed cabins Nkr375/450, s/d with bathroom Nkr400/535; [P]) Run by a Sami lady, this place serves no meals but rooms have TV and kitchen access. Prices leap if you don't have your own sheets or sleeping bag. Anne, who's no longer young, may be retiring in 2005 so do ring in advance.

Rica Hotel Karasjok (☎ 78 46 74 00; www.rica.no; Porsangerveien; s/d Nkr780/980 mid-Jun–mid-Aug, Nkr1220/1330 Sun-Thu, Nkr745/930 Fri & Sat rest-of-year; [P] [≣]) Adjacent to Sápmi Park, this is Karasjok's premier lodging, with handsome

---

AUTHOR'S CHOICE

Engholm's Husky (☎ 78 46 71 66; www.engholm.no; cabins Nkr200-300 plus per person Nkr100) Six kilometres from town on the Rv92, it is a wonderful haven in the forest that Sven Engholm and his partner Bodil have built from nothing over two decades. Each rustic cabin is individually furnished with great flair, all have well-equipped kitchens and one has a bathroom. You sink into sleep to the jangle of horses' harnesses and the odd bark and yelp from the sled dogs, and in summer, you can wake to a breakfast (Nkr70) of eggs from Bodil's free-range hens that scratch around the compound. A plentiful dinner costs Nkr200 in your cabin or Nkr350 if you take it in their traditional Sami turf hut. There are signed trails in the forest and a salmon stream with a fine beach a five-minute stroll away.

Sven's place also serves as Karasjok's HI-affiliated **youth hostel** (dm/s/d Nkr175/300/450).

rooms and Sami motifs throughout and an impressive Arctic Menu restaurant. It also runs the substantially cheaper **Gjestehus** (s/d Nkr600/800 Sun-Thu, Nkr550/650 Fri & Sat), also in the park grounds, for which you need to reserve at least a day in advance.

Gammen (☎ 78 46 74 00; mains Nkr200-310; ⓨ mid-Jun–mid-Aug) It's very much reindeer or reindeer, with a token trout dish, at this rustic complex of four large interconnected Sami huts run by the Rica Hotel. Although it may be busy with bus tours, it's an atmospheric place to sample traditional Sami dishes from reindeer stew to fillet of reindeer. And hey, cigarettes may be banned from all Norwegian eateries but tenacious puffers may derive more than cold comfort from this dark, smoky environment.

Shopping

Knivsmed Strømeng (☎ 78 46 71 05; Badjenjárga) This craft shop calls on four generations of local experience to create unique and original handmade Sami knives for everything from outdoor to kitchen use. Similar Sami crafts are sold at the Sápmi Park Gift Shop.

Getting There & Away

Daily buses connect Karasjok with Alta (Nkr350, 4¾ hours) via Lakselv (Nkr110, 1½ hours), Hammerfest (Nkr308, 4¼ hours) and Kirkenes (Nkr452, 5½ hours).

A daily Finnish Lapin Linjat bus to Rovaniemi (Nkr350, eight hours) via Ivalo (Nkr160, 2½ hours), in Finland, also runs from Karasjok, year-round.

THE FAR NORTH

Svalbard

CONTENTS

SVALBARD

Svalbard is an assault on the senses. This wondrous archipelago is the world's most readily accessible bit of the polar north and one of the most spectacular places imaginable. Vast icebergs and floes choke the seas, and icefields and glaciers frost the lonely heights. But under close scrutiny, the harsh conditions reveal tiny gems as the Arctic desert soil, however barren-looking, manages to sustain lichens, miniature grasses and delicate little flowers. The environment supports larger creatures too: whales, seals, walruses, Arctic foxes, squat Svalbard reindeer – and polar bears aplenty.

Svalbard doesn't come easy – especially on the pocket. It's nearly a 1000km flight from Tromsø, the nearest major airport on the mainland. This said, it's actually cheaper than ever to fly to the archipelago these days. Budget accommodation, however, is very much at a premium. If you arrive as an independent traveller, you'll be rather rarer than polar bears on these islands; the vast majority of visitors come as members of an organised tour or, as we too recommend, sign up for group visits once they arrive in Longyearbyen, the usual point of entry for all except those who come by cruise ship.

What really bumps the cost up is the price of organised tours and activities. Since travel outside Longyearbyen is difficult at best and can be downright dangerous, you miss out on a lot if you don't sign up for one or two. So, when you're doing your pre-holiday sums, budget for a glacier walk, a boat trip or a mine visit and see if you can still make ends meet.

HIGHLIGHTS

- **Cruising** (p356) around ice floes, hoping to spot seals, walruses and polar bears
- Experiencing pristine Arctic nature on an **organised hiking expedition** (p356)
- Penetrating deep into disused **Mine No 3** (p359) outside Longyearbyen and being glad you're not a collier
- Visiting the Russian mining village of **Barentsburg** (p362)
- Spending a sunny morning surrounded by the brilliant glaciers and turquoise waters of **Magdalenefjord** (p366)

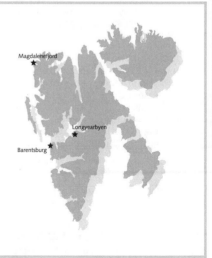

SVALBARD

| AREA: 61,400 SQ KM | HIGHEST ELEVATION: NEWTONTOPPEN (1713M) | POPULATION: 2700 |

History

The first mention of Svalbard occurs in an Icelandic saga from 1194. Officially, however, the Dutch voyager Willem Barents, in search of a northeast passage to China, is considered to be the first visitor from the European mainland (1596). He named the islands Spitsbergen, or 'sharp mountains'; the Norwegian name, Svalbard, comes from the old Norse for 'cold coast'; the sagas referred to 'a land in the far north at the end of the ocean'. Today, Spitsbergen is the name of Svalbard's largest island. In 1920 the Svalbard Treaty granted Norwegian sovereignty over the islands and restricted military activities. Initially signed by nine nations, it now has over 40 adherents, whose citizens enjoy the same rights and obligations on the islands as Norwegians themselves.

POLAR EXPLORATION

Longyearbyen is precisely 1338km from the North Pole (or not quite precisely; by the time you read this, it will be fractionally nearer as Svalbard inches northwards by 2mm per year). In the late 19th and early 20th centuries, a series of explorers attempted to reach the North Pole using airships and balloons, and most met with failure. Roald Amundsen and Umberto Nobile were successful in 1926, but two years later Amundsen and his crew died while on a rescue mission to find Nobile, who had disappeared on a similar expedition and was later rescued.

WHALING & HUNTING

At the time of Barents' discovery, the archipelago was uninhabited, as the early Inuit migrations eastward from Siberia and Alaska halted in Greenland. There's archaeological evidence of Russian overwintering around the beginning of the 17th century, but the first confirmed western European activities in Svalbard didn't begin until a decade later. From 1612 to 1720, English, Dutch, French, Norwegian and Danish ships engaged in whaling off the western coast of Spitsbergen Island; it's estimated that the Dutch alone took 60,000 whales.

The first known overwintering took place at Bellsund in 1630 by an English group, followed by a Dutch group at Smeerenburg in 1633; the following winter, however, scurvy took its toll and the settlement was abandoned for winter, but for a small caretaker team, who all perished. From the early 18th century, Russian Pomor (coast-dwelling) hunters and traders focused their attentions on Svalbard and began hunting walrus, moose, seals and belugas. From around 1795, Norwegians too took notice of the islands' wildlife resources and began hunting both polar bears and Arctic foxes.

COAL MINING

Perhaps as early as 1612, whalers had discovered coal at Ny Ålesund (p363), but the first modern mine wasn't opened until 1906, when the Arctic Coal Company (ACC) began extracting coal from a rich seam. The settlement that grew up around this mine was named for the ACC's US owner, John Munroe Longyear. In 1916, ACC sold out to the Store Norske Spitsbergen Kull Compani (SNSK). Over the next few years, two other Norwegian companies set up operations on the archipelago's southernmost island, Bjørnøya, and the Kings Bay Kull Compani opened a mine at Ny Ålesund.

During WWII, mining was halted, and on 3 September 1941 the islands were evacuated. Still, the Germans bombed Longyearbyen and the settlements of Barentsburg and Sveagruva (Mine No 2, on the hillside just east of Longyearbyen, was shelled and set alight and continued to burn for 14 years). When the Germans surrendered in 1945, Norwegian civilians returned, Longyearbyen was rebuilt and the Russians resettled and again mined in Pyramiden and Barentsburg.

Ny Ålesund also re-opened, but was closed down after a mine explosion in 1962 and converted into a scientific post.

Nowadays, Mine No 7 is the only one around Longyearbyen still producing, as it has been for nearly 40 years, yielding around 70,000 tonnes per year for firing the town's power station or for export to Germany.

The big one these days is the Svea North coalfield, 44km from Longyearbyen. The scale of the operation boggles the mind. In 2003, it gave up 2.7 million tonnes – more in a week than Mine No 7 in a year – most of which was exported to Finland, Germany and Denmark. There are estimated reserves of 40 million tonnes and the project will extend until at least 2013. At the other

SVALBARD

end of the scale, the workforce, based in Longyearbyen and flown into Sveagruva for one-week shifts, is small, operating colossal, state-of-the-art machinery that chews its way through the mountain.

OTHER NATURAL RESOURCES
The most sanguine predictions of Svalbard's gold reserves beneath the Arctic soil put them on a level with South Africa's. There's also the potential for oil extraction and the Russians were due to sink their first bore hole as we went to print.

Geography & Climate
The archipelago, about the size of Ireland, consists mainly of glaciated and eroded

sedimentary layers laid beneath the sea up to 1.2 billion years ago. Between 300 million and 60 million years ago, Svalbard lay in the tropics, where rich layers of organic matter built up on the surface and metamorphosed under great heat and pressure into coal. The continental drift shifted it to its polar location, and most of its present-day landforms were created during the ice ages of the past two million years. Its highest points are Newtontoppen (1713m) and Perriertoppen (1712m).

Svalbard's latitude ranges from latitude 74°N at Bjørnøya in the south to over 80°N on northern Spitsbergen and Nordaustlandet. In Longyearbyen the midnight sun lasts from 19 April to 23 August, while

---

BOOKS

As we went to press, *Svalbard: Spitsbergen, Franz Josef Land, Jan Mayen*, a new travel guidebook title in English written by longtime Svalbard resident Andreas Umbreit (see p357), was about to be published by the excellent Bradt Publications.

Svalbard & the Life in Polar Oceans by Bjorn Gulliksen and Erling Svensen deals specifically with the marine life and ecology of the region but it's also of interest to the more general reader and has stacks of stunning photos.

The Governor of Svalbard's office publishes some excellent booklets in English, both for guiding and for background reading. *Isfjorden* by Kristin Prestvold is an impressive guide to the fjord that runs between Longyearbyen, Barentsburg and west to the headland of Kap Linné. It comes with a reliable map at a scale of 1:250,000. More general titles include *Smeerenburg & Gravneset*, the fascinating history of a whaling community, and *Virgohamna*, an equally compelling description of this one-time base for North Pole expeditions, a spot described by the usually more positive Nansen as 'a desolate, dismal place...an isolated, disagreeable bay'.

---

the polar night lasts from 28 October to 14 February.

The archipelago enjoys a brisk polar desert climate, with only 200mm to 300mm of precipitation annually. Although the west coast remains ice-free for most of the summer, pack ice hovers just north of the main island year-round, and sheets and rivers of ice cover approximately 60% of the land area. Snow and frost are possible at any time of year; the mean annual temperature is -4°C, and in July, it's only 6°C. On occasion, however, you may experience temperatures of up to 20°C or higher. In January, the mean temperature is -16°C, but temperatures of -30°C aren't uncommon.

Dangers & Annoyances

In real life, Svalbard's symbol, the polar bear, is not the cute fuzzy you see in the zoo. Nobody really knows how many there are on the archipelago – the only place in Norway where they live in the wild. Estimates vary between 2000 and 5000 and the first bear census since 1973, scheduled for 2005, should lead to more precision – and probably confirmation that the region's bear population indeed still exceeds the number of humans.

But even one bear at close quarters is one too many. While it's most unlikely that you'll have a Close Encounter of the Furred Kind in the environs of Longyearbyen, the best advice is, if you're trekking, go with an organised tour. Walk leaders will normally carry a gun and know how to use it. Standard equipment too, especially if you'll be camping out, are trip wires with flares and

distress flares too – to fire at the ground in front of the bear, not to summon help, which could be hours away.

If, despite this, you're determined to set out without a guide, carry the same equipment; you'll come across several places in town that rent kits out – and make sure you get in some practice shooting before you travel if one end of a gun is much the same as another to you. Spitsbergen Guesthouse and Svalbard Snøscooterutleie both rent guns (Nkr100 per day).

And don't get over-alarmed. Since people *do* take great care, it's now nearly a decade since the last 'exit Knut pursued by a bear' line was acted out, when a Swedish teacher came to a dramatic end.

Tours

It's no simple matter to arrange an independent journey to Svalbard or to set up independent trips once you're there, so most visitors book organised tours. Fortunately, there are lots of options from winter

---

A POLAR BEAR IN YOUR COMPUTER

An altogether safer way to track polar bears is to log onto the website of **World Wildlife Fund** (www.panda.org/polarbears). Here, you can track the movements of Samantha and Marianne, a couple of mature females that scientists have equipped with a collar and satellite transmitter. You'll also learn a whole lot more about how these magnificent, resilient creatures survive in such tough conditions.

dog-sledding or snowmobiling day trips to two-week excursions to the North Pole. The **tourist information website** (www.svalbard.net) lists dozens of tours and we detail but a sample of the most popular ones below. For more day trip ideas, see p359.

SPITSBERGEN TRAVEL
The giant of the Svalbard travel scene, **Spitsbergen Travel** (☎ 79 02 61 00; www.spitsbergentravel .no; Postboks 548, N-9171 Longyearbyen), runs six-day journeys between mid-June and mid-September aboard the former Hurtigruten coastal steamer *Nordstjernena* with a four-day guided cruise that puts ashore at both Barentsburg and Ny Ålesund. Prices, not including the round-trip airfare from Tromsø are from Nkr7100 to Nkr11,700 per person without/with private shower.

SVALBARD WILDLIFE SERVICE
Offering many of the usual and several unusual trips, **Svalbard Wildlife Service** (☎ 79 02 56 60; www.wildlife.no; Postboks 164, N-9171 Longyearbyen) can take you on three days of camping, hiking and kayaking around the Esmark glacier exploration (Nkr4950), or seven days among the glaciers, seals and walruses of Prins Karls Forland island (Nkr12,800).

SPITSBERGEN TOURS
Svalbard's first locally based tour operator, **Spitsbergen Tours** (☎ 79 02 10 68; www.terrapolaris .com; Postboks 6, N-9171 Longyearbyen), has operated since 1987. Owner Andreas Umbreit has written the standard text in English about the archipelago (see the boxed text, p356).

The range of adventurous options includes an Arctic week in three versions, based in Longyearbyen: during the long, dark polar night (Nkr10,200), in April's wintry springtime (Nkr13,800), or during the summer high season, when prices range from Nkr7650 if you camp to Nkr19,000 in single room accommodation. The price includes day excursions from the settlements (eg two days of dog-sledding, a snow machine tour, boat cruises and walks, during the applicable seasons). Winter dog-sledding tours cost between Nkr1000 and Nkr2000 per day and it's advisable to book well in advance. For the hardy, there are also winter snowshoe and hiking weeks (Nkr12,800) with accommodation in tents (make sure you bring a four-season sleeping bag) and the opportunity to build – and sleep in, if you choose – an igloo.

Spitsbergen Tours also organises modular hiking tours, within the capacity of anyone who's reasonably fit, that mix day-walks with linear treks. All-in prices for one/two/three weeks are Nkr7,300/13,200/21,000.

BASECAMP
Basecamp (☎ 79 02 46 00; www.basecampexplorer.com; Postboks 316, N-9171 Longyearbyen) mainly offers winter activities, including a stay aboard the *Noorderlicht*, a Dutch sailing vessel that's set into the fjord ice as the long freeze begins each autumn.

SVALBARD VILLMARKSSENTER
The experts in dog mushing are **Svalbard Villmarkssenter** (☎ 79 02 19 86; www.svalbard-adven ture.com; Postboks 396, N-9171 Longyearbyen), whether by sledge over the snow or – OK, it's not the same thing but it gives you a feel of what a wintertime dog-sled experience must be like – on wheels during summer.

LONGYEARBYEN
pop 1500
The capital and 'metropolis' of Svalbard, this down-to-earth community had its beginnings as the main export site for the rich coal seams that thread the island.

The modern town, strewn with abandoned coal mining detritus (most of which enjoys protected status as part of the island's industrial heritage), enjoys a superb backdrop including two glacier tongues, Longyearbreen and Lars Hjertabreen. Construction here takes into account the harsh Arctic climate; most structures are built on pilings to prevent heated buildings from melting the permafrost that's never more than a metre deep, then simply sinking into it! The heavily insulated plumbing pipes also run above ground.

Reflecting the days when miners would remove their coal-dust-encrusted boots at the threshold, local decorum still dictates that people take off their shoes upon entering most buildings in town. Exceptions include the majority of shops and places to eat.

Information
Basecamp (per 10min Nkr20) The Internet can be accessed here (one terminal).

SVALBARD

LONGYEARBYEN

0 —————— 600 m
0 —————— 0.4 miles

INFORMATION
Library.............................(see 15)
Longyearbyen Hospital Casualty
  Clinic.............................**1** C2
Norwegian Polar Institute.........(see 4)
Post Office.........................**2** C2
Sparebanke 1 Norge................(see 2)
Telenor Office.....................**3** C1
Tourist Office.....................**4** C2

SIGHTS & ACTIVITIES   (pp360–1)
Galleri Svalbard...................**5** B4
Historic Graveyard................**6** B3
Sports Hall & Swimming Pool......**7** B3
Svalbard Museum...................**8** C2

SLEEPING   (pp361–2)
Basecamp Spitsbergen..............**9** C2
Gjesthuset 102....................**10** B4
Mary-Ann's Polarrigg..............**11** C1
Radisson SAS Polar Hotel..........**12** D1
Spitsbergen Guesthouse............**13** B4
Spitsbergen Hotel.................**14** C3

EATING   (p362)
Fruene Kaffe og Vinbar............**15** C2
Funktionærmessen Restaurant..(see 13)
Huset.............................**16** B3
Kafé Busen........................(see 15)
Kroa Pub & Restaurant.............(see 9)
Restaurant Nansen.................(see 12)
Svalbardbutikken Supermarket...**17** C2

DRINKING   (pp362–3)
Barents Pub.......................(see 12)
Funken Bar........................(see 14)
Huset.............................(see 16)
Kroa Pub & Restaurant.............(see 9)

TRANSPORT   (p363)
Svalbard Snøscooterutleie.........**18** D1

OTHER
Lompensenteret....................(see 15)
Nordpolet.........................(see 17)
Næringsbrygget....................(see 4)
Spitsbergen Travel................**19** D1
Svalbard Wildlife Service.........(see 4)
Sysselmann's (Governor's)
  Office............................**20** C1
UNIS University....................**21** D1

To Airport (4.5km);
Longyearbyen
Camping (4.5km);
New Cruise Ship Wharf

Burma Road
To Airport &
Longyearbyen
Camping

Skjæringa

Sentrum

To Adventdalen

Haugen

Nybyen

To Fossils

Walking Route
to Longyearbreen

Library (Lompensenteret; free Internet; ⏱ 11am–6pm Mon, Wed, Thu; 11am–2pm Tue–Sat)

Longyearbyen Hospital casualty clinic (☎ 79 02 42 00)

Norwegian Polar Institute (Næringsbrygget) Good for books on the region, posters and maps.

Post office On the main street.

Sparebanke 1 Norge For money-related queries contact this bank, in the Post Office building.

Telenor office Near the Sysselman's office.

Tourist office (☎ 79 02 55 50; www.svalbard.net; Næringsbrygget; ⏱ 8am–6pm Mon–Fri, 9am–4pm Sat, noon–4pm Sun mid-Jun–Aug, 8am–4pm Mon–Fri rest-of-year plus 10am–noon Sat Sep & Easter–mid-Jun) Produces *Svalbard*, an excellent guide (English version available) to the archipelago and the infinite range of outdoor activities you can pursue.

Sights & Activities
SVALBARD MUSEUM

Longyearbyen's little **museum** (☎ 79 02 13 84; Skjæringa; adult/child Nkr30/15; ⏱ 11am–6pm Mon–Sat, 1–6pm Sun Jun–Aug, shorter hours rest-of-year) occupies a former pig sty, one of the oldest buildings in town. Exhibits cover the history, climate, geology, wildlife and exploration of the archipelago, and include Svalbard's economic mainstay, mining – the sculpted miner gives a vivid sense of how uncomfortable it was to lie in low, narrow mine shafts. If you want more of the real thing, you can pull on miners' gear and crawl into a replica tunnel. In 2006, the museum is expected to move to larger premises near the University UNIS site.

MINE NO 3

To get an idea of working life in Longyearbyen before tourism really began to bite, sign on with Svalbard Wildlife Service or Spitzbergen Travel (see p357) for a journey deep into **Mine No 3** (Nkr590 incl transport from your lodging, around 3hr, minimum age 14). Productive from 1971 to 1996, it was the last shaft to be worked manually, thrusting itself for 5.5km deep into the heart of the mountain. The side spurs, from whose veins the coal was hacked, were only 80cm high and you can crawl into one to sense what life at the coal face was really like.

Coal may no longer be extracted but the mine is far from dead. Immured within a gallery is a gene bank containing over 7000 varieties of seed, kept down there in the permafrost at a perfect ambient temperature for storage.

GRAVEYARD

The haunting little graveyard on the hillside above town dates from the early 20th century. In a few days in October 1918, seven young men in Longyearbyen were struck down by the Spanish flu, a virus that killed 40 million people in Europe, Asia and North America.

GALLERI SVALBARD

The nearest thing Longyearbyen has to an art museum is **Gallery Svalbard** (☎ 79 02 23 40; Nybyen; admission Nkr40; ☼ 11am-5pm daily Jun-Aug, noon-5pm Fri-Mon, 2-5pm Tue-Thu rest-of-year), which features historic maps and books, the mainly Svalbard-themed works of artist Kåre Tveter and a short slide show on the magic of the polar light.

SWIMMING

If you've energy left at the end of the day, plunge into Longyearbyen's pool at the Sports Hall.

Tours

Visitors to Longyearbyen can choose from a dizzying array of short trips and day-tours that vary with the season, including fossil hunting (Nkr300), mine tours (Nkr590), boat trips to Barentsburg (Nkr990), dog-sledding (Nkr800), dog-sledding on *wheels* (Nkr550), glacial crossing (from Nkr490), ice-caving (from Nkr520), kayaking (from Nkr550), horse riding (Nkr550), and also snowmobiling (Nkr1000 to Nkr1400). The *Svalbard* brochure lists many more and, if you don't see something you want, just ask.

For further information on longer tours, see p356.

Courses

The local university, **UNIS** (☎ 79 02 33 00; www .unis.no), offers courses in Arctic technology, geology, biology and geophysics.

Sleeping

Longyearbyen has a couple of reasonably priced – for the island – options at the southern extremity of town, about a 20-minute walk from the centre. Each, formerly miners' accommodation, is identical, with corridor bathrooms, a kitchen for self-caterers and small lounge, and each now belongs to a tour company.

Gjesthuset 102 (☎ 79 02 57 16; 102@wildlife.no; Nybyen; dm/s/d Nkr295/450/750; ☼ Mar-Oct) The most recent of Lonyearbyen's limited sleeping options, Guesthouse 102 (which, to confuse things, occupies building No 7) belongs to Svalbard Wildlife Service and was once sardonically nicknamed 'Millionaire's Residence'.

Spitsbergen Guesthouse (☎ 79 02 63 00; www .spitsbergentravel.no; Nybyen; s/d/tr Nkr495/840/985; ☼ Mar-Sep) Spread over four buildings, one of which houses the large breakfast room (once the miners' mess hall), this guesthouse, a subsidiary of Spitsbergen Travel, can accommodate up to 136 in large rooms spread over three residential cabins.

Longyearbyen Camping (☎ 79 02 10 68; www.long yearbyen-camping.com; tent site per person Nkr80; ☼ late Jun-early Sep) Near the airport, with a nice, marshy bit of turf, this is by far your cheapest option. Guests have use of the service building, including kitchen, showers, laundry and heated toilets. It's about an hour's walk from town. You can also rent a tent (per night Nkr100) and sleeping bag (first/subsequent nights Nkr50/20). There are no cabins.

Mary-Ann's Polarrigg (☎ 79 02 37 02; www.polar riggen.com; Skjæringa; s/d Nkr595/850, with bathroom Nkr1500) The majority of the 43 rooms at this guesthouse have shared facilities and there's a kitchenette, available to all.

Spitsbergen Hotel (☎ 79 02 62 00; www.spitsber gentravel.no; s/d from Nkr1260/1485; ☼ mid-Mar–mid-Oct; ▣) Between the centre and Nybyen,

---

AUTHOR'S CHOICE

Basecamp Spitsbergen (☎ 79 02 46 00; www.basecampexplorer.com; s/d Nkr800/950 Oct-Jan, Nkr1150/1360 Jun-Sep, Nkr1350/1550 Mon-Thu, Nkr1550/1750 Fri-Sun Mar-May; 🖳) Imagine an old sealing hut, built in part from recycled beams, planks and flotsam. Add in a few artefacts and decorations, culled from the local refuse dump and mining cast-offs. Graft on 21st-century plumbing, an Internet point, design flair, free sauna and a friendly, informal team and you've got this place. Its 15 cabin-like rooms are cosiness and comfort defined, the breakfasts are splendid and it's bang next door to the equally evocative Kroa pub and restaurant.

---

this comfortable place – sink yourself low into the leather chairs of its salon – was originally the living quarters of the mine bosses, contrasting to this day with the two guesthouses, previously the more spartan accommodation of the miners.

Radisson SAS Polar Hotel (☎ 79 02 34 50; www.radissonsas.com; s/d Nkr1145/1275 mid-May–Dec, Nkr1280/1500 Jan–mid-May; 🖳) This 95-room chain hotel ('the world's northernmost full-service hotel') is the town's most luxurious and comes with free sauna, plus solarium. Planted right beside Advent Fjord, its rooms are stylishly furnished; it's well worth paying Nkr100 extra for one with views of the fjord and Hiorthfjellet mountain beyond. Its annexe was used as accommodation for the Lillehammer winter Olympic games and transported here.

Eating

There are two excellent hotel places to dine (Restaurant Nansen at the Radisson SAS Polar and Funktionærmessen Restaurant in the Spitsbergen Hotel). These apart, locals will tell you that the two best places to eat and drink are the pub and the house. But not just any old pub or house.

Huset (The House; ☎ 79 02 25 00) It's something of a walk to work up an appetite for the Huset's fine food and bar meals. The highly regarded restaurant does a regularly changing menu for Nkr360 and Nkr425. For a real treat, savour the very special 'Touch of the Arctic' menu, which begins with Arctic char, followed by scallops, reindeer and

grouse and house dessert. A curiosity for a place so far from the nearest vineyard: its wine cellar has over 30,000 bottles. For more modest fare, the bar serves up the usual quick-fare stuff, plus whale in pepper sauce (Nkr135) and seal pot (Nkr118).

Fruene Kaffe og Vinbar (☎ 79 02 76 40; Lompen-senteret) 'The Missus', run by three sprightly young women, is a welcoming place that functions as a café, serving decent coffee, pasta, pizza and snacks. Then, at 5pm each evening, it puts on its glad rags and metamorphoses into a wine bar.

Kafé Busen (☎ 79 02 36 50; Lompensenteret) In the same complex as Fruene Kaffe og Vinbar, the Busen has daily specials and cafeteria fare.

The supermarket in Svalbardbutikken carries a good selection of groceries.

Drinking & Entertainment

The Kroa is normally bustling and the choice of younger locals. Its metal bar stools are fashioned from old mine stanchions. More formal are the Radisson's Barents Pub, recently refurbished and the Funken Bar, up the hill at the Spitsbergen Hotel.

Huset (☎ 79 02 25 00) is your all-purpose nightspot, with a bar and a nightclub (cover charge Nkr50) with music and, at weekends, a lively scene. It also houses the town cinema, screening features a couple of nights a week.

Although alcohol is duty-free in Svalbard, it's rationed for locals, and visitors must present a valid onward airline ticket to prove they're leaving the archipelago in order to

---

AUTHOR'S CHOICE

Kroa (The Pub; ☎ 79 02 13 00; mains around Nkr175) This place was reconstructed less than a decade ago from the elements of a building that were hauled over here from the Russian settlement of Barentsburg (the giant white bust of Lenin peeking from behind the bar gives a clue). All the same, this cheerful, all-wood place gives every appearance of having been around for ages. Service is friendly and mains portions verge on the gargantuan. Starters are more modest in size; we particularly enjoyed the reindeer carpaccio (Nkr72) and marinated Arctic char (Nkr79).

---

buy it. The Nordpolet beer, wine and spirits outlet is at the back of Svalbardbutikken.

Getting There & Away

In clear weather, the descent to Longyearbyen provides otherworldly views. SAS Braathens and Norwegian cover the 957km between Tromsø and Longyearbyen. SAS Braathens has flights to/from Oslo, direct in summer, via Tromsø for the rest of the year. Prices have recently fallen substantially and can be as low as Nkr1700 return from Tromsø.

Getting Around

Svalbard Maxi Taxi (☎ 79 02 13 05) and **Longyearbyen Taxi** (☎ 79 02 13 75) charge Nkr80 to Nkr120 for a cab trip between town and airport. The airport bus (Nkr40) connects with flights and runs up to the two guesthouses at the southern extremity of town, calling by the hotels.

Possibilities for car hire include **Longyearbyen Bilutleie** (☎ 78 02 11 88) and **Svalbard Auto** (☎ 79 02 13 30). You'll tank up on the cheapest petrol in Norway (around Nkr5 per litre) but there are only 45km of road and not much to see from a vehicle.

Bicycles (per half/full day around Nkr75 to Nkr100) are a better bet. You can rent one from **Basecamp** (☎ 79 02 46 00) or **Spitsbergen Guesthouse** (☎ 79 02 63 00) – useful for coasting down the hill to the centre of town if you're staying at that end of town.

To scoot around Svalbard on a snowmobile in winter, you'll need to flash your home driving licence. Also, pick up a copy of the free leaflet, *Visiting Svalbard*, from the tourist office. This, in addition to other advice about how to protect the environment, has a map indicating where snowmobiles are permitted; many areas are off-limits to allow wildlife a little peace and quiet. Rental agencies include **Svalbard Snøscooterutleie** (☎ 79 02 16 66; www.scooterutleie.svalbard.no) and **Svalbard Reiser** (☎ 79 02 56 50). Expect to pay Nkr1000 to Nkr1400 per day.

AROUND LONGYEARBYEN
Platåberget & Bjørndalen

The vast upland region overlooking Longyearbyen to the west is known as Platåberget (commonly called the Plateau), and it makes a popular day hike. You can either ascend from near the Sysselmann's office (Map p358) in town, which is a steep and scree-covered route, or preferably, sneak up Blomsterdalen, not far from **Mine No 3**. You can also get onto Platåberget via Bjørndalen (yes, it means 'bear valley'), south of the airport. Once on Platåberget, you can continue to the summit of Nordenskiöldsfjellet (1050m), where a Swedish observatory once operated.

Longyearbreen

The prominent glacier tongues licking at the upper, southwestern outskirts of Longyearbyen have scoured and gouged through many layers of sedimentary material, including fossil layers, created when Svalbard enjoyed a more tropical climate. As a result, the terminal moraine throws up plant fossils – leaves and twigs that left their marks 40 to 60 million years ago. From mid-June to September, **Nox Polaris** (☎ 91 71 70 72; www .nox.no) does 2½-hour guided walks (Nkr295) up to the fossil fields where you've a chance of finding one or two or your own.

To get there under your own steam, pass the Huset and head up the river's true left bank, past the abandoned mine buildings, and onto a rough track. After the remains of a bridge (on your left), you'll approach the terminal moraine and cross a stream that flows down from your left. The track then traverses some steep slopes, crosses the river (sometimes there's a bridge) and continues upstream to its end at the fossil fields. The 5km return hike from Huset takes about 1½ hours, not counting fossicking time.

Burma Road

The Burma Rd, which is now a walking track, follows the old coal mine Taubanen cableway to the processing plant and Mine No 3, near the airport. It makes an easy half-day hike.

Adventdalen

Stark, wide-open Adventdalen beckons visitors with wild Arctic landscapes. There's pleasant hiking, but as you'll know from the polar bear crossing sign at the town end of the valley, you should carry a firearm outside the town.

After leaving town, you'll pass the pungent husky kennels; Isdammen, a freshwater lake that provides drinking water for Longyearbyen; and a Northern Lights station, linked to similar facilities in Alaska and Tromsø.

SVALBARD

In 1996 a Russian Tupolev aircraft crashed into the slopes of Operafjellet, the mountain north of the valley, killing 140 Russian and Ukrainian passengers and crew. With a car, you can also cruise out to the defunct **coal mine Nos 5 and 6** and have a look at **No 7** (the only one that still functions) in an hour or so. It's also quite feasible by bicycle.

BARENTSBURG

pop 800

The first thing you see of Barentsburg, Svalbard's only remaining Russian settlement, is its power-station chimney, belching dark black smoke into the blue sky. This isolated village continues to mine coal against all odds and still produces up to 350,000 tonnes per year, though selling it on the open market is a constant problem and stockpiles are huge. Everything's a bit run down, dishevelled and sooty but, with its signing in Cyrillic script, a still-standing bust of Lenin and murals of muscly workers in heroic pose, you get the feel of this unique community, implanted on the island.

History

Barentsburg, on Grønfjorden, was first identified as a coal producing area around 1900, when the Kullkompaniet Isefjord Spitsbergen started operations. Several other companies also sank shafts and in 1920, the town was founded by the Dutch company Nespico. Twelve years later it was passed to the Soviet Trust Arktikugol.

Like Longyearbyen, Barentsburg was partially destroyed by the British Royal Navy in 1941 to prevent it falling into Nazi hands (ironically, the German navy itself finished the job later). In 1948, it was rebuilt by Trust Arktikugol and embarked on a period of growth, development and scientific research that lasted until the fall of the Soviet Union.

Barentsburg, like every other pit on Svalbard, has known tragedy. In 1996, many of those who perished in a plane crash during a blizzard near Adventdalen (p361) were miners' families from the Ukraine. Then, in 1997, only a year later, 23 miners died in a devastating mine explosion and fire.

These days, most of Trust Arktikugol's coal shipments go directly to the west, notably to power stations in the Netherlands. Paycheques are now being eaten up by Russian inflation, there are no longer flights to or from Murmansk and obsolete mining equipment is breaking down. The scientific community has gone and the population has dwindled to around 800.

Supplies are sparse and Barentsburg continues to grow some of its own produce, including tomatoes, onions and peppers. However, most of the former pig farm has ended up in the cooking pot – though you may see a few of the community's very last cows clomping around. For most people, conditions here are preferable to those at home in Russia (or the Ukraine, which around half of Barentsburg's people call

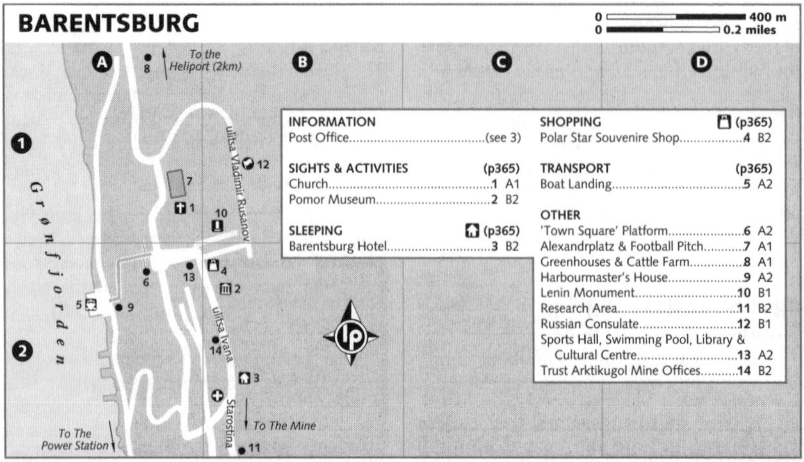

home) and quite a lot choose to remain in Barentsburg beyond their standard initial two-year contracts.

Sights & Activities
You'll probably be visiting Barentsburg as part of an organised tour. Once the guiding is over, do rush around in the short time left before the boat weighs anchor and fit in a visit to the bijou Pomor Museum and the community's tiny church.

POMOR MUSEUM
This simple, appealing little **museum** (☎ 79 02 18 14; admission Nkr35; ♈ when tour boats are in port) outlines (in Russian only) the historical Pomor trade with mainland Russia, plus Russian mining and history on Svalbard. Especially worthwhile are the excellent geological exhibits and the collection of impressive artefacts suggesting Russian activity in Svalbard even prior to the archipelago's accepted European 'discovery' by Willem Barents.

CHAPEL
The small wooden Orthodox **chapel** commemorates the twin disasters of 1996–97 (see p362). Above the football pitch and set aside from the community's other buildings, it merits poking your nose inside.

Sleeping & Eating
Barentsburg Hotel (☎ 79 02 10 80, 79 02 18 14; d Nkr550) The Barentsburg Hotel (the settlement's only accommodation for visitors) serves traditional Russian meals, featuring such specialities as boiled pork with potatoes and Arctic sorrel, parsley and sour cream. If you're overnighting, sign on for the gourmet dinner, offering both Russian and Ukrainian cuisine, lubricated with Russian champagne and vodka.

In the bar, you can enjoy a deliciously affordable and generous slug of vodka (Nkr10) or a Russian beer (Nkr33). It also sells large tins of real McCoy caviar at prices you'll never find elsewhere in the West, let alone Norway.

Shopping
This shop, Polar Star Souvenire (sic) Shop, is conveniently positioned as you begin to descend the 238 steps to the quayside, is worth dropping into if you should be after a babushka doll, Lenin lapel badge or some Soviet army surplus.

Getting There & Away
Several tour operators (p359) do summertime nine- to 10-hour **boat trips** (adult/child Nkr990/690) to Barentsburg from Longyearbyen. The cruise, which is half the fun, passes by the one-time Russian colliery of Grumantbyen, abandoned in the 1960s, and also approaches the vast Esmark glacier on the homeward journey. The price includes a light lunch and around 1½ hours in Barentsburg, mostly occupied by a guided tour. Most longer cruises also call in at Barentsburg.

In winter, you can belt across the snow and ice on a snowmobile guided tour (from per person Nkr1950). The record for the trip between Longyearbyen and Barentsburg is precisely 22 minutes, but tours stretch the journey to a more leisurely, much more enjoyable three hours each way.

PYRAMIDEN
Pyramiden, Russia's other settlement in Svalbard, was named for the impressive pyramid-shaped mountain that rises nearby. In the mid-1910s, coal was discovered here and operations were set up by the same Swedish concern that exploited Sveagruva. In 1926, it was taken over by a Soviet firm, Russkiy Grumant, which sold out to another Soviet company, Trust Arktikugol, in 1931. In the 1950s, the settlement counted 1100 residents, and during its heyday in the early 1990s had 60kms of shafts, 130 homes, agricultural enterprises similar to those in Barentsburg and the world's most northerly hotel and swimming pool.

In the late 1990s, this region ceased yielding enough coal to make the operation profitable, and Russia was no longer willing or able to subsidise the mine and Pyramiden was abandoned completely in 2001. Various Longyearbyen-based tour agencies and cruises take in Pyramiden.

NY ÅLESUND
pop 40–150
Despite its inhospitable latitude (79°N), you'd be hard pressed to find a more awesome backdrop anywhere on earth than the scientific post of Ny Ålesund, founded in 1916 by the Kings Bay Kull Compani. Ny Ålesund likes to claim that it's the world's

ROALD AMUNDSEN

If Fridtjof Nansen (see the boxed text, p339) had the biggest heart of any polar explorer, fellow Norwegian Roald Amundsen had the most determination and grit. Born in 1872 at Borge, near Sarpsborg, he dreamed of becoming a polar explorer and devoured every bit of literature he could find on the subject. Following his mother's wishes, he dutifully studied medicine, but when she died in 1893 he returned to his polar dreams and never looked back.

By 1897 he was sailing to the Antarctic as first mate on the Belgian *Belgica* expedition. That ship froze fast in the ice near Peter I's Island and became – unintentionally – the first expedition to overwinter in the Antarctic. When the captain fell ill with scurvy, Amundsen took command, displaying his ability in a crisis.

Having gained a reputation as a captain, Amundsen set his sights on the North-West Passage and study of the Magnetic North Pole. The expedition set out from Oslo in June 1903 aboard the 47-tonne sloop *Gjøa* and overwintered in a natural harbour on King William Island, which they named Gjøahavn. For two years they built observatories, took magnetic readings establishing the position of the Magnetic North Pole, studied the lives of the Inuit and learned how to drive dog teams. By August 1905 they emerged into waters that had been charted from the west, becoming the first vessel to navigate the North-West Passage. When the *Gjøa* again froze fast in the ice, Amundsen and an American companion set off by dog-sled to the telegraph station at Eagle, Alaska, over 900km away, to announce the success.

Amundsen had wanted to be the first man to reach the North Pole, but in April 1909 Robert Peary announced that he'd already been. So in 1910, Amundsen headed instead for the South Pole, only to learn that Britain's Robert Falcon Scott's *Terra Nova* expedition was setting out from New Zealand with the same goal.

Amundsen's ship dropped anchor in January 1911 at Roosevelt Island, 60km closer to the South Pole than Scott's base. With four companions and four 13-dog sleds, Amundsen reached the South Pole on 14 December 1911, and Scott – who, together with four members of his expedition, died of cold and starvation on the return journey – arrived on 17 January 1912 to discover the Norwegian flag already flying.

In 1925, Amundsen set about becoming the first man to fly over the North Pole. American Lincoln Ellsworth sponsored the expedition, and two planes took off from Svalbard bound for Alaska, but faulty equipment forced them to land on sea ice about 150km from the Pole. The pilot, Hjalmar Riiser-Larsen, hewed a runway with hand tools, managed to take off with all six crew members, and returned one plane to Nordaustlandet, in Svalbard, where they ditched at sea but were rescued.

Amundsen tried again the following year, aboard the airship *Norge* with Ellsworth, Riiser-Larsen and the Italian explorer Umberto Nobile. They left Spitsbergen on 11 May 1926 and, 16 hours later, dropped the Norwegian, American and Italian flags on the North Pole. On 14 May they landed triumphantly at Teller, Alaska, having flown 5456km in 72 hours – the first flight between Europe and North America.

In May 1928, Nobile attempted another expedition in the airship *Italia* and, when it crashed in the Arctic, Amundsen joined the rescue. Although Nobile and his crew were rescued, Amundsen's last signals were received just three hours after take-off, and he was never seen again.

northernmost, permanently inhabited civilian community (although you could make a case for three other spots in Russia and Canada).

Through much of the 20th century, Kings Bay mined local low-altitude coalfields. As many as 300 people once lived and worked here, but after the last of several lethal explosions resulted in 21 deaths,

mining stopped in 1963. Ny Ålesund has since emerged as a prominent scientific post with a year-round population of about 40, belonging to research stations of several nations, including Japan, France, the British Antarctic Survey and, since July 2004, China. Numbers swell to around 100 in summer as researchers from around the world visit to work on their own projects.

Information

Kings Bay (☎ 79 02 72 00; www.kingsbay.no) is your official tourist contact, though its real purpose is to serve the local scientific community, which has priority on both flights and accommodation, and it cannot confirm tourist bookings more than five days in advance.

The scientific community doesn't seem to think very highly of tourists either. Some of the coolness is probably warranted, as careless visitors can unwittingly affect instrument readings, alter the environment or damage sensitive equipment. So stick to the roads, steer clear of the scientific instruments with which the community bristles and don't drop a single shred of litter.

You'll also receive a less than friendly reception from the Arctic terns that nest in town, so it's wise to pick up a tern stick (available free at the dock) to waggle over your head and prevent a vicious pecking by a paranoid mother.

Visitors can buy a postcard at the world's northernmost gift shop and drop it off at the world's northernmost post office.

Sights

There's a 1.5km trail with multilingual interpretive panels that takes you around the main sites of this tiny settlement.

In the early 20th century, several polar explorers set off from Ny Ålesund, including the likes of Roald Amundsen, Lincoln Ellsworth, Admiral Byrd and Umberto Nobile. The anchor pylon was used by Nobile and Amundsen to launch the airship *Norge* on their successful flight over the pole to Alaska in 1926 and came in handy again two years later, when Nobile returned to launch the *Italia* on his ill-fated repeat attempt. You'll see **memorials** to these missions around town.

Perhaps the most unusual sight is the stranded **steam locomotive** near the dock. In 1917, a narrow-gauge railway was constructed to connect the coalfields with the harbour and it remained in use until 1958. The restored locomotive is, naturally, the world's northernmost railway relic.

The town also supports a very nice little **Mine Museum** (Gruvemuseum; donation suggested; ⌚ 24hr) in the old Tiedemann's Tabak (tobacco) shop, relating the coal-mining history of this area.

Sleeping & Eating

Very few travellers overnight in Ny Ålesund, where full board (around Nkr500) is compulsory, even for campers.

Nordpolhotellet (☎ 79 02 72 00; www.kingsbay.no; s/d with full board Nkr1390/2060) The settlement's hotel opened on 3 September 1939; then WWII came along and it closed the very next day. Long ago re-opened, its guests have to take full board and reservations (booking@kingsbay.no) are essential, year-round.

The extremely bare-bones camping ground (per person Nkr100) is near Nobile's airship pylon.

The Mess offers breakfast/lunch/dinner for Nkr80/220/220 for both the scientific community and guests.

Getting There & Away

As with most places in Svalbard, nearly all non-professional visitors arrive in Ny Ålesund on tourist cruises and linger for only an hour or two. Alternatively, **Kings Bay** (☎ 79 02 72 00; www.kingsbay.no) flies 16-seater planes to/from Longyearbyen (one-way/return Nkr1496/2992, 25 minutes) on Monday and Thursday, year-round, with one or more supplementary flights each week in summer.

AROUND NY ÅLESUND
Kongsfjorden

Ny Ålesund's spectacular backdrop, Kongsfjorden (the namesake for the Kings Bay Kull Compani), contrasts bleak grey-brown shores with expansive white icefields. The distinctive Tre Kroner peaks, Dana (1175m), Svea (1226m) and Nora (1226m) – named in honour of Denmark, Sweden and Norway, respectively – jut from the ice and are among Svalbard's most recognised landmarks.

Blomstrandhalvøya

Gravelly Blomstrandhalvøya was once a peninsula but, in the early 1990s, it was released from the icy grip on its northern end and it's now an island. In summer, the name Blomstrand, or 'flower beach', would be appropriate, but it was in fact named for a Norwegian geologist. Ny London, at the southern end of the island, recalls one Ernest Mansfield of the Northern Exploration Company, who attempted to quarry marble

SVALBARD

in 1911 only to discover that the stone had been rendered worthless by aeons of freezing and thawing. A couple of buildings and some forlorn machinery remain.

AROUND SPITSBERGEN

Sveagruva

Coal was first discovered at Sveagruva in the early 1910s and exploited by a Swedish company. It changed hands several times, survived a fire and was yielding 400,000 tonnes of coal annually by the time SNSK took it over in 1934. The operations were levelled by a submarine attack in 1944, but activity snapped back after the war and by the late 1970s Sveagruva had grown into a settlement of 300 workers that enjoyed nearly as many amenities as Longyearbyen.

Over the following years, increased production around more-accessible Longyearbyen resulted in declines at the original Sveagruva pit, and by the mid-1990s it had dwindled to just a handful of miners and administrators. Nowadays, the nearby Svea Nord (see p354) has taken over its mantle and is one of Europe's biggest producing mines.

Prins Karls Forlandet

On the west coast of Spitsbergen, the oddly shaped 86km-long island of Prins Karls Forlandet is a national park set aside to protect breeding pinnipeds. The alpine northern reaches, which rise to Grampianfjellet (1084m), are connected to Saltfjellet (430m), at the southern end, by a long flat plain called Forlandsletta.

Krossfjorden

Thanks to its grand tidewater glacier, Lillehöökbreen, and several cultural relics, Krossfjorden also attracts quite a few cruise ships. At Ebeltoftbukta, near the mouth of the fjord, you can see several whalers' graves as well as a heap of leftover junk from a 1912 German telegraph office that was shifted wholesale to Ny Ålesund in 1914. Opposite the entrance rise some crowded bird cliffs overlooking one of Svalbard's most verdant spots, with flowers, moss and even grasses.

Magdalenefjord

The lovely blue-green bay of Magdalenefjord, flanked by towering peaks and intimidating tidewater glaciers, is the most popular anchorage along Spitsbergen's western coast. In the 17th century, this area saw heavy Dutch whaling, and at Graveneset, near the mouth of the fjord, you can still see the remains of two stoves used to boil down the blubber. There are numerous graves of 17th- and mid-18th-century whalers, now protected as a cultural monument and marked with a 1930 memorial.

If you're there with (or at the same time as) a large cruise ship, your experience will probably be, shall we say, altered. Cruise-line crew members have been known to add spice to beach barbecues by dressing up as polar bears, or even penguins, and dancing on a convenient ice floe. On the other hand, the better cruise ships contract reputable historians and scientists to enrich their tours.

Danskøya

One of the most intriguing sites in northwest Spitsbergen is Virgohamna, on the bleak, gravelly island of Danskøya, where the remains of several broken dreams now lie scattered across the lonely beach. Among them are the ruins of three blubber stoves from a 17th-century whaling station, as well as eight stone-covered graves from the same era. You'll also find the remains of a cottage built by English adventurer Arnold Pike, who took a notion to sail north in the yacht *Siggen* and spend a winter subsisting on polar bears and reindeer.

The next adventurer at Virgohamna was Swedish engineer Salomon August Andrée, who in the summer of 1897 set off from Virgohamna in an airship, hoping to reach the North Pole. The fate of this expedition, which also included his colleagues Frænkel and Strindberg, wasn't known until 1930, when sailors from a seal-hunting ship put ashore and stumbled across their last site on Kvitøya.

Then, in 1906, journalist Walter Wellman, who was sponsored by a US newspaper, attempted to reach the North Pole in an airship but failed. He returned to try again the next year, when his ship was unfortunately quite badly damaged in a storm. On his third attempt, in 1909, he floated to within 60km of the pole, met with technical problems and gave up for good, mainly because he'd heard that Robert Peary had already reached the pole anyway. All of the

OUTER ISLANDS

The following islands are extremely remote and accessible only via organised tour. Even then, climate and geography make them expensive and difficult to reach.

Bjørnøya

Svalbard's southernmost island, 178-sq-km Bjørnøya, is occasionally visited mainly by private yachts and cruise ships. There's little to see but a tiny museum, the Norwegian Bjørnøya Radio meteorological station and a couple of historic buildings. The most interesting is a former pig sty known as Hammerfesthuset, constructed in 1823 and Svalbard's oldest surviving building. The island's name is derived from an errant bear who inhabited the island when Willem Barents first landed there.

Hopen

In 1942, the narrow and lonely island of Hopen saw the wreck of the Soviet freighter *Dekabrist* (Decembrist) and only three of the 80 passengers and crew survived the near-impossible winter conditions. The following year, the island was occupied by a German meteorological station, which was later rebuilt by the Norwegians to monitor climatic conditions and later, to study ice movements and the Aurora Borealis. It still functions as a meteorological station with a small resident team.

Nordaustlandet

Vast Nordaustlandet, Svalbard's second largest island, takes in over 14,700 sq km, about 75% of which is covered with ice. The lonely eastern coast is dominated by the Austfonna ice sheet, which forms the longest tidewater glacial face in the Arctic region.

remaining junk (including dozens of rusted 44-gallon fuel drums) is protected. Erosion damage, caused by the few visitors who manage to get here, has been considerable so make sure you do the right thing and stick strictly to the marked paths.

Amsterdamøya & Fairhaven

The island of Amsterdamøya was the site of the large Smeerenburg (meaning 'blubber town' in Dutch) whaling station. Co-founded in 1617 by Dutch and Danish concerns, all that remains of it today are

seven ovens and some graves. There are more whalers' graves, scattered around the nearby sound, Fairhaven.

Moffen

Most tourist cruises attempt to approach flat, gravelly Moffen Island, known for its walrus population, but so often are turned back by pack or drift ice. In any case, between mid-May and mid-September, boats are not allowed to approach within 300m of the island, lest they disturb the walruses' breeding activities.

Directory

CONTENTS

ACCOMMODATION

Norway has a wide range of accommodation, from camping, hostels and *pensions* to international-standard hotels. There's little doubt that you'll pay a lot more for what you get than in other countries, but standards are generally quite high. Remember also that if you're making enquiries in advance about prices, they're sometimes quoted *per person*, so always check.

Throughout this book, quoted prices are for a room with private bathroom unless stated otherwise, except for hostels and camping where you can expect most rooms to come with a shared bathroom.

By law, all bars and restaurants and 50% of hotel bedrooms must be nonsmoking and some hotels have no smoking rooms at all, so smokers will need to get used to puffing away in a community of pariahs outside.

A good source of information (and discounts) for those trying to save their kroner is **VIP Backpackers** (☎ 22 17 37 70; www.vipbackpackers.no; 3rd fl, Schweigaardsgate 34E, Oslo).

Throughout this book, budget accommodation generally ranges from Nkr80 to Nkr130 (camping) and up to Nkr300/500 for other types of accommodation. Midrange accommodation, usually in hotels, refers to singles/doubles up to Nkr725/925, while top-end accommodation can reach as high as Nkr2000 for a double.

B&Bs, Pensions & Private Homes

Tourist offices in most medium-sized towns have lists of private rooms which are among

---

PRACTICALITIES

- Norway currents are 220V AC and 50Hz (train sleeping cars 110V or 220V AC) with round, continental-style, two-pin plugs.

- Major international newspapers and magazines are available a day after publication in larger towns. Norwegian-language dailies include *Aftenposten*, *Dagbladet*, *Verdens Gang* and *Bergens Tidende*.

- The government-run NRK (one TV and three radio channels) competes with TV2 and TV Norge networks and the satellite broadcasts of TV3. Foreign-language programmes are subtitled, not dubbed. Hotels with cable TV often have CNN and English-language sports channels.

- Like most of Western Europe (but not France or the USA), Norway uses the PAL system.

- Norway uses the metric system. Watch out for the frequent use of *mil* (mile), which is not 1.6km but rather a Norwegian mile, which is 10km.

the cheapest places to stay. In some cases, they allow you to stay with a Norwegian family, which offers a far more intimate option than the hostel or hotel experience. Prices vary, but you'll rarely have to pay more than Nkr250/375 for a single/double; breakfast isn't normally included. Showers sometimes cost Nkr5 to Nkr10 extra.

Some places operate as B&Bs, where prices start from singles/double Nkr200/400 and can go up to Nkr450/750. These options can be tracked down through **Bed & Breakfast Norway** (www.bbnorway.com), which has listings for Oslo and Bergen, and sells *The Norway Bed & Breakfast Book*, with listings throughout the country.

Many towns also have *pensjonat (pensions)* and *gjestehus* (guesthouses). Prices usually start at Nkr300/500, but linen and/or breakfast will only be included at the higher-priced places. Some of these, particularly in Oslo, are very good.

Along highways, you'll also see a few *rom* signs, indicating inexpensive informal accommodation typically costing from Nkr125 to Nkr250 per room (without breakfast); those who bring their own sheets or sleeping bags may get a discount.

Camping

Norway has around 1000 camping grounds. Tent space ordinarily costs from Nkr80 at basic camping grounds up to Nkr130 for those with better facilities or in popular or expensive areas, such as Oslo and Bergen. Quoted prices usually include your car, motorcycle or caravan, although sites with the last can cost up to Nkr150. A per-person charge is also added in some places, electricity often costs a few kroner extra and some places charge Nkr5 to Nkr10 for showers.

Most camping grounds also rent simple cabins with cooking facilities starting at around Nkr250 for a very basic two- or four-bed bunkhouse. Bring a sleeping bag, as linen and blankets are provided only at an extra charge, which is anywhere from Nkr50 to Nkr80 per visit.

Unless you opt for a more expensive deluxe cabin with shower and toilet facilities (Nkr450 to Nkr1000), you'll normally also have to pay for showers and washing water (there are, however, a few enlightened exceptions). Normally, cabin occupants must clean their cabin before leaving or pay an additional cleaning charge, which averages around Nkr120.

Note that although a few complexes remain open year-round, tent and caravan sites are closed in the off season (normally early September to mid-May).

For a comprehensive list and descriptions of Norwegian camping grounds, pick up a copy of the free *Camping* (available at most tourist offices) or visit www.camping.no.

MINIMUM-IMPACT CAMPING

Campers pitching a tent away from a dedicated campground must remember the following:

- If it's raining, select a well-drained camp site and use a waterproof groundsheet to prevent having to dig trenches.

- Along popular routes, particularly in the Jotunheimen or Rondane National Parks, set up camp on previously used sites.

- Carry out all your rubbish, including cigarette butts. Biodegradable items may be buried, but anything with food residue should be carried out, lest it be dug up and scattered by animals.

- Use established toilet facilities if they're available. Otherwise, select a site at least 50m from water sources and bury waste at least 20cm below the surface. Carry out (it's probably wise to carry a sturdy, leak-proof plastic bag for this purpose) or bury used toilet paper.

- Use only biodegradable soap products and use natural-temperature water if possible. When washing with hot water, avoid damage to vegetation either by letting the water cool before pouring it out or by dumping it in a gravelly, nonvegetated place.

- In times when you're permitted to build a fire (15 September to 15 April), try to select an established site and keep fires as small as possible. Use only fallen, dead wood and, when you're finished, make sure ashes are cool and buried before you leave the site.

- Caravans and camper vans must use signed waste-disposal points.

Norway also has an age-old tradition known as *allemannsretten* (every man's right), which is often referred to as 'right of access'. Under this ancient law, anyone is free to camp in any uncultivated area for up to two days, provided you remain at least 150m (preferably further and out of sight) from any hut or house. Doing so is a great option for cutting costs, especially given the extremely low crime rate in Norway. Above all, the golden rule is to leave no trace of your passing and to preserve the country's beauty and foster goodwill among the locals. To do this, you should follow the protocols which are attached to free camping – see the boxed text, p369, for details.

DNT & Other Mountain Huts

Den Norske Turistforening (Map p74; DNT; Norwegian Mountain Touring Club; ☎ 22 82 28 22; www.turistforeningen.no; Storgata 3) maintains a network of over 378 mountain huts a day's hike apart, all along the country's 20,000km of well-marked and maintained wilderness hiking routes. These range from unstaffed huts (335 around the country) with two beds, to large staffed lodges (43) with more than 100 beds and renowned standards of service. All unstaffed huts offer cooking facilities but, in most places, you must have your own sleeping bag or a hostel-style sleeping sheet; sleeping sheets are often sold or included in the price at staffed huts. Staffed lodges do not normally have cooking facilities for guests, but a self-service section with cooking facilities is available at some lodges when unstaffed.

At staffed huts, which are concentrated in the south, you can simply turn up and pay your fees. In compliance with international mountain courtesies, no-one is turned away, even if there's only floor space left; DNT members over 50 years of age are guaranteed a bed, even if it means displacing a younger hiker! Huts tend to be packed at Easter and consistently busy throughout summer.

For details of becoming a DNT member, see p374.

In the staffed huts, nightly fees for DNT members/nonmembers in a room with one to three beds are Nkr185/240; rooms with four to six beds Nkr145/210; dormitories Nkr95/160; and overflow on the floor Nkr70/135. Lodging and full board (for DNT members only) in one- to three-bed

rooms/dorms costs Nkr480/445 in low season, Nkr500/460 in summer and Nkr550/510 during Easter. Otherwise, a full breakfast (members/nonmembers Nkr75/95) or dinner (Nkr175/210) is available, as are sandwiches (Nkr10/15), a thermos of tea or coffee (Nkr25/40) and lighter dinners (Nkr110/130). Dinners, often including local specialities, can be excellent.

Members/nonmembers who prefer to camp outside the huts and use their facilities will pay Nkr45/55. Otherwise, tenters must camp at least 150m from the hut and may not use the facilities. Breakfasts are Nkr70/90, a thermos of coffee or tea is Nkr20/25, sandwiches are Nkr10/13, light dinners cost Nkr105/120, and three-course meals cost Nkr155/185. A sleeping sheet costs Nkr45/55.

For unstaffed huts, you must pick up keys (Nkr100 to Nkr150 deposit) in advance from a DNT office or a staffed hut. To pay, fill out a Once-Only Authorisation slip and leave either cash or a valid credit-card number in the box provided. There are two classes of unstaffed huts. Self-service chalets are stocked with blankets and pillows and have wood stoves, firewood, gas cookers and a wide range of tinned or freeze-dried food supplies for sale (on the honour system). In these, DNT members/nonmembers pay Nkr145/240 for a bed. At other unstaffed huts, users must carry in their own food.

At all huts, whether staffed or unstaffed, children pay less.

Most DNT huts are closed between 15 October and 15 February. In winter, staffed DNT lodges are open between the Saturday before Palm Sunday and Easter Monday, but huts along the Oslo–Bergen railway and a few others open for the cross-country ski season as early as late February. DNT can provide lists of opening dates for each hut.

There are also numerous private hikers' huts and lodges peppered around most mountain areas, but not all are open to the public. Some places offer DNT members a discount.

Hostels

In Norway, reasonably priced hostels *(vandrerhjem)* offer a bed for the night, plus use of communal facilities that usually include a self-catering kitchen (but you're advised to take your own cooking and eating utensils), Internet access and bathrooms. Hostels vary widely in character, but increasingly, they're open longer hours and family-run places have largely replaced those presided over by 'wardens' with a sergeant-major mentality. (Note, however, that consumption of alcohol on hostel premises is prohibited.) The trend has also been towards smaller dormitories with just two to six beds. Guests must bring their own sleeping sheet and pillowcase, although most hostels hire sleeping sheets for around Nkr50 for as long as you stay at that hostel.

Several hostel guides are available, including HI's annually updated Europe guide. The Norwegian hostelling association, **Norske Vandrerhjem** (☎ 23 13 93 00; www .vandrerhjem.no; Torggata 1, Oslo), also publishes a free six-page booklet, *Hostels in Norway*, which contains a full listing of hostels and updated prices.

Some hostels are quite comfortable lodge-style facilities and are open year-round, while others occupy school dorms and are open in summer only. Most have two- to six-bed rooms and cost from Nkr130 to Nkr220. The higher-priced hostels usually include a buffet breakfast, while other places may charge from Nkr40 to Nkr60 for breakfast. Some also provide a good-value evening meal for around Nkr100.

In summer, reservations are recommended, particularly for popular destinations. Most places in Norway accept phone reservations and are normally happy to book beds at your next destination for a small fee (around Nkr20). Note, however, that popular hostels in Oslo and Bergen are often heavily booked in summer.

Prices listed in this book are those for HI members; nonmembers pay an additional Nkr25 per night. Even if you haven't bought a membership in your own country, you can pick up a Welcome Card; after six nights at nonmember prices, you'll qualify for the lower HI-member rates. Be sure to request the card on your first night and pick up stamps to fill it on each consecutive night.

There are very few private hostels in Norway.

Hotels

Although normal hotel prices are high, most hotels offer substantially discounted rates on w___
son (usual___
sometimes ___
ods for bus___

Although ___
consistent ___
exorbitant ___
Nkr1050/1___
day outside ___
largely bec___
are busines___ ___ ___ accounts. If you're travelling at this time, ask the hotel about special offers to see if discounts are available.

Nationwide chains offer such deals, usually upon payment for a chain hotel pass (up to Nkr100, summer only), which can entitle you to a free night if you use the chain enough times. Another significant consideration in this land of daunting food prices is that hotels, unlike *pensions*, normally offer an enormous all-you-can-eat breakfast buffet. The main nationwide chains (whose discounts sometimes also apply in other Scandinavian countries):

Best Western (www.bestwestern.no; s/d 695/830Nkr) Offers a free pass available at Best Western hotels from June to August; entitles you to third consecutive night at same hotel free.

Fjord Pass (www.fjordpass.no; s/d 470/580Nkr) This pass costs 100Nkr and is available at 225 hotels year-round; no free nights, but discounted rates.

Nordisk Hotellpass (www.choicehotels.no; s/d 550/640Nkr) This pass costs 100Nkr and is available at Comfort, Quality and Clarion hotels from mid-June to mid-August and weekends; entitles you to fifth night free at any hotel within the network.

Rica Feriepass (www.rica.no; s/d 695/945Nkr) Offers a free pass available at Rica hotels from mid-June to mid-August; entitles you to fifth night free at any hotel within the network.

Skanplus (www.skanplus.com; s/d 495/625Nkr) This pass costs 100Nkr and is available at Rainbow, Norlandia and Golden Tulip hotels from mid-June to mid-August; entitles you to sixth night free at any hotel within the network.

In some Comfort Hotels, you'll also get a light meal included in the price, which usually replicates the breakfast buffet.

Summer Homes & Cabins

Most tourist offices in popular holiday areas keep lists of private huts, cabins and summer homes that are rented out to holiday-makers when the owners aren't using them.

…eek's rental starts from … for a simple place in the … about Nkr13,500 for the most …halet in midsummer. Most cab… … at least four people, and some ac… …odate as many as 12, so if you have … group and want to spend some time in a certain area, it's a very economical option. Advance booking is normally required, and you'll probably have to pay a deposit of around Nkr500 or 20% of the total fee, whichever is less.

For further information, contact **Novasol** (☎ 81 54 42 70; www.novasol.com), which publishes an English-language photo catalogue describing nearly 2000 self-catering cabins and chalets in Norway. A similar scheme is offered by the Danish company **Dansommer** (☎ +45 86 17 61 22; www.dansommer.com).

ACTIVITIES

Norway is one of the best wilderness destinations in the world, renowned for its combination of spectacular scenery and a well-organised adventure industry. Possibilities range from the relatively contemplative art of fishing, through hiking, skiing and rock climbing all the way up to high-adrenaline white-water rafting, bungee jumping and parasailing. Throughout this book, look out for boxed texts highlighting some of the best the local regions have to offer, while we've also designed an itinerary (p17) for those seeking one of Norway's more active holidays.

Thanks to Norway's 1000-year-old *allemannsretten* tradition and the Friluftsleven (Outdoor Recreation Act), anyone is legally entitled to hike or ski across uncultivated, wilderness areas, including outlying fields and pastures; camp anywhere for up to two days, as long as it's more than 150m from a dwelling; cycle or ride on horseback on all paths and roads; and canoe, kayak, row and sail on all rivers and lakes. However, these freedoms come with some responsibilities: not to light fires between 15 April and 15 September; not to litter; to avoid damaging plant or animal life; to leave cultural sites perectly intact; and to leave the countryside as pristine as it was found.

Cycling

Exploring Norway by bicycle is an excellent way to see the country, although it requires quite high levels of fitness as roads can be decidedly steep. Although Norwegian drivers are accustomed to cyclists and take them into consideration when driving, many rural roads can be very narrow, requiring extra vigilance.

Most tourist offices can offer advice on cycling trails (and some offer maps) in their local area, while **Syklistenes Landsforening** (☎ 22 47 30 30; post@slf.no; Storgata 23C, Oslo) is the place for maps and advice for longer expeditions throughout Norway and across Scandinavia.

One of the most rewarding cycling experiences is across the Hardangervidda Plateau near Rjukan; see the boxed text, p138, for details.

Dog-sledding

Although dog-sledding isn't an indigenous Norwegian sport, this Inuit means of transport readily transfers to the Norwegian wilds, and several operators can take you on a range of winter adventures. While many people are content with just a half-day taster of the sport – the tourist office in Røros organises two- to five-hour expeditions (p155) – keen prospective 'mushers' can jump in the deep end and opt for a two-week dog-sled safari through Troms, Finnmark or Svalbard. Any Svalbard operator (p356) worth their salt can organise dog-sled expeditions. Elsewhere, among the best companies offering tours are Arcturus Expeditions (p395), Bjørn Klauer (p324), Den Norske Turistforening (p71) and Engholm's Husky (p350).

Fishing

Norway's rivers and lakes have drawn European aristocrats, English lords and avid American anglers since the 19th century. Norway's salmon runs are still legendary and, in June and July, you can't beat the rivers of Finnmark. In addition to salmon, 41 other fish species inhabit the country's 200,000 rivers and lakes. In the south, you'll normally find the best fishing from June to September, and in the north, in July and August. In Svalbard, the best fishing holes are well-kept secrets, but Arctic char inhabit some rivers and lakes. The 175-page book *Angling in Norway*, available from tourist offices for Nkr185, details the best salmon- and trout-fishing areas, fees and

11 COMMANDMENTS FOR ANGLERS

1   Foreigners may fish for free on the Norwegian coast but can't sell their catch.
2   Fishing is prohibited within 100m of fish farms, cables and nets that are anchored or fastened to the shore.
3   Anyone who damages fishing equipment must pay compensation for the damage.
4   Anchoring is prohibited in the vicinity of drift nets or line-fishing sites.
5   It's forbidden to shoot off firearms or make noises that can disturb the fish.
6   Fishing with live bait is prohibited.
7   It's forbidden to abandon fishing tackle or other rubbish that can disturb, delay or damage fish catches or fishing boats.
8   Only Norwegian citizens or permanent residents may catch lobsters.
9   Salmon, trout and char fishing with a rod is permitted year-round. For rivers with fishing bans, you may still fish within 100m of the river mouth. From 1 June to 4 August, between 6pm on Friday and 6pm on Monday, you can fish for salmon, trout and char with a hook and troll. All anglers for these fish must have a national fishing permit, and must also follow other local fishing regulations (which may include compulsory disinfection of fishing equipment).
10 All anglers from boats must wear life jackets.
11 Don't throw rubbish or pollute the waters in any way.

regulations. In the UK, it's available from the **Scandinavia Connection** (www.scandinavia-connection.co.uk).

Regulations vary between rivers but, generally, from mid-September to November, fish under 20cm must be thrown back. At other times between August and May, you can't keep fish less than 30cm in length.

All river and lake fishing in Norway requires an annual licence (Nkr200 for salmon, trout and char and Nkr100 for other fish), which is sold at post offices. A weekly licence is also available for Nkr50. To fish on private land, you must also purchase a local licence (Nkr50 to Nkr350 per day), which is available from sports shops, hotels, camp sites and tourist offices. Some areas require a compulsory equipment disinfection certificate (Nkr100).

Hiking

Norway has some of Europe's best hiking, including a network of around 20,000km of marked trails that range from easy strolls through the green zones around cities, to long treks through national parks and wilderness areas. Many of these trails are maintained by DNT and are marked either with cairns or red Ts at 100m or 200m intervals.

The hiking season runs roughly from late May to early October, with a much shorter season in the higher mountain areas. In the highlands, the snow often remains until June and returns in September. The most popular wilderness hiking areas are the Jotunheimen (p167) and Rondane (p161) National Parks and the Hardangervidda plateau (see the boxed text, p138). If you're after a wilder experience, try such national parks as Dovrefjell-Sunnsdalfjella (p163), Stabbursdalen (p334), Rago (p277), Reisa (p349), Saltfjellet-Svartisen (p274) and Øvre Dividal (p323), or any of the vast number of unprotected areas throughout the country, such as Trollheimen (p159) near Oppdal. Avid hikers will never run out of options!

There are many excellent books for hikers in Norway. Erling Welle-Strand's *Mountain Hiking in Norway* includes hiking itineraries, sketch maps and details on trail huts. A better choice for avid hikers is probably *Norwegian Mountains on Foot* by DNT, which is the English edition of the Norwegian classic, *Til Fots i Fjellet*. Other hiking books include *Great Hikes & Treks in Norway* by Graeme

WARNING

When scrambling, travelling cross-country or hiking through any exposed area, be prepared for sudden inclement weather and stay aware of potential avalanche dangers, which are particularly rife in Jotunheimen. Also, never venture onto glacial ice without the proper equipment and experience.

Cornwallis (only available on the Internet from www.ablibris.com) and *Walking in Norway* by Connie Roos.

For a full list and description of Norway's national parks, see p55.

DEN NORSKE TURISTFORENING

Den Norske Turistforening and its various chapters maintain a network of over 370 mountain huts and lodges throughout the country. For details and prices for the use of these huts, see p370.

If you're doing lots of hiking, it's certainly worth joining DNT. The standard annual membership starts at Nkr410, or Nkr470 to also receive the DNT book and seven *Fjell og Vidde* magazines. Memberships for children/under-23/seniors cost Nkr50/200/240; members' families pay Nkr140 per person. For further information, contact **DNT** (Map p74; ☎ 22 82 28 22; www.turistforeningen.no) in Oslo. DNT also sells hiking maps and topographic sheets (see p382).

Paragliding, Parasailing & Bungee Jumping

Those who either have no fear or would simply love a bird's-eye view of some of Europe's most spectacular country should head to Voss, where **Nordic Ventures** (☎ 56 51 00 17; www.nordicventures.com) organises tandem paragliding flights, parasailing and bungee jumping; see the boxed text, p192, for details. Bungee jumping is also possible in Rjukan (see the boxed text, p138).

If plummeting towards the earth at breakneck speed is your thing, base jumping is possible from the precipitous cliffs of Lysefjord (p206).

Rock Climbing & Mountaineering

As one would imagine, a country with the astounding vertical topography of Norway is a paradise for climbers interested in rock, ice and alpine pursuits. In fact, outside the Alps, Norway is probably Europe's finest climbing venue. However, due to Norway's topographic and climatic extremes, technical climbers face harsher conditions, shorter seasons and many more restrictions than hikers and backpackers. The most popular alpine venues include the area around Åndalnes (p232), the Lyngen Alps (p322) and Lofoten (p295); the last has a good climbing school that also organises expeditions

within Norway and further afield. In addition to wonderful surrounding peaks, Åndalsnes has a mountaineering museum (p232) and a very popular mountaineering festival, Norsk Fjellfestivalen (p232). Lom also has the Norwegian Mountain Museum (p165) that is worth checking out.

For general information on climbing in Norway, contact **Norsk Tindeklub** (☎ 22 50 54 66; www.ntk.no; c/o Egil Fredriksen, Sorkedalsveien 202b, N0754, Oslo).

In addition to the rock climbers' classic *Climbing in the Magic Islands* by Ed Webster, which describes most of the feasible routes in the Lofoten Islands, prospective climbers may want to look for *Ice Fall in Norway* by Sir Ranulph Fiennes, which describes a 1970 jog around Jostedalsbreen. The more practical *Scandinavian Mountains* by Peter Lennon introduces the country's finest climbing venues.

Skiing

'Ski' is a Norwegian word and thanks to aeons-old rock carvings depicting hunters travelling on skis, Norwegians make a credible claim to having invented the sport. Interest hasn't waned over the years and these days, it's no exaggeration to say it's the national pastime. Most skiing is of the cross-country (nordic) variety, and Norway has thousands of kilometres of maintained cross-country ski trails. However, visitors should only set off after studying the trails/routes (wilderness trails are identified by colour codes on maps and signposts) and ensuring that they have appropriate clothing, sufficient food and water, and emergency supplies, such as matches and a source of warmth. You can either bring your own equipment or rent or purchase skis, poles and boots on site. You'll probably find the best deals on second-hand gear at weekend flea markets.

Most towns and villages provide some illuminated ski trails, but elsewhere it's still worth carrying a good torch, as winter days are very short and in the north there's no daylight at all in December and January. The ski season generally lasts from early December to April. Snow conditions vary greatly from year to year and region to region, but February and March, as well as the Easter holiday period, tend to be the best (and busiest) times.

CROSSING STREAMS

Fortunately, most large rivers along major Norwegian hiking routes are bridged, but trekkers and mountaineers are still bound to face the odd swollen stream or unbridged river. In most cases, however, you need not be put off.

Normally, the sun and heat of the day melt the snow and glacial ice in the high country and cause water levels to rise, so the best time to cross is early in the morning, preferably no sooner than 24 hours after a rainstorm. Remember that constricted rivers passing through narrow passages run deep, so the widest ford is likely to be the shallowest. The swiftest and strongest current is normally found near the centre of straight stretches and at the outside of river bends. Observe the character of the water as it flows and choose a spot with as much slack water as possible.

Never try to cross just above a waterfall and avoid crossing streams in flood – identifiable by dirty, smooth-running water carrying lots of debris and vegetation. A smooth surface suggests that the river is too deep to be crossed on foot. Anything over knee-deep shouldn't be considered 'crossable' without experience and extra equipment.

Before attempting to cross deep or swift-running streams, be sure that you can jettison your pack in midstream if necessary. Put anything that mustn't get wet inside sturdy waterproof bags. Unhitch the waist belt and loosen shoulder straps, remove any bulky clothing that will inhibit swimming, and remove long trousers. Lone hikers should use a hiking staff to probe the river bottom for the best route and to steady themselves in the current.

Never try to cross a stream barefoot. While crossing, face upstream and avoid looking down or you may risk losing your balance. Two hikers can steady each other by resting their arms on each other's shoulders. More than two hikers should cross forming a wedge pointed upstream, with the people behind holding the waist and shoulder of the person at the head of the wedge.

If you do fall while crossing, don't try to stand up. Remove your pack (but don't let go of it), roll over onto your back, and point your feet downstream, then try to work your way to a shallow eddy or to the shore and attempt to regain your footing.

There are also scores of resorts with downhill runs, but these are quite expensive due to the costs of ski lifts, accommodation and the après-ski drinking sessions. The spring season lasts longer than in the Alps and the snow is better quality too. Popular spots include the Holmenkollen area (p84) near Oslo, Geilo (p170) on the spectacular Oslo–Bergen railway line, Voss (see the boxed text, p192), Lillehammer (p148) and Hovden (p142). Summer skiers can head for Stryn (p224), Folgefonn (p195) or Jotunheimen National Park (p168).

For general information on skiing in Norway, contact DNT (p374), or visit www .skiingnorway.com.

White-Water Rafting

Norway's steep slopes and icy, scenic rivers create an ideal environment for avid rafters, and a number of reputable operators offer trips. These range from short, Class II doddles to Class III and IV adventures and rollicking Class V punishment. While these trips aren't especially cheap, most are guaranteed to provide an adrenaline thrill,

and the rates include all requisite equipment and waterproofing. Among the finest venues are Evje (Setesdalen; see the boxed text, p141), Sjoa (Heidalen; see the boxed text, p160), Oppdal (Drivadalen; see the boxed text, p158) and Voss (see the boxed text, p192).

Norges Padleforbund (☎ 21 02 98 35; www .padling.no; Service boks 1, Ullevål stadion, 0840 Oslo) provides a comprehensive list of rafting operators in Norway, many of which can also organise sea-kayaking and river-boarding.

BUSINESS HOURS

Opening hours for shops are 10am to 5pm weekdays, 10am to 2pm on Saturday; post offices 9am to 5pm weekdays, 10am to 2pm on Saturday; banks 8.15am to 3pm weekdays; offices 9am to 5pm; supermarkets 9am to 9pm weekdays, 9am to 6pm on Saturday; and restaurants 8am to 11am, noon to 3pm and 6pm to 11pm. The opening hours for tourist offices are listed under each city throughout the book. See the inside cover for a summary of the country-wide opening hours.

DIRECTORY

CHILDREN

Travelling through Norway with children couldn't be easier, although successful travel with young children requires planning and effort. Don't try to overdo things; packing too much into the time available causes problems, even for adults. Make sure the activities include the kids as well; if they've helped to work out where you're going, chances are they'll still be interested when you arrive. Lonely Planet's *Travel with Children* by Cathy Lanigan is a useful source of information.

Practicalities

Car-rental firms hire out children's safety seats at a nominal cost, but it's essential that you book them in advance. The same goes for highchairs and cots (cribs); they're standard in many restaurants and hotels, but numbers may be limited. Norway offers a relatively wide choice of baby food, infant formulas, soy and cow's milk, disposable nappies (diapers) etc; after the supermarkets close, you'll have to resort to more expensive convenience stores.

Children aged under two travel for 10% of the full fare (or free on some airlines), as long as they don't occupy a seat. They don't get a baggage allowance in this case. 'Skycots', baby food and nappies (diapers) should be provided by the airline if requested in advance. Children aged between two and 12 can usually occupy a seat for half to two-thirds of the full fare and get a standard baggage allowance.

Hotels, HI hostels, camping grounds and other accommodation options often have 'family rooms' or cabins that accommodate up to two adults and two children. In hotels, this may cost little more than the price of a regular double. For information on child-friendly restaurants, see p63.

Sights & Activities

In many ways, Norway is a children's country, and most towns have attractions and museums specifically targeted for the younger crowd. Domestic tourism is largely organised around children's interests: regional museums invariably have a children's section with toys and activities, and there are also numerous public parks for kids to play at. Most attractions are generous and allow free admission for young children up to about six years of age and half-price (or substantially discounted) admission for those up to 16 or so. Family tickets are usually available at Norway's sights.

For more specific advice on the best places in Norway for kids, see p11.

THE VIRTUES OF SKINNY SKIS

Not only do nordic skiing, ski jumping and biathlon (skiing and target-shooting) competitions dominate Norwegian Olympic efforts, they also provide a recreational foundation among people for whom winter is the dominant season of the year. Nearly everyone outside the big cities skis and all villages have a floodlit ski track for winter use. Nordic skiing isn't only a great source of exercise, but it's also a ticket into the wilderness when few are prepared to venture far from the home fires.

The concept sounds easy, but it's actually fairly difficult for adults to learn. Most of the propulsive effort is made by kicking downwards on the stationary ski, so that the waxed under-surface comes into contact with and grips the snow, even on gentle uphill gradients. As the skier kicks with one foot, the weight decreases on the other ski, which arches slightly upwards in the middle, so the waxed section is above the snow and the ski can glide forward. Movement and rhythm is augmented by the ski poles. The process is often made easier in popular areas with prelaid parallel tracks cut into the snow.

For steeper gradients, you may have to apply skins – strips of brushed nylon which attach to the bottom of the skis and ensure maximum gripping power.

The Telemark region of Norway has lent its name to the graceful turn that has made nordic skiing popular around the world. Nordic ski bindings attach the boot at the toes, allowing free movement of the heel; to turn, one knee is dropped to the surface of the ski while the other leg is kept straight. The skis are positioned one behind the other, allowing the skier to smoothly glide around the turn in the direction of the dropped knee.

CLIMATE CHARTS

Although Norway covers the same latitude range as Alaska (and much further north when you include Svalbard), most of the country enjoys a surprisingly temperate climate. For this you can thank the Gulf Stream, which flows north along the coast. Average maximum temperatures for July hovering around 16°C in the south and around 13°C in the north. In January, the average maximum temperature is 1°C and -3°C respectively. Bergen, on the southwest coast, is the wettest city, with 2250mm of annual precipitation, while Rondane and Gudbrandsdal, protected by coastal mountain ranges from the moisture-laden prevailing southwesterly winds, are among the driest districts of Norway, with less than 500mm of precipitation annually.

Extreme temperatures are possible even in the Arctic region. In July 1998, even Narvik rose above 30°C and Svalbard positively soared to over 20°C a month later. At the other end of the scale, winter temperatures can plummet – in January 1999, the temperature in Kirkenes dropped for a short time to a decidedly chilly -56°C – and snow up to 10m deep can accumulate in the mountains; accumulations of a mere 2m to 3m are more usual in the lower areas.

Just when you think you understand the vagaries of Norway's climate, remember that Alta in the country's far north receives less rain than the Sahara!

The **Norwegian Meteorological Institute** (www.dnmi.no) is the place to go for the latest weather information.

CUSTOMS

Alcohol and tobacco are extremely expensive in Norway, so, to at least get you started, it's worth importing your duty-free allotment: 1L of spirits and 1L of wine

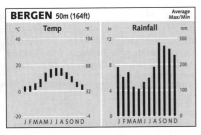

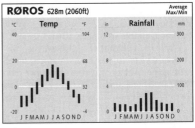

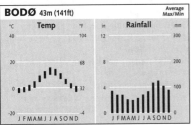

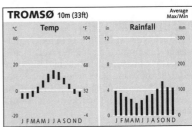

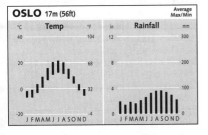

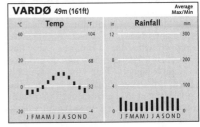

DIRECTORY

(or 2L of wine), plus 2L of beer. Note that drinks with an alcohol content of over 60% may be treated as narcotics! Even if you don't drink, it will normally be a welcome gift for Norwegian friends. You're also allowed to import 200 cigarettes duty-free. Importation of fresh food and controlled drugs is prohibited.

DANGERS & ANNOYANCES

Your personal belongings are safer in Norway than in many people's home countries, and the cities – even east Oslo, which has a relatively poor reputation – are reasonably safe at all hours of the night. However, don't become blasé about security: be careful near the nightclubs in the Rosenkrantz gate area of Oslo and beware of pickpockets around the Torget area of Bergen. Normally, the greatest nuisance value will come from drug addicts, drunks and/or beggars – mainly in Oslo – who can spot a naive tourist a block away. Oslo and other larger cities suffer from a growing drug problem. Although dope may be readily available in places, it isn't legal.

While the risk of theft in Norway is minimal, it's wise to keep photocopies of all your important documents (passport data page, air tickets, insurance policy, travellers cheques serial numbers) in a separate place in case of theft; stash US$100 alongside, just in case. Leave copies of these documents at home, too.

DISABLED TRAVELLERS

Although Norway is better than most countries in catering for disabled travellers and all newly constructed public buildings are required by law to have wheelchair access, it can still be a challenging destination. As a result, anyone with special needs should plan ahead.

Most Norwegian tourist offices carry lists of wheelchair-accessible hotels and hostels, but your best bet is to contact the Norwegian Association for the Disabled (see right). Nearly all street crossings are equipped with either a ramp or a very low kerb (curb), and crossing signals produce an audible signal – longer beeps when it's safe to cross and shorter beeps when the signal is about to change. Most (but not all) trains have carriages with space for wheelchair users.

Organisations

For information on disabled travel and sites of special interest to disabled travellers in Norway, contact the **Norwegian Association for the Disabled** (Norges Handikapforbund; ☎ 22 17 02 55; www.nhf.no; Schweigaards gate 12, Grønland, Oslo).

Other national associations in other countries that can offer (often Norway-specific) advice:
Royal Association for Disability & Rehabilitation (RADAR; ☎ 020-7250 3222; www.radar.org.uk; 12 City Forum, 250 City Rd, London, EC1V 8AF)
Society for Accessible Travel and Hospitality (☎ 212-447 7284; www.sath.org; 347 5th Ave, Suite 610, New York, NY 10016)
Mobility International USA (☎ 541-343 1284; fax 343 6812; www.miusa.org)
Canadian Transportation Agency (☎ 1-888 222 2592; www.cta-otc.gc.ca; 15 Eddy St, Gatineau, Quebec K1A 0N9) On the website, click on 'Accessible Transportation'.

Tours

A number of American-based tour companies offered tailored trips to Norway for travellers with a disability, with a special focus on wheelchair travellers.
Accessible Journeys (☎ 610-521 0339; www.disability travel.com; 35 West Sellers Ave, Ridley Park, PA 19078)
Easy Access Adventures (☎ 651-770 1956; www .easyaccessadventures.com)
Flying Wheels Travel (☎ 507-451 5005; www.flying wheelstravel.com; 143 W Bridge St, Owatonna, MN 55060)

DISCOUNT CARDS

For details on benefits of purchasing a HI card before you leave home, see p370.

Senior Cards

Honnør (senior) discounts are the same as those for students and are normally available to those 67 years of age and over for admission to museums, public pools, transport etc. The discounts are usually less than for children (entry usually amounts to 75% of the full price). You don't require a special card, but those who look particularly youthful may, apart from enjoying the compliment, need proof of their age to qualify, as the ever-friendly Norwegian ticket-sellers won't believe you're a day over 39.

Student & Youth Cards

The most useful student card is the International Student Identity Card (ISIC), a plastic ID-style card with your photograph. Some travellers have reported being refused access with their normal university cards (unless it's from a Norwegian university) so the ISIC card is a good investment. It can provide discounts on many forms of transport (including airlines, international ferries and local public transport) and in Internet cafés, reduced or free admission to museums and sights and cheap meals in some student restaurants – a worthwhile way of cutting costs.

EMBASSIES & CONSULATES
Norwegian Embassies & Consulates

You'll find an up-to-date listing of Norwegian embassies and consulates on the Internet at www.embassies.mfa.no.

Australia & New Zealand (☎ 02-6273 3444; emb .canberra@mfa.no; 17 Hunter St, Yarralumla, ACT 2600)

Canada (☎ 613-238 6571; www.emb-norway.ca; Royal Bank Centre, 90 Sparks St, Suite 532, Ottawa, Ontario K1P 5B4)

Denmark (☎ 33 14 01 24; emb.copenhagen@mfa.no; Amaliegade 39, DK-1256 Copenhagen K)

Finland (☎ 09-686 0180; emb.helsinki@mfa.no; Rehbindervägen 17, FIN-00150 Helsinki/Helsingfors)

France (☎ 01 53 67 04 00; emb.paris@mfa.no; 28 Rue Bayard, F-75008 Paris)

Germany (☎ 030-505050; emb.berlin@mfa.no; Rauchstrasse 1, D-10787 Berlin)

Ireland (☎ 01-662 1800; emb.dublin@mfa.no; 34 Molesworth St, Dublin 2)

Japan (☎ 3-3440 2611; emb.tokyo@mfa.no; Minami Azabu 5-12-2, Minato-ku, Tokyo 106-0047)

Netherlands (☎ 070-311 7611; emb.hague@mfa.no; Lange Vijverberg 11, NL-2513 AC The Hague)

Russia Moscow (☎ 0501-421 1220; emb.moscow@mfa .no; Ulitsa Povarskaya 7, RU-131940); Murmansk (☎ 51295 10037; Ulitsa Sofji Perovskoj 5, RU-183038)

Sweden (☎ 08-665 6340; emb.stockholm@mfa.no; Skarpögatan 4, SE-11593 Stockholm)

UK (☎ 020-7591 5500; emb.london@mfa.no; 25 Belgrave Sq, London, SW1X 8QD)

USA (☎ 202-333 6000; www.norway.org; 2720 34th St NW, Washington, DC, 20008)

Embassies & Consulates in Norway

Australia Refer to the UK embassy, which handles Australian consular affairs in the absence of an embassy.

Canada (☎ 22 99 53 00; www.dfait-maeci.gc.ca; Wergelandsveien 7, N-0244 Oslo)

Denmark (☎ 22 54 08 00; www.denmark-embassy.no; Olav Kyrres gate 7, N-0244 Oslo)

Finland (☎ 22 12 49 00; www.finland.no; Thomas Heftyes gate 1, N-0244 Oslo)

France (☎ 22 28 46 00; www.ambafrance-no.org; Drammensveien 69, N-0244 Oslo)

Germany (☎ 22 27 54 00; www.deutschebotschaft .no/de/home; Oscars gate 45, N-0244 Oslo)

Ireland (☎ 22 01 72 00; 4th Fl, Håkon VII's gate 1, N-0212 Oslo)

Japan (☎ 22 99 16 00; www.no.emb-japan.go.jp; Wergelandsveien 15, N-0244 Oslo)

Netherlands (☎ 23 33 36 00; www.netherlands -embassy.no; Oscars gate 29, N-0244 Oslo)

New Zealand (☎ 66 77 53 30; fax 66 77 53 31; Billingstadsletta 19B, Postboks 113, N-1361 Billingstad)

Russia (☎ 22 55 32 78; www.norway.mid.ru; Drammensveien 74, N-0271 Oslo)

Sweden (Map p72; ☎ 24 11 42 00; www.swedena broad.com; Nobelsgata 16A, N-0244 Oslo)

UK (Map p72; ☎ 23 13 27 00; www.britishembassy.gov .uk; Thomas Heftyes gate 8, N-0244 Oslo)

USA (☎ 22 44 85 50; www.usa.no; Drammensveien 18, N-0244 Oslo)

FESTIVALS & EVENTS

Norway is chock-a-block with special festivals, which take place at all times of year in every city, town and village. Large and popular ones are covered in most regional chapters of this book, but for a listing of almost 50 of Norway's larger extravaganzas, contact **Norway Festivals** (Norske Festivaler; www .norwayfestivals.com).

There are some events which take on a nationwide significance, most notably Norway's Constitution Day national holiday, 17 May, when people take to the streets in traditional dress and attend celebratory events throughout the country. The biggest bash is in Oslo, where marching bands and thousands of schoolchildren parade down Karl Johans gate to the Royal Palace, to be greeted by the royal family.

Midsummer's Eve, or *Jonsok*, is generally observed on St Hans Day (23 June) and is celebrated with much fanfare and bonfires in every community from Halden to Grense Jakobselv.

On 13 December, Christian children celebrate the feast of Santa Lucia by dressing in white and holding a candlelit procession. Boys generally wear cone-shaped hats and girls put silver tinsel and glitter in their hair.

For some of our favourite regional festivals and events, see p11.

FOOD

For a comprehensive insight into eating in Norway for both carnivores and vegetarians, see p60.

Throughout this book, restaurant information includes whether the restaurant is open for breakfast, lunch and/or dinner.

Generally meal times in Norway are from 8am to 11am, noon to 3pm and 6pm to 11pm.

Throughout the book, we also provide a range of prices for starter dishes, main courses, light meals and/or the average cost of a meal at each restaurant.

GAY & LESBIAN TRAVELLERS

Norwegians are generally tolerant of alternative lifestyles, and Norway, along with several neighbouring countries, allows gay and lesbian couples to form 'registered partnerships' that grant every right of matrimony, except access to church weddings, adoption and artificial insemination. However, public displays of affection (regardless of sexual preference) are not common practice.

Gay and lesbian travellers can find gay entertainment spots in larger cities and towns. The *Spartacus International Gay Guide*, published by Bruno Gmünder Verlag (Berlin), is an excellent international directory of gay entertainment venues, but it's now well out of date and is best used in conjunction with up-to-date listings in local papers, as popular places tend to change quickly.

Oslo has the liveliest gay scene (see the boxed text, p93), with the latest Oslo information available in the 'Gay Guide' section of the excellent *Streetwise* booklet published annually by Use-It (p71).

For local information on gay issues, contact **Landsforeningen for Lesbisk og Homofil frigjøring** (LLH; ☎ 22 36 19 48; www.llh.no in Norwegian; St Olavs plass 2, Oslo).

HOLIDAYS
Public Holidays

The following public holidays are observed in Norway:

New Year's Day (Nyttårsdag) 1 January
Maundy Thursday (Skjærtorsdag) March/April
Good Friday (Langfredag) March/April
Easter Monday (Annen Påskedag) March/April
Labour Day (Første Mai, Arbeidsdag) 1 May
Constitution Day (Nasjonaldag) 17 May
Ascension Day (Kristi Himmelfartsdag) Fortieth day after Easter, May/June
Whit Monday (Annen Pinsedag) Eighth Monday after Easter, May/June
Christmas Day (Første Juledag) 25 December
Boxing Day (Annen Juledag) 26 December

School Holidays

Norwegian children enjoy the following school holidays: eight weeks from mid-June to mid-August; two weeks over Christmas and New Year; one week at the end of September or early October; one week at the end of February; and one week at Easter.

INSURANCE

You should seriously consider taking out travel insurance that covers not only medical expenses and luggage theft or loss, but also cancellation or delays in your travel arrangements (due to illness, ticket loss, industrial action etc). It's a good idea to buy insurance as early as possible, as late purchase may preclude coverage of industrial action that may have been in force before you bought the policy. Note that some policies specifically exclude 'dangerous activities' such as motorcycling, skiing, mountaineering, scuba diving or even hiking. Make sure the policy covers ambulances and an emergency flight home. A policy that pays doctors or hospitals directly may be preferable to one where you pay on the spot and claim later. If you have to claim later, make sure you keep all documentation.

CHRISTMAS IN NORWAY

Christmas, or *jul*, is a wonderful time to be in Norway. The name *jul* is derived from *joulu* or *lol*, a pagan fertility feast that was celebrated all over Europe in pre-Christian times and synchronised nicely with the holiday to honour the birth of Christ. Currently, most people celebrate between Christmas Eve and Epiphany, or 12th night, although some continue until the Feast of St Canute, which is the 20th day of Christmas.

A Christmas tree is a requisite part of the décor in most homes, and gifts are exchanged on Christmas Eve. In the countryside, sheaves of oats known as *julenek* are mounted on a pole and left out for the birds. In gratitude for past blessings, a bowl of porridge is also left out for the *nisse*, the gnome that historically brought good fortune to farmers. This concept has now been merged with the international tradition of Santa Claus in the personage of Jule-nissen, whom Norwegians believe makes his home in Drøbak (p96), south of Oslo (and there's a Santa Crossing road sign there to prove it!).

There are all sorts of special Christmas confections and concoctions. Among them are *rømmegrøt*, an extremely sweet cream porridge; *rupa*, ptarmigan or grouse; *lutefisk*, a glutinous fish dish that's definitely an acquired taste; *pinneribbe*, mutton ribs steamed over birch or juniper branches; and pork roast, which stems from the Viking tradition of sacrificing a pig at yuletide. Children like to munch raisin buns and a variety of biscuits, including *strull*, *krumkake* and *goro*. And then everyone drinks *gløgg*, readily translated as 'grog'. Good *gløgg* blends cinnamon, raisins, almonds, ginger, cloves, cardamom and other spices with juice, which may or may not be fermented. Many people also imbibe *julaøl*, or 'holiday beer', which dates from the Viking days, when it was associated with pagan sacrifices; as with the *lutefisk*, not all foreigners fully appreciate it. Die-hard alcohol fans celebrate the season with generous quantities of Norway's own potato power brew, *aquavit* (see the boxed text, p61).

A great place to be around Christmas is Lillehammer for the Christmas Festival; see p148 for details. Bergen is another fantastic place to be for the festive season. Look out also for *Christmas in Norway*, a free brochure available from tourist offices and which contains loads of historical background.

In Norway, EU citizens may be required to pay a service fee for emergency medical treatment, but presentation of an E111 form will certainly expedite matters and minimise the amount of paperwork involved. Inquire about these at your national health service or travel agent well in advance. Travel insurance is still advisable, however, as long as it allows treatment flexibility and will also cover ambulance and repatriation costs.

For details of health insurance see p407, and for car insurance see p401.

INTERNET ACCESS

Apart from in larger towns, there are fewer Internet cafés around Norway than you might expect. However, that is more than compensated for by the fact that free Internet access is available in most municipal libraries. As it's a popular service, you normally have to reserve a time slot earlier in the day; in busier places, you may be restricted to a half-hour slot. Internet access is also available at many tourist offices around the country (Nkr40 to Nkr80 per hour). At private Internet cafés, expect to pay around Nkr30/50 per 30/60 minutes; students receive a discount of around 25%.

If you're bringing a laptop and hope to access the Internet while in Norway, a good source of information on plugs is **Tele-Adapt** (www.teleadapt.com). Both **AOL** (www.aol.com) and **Compuserve** (www.compuserve.com) have local ISDN modem access numbers.

If your laptop has a wireless Internet facility, connecting couldn't be easier. You can access the Internet using wireless technology at almost all hotels, and even some hostels and guesthouses. To do so, you need to purchase an access scratchcard from either the hotel or local tourist office; the cards typically cost Nkr150 for 24 hours. Some of the more pleasant and unusual places which are also in the wireless loop are at the very cool QBA café in Oslo (p69) or on board your yacht in the Grimstad Guest Harbour (p119).

LAUNDRY

Myntvaskeri (coin laundries) are expensive and hard to find, with two exceptions. The guest-harbour facilities in most towns along Norway's coast (particularly in the south) have coin-operated machines (Nkr35 to Nkr50 per wash-and-dry). Some of these are listed under the individual town entries in the regional chapters. In addition, hostels and camping grounds often have coin-operated washers and dryers available to guests. The prices are usually very reasonable, though you may want to bring a supply of laundry soap for washing by hand.

In both Oslo (p70) and Bergen (p175), you'll find laundries where they'll provide detergent, wash, dry and even fold your clothes nicely; expect to pay around Nkr60 for the full service and to wait for two to three hours. Some of these places also let you do it yourself (cheaper) or even deliver to your hotel (more expensive). Unless you're on an expense account, avoid hotel laundry and dry-cleaning services.

MAPS

For all travellers, Nortrabooks has produced the colourful and popular *Bilkart over Norge*. This detailed map includes useful topographic shading and depicts the entire country on one sheet at a scale of 1:1,000,000.

Statens Kartverk covers the country in 21 sheets at a scale of 1:250,000, and also produces hiking maps at a scale of 1:50,000 (Nkr90). You'll find the index on the Internet at http://showcase.netins.net/web/travelgenie/norway.htm.

Most local tourist offices distribute user-friendly and free town plans.

Hiking Maps

The best source of hiking maps is **Den Norske Turistforening** (Map p74; DNT; Norwegian Mountain Touring Club; ☎ 22 82 28 22; www.turistforeningen.no; Storgata 3, Oslo) and hikers can pick up topographic sheets at any DNT office, although the offices in larger cities have a wider selection beyond the local area.

Map Shops

General maps are available in Norway in bookshops, Narvesen kiosks, rural general stores, DNT offices and most large tourist offices. If you want to pick maps before

you leave home, the following places have comprehensive catalogues and some allow you to order online:

The Map Shop (☎ 01684-593146; fax 01684-594559; 15 High St, Upton-upon-Severn, Worcester, WR8 0HJ)

Stanfords (☎ 020-7836 1321; www.stanfords.co.uk; 12-14 Long Acre, London, WC2E 9LH)

Omni Resources (☎ 336-227 8300; www.omnimap.com; 1004 S Mebane St, Burlington, NC 27216-2096)

Map Land (☎ 03-9670 4383; www.mapland.com.au; 372 Little Bourke St, Melbourne, VIC 3000)

Travel Bookshop (☎ 02-9261 8200; Shop 3, 175 Liverpool St, Sydney, NSW 2000)

Road Maps

The best road maps for drivers are the Cappelens series, which are sold in Norwegian bookshops for Nkr95. There are three maps at 1:335,000 scale: *No1 Sør-Norge Sør, No2 Sør-Norge Nord* and *No3 Møre og Trøndelag*. Northern Norway is covered in two sheets at 1:400,000 scale: *No4 Nordland og Sør-Troms* and *No5 Troms og Finnmark*. The *Veiatlas Norge* (Norwegian Road Atlas; Nkr235), published by Statens Kartverk (the national mapping agency), is revised every two years.

MONEY

The Norwegian krone is most often represented as Nkr (preceding the number, as in this book), NOK (preceding the number) or simply kr (following the amount). One Norwegian krone (Nkr1) equals 100 øre. Coins come in denominations of 50 øre and Nkr1, Nkr5, Nkr10 and Nkr20, and notes can be worth Nkr50, Nkr100, Nkr200, Nkr500 and Nkr1000.

For exchange rates at the time of publication, see inside the front cover of this book.

ATMs

Norwegian ATMs will allow you to access cash in your home account with an ATM card from your home bank. 'Mini-Banks' (the Norwegian name for ATMs) are found adjacent to many banks and around busy public places, such as shopping centres. They accept major credit cards as well as Cirrus, Visa Electron and/or Plus bank cards.

Cash & Travellers Cheques

Post offices, some tourist offices and banks exchange major foreign currencies and accept all brands of travellers cheques, which

---

MAY I SEE YOUR ID, PLEASE?

For the record:

■ The legal age for drinking beer is 18, but for spirits and wine it is 20.

■ The legal age for voting in Norway is 18.

■ You can drive when you are 18.

■ The legal age of sexual consent is 16 (whether heterosexual or homosexual).

---

command a better exchange rate than cash by about 2%. Rates at post offices and tourist offices are generally slightly worse than at banks, but can be convenient outside banking hours. Post offices charge a service fee of Nkr10 per travellers cheque (minimum Nkr25, maximum Nkr100) or Nkr30 per cash transaction. Some banks, including Kreditkassen and Den Norske Bank, have slightly higher fees but similar exchange rates. Other banks tend to charge steeper travellers cheque commissions (1% to 5%).

Credit Cards

Visa, Eurocard, MasterCard, American Express and Diners Club cards are widely accepted throughout Norway and generally you'll be better off using a credit card (particularly a 'credit' card tied to a debit account in your home country) as you avoid the fees charged for changing cash or travellers cheques. Credit cards can be used to buy train tickets and are accepted on some (eg Hurtigruten), but not all, domestic ferries.

If your card is lost or stolen in Norway, report it to the appropriate agency:

American Express (☎ 80 03 32 44)
Diners Club (☎ 23 00 10 00)
Eurocard/MasterCard (☎ 80 03 02 50)
Visa (☎ 22 01 34 20, 80 03 02 50)

Tipping

Service charges and tips are included in restaurant bills and taxi fares, and no additional gratuity is expected, but there's no problem if you want to reward exceptional service with a tip.

PHOTOGRAPHY
Film

Although print and slide film are readily available in major cities, prices are high and you're better off buying before you come. A 24-/36-exposure roll of Fuji Superia costs around Nkr55/65 and processing costs from Nkr59/79, but can go as high as Nkr129/149 for a one-hour turnaround. Fujichrome Sensia/Velvia 36-exposure slide film costs Nkr62/90. The best value by far is offered by the chain Japan Photo, which offers discounts on bulk orders.

Photographing People

Although most Norwegians enjoy being photographed and few are camera-shy, it's still a courtesy to ask permission before snapping away. This is especially important in the Sami areas, where you may encounter some camera sensitivity, as well as in villages where whaling is a mainstay – people may be concerned that the photos will be used against them in environmental pieces.

Technical Tips

Photographers worldwide sing the praises of the magical northern light, and the crystalline air combined with the long, red rays cast by a low sun create excellent effects on film. Add spectacular scenery with a picturesque fishing village and you have a photographer's paradise. However, taking home photographs that do justice to your memories requires some care. Due to the clear northern light and glare from water, ice and snow, photographers may want to use a UV or skylight filter and a lens shade. In winter, you may want to polar oil your camera so that the mechanism doesn't freeze up. In temperatures below around -20°C, electronic/digital cameras may fail altogether.

For general advice on taking good pictures, consult Lonely Planet's *Travel Photography*, by Richard I'Anson.

POST

Norway has an efficient postal service, but postal rates have soared in recent years. Postcards and letters weighing up to 20g cost Nkr6.50 within Norway, Nkr8.50 to other Nordic countries, Nkr9.50 to elsewhere in Europe and Nkr10.50 to the rest of the world. For sending larger parcels, the good-value Verdenspakke rate (up to 20kg) will provide delivery anywhere in the world within 15 working days. Poste restante services are available at all but a handful of Norwegian post offices.

For information on post office opening hours, see p375.

SHOPPING

Given the prices, few people would consider a shopping holiday in Norway. While items in shops are mostly high quality, beware of cheaper kitsch in tourist areas. Specialities include wool sweaters and other hand-knitted clothing, pewter ware, intricate silver jewellery, Sami sheath knives, reindeer-leather products, troll figurines, wooden toys and woodwork adorned with *rosemaling* (painted or carved floral motifs). For the best quality Norwegian handicrafts – at corresponding prices – look for the Husfliden shops, which exist in most large cities and towns.

If you're shipping purchases back home, a good option is the post office's Verdenspakke option (see p383).

Bargaining

As for bargaining, it's as rare in Norway as bargains themselves. However, if you are spending lots of money at a tourist shop, you can reasonably expect some sort of high-volume discount.

Taxes & Refunds

The 24% MVA (the equivalent of value-added or sales tax), locally known as MOMS, is normally included in the marked prices for goods and services, including meals and accommodation. One exception is car hire, where quoted rates may or may not include MVA.

At shops marked 'Tax Free for Tourists', goods exceeding Nkr318 are eligible for an MVA refund, less a service charge (11% to 18.5% of the purchase price). At the point of sale, ask the shop for a 'Tax-Free Shopping Cheque', which should be presented along with your purchases at your departure point from the country (ferry passengers normally collect their refund from the purser during limited hours once the boat has sailed).

Most tourist offices and some tourist shops have the brochure *How to Shop Tax Free in Norway*, which explains the procedure and lists border crossings at which refunds can be collected.

TELEPHONE & FAX

All Norwegian telephone numbers consist of eight digits. Most pay phones accept Nkr1, Nkr5, Nkr10 and Nkr20 coins and will return unused coins but won't give change, so only insert the minimum amount (Nkr5 for all calls) to ensure a connection. There are no local call rates in Norway – to call anywhere in the country from anywhere else costs a fixed national rate. National calls get a 33% discount on standard phone rates between 5pm and 8am on weekdays, and any time on weekends. Directory assistance (☎ 180) is available throughout the country and costs Nkr9 per minute.

A peak-rate national call costs Nkr7 then Nkr0.60 per minute. International calls can be prohibitively expensive, so you're in a better position by purchasing a dedicated international phonecard issued by private companies (see p385).

Fax

Faxes can be received and sent from most hotels, but it's considerably cheaper to send from any post office.

Mobile Phones

GSM mobile telephone networks cover over 80% of populated areas in Norway. There are two main service providers: **Telenor Mobil** (☎ 22 78 50 00) and **NetCom** (☎ 23 88 80 00).

To use your home-country mobile in Norway, always check with your carrier about the cost of roaming charges to avoid a nasty surprise when your next bill arrives; although agreements between European countries have substantially reduced calling costs in recent years, prices remain high.

If you wish to use your mobile, but with a Norwegian SIM card, check with your network before leaving home as some phones sold by some networks (eg Vodafone) are blocked from using other carriers. If your phone will accept a foreign SIM card, these can be purchased from any 7-Eleven store and some Narvesen kiosks. However, as the connection instructions are entirely in Norwegian, you're better off purchasing the card from any Telehuset outlet, where they'll help you connect on the spot. SIM cards start from Nkr200, which includes Nkr100 worth of calls.

Mobile-phone rental isn't possible in Norway but you can buy one from any

Telehuset shop (from Nkr399, including charge card).

Phone Codes
There are no regional area codes in Norway.

To make international calls from Norway call ☎ 00.

Phonecards
Card phones accept Telenor phonecards and most also accept credit cards. Card and coin phones are found at post offices, transport terminals, kiosks and other public places, but they're not as ubiquitous elsewhere as you might expect. *Telekort* (Telenor phonecards) are sold in Nkr40, Nkr90 and Nkr140 denominations and work out slightly cheaper than using coins. Cards can be purchased at post offices and Narvesen kiosks. Beware of 'freephones' which will soak you for Nkr5 every time you access a so-called 800 number from a public telephone.

For making international calls, you're best bet is to forsake Telenor altogether and go for one of the phonecards issued by a private company. Usually costing Nkr100, they can allow you to make over six hours of calls. These cards aren't inserted into phones – on the back are local access numbers (usually a freephone 800 number) and a PIN which you dial after following the prompts. Instructions once you connect are in a variety of languages. The cards can be used from a payphone (Nkr5) or private or hotel phone (free). Some of the better cards for calling Western Europe, Australasia or North America are EuroCity and Unity, but ask where you buy them for a list of destinations and corresponding call length covered by the card. The only drawback with these cards is that they can be difficult to find – we found them only in Oslo, Bergen and Kristiansand. Some kiosks sell them, but the easiest place to look is an 'ethnic' grocery store.

TIME
Time in Norway is one hour ahead of GMT/ UTC, the same as Sweden, Denmark and most of Western Europe. To make the most of lengthening days, clocks go forward one hour on the last Sunday in March and back an hour on the last Sunday in October.

When telling the time, note that in Norwegian the use of 'half' means *half before* rather than half past. Always double check

which time is required unless you wa. be an hour late!

TOILETS
Toilets are Western style and nearly every town has public facilities. However, at most shopping malls, train stations, bus terminals and even some (but not many) restaurants (!) you may have to pay up to Nkr10. If you resent paying for an entirely necessary and natural bodily function, hang on until lunch time or until you reach your hotel. For tracking down free points of relief in Oslo, see p71.

TOURIST INFORMATION
Local Tourist Offices
It's impossible to speak highly enough of tourist offices in Norway. Most serve as one-stop clearing houses for general information and bookings for accommodation and activities. Nearly every city and town – even the tiniest place – has its own tourist office, and most publish comprehensive annual booklets giving the complete, up-to-date lowdown on their town.

Offices in smaller towns may be open only during peak summer months, while in cities they're open year-round but with shorter hours in the off season. Opening hours and contact details are listed under each city throughout the book.

Tourist offices operate under a variety of names – *turistkontor* and *reiseliv* are among the most common – but all have the information symbol (i) prominently displayed outside and are easy to identify and find.

For general information on travelling in Norway, contact the **Norwegian Tourist Board** (Norges Turistråd; ☎ 24 14 46 00; www.visitnorway.com; PO Box 722, Sentrum, N-0105 Oslo).

Tourist Offices Abroad
For the nearest Norwegian tourist office in your country, contact the nearest Norwegian embassy; see p379 for details.

Australia & New Zealand (Royal Norwegian Embassy; ☎ 02-6273 3444; emb.canberra@mfa.no; 17 Hunter St, Yarralumla, ACT 2600)

France (Office National du Tourisme de Norvége; ☎ 01 53 23 00 50; www.visitnorway.com/foreign_offices /france/; Paris)

Germany (Norwegisches Fremdenverkehrsamt; ☎ 01-80 50 01 54 8; germany@ntr.no; Postfach 113317, D-20433 Hamburg)

urist Board; ☎ 3-5212 1121;
Gobancho 4F, Gobancho 12-11,
)076)

erkeersbureau; ☎ 0900 899 1170;
s 101, NL-2460 AC, Ter Aar)
UK & Ireland (Norwegian Tourist Board; ☎ 0906-302
2003; www.norway.org.uk; 5th fl, Charles House, 5 Lower
Regent St, London, SW1Y 4LR)
USA & Canada (Norwegian Tourist Board; ☎ 212-885
9700; www.norway.org; 655 Third Ave, New York, NY 10022)

VISAS

Citizens of Denmark, Finland, Iceland and
Sweden may enter Norway freely without a
passport. Citizens of the USA, Canada, the
UK, Ireland, Australia and New Zealand
need a valid passport to visit Norway, but
do not need a visa for stays of less than three
months. The same is true for EU and European Economic Area (EEA) countries, most
of Latin America and most Commonwealth
countries. Norway belongs to the Schengen
group of countries (named after the treaty
which allows free movement within EU
countries), so there are only limited border
controls at Norwegian frontiers.

WOMEN TRAVELLERS

Women travellers have few worries in Norway, and sober Norwegian men are normally the very picture of decorum. While
alcohol-impaired men may become tiresome or obnoxious, they're probably no different from the same breed you'll encounter
in your home country.

Norway's main feminist organisation is
Kvinnefronten (Women's Front; ☎ 23 01 03 13; kvinne
fronten@online.no; Storgata 11, Oslo). Women who

have been attacked or abused can contact
the **Krisesenter** (☎ 22 37 47 00) in Oslo or dial
☎ 112 nationwide.

First-time women travellers should track
down the eminently practical *Handbook for
Women Travellers* by Maggie and Gemma
Moss, although remember that most of the
situations described are no more likely to
confront you in Norway than they are in
your home country.

Of the general websites dedicated to
women travellers, **Journeywoman** (www.journey
woman.com) is outstanding. There's also a
women's page on Lonely Planet's **Thorn Tree**
(www.thorntree.lonelyplanet.com).

WORK

In order to work in Norway, knowledge
of basic Norwegian is required at the very
least. As a member of the EEA, Norway
grants citizens of other EEA countries (essentially EU countries, plus Switzerland,
Liechtenstein, Greenland and the Faroe Islands) the right to look for work for a three-
month period without obtaining a permit;
those who find work have a right to remain
in Norway for the duration of their employment. For other foreigners, it's very difficult
and application for a work permit must be
made through the Norwegian embassy or
consulate in their home country before entering Norway.

For help with looking for work, the
EURES Department of the **Directorate of Labour** (www.aetat.no), which distributes two free
booklets, *Looking for Work in Norway* and
Norway – Access to Job Vacancies, or Use-It
(p71) are the best places to start.

Transport

GETTING THERE & AWAY

ENTERING THE COUNTRY

Crossing most borders into Norway is usually hassle-free, particularly if you're arriving by road, although if you're Black you may find yourself and your baggage under greater scrutiny than other travellers. If you're arriving in Norway from a non-EU country, expect your papers to be checked very carefully.

For details on visa requirements for entering Norway, see p386.

AIR
Airports & Airlines

The main Norwegian airports that handle international traffic:

Flesland Airport, Bergen (airport code BGO; ☎ 55 99 80 00; infosenteret.bergen@avinor.no)
Gardermoen Airport, Oslo (airport code OSL; ☎ 64 81 20 00; www.osl.no)
Karmøy Airport, Haugesund (airport code HAU; ☎ 52 85 79 00; haugesund.lufthavn@avinor.no)
Kjevik Airport, Kristiansand (airport code KRS; ☎ 38 06 56 00; fax 38 06 31 22)

THINGS CHANGE....

The information in this chapter is particularly vulnerable to change: prices for international travel are volatile, routes are introduced and cancelled, schedules change, special deals come and go, and rules and visa requirements are amended. The details given in this chapter should be regarded as pointers and are not a substitute for your own careful, up-to-date research.

Sola Airport, Stavanger (airport code SVG; ☎ 51 65 80 00; stavanger.lufthavn@avinor.no)
Torp Airport, Sandefjord (airport code TRF; ☎ 33 42 70 02; www.torp.no)
Værnes Airport, Trondheim (airport code TRD; ☎ 74 84 30 00; info.vaernes@avinor.no)

Airlines which use Norway as their primary base:
Coast Air (airline code BX; ☎ 52 84 85 00; www.coastair .no) Flies to Aberdeen from Haugesund.
Norwegian Air Shuttle (airline code DY; ☎ 81 52 18 15; www.norwegian.no) Low-cost airline flying to 14 European cities.
SAS Braathens (airline code BU or SK; ☎ 81 52 00 00, 81 52 40 00, 05400; www.sasbraathens.no) Over 30 destinations around Europe, including Heathrow and Gatwick, with hundreds more cities around the world.
Widerøe (airline code WF; ☎ 81 00 12 00; www.wideroe .no) Flies to Aberdeen, Manchester, Newcastle, Copenhagen, Gothenburg and Stockholm from four Norwegian airports.

Other international airlines which fly to/ from Norway:
Aeroflot (airline code SU; ☎ 22 83 44 47; www .aeroflot.org; hub Moscow)
Air France (airline code AF; ☎ 23 50 20 01; www.air france.com; hub Paris)
British Airways (airline code BA; ☎ 81 53 31 42; www .british-airways.com; hub London)
British Midland Airways (airline code BD; www.flybmi .com; hub London)
Finnair (airline code AY; ☎ 81 00 11 00; www.finnair.fi; hub Helsinki)
Iberia (airline code IB; www.iberia.com; hub Madrid)
Icelandair (airline code FI; ☎ 22 03 40 50; www.iceland air.com; hub Reykjavík)

KLM-Royal Dutch Airlines (airline code KL; ☎ 22 64 37 52; www.klm.com; hub Amsterdam)
Lufthansa (airline code LH; ☎ 23 35 54 00; www.lufthansa.com; hub Frankfurt)
Maersk (airline code DM; ☎ 81 50 07 40; www.maersk-air.com; hub Billund, Denmark)
Nordic Airlink (airline code LF; ☎ 24 14 87 58; www.flynordic.com; hub Stockholm)
Ryanair (airline code XY; ☎ 33 42 75 00; www.ryanair.com; hub Dublin) Budget airline.
Spanair (airline code JK; ☎ 81 52 40 00; www.spanair.com; hub Majorca)
Sterling (airline code NB; www.sterling.dk; hub Copenhagen) Budget airline.

For details of these and other airline safety records, visit www.airsafe.com or www.waasinfo.net.

Tickets

For bargain air fares, go to a travel agent rather than directly to the airline who generally only sell fares at the official listed price. One exception to this rule is the expanding number of 'no-frills' carriers operating in the USA and Europe, which sell direct to travellers (many sell tickets over the Internet); see p387 for low-cost airlines, marked as budget airlines.

Reliable online flight-booking sites:
Cheap Flights (www.cheapflights.co.uk)
eBookers UK Group (www.ebookers.co.uk)
Last Minute (www.lastminute.com)
Opodo (www.opodo.com)
Travelocity (www.travelocity.co.uk)

However, online superfast fare generators are no substitute for a travel agent who knows all about special deals and can offer advice on other aspects of your trip.

The first step for anyone headed for Norway is to get to Europe and, in these days of airline competition, you'll find plenty of deals to European 'gateway' cities, particularly London, Paris, Frankfurt, Berlin or even Copenhagen. The only intercontinental flights available to Norway are from the USA.

Africa

Nairobi and Johannesburg are the best places in Africa to buy tickets to Europe, thanks to the strong competition between their many bucket shops. Several West African countries offer cheap charter flights to

France, and charter fares from Morocco can be incredibly cheap if you're lucky enough to find a seat.

Rennies Travel (www.renniestravel.com) and **STA Travel** (www.statravel.co.za) have offices throughout Southern Africa. Check their websites for branch locations.

Asia

STA Travel (www.statravel.com; Bangkok ☎ 0 2236 0262; www.statravel.co.th; Singapore ☎ 6737 7188; www.statravel.com.sg; Hong Kong ☎ 2736 1618; www.statravel.com.hk; Japan ☎ 03 5391 2922; www.statravel.co.jp) proliferates in Asia, with branches just about everywhere. Another resource in Japan is **No 1 Travel** (☎ 0332-05 6073; www.no1-travel.com); in Hong Kong try **Four Seas Tours** (☎ 2200 7760; www.fourseastravel.com/English).

In India, **STIC Travels** (in Delhi ☎ 11-233 57 468, in Mumbai ☎ 22-221 81 431; www.stictravel.com) has offices in dozens of cities. Another possible agency is **Transway International** (www.transwayinternational.com).

Australia & New Zealand

If coming from Australasia, there's a large difference between low- and high-season fares and, unlike transatlantic flights, where prices rise and fall gradually on either side of the high season, the change in fares for travel from Australia and NZ is more sudden.

From Australia, flights to Oslo require a couple of stopovers on the way, usually Singapore or Bangkok and another European city. In the low season, expect to pay around A$1750 for a return fare with Air France/Qantas or KLM. Air France/Qantas and Cathay Pacific have high-season return fares starting from A$2300. From New Zealand, Lufthansa offers some of the best deals for travel to Oslo. Return fares start from NZ$2250/2700 in low/high season.

Both **STA Travel** (☎ 1300 733 035; www.statravel.com.au) and **Flight Centre** (☎ 133 133; www.flightcentre.com.au) have offices throughout Australia. For online bookings, try www.travel.com.au.

In New Zealand, both **Flight Centre** (☎ 0800 243 544; www.flightcentre.co.nz) and **STA Travel** (☎ 0508 782 872; www.statravel.co.nz) have branches throughout the country. The site www.travel.co.nz is recommended for online bookings.

Continental Europe

Although London is the travel discount capital of Europe, there are several other cities where you'll find a range of good deals. Generally, there's not much variation in air fare prices for departures from the main European cities. All the major airlines are usually offering some sort of deal and travel agents generally have a number of special offers, so shop around.

Recommended agencies in France:

Anyway (☎ 0892 893 892; www.anyway.fr)
Nouvelles Frontières (☎ 0825 000 747; www.nouvelles -frontieres.fr)
Voyageurs du Monde (☎ 01 40 15 11 15; www.vdm .com)

In Germany, try:

Expedia (www.expedia.de)
Just Travel (☎ 089 747 3330; www.justtravel.de)
STA Travel (☎ 01805 456 422; www.statravel.de)

Elsewhere, one recommended agent in Italy is **CTS Viaggi** (☎ 06 462 0431; www.cts.it), while in the Netherlands, **Airfair** (☎ 020 620 5121; www .airfair.nl) is recommended.

UK

If you're looking for a cheap way into or out of Scandinavia, London is Europe's major centre for discounted fares. You can fly from London to Oslo for as little as UK£25 one way, although if you're lucky you may pick up one of Ryanair's UK£1 one-way fares! Most air fares from London now beat surface alternatives in terms of cost.

Airline ticket discounters are known as bucket shops in the UK. Despite the somewhat disreputable name, there's nothing under-the-counter about them. Discount air travel is big business in London. Advertisements for many travel agents appear in the travel pages of the weekend broadsheets, such as the *Independent* on Saturday and the *Sunday Times*. Look out for the free magazines, such as *TNT*, which are widely available in London – start by looking outside the main railway and underground stations.

Recommended travel agencies:

Flightbookers (☎ 0870 010 7000; www.ebookers.com)
Flight Centre (☎ 0870 890 8099; flightcentre.co.uk)
North-South Travel (☎ 01245 608 291; www.north southtravel.co.uk) North-South Travel donates part of its profit to projects in the developing world.
STA Travel (☎ 0870 160 0599; www.statravel.co.uk)

USA & Canada

The North Atlantic is ⌐
long-haul air corridor ar⌐
are bewildering. Larger ⌐
the *New York Times*, *Ch*⌐
Francisco Chronicle and *Los Angeles Times* all produce weekly travel sections in which you'll find any number of travel agents' ads for air fares to Europe.

Thanks to the large ethnic Norwegian population in Minnesota, Wisconsin and North Dakota, you may find small local agencies specialising in travel to Scandinavia and offering good-value charter flights in those areas. Otherwise, you should be able to fly return from New York or Boston to Oslo for around US$650 in the low season and US$1100 in the high season. With most tickets you can usually travel 'open jaw', allowing you to land in one city (Copenhagen, for example) and return from another (such as Oslo) at no extra cost.

Many European destinations, including Oslo, are serviced by **Icelandair** (☎ 800 223 5500; www.icelandair.net), via Reykjavík, from New York, Boston, Baltimore-Washington, Minneapolis and Orlando. It offers some of the best deals, and on its transatlantic flights it allows a free three-day stopover in Reykjavík. Return fares start at around US$800 (including taxes), but special fares are sometimes available.

If you're planning on flying within Norway (or around Scandinavia), **SAS** (☎ 800 221 2350; www.sas.no) has some interesting regional discounts available to passengers who fly on its transatlantic flights.

Airhitch (☎ 800 326 2009; www.airhitch.org) specialises in cheap stand-by tickets to Europe, but the destinations are by region (not a specific city or country), so you'll need a flexible schedule.

Discount travel agents in the USA are known as consolidators and San Francisco is the ticket consolidator capital of America, although some good deals can be found in Los Angeles, New York and other big cities.

The following agencies are recommended for online bookings:

Cheap Tickets (www.cheaptickets.com)
Expedia (www.expedia.com, www.expedia.ca)
ITN (www.itn.net)
Lowest Fare (www.lowestfare.com)
Orbitz (www.orbitz.com)

TRANSPORT

∴vel (www.sta.com)
relocity (www.travelocity.com, www.travelocity.ca)

Other recommended agencies:
Air-Tech (☎ 212-219 7000; www.airtech.com; 588 Broadway, Suite 204, New York, NY 10012-5405)
Educational Travel Centre (☎ 800 747 5551; www.edtrav.com; 438 N Frances St, Madison, WI 53703-1084)
Travel Cuts (☎ 1866-246-9762; www.travelcuts.com) Canada's national student travel agency.

LAND
Border Crossings
Border crossings between Norway and Sweden or Finland are straightforward; passports are rarely checked and half the time you aren't even aware that you've crossed a border. If you're travelling by bus, some bags may be checked by customs, but you'll rarely stop for more than a few minutes. For Russia, however, everyone needs a visa and travellers will face greater scrutiny.

Bus
For almost all international bus services to/from Norway, the best website is www.eurolines.nu, which acts as a feeder for national companies.

Train
International trains from Norway were in a state of flux at the time of research as the main company servicing international routes had gone bankrupt and was due to close at the end of 2004. We were assured that another company would take up the reins, but the information contained in this section is particularly vulnerable to change. Contact **Norwegian Railways** (NSB; ☎ 81 50 08 88; www.nsb.no) for the latest information.

TRAIN PASSES
The ScanRail pass is generally a better deal than the Eurail pass.

Eurail
Eurail passes (www.eurailpass.com) can only be bought by residents of non-European countries (residents of Morocco, Algeria, Tunisia, Turkey and Russia are also excluded), and are supposed to be purchased before arriving in Europe. However, Eurail passes can be purchased within Europe as long as your passport proves you've been there for less than six months. The outlets

where you can do this are limited, and the passes will be more expensive than getting them outside Europe. Oslo is the only place in Norway where you can buy Eurail passes and this is at the **Oslo S train station** (☎ 23 15 24 48). In London, try **Rail Europe** (☎ 0870 584 8848; www.raileurope.com) and the **German Rail UK Booking Centre** (☎ 0870 243 5363).

If you've lived in Europe for more than six months, you're eligible for an Inter-Rail pass; see p391 for details.

Eurail passes are valid for unlimited travel on national railways and some private lines in 17 European and Scandinavian countries. The passes do not cover the UK or the Baltic countries.

Eurail is also valid for some ferries between Ireland and France (but not between the UK and France), and from Sweden to Finland, Denmark or Germany. Reductions are given on some other ferry routes and on steamer services in various countries.

Eurail passes offer reasonable value to people aged under 26. A Youthpass is valid for unlimited 2nd-class travel for 15 days (US$414), 21 days (US$534), one month (US$664), two months (US$938) or three months (US$1160). The Youth Flexipass, also for 2nd class, is valid for freely chosen days within a two-month period: 10 days for US$488 or 15 days for US$642.

For those aged over 26, a standard Eurail-pass is valid for 15 days (US$588), 21 days (US$762), one month (US$946), two months (US$1338) or three months (US$1654). The Flexipass (available in 1st class only) costs US$694 for 10 days and US$914 for 15 days. Two to five people travelling together can get good discounts on a Saverpass, which works like the standard Eurail pass. A 15-day Saverpass costs US$498 per person, up to US$1408 for three months. Children under four travel free and those between four and 11 pay half-price.

The Eurail Select Pass allows you to travel within three to five bordering countries by rail or sea. It covers between five and 10 days travel over two months and you must use the pass within six months of purchase. It costs from US$356/394/470/542 for five/six/eight/10 days of travel for an adult in first class. There are greater discounts for groups of two to five people under the Eurail Selectpass Saverpass (US$304/336/400/460 in 1st class) and people under 25 years of age (US$249/276/329/379 in 2nd class). Reservations are required. The pass also offers various discounts on some ferry crossings and car rental.

Inter-Rail

Inter-Rail passes (www.inter-rail.com) are available to European residents of six-months standing (passport identification and evidence is required). Terms and conditions vary from country to country, but in the country of origin there's only a discount of around 50% on normal fares.

Travellers over 26 can get the Inter-Rail 26+, valid for unlimited rail travel in many European and Scandinavian countries, although most price structures are split into regional zones; Norway is in Zone B along with Sweden and Finland. The pass also gives 30% to 50% discounts on various other ferry routes (more than covered by Eurail) and certain river and lake services. A one-zone, 22-day pass costs UK£223 and an all-zone, one-month pass costs UK£415.

The Inter-Rail pass for those under 26 costs for any one zone UK£159 for 16 days; a two-zone, 22-day pass costs UK£215; and an all-zone, one-month pass cost is UK£295.

The Baltics are expected to join the Inter-Rail system at some future date. Check for the latest information if considering buying a pass.

Euro Domino

A Euro Domino pass for adults (travelling 1st or 2nd class) and youths under 26 is valid for travel within one country on any three to eight days during one month. In Norway, adult/youth prices for seven days in 2nd class are UK£290/220.

ScanRail

The flexible **ScanRail pass** (www.scanrail.com) covers travel in Denmark, Norway, Sweden and Finland.

There are three versions. For 2nd-class travel on any five days within a two-month period, the pass costs UK£230 (UK£160 for travellers under age 26). For travel on any 10 days within a two-month period, the pass costs UK£308 for 2nd class (UK£215 for those under 26). For a pass allowing unlimited travel during 21 consecutive days, the cost is UK£358 (UK£249 for those under 26).

If you're aged 55 or over, then you're eligible for the ScanRail 55+ pass, which will allow 2nd-class travel over five days in a two-month period for UK£204, 10 days in a two-month period for UK£274 and 21 consecutive days for UK£316.

To get ScanRail passes at these prices they must be purchased before you arrive in Scandinavia (the ScanRail website has a list of worldwide agents, or you can purchase the pass from most European train stations). ScanRail passes can also be purchased in Scandinavia, but they'll cost roughly 10% to 20% more, depending on exchange rates.

The pass also includes free travel on a number of internal Norwegian bus routes, including Grong–Brønnøysund, Åndalsnes–Ålesund, Oppdal–Kristiansund, Åndalsnes–Molde and Mosjøen–Sandnessjøen. You'll also get a 30% discount on the Flåm–Myrdal Flåmsbanen (p231) and discounts on the following ferry services: Frederikshavn–Oslo (30%; Stena Lines), Larvik–Hirtshals (50%; Color Line), Bergen–Stavanger (50%; Flaggruten), Newcastle–Bergen (25% to 50%; Fjordline), and Hardangerfjord and southern Hordaland ferries (50%; HSD Snoggbåtene).

Denmark
BUS

Nor-Way Bussekspress (www.nor-way.no) buses travel between Copenhagen and Oslo (Dkr305, eight hours, at least twice daily). Buses travel via Göteborg, Malmö and the Øresund bridge. Three **Swebus Express** (☎ 8070 3300) buses also run to/from Copenhagen each day.

TRAIN

There are at least two daily services running between Copenhagen and Oslo (Dkr610, from 8¾ hours). Trains run via the Øresund bridge and Malmö and you may be required to change in Malmö or Gothenburg for Oslo.

For details of the uncertainty of international train services from Norway, see p390.

Finland
BUS

The E8 highway runs from Tornio, in Finland, to Tromsø and secondary highways connect Finland with the northern Sami

TRANSPORT

BUS TRAVEL FROM FINLAND				
From	**To**	**Price**	**Duration**	**Period**
Oulu	Tromsø	€88.55	8hr	1 Jun-18 Sep
Rovaniemi	Tana Bru	€65.60	7hr	1 Jun-5 Oct
Rovaniemi	Kautokeino	€74.10	6½hr	1 Jun-14 Aug
Rovaniemi	Karasjok	€55.20	7hr	4 Jun-30 Sep
Rovaniemi	Lakselv	€65.90	12½hr	4 Jun-30 Sep
Rovaniemi	Nordkapp	€101.50	12hr	4 Jun-30 Sep
Ivalo	Kirkenes	€35.20	3¼hr	28 Jun-8 Aug

towns of Karasjok and Kautokeino. Regular buses serve all three routes.

See the table above for details of cross-border services (one daily service only) offered by the Finnish company **Eskelisen Lapin Linjat** (☎ 016-342 2160; www.eskelisen-lapin linjat.com).

Nor-Way Bussekspress (www.nor-way.no) also has one service a day between Oslo and Helsinki (Nkr662, 25 hours), which requires a change in Stockholm.

Germany
BUS
Nor-Way Bussekspress (www.nor-way.no) buses connect Berlin with Oslo (€83.90, 15¼ hours) every day, via Rostock, Germany and Gothenburg (Göteborg), Sweden.

TRAIN
Hamburg is the central European gateway for Scandinavia, with up to five daily trains to Copenhagen or Malmø; connections for Oslo are available for two of these services.

Berlin Night Express (www.berlin-night-express .com) has a daily overnight train from Berlin to Oslo (from €165 including couchette, 17¾ hours) via the Sassnitz (Germany) to Trelleborg (Sweden) ferry and Malmö. Travelling to/from Oslo always requires changing trains in Malmö, and in Gothenburg from late August until mid-June.

For these and services and online booking, contact **Deutsche Bahn** (www.bahn.de).

Russia & Asia
BUS & TRAIN
Russia has a short border with Norway and buses run daily between Kirkenes and Murmansk. The rail link to/from eastern Asia via Russia can work out at about the same price as flying, depending on how much time and

money you spend along the way, and it can be a lot more fun. Russian trains run as far as Murmansk (from St Petersburg).

For more details on overland travel to/from Russia, see p343. Check out Lonely Planet's comprehensive *Trans-Siberian Railway* for detailed information on trans-Siberian travel.

Sweden
BUS
Nor-Way Bussekspress (☎ 08-762 59 60) runs express buses from Oslo to Gothenburg (Göteborg; Skr225, 4½ hours, six daily) and Malmö (Skr365, 7¼ hours, three daily). Three daily **Swebus Express** (☎ 0200 218 218; www.swebusexpress.se) buses run between Stockholm and Oslo (Skr365, eight hours).

There are also buses between Bodø and Skellefteå (Skr510, 8¾ hours, once daily except Saturday) and along the Blå Vägen, or 'Blue Highway', between Mo i Rana and Umeå (Skr268, eight hours, once daily).

CAR & MOTORCYCLE
The main highways between Sweden and Norway are the E6 from Gothenburg to Oslo, the E18 from Stockholm to Oslo, the E14 from Sundsvall to Trondheim and the E12 from Umeå to Mo i Rana. Many secondary roads also cross the border.

TRAIN
There are daily trains from Stockholm to Oslo (from Skr695, seven hours) and Narvik (Skr1450, 18¾ hours). Journeys from Trondheim to Sweden via Storlien and Östersund require changing trains at the border. Trains also run between Oslo and Malmö (Skr698, 8¼ hours, twice daily), via Gothenburg (Skr537, four hours, four daily).

For details of the uncertainty of international train services from Norway, see p390.

UK
BUS
If you like long and arduous journeys, you can bus it between London and Oslo in about 36 hours, but you may have to change buses as often as four times! This year-round service operates three to five times weekly via Brussels, Copenhagen and Gothenburg. Reservations are compulsory. Contact **National Express** (☎ 0870 580 8080; www.nationalexpress.com) or **Nor-Way Bussekspress** (☎ 81 54 44 44; www.nor-way.no). One-way fares start at UK£108, so it's usually cheaper to fly!

TRAIN
Travelling by train from the UK to Oslo (29 hours) can also be more expensive than flying. From London, a return 2nd-class train ticket to Oslo, valid for two months, costs around UK£380 including couchettes and a ScanRail Pass valid for any five days in the two months. For tickets, contact **Deutsche Bahn UK** (☎ 0870 243 5363; www.bahn.de) or **Euro Railways** (☎ 1-866-768 8927; www.euro railways.com).

SEA
Transatlantic Passenger Ships & Freighters
Regular, long-distance passenger ships disappeared with the advent of cheap air travel and were replaced by a small number of luxury cruise ships. **Cunard Line** (in US ☎ 800 728 6273, in UK ☎ 0845 071 0300; www.cunardline.com) has sailings on the *QE2* between New York and Southampton up to twice a month, taking five nights/six days per crossing. The cost of a one-way crossing starts at around UK£999, but there are always special offers; check the website. Cunard Line also offers around six summer cruises (late April to mid-August) from Southampton to the Norwegian coast (even as far up as Nordkapp) and back again. Basic prices for seven-day cruises start at UK£669, up to UK£1269 for 13 days; remember that the trip's duration also includes getting to and from Norway.

A more adventurous – but not necessarily cheaper – alternative is as a paying passenger on a freighter. Freighters are far more numerous than cruise ships, and there are many more routes from which to choose. With a bit of homework, you'll be able to sail to Europe from just about anywhere else in the world, with stopovers at exotic little-known ports. The book *Travel by Cargo Ship* (Cadogan, London, 1995) covers the subject. Passenger freighters typically carry six to 12 passengers (more than 12 would require a ship's doctor aboard) and, although they're less luxurious than dedicated cruise ships, they provide a real taste of life at sea. Schedules tend to be flexible and costs vary, but normally hover around US$100 a day; vehicles can often be included for an additional charge.

Ferry
Ferry connections between Norway and Denmark, Germany, Iceland, the Faroe Islands, Sweden and the UK provide straightforward links, especially for anyone bringing their own vehicle. There may be special deals for four people travelling with a car and most lines offer substantial discounts for seniors, students and children, so it pays to ask when booking. Taking a bicycle incurs a small extra fee.

If you're travelling by international ferry, consider picking up your maximum duty-free alcohol allowance on the boat, as alcohol is prohibitively expensive in Norway and, even if you don't drink, it will make a welcome gift for Norwegian friends.

DENMARK
The following companies operate ferries between Norway and Denmark.
Color Line (in Denmark ☎ 99 56 19 77, in Norway ☎ 81 00 08 11; www.colorline.no)
DFDS Seaways (in Denmark ☎ 33 42 33 42, in Norway ☎ 22 41 90 90; www.dfdsseaways.com)
Fjord Line (in Norway ☎ 81 53 35 00, in Denmark ☎ 97 96 14 01; www.fjordline.com)
Stena Line (in Norway ☎ 02010, in Denmark ☎ 96 20 02 00; www.stenaline.no)

The table on p394 lists the possible routes accompanied by high-season (mid-June to mid-August) fares and frequency of departure; at other times, fares can be half the high-season price but departures are much less frequent.

Most ferry operators offer package deals which include a car and passengers. On all

FERRY ROUTES BETWEEN DENMARK & NORWAY

To	From	One-way fare per person	Duration	Times per week	Ferry operator
Bergen	Hanstholm	€110	15½hr	3	Fjord Line
Egersund	Hanstholm	€70	6¾hr	7	Fjord Line
Kristiansand	Hirtshals	€58	4½hr	6	Color Line
Larvik	Fredrikshavn	€58	6¼hr	11	Color Line
Olso	Copenhagen	€80	16hr	7	DFDS Seaways
Oslo	Fredrikshavn	€47	12½hr	6	Stena Line
Oslo	Hirtshals	€58	8½hr	4	Color Line

of the above Color Line routes, a car with up to five people costs €252, while DFDS Seaways charges €195, including two passengers. On Stena Line, a car with driver included costs up to €160, while to Bergen with Fjord Line costs around €165, including driver and one passenger, and there's a special high-season return fare to Egersund for a car and five persons for €199 from Monday to Wednesday or €279 Thursday to Sunday.

GERMANY
Color Line (in Germany ☎ 0431-7300 300, in Norway ☎ 81 00 08 11; www.colorline.no) has a daily ferry link between Kiel and Oslo (20 hours). From mid-June to mid-August, reclining chairs start at €92 (Sunday to Thursday) or €102 (Friday and Saturday). The cheapest equivalent per-person fare in a two-berth cabin is €114 or €124. Cars cost €80. Outside high season, one-way/return packages are available for a car and basic cabin for two people for €188/342.

ICELAND & THE FAROE ISLANDS
Smyril Line (in the Faroes ☎ 345900, in Norway ☎ 55 59 65 20; www.smyril-line.fo) runs once weekly from May to mid-September between Bergen and Seyðisfjörður (Iceland), via Lerwick (Shetland) and the Faroe Islands. One-way fares from Bergen begin at €180 to Tórshavn (25 hours) in the Faroes and €275 to Seyðisfjörður (46 hours), Iceland.

SWEDEN
The following companies or boats all operate ferry services between Sweden and Norway:
Color Line (in Sweden ☎ 0526-62000, in Norway ☎ 81 00 08 11; www.colorline.no)

DFDS Seaways (in Sweden ☎ 031-650 600, in Norway ☎ 22 41 90 90; www.dfdsseaways.com)
Fjordlink & M/S Silverpilen (in Sweden ☎ 052-661 560, in Norway ☎ 69 39 65 04; www.silverpilen.com)

The table on p395 describes ferry routes between Sweden and Norway, with high-season fares and frequency of departures.

Car fares start at €27 on the Gothenburg–Kristiansand–Gothenburg route, while between Strömstad and Sandefjord car fares cost €22.

The ferry **M/S Sagasund** (☎ 90 99 81 11) connects Halden with Ströstad (Skr115, two hours). These services are more like Swedish-Norwegian 'booze cruises' rather than real transport links (duty-free goods are available on board).

UK
Fjord Line (in UK ☎ 0191-296 1313, in Norway ☎ 81 53 35 00; www.fjordline.co.uk) sails from Newcastle to Bergen (23 hours) twice weekly in winter and thrice weekly in summer (mid-May to early September). The winter sailings and two of the summer sailings go via Stavanger (19½ hours) and Haugesund (21 hours). For a bunk in a basic four-berth cabin below the car deck, fares range from UK£60 for some sailings between January and March, and up to UK£120 on summer weekends; a range of cheaper fares are available for early advance booking and through a range of special offers. For cars and up to four passengers, packages are available for UK£240.

Smyril Line (in UK ☎ 01595-690845, in Norway ☎ 55 59 65 20; www.smyril-line.fo) sails between Lerwick (Shetland) and Bergen, from May to mid-September, and takes from 10½ hours. Couchette fares in low/high-season are

FERRY ROUTES BETWEEN SWEDEN & NORWAY

To	From	One-way fare per person	Duration	Times per week	Ferry operator
Fredrikstad	Strömstad	€12	1¼hr	up to 10	Fjordlink
Kristiansand	Gothenburg	€22	9hr	3	DFDS Seaways
Olso	Helsingborg	€65	14hr	7	DFDS Seaways
Sandefjord	Strömstad	€24	2½hr	14	Color Line

UK£48/68 and cars up to 5m long cost UK£38/57. See also p394.

The popular **DFDS Seaways** (in UK ☎ 01255-240240, in Norway ☎ 22 41 90 90; www.dfdsseaways .com) service between Newcastle and Kristiansand sails twice weekly from mid-January to mid-November and takes from 16½ hours. One-way high-season fares start at UK£70 for pedestrians and UK£150 for four people in a car.

TOURS

Given the expenses involved in Norwegian travel, it may be worth looking into an organised tour. Several reputable operators offer affordable itineraries concentrating either on Scandinavia in general or Norway in particular.

Australia

Bentours International (☎ 02-9241 1353; www.bentours.com.au; Level 7, 189 Kent St, Sydney) is the only Australian travel agency specialising in Scandinavian travel.

France

Grand Nord Grand Large (☎ 01 40 46 05 14; www.gngl .com; 15 rue du Cardinal Lemoine, F-75005 Paris) is one of the world's most adventurous agencies. GNGL seeks out the locations and activities that are noticed by only a handful of other companies. In Norway, it offers cruises and hiking in Svalbard and Lofoten.

North America

Backroads (☎ 800 462 2848; www.backroads.com; 801 Cedar St, Berkeley, CA 94710-1800) offers all-inclusive and generally upmarket six-day hiking, rail and ferry tours between Geilo and Bergen, via the Hardangervidda plateau, Aurlandsdalen, Flåm and Sognefjorden (US$2198).

Borton Overseas (☎ 800 843 0602; www.bortonoverseas.com; 5412 Lyndale Ave S, Minneapolis, MN 55419)

specialises in adventure outdoor travel. It offers seven- to 18-day escorted tours and can arrange independent tours including Hurtigruten and train trips.

Brekke Tours (☎ 800 437 5302; www.brekketours .com; 802 N 43rd St, Grand Forks, ND 58203) caters mainly for North Americans of Norwegian descent, and has excellent escorted and independent Norwegian and Scandinavian tours. The 'Ultimate Fjord Adventure', a four-day unescorted tour from Oslo to Bergen (or back to Oslo) via the best of the Western Fjords, costs US$770 excluding flights.

Scanam World Tours & Cruises (☎ 800 545 2204; www.scanamtours.com; 108 N Main St, Cranbury, NJ 08512) organises cruises and shorter upmarket tours, including an eight-day fjord tour (from US$1075 per person excluding airfares).

Scantours (☎ 800 223 7226; www.scantours.com) offers an extensive range of short tours in Norway, from one day around Sognefjord ('Norway in a Nutshell') to 12 days aboard the Hurtigruten coastal ferry.

UK

Arctic Experience (☎ 01737-214214, www.arctic-experience.co.uk; 29 Nork Way, Banstead, Surrey, SM7 1PB) is a friendly agency and one of the most popular British tour operators to Scandinavia and the North Atlantic. It offers a range of hiking tours, skiing expeditions, snowmobile safaris and short breaks, mostly in Svalbard.

Arcturus Expeditions (☎ 01389-830204; www.arcturusexpeditions.co.uk; PO Box 850, Gartocharn, Alexandria, Dunbartonshire, G83 8RL) is one of Britain's most inventive operators and organises hiking, trekking, dog-sledding and cruising tours through the furthest reaches of the polar regions. In Norway, it offers hiking and dog-sledding in Finnmark and Dividalen, visits to Jan Mayen and Bjørnøya, and ice-breaker cruises and trekking in and around Svalbard. Highly recommended.

Go Fishing Worldwide (☎ 020-8742 8299; www.go fishingworldwide.co.uk; 2 Oxford House, 24 Oxford Rd N, London, W4 4DH) is the company to go with if you're a fishing fan. It can organise tailor-made fishing trips to Norway on request.

Scantours (☎ 020-7839 2927; www.scantoursuk .com; 47 Whitcomb St, London, WC2H 7DH) offers a wide range of options throughout Norway and Svalbard, lasting from five to 13 days. The prices and details are listed on the company's website.

Taber Holidays (☎ 01274-594642; www.taberhols .co.uk; 30A Bingley Rd, Shipley, West Yorkshire, BD18 4RS) offers a range of highlight-oriented, all-inclusive tours around Norway, including cruises, coach tours and self-drive possibilities.

Tangent Expeditions International (☎ 01539-737757; www.tangent-expeditions.co.uk; 3 Millbeck, New Hutton, Kendal, Cumbria, LA8 0BD) runs well-organised ski mountaineering expeditions to Newtontoppen and Perriertoppen in Svalbard (23 days, UK£2950).

Waymark Holidays (☎ 01753-516477; www.way markholidays.com; 44 Windsor Rd, Slough, SL1 2EJ) specialises in nordic skiing and hiking holidays in the Gol and Oslo areas.

GETTING AROUND

Norway's efficient domestic public transport systems include trains, buses and ferries and they're often timed to link with each other. The handy *NSB Togruter*, available free at train stations, details rail timetables and includes information on connecting buses. Boat and bus departures vary with the season and the day (services on Saturday are particularly sparse), so pick up the latest *ruteplan* (timetables) from regional tourist offices.

Rail lines extend as far north as Bodø (you can also reach Narvik by rail from Sweden); further north you're limited to buses and ferries. Thanks to the great distances, bus fares can add up, but Inter-Rail and Scan-Rail pass holders are entitled to discounts on some northern routes. Some express boats and buses offer a 50% discount for the second person when two people travel together, so it pays to ask. A fine alternative to land travel is the Hurtigruten coastal ferry, which calls in at every sizable port between Bergen and Kirkenes and provides stunning views of some of Europe's finest coastal scenery.

AIR
Airlines in Norway

Norway has nearly 50 airports with scheduled commercial flights, from Kristiansand in the south to Longyearbyen and Ny Ålesund in the north. Thanks to the time and distances involved in overland travel, even budget travellers may want to consider doing some segments by air.

The four airlines operating on domestic routes:

Coast Air (☎ 52 84 85 00; www.coastair.no)
Norwegian Air Shuttle (☎ 81 52 18 15; www .norwegian.no)
SAS Braathens (☎ 81 52 00 00, 81 52 40 00, 05400; www.sasbraathens.no)
Widerøe (☎ 81 00 12 00; www.wideroe.no)

The major Norwegian domestic routes are quite competitive, meaning that it is possible (if you're flexible about departure dates and book early) to travel with SAS Braathens from Oslo to Bergen (Nkr739), Stavanger (Nkr739), Tromsø (Nkr808), Trondheim (Nkr553) or Ålesund (Nkr553) for little more than the equivalent train fare. Widerøe offers similar fares and a similarly extensive network, although standard fares are considerably lower than on the big airlines. Coast Air, based in Haugesund, flies small planes and concentrates on the main airports in Southern Norway.

Air Passes

Air passes have become less important in recent years as most airline companies have slashed the prices of their regular one-way or return tickets. With SAS Braathens, standard '*minipris*' return tickets cost only about 10% more than full-fare one-way tickets and there are sometimes promotional fares that make return tickets even cheaper than one-way tickets. In addition, spouses (including gay partners), children aged two to 15 and senior citizens over 67 years of age are eligible for 50% discounts. There are also special summer fares, valid on return tickets between mid-June and mid-August.

Both SAS Braathens and Widerøe offer significant discount deals for travellers aged under 26 (and students under 32).

SAS Braathens offers its international passengers (who aren't resident in Scandinavia) advance-purchase coupons for Nkr850 to Nkr1200, which allow travel on direct flights between any two Scandinavian airports it serves, including several in Norway. Coupons are valid on most SAS flights within the region and must be purchased at least seven days in advance. You can buy up to eight coupons, which are good for one segment each.

There are also some good-value air passes and other tickets. Widerøe offers good-value Summerpass tickets (valid from June to August) which cost Nkr550 for one-way flights within any one of four zones, divided at Trondheim, Bodø and Tromsø (some short flights cost Nkr400). Multi-sector flights cost Nkr1000/1500/2000 for two/three/four zones. These tickets must be purchased outside of Norway. Widerøe's *minipris* ticket, valid one month, costs 40% less than the normal return fare, but you'll either have to stay at least one Saturday night or complete your return journey on Saturday or Sunday.

BICYCLE

Given Norway's great distances, hilly terrain and narrow roads, only serious cyclists engage in extensive cycle touring. Assuming that you've steeled yourself for the challenge of ascending mountain after mountain, the long-distance cyclist's biggest headache will be tunnels (see the boxed text, p402), and there are thousands of them. Many of these, especially in the Western Fjords, are closed to nonmotorised traffic due to the danger from hydrocarbon emissions and carbon monoxide fumes. This severely limits where cyclists can go and, even when alternative routes are available, they may involve a few days pedalling around a long fjord or over a high mountain pass.

An excellent website with route descriptions of some of the better long-distance cycling routes in Norway and cycling maps available for sale online is www.bike-norway.com. For further information on long-distance cycling routes and tunnels, contact **Syklistenes Landsforening** (☎ 22 47 30 30; post@slf.no; Storgata 23C, Oslo), the main contact point for Norway's cycling clubs. The map *Sykkelruter i Norge* (Nkr120) is sold by Syklistenes Landsforening; it's only available in Norwegian, but the English-text *Sykkelguide* series of booklets with maps are available for Nkr125 each and include Lofoten, Rallarvegen, the North Sea Cycleway from the Swedish border at Svinesund to Bergen, and other routes.

Rural buses, express ferries and non-express trains carry bikes for various additional fees (around Nkr100), but express trains don't allow them at all and international trains treat them as excess baggage (Nkr250). Nor-Way Bussekspress charges half the adult fare to transport a bicycle!

If cycling is more a hobby than a mode of transport, there are hundreds of regional cycling venues. Tourist offices across the country have devised suggested cycling tours and most have produced maps of the best routes.

For further information on cycling in Norway, see p372.

Hire

Although there are few dedicated bicycle hire places, most tourist offices and many hostels and camping grounds rent out bicycles; if they don't chances are that they'll know someone who does. Rental usually starts at around Nkr30 to Nkr50 for an hour and is rarely more than Nkr200 per day, although this can drop to as little as Nkr100 if you rent for a few days.

BOAT

If it weren't for Norway's excellent system of ferries, much of coastal Norway would consist of inaccessible, isolated communities separated by large stretches of water and rugged mountains. Indeed, they're the very lifeblood of much of western Norway, with an extensive network of reasonably frequent car ferries crisscrossing the fjords, while express boats link the country's offshore islands to the mainland. Most ferries along the highway system accommodate motor vehicles, but express coastal services normally take only foot passengers and cyclists, as do the lake steamers. See individual entries for specific destinations throughout this book for details.

Highway ferries are subsidised and therefore aren't overly expensive (at least in a universally expensive Norwegian context), but long queues and delays are possible at popular crossings in summer and reservations are rarely possible. They do, however, run deep into the night, especially in summer, and some run around the clock, although departures in the middle of the night are less frequent. Details on schedules and prices for vehicle ferries and lake steamers are provided in the timetables published by the Norwegian Tourist Board, or *Rutebok for Norge*, while tourist offices can provide timetables for ferries in their local area.

Canal Trips

Southern Norway's Telemark region has an extensive network of canals, rivers and lakes. There are regular ferry services or you can travel using your own boat. See p133 for details.

Hurtigruten Coastal Ferry

For more than a century, Norway's legendary **Hurtigruten coastal ferry route** (☎ 810 30 000; www.hurtigruten.com) has served as a lifeline linking coastal towns and villages and it's now one of the most enjoyable (and most popular) ways to explore Norway. Year-in, year-out, one of 11 Hurtigruten ferries heads north from Bergen almost every night of the year, pulling into 34 ports on its six-day journey to Kirkenes, where it then turns around and heads back south. The return journey takes 11 days and covers a distance of 2500 nautical miles. In agreeable weather the fjord and mountain scenery along the way is nothing short of spectacular. Most of the ships are modern and some even have the comforts of a cruise liner. Others are showing their age; the oldest ship dates from 1982, but all were substantially remodelled in the 1990s.

If you're travelling as a deck-class passenger, there are baggage rooms, a shower room, a 24-hour cafeteria and a coin laundry available. Meals are served in the dining room and you can buy snacks and light meals in the cafeteria. At night, some people roll out a sleeping bag on the floor in one of the lounges, but all-night activity will mean short nights of little sleep, especially in the 24-hour summer daylight; at least one LP author has been known to have enjoyed a blissful sleep curled up in a cupboard.

Sample deck-class fares from Bergen are Nkr1488 to Trondheim, Nkr2536 to Stamsund, Nkr3053 to Tromsø, Nkr384(to Honningsvåg and Nkr4736 to Kirkenes Cars can also be carried for an extra fee Children aged four to 16, students, an(seniors over the age of 67, all receive 50% discount, as do accompanying spouses an(accompanying children aged 16 to 25.

There are also some great off-seasor deals. From 1 September to 30 April, pas sengers get 40% discount off basic fares fo. sailings on any day except Tuesday an(receive a further 50% reduction on the re turn portion of the ticket. Also, betweer September and April, passengers aged 1(to 26 years may buy a 21-day coastal pas: for Nkr1875.

If you prefer an en suite cabin – and mos1 people do – you'll pay an additional Nkr30(to Nkr1000 per night from mid-April tc mid-September and Nkr135 to Nkr435 ir the low season. Basic cabins with sharec bathroom start at Nkr90 per night all year Cabins are extremely popular, so be sure tc book well in advance.

You may want to break up the trip with shore excursions, especially if you're travelling the entire route. The possibilities, which are organised by the shipping company include the following (northbound/southbound excursions are denoted by N/S): an overland tour between Geiranger and Ålesund or Molde (N; three or seven hours) a short tour of Trondheim (S; two hours); a day trip to Svartisen (N; six hours); spins around Lofoten (S; three hours) and Vesterålen (S; four hours); a haul from Honningsvåg up to Nordkapp (N; four hours); an overland tour between Honningsvåg and Hammerfest, via Nordkapp (S; seven hours); and a tour from Kirkenes, at the end of the line, to the Russian border (two hours). These offer fairly good value (contact the operators for prices) but, in some cases, you'll miss segments of the coastal scenery.

In addition to using the toll-free number or website given above, you can contact either **Troms Fylkes Dampskibsselskap** (☎ 77 64 82 00; booking@tfds.no) in Tromsø or **Ofotens og Vesterålens Dampskibsselskab** (☎ 76 96 76 96; booking@ovds.no) in Narvik.

In North America, you can book through **Norwegian Coastal Voyages** (☎ 800 323 7436; www .coastalvoyage.com); in the UK, contact **Norwegian Coastal Voyage** (☎ 020-8846 2600; www.norwegian

oastalvoyage.com); and in Australia, **Bentours International** (☎ 02-9241 1353; www.bentours.com au). The Hurtigruten website carries a full ist of international sales agents.

Yacht

Exploring the Norwegian coastline aboard your own yacht is one of life's more pleasurable experiences, although harsh weather conditions will restrict how far north you go. Almost every town along Norway's southern coast has an excellent *gjestehavn* (guest harbour) where the facilities include showers, toilets, electricity and laundries as a bare minimum, while some, such as Grimstad (p119), offer free bicycle hire and a wireless Internet zone. Standard mooring fees generally range from Nkr75 to Nkr125 per 24 hours.

BUS

Buses on Norway's extensive long-distance bus network are quite comfortable and make a habit of running on time.

Nor-Way Bussekspress (☎ 82 02 13 00; www.nor way.no) operates the largest network of express buses in Norway, with routes connecting most towns and cities, from Mandal in the far south to Alta in the far north. There are also a number of independent long-distance companies which provide similar prices and levels of service.

In northern Norway, several Togbuss (train-bus) routes offer half-price fares to Eurail, Inter-Rail and ScanRail pass holders. See p390 for details.

There's also a host of local buses, most of which are confined to a single *fylke* (county). Each of these routes has a designated number, but it's rarely marked on the bus, which is identified by its destination. To confuse matters, some buses also have a second route number, which is used in the specific area where it circulates. This number normally does appear on the bus.

Travellers are warned that most local and even some long-distance bus schedules are drastically reduced everywhere in Norway on Saturday. Sunday and off-season (usually mid-August to mid-June) schedules may also be reduced – and nonexistent in some cases.

To get a complete listing of bus timetables throughout the country (including

prices for major stops on most routes), pick up a copy of the free and nationwide *Rutehefte* from any reasonably sized bus station and some tourist offices. All bus stations and tourist offices also have smaller timetables for the relevant routes passing through town.

For information on city and town buses, see p404.

Bus Passes

Nor-Way Bussekspress offers the nontransferable Nor-Way BusPass (Nkr2300), which entitles you to unlimited domestic bus travel for 21 consecutive days; children between four and 15 years pay Nkr1725. With the pass, you can also travel on the Oslo airport bus for free. Tickets can be purchased in Norway from most bus stations, but most assuredly at the Oslo's central bus station. International sales agents are listed at www.nor-way.no; follow the 'Nor-Way BusPass' links.

Costs

Tickets are sold on the buses or in advance at the bus station and fares are based on the distance travelled, averaging Nkr145 for the first 100km. Many bus companies quote bus fares excluding any ferry costs. However, bus fares given in this book include ferry tickets where appropriate.

Many bus companies offer student, child, senior and family discounts of 25% to 50%, so it pays to inquire when purchasing. Groups (including two people travelling together) may also be eligible for discounts. In northern Norway, holders of Inter-Rail and ScanRail passes (see p390) are also often eligible for discounts on some routes.

In summer, special '*minipris*' tickets are frequently offered for some of the more popular long-distance services, including from Oslo to Bergen (*minipris*/normal fare Nkr265/640), Trondheim (Nkr290/610) and Røros (Nkr290/465).

Reservations

Advance reservations are almost never required in Norway and Nor-Way Bussekspress even has a 'Seat Guarantee – No Reservation' belief in its ability to get you where you want to go at the time of your choosing.

TRANSPORT

TRANSPORT

CAR & MOTORCYCLE
Automobile Associations

By reciprocal agreement, members of AIT-affiliated (Alliance Internationale de Tourisme) national automobile associations are eligible for 24-hour breakdown recovery assistance from the **Norges Automobil-Forbund** (NAF; breakdown ☎ 81 00 05 00, enquiries ☎ 22 34 14 00). NAF patrols ply the main roads from mid-June to mid-August. Emergency telephones can be found along motorways, in tunnels and at certain mountain passes.

Another recommended company to call if you break down is **Falken Redningskorps** (☎ 80 03 00 50).

Bring Your Own Vehicle

There are no special requirements for bringing your car to Norway. For details on ferry services to Norway from other European countries, see p393.

Driving Licence

Short-term visitors may hire a car with only their home country's driving licence. Also ask your automobile association for a *lettre de recommendation* (letter of introduction), which entitles you to services offered by affiliated organisations in Norway, usually free of charge. These services may include touring maps and information, help with breakdowns, technical and legal advice etc.

For advice on driving your own vehicle in Norway, see p403.

Fuel & Spare Parts

Leaded and unleaded petrol, as well as diesel, is available at most petrol stations. Although prices can vary from day to day in keeping with fluctuating international oil prices, prevailing prices at the time of research ranged between Nkr9.50 per litre up to Nkr10.75. Diesel usually costs around Nkr1 per litre less. Credit cards are accepted at most places. In towns, petrol stations may be open until 10pm or midnight, but there are some 24-hour services. In rural areas, many stations close in the early evening and don't open at all on weekends. Some have 24-hour automatic pumps operated with credit cards or cash notes.

Make sure that your car is in peak condition before you travel to Norway, because spare parts, although widely available, are expensive.

Hire

Norwegian car hire is costly and geared mainly to the expense-account business traveller. Walk-in rates for a compact car with 200km free start are typically over Nkr1000 per day (including VAT, but insurance is Nkr50 per day extra).

You'll always get a better daily rate the longer you rent. In summer, always ask about special offers, as you may be able to get the smallest car (eg VW Lupo) for a three- to five-day period for Nkr440 per day with 50km free, or Nkr555 per day with 200km free; each extra kilometre costs Nkr2.50. The equivalent rates for eight- to 13-day hire start at Nkr378 and Nkr478, while for 14 days or more, the daily rate drop to Nkr351 and Nkr444.

Some major rental agencies also offer weekend rates, which allow you to pick up a car after noon on Friday and keep it until 10am on Monday for around Nkr1200 – be sure it includes unlimited kilometres.

All major firms, such as Hertz, Avis, Budget and Europcar, have desks at Oslo's Gardermoen International Airport, as well as other airports around the country. They're also represented in city centres. If you have hired a car, any speed-camera tickets are automatically paid through your credit card. Beware – some Scandinavian car-hire companies have been known to charge 'extras' to customers' credit-card bills so always scrutinise your credit-card statements for a few months afterwards.

In general, local companies will offer better deals than larger international firms, although their offers aren't always as good. The following is a partial list of firms:

Avis (www.avis.no) Oslo (☎ 81 56 90 44; Munkedamsveien 27); Bergen (☎ 55 55 39 55; Lars Hilles gate 20B)
Bislet Bilutleie (☎ 22 60 00 00; www.bislet.no; Pilestredet 70, Oslo)
Budget (www.budget.no) Oslo (☎ 81 56 06 00; Hedgehaugsveien 4); Bergen (☎ 55 27 39 90; Storetveitveien 58)
Europcar (☎ 22 83 12 42; www.europcar.no; Haakon VIIs gate 9, Oslo)
Hertz (☎ 22 21 00 00; www.hertz.no; SAS Hotel, Holbergs gate 30, Oslo)
Rent-a-Wreck (☎ 81 52 20 50; www.rent-a-wreck.no; Filipstadveien 5, Oslo)

Such are the prohibitive costs of car rental in Norway, that you should seriously consider hiring your car just across the border in

Sweden and either return it there afterwards, or negotiate a slightly more expensive one-way deal whereby you pick up in Sweden and leave it in Norway. By far the best online rental agency is the highly recommended **Auto Europe** (www.autoeurope.com), which acts as a clearing house for cheap rates from major companies and offers a host of pick-up and drop-off options in Norway and across Europe.

Insurance
Third-party car insurance (unlimited cover for personal injury and Nkr1,000,000 for property damage) is compulsory and, if you're bringing a vehicle from abroad, you'll have fewer headaches with an insurance company Green Card. Ensure that your vehicle is insured for ferry crossings.

Road Conditions
If Norway was Nepal they would have built a road to the top of (or underneath) Mt Everest. There are roads which can inspire nothing but profound admiration for the engineering expertise involved. To get an idea of just how hard-won were Norway's roads and tunnels through the mountains, visit the Norwegian Museum of Road History (p148) in Lillehammer.

Main highways, such as the E16 from Oslo to Bergen and the entire E6 from Oslo to Kirkenes, are open year-round. The quality of the road network is constantly improving and more bridges and tunnels are constructed every year. The longest tunnels link adjacent valleys, while shorter tunnels drill through rocky impediments to straighten routes. Most tunnels are lit and many longer ones have exhaust fans to remove fumes, while others are lined with padded insulation to absorb both fumes and sound. Motorcyclists must be wary of fumes in longer tunnels and may want to avoid them. At the time of writing, Lærdalstunnelen (between Lærdal and Aurland) is the longest road tunnel in the world at 24.51km; see the boxed text, p402, for more information.

We do, however, have two complaints. For all their considerable expertise in road-building, Norway's transport authorities

ROAD DISTANCES (KM)

	Ålesund	Alta	Bergen	Bodø	Florø	Hammerfest	Harstad	Kautokeino	Kirkenes	Kristiansand	Kristiansund	Lillehammer	Narvik	Odda	Oslo	Røros	Stavanger	Tromsø	Trondheim
Ålesund	---																		
Alta	1701	---																	
Bergen	384	2071	---																
Bodø	1008	814	1378	---															
Florø	201	1970	248	1277	---														
Hammerfest	1845	144	2215	959	2114	---													
Harstad	1186	557	1556	300	1455	701	---												
Kautokeino	1827	131	2197	941	2096	276	684	---											
Kirkenes	2215	519	2585	1329	2484	498	1072	451	---										
Kristiansand	811	2226	492	1533	652	2370	1711	2352	2740	---									
Kristiansund	142	1609	517	916	329	1753	1094	1735	2123	867	---								
Lillehammer	382	1756	439	1063	466	1900	1241	1882	2270	473	396	---							
Narvik	1190	511	1560	304	1459	655	119	637	1025	1715	1098	1245	---						
Odda	416	2064	159	1371	320	2208	1549	2190	2578	333	549	362	1553	---					
Oslo	533	1909	478	1216	512	2053	1394	2035	2423	322	562	168	1398	357	---				
Røros	401	1569	635	876	535	1713	1054	1695	2083	704	327	263	1058	624	382	---			
Stavanger	603	2251	179	1558	426	2395	1736	2377	2765	245	736	587	1740	187	453	836	---		
Tromsø	1440	290	1810	554	1709	435	296	417	805	1965	1348	1495	250	1803	1648	1308	1990	---	
Trondheim	287	1414	657	721	556	1558	899	1540	1928	812	195	342	903	650	495	155	837	1153	---

TRANSPORT

TRANSPORT

TUNNELS IN NORWAY

Visitors to Norway are usually (and rightly) impressed by the civil-engineering wonders that dominate road transport around the country, particularly in the Western Fjords, Nordland and the Far North. The most extraordinary road tunnels include ones that spiral upwards through mountains, pass deep under the sea to reach offshore islands or bore through mountains which are buried underneath glaciers.

In November 2000, after nearly six years of construction, the world's longest road tunnel, from Lærdal to Aurland (24.51km long, 7.59km longer than the St Gotthard tunnel in Switzerland), was completed at a total cost of Nkr1082 million. There are no tolls to use the tunnel since it was paid for entirely by the national government. The two-lane tunnel, part of the vital E16 road connecting Oslo and Bergen, reduces the difficulties of winter driving and replaces the lengthy Gudvangen–Lærdal ferry route. It was drilled through very hard pre-Cambrian gneiss, with over 1400m of overhead rock at one point. There's a treatment plant for dust and nitrogen dioxide in the tunnel, 34 gigantic ventilation fans, emergency telephones every 500m and three bizarre 'galleries' with blue lighting to 'liven up' the 20-minute trip.

Motorists should tune into NRK radio P1 when driving through the tunnel (yes, there are transmitters inside!) in case of emergency.

Other long road tunnels in Norway include: Gudvangentunnelen in Sogn og Fjordane (11.43km, also on the E16); Folgefonntunnelen in Hardanger (11.15km, on Rv551 and passing beneath the Folgefonn icecap); Steigentunnelen in Nordland (8.06km, Rv835); and Svartisentunnelen in Nordland (7.61km, on Rv17 and passing beneath the Svartisen icecap).

Interesting undersea tunnels, which typically bore around 40m below the sea bed, include: Oslofjordtunnelen (7.2km, on Rv23, south of Oslo); Nordkapptunnelen (6.87km, on the E69 and connecting Magerøya Island to the mainland); Byfjordtunnelen (5.86km, on the E39 just north of Stavanger); and Nappstraumen tunnel (1.78km, on the E10 and linking Vestvågøy and Flakstadøy in Lofoten).

---

seem incapable of understanding the frustration of sitting behind a slow vehicle for an hour or more and instead widening some of the roads, at least in flat areas where it is feasible. For all but a few kilometres around the major cities, Norway's highways are single lane in either direction, with precious few overtaking lanes.

Which brings us to our other complaint. When you've just spent three hours going 200km along a major highway, it's galling to say the least to have to pay a toll (up to Nkr150) for the privilege. Road tolls are a particular problem in the south. Keep a stack of coins handy. New segments of highway and recently built tunnels and bridges must be paid off in user tolls and these can be as high as Nkr145 per car. In theory, the tolls are dropped when the construction project is paid off although some privately funded facilities become quite lucrative so this doesn't always happen. Oslo, Bergen, Trondheim, Stavanger and Kristiansand impose tolls on drivers every time they cross the city limits – this is just a tax for visiting, since no attempt is made

to encourage people to switch from cars to buses. Note that there's a Nkr325 fine if you use a lane reserved for vehicles with *abonnement* (subscription) passes. Motorcycles aren't subject to the tolls.

For details of road conditions which require more care, see below.

A good guide for those wanting to know more is Erling Welle-Strand's concise *Motoring in Norway*.

Road Hazards

Older roads and mountain routes are likely to be narrow with multiple hairpin bends and very steep gradients. Although most areas are accessible by car, some of the less-used routes have poor or untarred surfaces only suitable for 4WD vehicles and some seemingly normal roads can narrow sharply with very little warning. On some mountain roads, caravans and motorhomes are forbidden or advisable only for experienced drivers, as it may be necessary to reverse in order to allow approaching traffic to pass. Restricted roads for caravans are outlined on a map published by **Vegdirektoratet**

(☎ 22 07 35 00; www.vegvesen.no; Brynsengfaret 6A, 0667 Oslo).

In winter, spring or early summer, check beforehand to make sure the passes are open, as many remain closed until May or June. **Vegmeldingssentralen** (☎ 175), Statens Vegvesen's 24-hour Road User Information Centre, provides up-to-date advice on road closures and conditions throughout the country. If you're expecting snowy or icy conditions, it's wise to use studded tyres or carry snow chains. In Oslo, snow chains can be hired from **Hakres** (☎ 35 51 48 57; fax 35 51 52 50) for Nkr1000/1300 for one/two weeks, including changing of tyres. Your ordinary tyres are kept as a deposit. Snow chains can also be obtained in the UK from **Snowchains Europroducts** (☎ 01732-884408; www .snowchains.co.uk).

Road Rules

In Norway, traffic keeps to the right. The use of seat belts is obligatory at all times and children under the age of four must have their own seat or safety restraint. The use of dipped headlights (including on motorcycles) is required at all times and right-hand-drive vehicles must have beam deflectors affixed to their headlight in order to avoid blinding oncoming traffic. Drivers must carry a red warning triangle to use in the event of a breakdown; motorists must always give way to pedestrians at zebra crossings; and vehicles from other countries must bear an oval-shaped nationality sticker on the back. Motorcycles may not be parked on the pavement (sidewalk) and are subject to the same parking regulations as cars.

Drunk-driving laws are strict in Norway: the maximum permissible blood alcohol content is 0.02% and violators are subject to severe fines and/or imprisonment. Because establishments serving alcohol may legally share liability in the case of an accident, you may not be served even a small glass of beer if the server or bartender knows you're driving a car.

UK-registered vehicles must carry a vehicle registration document (Form V5), or a Certificate of Registration (Form V379, available from the DVLA in the UK). For vehicles not registered in the driver's name, you'll require written permission from the registered owner.

HASTE MAKES WASTE

The national speed limit is 80km/h on the open road, but pass a house or place of business and the limit drops to 70km/h or even 60km/h. Through villages, limits range from 50km/h to 60km/h and, in residential areas, they're 30km/h. A few roads have segments allowing 90km/h and you can drive at 100km/h on a small part of the E6. The speed limit for caravans (and cars pulling trailers) is usually 10km/h less than for cars.

The lethargy-inspiring national speed limits may seem laborious by your home standards, but avoid the temptation to drive faster as they're taken very seriously. Mobile police units lurk at the side of the roads. Watch for signs designating *Automatisk Trafikkontrol*, which means that there's a speed camera ahead; these big and ugly grey boxes have no mercy at all.

You'll be nabbed for even 5km/h over the limit – there's no leniency, no compromises, and fines range from Nkr1000 to well over Nkr10,000. Norwegian nationals risk losing their driving licence and could even land in jail.

If you like tempting fate, head to the roads around the Nordland town of Fauske (p275), which is known as the speed-trap capital of the country.

Most road signs are international, but a white M on a blue background indicates a passing place on a single-track road (the 'm' stands for *møteplass*). *All Stans Forbudt* means 'No Stopping', *Enveiskjøring* is 'One Way'; *Kjøring Forbudt* is 'Driving Prohibited' or 'Do Not Enter'; *Parkering Forbudt* is 'No Parking'; and the cryptic *Rekverk Mangler* is 'Guardrail Missing'.

Vehicle Ferries

Travelling along the scenic but mountainous and fjord-studded west coast may be spectacular, but it also requires numerous ferry crossings, which can prove time-consuming and costly. Reservations aren't usually possible and are rarely needed anyway. For a complete list of ferry schedules, fares and operators' phone numbers, get hold of the Nkr225 *Rutebok for Norge*, a telephone-book-sized transport guide sold in bookshops and larger Narvesen kiosks. Otherwise, order directly from **Norsk Reisein-formasjon** (☎ 22 47 73 40; www.reiseinfo.no; Karl Johans gate 12A, 0154 Oslo), or download it at www .rutebok.no.

HITCHING

Hitching isn't entirely safe and we don't recommend it. Travellers who decide to hitch should understand that they're taking a small but potentially serious risk. People who choose to hitch will be safer if they travel in pairs and let someone know where they're planning to go. What's more, the Norwegian government generally considers car ownership a luxury and sets up its tax structure accordingly, so motorists may look askance at anyone who can't afford a vehicle. For that reason, hitching isn't especially popular.

That said, if you're determined to hitch, you will find Norwegians generally friendly, and they understand that not all foreigners enjoy an expense-account budget. With a measure of luck and patience, most hitch-hikers do manage to find lifts. Your chances of success are better on main highways, but you still may wait for hours in bad weather. Western Norway is generally the most difficult area for hitching, while the more laid-back north is probably the best. One good approach is to ask for rides from truck drivers at ferry terminals and petrol stations; that way, you'll normally have a place to keep warm and dry while you wait.

LOCAL TRANSPORT
Bus, Tram, Underground & Ferry

Nearly every town in Norway supports a network of local buses and ferries, which circulate around the town centre and also connect it with outlying areas. In many smaller towns, the local bus terminal is adjacent to the train station, ferry quay and/ or long-distance bus terminal. Fares range from Nkr15 to Nkr23 per ride. Day- or multi-trip tickets are also available.

Taxi

Taxis are best hailed around taxi ranks, but you can also reserve one by telephone. If you're phoning for a taxi immediately, remember that charges begin at the moment the call is taken. Daytime fares, which apply from 6am to 7pm on weekdays and from 6am to 3pm on Saturday, cost from Nkr29.70 at flagfall (more in larger cities), plus Nkr12 to Nkr18 per kilometre. Weekday evening fares are 22% higher, and in the early morning, on Saturday afternoon and evening, and on Sunday, they're 30% higher. On holidays, you'll pay 45% more. These fares are good for up to four passengers, but in some places, you may find 'maxi-taxis', which can carry up to eight passengers for about the same price.

TOURS

Numerous local tour companies operate in Norway and in every tourist office you'll find an exhaustive collection of leaflets, folders and brochures outlining their offerings in the immediate area.

Fjord Tours
NORWAY IN A NUTSHELL

A very popular option is the year-round 'Norway in a Nutshell' tour, organised through travel agencies, NSB rail services and tourist offices around southern Norway. To find out more, contact **Fjord Tours** (☎ 81 56 82 22; www.fjordtours.no). Itineraries vary, but most involve a one- or two-day excursion taking in the rail line between Oslo and Myrdal, the Flåmbanen line to Flåm, a cruise along Nærøyfjord to Gudvangen, a bus to Voss, and then rail trips to Bergen and back to Oslo (overnight or otherwise). The full tour from Oslo to Bergen costs Nkr1065, or Nkr1735 with a return to Oslo. There are cheaper (and shorter) options from Bergen (Nkr750) and Voss (Nkr480). An alternative to this route involves the rail line between Oslo and Stavanger. For more information, see the entries for Oslo (p85), Bergen (p183), Flåm (p211), Voss (p191) and Stavanger (p198).

OTHER TOURS

Fjord Tours also organises a number of other, similar self-guided tours around southern and western Norway. These include: the Triangle Tour (round trip to/ from Oslo via Kristiansand, Stavanger, Haugesund, Bergen and Geilo; Nkr1585); Golden Route (round trip to/from Oslo via Lillehammer, Otta, Geiranger, Åndalsnes, Trondheim and Dombås; Nkr1597); Explore Hardangerfjord (round trip to/ from Bergen via Voss, Ulvik, Eidfjord and

Norheimsund; Nkr610); and Polar Tour (round trip to/from Trondheim via Mo i Rana, Fauske, Svolvær, Bodø and the Hurtigruten Coastal Ferry; Nkr3840). Each of these tours can, like 'Norway in a Nutshell', be taken in whole or in part. Only 'Norway in a Nutshell' and the Triangle Tour may be purchased outside Norway.

Full details on all of these tours are available on the Fjord Tours website, or in its *Combination Tours in Norway* booklet (available from most larger tourist offices).

Den Norske Turistforening

Den Norske Turistforening (DNT; Norwegian Mountain Touring Club; ☎ 22 82 28 22; www.turistforeningen.no; Storgata 3) organises hundreds of year-round adventure trips in the Norwegian mountains, including cycling, fishing, hiking, skiing, glacier hiking, rock and ice climbing, family activities, hut-to-hut trekking, Svalbard tours, and so on. Five-/eight-day hiking tours cost from around Nkr3090/4170 (round trip from Oslo). Information on the tours is available on the DNT website, or you can pick up the brochure *Norwegian Summer* from any DNT office.

TRAIN

Norwegian State Railways (Norges Statsbaner; NSB; ☎ 81 50 08 88; www.nsb.no) operates an excellent, though limited, system of lines connecting Oslo with Stavanger, Bergen, Åndalsnes, Trondheim, Fauske and Bodø; there are also lines between Sweden and Oslo, Trondheim and Narvik. Most train stations offer luggage lockers for Nkr15 to Nkr50 and many also have baggage storage rooms.

Most long-distance day trains have 1st- and 2nd-class seats and a buffet car or refreshment trolley service. Public telephones can be found in all express trains and most Inter-City trains. Doors are wide and there's space for bulky luggage, such as backpacks or skis.

Classes

On long-distance trains, 2nd-class coaches provide comfortable reclining seats with footrests. First-class coaches, which cost 50% more, offer marginally more space and often a food trolley, but they're generally not worth the extra expense.

Costs

'*Minipris*' tickets cover all long-distance services with one ticket for each direct route and must be purchased at least five days in advance. Regular/*minipris* fares from Oslo are Nkr670/390 to Bergen, Nkr644/325 to Åndalsnes and Nkr783/400 to Stavanger (all prices include the Nkr35 seat reservation fee).

There's a 50% discount on rail travel for people aged 67 and older and for children under 16. Children under four travel free. Students get a 60/40% discount on departures marked green/white in timetables.

Second-class sleepers offer a good, cheap sleep: a bed in a three-berth cabin costs Nkr125; two-berth cabins cost Nkr210/270 per person in old/new carriages.

Reservations

Reservations cost an additional Nkr35 and are mandatory on a number of long-distance routes, including between Oslo and Bergen.

Train Passes

For details of international rail passes which can be used in Norway (but which are best bought before you arrive in the country), see p390.

Details about rail passes can also be found at www.railpass.com.

TRANSPORT

Health

CONTENTS

Travel health depends on your predeparture preparations, your daily health care while travelling and how you handle any medical problem that does develop. If you do fall ill while in Norway you will be very well looked after as health care is excellent.

Norway is, in general, a very healthy place and no special precautions are necessary when visiting. The biggest risks are likely to be viral infections in winter, sunburn and insect bites in summer, and foot blisters from too much hiking.

For a medical emergency dial ☎ 113; visit a local pharmacy or medical centre if you have a minor medical problem and can explain what it is. Hospital casualty wards will help if the problem is more serious. Nearly all health professionals in Norway speak English; tourist offices and hotels can make recommendations.

BEFORE YOU GO

Prevention is the key to staying healthy while abroad. A little planning before departure, particularly for pre-existing illnesses, will save trouble later – see your dentist before a long trip, carry a spare pair of contact lenses and glasses, and take your optical prescription with you. You will have no problem getting new glasses or contact lenses made up quickly and competently in Norway, but you will pay for the privilege. Bring medications in their original, clearly labelled containers. A signed and dated letter from your physician describing your medical conditions and medications is also a good idea. Most medications are available in Norway, but may go by a different name than at home, so be sure to have the generic name, as well as the brand name. If carrying syringes or needles, be sure to have a physician's letter documenting their medical necessity.

INSURANCE

If you're an EU citizen, an E111 form (available from health centres, or post offices in the UK) covers you for most medical care, except nonemergencies or emergency repatriation home. Citizens from other countries should find out if there is a reciprocal arrangement for free medical care between their country and the country visited. If you do need health insurance, strongly consider a policy that covers you for the worst possible scenario, such as an accident requiring an emergency flight home. Find out in advance if your insurance plan will make payments directly to providers or reimburse you later for overseas health expenditures. The former option is generally preferable, as it doesn't require you to pay out of pocket in a foreign country.

RECOMMENDED VACCINATIONS

The World Health Organization (WHO) recommends that all travellers should be covered for diphtheria, tetanus, measles, mumps, rubella and polio, regardless of their destination. Since most vaccines don't produce immunity until at least two weeks after they're given, visit a physician at least six weeks before departure.

ONLINE RESOURCES

The WHO's publication *International Travel and Health* is revised annually and is available online at www.who.int/ith. Other useful websites include www.mdtravelhealth.com

MEDICAL KIT CHECK LIST

Following is a list of items you should consider including in your medical kit – consult your pharmacist for brands available in your country.

- antibiotics – consider including these if you're travelling well off the beaten track; see your doctor, as they must be prescribed, and carry the prescription with you
- antifungal cream or powder – for fungal skin infections and thrush
- antihistamine – for allergies, eg, hay fever; to ease the itch from insect bites or stings; and to prevent motion sickness
- antiseptic (such as povidone-iodine) – for cuts and grazes
- aspirin or paracetamol (acetaminophen in the USA) – for pain or fever
- bandages, band-aids (plasters) and other wound dressings
- calamine lotion, sting relief spray or aloe vera – to ease irritation from sunburn and insect bites or stings
- cold and flu tablets, throat lozenges and nasal decongestant
- eye drops
- insect repellent
- loperamide or diphenoxylate –'blockers' for diarrhoea
- multivitamins – consider for long trips, when dietary vitamin intake may be inadequate
- prochlorperazine or metaclopramide – for nausea and vomiting
- rehydration mixture – to prevent dehydration, which may occur, for example, during bouts of diarrhoea; particularly important when travelling with children
- scissors and tweezers
- sunscreen and lip balm
- thermometer – note that mercury thermometers are prohibited by airlines
- water purification tablets or iodine

CHECK BEFORE YOU GO

It's usually a good idea to consult your government's travel-health website (if available) before departure:
Australia www.dfat.gov.au/travel
Canada www.travelhealth.gc.ca
United Kingdom www.doh.gov.uk/traveladvice
United States www.cdc.gov/travel

(travel-health recommendations for every country, updated daily), www.fitfortravel .scot.nhs.uk (general travel advice), www .ageconcern.org.uk (advice on travel for the elderly) and www.mariestopes.org. uk (information on women's health and contraception).

FURTHER READING

Health Advice for Travellers (currently called the 'T6' leaflet) is an annually updated leaflet by the Department of Health in the UK available free in post offices. It contains some general information, legally required and recommended vaccines for different countries, reciprocal health agreements and an E111 application form. Lonely Planet's *Travel with Children* includes advice on travel health for younger children. Other recommended references include *Traveller's Health,* by Dr Richard Dawood (Oxford University Press), and *The Traveller's Good Health Guide,* by Ted Lankester (Sheldon Press).

IN TRANSIT

DEEP VEIN THROMBOSIS (DVT)

Blood clots may form in the legs during plane flights, chiefly because of prolonged immobility – the longer the flight, the greater the risk. The chief symptom of DVT is swelling or pain of the foot, ankle or calf, usually but not always on just one side. When a blood clot travels to the lungs, it may cause chest pain and breathing difficulties. Travellers with any of these symptoms should immediately seek medical attention.

To prevent the development of DVT on long flights you should walk about the cabin, contract and move leg muscles by completing exercises while sitting, drink plenty of fluids and avoid alcohol and tobacco.

JET LAG & MOTION SICKNESS

To avoid jet lag (common when crossing more than five time zones) try drinking plenty of nonalcoholic fluids and eating light meals. Upon arrival, get exposure to natural sunlight and readjust your schedule (for meals, sleep and so on) as soon as possible.

Antihistamines such as dimenhydrinate (Dramamine) and meclizine (Antivert, Bonine) are usually the first choice for treating motion sickness. A herbal alternative is ginger.

IN NORWAY

AVAILABILITY & COST OF HEALTH CARE

Good health care is readily available, and for minor, self-limiting illnesses, pharmacists can dispense valuable advice and over-the-counter medication. They can also advise when more specialised help is required. The standard of dental care is usually good; however, it is sensible to have a dental checkup before a long trip. However, remember that, like almost everything else, medical care can be prohibitively expensive in Norway.

INFECTIOUS DISEASES

Tick-borne encephalitis is spread by tick bites. It is a serious infection of the brain and vaccination is advised for those in risk areas who are unable to avoid tick bites (such as campers, forestry workers and ramblers). Two doses of vaccine will give a year's protection; three doses up to three years.

TRAVELLER'S DIARRHOEA

Stomach upsets are as possible in Norway as they are at home and the same rules apply. Take great care when eating fish or shellfish (for instance, cooked mussels that haven't opened properly can be dangerous). As autumn approaches, collecting mushrooms is a favourite pastime in this part of the world, but don't eat any mushrooms until they have been positively identified as safe.

If you develop diarrhoea, be sure to drink plenty of fluids, preferably an oral rehydration solution (eg dioralyte). A few loose stools don't require treatment, but if you start having more than four or five stools a day, you should start taking an antibiotic (usually a quinoline drug) and an anti-diarrhoeal agent (such as loperamide). If diarrhoea is bloody, persists for more than 72 hours or is accompanied by fever, shaking, chills or severe abdominal pain, you should seek medical attention.

ENVIRONMENTAL HAZARDS
Giardia

Giardia is an intestinal parasite which lives in the faeces of humans and animals and is normally contracted through drinking water. Problems can start several weeks after you've been exposed to the parasite and symptoms may sometimes remit for a few days and then return; this can go on for several weeks or even longer.

The first signs are a swelling of the stomach, followed by pale faeces, diarrhoea, frequent gas and possibly headache, nausea and depression. If you exhibit these symptoms you should visit a doctor for treatment.

Tap water is always safe to drink in Norway, but it's wise to beware of drinking from streams, as even the clearest and most inviting water may harbour giardia and other parasites. For extended hikes where you must rely on natural water, the simplest way of purifying water is to boil it thoroughly. Vigorous boiling should be satisfactory; however, at high altitude water boils at a lower temperature, so germs are less likely to be killed. Boil it for longer in these environments (up to 10 minutes).

If you cannot boil water it should be treated chemically. Chlorine tablets (Puritabs, Steritabs or other brands) will kill many pathogens, but not giardia and amoebic cysts. Iodine is more effective in purifying water and is available in tablet form (such as Potable Aqua). Follow the directions carefully and remember that too much iodine can be harmful.

Although some unpopulated lands in Norway serve as sheep pastures, there seems to be little giardia. However, while most people have no problems drinking untreated surface water, there's still a possibility of contracting it.

Hypothermia & Frostbite

Proper preparation will reduce the risks of getting hypothermia. Even on a hot day in the mountains, the weather can change rapidly – carry waterproof garments and warm layers, and inform others of your route.

Acute hypothermia follows a sudden drop of temperature over a short time. Chronic hypothermia is caused by a gradual loss of temperature over hours.

Hypothermia starts with shivering, loss of judgment and clumsiness. Unless re-warming occurs, the sufferer deteriorates into apathy, confusion and coma. Prevent further heat loss by seeking shelter, wearing warm, dry clothing, drinking hot, sweet drinks and sharing body warmth.

Frostbite is caused by freezing and subsequent damage to bodily extremities. It is dependent on wind-chill, temperature and length of exposure. Frostbite starts as frostnip (white, numb areas of skin) from which complete recovery is expected with rewarming. As frostbite develops, the skin blisters and becomes black. Loss of damaged tissue eventually occurs. Wear adequate clothing, stay dry, keep well hydrated and ensure you have adequate calorie intake to prevent frostbite. Treatment involves rapid rewarming. Avoid refreezing and rubbing the affected areas.

Insect Bites & Stings

In northern Norway, the greatest nuisances are the plagues of blackflies and mosquitoes that swarm out of tundra bogs and lakes in summer. Fortunately, malaria is unknown, but the mental risks can't be underestimated, as people have literally been driven insane by the ravenous hordes. Mid-summer is the worst, and regular mosquito coils and repellents are scarcely effective; hikers must cover exposed skin and may even need head nets to keep the little buggers from making kamikaze attacks on eyes, nose, ears and throat. If you're camping, a tent with mosquito netting is essential. Most people get used to the mosquito bites after a few days as their bodies adjust and the itching and swelling become less severe. An antihistamine cream should help alleviate the symptoms. Use a DEET-based insect repellent.

Bees and wasps cause real problems only to those with a severe allergy (anaphylaxis.) If you have such an allergy, make sure you carry EpiPen or similar adrenaline injections at all times.

Rabies

Rabies, caused by a bite or scratch by an infected mammal, is found in Svalbard and (occasionally) in eastern Finnmark. Dogs are a noted carrier, but cats, foxes and bats can also be infected. Any bite, scratch or even lick from a warm-blooded, furry animal should be cleaned immediately and thoroughly. Scrub with soap and running water, and then apply alcohol or iodine solution. If you've been infected by a rabid animal, medical help should be sought immediately.

Snakes

Snakes are rarely seen in Norway and adders (the only poisonous variety) don't exist north of Tysfjorden in Nordland. To minimise your chances of being bitten always wear boots, socks and long trousers when walking through undergrowth where snakes may be present. Don't put your hands into holes and crevices, and be careful when collecting firewood.

Adder bites aren't normally fatal and antivenins are available. Immediately wrap the bitten limb tightly, as you would for a sprained ankle, and then attach a splint to immobilise it. Keep the victim still and seek medical help, if possible with the dead snake for identification. Don't attempt to catch the snake if there is a possibility of being bitten again. Tourniquets and sucking out the poison are now comprehensively discredited.

Sunburn

You can get sunburnt surprisingly quickly, even through cloud. Use a sunscreen, a hat, and a barrier cream for your nose and lips. Calamine lotion or Stingose are good for mild sunburn. Protect your eyes with good-quality sunglasses, particularly if you will be near water, sand or snow.

Ticks

Check your body after walking through tick-infested areas, as ticks can cause skin infections and other more serious diseases. If a tick is found, press down around the tick's head with tweezers, grab the head and gently pull upwards. Avoid pulling the rear of the body as this may squeeze the tick's

HEALTH

gut contents through the attached mouth parts into the skin, increasing the risk of infection and disease.

TRAVELLING WITH CHILDREN

All travellers with children should know how to treat minor ailments and when to seek medical treatment. Make sure the children are up-to-date with routine vaccinations and discuss possible travel vaccines well before departure, as some vaccines are not suitable for children under a year.

Remember to avoid contaminated food and water. If your child has vomiting or diarrhoea, lost fluid and salts must be replaced. It may be helpful to take rehydration powders for reconstituting with boiled water.

Children should be encouraged to avoid and mistrust any dogs or other mammals because of the risk of rabies and other diseases. Any bite, scratch or lick from a warm-blooded, furry animal should immediately be thoroughly cleaned. If there is any possibility that the animal is infected with rabies, immediate medical assistance should be sought.

SEXUAL HEALTH

Condoms are widely available at *apótek* (pharmacies). When buying condoms, look for a European CE mark, which means they have been rigorously tested, and then keep them in a cool, dry place or they may crack and perish.

Emergency contraception is most effective if taken within 24 hours after unprotected sex. The **International Planned Parent Federation** (www.ippf.org) can advise about the availability of contraception in different countries.

HEALTH

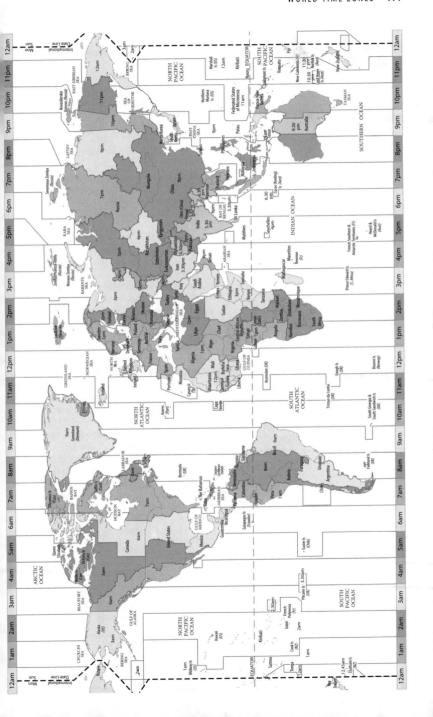

Language

CONTENTS

LANGUAGES OF NORWAY
Bokmål & Nynorsk

Norway's two official languages, Bokmål (BM) and Nynorsk (NN), are quite similar and spoken or understood by all Norwegians. However, rural regional dialects vary tremendously and people from one side of the country may have difficulty understanding people from the other side.

Bokmål, literally 'book-language' (also known as Riksmål, the 'national language') is the modern urbanites' version of the language of the former Danish rulers. As the predominant language in Norwegian cities, it's used by over 80% of the population. It's also the language of instruction for most school children and the predominant language of the media.

Nynorsk or 'New Norwegian' (as opposed to Old Norwegian, the language used prior to Danish rule) predominates in the Western Fjords and parts of central Norway; it also serves as a lingua franca (common language) in those regions which may have one or more dialects. Prior to WWII, Nynorsk was the first language of nearly one-third of all Norwegian school children;

growing urbanisation has seen this figure reduced to about 15% today.

Perhaps the most striking oddity of Norway's linguistic dichotomy is that many words and place names have two or more authorised spellings. Today, Nynorsk is the official administrative language in the counties of Møre og Romsdal and Sogn og Fjordane. Interestingly, the national government has decreed that a certain percentage of television subtitles be translated into Nynorsk.

Fortunately for most visitors, English is also widely spoken in Norway, even in rural areas. Nevertheless, it's still a good idea to learn a few Norwegian phrases to help you establish contact with people – and if you're having obvious trouble with your Norwegian, most people will be happy to switch to English.

Sami

In northern Norway, quite a few people speak Sami, a language of the Finno-Ugric group. It's related to Samoyed (among other northern Russian ethnic dialects), Finnish, Estonian and Hungarian.

Sami is spoken by around 20,000 people in Norway (there are also Sami speakers in Finland, Sweden and Russia). Although most of them can also communicate in Norwegian (and some even speak English), visitors who know even a few words of the local language will be able to access this unique culture more readily (see p418 for some basic Sami words and phrases).

There are three distinct Sami dialects in Norway – the Fell (also called Eastern or Northern) Sami, Central Sami and South Sami – but a total of 10 different dialects are used within the Sápmi region: Ume, Pite, Lule, Inari, Skolt, Kildin and Ter (see the map on p34). Fell Sami is considered the standard Sami language.

NORWEGIAN

While Norway has two official languages guide we've used Bokmål only – it's by far the most common language that travellers to Norway will encounter.

Lonely Planet's *Scandinavian Phrasebook* offers a more comprehensive guide to Norwegian. A number of Norwegian language course books are available internationally – most also come with audio cassettes. If you're interested in learning Bokmål, the two best Norwegian books are *Ny i Norge* and *Bo i Norge*; both are available locally.

The Norwegian alphabet has 29 letters: those used in English, plus the vowels **æ**, **ø** and **å** (which are listed at the end of the alphabet). While the consonants **c**, **q**, **w**, **x**, and **z** are included, they are used mainly in foreign words. In many Norwegian place names, the definite article 'the' – which may be masculine *(-en)*, feminine *(-en/-a)* or neuter *(-et)* – is appended to the end, eg Jotunheim becomes Jotunheimen, and Horningdalsvatn becomes Horningdalsvatnet. Plurals of nouns are usually formed by adding the suffix *-e* or *-er*.

PRONUNCIATION

Norwegian pronunciation is a complex affair for native English speakers. We've included pronunciation guides in this chapter to simplify things, but the best way to improve your pronunciation is to employ the 'listen and learn' method.

Vowels

As in English, Norwegian vowels can have many permutations. The length of vowels is a very important feature in the pronunciation of Norwegian. When occurring in a stressed syllable every vowel has both a (very) long and a (very) short counterpart. Generally, a vowel is short when followed by one consonant, and when followed by two or more consonants, it's long.

Pronunciation Guide

a	**a/aa** – short, as the 'u' in 'cut'; long, as in 'father'
å	**o/aw** – short, as the 'o' in 'pot'; long, as in 'law'
e/æ	**e/ay/ə** – short, as in 'bet'; long, as in posh British 'day'; in unstressed syllables, as the 'a' in 'ago'
i	**i/ee** – very short, as in 'police'; long, as in 'seethe'
o	**o/oo/u/or** – short, as in British 'pot'; long as in 'zoo'; short, as the 'u' in put; long, as in 'or'
ø	**er** – as the 'e' in 'her'
u	**u/oo** – short, as in 'put'; long, as in 'soon'
y	**ew/y** – produced as if pursing your lips and saying 'ee'

Consonants & Semivowels
Pronunciation Guide

d	**d** – often silent at the end of a word, or when between two vowels
g	**g/y** – as in 'go' except before **ei**, **i**, **j**, **øy** and **y** when it's pronounced as the 'y' in 'yard'
h	**h** – as in 'her'; silent before **v** and **j**
j	**y** – always as the 'y' in 'yard'
k	**k/ch** – a hard sound, as in 'kin'; before the letters or combinations **ei**, **i**, **j**, **øy** and **y** it's mostly pronounced as the 'ch' in 'chin'. (In many areas, these combinations are pronounced as the 'h' in 'huge', or as 'ch' in Scottish *loch*.)
l	**l/ll** – pronounced thinly, as in 'list', except after 'ah', 'aa', 'o' and 'or' sounds, when it's like the 'll' in 'all'
ng	**ng** – in most areas, as the 'ng' in 'sing'
r	**r** – trilled, like Spanish 'r'; in southwest Norway the **r** has a guttural pronunciation, as in French *rien*. The combinations **rd**, **rl**, **rn**, **rt** sound a little as they do in American 'weird', 'earl', 'earn' and 'start', but with a much weaker 'r'. The combination **rs** is pronounced 'sh' as in 'fish'.
s	**s/sh** – as in 'so'; when **sk** is followed by **ei**, **i**, **j**, **øy** and **y**, it's pronounced as 'sh', eg the Norwegian word *ski* sounds like English 'she'
t	**t** – as in 'top', except in two cases where it's silent: in the Norwegian word *det* (it, that) – roughly pronounced like British English 'dare' – and in the definite singular ending *-et* of Norwegian neutral nouns
v	**v** – a cross between English 'v' and 'w' but without rounding the lips

ACCOMMODATION

I'm looking for a ...
Jeg leter etter ...
yay le·tər et·tər ...
   campground
   camping-plass   kam·ping plaas

guesthouse
gjestehus yes·tə·hoos
hotel
hotell hu·tel
youth hostel
vandrehjem vun·dra·hyem

Where is a cheap hotel?
Hvor er et billig hotell? voor ar et bil·li hu·tel?
What is the address?
Hva er adressen? vaa ar a·dres·en?
Could you write it down, please?
Kan du skrive det ned? kan do skree·va də ned?
Do you have any rooms available?
Har du ledige rom? har du lay·di·ə rum?

I'd like a ...
Jeg vil gjerne ha ...
yay vil yar·nə haa ...
　bed
　en seng en seng
　single room
　et enkeltrom et eng·kəlt·rum
　double-bed
　en dobbeltseng en dob·elt·seng
　room
　et rom et rom
　double room
　et dobbeltrom et dob·əlt·rum
　room with a bathroom
　et rom med bad et rom med baad

I'd like to share a dorm.
Jeg vil gjerne ligge på sovesalen.
yay vil yar·nə lig·gə paw sor·və·saa·lən

How much is it ...?
Hvor mye er det ...?
vor mew·yə kos·tər de ...
　per night
　pr dag par daag
　per person
　pr person par pa·shoon

May I see it?
Kan jeg få se det? kan yay for se de?
Where is the toilet?
Hvor er toalettene/wc? voor ar too·a·let·tə·nə/ve·se?
I'm leaving now/tomorrow.
Jeg reiser nå/i morgen. yay ray·sər nor/i·mo·rn

CONVERSATION & ESSENTIALS
Hello.
Goddag. gud·daag
Goodbye.
Ha det. ha·de

Yes.
Ja. yaa
No.
Nei. nay
Thank you.
Takk. taak
You're welcome.
Ingen årsak. ing·ən aw·shaak
Excuse me.
Unnskyld. un·shewl
Sorry.
Beklager. bek·laga
What's your name?
Hva heter du? vaa hay·tə du?
My name is ...
Jeg heter ... yay hay·tər ...
Where are you from?
Hvor er du fra? voor ar du fraa?
I'm from ...
Jeg er fra ... yay ar fraa ...
I like ...
yay lee·kər ... Jeg liker ...
I don't like ...
yay lee·kər ik·kə ... Jeg liker ikke ...
Just a minute.
Vent litt; vent lit;
Et øyeblikk. et ə·yew·blik

DIRECTIONS
Where is ...?
Hvor er ...? voor ar ...?
Go straight ahead.
Det er rett fram. de ar ret fraam
Turn left.
Ta til venstre. taa til vens·trə
Turn right.
Ta til høyre. taa til hə·yew·rə
at the next corner
ved neste hjørne ve nes·tə yayr·nə
at the traffic lights
ved lyskrysset ve lews·krew·sə

SIGNS

Inngang	Entrance
Utgang	Exit
Opplysninger	Information
Åpen	Open
Stengt	Closed
Forbudt	Prohibited
Politistasjon	Police Station
Toaletter	Toilets
Herrer	Men
Damer	Women

LANGUAGE

behind	*bak*	bak
in front of	*foran*	fo·raan
far	*langt*	laangt
near (to)	*nær*	nar
opposite	*overfor*	or·vər·for
beach	*strand*	straan
bridge	*bru*	broo
castle	*slott*	slot
cathedral	*katedral*	ka·te·draal
church	*kirke*	chir·kə
island	*øy*	əy
lake	*vann/vatn*	vunn/vutt·en
main square	*(stor)torget*	(stoo·r)·to·rgə
market	*torget*	to·rgə
old city (town)	*gammel by*	gam·məl bew
palace	*slott*	slot
quay	*brygge*	brew·gə
riverbank	*elvebredd*	el·və bred
ruins	*ruiner*	roo·ee·nər
sea	*sjø*	shə
square	*torget*	tor·gə
tower	*tårn*	torn

EMERGENCIES

Help!
Hjelp! yelp!
It's an emergency!
Det er en nødsituasjon! de aa en nərd·see·tyoo·ay·shon
There's been an accident!
Det har skjedd en ulykke! de haar shed en oo·lew·kə!
I'm lost.
Jeg har gått meg vill. yay haar gawt me vil
Go away!
Forsvinn! fo·shvin!

Call ...!	*Ring ...!*	ring ...
a doctor	*ein lege*	ayn lay·gə
the police	*politiet*	pu·li·tee·ə

HEALTH

I'm ill.
Jeg er syk. yay ar sewk
It hurts here.
Dette gjør vondt. de yer·r vunt har

I'm ...
Jeg har ... yay haar ...
asthmatic	*astma*	aast·ma
diabetic	*sukkersyke*	suk·kər·sew·kə
epileptic	*fallesyke*	faal·lə·sew·kə

I'm allergic to ...
Jeg er allergisk mot ... yay ar a·ler·gisk moot ...
antibiotics	*antibiotika*	aan·ti·byoo·ti·ka
penicillin	*penicillin*	pen·ni·si·leen
bees	*bier*	bee yər
nuts	*nøtter*	nə tər
peanuts	*peanøtter*	pee·ya·nə tər

antiseptic
sårsalve so·ar sal·va
aspirin
aspirin/parasett/dispril a·spe·reen/pa·ra·set/dis·preel
condoms
kondomer kon·dom·ma
contraceptive
prevensjons middel pre ven·syons mi·del
contraceptive pill
P-Pille peh pil·lə
diarrhoea
diare dee·ya·ray
medicine
medisin me·dee·sin
nausea
kvalm kvarm
sunblock cream
solfaktor sool fak·tor
tampons/pads
tamponger/bind tam·pon·gər/bind

LANGUAGE DIFFICULTIES

Do you speak English?
Snakker du engelsk? sna·kə du eng·əlsk?
Does anyone here speak English?
Er det noen som snakker engelsk? ar de noon som sna·kər eng·əlsk?
How do you say ... in Norwegian?
Hva heter ... på norsk? vaa hay·tər ... por noshk?
What does ... mean?
Hva betyr ...? vaa bə·tewr ...?
I understand.
Jeg forstår. yay for·shtawr
I don't understand.
Jeg forstår ikke. yay for·shtawr ee·kə
Could you speak more slowly, please?
Kan du snakke sakte? kan du sna·kər sak·tə?
Can you show me (on the map)?
Kan du vise meg (på kartet)? kan du vee·sə ma (po kaar·tə)?

NUMBERS

0	*null*	nul
1	*en*	en
2	*to*	too
3	*tre*	tre
4	*fire*	fee·rə
5	*fem*	fem
6	*seks*	seks
7	*sju/syv*	shu/sewv
8	*åtte*	ot·tə
9	*ni*	nee
10	*ti*	tee
11	*elleve*	el·və
12	*tolv*	tol
13	*tretten*	tre·ten
14	*fjorten*	fyor·ten
15	*femten*	fem·ten
16	*seksten*	seks·ten
17	*sytten*	sew·ten
18	*atten*	at·ten
19	*nitten*	ni·ten
20	*tjue*	chu·ə
21	*tjueen*	chu·en
30	*tretti/tredve*	tret·te/tred·və
40	*førti*	fer·rti
50	*femti*	fem·ti
60	*seksti*	seks·ti
70	*sytti*	sew·ti
80	*åtti*	ot·ti
90	*nitti*	nit·ti
100	*hundre*	hun·drə
1000	*tusen*	tus·ən

PAPERWORK

name
navn — naavn
nationality
nasjonalitet — naa·shu·naa·li·tayt
date of birth
fødselsdato — fert·səls·daa·tu
place of birth
fødested — fayr·də·stay
sex/gender
kjønn — chern
passport
pass — paas
visa
visum — vee·sum

QUESTION WORDS

Who?	*Hvem?*	vem?
What?	*Hva*	vaa?
What is it?	*Hva er det?*	vaa ar de?
When?	*Når?*	nor?
Where?	*Hvor?*	vor?
Which?	*Hvilken?*	vil·ken?
Why?	*Hvorfor?*	vor·for?
How?	*Hvordan?*	vor·dan?

SHOPPING & SERVICES

I'd like to buy ...
Jeg kan få ... — yay kan faw ...
How much is it?
Hvor mye koster det? — vor mew·yə kos·tər de?
I don't like it.
Det liker jeg ikke. — de lee·kər yay ik·kə
May I look at it?
Kan jeg få se på det? — kan yay for say po de?
I'm just looking.
Jeg bare ser meg rundt. — yay ba·rə sayr ma roont
I'll take it.
Jeg tar det. — yay taar de

Do you accept ...?
Tar du imot ...?
taar du i·moot ...?
  credit cards
  kredittkort — kray·dit·kort
  travellers cheques
  reise-sjekk — ray·se shek

more	*mer*	mer
less	*mindre*	min·drə
small	*liten*	lee·tən
big	*stor*	stoor

I'm looking for ...
Jeg leter etter ...
yay le·tər et·tər ...
  a bank
  banken — baang·kən
  the church
  kirken — chir·kən
  the city centre
  sentrum — sen·trum
  the ...embassy
  den ... ambassade — den ... am·ba·saa·də
  the hospital
  sykehus — sew·kə·hoos
  the market
  torget — tor·gə
  the museum
  museet — mu·say·ə
  the police
  politiet — pu·lee·tee·ə
  the post office
  postkontoret — post·kun·too·rə
  a public toilet
  et offentlig toalett — et of·fənt·lee too·a·let

LANGUAGE

the tourist office
turistinformasjon   tu·rist·in·for·ma·shoon

TIME & DATES
What time is it?
Hva er klokka?   vaa ar klok·ka?
It's ... o'clock.
Klokka er ...   klok·ka ar ...
in the morning
om formiddagen   um for·mid·daa·gən
in the afternoon
om ettermiddagen   um et·tər·mid·daa·gən
in the evening
om kvelden   um kve·lən

When?	*Når?*	nawr?
today	*i dag*	i·daag
tomorrow	*i morgen*	i·mor·ən
yesterday	*i går*	i·gawr

Monday	*mandag*	man·daa(g)
Tuesday	*tirsdag*	teesh·daa(g)
Wednesday	*onsdag*	uns·daa(g)
Thursday	*torsdag*	toosh·daa(g)
Friday	*fredag*	fre·daa(g)
Saturday	*lørdag*	lər·daa(g)
Sunday	*søndag*	sərn·daa(g)

January	*januar*	ya·noo·waar
February	*februar*	feb·roo·waar
March	*mars*	maash
April	*april*	a·pril
May	*mai*	maa·i
June	*juni*	yoo·ni
July	*juli*	yoo·li
August	*august*	ow·gust
September	*september*	sep·tem·bər
October	*oktober*	uk·too·bər
November	*november*	no·vem·bər
December	*desember*	de·sem·bər

TRANSPORT
Public Transport
What time does the ... leave/arrive?
Når går/kommer ...?
naw gaw/kom·mər ...?

boat	*båten*	baw·tən
(city) bus	*(by)bussen*	(bew)bu·sən
plane	*flyet*	flew·yə
train	*toget*	tor·gə
tram	*trikken*	trik·kən

I'd like a ... ticket.
Jeg vil gjerne ha ... billett.
yay vil ya·rnə haa ... bil·let

one-way	*enkelt*	en·kelt
return	*tur-retur*	too·rə·toor
1st class	*første klasse*	fərsh·tə klaa·sə
2nd class	*annen klasse*	aan·ən klaa·sə

I want to go to ...
Jeg skal til ...
yay skaal til ...
The train has been delayed/cancelled.
Toget er forsinket/innstilt.
tor·gə ar fo·shing·ket/in·stilt

the first	*første*	fersh·tə
the last	*siste*	sis·tə
next	*neste*	nes·tə
platform	*perrong*	pə·rong
ticket office	*billettluka*	bi·let·lu·ka
timetable	*tidtabell*	teed·taa·bel
train station	*stasjon*	sta·shoon

Private Transport
Where can I rent ...?
Hvor kan jeg leie ...?
voor kan yay lay·ə ...?

a car	*en bil*	en beel
a 4WD	*firehjulstrekk*	fee·rə·hyools·trek
a motorbike	*(motor)sykkel*	(maw·tor·)sew·kel
a bicycle	*tråsykkel*	traw·sew·kel

ROAD SIGNS	
Vikeplikt	Give Way
Parkering Forbudt	No Parking
Omkjøring	Detour
Inngang	Entry
Utgang	Exit
Selvbetjent	Self Service
Veiarbeid	Roadworks

Is this the road to ...?
Er dette veien til ...?
ar de·tə vay·yən til ...?
Where's the next service station?
Hvor er nærmeste bensinstasjon?
voor ar nar·məs·tə ben·seen·sta·shoon?

diesel
diesel   dee·sel
(unleaded) petrol
blyfri   blew·free

(How long) Can I park here?
(Hvor lenge) Kan bilen min stå her?
(voor leng·ə) kan bee·lən min staw har?

LANGUAGE

Where do I pay?
Hvor betaler jeg?
voor be·ta·lər yay?

I need a mechanic.
Jeg trenger en bilmekaniker.
yay treng·ər en bil·me·kaa·ni·kər.

The car/motorbike has broken down at ...
Bilen/Sykkelen har fått motorstopp ...
bee·lən/sew·ke·lən har fawt mo·tor·stop ...

The car/motorbike won't start.
Bilen/Sykkelen starter ikke.
bee·lən/sew·ke·lən star·tər ik·kə

I have a flat tyre.
Hjulet er punktert.
yoo·lə aar pung·tayrt

I've run out of petrol.
Jeg er tom for bensin.
yay ər tom for ben·seen

I've had an accident.
Jeg har vært i en ulykke.
yay haar vart ee en u·lew·kə

TRAVEL WITH CHILDREN
Is there (a/an) ...?
Finnes det ...?
fin·nes de ...?

I need (a/an) ...
Jeg trenger ...
yay tren·ga ...

   baby change room
   et stellerom   et stel·la·room
   car baby seat
   et barnesete   et bar·na·say·tə
   child-minding service
   en barnevakt   en bar·nə·vaakt
   children's menu
   en barnemeny   en baar·nə·me·new
   disposable nappies/diapers
   bleier   blay·yər

Also available from Lonely Planet:
Scandinavian Phrasebook

formula
morsmelktillegg   mors·melk·til·eg
(English-speaking) babysitter
en engelsktalende   en en·gelsk·ta·len·də
  barnevakt   bar·na·vaakt
highchair
en høy barnestol   en høy bar·na·stool
potty
en potte   en po·tə
stroller
en sportsvogn   en spawts·von

Do you mind if I breastfeed here?
Kan jeg amme her?   kan yay am·mə haar?
Are children allowed?
Er det tillat for barn?   aar de til·lat faw baarn?

SAMI

Although written Fell Sami includes several
accented letters, it still doesn't accurately
represent the spoken language – even some
Sami people find the written language difficult to learn. For example, *giitu* (thanks)
is pronounced '*gheech*-too', but the strongly
aspirated 'h' is not written.

Here are a few Sami phrases. To learn the
correct pronunciation, it's probably best to
ask a local to read the words aloud.

Hello.	*Buorre beaivi.*
Hello. (reply)	*Ipmel atti.*
Goodbye. (to person leaving)	*Mana dearvan.*
Goodbye. (to person staying)	*Báze dearvan.*
Thank you.	*Giitu.*
You're welcome.	*Leage buorre.*
Yes.	*De lea.*
No.	*Li.*
How are you?	*Mot manna?*
I'm fine.	*Buorre dat manna.*

1	*okta*
2	*guokte*
3	*golbma*
4	*njeallje*
5	*vihta*
6	*guhta*
7	*cieza*
8	*gávcci*
9	*ovcci*
10	*logi*

Glossary

You may encounter some of the following terms and abbreviations during your travels in Norway. See also p60 for all food-related Norwegian words

Note that the letters æ, ø and å fall at the end of the Norwegian alphabet.

abonnement – subscription
allemannsretten – 'every man's right'; a tradition (now a law) allowing universal access to private property (with some restrictions), public lands and wilderness areas
apótek – pharmacy
Arctic Menu – scheme to encourage the use of the region's natural ingredients in food served by 0restaurants
arête – a sharp ridge between two valley glaciers
arsamerit – name given by Inuit (Eskimos) in reference to aurora borealis (northern lights)
automatisk trafikkontrol – speed camera

bakke – hill
berg – mountain
bever – beaver
bibliotek – library
bilutleie – car hire company
billett – ticket
bird cliffs – sea cliffs inhabited by colonies of nesting birds
Bjørnstein – bear rock
blodveien – literally 'blood road'; nickname given to Artic Highway during construction due to high number of worker fatalities
blåsel – bearded seals
bokhandel – bookshop
bru, bro – bridge
brygge – quay, wharf
bryggeri – brewery
bukt, bukta – bay
bunad – the Norwegian national costume; each region has its own version of this colourful affair
by – town

calving – breaking off of icebergs from tidewater glaciers
cirque – an amphitheatre scoured out by a glacier
crevasse – a fissure in moving ice, which may be hidden under snow, caused by various strains as the ice flows downhill

dal – valley
DNT – Den Norske Turistforening (Norwegian Mountain Touring Club)
domkirke – cathedral

dressin – rail bikes or bicycles on bogies

elg – elk, moose
elv, elva – river

fast ice – a solid sheet of pack ice frozen to some land
femboring – small Norland boat measuring 11m to 13m
ferje – ferry
festning – fort, fortress
firroing – small Norland boat measuring up to 5m
fiskeskrue – fish press
fjell, fell, fjall – mountain
fjord – drowned glacial valley
fonn – glacial *icefield*
forening – club, association
foss – waterfall
Fv – Fylkesvei; county road
fylke – county
fyr, fyrtårn – lighthouse
færing – small Norland boat measuring up to 5m

galleriet – gallery or shopping arcade
gamma, gammen – Sami turf hut, sometimes partially underground
gamle, gamla, gammel – old
gamlebyen – the 'old town'; the historic portion of a city or town
gate, gata – street (often abbreviated to g or gt)
gatekjøkken – literally 'street kitchen'; street kiosk/stall/grill selling greasy fast food
gjestehavn – 'guest harbour'; the area of a port town where visiting boats and yachts moor; washing and cooking facilities are normally available
gjestehus – guesthouse
gravlund, gravplass – cemetery
grevling – badges
grindhval – pilot whale
gruve, gruva – mine
grønlandssel – harp seals
gård, gard – farm or courtyard

hage – garden
halvfemterømming – small Norland boat measuring up to 9m
halvfjerdomning – small Norland boat measuring up to 7.5m
halvøya – peninsula
Hanseatic League – association of German traders who dominated trade in Bergen from the 12th to the 16th centuries

hare – Artic hares
hav – ocean
havert – grey seals
havn – harbour
honnør – senior citizen
hulder – elusive mythical Norwegian creature who steals milk from summer pastures
Hurtigruten – literally 'the Express Route'; system of coastal steamers plying the route between Bergen and Kirkenes
hus – house
husmannskost – traditional Norwegian food; home-cooking
hval – whale
hvalross – walrus
hvithal – Beluga whales
hytte – cabin, hut or chalet
hytteutleie – hut hire company
høvedmann – captain of a Norland boat

ice floe – a flat chunk of floating sea ice, normally pack ice, but it may also refer to a small iceberg
icecap, icefield – a stable zone of accumulated and compressed snow and ice, and a source of valley glaciers. An icecap generally covers a larger area than an icefield. When the entire interior of a landmass is covered by an icecap (as in Greenland or Antarctica), it's known as a continental glacier.
iddis – colourful sardine tin label; Stavanger dialect for 'etikett' or label
isbjørn – polar bear

jarls – earls
jernbanestasjon – train station
jerv – wolverine
joik – 'song of the plains'; religious Sami tradition
jul – Christmas

kai, kaia – quay
kanoutleie – canoe hire company
kappleiker – dance competitions
kart – map
kirke, kirkja, kirkje, kerk – church
klappmyss – hooded seals
knolhavl – humpback whales
knörr – small cargo boats, plural knerrir
kort – card
krambua – general store
krone – Norwegian currency unit
Kulturhus – translates literally as Culture House, a large complex containing everything from cinemas and public library to museums etc
kvadraturen – the square grid pattern of streets measuring six long blocks by nine shorter blocks
kyst – coast

landsmål – Norwegian dialect
lavvo, lavvu – tepee; Sami tent dwelling
legevakten – clinic
leikarringer – folk dancers
lemen – lemmings
lettre de recommendation – letter of introduction; letter written by automobile association that entitles the bearer to services offered by affiliated organisations in Norway
libris – books; indicates a bookshop
lufthavn – airport

magasin – department store
mil – Norwegian mile measuring 10km
minkehval – minke whales
MOMS – Value Added Tax/sales tax
moskus-okse – musk oxen
M/S – motorship or motor ship, used to designate ship names
museum, museet – museum
mush – to drive a dog-sled (word of Alaskan origin)
MVA – see *MOMS*
myntvaskeri – coin laundry

nartival – narwhal whales
nasjonalpark – national park
naturreservat – nature reserve
navvy – railway worker
nessekonger – early 19th century merchant squires
nord – north
nordlys – northern lights, aurora borealis
Norge – Norway
Norges Turistråd – Norwegian Tourist Board, formerly NORTRA
Norsk – Norwegian
Norway in a Nutshell – a range of tours which give high-speed travellers a glimpse of the best of Norway in one or two days
NSB – Norges Statsbaner (Norwegian State Railways)
nunatak – Greenlandic word referring to a mountain peak that protrudes through a glacier or *icecap*
ny – new
Nynorsk – see *landsmål*

og – and
oter – otter

pack ice – floating ice formed by frozen seawater, often creating an impenetrable barrier to navigation
pensjonat – pension or guesthouse
pinnsvin – hedgehogs
plass – plaza, square
polarsirkelen – Arctic Circle; 66°33'N latitude
Polynya – Russian word referring to an area of open water surrounded by pack ice

Pomor – the Russian trading and fishing community from the White Sea area, which prospered in northern Norway in the 17th century
postkontor – post office

reinsdyr – reindeer
reiseliv – local tourist office
riksdaler – old Norwegian currency
ringsel – ringed seals
rom – signs on roads indicating private rooms/cabins for rent
rorbuer – cabin/fishing hut
rosemaling – painted floral motifs
russ – to run amuck; students graduating from high-school dress in a red beret and overalls and have permission to get into mischief
rutebilstasjon – bus terminal
ruteplan – transport timetable
Rv – Riksvei; national highway
rådhus – town hall
rødruss – see *russ*
røyskatt – stoats

schøtstue - large assembly room where employees of the Hanseatic League met and ate
seksring – small Norland boat measuring up to 7m
selskap – company
sentrum – town centre
siida – small Sami communities or bands that hunted and trapped together
sjø – sea, ocean
sjøhus – fishing bunkhouse on the docks; many are now available for tourist accommodation
skalds – metaphoric and alliterative works of Norwegian court poets in the 9th and 10th centuries
skerries – offshore archipelago of small rocky islets
skog – forest
skoglemen – forest-dwelling version of lemmings
skogmår – pine martens
sla låm – slope track
slott – castle, palace
snø – snow
solarsteim – Viking navigational tool used when the sky was overcast or the sun below the horizon
spekkhogger – killer whales
stabbur – raised storehouse
stasjon – station
Statens Kartverk – State Mapping Agency
stavkirke – stave church
steinkobbe – harbour seals

stige – ladder
stoll – tunnel chipped
storting – parliament
strand – beach
stuer – trading firms
sund – sound, strait
Svalbard rein – Svalbard caribou
Sverige – Sweden
svømmehall, svømmebad – swimming pool
sykehus – hospital
sykkel – bicycle
sykkelutleie – bicycle hire company
sæter – summer dairy
sør – south
søyle – column, pillar

taiga – marshy forest
teater – theatre
telekort – Telenor phonecards
tog – train
togbuss – bus services in Romsdalen and Nordland run by NSB to connect railheads with other popular destinations
torget, torvet – town square
tran – cod-liver oil
turistkontor – tourist office
tårn – tower

utleie – hire company

vandrerhjem – youth hostel
vann, vatn, vannet, vatnet – lake
vaskeri – laundry
vei, veg – road (often abbreviated to v or vn)
vesel – weasels
vest – west
vetter – mythical Norwegian guardian spirits of the wildest coastline
vidde, vidda – plateau
vinmonopolet – 'wine monopoly shop'; government-run shop selling wine and liquor

yoik – see *joik*

øl – beer
ølutsalg – beer sales outlet
øst – east
øvre – upper
øy – island

åttring – small Norland boat measuring 10m to 11m

Behind the Scenes

THIS BOOK

This 3rd edition of *Norway* was coordinated by Anthony Ham, who also wrote the introductory, Directory, Transport, Health, Oslo, Southern Norway, Central Norway and Bergen & The Southwestern Fjords chapters. He was ably assisted by co-author Miles Roddis, who wrote the Western Fjords, Trøndelag, Nordland, The Far North and Svalbard chapters. The Health chapter was adapted from material written by Dr Caroline Evans.

The 2nd edition of *Norway* was written by Graeme Cornwallis and Andrew Bender, while Deanna Swaney wrote the 1st edition using material from the Norway chapter of *Scandinavian & Baltic Europe* (3rd edition), originally researched by Glenda Bendure and Ned Friary.

THANKS from the Authors

Anthony Ham Above all others, special thanks to Marina for, as always, making a place special through her presence, tolerating my long absences and making the welcome home so wonderful.

If I could write all my books with my co-author, Miles Roddis, and commissioning editor, Alan Murphy, I would be a very happy man – both were wonderful, wise companions along the way. Thanks also to Stefanie Di Trocchio, Danielle De Maio and Tony Fankhauser for a smooth and trouble-free editorial process.

The staff at Norway's countless tourist offices should take a bow – few countries have better or more helpful ambassadors. Those who were particularly generous with time and information include Cécile Poppe (Gamlebyen, Fredrikstad); Beathe Romsdalen (Risør); Nancy Thomsen (Grimstad); Mette Olsson (Hovden); Kari Kluge (Røros); Lene (Kristiansand); Martin Henriksen (Oslo); and Johannes Berg and Moussa Masumbuko (Use-It, Oslo).

It was a pleasure to meet both Tony Stewart and Bjoern Kolberg on the journey up Lysefjord, while Piers Crocker at the Canning Museum in Stavanger deserves a special mention for his inspirational rendition of the perfect host.

Special thanks also to Ron, Lisa, Greg, Alex, Greta, Marina, Alberto, Paco, Esperanza, Eva, Nacho, Alex and Dulce and all my friends and family in Madrid, Melbourne and so many other ports-of-call. And a special dedication to Antonio, who was born while this book was being written – may your world be a wonderful place.

Miles Roddis Huge thanks to Ingrid for being there, night after night, cabin after cabin, and for bearing the lioness' share of the driving around Norway's vast north. Anthony Ham, my companion in successive literary crimes, was sheer pleasure to work with and Alan Murphy, a genial commissioning editor, brimful of common sense. Special thanks too to Andreas Umbreit for sharing his wisdom and deep knowledge of Svalbard.

Readers Karoline Winkler, Jochen Domscheit, Mariska Schrever and Donny Thieme sent in particularly informative email letters. And Neroli Foster passed on a couple of much appreciated outdoor activity tip-offs.

Sadly, there's no room to mention by name all the hyper-efficient tourist office staff the length and breadth of northern Norway who so willingly pitched in with information. Many were themselves

---

THE LONELY PLANET STORY

The story begins with a classic travel adventure: Tony and Maureen Wheeler's 1972 journey across Europe and Asia to Australia. There was no useful information about the overland trail then, so Tony and Maureen published the first Lonely Planet guidebook to meet a growing need.

From a kitchen table, Lonely Planet has grown to become the largest independent travel publisher in the world, with offices in Melbourne (Australia), Oakland (USA) and London (UK).

Today Lonely Planet guidebooks cover the globe. There is an ever-growing list of books and information in a variety of media. Some things haven't changed. The main aim is still to make it possible for adventurous travellers to get out there – to explore and better understand the world.

At Lonely Planet we believe travellers can make a positive contribution to the countries they visit – if they respect their host communities and spend their money wisely.

avid, seasoned Lonely Planet travellers in their vacation time, so we would immediately find ourselves on the same wavelength. And most spoke with infectious enthusiasm about their towns.

Some were outstandingly helpful. My special thanks to Anja Jenssen and Florian Pfeiffer (Tromsø), Camilla Sandnes Holvim and Birgitte Bjørkno (Mo i Rana), and Monica Buan and Lise Rechsteiner (Trondheim).

Lastly, thank you, Robert Ptacnik, for helping Ingrid when the going got tough on a trek.

CREDITS

This title was commissioned and developed in Lonely Planet's London office by Alan Murphy, with assistance from Stefanie Di Trocchio (Melbourne office). Cartography for this guide was developed by Mark Griffiths and Jolyon Philcox.

Coordinating the production for Lonely Planet were Helen Rowley and Tony Fankhauser (cartography) with assistance from Adrian Persoglia, Anthony Phelan, Barbara Benson, Louise Klep and Sarah Sloane (cartography), James Hardy (cover design), Indra Kilfoyle (cover artwork), Quentin Frayne, Lee Frayne, Tone Frayne (language) and Charles Rawlings-Way (project management).

Coordinating the production for Palmer Higgs Pty Ltd were Danielle De Maio, Tony Davidson, Jane Fitzpatrick, Rod Faulkner (editorial), Andrew Seymour (layout design and photo research), Selina Brendish (project management) and John Simkin (indexing), with assistance from Simon Longstaff (editorial production support).

THANKS from Lonely Planet

Many thanks to the travellers who used the last edition and wrote to us with helpful hints, useful advice and interesting anecdotes:

A Kristin Alberti **B** Ann Best, Alan Bowring, Robert L Brown, Marianne Bruvoll, Johan Burman **C** Ken & Diana Campbell, John Carmody, Denise Cheng, Emmelena Christiansen, Guido Claessen **D** Karinna Damo, Edward Dang, Iestyn Davies, Geert De Coninck, Ron Deacon, Daniele Defranchis, Jochen Domscheit,

SEND US YOUR FEEDBACK

We love to hear from travellers – your comments keep us on our toes and help make our books better. Our well-travelled team reads every word on what you loved or loathed about this book. Although we cannot reply individually to postal submissions, we always guarantee that your feedback goes straight to the appropriate authors, in time for the next edition. Each person who sends us information is thanked in the next edition – and the most useful submissions are rewarded with a free book.

To send us your updates – and find out about LP events, newsletters and travel news – visit our award-winning website: **www.lonelyplanet.com**.

Note: We may edit, reproduce and incorporate your comments in Lonely Planet products such as guidebooks, websites and digital products, so let us know if you don't want your comments reproduced or your name acknowledged. For a copy of our privacy policy visit www.lonelyplanet.com/privacy.

John Donovan, Sarah Dyer **E** Moray Easdale, Oivind Egeland, David Eklund, Giorgos Epitidios, Tor Ercleve **F** Katina Fossum, Les Fraser, Sarah Fuell **G** Esther Goldsby, Annie & Lawrence Green, Liese Greensfelder **H** Paal Hangeraas, Tanja Heller, Nora Holst **J** Nils Jacobsen **K** Wendy King, Jan Klovstad, Ole Bjoern Kolflaath **L** Foh Lin Lim, Kai Roger Lindberget **M** Duncan Maggs, Hank Manning, Suzanne Martin, Brian McConaghy, JS McLintock, Joanna Miller, Ove Mjatveit, Hakon Mosseby, Clemens Muller-Landau, Tatu Myohanen **N** Pearl Ng, Thorkild Nielsen, Sarah Nortcliffe, Sally Ann Northcliffe **O** Dag Oien, Phil Olsen **P** Stéphan Paccou, Annie Paterson, Michael & John Patrick Plunkett, Jack Priestley **R** Mace Ramsay, Hank Raymond, Finn Roed **S** Fay Sampson, Sabrina Scaravetti, Dr K Sewell, J Sharp, David K Smith, Riccardo Soffritti, Jean Stanyon, Susan Stevens, David Szylit **T** Kevin Taylor, Sanchia Templar, Alessandro Turato, Juha Turpeinen **V** Karin Vaagen **W** Ulli Waas, Christine Weber, Brent Weston, Kristin Wilhelmsen, Karoline Winkler **Z** Peter Zombori

424

Index

432

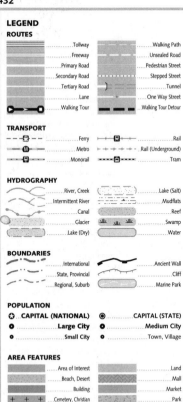

LONELY PLANET OFFICES

Australia
Head Office
Locked Bag 1, Footscray, Victoria 3011
☎ 03 8379 8000, fax 03 8379 8111
talk2us@lonelyplanet.com.au

USA
150 Linden St, Oakland, CA 94607
☎ 510 893 8555, toll free 800 275 8555
fax 510 893 8572, info@lonelyplanet.com

UK
72–82 Rosebery Ave,
Clerkenwell, London EC1R 4RW
☎ 020 7841 9000, fax 020 7841 9001
go@lonelyplanet.co.uk

Published by Lonely Planet Publications Pty Ltd
ABN 36 005 607 983

© Lonely Planet 2005

© photographers as indicated 2005

Cover photographs: Harbour at Bergsfjord on Loppa Island off the Finnmark coast, John Cleare/Alamy (front); Waterfront warehouses in Tondheim, Norway, Ned Friary/Lonely Planet Images (back). Many of the images in this guide are available for licensing from Lonely Planet Images: www.lonelyplanetimages.com

All rights reserved. No part of this publication may be copied, stored in a retrieval system, or transmitted in any form by any means, electronic, mechanical, recording or otherwise, except brief extracts for the purpose of review, and no part of this publication may be sold or hired, without the written permission of the publisher.

Printed through SNP SPrint Singapore Pte Ltd at
KHL Printing Co Sdn Bhd Malaysia

Lonely Planet and the Lonely Planet logo are trademarks of Lonely Planet and are registered in the US Patent and Trademark Office and in other countries.

Lonely Planet does not allow its name or logo to be appropriated by commercial establishments, such as retailers, restaurants or hotels. Please let us know of any misuses: www.lonelyplanet.com/ip.

Although the authors and Lonely Planet have taken all reasonable care in preparing this book, we make no warranty about the accuracy or completeness of its content and, to the maximum extent permitted, disclaim all liability arising from its use.